Mormonism in Dialogue with Contemporary Christian Theologies

Mormonism in Dialogue with Contemporary Christian Theologies

Edited by

DAVID L. PAULSEN,
Brigham Young University

DONALD W. MUSSER,
Stetson University

Mercer University Press
Macon, Georgia

2007

ISBN 0-88146-083-4 | 978-0-88146-083-4 | MUP/H743
ISBN 0-88146-116-4 | 978-0-88146-116-9 | MUP/P378

© 2007 Mercer University Press
1400 Coleman Road
Macon, Georgia 31207

First Edition

The paper used in this publication meets
the minimum requirements of American National Standard
for Information Sciences—Permanence of Paper for Printed
Library Materials, ANSI Z39.48-1984.

Library of Congress Cataloging-in-Publication Data

Mormonism in dialogue with contemporary Christian theologies
edited by David L. Paulsen, Donald W. Musser.
p. cm.

Includes bibliographical references and index
ISBN-13: 978-0-88146-083-4 (hardback : alk. paper)
ISBN-10: 0-88146-083-4 (hardback : alk. paper)
ISBN-13: 978-0-88146-116-9 (pbk. : alk. paper)
ISBN-10: 0-88146-116-4 (pbk. : alk. paper)
1. Theology–History–20th century
2. Church of Jesus Christ of Latter-day Saints–Doctrines
3. Mormon Church–Doctrines
I. Paulsen, David L. (David Lamont), 1936-
II. Musser, Donald W., 1942-
BT28.M67 2007
230'.93–dc22

2007039607

Contents

Foreword

Wʜʏ ʙᴏᴛʜᴇʀ? Tʜᴀᴛ ɪꜱ ᴀ ɢᴏᴏᴅ ᴀɴᴅ ɴᴀᴛᴜʀᴀʟ ǫᴜᴇꜱᴛɪᴏɴ for potential readers to ask the editors and authors of a book like this one. Those who are curious about religion, whether as professionals or not, are likely to be busy readers, who have to budget the time they devote to selected topics. No doubt most readers in religion would not have selected a work that conjoins and juxtaposes Christian—in this case mainly Protestant—theology and Mormon or Latter-day Saint thought.

Notice even the two words I just used, "theology" for Christians and "thought" for Mormons. That terminological tipping of the hat was a preliminary courtesy to those Mormons who note and sometimes even brag that they do not have a theology, nor do they "do" theology. Numbers of essayists in this book test the accuracy of that note or claim, and as I read the response of Mormons in this book, I have to say that they indeed have a theology or make theological statements, albeit with a slightly broader definition of that term than the conventional ones. *Conventional* here means the Christian modes that combine the language of the Hebrew Scriptures with mainly Greek philosophical concepts as filtered through academic experiences in Western Europe, most notably Germany. Were Catholics more represented here we might add "and also, notably, France and Italy, etc. . ."

If *logos* means word or statement and *theos* refers to God, Mormon thought overflows with theology, of a sort rooted in narrative. It may be that the dialogue in this book will remind more Christians that their theology is also born of story and stories—of God's dealing with the people of Israel and those who witness of Jesus Christ. And if theology is a reflection on a canon, an accepted documentary standard of a faith-community, we can find scholars here firing more than one canon at each other from the Hebrew Scriptures, the New Testament, to the Book of Mormon.

Still, supposing we establish that there is theology of different sorts on both sides of the conventionally Christian/LDS divides, we still have to ask, "Why bother?" Scholars in most disciplines recognize that doing comparative work illuminates particulars. Scientists classify insects and compare them; humanists label philosophies and histories and contrast them.

Still, such comparisons, to make sense and be profitable, have to have some common features if there is to be intelligibility and point. To coin a cliché: Comparing apples and oranges is not always the best way of learning which apples or which oranges are most appropriate or pleasing to the taste.

Most profitably, one compares phenomena from similar neighborhoods. Polemicists in both camps often regard aggressive articulators of ideas in the other as being far removed from their respective neighborhoods. Being Latter-day Saint meant a strong judgment—the prophet Joseph Smith could not have been more emphatic—on the limits and spent-ness of the Christian churches. Most Christian churches in the 1840s and many in the twenty-first century return the favor by insisting that they know Mormons are not Christian and should not be confused as having common features with Christianity.

Whoever reads the following essays will find good reason to see that the two camps do indeed live in the same neighborhood, and that carrying on conversation across the lines that separate them has promise. So, the scholars converse and compare. The moment one hears about such inter-faith (or, some here might contend, intra-faith) dialogue, two temptations arise. On the one hand, those who venture into such conversations get dismissed as syncretists, superficial synthesizers who belong in the indifferently tolerant school, whose adherents profess, despite all appearances, that "after all, we are in different boats heading for the same shore." On the other, pacifiers will read some sharp differentiations and exchanges here and assume that the only way to deal with "the other" is to evidence the *odium theologicum*, the hatred that theologians often have manifested.

Sorry, one will not find these extremes either. To explain what I see or read going on here, let me shift metaphors from neighborhoods to worlds, mental and spiritual worlds, conceived of as rooms. In my own work in these fields, a paragraph of George Santayana in his *Reason in Religion* provides a helpful framework:

> Any attempt to speak without speaking any particular language is not more hopeless than the attempt to have a religion that shall be no religion in particular. . . . Thus every living and healthy religion has a marked idiosyncrasy. Its power consists in its special and surprising message and in the bias which that revelation gives to life. The vistas it opens and the mysteries it propounds are another world to live in; and another world to live in—whether we expect ever to pass wholly over into it or no—is what we mean by having a religion.[1]

Latter-day Saints and Christians do in their spiritual lives live in "different worlds" theologically. The writers of these essays, however, show the

---

1. Quoted in Clifford Geertz, *The Interpretation of Cultures* (New York: Basic, 1973), 87.

benefits of at least entering and visiting in the figurative other rooms, different worlds. Since the authors are all clear about their purposes and their expositions, it would be presumptive and redundant were I to try to condense them. Let me just point to some themes that leaped out at me as I read the manuscript.

1. In general, the LDS scholars are far more at home with (think the word "conventional" each time) Christian thought than vice versa. They earn their doctorates at Harvard or other graduate schools permeated with the concepts of Christian theology, even if and though they often return "home" to Brigham Young & Company. The Christians here with few exceptions give little evidence that they boned up on LDS thought with the present project in view. This may be because they were invited to lecture solely on twentieth-century Christian theology at the conference. Either way, these factors and the book format necessarily keep the Latter-day Saint scholars in a kind of responsive-defensive mode. There is no way of getting around this inevitable distortion, but working through it has, I think, great hermeneutical and pedagogical value.

2. For a scholar to become adept at theological traditions as complex as these takes years, and to be selected for this task implies achievement of the sort that senior scholars alone pile up. That has meant here, at least in most Christian cases, that the authors are emeriti who were shaped in a world that differs considerably from what scholars-in-the-making begin to take for granted. Writers on Barth, Niebuhr, and Tillich in this book reckon with the fact that they represent an era regarded as historic by today's believers and scholars. The essay on thought of Langdon Gilkey illustrates this well, since it takes seriously his own sense that an era he was going to take for granted had ended. There are exceptions, of course: Gary Dorrien brings newer-generation perspective to his exposition of Christian theological development, and the Hopkins's essays come from a new generation and reflect life in a pluralist society more expansive and confusing than that known in the time when the language "Protestant-Catholic-Jew" was to suffice for America. Muslims were hardly known and Mormons were known about, but at a safe distance. One hopes that the richness of the essays in this book will inspire study in theological schools and schools of religion so that a new generation can be poised to do as well as this one in dealing with "the other."

3. For all the good will and good manners shown among the gentlepersons who write here, they serve us well by showing how difficult

it is to be at home with "another world to live in." The writers bend forwards and sideways to find bridges and bonds, and they do find some. Sooner or later, however, they are honest and bold enough to say: "Stop! We can't make it across the divide." Examples appear in every chapter, for example in talk about conceptions of life beyond the grave, or deification. Rather than being paralyzed at the point of disruption or frustration, readers of all the chapters in this book are likely to be inspired—bracing as the cold winds of the spirit that whips their way may be—to probe more deeply. In some cases—I think of the process theology chapters—they are likely to use the voice of the other, both in its sameness and in its differences—to engage in reflection, revising, and forming new resources.

4. One can get a distance-learning education by reading these chapters. While I have been on theological faculties for decades, I cannot claim to have kept up on all the movements described here—I am thinking of the Christian chapters—and learned from the ways most of the authors concisely re-educated me. As for the LDS writers: while I have taught about Mormons in American religious history, I found almost every LDS response capable of imparting what I had not known or connected previously. At our house, we often talk about "Mother-God" as a concept and then back off in bewilderment. Here one reads Mormons throwing light on such subjects by setting them in context.

5. Some of the essayists and respondents amaze scholars "on the other side" by the way they engage in self-critique. It may be easy to get by without such critique when there is no conversation going on, or there may be denial when one suspects that the partner in dialogue may exploit what is revealed in such criticism. Here readers are likely to agree that the scholars are forthright in stating their differences, open to listening to the other, and courteous about the way they handle both the self-assurance and the self-criticism of the other.

When I agreed to read the manuscript and write a foreword, I don't think I anticipated the scope, detail, and depth of this one. Now I pass it along to other readers who will find that such scope, detail, and depth represent gifts to everyone who has interest in and concern for "the other" in religious thought. In our crowding and conflict-filled world, there are more reasons than ever to accept such gifts and work to develop them and pass the results of new thinking on to others.

MARTIN E. MARTY
Fairfax M. Cone Distinguished Service Professor Emeritus,
The University of Chicago

Acknowledgments

This project has its origin in David Paulsen's appointment as the Richard L. Evans Professor of Religious Understanding at Brigham Young University (1994–1998). Holders of this chair are charged with the enjoyable task of increasing mutual understanding and building bridges between Latter-day Saints and other Christians. In pursuing these ends, Paulsen consulted with Martin Marty, Fairfax M. Cone Distinguished Service Professor Emeritus at the University of Chicago Divinity School, to discuss the possibility of a conference on Christian theology and Mormonism. Marty promptly introduced Paulsen and Donald Musser to each other, helped identify topics for dialogue, and recommended presenters and discussants for the conference. Coming full circle, Professor Marty has now graciously provided a foreword to this resulting volume.

This work would not exist without the contributions of many people. We thank the several dialogue partners who have provided clear and enlightening presentations of their respective theological viewpoints and who, in the form of replies and rejoinders, have interacted vigorously and respectfully with each other's views.

Many have contributed to the polishing of this book, belying, we believe, the old adage that many hands spoil the pot. These include John W. Welch, editor in chief, and his dedicated staff at BYU Studies. Besides making invaluable inputs to the form and substance of the several dialogues, he has overseen bringing this book to press from the beginning. His associate editors Anastasia Sutherland, Jennifer Hurlbut, Josh Probert (who also helped design the cover), and Katy Worlton Pulham have creatively polished both form and substance. Catharine Verhaaren helped design the layout and page formatting.

Current and former student research assistants Brent Alvord, Ari Bruening, Robb Duffin, Matthew G. Fisher, Marc-Charles Ingerson, Jeff Johnson, Brett McDonald, Jason Scoffield, Tyler Stoehr, Craig Atkinson, Carl Cranney, Nathan Westbrook, and J. Andrew West each all tirelessly and meticulously worked to proofread, edit, and source-check each paper. Brett and Tyler collaborated on first drafts of coeditor Paulsen's pieces in this book, and Jeff prepared the indices. Karen Steineckert, secretary of the BYU philosophy department, has gone the second mile in cheerfully and capably performing sundry tasks.

The religious studies faculty at Stetson University provided the amiable congeniality and intellectual "space" for co-editor Musser during the project, and departmental secretary, Lisa Guenther, provided solid clerical assistance.

In addition to the support received from the Richard L. Evans Chair, funding for various stages of this project have been provided, directly or indirectly, by Brigham Young University's Neal A. Maxwell Institute for Religious Scholarship, College of Humanities, Department of Philosophy, and other academic units.

To all of the above, we express our profound gratitude.

DONALD MUSSER
DAVID PAULSEN

Preface

On a flight from Atlanta to Salt Lake City where I was to be met by my co-editor, Professor David Paulsen of Brigham Young University, I settled back for a leisurely read of the Sunday edition of *The Atlanta Journal-Constitution*. This significant newspaper provides lively coverage of religion quite frequently. Not to disappoint me, one feature story focused on the topic "Christianity at 2000."[1]

An entire page enumerated basic facts and current statistics of "the major Christian sects in the United States." Covered were Adventists, Baptists, Catholics, Congregationalists, Disciples and Churches of Christ, Episcopalians, Lutherans, Methodists, Orthodox, Pentecostals, and Reformed Christians.

However, there was not a word of reference to The Church of Jesus Christ of Latter-day Saints. Why were there no facts and statistics on a religious body that easily outnumbers many of the "major" groups covered in the article?

Most people would not have even noticed this exclusion. Prior to my intersection with scholars at BYU, and especially the congenial faculty in the Philosophy Department, I would have not noticed either. At one time, my image of Latter-day Saints consisted mainly of two young men in white shirts riding their bicycles around my community faithfully serving their Mormon mission. I ducked any duo that I thought had a "Mormon missionary" look. Since then, my image of Latter-day Saints and my interest in Mormon thought and practice has changed significantly as I have become engaged in the conversations contained in this volume.

The present volume aims to foster conversations between Latter-day Saints and others in the Christian world. One of the immediate problems was how to begin to talk with one another, especially how we would refer to one another. Latter-day Saints, who see themselves as recipients of a "latter-day" revelation and the progenitors of a "restored" Christian church, sometimes refer to us other Christians as "gentiles" and to our churches as

---

1. "One Nation, Many Creeds," *Atlanta Journal-Constitution,* August 22, 1999.

"apostate," while we often refer to them as "cultists." These sorts of designators are hardly conducive to conversation, let alone to fruitful exchanges. Professor Paulsen and I have chosen nonpejorative language to refer to one another. We have agreed that referring to the followers of the restoration movement of Joseph Smith as "Mormons," "Latter-day Saints," or even "LDS-Christians" would be fine with all discussants. We are not sure everyone reading this book will approve referring to those outside the Mormon Church as "non-LDS Christians," but we have agreed that this designation is inoffensive.

Another point of perspective that informs this volume is that these conversations are not between LDS scholars and representatives of non-LDS scholars, popularly designated as "evangelical" or "conservative." Other recent forums have brought "evangelical" Protestants and LDS scholars into conversation.[2] With one exception,[3] the discussions in the present volume occur between Latter-day Saint scholars and non-evangelical, non-fundamentalist Christian scholars, Roman Catholic and Protestants academics popularly known as "mainline," "progressive," or "liberal." These scholars represent Christian groups connected with national and global ecumenism. For the most part these Christian scholars take the Bible seriously but not literally, affirm the significance of the ecumenical councils of the early church, stand "within" Western culture more than "outside" of it, and find dialogue with faith traditions different from their own to be stimulating and enriching. Thus, they have avidly participated in these conversations.

DONALD W. MUSSER

2. See, for example, Craig L. Blomberg and Stephen E. Robinson, *How Wide the Divide? A Mormon and an Evangelical in Conversation* (Downers Grove, Ill.: Intervarsity, 1997); and Francis J. Beckwith, Carl Mosser, and Paul Owen, eds., *The New Mormon Challenge: Responding to the Latest Defenses of a Fast-Growing Movement* (Grand Rapids, Mich.: Zondervan, 2002). For reviews of *How Wide the Divide?* see, for example, *FARMS Review of Books* 11, no. 2 (1999); and Francis J. Beckwith, "With a Grain of Salt: Assessing a Mormon-Evangelical Dialogue," *Christianity Today,* November 17, 1997, 57–59. For a detailed summary of responses to *How Wide the Divide?* see Matthew R. Connelly, Stephen E. Robinson, Craig L. Blomberg, and BYU Studies Staff, "Sizing Up the Divide: Reviews and Replies," *BYU Studies* 38, no. 3 (1999): 163–90. For responses to *The New Mormon Challenge,* see *FARMS Review of Books* 14, no. 1–2 (2002): 99–221; and *The FARMS Review* 15, no. 1 (2003), 97–258.

3. See Clark H. Pinnock's essay in present volume. Although Openness thinkers consider themselves to be evangelical, they differ substantially on a number of theological positions from more conservative thinkers. For an excellent introduction to openness theology see Clark H. Pinnock, *Most Moved Mover: A Theology of God's Openness* (Grand Rapids, Mich.: Baker Academic, 2001).

Introduction

Joint Perspective

David L. Paulsen and Donald W. Musser

THE TWO MODES of APOLOGETICS (explaining and defending one's own theological position) and polemics (critiquing another's theological position) have dominated the frequent interchanges between Latter-day Saints and other Christians. Differences and disagreements have been discussed and distinguished. Typically, discussants have found a wide divide between one another.

Not surprisingly then, when Professor Musser finished two days of lectures at Brigham Young University on twentieth-century Christian theologies, the first question from the audience was, "Do you think that we Mormons are Christians?"

His response to that question was that other questions need to be asked first. To ask a non-LDS Christian scholar if Latter-day Saints are Christian is the wrong place to start. It stifles productive conversation. Similarly, for Latter-day Saints to witness to and evangelize non-LDS Christians, without first entering into empathetic dialogue, is to invite resistance and resentment. Significant conversation must precede judgment, lest we misunderstand each other.

The series of discussions that this volume launches has pursued neither an apologetic nor a polemical tack. The discussants are interested in conversations—discussions that lead to understanding. Of course, differences and disagreements arise, but so do areas of commonality and agreement. Indeed, the similarities surprised both sides. Agreements were far more frequent than many discussants expected at the outset.

Donald Musser seeks to set the stage or prepare the context for these conversations. David Paulsen highlights some of the mutual benefits arising out of these lively interactions.

Christian Thought in the Twentieth Century

Donald W. Musser

TWENTIETH-CENTURY THEOLOGY BEGAN IN 1947 when Karl Barth published his commentary on St. Paul's Letter to the Romans.[1] This watershed study by the Swiss theologian brought the liberal theology[2] of the late nineteenth and early twentieth centuries to a close and ushered in Neo-Reformation (or Neo-orthodox) theologies.[3] These theologies dominated Western Christianity until the mid-1960s. The present essay provides a brief perspective on the context of twentieth-century Christian theologies, especially as they display connections to the conversations in the current volume.

What Is Theology?

To understand the conversations in this volume, one must have some notion of what "theology" is. Succinctly put, theology is disciplined reflection on the key concepts of a religious tradition.[4] A "religious tradition" refers to a particular faith community that cherishes the key concepts central to that tradition. Typically, a religious tradition has a disciplined history of thought about these key concepts. For example, both LDS and traditional Christians have a developed notion of God, a perspective on the creation and salvation of human beings, and a sense of the nature of nature. Both groups have some ideas about the creation of the heaven and the earth, the purpose and path of human life, and the future of humanity and the earth. The intersections of the concepts of God, human beings, and nature provide the "stuff," the key concepts, out of which theologies emerge. Disciplined

---

Practically every sentence in this essay is a "window" that opens further paths of inquiry. To help readers see the landscape of twentieth-century theology more vividly, copious references will be made to two standard handbooks where pertinent articles can be assessed. Co-edited by Donald W. Musser and Joseph L. Price, both non-LDS theologians, the volumes are *A New Handbook of Christian Theology* (Nashville, Tenn.: Abingdon, 1992) and *A New Handbook of Christian Theologians* (Nashville, Tenn.: Abingdon, 1996). Both handbooks appear in electronic format on CD-ROM as *The Abingdon Dictionary of Theology* (Nashville, Tenn.: Abingdon, 1998).

1. "Karl Barth," *New Handbook of Christian Theologians*, 49–59.

2. See John P. Crossley, Jr., "Liberalism," and Douglas F. Ottati, "Social Gospel," in *New Handbook of Christian Theology*, 285–87 and 447–49.

3. See Langdon Gilkey, "Neoorthodoxy," in *New Handbook of Christian Theology*, 334–37.

4. See James B. Wiggins, "Religion," and E. Glenn Hinson, "Tradition," in *New Handbook of Christian Theology*, 397–402 and 489–92.

thought leads to theological formulations; the subject headings are: God,[5] creation,[6] human beings,[7] sin,[8] salvation,[9] eschatology,[10] and nature.[11] Theology is disciplined thought about these subjects.[12]

Why Have Theology?

Clarity of thought and expression is a basic human goal. We want to understand one another. People who believe they have encountered God not only cherish their religious experiences but also seek to understand the implications of those experiences and communicate them to others.[13] These aims provide a first impulse to do theology.[14] A second impulse for thinking theologically is to define your own group. Creating a set of official or "orthodox" beliefs provides a basis for gathering persons into a united community and provides a basis for excluding deviate thinking (heresy).[15] As a downside, it also often has the consequence of dividing groups against one another.

A third impulse of theology is to relate the concepts of a religious tradition to a new and changing cultural context. Examples of this might include the translation of scriptures and liturgies into vernacular languages, the democratization of church authority in Western democracies, and the artistic expressions of Jesus in the image of a particular people.

What Are the Sources for Theology?

Four streams have fed Christian theology from the beginning: tradition, sacred texts, religious and social experience, and reason. Initially, Christian theology inherited Jewish traditions, such as the notions of righteousness

---

5. See Langdon Gilkey, "God," in *New Handbook of Christian Theology*, 198–209.

6. See Langdon Gilkey, "Creation," in *New Handbook of Christian Theology*, 107–13.

7. See Mark Kline Taylor, "Anthropology," in *New Handbook of Christian Theology*, 28–34.

8. See James Wm. McClendon Jr., "Sin," in *New Handbook of Christian Theology*, 442–47.

9. See Jeffery Hopper, "Soteriology," in *New Handbook of Christian Theology*, 452–56.

10. See Hans Schwarz, "Eschatology," in *New Handbook of Christian Theology*, 156–60.

11. See Lois K. Daly, "Ecology," in *New Handbook of Christian Theology*, 138–40.

12. The *New Handbook of Christian Theology* contains 148 introductory articles on core topics in contemporary theology.

13. The idea of theology as "faith seeking understanding" goes back to Augustine and Anselm, among others.

14. See Thomas E. Hosinski, "Epistemology," in *New Handbook of Christian Theology*, 150–56.

15. See David J. Gouwens, "Heresy," in *New Handbook of Christian Theology*, 216–19.

before God, the coming of a Messiah, and the building up of the kingdom of God. Every primitive Christian idea had roots in Judaism. Later, Christian theology inherited ideas from Platonic and Aristotelian philosophy and Roman legal thought. In time, the church's own history of thought was food for further reflection. Early confessions of faith (the Apostles' Creed) and declarations of Church councils (for example, at the councils of Nicea and Chalcedon) became honored guides for later generations. Today, each of the three central family traditions of historic Christianity—Catholic, Orthodox, and Protestant—draws on these traditional sources in articulating their own particular views, asking what past traditions teach that is essential for the present time.

Sacred texts have provided a second source of nourishment for Christian theology. Initially, the Hebrew Scriptures were the scriptures of the church. Later, by the fourth century, a distinctive set of texts from the life of the early church until about the end of the first century, the New Testament, became authoritative. Although Catholics, Orthodox, and Protestants all use the Old and New Testaments, they disagree over which books constitute the official "canon."[16] When doing theology, Christians ask what the sacred texts teach about the subject under discussion.

Experience has provided a third source for Christian theology. Personal religious experiences such as St. Paul's conversion on the Damascus Road, the appearance of Jesus to the disciples in the Upper Room, Martin Luther's conversion, the visions of mystics, or the sense of the presence of God in the quiet of a Quaker meetinghouse provide both emotional assurance and conceptual soil for theological reflection. Social experience also feeds theological reflection. One's relationship with other persons provides an understanding of human relatedness to God. The love of a parent for children, for example, gives insight into the biblical basis of God's love for human beings. Again, one's status in society may provide experiences of "bondage" or "liberation" that elucidate biblical themes of slavery and exodus. Theology asks how our personal and social experiences inform our inherited beliefs.

Reason is the fourth source that has nourished theology. In light of tradition, sacred scriptures, and human experience, disciplined thinkers seek to develop coherent and sometimes systematic worldviews. In the tradition of Anselm, the use of reason in theology is "faith seeking understanding." Theology therefore has a positive intention—it clarifies, defines, and relates. When it succeeds, believers assent with their minds and are confident in their hearts that their faith has substance.

---

16. See Frank Anthony Spina, "Canon," in *New Handbook of Christian Theology*, 75–78.

Theology in the Twentieth Century

Twentieth-century theology may be understood with direct reference to the three previous sections of this essay. Contemporary theology remains devoted to thinking clearly about the central theological topics—God, human beings, and nature. It continues to define, distinguish, and develop normative beliefs and to render affirmations of faith in terms relevant to believers who live in the modern world.

The central challenge for contemporary theology is how to remain consistent with the past (that is, in continuity with scripture and tradition) while being relevant and intelligible to personal and social experience and reason in the modern world.[17]

One can distinguish between contemporary theologies based on how they utilize the four sources. "Traditionalist" theologies tend to place more weight on the authority of scripture and tradition and less authority on experience and reason, while "modern" theologies place more emphasis on the authority of experience and reason and less on tradition and scripture. Traditional theologies emphasize the conservation of the historic statements of faith and are therefore "conservative." Generally, Eastern Orthodox, Roman Catholic, and evangelical and fundamentalist Protestant theologians tend to "look back," seeking to conserve the essentials of scripture and tradition. On the other hand, modern theologies tend to "look around" at current personal and social experiences and contemporary ways of thinking, seeking to confirm the essentials of scripture and tradition in the light of the present age.

To be sure, the actual situation in a particular faith group may be much more complex. It would be a mistake to conceive of twentieth-century theology in terms of polar opposites, with traditionalist theologies on the right and modern theologies on the left. Rather than think in terms of polarities, one ought to think of contemporary theology in terms of a continuum bridging extreme modernists on the left and extending across a spectrum to extreme traditionalists on the right. Most theologies, especially those represented by the non-LDS Christians in this volume, fall on the continuum somewhere between these two extremes.

The central difference among twentieth-century theologies lies in the issue of the relative authority of theological sources. These sources—scripture, tradition, experience, and reason—are affirmed by all theologians. Differences occur with regard to the weight or emphasis given to each authoritative source.

---

17. See Donald K. McKim, "Authority," in *New Handbook of Christian Theology*, 44–49.

The current emphasis on theological hermeneutics[18] is a case in point. Hermeneutics attempts to articulate how one re-presents the essence of scripture and tradition in terms of modern experience and thinking. The way current theology proceeds to use theological sources constitutes "theological method."[19] Each of the non-LDS theologies represented in this volume has toiled to clarify its method as a means to re-present the biblical message for today's believers.

Neo-orthodoxy, the most dominant of the Protestant approaches to theology in the twentieth century, is focally represented in this volume. In many respects the neo-orthodox theologians sought a 'middle' way between traditionalist and modernist approaches. They sought to be traditional (orthodox) by taking scripture and the early theological traditions seriously and also sought to be modern (neo-) by expressing the meanings of the early symbols and ideas in twentieth-century language and ideas. The four individual Protestant theologians treated in the first set of essays in this work—Barth, Niebuhr, Tillich, and Gilkey[20]—have all relied on scripture and tradition while seeking to render the essence of these sources relevant to the lives and thought of modern persons. Barth initiated a return to biblical, patristic, and Reformation formulations and emphases (a retrieval of essentials from scripture and tradition) while critiquing the "liberalism" of the late nineteenth and early twentieth centuries (especially the theologies of F. D. E. Schleiermacher, A. Ritschl, and A. Harnack). He saw these theologies as an attempt to replace (or at least dilute) the authority of scripture and tradition with the authority of modern culture—namely, Enlightenment reason and the methods and results of the natural and social sciences. Over against liberal theologies that began "from below" with an attempt to understand the divine within the parameters of human experience, Barth began "from above" in an attempt to understand human experience within the context of God's revealed presence in Word and Scripture.

For Reinhold Niebuhr the modern world had become overly captivated by the ideas found in the movements of rationalism, romanticism, individualism, and naturalism, which led it to unrealistic assumptions and hopes. His "Christian realism" about humanity, culture, and history was rooted in classical Christian formulations and scriptural symbols. Niebuhr recast the social ethics of nineteenth-century liberalism using a "realistic" philosophy and what he considered the core biblical symbols. Biblical texts provided an

---

18. See John McCarthy, "Hermeneutics," in *New Handbook of Christian Theology*, 219–24.

19. See Werner G. Jeanrond, "Theological Method," in *New Handbook of Christian Theology*, 480–86.

20. See the articles on these four theologians in the *Handbook of Christian Theologians*.

authoritative basis for understanding and interpreting contemporary culture. Biblical ideas about God, human beings, and sin were "symbols." For him, neither a literal nor a traditionalist reading of them was intelligible. Nevertheless, they illuminated personal and, especially, social and political situations in twentieth-century America.

Paul Tillich sought to mediate between the present and the past with the tools of modern philosophy. Tillich began with existential questions of meaning ("Who am I?" and "Who is God?") and value ("What is good?" and "What is just?") and proposed answers that used the biblical symbols as interpreted through the Idealistic philosophy of Schelling and the Existentialism of Heidegger and Kierkegaard. He used traditional sources to answer contemporary questions via a correlating bridge of modern thought.

Langdon Gilkey grew to theological maturity under the tutelage of both Niebuhr and Tillich and was also vastly influenced by Barth. Gilkey represents the generation of theologians who followed Barth, Niebuhr, and Tillich in the second half of the twentieth century. Gilkey's approach to theology finds intimations of the sacred in secular experience reflected through the lenses of classical Christian and biblical themes.[21]

In the perspective of the continuum of theologies proposed earlier in this essay, the theologies of Barth, Niebuhr, Tillich, and Gilkey are, strictly speaking, neither traditionalist nor modernist. They neither take the language and meaning of scripture and tradition to be controlling and normative nor do they sanctify modern experience and modes of meaning. They are, however, both traditional and modern. All four theologians take seriously the traditional topics or symbols of theological thinking while at the same time giving credence to modern experience and thinking. They all seek to mediate between the past and the present, conserving the essentials of traditional revelation and meaning in the fresh wine skins of modern thought.

The second set of essays in this book focuses on the issues of revelation[22] and reason.[23] In Christian theology "revelation" designates the disclosure or unveiling of the truth about God, human beings, and nature. Christians receive revelation in their lived experience, both as an encounter with the Divine (in experience) and as concepts about sacred reality (with reason). In theology "reason" is the conceptual tool by which believers appropriate revelation and come to an understanding of divine truth.

---

21. Langdon Gilkey's *Message and Existence: An Introduction to Christian Theology* (New York: Seabury, 1979) is a good illustration of his method in practice.

22. See Carl E. Braaten, "Revelation," in *New Handbook of Christian Theology*, 408–13.

23. See Hosinski, "Epistemology," and David L. Mueller, "Natural Theology," in *New Handbook of Christian Theology*, 150–56 and 328–31.

The essays by David Tracy and David Ray Griffin clarify, among other important matters, two different ways of coming to human knowledge of the sacred. Tracy, writing from the viewpoint of Roman Catholic theology, explores how understanding the revelation of God in the event and person of Jesus Christ can be aided by philosophy. Noting how early Christianity utilized Platonic philosophy to understand the meaning of the biblical revelation in that cultural milieu, he advocates a "hermeneutical philosophy [that] provides the kind of contemporary philosophy needed by revelational theology" (Tracy, 461). In formulating his method, Tracy rejects both theological rationalism, which holds that "only reason is relevant for understanding and judging any cognitive claims implicit in Christian faith" (Tracy, 453) and theological fideism, which claims that "faith is the only relevant form of knowledge" (Tracy, 452).

In the tradition of theology using a philosophical framework to bring the content of Christian faith into a contemporary mode of thinking, Griffin rethinks theology through the lenses of the process philosophies of Alfred North Whitehead and Charles Hartshorne. He writes that "Christian process theologians . . . seek to articulate Christian faith on the basis of the process philosophy of Whitehead and/or Hartshorne, employed as a 'natural' or 'philosophical' theology" (Griffin, 164). One of the central features of his approach to theology is to work within a natural or empirical thought-world in which "hard-core common sense," as opposed to an allegedly revealed set of propositional truths, is authoritative (Griffin, 165–68).

The third block of essays, those by Robert McAfee Brown, Rosemary Radford Ruether,[24] Dwight Hopkins, and Linda Thomas, introduce liberation theologies that have emerged in the latter third of the twentieth century and promise to be of importance throughout the twenty-first century. Each of these theologies is "contextual" in the sense that it focuses theologically on a social context that oppresses a particular group of people. They may, and often do, have considerable relevance for persons in other contexts, but liberation theologies find their primary relevance for the economically and socially oppressed.

For example, South American liberation theology[25] begins with the social and economic oppression of the poor in Latin America. Feminist the-

---

24. See "Rosemary Radford Ruether," *New Handbook of Christian Theologians*, 399–410.

25. See Otto Maduro, "Liberation Theology," in *New Handbook of Christian Theology*, 287–93. In the *New Handbook of Christian Theologians* see "Leonardo Boff," 74–84; "Gustavo Gutiérrez," 189–99; "Juan Luis Segundo," 419–26; and "Jon Sobrino," 427–33.

ology[26] targets the oppressive legacy of sexism and patriarchy in Western culture and Christianity. Black theology[27] assesses the oppressive results of racism in Western culture, particularly in North America. Womanist theology[28] pinpoints the triple-pronged oppression of race, sex, and class on poor black women in North America. In all four cases these theologies look from an oppressed present situation to resources for resolution and redemption in the Bible and tradition.[29]

Theological voices at the turn of the twenty-first century, as the discussions in this book show, have been lively and diverse. Using the sources of scripture, tradition, experience, and reason, these voices have sought to enunciate the truths of Christian faith in an increasingly diverse world. With this volume, these Protestant theologians venture into new and previously uncharted areas of religious exchange, entering into dialogue with the thought of Latter-day Saints and encountering, often for the first time, scriptures, practices, experiences, and thinking that in many ways differ, but, as we shall see, have surprising similarities with their own concerns and approaches.

---

26. See Rebecca S. Chopp, "Feminist Theology," in *New Handbook of Christian Theology*, 185–91. In the *New Handbook of Christian Theologians* see "Rosemary Radford Ruether," 399–410; "Mary Daly," 127–34; and "Sallie McFague," 278–86.

27. See James H. Evans, Jr., "Black Theology," in *New Handbook of Christian Theology*, 69–75. See "James Hal Cone," in the *New Handbook on Christian Theologians*, 118–26; "Howard Thurman," 440–48; "Desmond Tutu," 479–88; and "Cornel West," 505–12.

28. See Toinette M. Eugene, "Womanist Theology," in *New Handbook of Christian Theology*, 510–12. See Jacquelyn Grant and Delores Williams, "Womanist Theologians," in the *New Handbook of Christian Theologians*, 513–19.

29. Various contexts of oppression evoke other "contextual" theologies. Among emerging theologies are Asian, Minjung, Hispanic, Mujerista, red (Native American), and gay theologies. See Kosuke Koyama and others, "Asian Theologians," in the *New Handbook of Christian Theologians*, 22–48, and "Ada Maria Isasi-Diaz," in the *New Handbook of Christian Theologians*, 236–43.

Polemics, Apologetics and the Fruits of Dialogue

David L. Paulsen

Beginning with the emergence of The Church of Jesus Christ of Latter-day Saints (hereafter LDS church or Mormonism) as a distinct and growing religion, the relationship between Mormonism and other Christian traditions in regard to theological discussion has been tenuous at best. Historically, polemics, proselytizing, and prejudice have dominated interaction rather than genuine attempts to understand and learn from one another through dialogue. Non-LDS scholars have rarely taken seriously the ideas and potential contributions to their respective theologies of LDS thought. Meanwhile, on the LDS side, a tendency to publish for and to the LDS community has fostered isolation rather than interaction. The reasons for the historically feeble interaction between these two groups are varied, ranging from geographical separation to theological methodology.

Where Have We Been?

From the early 1830s and continuing throughout his life, Joseph Smith sought to establish cities where his followers could gather. Joseph's cities were to provide a home for those who "confessed that they were strangers and pilgrims on the earth" (D&C 45:13). The LDS communities' trouble with the citizens of Missouri and Illinois is well documented, as is their migration westward under the leadership of Brigham Young. With their relocation to the Rocky Mountains, the Latter-day Saints' main intellectual interaction with the rest of Christianity came in the form of missionary tracts. Written for the propagation of the faith, these tracts often dealt harshly with the doctrines of conventional Christianity. Meanwhile, the anti-Mormon genre begun in 1834 by Eber D. Howe's exposé *Mormonism Unvailed* sought to attack and discredit rather than dialogue with LDS theology.

Geographical isolation was exacerbated by methodological differences between LDS and traditional Christian scholars. The early animosity between the Latter-day Saints and those not of their faith was due in large part to the LDS ascription of divine and authoritative revelation to Joseph Smith. All subsequent revelations and doctrinal explications build upon the foundation of Joseph Smith's First Vision in making revelation the chief constituent of Latter-day Saint doctrine. The bold dynamism of the LDS understanding of revelation is found succinctly expressed in the Ninth Article of Faith, written by Joseph Smith: "We believe all that God has revealed, all that he does now reveal, and we believe that he will yet reveal many great and important things pertaining to the kingdom of God." Thus, while the rest of Christianity takes the Bible as its point of departure, the Mormon tradition claims continual direction from God himself through a living prophet. As a result of these differing methodologies, scholars from both groups faced difficulties in approaching one another.

Despite this troubled past, recent engagements between LDS and non-LDS scholars have been promising and progressive. In the groundbreaking *How Wide the Divide*, an LDS scholar and an Evangelical scholar *talk* through a number of theological issues in a respectful and honest manner. This work has as its goal "to explain and to educate—at last to hear and to tell the truth about each other."[30] Even the recent *The New Mormon Challenge*, which encourages evangelicals to "significantly retard the spread and growth of the LDS faith,"[31] is generally respectful in tone and takes seriously the theological ideas of the LDS tradition. Perhaps more remarkable is the fact that recently, influential spokesmen and writers in the major wings of Christendom are beginning to appropriate and teach theological insights that a century ago Joseph Smith almost alone taught.[32]

On the LDS side, the former reclusiveness has been replaced by a desire to produce scholarly works addressed to a wider audience. The most recent examples include Robert Millet's *A Different Jesus? The Christ of the Latter-day Saints*, Richard Bushman's biography *Joseph Smith: Rough Stone Rolling*, and Terryl Givens's *By the Hand of Mormon*.[33] These and other works have signaled the emergence of "gifted Mormon intellectuals" who, according to Richard Mouw, "have earned the right to be taken seriously in the larger academic community."[34] Furthermore, theological and historical articles have appeared by Protestant scholars such as Mark Noll, Richard Mouw, and Jan Shipps in the leading LDS academic journal, *BYU Studies*. The emergence of Mormon Studies conferences hosted by academic institutions such as Yale Divinity School, Claremont Graduate School of Religion, the University of Nottingham, and the University of Durham has highlighted

---

30. Craig L. Blomberg and Stephen E. Robinson, *How Wide the Divide? A Mormon and an Evangelical in Conversation* (Downers Grove, Ill..: InterVarsity, 1997), 21.

31. Carl Mosser, "And the Saints Go Marching On," in *The New Mormon Challenge*, ed. Francis J. Beckwith, Carl Mosser, and Paul Owen (Grand Rapids, Mich.: Zondervan, 2002), 69.

32. I have pointed out areas of non-LDS Christianity's convergence with Mormon thought in "Are Christians Mormon? Reassessing Joseph Smith's Theology in His Bicentennial," *BYU Studies* 45, no. 1 (2006): 35–128.

33. Robert Millet, *A Different Jesus? The Christ of the Latter-day Saints* (Grand Rapids, Mich.: Eerdmans, 2005); Richard Lyman Bushman, *Joseph Smith: Rough Stone Rolling* (New York: Knopf, 2005); and Terryl L. Givens, *By the Hand of Mormon* (New York: Oxford University Press, 2002).

34. As stated by Richard Mouw in his foreword to *The New Mormon Challenge*, 12.

the fact that LDS theology has much to contribute to the Christian theological landscape.

Do Latter-day Saints Do Theology?

Another problem that has impeded theological discourse between Latter-day Saints and those of other religious faiths is that many Latter-day Saints do not think of themselves as doing theology. There are several reasons for this attitude. For example, theology is taught at schools of divinity and studied by professional clergy, while Latter-day Saints have a lay ministry.

If by "theology," however, one means "thinking and talking about God," then Latter-day Saints obviously do pursue theology. They explore the implications of their faith and give reasons for the hope that is in them. What Latter-day Saints want to avoid is not theology in this sense but the problems of doing theology badly or improperly, and thus many of them would add that theology is a dangerous enterprise that must be handled with great caution.

At least five arguments against theology are commonly heard among Latter-day Saints. First, Latter-day Saints believe that God will yet reveal many things pertaining to his kingdom (Article of Faith 9), and since a systematic theology might close one to the possibility of further revelation being received, systematic theology should be eschewed. Hugh Nibley and others have argued that theology corrupted and ossified the early Christian church and that it would corrupt the modern one, too. "It is thus abundantly clear that the whole philosophical theological enterprise, however well intended, is incompatible with the existence of continuing revelation." For that reason, as R. Douglas Phillips sees it, "there can never be a theology, a systematic theology as such, in the true Church."[35] Second, some Latter-day Saints point out that Mormonism focuses more on praxis than on theory or orthodoxy. Since theology is often abstract and can distract from practice, Latter-day Saints are understandably apprehensive about theology. Third, in a similar vein, Mormonism claims to be a restoration of the simple faith of early Christianity, but theology tends to complicate and create problems for that simplicity. Fourth, for Latter-day Saints, knowledge about God is not to be found at the end of a syllogism but in the visions of God received by his prophets, ancient and modern. In Joseph Smith's First Vision, the Lord was critical of creeds, which makes theology suspect to the extent that it contributed to the formulation or adoption of creeds. Fifth, Joseph Smith was also told in his First Vision that the Lord condemned contention and

---

35. R. Douglas Phillips, Foreword to *The World and the Prophets*, vol. 3 of Collected Works of Hugh Nibley (Salt Lake City: Deseret; Provo, Utah: FARMS, 1987), xii.

disputations that theology is prone to incite, a concern that is echoed by Latter-day Saint scholars.[36]

All of these are legitimate concerns, but they all can be addressed as cautions rather than as absolute barriers. Some of this hesitancy is openly articulated by the Latter-day Saint contributors to this book, all of whom acknowledge that theology has its risks and thus has its limits. We hope that an awareness of these concerns will help theologians and others as they dialogue with Latter-day Saints.

Indeed, Mormonism brings a flood of fresh ideas to the table on many topics, including divine authority, ecclesiology, Christology, soteriology, the nature of the Godhead, salvation for the unevangelized, divine process, the divine feminine, and deification. As illustrated by the sustained conversations in this volume, Mormon thought is laden with ideas relevant to each of the varied expressions of Christian theology represented in this book. And, reciprocally, each of these theologies can illuminate aspects of LDS thought.

A Model for Fruitful Exchange

Interfacing with each other's ideas promises to be very beneficial not only for bridge building, but also for helping Latter-day Saints and other Christians clarify and refine their respective theological formulations. One such example of clarification and refining occurs in "A Dialogue on Philosophy," which focuses upon the interaction between reason and revelation (Tracy, 451–64). In this dialogue, David Tracy attempts an "inner-Catholic clarification" of the relationship between philosophy and theology in hopes that it may encourage a similar articulation in Mormon thought. In their responses, James Siebach, James Faulconer, and Benjamin Huff disclose the diversity of LDS perspectives on the issues Tracy poses, in the process laying the ground for continuing dialogue not only with other Christians but within their own community.

As a volume that pleads for a volume two, this book contains some first-time interactions. For example, an important first interaction comes between Dennis P. McCann and Richard Sherlock concerning the public theology of one of the twentieth century's most influential theologians—Reinhold Niebuhr. Just note what McCann has to say regarding the new and unique LDS contribution to this field: "Those who still find merit in Niebuhr's Christian realism, as I do, are in Sherlock's debt; for coming to a better understanding of the LDS interpretation of 'prophetic Christianity'

---

36. See James E. Faulconer, "Scripture as Incarnation," in *Historicity and the LDS Scriptures*, ed. Paul Y. Hoskisson, (Provo, Utah: Religious Studies Center, Brigham Young University, 2001), 17–61.

may help us to see more clearly what precisely it means for public theology to be practical" (McCann, 115).

Another, perhaps even more original, example, "A Dialogue on Myth Theology" exhibits all of the elements of a first interaction between two religious traditions: misunderstandings, clarifications, and proposals for a continuation of the dialogue. One especially interesting exchange deals with the ultimate dimension of one's existence. In his essay, Gary Dorrien explains Langdon Gilkey's proposal that the ultimate dimension of one's existence is not secularism's interpretation of human life "as though it should be understood solely in terms of biology, chemistry, social environment, and other measurable finite forces" but "the dimension of ultimacy," wherein the individual "faces mortality and embraces its relative meanings" (Dorrien, 393). According to Dorrien, "It is the reality of this dimension of human life that makes religious language meaningful and necessary" (Dorrien, 394). In Kent Robson's response, this LDS thinker expresses appreciation for Gilkey's insights into the ultimate dimension of human existence but suggests that LDS doctrine moves "a step beyond Gilkey in that it assigns the origin of this dimension of ultimacy" (Robson, 415).

This pattern of appreciation and suggestion of ideas from the LDS respondents is repeated throughout the volume. For example, in "A Dialogue on the Theology of Karl Barth," Roger Keller highlights the role of Joseph Smith's First Vision as the foundational revelatory precedent upon which the basic LDS understanding of God and Trinity are grounded (Keller, 39). As Keller notes, the LDS understanding of the Trinity diverges from the "more classical understanding of the Godhead in favor of what theologians call the social Trinitarian model" (Keller, 39). Historically, mainstream Christian theologians have disparaged LDS thought concerning the Trinity or simply ignored it. But now, with the relatively recent emergence or reemergence of the social Trinitarian model, Christians are exploring within their own tradition ideas with significant Mormon parallels. In cases like this, LDS and conventional Christian dialogic interactions may be especially beneficial to both parties. Indeed, this volume contains numerous examples of the mutual benefit that occurs when religious traditions interface in a respectful and open manner.

One such example is the dialogue between process and LDS theologies. In this dialogue, Jim McLachlan points out that one point of departure between LDS theology and process theology is the doctrine of the fate of the soul after death. Whitehead and Hartshorne (the originators of process theology) believe that the soul has "objective immortality" after death, meaning that the soul continues to exist merely as a memory in God's mind. Latter-day Saints reject this notion in favor of a doctrine of personal immortality. Indeed, as McLachlan points out, modern revelation affirms not only that individuals continue to exist after death, but as "intelligences" are uncreated, self-existent, and co-eternal with God. David Ray Griffin hastens to explain that the Whitehead-Hartshorne notion of immortality is not a "core doctrine" and can therefore be discarded without compromising the fundamental doctrines of process theology. Given this possibility, McLachlan suggests that process theologians seriously consider the LDS doctrine of the eternal nature of the human soul. It would fit well with their denial of creation ex nihilo, their belief in the radical freedom of the human soul, and their idea that there are ontological limits and conditions on God's power.

Griffin himself acknowledges that LDS theology has contributions to make that could benefit theology broadly, as well as process theology specifically. One point of LDS doctrine that he believes has great potential for contributing to theology is our emphasis on the perpetuation of sociality and loving relationships beyond the grave. He says, "I agree that process theology's attempt to account for our sense that life is ultimately meaningful could be enriched by considering the importance of our mutual love in a life that continues far beyond this present one" (Griffin, 205). Another doctrine that he considers potentially beneficial, though not without reservations, is the LDS doctrine of deification, or as Latter-day Saints typically refer to it, exaltation. He says in reference to this doctrine, "It would be . . . a good term to describe the process through which God creates and saves us, in that God becomes incarnate in each moment of experience in such a way that the divine forms that are possibilities for our existence enter into us, literally transforming us" (Griffin, 206).

Reciprocally, McLachlan acknowledges that process theology can make contributions to LDS theology as well. He says, "Latter-day Saint scholars interested in theology have already begun an interchange with process thinkers, and it is evident that process theology offers much to LDS scholars interested in explicating the theological implications of LDS teachings" (McLachlan, 201).

Another interchange that produces much by way of convergence is the dialogue on liberation theology. In this dialogue, Robert McAfee Brown and Warner Woodworth engage in an exciting discussion based on the mutually shared starting point elucidated by Brown in his rejoinder, "The world should not be the way it is" (Brown, 239). Throughout the dialogue the reader will discover that both LDS and liberation theologies accept this statement as significant in their doctrine and practice. The ensuing dialogue explores how each tradition has historically gone about responding to this shared outlook on the present world. The convergence between the two theologies is striking, as is the opportunity for cooperation which this dialogue hopes to engender.

On the other hand, there are some dialogues that produce much by the way of divergence. For example, while LDS writer Camille S. Williams and feminist theologian Rosemary Radford Ruether each focus on the relationship between God and human beings, they differ sharply in their respective analyses of that relationship. Williams's assertion that "For Latter-day Saints, the maleness of god the Father and Christ the Son is part of their eternal identity, not the outgrowth of misogynist . . . imagery" (Williams, 279) is a view characterized by Ruether as unique not only to her as a feminist theologian—calling it a kind of "idolatry"—but also to the view of the mainstream Christian tradition (Ruether, 299). Ruether's "re-envisioning of God," as "the divine matrix of being and new being," (Ruether, 275) is seen by Williams as a species of Gnosticism that undercuts her efforts "to correct the authoritarian, antimaterial concept of God's transcendence with incarnational and interactive views of divine-world relations" (Ruether, 271). Ruether's poetic conclusion that "God cannot redeem the world apart from our free and loving response to God, which is, simultaneously, a choice to love and support one another" (Ruether, 275) would not contradict Mormon doctrine, and provides one intriguing example of why these conversations between ostensibly different theological positions also reveal deep similarities.

Perhaps one of the greatest contributions that LDS theology offers to all schools of thought is its vast resource of other scriptures. The rich content of this expanded canon of specifically LDS scripture remains one of the best kept secrets within the larger Christian theological world. Few Christian scholars have been willing to seriously examine any sacred writings which purport to be canonically on par with the Bible. Consequently, Book of Mormon scholarship has largely been written by Mormons for Mormons. In the twentieth century, the question of "canonicity" has grown more complex. The Bible's role as the sole depository of sacred writ is being more closely and critically examined than ever before. Perhaps this trend will lead more Christian scholars to look more closely at LDS-specific scripture. Indeed, as a result of the dialogues in this collection, the non-LDS contributors found themselves more widely exposed to LDS scripture with promising results. In his rejoinder to the late LDS scholar Eugene England, Dwight Hopkins points out how LDS scripture is especially parallel and pertinent to black theology: "I was also struck by the occurrence of liberation themes in LDS tradition, especially when Eugene England cites the unique LDS testaments. And it is in the revelations and words found in such books as Moses and Nephi that we encounter texts that could be lifted directly from some of the standard black theology essays from 1996 to the present" (Hopkins, 383). I think it is reasonable for me to say that most LDS scholars would delight in the fact that a distinguished theologian of another faith does not immediately dismiss LDS scripture, but instead cites it to strengthen his argument. Other non-LDS scholars would do us an honor by following Hopkins's example. In doing so, they, like Hopkins, could find something of benefit to their respective fields. What is more promising, however, is that we as Latter-day Saints could benefit greatly from "outsider" perspectives on our own scripture.

In this volume, one will find sincere and thoughtful discussions on a variety of theological issues across a wide spectrum of theological viewpoints. Like other recent works of its kind, it does not seek to be the final word on any of the issues covered, but to continue a fruitful dialogue. Opinions expressed in this book are solely the opinions of contributors. Their views should not necessarily be attributed to The Church of Jesus Christ of Latter-day Saints, Brigham Young University, Mercer University Press, or any others.

In doing so, this book uses a format that might be used in future, continuing dialogue. First, both sides are given a voice in their own words. In this book, our Protestant and Catholic scholars launch each discussion by introducing the main ideas of an important twentieth-century theologian or theology. Latter-day Saint respondents then seek to point out areas of convergence or divergence. In future dialogues, this order might be reversed. For better or worse, any opening statement tends to define the scope, set the tone, and shape the contours of the ensuing discussion. Careful speaking and attentive listening on both sides, however, can overcome this problem, as we believe has been the case in this book.

Secondly, the given topics are focused enough to allow for meaningful, in-depth discussion. Conversations are more satisfying when they have a center of gravity. This is not to say that each of the dialogue sequences in this book begins or ends at the best of all possible places. Liberal and evangelical theologians have something of an advantage over Latter-day Saint thinkers in that traditional Christianity has a longer record of specialized analysis. Mormonism is still a young religion by world standards. With this in mind, the willingness of the theologians in this book to come to Brigham Young University and to try to relate their thinking to the doctrines and religious practices of Latter-day Saints made this book uniquely possible. On subsequent occasions, different topics might be taken by LDS thinkers into other Christian forums that will there host equally focused and fruitful exchanges.

Thirdly, this book contains responses, rejoinders to those responses, and often replies to the rejoinders, thus offering ample room for authentic give and take. The point is not to give one or the other the final word. The format is to encourage sincere inquiry and interest in each other. Whether readers will always be able to sense this or not, in many cases genuine friendships have come out of these pairings.

As Donald Musser points out above, four streams (perhaps a subliminal allusion to Eden) have fed Christian theology for many centuries: tradition, scripture, experience, and reason. Particular theologies have tended to emphasize one or another, or perhaps to seek a middle ground between two of these streams. Mormonism has much to say about all four of these sources, with a strong impulse to adjust or add to the course and flow of these streams. Mormonism seeks to optimize the fullness of all four of these currents and perhaps uncover even more streams of the waters of life flowing from the fountain of righteousness.

It is past time for Mormon thinkers to be among the players on the Christian theological stage. This book hopes to firmly place them there.

A Dialogue on the Theology of Karl Barth

The Theology of Karl Barth

Donald K. McKim

Karl Barth (1886–1968) was one of the giants of twentieth-century Christian theology.[1] His thought was forged in the wake of World War I and was highly influential in post–World War II Europe and then in America. His numerous writings made him one of the most prolific theologians in Christian history. His basic view that "theology means rational wrestling with mystery" led to a dogmatics that was always developing, never a "caged bird" but always a "bird in flight."[2] Barth spoke of the need for each theological topic to "begin again at the beginning."[3] Thus he wrestled afresh with traditional Christian doctrine, recognizing the fallible nature of all theological formulations and seeking to provide a faithful "ongoing response to divine mystery."[4]

Context

Barth was born in Basel, Switzerland, and was the first son of Fritz Barth, a minister in the Swiss Reformed Church and later a professor of New Testament and church history. Karl attended the universities of Bern, Berlin, Tübingen, and Marburg where he studied under leading liberal theologians such as Wilhelm Herrmann (1846–1922) and Adolf von Harnack (1851–1930).

---

1. As a small indication of Barth's influence, see Donald K. McKim, ed., *How Karl Barth Changed My Mind* (Grand Rapids: Eerdmans, 1986) in which contemporary theologians reflect on their relationship to Barth's thought a century after his birth.

2. Karl Barth, *The Doctrine of the Word of God,* part 1, ed. G. W. Bromiley and T. F. Torrance, trans. G. W. Bromiley, *Church Dogmatics,* I/1, 2d ed. (Edinburgh: T. and T. Clark, 1975), 368 (*Church Dogmatics* hereafter cited as *CD*); Karl Barth, *Evangelical Theology: An Introduction,* trans. Grover Foley (London: Collins, 1963), 15.

3. William Stacy Johnson, *The Mystery of God: Karl Barth and the Postmodern Foundations of Theology* (Louisville: Westminster John Knox, 1997), 1–3.

4. Johnson, *Mystery of God,* 5.

Barth was ordained and, in 1911, became pastor in Safinwil, a village in north-central Switzerland.

A major shock for Barth occurred in August 1914 when he discovered that many of his former theological professors were supporting the war policy of Kaiser William II. Upon that discovery, Barth responded, "a whole world of exegesis, ethics, dogmatics and preaching which I had hitherto held to be essentially trustworthy, was shaken to the foundations, and with it, all the other writings of the German theologians."[5]

Barth embarked on a life-long attempt to set theology on a new footing from that of his professors and their mentors, particularly Friedrich Schleiermacher (1768–1834) and Albrecht Ritschl (1822–89). Barth turned to the Bible and found within it a "strange new world." He wrote:

> It is not the right human thoughts about God which form the content of the Bible, but the right divine thoughts about men. The Bible tells us not how we should talk with God but what he says to us; not how we find the way to him, but how he has sought and found the way to us; not the right relation in which we must place ourselves to him, but the covenant which he has made with all who are Abraham's spiritual children and which he has sealed once and for all in Jesus Christ. It is this which is within the Bible. The word of God is within the Bible.[6]

The first results of Barth's newfound interest in the Bible, over against the ethics-oriented approaches of his teachers, were in his commentary on Paul's letter to the Romans *(Der Römerbrief)*, published in 1919. Here Barth sought a theological exegesis in which he wished "to see through and beyond history into the spirit of the Bible, which is the Eternal Spirit."[7]

Also influenced by the thought of Kierkegaard, Barth began to stress the transcendence and majesty of God. The God of the Bible is a God who is "wholly Other" from humans, the "hidden One" who is made known only by the divine revelation in Jesus Christ. The world is in a "crisis" situation because in Jesus Christ, God has entered human history as both grace and judgment.[8]

---

5. Eberhard Busch, *Karl Barth: His Life from Letters and Autobiographical Texts*, trans. John Bowden (Philadelphia: Fortress, 1976), 81.

6. Karl Barth, "The Strange New World within the Bible," chap. 2 in *The Word of God and the Word of Man*, trans. Douglas Horton (New York: Harper and Row, 1957), 43.

7. Karl Barth, *The Epistle to the Romans*, trans. Edwin C. Hoskyns, 6th ed. (London: Oxford University Press, 1933), 1.

8. Thus Barth's theology at this point was called "crisis" or "dialectical" theology, stressing the absolute contrast between God and humanity instead of their essential continuity as found in the ideas of nineteenth-century theologians.

Barth's subsequent appointments as a professor of theology at Göttingen (1921), Münster (1925), Bonn (1930), and Basel (1935) led him to develop further his "theology of the Word" as he immersed himself in the study of the sixteenth-century Protestant Reformers, especially Luther, Calvin, and Zwingli. In addition, his study of the theologian Anselm of Canterbury led him to adopt the Anselmic method: Faith seeking understanding (Lat. *Fides quaerens intellectum* or *Credo ut intelligam*, "I believe in order to understand").[9] Sequentially, God's revelation is given, faith occurs, and that faith propels one to seek further understanding. Christian theology is the quest for understanding. Theology does not create faith; faith begins with the Word of God and perceives the reality behind the words of the scriptures.[10] That reality is God's revelation in Jesus Christ. Christian theology is carried out within the circle of faith that acknowledges God's revelation and actions.

Barth's major theological project for his last thirty-five years of life was his *Church Dogmatics*. He worked from the concept of the "analogy of faith" in which he recognized that humans may speak of God in faith on the basis of God's grace in allowing human knowledge to conform to its divine object through revelation.[11] His work ran to thirteen books published between 1932 and 1967. They were divided into four volumes: "The Doctrine of the Word of God" (2 parts), "The Doctrine of God" (2 parts), "The Doctrine of Creation" (4 parts), and "The Doctrine of Reconciliation" (4 parts in 5 books). A fifth volume on redemption was contemplated but never written.

Church Dogmatics I: "The Doctrine of the Word of God"

Barth begins his *Church Dogmatics* with two volumes of prolegomena entitled "The Doctrine of the Word of God." For him, "Word of God" refers to God's self-revelation.[12] This revelation is found supremely in Jesus Christ. Barth writes succinctly, "Revelation in fact does not differ from the person of Jesus Christ nor from the reconciliation accomplished in Him. To say revelation is to say 'The Word became flesh.'"[13] In other words, "God's Word means that God speaks."[14]

Barth emphasizes that the Word of God comes in a threefold form. The Word is revealed (Jesus Christ), written (scripture), and proclaimed

9. See Karl Barth, *Anselm: Fides quaerens intellectum: Anselm's Proof of the Existence of God in the Context of His Theological Scheme*, trans. Ian W. Robertson (Pittsburgh: Pickwick, 1975).

10. See John 1:1–3.

11. See Bruce L. McCormack, *Karl Barth's Critically Realistic Dialectical Theology: Its Genesis and Development, 1909–1936* (Oxford: Clarendon, 1995).

12. Barth, *Doctrine of the Word of God*, CD, I/1, 295; 117–20.

13. Ibid., 119; see also 137, 157.

14. Ibid., 132; see also 136, 141, 150.

(preaching).[15] These forms are mutually interrelated and cannot be severed from each other. They do not constitute three "different" Words of God. Ultimately, there is one Word of God (Jesus Christ) that is encountered in this threefold way.[16]

Scripture becomes the Word of God in Barth's thought in that it witnesses to the revealed Word, Jesus Christ.[17] For Barth, "The Bible is God's Word to the extent that God causes it to be His Word, to the extent that He speaks through it."[18] The scriptures are the "witness" to God's revelation of Christ, the only source of our knowledge of Jesus. The Bible points beyond itself to Jesus Christ as the Word of God; however, Barth does not directly equate the Bible with God's revelation. Rather, "Scripture is holy and the Word of God, because by the Holy Spirit it became and will become to the Church a witness to divine revelation."[19] The canonical scriptures, as accepted by the universal church, are the authoritative sources of the knowledge of Jesus Christ. The written Word directs its readers to the revealed and living Word, Jesus Christ.

Barth's emphasis here also distinguishes the Christian revelation in Jesus Christ from all other revelations. Barth strongly rejects any forms of "natural theology" or any approach which seeks to know the true God by means of a "general" or a "natural" revelation.[20] No concept external to God's revelation in Jesus Christ can determine God's revelation or self-manifestation. The uniqueness of the biblical revelation that begins with the actuality of the incarnate Word is paramount for Barth. As Barth often puts it, "Through God alone may God be known."

This position also highlights another of Barth's emphases: God's freedom. Humans cannot prescribe to God what God should do or how God should do it. Humans cannot coerce God's revelation or dictate the form it should take. Barth believed theology since the time of Schleiermacher had become "anthropological theology" with humans as the main focus instead of God. Barth's emphasis on the "Godness of God" countered

---

15. Ibid., 88–124.

16. Ibid., 120–21.

17. On Barth's views, see Jack B. Rogers and Donald K. McKim, *The Authority and Interpretation of the Bible: An Historical Approach* (San Francisco: Harper and Row, 1979), 406–26; and Donald K. McKim, "Neo-Orthodox Theology: Scripture as Witness," chap. 6 in *The Bible in Theology and Preaching* (Nashville: Abingdon, 1994).

18. Barth, *Doctrine of the Word of God, CD*, I/1, 109.

19. Karl Barth, *The Doctrine of the Word of God*, ed. G. W. Bromiley and T. F. Torrance, trans. G. T. Thomson and Harold Knight, *CD*, I/2 (New York: Charles Scribner's Sons, 1956), 457.

20. This was illustrated most strongly in Barth's famous exchange on natural theology with Emil Brunner. See *Natural Theology*, trans., Peter Fraenkel (London: Geoffrey Bles: Centenary, 1946).

Schleiermacher's theology, giving humans no standing or status before the transcendent Lord from which to insist upon or to judge God's revelation. For Barth, "Divine determination and revelation, and not man's approval, are the criterion of what is appropriate to God and salutary for us."[21]

Barth further develops his doctrine of revelation in relation to the doctrine of the Trinity. The Trinity becomes the key for understanding God and the divine revelation. God is "Revealer, Revelation, and Revealedness."[22] The God who reveals is the Father of Jesus Christ, Jesus Christ himself, and the Spirit of the Father and Son. Barth does not begin with a general doctrine of God or a "natural theology" of an abstract philosophical viewpoint. He will not admit to any analogies for the Trinity in nature, culture, history, or human existence. Instead, he firmly contends that "the doctrine of the Trinity is what basically distinguishes the Christian doctrine of God as Christian, and therefore what already distinguishes the Christian concept of revelation as Christian, in contrast to all other possible doctrines of God and concepts of revelation."[23]

In agreement with the early church, Barth stresses that there is no subordinationism in the doctrine of the Trinity. Neither the Son nor the Spirit is subordinate to the Father. Barth also rejects modalism, the view that the Son and Spirit are only "temporary roles" assumed by God. Instead, Barth argues that God is one in God's essential substance (essence), being, or nature. He rejects tritheism, the view that there are three Gods. He goes on to assert, with the early church, that "the God who reveals Himself according to Scripture is One in three distinctive modes of being subsisting in their mutual relations: Father, Son, and Holy Spirit."[24] There is a triunity or "threeness" which is essential to God's nature as God. Thus, there is a "oneness in threeness" and a "threeness in oneness" for Barth, which leads him to speak of a "Three-in-Oneness" in God.[25] Yet God's full and undivided essence is found equally in each of the three modes of God's being. This is the "mutual indwelling" or "mutual interpenetration" of the three modes of God's being. In this, Barth is affirming that God is equally and fully present in each of the three modes of being.

Parts 2 and 3 of Barth's doctrine of revelation concern the incarnation of the Word and the outpouring of the Holy Spirit, respectively. Barth's approach is to deal with the concrete reality of God's revelation in Jesus Christ rather than with general questions such as "Is revelation possible?" or "Is there a God?" These questions, Barth claims, are anthropological rather

---

21. Barth, *Doctrine of the Word of God, CD*, I/2, 5.
22. Barth, *Doctrine of the Word of God, CD*, I/1, 295.
23. Ibid., 301.
24. Ibid., 348.
25. Ibid., 368–75.

than Christological starting points. Christology is where theology must begin for Barth, because it is in Jesus Christ that God's revelation is known. For Barth, "According to Holy Scripture God's revelation takes place in the fact that God's Word became a man and that this man has become God's Word. The incarnation of the eternal Word, Jesus Christ, is God's revelation. In the reality of this event God proves that He is free to be our God."[26] The concrete reality of Jesus Christ is the concrete reality of God's revelation: "The Word or Son of God became a Man and was called Jesus of Nazareth; therefore this Man Jesus of Nazareth was God's Word or God's Son."[27]

Barth argues that theology must begin with the person of Jesus and not with a preconception of God or of the nature of the incarnation. It is Jesus Christ and he alone who determines what incarnation means. Barth stands against both Docetism, which does not take the reality of Jesus' humanity seriously, and Ebionitism (for him, a fault of nineteenth-century liberal theology), which does not take Jesus' divinity seriously enough and views it as simply the highest expression of human nature. Either of these two heretical tendencies would deny God's true revelation in Jesus Christ who is "very God and very man."[28] The key biblical text for Barth is John 1:14: "The Word became flesh." This means that in Jesus of Nazareth, humanity is confronted by the Son of God (John 1:14; see also Heb. 1:2; Rev. 19:13).

God is present and free for humanity in Jesus Christ. God in his entire divinity became man.[29] Yet, at the same time, God did not cease to be God, for "by becoming flesh the Word is no less true and entire God than He was previously in eternity in Himself."[30] The incarnation is God's free choice. God was not coerced, nor was there any latent capacity within humans themselves that could call forth God's revelation. In Jesus, humans see what it means to be truly human. In him, the divine and human are united in one person. All of this is a divine mystery, says Barth:

> The mystery of the revelation of God in Jesus Christ consists in the fact that the eternal Word of God chose, sanctified and assumed human nature and existence into oneness with Himself, in order thus, as very God and very man, to become the Word of reconciliation spoken by God to man.[31]

This is the "miracle of Christmas" for Barth, who strongly defends the doctrine of the virgin birth of Jesus. For Barth, the virgin birth is a sign that

---

26. Barth, *Doctrine of the Word of God, CD*, I/2, 1.
27. Ibid., 13.
28. Ibid., 132; see also 132–71.
29. Ibid., 159.
30. Ibid., 38.
31. Ibid., 122.

God "justifies and sanctifies human nature in spite of its unrighteousness and unholiness to be a temple for His Word."[32]

Barth's treatment of the outpouring of the Holy Spirit emphasizes the Holy Spirit as the one who enables the subjective appropriation of Jesus Christ through faith. God's objective revelation in Jesus Christ becomes real by the work of the Spirit.

> The subjective reality of revelation consists in the fact that we have our being through Christ and in the Church, that we are the recipients of the divine testimonies, and, as the real recipients of them, the children of God. But the fact that we have this being is the work of the Holy Spirit. Therefore the Holy Spirit is the subjective reality of revelation.[33]

God's revelation meets humans in freedom by means of the outpouring of the Spirit, in which the Word of God is brought into human hearing. Humans have no possibility of meeting God on their own; they meet God in Jesus Christ solely through the Spirit. In this encounter, the Word of God becomes one's Master as one responds in faith such that "the knowledge of God occurs in the fulfillment of the revelation of His Word by the Holy Spirit, and therefore in the reality and with the necessity of faith and its obedience."[34] Faith is not assent to logical or divine propositions, but rather the acknowledgment of "the One whom the Bible attests and the Church as taught by the Bible proclaims, the living Jesus Christ Himself, none other."[35] Faith is the gift of the Holy Spirit.

Church Dogmatics II: "The Doctrine of God"

Barth's doctrine of God focuses on his thesis that God is "the one who loves in freedom."[36] God is interpreted through God's revelation in that through Jesus Christ, God establishes a "fellowship" between humanity and God as an act of divine love.[37] The doctrine of God is developed in relation to the divine perfections. These reflect the richness of God's being and do not contradict the essential oneness of God or the unity of the Godhead.

The perfections of the "divine loving" are seen by Barth as God's grace and holiness, mercy and righteousness, and patience and wisdom. In each

---

32. Ibid., 201.

33. Ibid., 242.

34. Karl Barth, *The Doctrine of God,* part 1, ed. G. W. Bromiley and T. F. Torrance, trans. T. H. L. Parker and others, *CD,* II/1 (New York: Charles Scribner's Sons, 1957), 3.

35. Karl Barth, *The Doctrine of Reconciliation,* ed. G. W. Bromiley and T. F. Torrance, trans. G. W. Bromiley, *CD,* IV/1 (Edinburgh: T. and T. Clark, 1956), 760.

36. Barth, *Doctrine of God, CD,* II/1, 257–321.

37. Ibid., 273.

of these pairings, the second member emphasizes the God, the one who is free, who loves. The divine freedom is developed in God's perfections of unity and omnipresence, constancy and omnipotence, and eternity and glory. In these, the first member accents God's freedom while the second indicates the way in which God is free. Ultimately, God's freedom "is the freedom of His love."[38] This love is expressed most fully in Jesus Christ, who himself determines every Christian affirmation about God's being and action. Jesus Christ "emerged as the perfect One, the fullness of the love and freedom of God Himself, the love and freedom of God in which all the divine perfections are neither more nor less than God Himself."[39]

Perhaps Barth's most intense Christological focus is in his development of the doctrine of election.[40] Barth calls this doctrine

> the sum of the Gospel because of all words that can be said or heard it is the best: that God elects man; that God is for man too the One who loves in freedom. It is grounded in the knowledge of Jesus Christ because He is both the electing God and elected man in One. It is part of the doctrine of God because originally God's election of man is a predestination not merely of man but of Himself. Its function is to bear basic testimony to eternal, free and unchanging grace as the beginning of all the ways and works of God.[41]

Barth's treatment of election is a unique approach.[42] He does not balance "election" and "reprobation" as equal divine decrees in the way developed by post-Reformation scholastic theologians in the seventeenth century. Barth believed he had discovered a more biblical approach to election than had earlier theologians such as Augustine and Calvin, who had developed a "double predestination" of election to salvation and reprobation to damnation.

For Barth, Jesus Christ is both electing God and the elected human being.[43] This means, says Barth, that God's decision in "primal history" was

---

38. Ibid., 441.

39. Karl Barth, *The Doctrine of God*, ed. G. W. Bromiley and T. F. Torrance, trans. G. W. Bromiley and others, *CD*, II/2 (New York: Charles Scribner's Sons, 1957), 5.

40. Barth, *Doctrine of God, CD*, II/2.

41. Ibid., 3.

42. Barth wrote on the issue of divine election: "As I let the Bible itself speak to me . . . I was driven irresistibly to reconstruction." Barth, Doctrine of God, pt. 2, x. As Johnson notes: "This reconstruction is summed up in the affirmation that, in Jesus Christ by the Spirit's power, God is fundamentally 'for' human beings. The divine 'for' is comprehensive in its scope. Everyone is elected to be reconciled with God in Jesus Christ, although whether everyone will fully realize her or his election is another matter." Johnson, *Mystery of God*, 59.

43. Barth, *Doctrine of God, CD*, II/2, 58.

to be "for" humanity in Jesus Christ. This forms the basis for Barth's later development of the covenant and God's covenant history. Jesus Christ is the election of God in God's inner being and outward expression.[44] God's election in grace is in Jesus Christ as the one in whom God wills to be gracious.

Jesus Christ is both the subject and the object of God's election. Jesus Christ as the Son of God is the subject of election. It is in him that God carries out the divine decision to be gracious. Jesus Christ as the Son of Man is the object of God's election. He is the one in whom all others are elected. This means, for Barth, that God in all God's ways is gracious. The election of Jesus Christ is an act of God's sheer grace as Jesus in his death becomes the representative substitute for sinful humanity. Human faith is the actualization of the divine election on behalf of humans.

If Jesus Christ is known as the subject and object of election, says Barth, then in him we know the eternal will of God. Election is not an "inscrutable decree" of an "unknown God" and an "unknown object." Rather, we concretely know of God's eternal will in Jesus Christ, who is God's decree of election. In Jesus Christ, God wills to become a covenant partner with humans. In his suffering and rejection, Jesus assumed the suffering of humans, taking upon himself what they ought to have suffered because of their sin. "Double predestination" for Barth would refer not to decrees of election and reprobation, but to God electing God's self for rejection and humans for election in Jesus Christ.

God's election in Christ takes shape in human history through the election of a community and through the election of individuals.[45] For Barth, the one community whom God has elected takes two forms: Israel and the church. The community, as the people of God, are to witness to Jesus Christ in the world and to "summon the whole world to faith in Him."[46] Israel, in its rejection of Jesus as the Messiah, represents the rejection dimension of election. The church, as the positive aspect of election, witnesses God's mercy, love, and grace seen most clearly in Jesus' resurrection from the dead.

Individual election takes shape only in light of the election of Jesus Christ and of the community. There is no election of individuals due to their merit or goodness. The work of the Holy Spirit is the basis for election. The elect person is one who has acknowledged, through faith, Jesus Christ as God's Word. The elect person participates in the ministry of the church in witnessing to the gospel—the good news of God's gracious love for the

---

44. See John 1:1.

45. Barth, *Doctrine of God, CD,* II/2, 195–449.

46. David L. Mueller, *Karl Barth, Makers of the Modern Theological Mind,* ed. Bob E. Patterson (Waco, Texas: Word, 1972), 107. Mueller's work has been helpful in highlighting important emphases in Barth's Church Dogmatics throughout this exposition.

world in Jesus Christ. There can be no outward determination of who are the "elect" either by the church or by individual believers.

Barth's view of election leads him to what has been described as the "brink of universalism."[47] In an important passage, Barth writes:

> The man who is isolated over against God is as such rejected by God. But to be this man can only be the godless man's own choice. The witness of the community of God to every individual man consists in this: that this choice of the godless man is void; that he belongs eternally to Jesus Christ and therefore is not rejected, but elected by God in Jesus Christ; that the rejection which he deserves on account of his perverse choice is borne and canceled by Jesus Christ; and that he is appointed to eternal life with God on the basis of the righteous, divine decision. The promise of his election determines that as a member of the community he himself shall be a bearer of its witness to the whole world. And the revelation of his rejection can only determine him to believe in Jesus Christ as the One by whom it has been borne and canceled.[48]

Yet, Barth rejects universalism in principle on the basis that humans cannot determine the breadth and scope of God's election. To insist on a "universalism" is to bind God to adhere to a principle, yet God is the one who loves in freedom. At the same time, one cannot rule out "in principle" the possibility that all will indeed be saved. The decision and action is God's—not ours. In the meantime, the mandate for the Christian church is clear: proclaim the gospel of Jesus Christ in the hope that God will extend the circle of the elect. Some do live as though they are rejected by God and do not believe in their salvation in Jesus Christ. Since Jesus Christ has borne the rejection for all, these are people who live a lie. They do not live as God desires. The message of the church to them is that on the basis of God's gracious love, they are elect in Christ.

Church Dogmatics III: "The Doctrine of Creation"

Barth's Christological approach to dogmatics continues in volume three of *Church Dogmatics* in which he deals with the doctrine of creation. This third volume features four parts: "The Work of Creation" (pt. 1), "The Creature" (pt. 2), "The Creator and His Creature" (pt. 3), and "The Command of God the Creator" (pt. 4). In these expositions, Barth opposes establishing a doctrine of creation from a universal, general revelation, natural theology standpoint or on the basis of philosophical or scientific speculation. Instead,

---

47. "In election God utters a 'yes' to humanity—all human beings are elect in Jesus Christ, even though not all human beings happen to live out their election." Johnson, *Mystery of God*, 61.

48. Barth, *Doctrine of God, CD*, II/2, 306.

he focuses on Jesus Christ: for "it is here [in Jesus Christ] that God Himself has revealed the relationship between Creator and creature—its basis, norm and meaning."[49]

In Barth's view, God's act of creation begins the series of divine works which have been, from eternity, oriented toward carrying out the divine, saving purpose. Jesus Christ as the eternal Word of God, being one with God the Father, also shares in the act of creation. Barth argues that creation is the external basis of God's covenant of grace with humanity and that this covenant of grace is the internal basis of creation.[50] In a real sense, "creation sets the stage for the story of the covenant of grace" for it is through creation that God wills to institute, preserve, and carry out the covenant of grace with humanity (See Gen. 1:1–2:4a). In his exegesis of the first creation story in Genesis, Barth (with Calvin) emphasizes the created world as the "theater of God's glory" where the divine intentions are carried out (See Gen. 2:4b).

Relatedly, for Barth, the covenant as the internal basis of creation is established through his interpretation of the second creation story in which he argues that the covenant of grace is the presupposition of creation and actually precedes creation in terms of God's eternal purpose.[51] This thesis leads to Barth's emphasis that the history of salvation is the world's "true history" and that salvation history is determinative of all other history: "The covenant of grace is *the* theme of history. The history of salvation is *the* history."[52] In short, God has spoken a divine "yes" to humanity. The creation and the creature are created "good" and are considered so by God as they live within history and as they are justified and reconciled to God in Jesus Christ. In Jesus Christ, humanity has received a covenant-partner as humans enter into this covenantal partnership with God. Humans may speak their "yes" to the divine "yes" by faith.

Barth's doctrine of humanity is developed in more than six hundred pages in volume 3, part 2 of *Church Dogmatics*. Again, his Christological emphasis is present, as was anticipated years before when Barth wrote that "there is a way from Christology to anthropology, but there is no way from anthropology to Christology."[53] So Barth rejected beginning anthropological understandings with non-theological approaches, such as in human self-understanding. Instead, he insists that a knowledge of humanity as

---

49. Karl Barth, *The Doctrine of Creation,* ed. G. W. Bromiley and T. F. Torrance, trans. J. W. Edwards, O. Bussey, and Harold Knight, *CD,* III/1 (Edinburgh: T. and T. Clark, 1958), 25.

50. Ibid., 42–329.

51. Ibid., 44.

52. Ibid., 60.

53. Barth, *Doctrine of the Word of God, CD,* I/1, 131.

creatures must come from the Word of God in Jesus Christ. With Calvin, Barth emphasizes that true self-knowledge is in correlation with the knowledge of God.

Jesus Christ is "the real man," for "as the man Jesus is Himself the revealing Word of God, He is the source of our knowledge of the nature of man as created by God."[54] True humanity is found not by looking at humans as "sinners" but at Jesus Christ, the "Man for God."[55] For Barth, "the ontological determination of humanity is grounded in the fact that one man among all others is the man Jesus."[56] The true intention of God for humanity is found not in the nature of the first Adam, but in the nature of the second Adam, Jesus Christ. Jesus expressed human nature perfectly.

Barth asserts that "to be a man is to be with God," derived from looking at Jesus Christ as the one who supremely sought to do God's will in all things and who lived in unbroken relationship with God.[57] As such, Jesus manifests his divinity. He is the "God-Man" reflecting "the transcendence of God" in the "hidden form" of his humanity. Humans may be with God because they are with Jesus. Sinning is "godlessness" since it is a "mode of being contrary to our humanity."[58]

Since Jesus is the supreme Word of God, true human nature "consists in the hearing of the Word of God."[59] Jesus confronts humans with God's actualized will for human creatures. Humans, as humans, are "addressed, called and summoned by God" in Jesus Christ.[60] Human nature cannot be abstracted from the human nature found in Jesus Christ as God's Word. Indeed, humanity's "true being" is as a history, a history "grounded in the man Jesus, in which God wills to be for [humanity] and [humanity] may be for God."[61]

Humanity's proper response is gratitude. Humans must live responsibly before God and in so doing come to know God and to know themselves. Their lives are characterized by invoking God through obedience and prayer, thus gaining freedom. Sin is the renunciation of this God-given freedom, the failure to live as the good creature God intended.[62]

54. Karl Barth, *The Doctrine of Creation*, ed. G. W. Bromiley and T. F. Torrance, trans. Harold Knight et al., *CD*, III/2 (Edinburgh: T. and T. Clark, 1960), 3.

55. Ibid., 55–71.

56. Ibid., 132.

57. Ibid., 135.

58. Ibid., 136.

59. Ibid., 142.

60. Ibid., 149.

61. Ibid., 162.

62. See Barth, *Doctrine of Creation, CD*, III/2, 164–202.

Barth continues and develops these emphases in the other parts of *Church Dogmatics III*. In his treatment of humans as the "covenant-partner of God," he begins by discussing Jesus, "man for other men," and argues that the essence of the humanity of Jesus was that he was the man who lived wholly for other persons. Jesus' humanity is "to be described unequivocally as fellow-humanity."[63] Jesus lives for others as their deliverer and savior. This indicates that humans themselves are created to live in fellowship with God as God's creaturely covenant-partner.

Every "I-Thou" encounter of persons with each other reflects the truth that humans are created for community with each other. Barth's exegesis of Genesis 2:18–25 on the relationship between man and woman seeks to establish this point. Whenever persons live in an I-Thou relationship, they are living in the image of God—of which Jesus is the supreme exemplar.[64] As humans realize they are created for community, they are also reminded that God in the divine, triune being is also a communal being. Even sin cannot erase this fundamental reality for humans. All of this is known by faith. The person of Jesus determines the basic structure of humanity (ontology) as well as how humanity is known (noetically).[65]

Church Dogmatics IV: The Doctrine of Reconciliation

The work of Jesus Christ is more fully expounded by Barth in volume 4 of Church Dogmatics on the doctrine of reconciliation and developed in three major parts plus a fragment.[66] The scope of this work is made clear when Barth writes:

---

63. Barth, *Doctrine of Creation, CD*, III/2, 208. For Barth, Jesus Christ is both a human being for God (*Doctrine of Creation, CD*, III/2, 55–71) and a human being for others (*Doctrine of Creation, CD*, III/2, 203–22). "These are not two essentially different and juxtaposed aspects of Jesus' humanity but a way of viewing the singularity of his action from two perspectives." Johnson, *Mystery of God*, 81.

64. In terms of Barth's view of the *imago Dei* ("image of God"), the image is "'the act of decision for God'" and "humanity is the image of God only when it is determined to be 'for' God in response to God's being 'for' humanity.... The image is a dynamic historical relationship." Johnson, *Mystery of God*, 85–86.

65. As Johnson indicates, for Barth, "Jesus is divine precisely by virtue of his being truly human." Jesus "enacts what all human beings were created to fulfill, for all humanity is supposed to be 'for' God in just the same way as Jesus. Jesus has achieved the 'real' or 'actual' (*wirklich*) humanity that all the rest of us are meant to become. Therefore, Jesus as 'human being for God' points the way forward to the fulfillment of our own human destiny." Johnson, *Mystery of God*, 82.

66. For an analysis, see John Webster, *Barth's Ethics of Reconciliation* (Cambridge: Cambridge University Press, 1995).

The subject-matter, origin and content of the message received and pro-claimed by the Christian community is at its heart the free act of the faithfulness of God in which He takes the lost cause of man, who has denied Him as Creator and in so doing ruined himself as creature, and makes it His own in Jesus Christ, carrying it through to its goal and in that way maintaining and manifesting His own glory in the world.[67]

Humans realize God's purposes for humanity not through their own efforts or knowledge but only through God's gracious, reconciling work for sinners in Jesus Christ. The covenant broken by human sinners is restored by the work of Jesus. While the sin of humanity contradicts God's desires and purposes, it is overcome by God's grace in Jesus Christ. In him, God humbles the divine self and assumes the judgment which human sin deserves, thereby substantiating reconciliation.

Humans appropriate this reconciliation in the work of God through the Holy Spirit. The Spirit gathers and builds up the church, equipping it for its mission of witnessing to the gracious gospel of Christ—the good news of reconciliation. It is by the Spirit's witness that humans receive the gift of faith so that they accept the justification they have in Christ Jesus, acknowl-edge their sanctification and growth in grace, and by the power of the Spirit are enabled to live lives of love and service. Christians within their individ-ual vocations are enlightened by the Spirit to live in hope as they anticipate the future consummation and redemption of all things in the reign of God through Jesus Christ. Barth's Christology is crucial here as he explains the way by which the reconciliation of the world in Jesus Christ takes place.

In accord with classical Christian orthodoxy, Barth affirms Jesus Christ as "true God" and "true man." As "true God," Jesus Christ performs a priestly work in humanity's justification by humbling himself and becom-ing a servant who reconciles humanity to God.[68] As "true man," Christ is the Son of Man who is exalted by God and is thus the "reconciled man" through whom all other humans are exalted. This is Christ's work as king and brings about humanity's sanctification.[69] In his fullness, Jesus Christ is the "God-human" who, as truly God and truly human, is the mediator of humanity's reconciliation. He is "guarantor and witness" of the atonement he accomplishes. In this, Jesus Christ carries out a prophetic work through which he equips humans to live out their vocations or callings as witnesses

67. Barth, *Doctrine of Reconciliation*, CD, IV/1, 3.

68. Ibid., CD, IV/1.

69. Karl Barth, *The Doctrine of Reconciliation*, ed. G. W. Bromiley and T. F. Torrance, trans. G. W. Bromiley, CD, IV/2 (Edinburgh: T. and T. Clark, 1958).

of Christ's reconciling work.[70] This Christological focus is the key to the doctrine of reconciliation for Barth since Jesus Christ is the "beginning and the middle and the end" of the doctrine of reconciliation.[71] It is through God's grace in Jesus Christ that the reconciliation of humanity with God takes place, thus reconstituting man in authentic humanity and freedom.

This is possible, as Barth develops the doctrine, by the work of Jesus Christ, who is himself one in being and action. He is the Son of God, who in his humiliation goes into the "far country," humbles himself, and dies on behalf of humanity, performing this priestly act to procure salvation.[72] This "downward" movement is by Jesus Christ who as Lord becomes a servant. By becoming "truly human," Jesus Christ does not cease to be "truly God" while incarnate. But it is in the incarnation, the condescension of the Son of God, that the true deity of God is revealed. Thus Barth rejects all speculations about God's deity apart from God's revelation in Jesus Christ.

Salvation is accomplished by Jesus Christ as he becomes the "brother" to humanity to indicate that God desires to save humanity and become a covenant-partner with men and women. Thus *Deus pro nobis* [God for us] means simply that God has not abandoned the world and man in the unlimited need of his situation, but that He willed to bear this need as His own, that He took it upon Himself, and that He cries with man in this need."[73] Barth's view is that an "exchange" took place on the cross. In the Atonement, the sinless Judge who alone is righteous takes the sin of humanity upon himself. Jesus, who is priest, becomes the victim. In the crucifixion is rejection, suffering, and death of the innocent Son of God, whom God—in His great mercy—permitted to be judged in the place of sinful humanity. For Barth, "What took place is that the Son of God fulfilled the righteous judgment on us men by Himself taking our place as man and in our place undergoing the judgment under which we had passed."[74]

In the resurrection of Jesus Christ, which Barth calls "the Verdict of the Father," God's saving purposes found in the cross are vindicated. For Barth, the resurrection of Christ of which the New Testament speaks is "an

---

70. See Barth, *Doctrine of God, CD*, II; Barth, *Doctrine of Reconciliation, CD*, IV/1, 79; and Karl Barth, *The Doctrine of Reconciliation*, ed. G. W. Bromiley and T. F. Torrance, trans. G. W. Bromiley, *CD*, IV/3/1 (Edinburgh: T. and T. Clark, 1961).

71. Barth, *Doctrine of Reconciliation, CD*, IV/1, 125–26.

72. Barth uses the parable of the prodigal son as an illustration of the humiliation and exaltation of Jesus Christ. See charts in appendixes A and B. See also Johnson, *Mystery of God*, 104–110. Johnson writes: "Reconciliation begins with the 'downward' movement from God to humanity in which God, operating in the mode of the divine 'Son,' becomes incarnate in Jesus Christ." Johnson, *Mystery of God*, 104.

73. Barth, *Doctrine of Reconciliation, CD*, IV/1, 215.

74. Ibid., 222.

event in time and space."[75] It is God's sovereign "yes" to the judgment of the cross for the purposes of divine grace and mercy. It is God's acceptance of the "act of [Jesus'] obedience which judges the world, but judges it with the aim of saving it."[76] In the person of Jesus is "the justification of all sinful men, whose death was decided in this event, for whose life there is therefore no more place. In the resurrection of Jesus Christ His life and with it their lives have in fact become an event beyond death: 'Because I live, ye shall live also.'"[77]

In the light of Jesus Christ, humans know their sinfulness: "Only when we know Jesus Christ do we really know that man is the man of sin, and what sin is, and what it means for man."[78] Barth interprets the doctrine of sin Christologically—in light of Jesus Christ—as he moves through volume 4 parts 1, 2, and 3 of the *Church Dogmatics*. Sin is seen as pride, sloth, and falsehood overcome by justification, sanctification, and knowing the truth in Jesus Christ. These are correlated as well with the calling, building up, and missionary actions of the Christian church and with the three theological virtues of faith, love, and hope.[79]

For Barth, the story of Adam and Eve is a saga which points to the experience of every living person. "No one has to be Adam. We are so freely and on our own responsibility. Although the guilt of Adam is like ours, it is just as little our excuse as our guilt is his."[80] Barth believes in a total and radical perversion of human nature, yet also maintains that even in this sin, humans still remain God's creatures: "However we may describe the fallen being of man, we cannot say that man is fallen completely away from God, in the sense that he is lost to Him or that he has perished."[81]

Only God, in Jesus Christ, can justify humanity. God's eternal decree is to save humanity in Jesus Christ. This is the ultimate ground of human justification. Humans can be justified only through what God has done in the life, death, and resurrection of Jesus Christ, the Son of God. This is made known by the work of the Holy Spirit who gives the gift of faith and reveals to humans that they are new beings in Jesus Christ. In him, humans have

---

75. Ibid., 336 (a view counter to Rudolf Bultmann's).

76. Ibid., 309.

77. Ibid.

78. Here Barth reverses traditional Christian dogmatics which have usually dealt with sin in relation to humans as God's creatures and in relation to their disobedience to the law of God. For Barth, "The doctrine of sin belongs to the context of the doctrine of reconciliation." Barth, *Doctrine of Creation, CD*, IV/2, 34; *CD*, IV/1, 389.

79. See chart in appendix C.

80. Barth, *Doctrine of Reconciliation, CD*, IV/1, 509–10.

81. Ibid., 480.

forgiveness of sins and become the children of God in an actualized sense (the priestly role of Christ).

But Jesus Christ, who is the Lord who became a servant, is also exalted as Lord—thus effecting what God has purposed to do.[82] In the exaltation of Jesus Christ, humanity is exalted. The human nature Jesus assumed in the incarnation is redeemed and moves "upward" or homeward to God in the resurrection and ascension of Jesus, in accord with God's divine, eternal purpose (the kingly role of Christ). Jesus Christ is the "royal man," the "second Adam." In sanctification, humans are turned in a new direction, living "Godward" and responding to God in Christ through obedience and love. But human "good works" alone do not merit justification as it is a gift from God. So also in sanctification humans are led into their works by God in Jesus Christ through the power of the Holy Spirit.

The "saints" (those being sanctified) share in Christ's holiness, yet know they are not completely redeemed in this life. But they serve Christ by the power of the Spirit. Sanctification means living in responsible discipleship to Jesus Christ, as a "witness" to God's love for the entire world.

These actions of God in Christ are communicated to the world by Jesus Christ, "the true Witness."[83] In this third act of the doctrine of reconciliation, Barth affirms Jesus' prophetic role as the Truth who overcomes the sin of falsehood and is "the Light of Life." Before him, all "lesser lights" in creation (nature, events in history, human existence) which may point to him pale. It is Jesus Christ who is "the one Word of God."[84] In his prophetic office, Jesus continues to call persons to faith and to recognize the reconciliation his death and resurrection has brought to the world. Christoph Blumhardt's phrase, "Jesus is Victor!" captures the message.[85] Jesus continues to call persons from darkness into light, confronting demonic powers and liberating those held captive to them. The final triumph of God's grace in Jesus Christ is yet to come, eschatologically. However, because of who Jesus is, this future victory is secured and assured.[86]

---

82. See Barth, *Doctrine of Reconciliation, CD*, IV/2.

83. See Johnson, *Mystery of God*, 112–15.

84. This formulation is from the "Theological Declaration of Barmen," a statement written by a group of church leaders against Nazi ideals in Germany during the time of Hitler. Barth is considered to be the primary author of the Barmen declaration. For the text, see Presbyterian Church (U.S.A.), *Book of Confessions, pt. 1 of The Constitution of the Presbyterian Church (U.S.A.)* (Louisville: Office of the General Assembly, 1996), 253–58.

85. See Donald G. Bloesch, *Jesus Is Victor! Karl Barth's Doctrine of Salvation* (Nashville: Abingdon, 1976).

86. Barth, *Doctrine of Reconciliation, CD*, IV/3/1, 165–274.

The period between Christ's resurrection and final victory is the time in which the Holy Spirit is operative in the world through the church. The church as the community of faith is gathered, built up, and sent into the world by the action of the Holy Spirit. The Spirit works in individuals by establishing faith, love, and hope.[87] The Spirit draws the church as the community of believers into missionary work and ministry in the world, to be witnesses to God's reconciling love in Jesus Christ.

Through the *Church Dogmatics,* we can see that Barth's views on "sacraments" (that is, baptism and the Lord's Supper) changed over the years. In 1943, he upheld the traditional Protestant view that the sacraments were mediators of divine grace. By the time he wrote on the doctrine of reconciliation (1959–60), he had rejected the traditional view and wrote that the so-called sacraments are

> not events, institutions, mediations, or revelations of salvation. They are not representations and actualizations, emanations, repetitions, or extensions, nor indeed guarantees and seals of the work and word of God; nor are they instruments, vehicles, channels, or means of God's reconciling grace. They are not what they have been called since the second century, namely, mysteries or sacraments.[88]

Rather, sacraments are

> actions of human obedience for which Jesus Christ makes his people free and responsible. They refer themselves to God's own work and word, and they correspond to his grace and commands. In so doing they have the promise of the divine good pleasure and they are well done as holy, meaningful, fruitful, human actions, radiant in the shining of the one true light in which they may take place and which they have to indicate in their own place and manner as free and responsible human action.[89]

Barth put it succinctly when he wrote in a letter: "I regard baptism, in brief, as an act, a confession, a prayer of faith, or of the obedience of faith— not as a 'means' of grace and salvation, not as a 'sacrament.'"[90] This shows that Barth rejected the practice of infant baptism.[91]

---

87. See John Thompson, *The Holy Spirit in the Theology of Karl Barth* (Allison Park, Penn.: Pickwick, 1991).

88. Karl Barth, *The Christian Life: Church Dogmatics* IV/4, Lecture Fragments, trans. Geoffrey W. Bromiley (Grand Rapids: Eerdmans, 1981), 46.

89. Ibid.

90. Karl Barth to Herman Bizer, March 29, 1963, in *Karl Barth: Letters, 1961–1968,* ed. Jürgen Fangmeier and Hinrich Stoevesandt, trans. and ed. Geoffrey W. Bromiley (Grand Rapids: Wm. B. Eerdmans, 1981), 96.

91. Barth, *Christian Life,* 164–94. Barth argued that infant baptism is without biblical foundation and has led to the assumption that persons are Christians purely by matter of their birth and that the practice of infant baptism weakens the link between

Significance

Barth's significance for contemporary theology has been variously assessed, just as the key points of his theology have been variously assayed.[92] Among the important contributions Barth made, three stand out.

1. **His Christological theological method.** His approach to theology was Christological intent, and he interpreted such important doctrines as revelation, election, anthropology, and ethics from a Christological starting point.

2. **His stress on the authority of scripture.** Barth's refocus on scripture as the "witness to the Word," Jesus Christ, gave his whole theological work an extensive engagement with scripture that has perhaps exceeded that of any contemporary theologian.

3. **His conviction that God is decentering mystery.** As Johnson has recently explored, Barth's trinitarian approach has maintained God as ultimate mystery, and as such, his theology holds many constructive possibilities for furthering theological dialogue in a postmodern age. Barth invites a "'nonfoundationalist' mode of theological inquiry" so that theology must always "begin again at the beginning."[93] All theological formulations are eminently revisable.

Karl Barth's theology will continue to elicit interest from the wider theological community. Because of the depth, profundity, and provocativeness of Barth's theology, theologians will be in dialogue with Barth's approach and views for years to come. As Barth himself writes, "In dogmatics . . . there are no comprehensive views, no final conclusions and no permanent results. There is only the investigation and teaching which take place in the act of dogmatic work and which . . . must continually begin again at the beginning in every point."[94]

baptism and Christian discipleship. See also Webster, *Barth's Ethics of Reconciliation*, chaps. 4–5.

92. See, for example, Hans Urs von Balthasar, *The Theology of Karl Barth*, trans. John Drury (New York: Holt, Rinehart and Winston, 1971); G. C. Berkouwer, *The Triumph of Grace in the Theology of Karl Barth*, trans. Harry R. Boer (Grand Rapids: Eerdmans, 1956); Herbert Hartwell, *The Theology of Karl Barth: An Introduction* (Philadelphia: Westminster, 1964); George Hunsinger, *How to Read Karl Barth: The Shape of His Theology* (New York: Oxford University Press, 1991).

93. See Johnson, *Mystery of God*, 2–3.

94. Barth, *Doctrine of the Word of God, CD*, I/2, 868.

Response to Professor McKim

Roger R. Keller

Professor Donald McKim has provided a lucid statement of the fundamental tenets of the theology of Karl Barth. Though Barth's theology is comprehensive and complex, it all spirals around its center, Jesus Christ, attempting in the explication of each doctrine to derive its content from God's self-revelation in Christ. Space does not allow me to examine all of the tenets summarized in McKim's essay in the light of Latter-day Saint thought, but there are some that bear critical reflection here, either because of their close parallels with Latter-day Saint theology or because of their significant differences. My response will follow McKim's four-part structure, selecting topics from each section for examination. In framing Latter-day Saint doctrine, I will rely as much as possible on the teachings of Joseph Smith, the founder of The Church of Jesus Christ of Latter-day Saints, and on the LDS church's standard works as supporting documentation.[95]

Doctrine of the Word of God

Revelation

Revelation is the starting point of all theology for Barth and the beginning point for Latter-day Saints. "Behold, great and marvelous are the works of the Lord. How unsearchable are the depths of the mysteries of him," Latter-day Saint scripture reads, "and it is impossible that man should find out all his ways . . . save it be revealed unto him; wherefore, brethren, despise not the revelations of God" (Jacob 4:8).[96]

According to Barth, nothing can be known of God apart from divine revelation. The primary locus of that revelation is found in Jesus Christ, who is the second person of the Godhead and who has become incarnate. Similarly, for Latter-day Saints, it is Jesus Christ who makes the Father known, for those who have seen the Son have seen the Father (John 14:9). However, Latter-day Saint knowledge of the nature of God and the Godhead

---

95. The standard works among Latter-day Saints are the Bible (King James Version), the Book of Mormon, the Doctrine and Covenants (revelations given primarily to the Prophet Joseph Smith), and a collection known as the Pearl of Great Price.

96. This is a reference to a book within the Book of Mormon. The citations from the Book of Mormon will appear much like biblical references, but the names do not duplicate biblical names. The books of Moses and Abraham, along with Joseph Smith–Matthew, Joseph Smith–History, and the Articles of Faith appear in the Pearl of Great Price.

is not derived solely from a knowledge of Jesus Christ. It comes also from the First Vision,[97] in which both the Father and the Son appeared to the fourteen-year-old Joseph Smith as fully embodied beings who were unified in purpose and love, and from subsequent revelations received by Joseph Smith.

While the Savior shows us the works and the love of God, the First Vision shows us the nature of God and the Godhead. The Father, the Son, and the Holy Ghost are three separate persons who constitute a perfectly harmonious social unit but are not one metaphysical substance or essence.[98] Thus, Latter-day Saints reject Barth's more classical understanding of the Godhead in favor of what theologians call the social Trinitarian model.

Latter-day Saints also reject Barth's assumption that revelation concerns only Jesus Christ and is no longer given now that Christ's earthly ministry is over. Instead, Latter-day Saints believe that God continues to reveal many things about his work, this world, human nature, and how his church is to be managed.[99] God spoke to Israel through prophets in the past and continues to speak through prophets today. The role that Isaiah, Jeremiah, and Ezekiel filled as they revealed God's will for Israel is precisely the same role that modern-day prophets fill as they reveal the will of the Lord for contemporary human beings. Prophets past and present bear witness of Jesus Christ, but they also bring God's word into contact with humanity. Latter-day Saints do not believe the pattern has changed simply because the Word became incarnate in Jesus Christ. It is true that the Word

---

97. "I saw a pillar of light exactly over my head, above the brightness of the sun, which descended gradually until it fell upon me. . . . When the light rested upon me I saw two Personages, whose brightness and glory defy all description, standing above me in the air. One of them spake unto me, calling me by name and said, pointing to the other—*This is My Beloved Son. Hear Him!*" (Joseph Smith—History 1:16–17; emphasis in original).

98. "The Father has a body of flesh and bones as tangible as man's; the Son also; but the Holy Ghost has not a body of flesh and bones, but is a personage of Spirit. Were it not so, the Holy Ghost could not dwell in us" (D&C 130:22).

99. "And the day cometh that the words of the book which were sealed shall be read upon the house tops; and they shall be read by the power of Christ; and all things shall be revealed unto the children of men which ever have been among the children of men, and which ever will be even unto the end of the earth" (2 Nephi 27:11).

"And not only this, but those things which never have been revealed from the foundation of the world, but have been kept hid from the wise and prudent, shall be revealed unto babes and sucklings in this, the dispensation of the fulness of times" (D&C 128:18).

"We believe all that God has revealed, all that He does now reveal, and we believe that He will yet reveal many great and important things pertaining to the Kingdom of God" (Articles of Faith 1:9).

is incarnate, but God continues to speak words of historical, doctrinal, and ecclesiastical import. The Doctrine and Covenants instructs, "In case of difficulty respecting doctrine or principle, if there is not a sufficiency written to make the case clear to the minds of the council, the president may inquire and obtain the mind of the Lord by revelation" (D&C 102:23).

Word of God

Barth's usage of the phrase "Word of God" is more exclusive than Latter-day Saint usage. For Latter-day Saints, Jesus is the Word of God, and scripture is also the Word of God because it bears witness of God. The idea of the preached word is not as central to Latter-day Saint thinking as it was to the reformers and their descendants, so the "proclaimed Word of God" is generally not mentioned. "Word of God" does not appear as an entry in the *Encyclopedia of Mormonism*, although it is treated therein as a title of Christ.[100]

The Trinity

As already suggested, there are differences in the way the Godhead is understood by Barth and the Latter-day Saints. Barth adheres to the more traditional Trinitarian formula of three persons constituting one essence, and, although he speaks of three "modes" of being, he rejects modalism.[101] As noted, Latter-day Saints believe that there are three distinct members of the Godhead. While these three persons are not physically or metaphysically one substance, a fact clearly revealed in Joseph Smith's First Vision, there are several ways in which Latter-day Saints would affirm that there is only one God.

First, although the Father, Son, and Holy Ghost are all divine, there is only one font of divinity, only one Father, only one God in the sense of being the ultimate source of all other godhood. Paul explains in the New Testament:

> We know that an idol is nothing in the world, and that there is none other God but one. For though there be that are called gods, whether in heaven or in earth, (as there be gods many, and lords many,) But to us there is but one God, the Father, of whom are all things, and we in him; and one Lord Jesus Christ, by whom are all things, and we by him. (1 Cor. 8:4–6)

---

100. See Stephen E. Robinson, "Jesus Christ, Names and Titles of," in *Encyclopedia of Mormonism*, ed. Daniel H. Ludlow, 4 vols. (New York: Macmillan, 1992), 2:740–42.

101. Modalism, a Christian heresy that stresses there is one God who reveals himself in three modes, but those modes are not simultaneously coexisting. In other words, when God reveals himself as the Son, the Father, and the Holy Spirit do not exist.

Second, although there are three divine persons, there is only one set of divine characteristics, one *divinitas* or *deitas* or *theotes,* one godhood or Godhead or godness. Latter-day Saints thus understand the divine essence not as a concrete substance, but as a set of excellent properties severally necessary and jointly sufficient for their possessor to be divine.[102] The Father, the Son, and the Holy Spirit each have the divine essence, though none is the divine essence. Note that Latter-day Saints also use the word "God" to designate the whole Trinity—three persons in their peculiar relations to each other. This particular usage is a favorite among social Trinitarians: there are three divine persons but only one divine family or monarchy or community—the Holy Trinity itself.

Christology

Barth states that theology must begin with the person of Jesus Christ. Latter-day Saints would agree with this view but would not feel limited to it, since

---

102. Uniquely Latter-day Saint scripture unmistakably declares the unity of the Godhead. Christ, for example, declared to Joseph Smith: "I am Jesus Christ, the Son of God, who was crucified for the sins of the world, even as many as will believe on my name, that they may become the sons of God, even one in me as I am one in the Father, as the Father is one in me, that we may be one" (D&C 35:2). Doctrine and Covenants 20:23–24 reads, "[Christ] was crucified, died, and rose again on the third day; And ascended into heaven, to sit down on the right hand of the Father, to reign with almighty power according to the will of the Father." In 3 Nephi 11:7, we read that as the resurrected Savior appears to the Nephites assembled on the American continent, they hear a voice from heaven announcing, "Behold my Beloved Son, in whom I am well pleased, in whom I have glorified my name—hear ye him." The resurrected Savior then appears and proceeds to minister unto the Nephites, demonstrating the individuality of the Father and the Son as well as their unity in purpose and will. Latter-day Saints also draw upon the Bible to support their unique understanding of the Godhead. In his great intercessory prayer on behalf of his disciples, Jesus Christ states, "And now I am no more in the world, but these are in the world, and I come to thee. Holy Father, keep through thine own name those whom thou hast given me, that they may be one, as we are" (John 17:11). Accordingly, as it is impossible for the apostles to be one metaphysical substance, the oneness referred to is a perfect unity of will and purpose, a perfect social unity. As James E. Talmage explains:

> The one-ness of the Godhead, to which the scriptures so abundantly testify, implies no mystical union of substance, nor any unnatural and therefore impossible blending of personality. Father, Son, and Holy Ghost are as distinct in their persons and individualities as are any three personages in mortality. Yet their unity of purpose and operation is such as to make their edicts one, and their will the will of God. (James E. Talmage, *Articles of Faith* [Salt Lake City: The Church of Jesus Christ of Latter-day Saints, 1982], 41. See also 2 Nephi 31:21; Mosiah 15:4; and Alma 11:28–29)

in their view the incarnation of Jesus Christ does not exhaust His revelation. They would agree with Barth that in Jesus of Nazareth humanity is confronted by the Son of God. Likewise, Latter-day Saints certainly understand that in Jesus Christ humanity also learns what it means to be truly human. But more than that, Latter-day Saints believe that God wishes humans to become like Christ in the fullest of senses. Christ not only shows us what it is to be human, he also shows us our divine potential, a step well beyond Barth's ideas. Latter-day Saints believe that through Christ human beings may become like God.[103]

The Holy Spirit

The Holy Spirit, or the Holy Ghost as Latter-day Saints tend to call the third member of the Godhead, is central to Latter-day Saint thought. As with Barth, they regard the Holy Ghost as the agent through whom individuals appropriate the Atonement into their lives. However, Latter-day Saints believe that God gives us the gift of the Holy Ghost in response to certain acts. First, we must have faith in Jesus Christ as Savior and Lord. Second, we must repent of our sins, for the Spirit cannot dwell in unclean vessels. We must turn away from sin to a new way of life. Third, we must be baptized by immersion by an individual who bears priesthood authority. Finally, we must receive the gift of the Holy Ghost, which is conferred upon believers through an ordinance by those with priesthood authority. Grace is, therefore, mediated by the Spirit through essential priesthood ordinances of the LDS church, which apply the atonement to individuals. In a similar manner, it is the Spirit who unlocks the scriptures and through whom revelation comes to individuals and to the prophet of the LDS church. Both Barth and

---

103. "What was the design of the Almighty in making man, it was to exalt him to be as God, the scripture says yet [sic—meaning "ye"] are Gods and it cannot be broken, heirs of God and joint heirs with Jesus Christ equal with him possesing [sic] all power &c." Andrew F. Ehat and Lyndon W. Cook, *The Words of Joseph Smith* (Provo, Utah: Religious Studies Center, Brigham Young University, 1980), 247, quoting from James Burgess's notebook.

In the Doctrine and Covenants, the following statement is found:

> They [those who will come forth in the resurrection of the just] are they who are priests and kings, who have received of his fulness, and of his glory; And are priests of the Most High, after the order of Melchizedek, which was after the order of Enoch, which was after the order of the Only Begotten Son. Wherefore, as it is written, they are gods, even the sons of God—Wherefore, all things are theirs, whether life or death, or things present, or things to come, all are theirs and they are Christ's, and Christ is God's. . . . These shall dwell in the presence of God and his Christ forever and ever. (D&C 76:56–59, 62)

Latter-day Saints affirm that "the knowledge of God occurs in the fulfillment of the revelation of His Word by the Holy Spirit, and therefore in the
reality and with the necessity of faith and its obedience."[104] Joseph Smith
underlines this when he says:

> We believe that the holy men of old spake as they were moved by the
> Holy Ghost, and that holy men in these days speak by the same prin-
> ciple; we believe in its being a comforter and a witness bearer, that
> it brings things past to our remembrance, leads us into all truth, and
> shows us of things to come; [we] believe that "no man can know that
> Jesus is the Christ, but by the Holy Ghost." We believe in it [this gift of
> the Holy Ghost] in all its fulness, and power, and greatness, and glory;
> but whilst we do this, we believe in it rationally, consistently, and scrip-
> turally, and not according to the wild vagaries, foolish notions and tra-
> ditions of men.[105]

Doctrine of God

Perfections

"Perfections" is not a Latter-day Saint word, but the ideas that the word
implies are very much Latter-day Saint. For Latter-day Saints, God is
unquestionably loving, righteous, wise, one, omnipresent, constant, omnipotent, eternal, and glorious. Out of those attributes grow his justice and
mercy, between which there is a delicate balance.

Alma, a Book of Mormon prophet, taught that mercy cannot rob justice (Alma 42:25). Latter-day Saints believe that God's law must be taken
seriously, and when a divine command is violated, a penalty must be paid.
Because sheer repentance does not atone for the breaking of divine laws,
forgiveness cannot be predicated solely upon repentance or sorrow.[106] It
must also entail the payment of a price, or God's justice is not satisfied and
the force of his law is nullified. Thus, for Latter-day Saints the atonement

---

104. Karl Barth, *The Doctrine of God,* trans. T. H. L. Parker, W. B. Johnston,
Harold Knight, J. L. M. Haire, vol. 2, bk. 1, *Church Dogmatics,* ed. G. W. Bromiley and
T. F. Torrance (New York: Charles Scribner's Sons, 1957), 3.

105. The words of Joseph Smith on June 15, 1842, as recorded in Joseph Smith Jr.,
History of The Church of Jesus Christ of Latter-day Saints, ed. B. H. Roberts, 2d ed.,
rev., 7 vols. (Salt Lake City: Deseret Book, 1971), 5:27 (hereafter cited as *History of
the Church*).

106. This is why repentance is not the first principle of the gospel. Rather, faith
in the Lord Jesus Christ is the first principle, for it is Christ that will pay the price for
our sins. The first principles of the gospel are stated in the fourth Article of Faith: "We
believe that the first principles and ordinances of the Gospel are: first, Faith in the
Lord Jesus Christ; second, Repentance; third, Baptism by immersion for the remission of sins; fourth, Laying on of hands for the gift of the Holy Ghost."

is absolutely necessary to satisfy the demands of justice. The atonement also embodies God's grace because it not only allows but empowers sinners to repent through Jesus Christ. Thereby, the balance between justice and mercy is maintained.[107]

Election

Barth's doctrine of election focuses on the election of Jesus Christ both to damnation and to salvation, thus correcting what he understood to be a misdirection in the theologies of the reformers and their successors. As with his other doctrines, Barth's doctrine of election begins with Jesus Christ and what can be learned there. It has affinities with Latter-day Saint thought found in the concept of agency and in the "plan of salvation."

Latter-day Saints believe that agency, or freedom of choice, is an eternal gift to humans that God never takes away.[108] Thus, even the Fall does not remove human beings' freedom to say yes or no to God. Any sense of predestination or determinism is totally absent from Latter-day Saint theology.[109] Instead, what holds a prominent place in Latter-day Saint thought

---

107. Alma 42:15, 24–26 reads:

And now, the plan of mercy could not be brought about except an atonement should be made; therefore God himself atoneth for the sins of the world, to bring about the plan of mercy, to appease the demands of justice, that God might be a perfect, just God, and a merciful God also. . . . For behold, justice exerciseth all his demands, and also mercy claimeth all which is her own; and thus, none but the truly penitent are saved. What, do ye suppose that mercy can rob justice? I say unto you, Nay; not one whit. If so, God would cease to be God. And thus God bringeth about his great and eternal purposes, which were prepared from the foundation of the world. And thus cometh about the salvation and the redemption of men, and also their destruction and misery.

108. C. Terry Warner stated:

Agency is an essential ingredient of being human . . . both in the premortal spirit existence (D&C 29:36) and in mortality. No being can possess sensibility, rationality, and a capacity for happiness without it (2 Nephi 2:11–13, 23; D&C 93:30). Moreover, it is the specific gift by which God made his children in his image and empowered them to grow to become like him through their own progression of choices. . . . Agency is such that men and women not only can choose obedience or rebellion but must. (C. Terry Warner, "Agency," in *Encyclopedia of Mormonism,* 1:26)

109. Joseph Smith stated:

The true version of predestination [is], namely, that the means of our redemption were predetermined in harmony with eternal law and as

similar to election in Barth's theology is the "plan of salvation." Essentially, the plan of salvation holds that Christ covenanted with the Father in the premortal world to enter history and atone through his suffering and death for the sins of all Heavenly Father's children. This atonement allows humans to return to the Father as they repent of their sins. Upon this foundation, premortal spirits were and are willing to enter earth life.[110] They know the plan of salvation before they enter mortality, but a veil of forgetfulness comes over them as they come to earth, and they must rediscover the plan once on earth. People find Christ, rediscover the plan of salvation, and learn of their divine destiny through the teachings and preachings of the LDS church:

> Such a learning process recollects more than it researches. It is the opposite of amnesia. It is less discovery than recovery. . . . One begins mortality with the veil drawn, but slowly he is moved to penetrate the veil within himself. He is, in time, led to seek the "holy of holies" within the temple of his own being.[111]

Without the plan of salvation, we could not penetrate the veil of forgetfulness into the presence of the Father, either in mortality or after this life. The center of the plan is the Atonement and Resurrection of Christ. "The fundamental principles of our religion are the testimony of the Apostles and Prophets, concerning Jesus Christ, that He died, was buried, and rose again the third day, and ascended up into heaven; and all other things which pertain to our religion are only appendages to it."[112]

Latter-day Saints believe that the Atonement, as part of the plan of salvation, has both unconditional and conditional aspects. Because of Adam and Eve's decision to leave the Garden of Eden and enter mortality, Christ has elected to unconditionally save humanity from both temporal death (the separation of the spirit from the body) and spiritual death (the separation of the spirit from God's presence). Christ's Resurrection saves us from

---

sanctioned voluntarily by us. But our own agency was not 'predetermined' except as its exercise carries over into our present tendencies. "God did predestinate that all who were saved would be saved through Jesus Christ, but unconditional election was not taught by the ancient apostles." (Joseph Fielding Smith, comp., *Teachings of the Prophet Joseph Smith* [Salt Lake City: Deseret Book, 1972], 189, quoted in Truman G. Madsen, *Eternal Man* [Salt Lake City: Deseret Book, 1970], 69 n. 14)

110. Note that Latter-day Saints hold that the Father clothed eternal intelligences with spirit form. These premortal spirit beings then live in the presence of God before they enter earth life, where they gain a body of flesh and blood that is subject to death.

111. Madsen, *Eternal Man*, 19–20.

112. Joseph Smith Jr., ed., *Elders' Journal of The Church of Jesus Christ of Latter-day Saints* 1, no. 3 (1838): 44; also recorded in *History of the Church*, 3:30.

temporal death, granting universal resurrection and immortality to all persons. His Atonement saves us from spiritual death, breaking the barrier between humanity and the Father and making it possible for all humans to return to the presence of the Father for judgment.[113]

Were we to stop at this point, we would be quite close to what many have understood to be a latent doctrine of universal salvation in Barth, as mentioned by McKim. Latter-day Saints, however, also believe in a conditional side to the Atonement. While all may return to the presence of God for judgment, only those who have repented of their sins will be able to stay in his presence. "No unclean thing can dwell with God" (1 Nephi 10:21). Thus, eternal life and exaltation with God are conditional aspects of the Atonement because they are obtained only through faith in the Lord Jesus Christ, repentance, and the grace appropriated by participating in the ordinances of the gospel: "And if they will not repent and believe in his name, and be baptized in his name, and endure to the end, they must be damned; for the Lord God, the Holy One of Israel, has spoken it" (2 Nephi 9:24).

A final significant difference exists between Barth's doctrine of election and Latter-day Saint theology. Barth's doctrine focuses strongly on Christ

---

113. 2 Nephi 9:6, 10–13, 15 states:

For as death hath passed upon all men, to fulfil the merciful plan of the great Creator, there must needs be a power of resurrection, and the resurrection must needs come unto man by reason of the fall; and the fall came by reason of transgression; and because man became fallen they were cut off from the presence of the Lord. . . . O how great the goodness of our God, who prepareth a way for our escape from the grasp of this awful monster; yea, that monster, death and hell, which I call the death of the body, and also the death of the spirit. And because of the way of deliverance of our God, the Holy One of Israel, this death, of which I have spoken, which is the temporal, shall deliver up its dead; which death is the grave. And this death of which I have spoken, which is the spiritual death, shall deliver up its dead; which spiritual death is hell; wherefore, death and hell must deliver up their dead, and hell must deliver up its captive spirits, and the grave must deliver up its captive bodies, and the bodies and the spirits of men will be restored one to the other; and it is by the power of the resurrection of the Holy One of Israel. O how great the plan of our God! For on the other hand, the paradise of God must deliver up the spirits of the righteous, and the grave deliver up the body of the righteous; and the spirit and the body is restored to itself again, and all men become incorruptible, and immortal, and they are living souls, having a perfect knowledge like unto us in the flesh, save it be that our knowledge shall be perfect. . . . And it shall come to pass that when all men shall have passed from this first death unto life, insomuch as they have become immortal, they must appear before the judgment-seat of the Holy One of Israel; and then cometh the judgment, and then must they be judged according to the holy judgment of God.

as the Elect One to whom persons must come in faith and repentance. Latter-day Saint thought also focuses strongly on Christ, as the center of the plan of salvation, to whom all persons must come in faith and repentance. However, in Latter-day Saint theology the object of God's "election" is not Jesus Christ but all God's children, who depend upon Christ and his merit for their salvation:

> And ye are called to bring to pass the gathering of mine elect; for mine elect hear my voice and harden not their hearts. (D&C 29:7; emphasis added)
>
> For whoso is faithful unto the obtaining these two priesthoods of which I have spoken, and the magnifying their calling, are sanctified by the Spirit unto the renewing of their bodies. They become the sons of Moses and of Aaron and the seed of Abraham, and the church and kingdom, and the elect of God. (D&C 84:33–34)

Israel

Latter-day Saints agree with Barth that God's gracious act in Jesus Christ for humanity takes the concrete form of community, but there is a much stronger tie to Israel for Latter-day Saints than for Barth. Latter-day Saints believe that there is no salvation outside of Israel. If persons do not belong to the house of Israel, either by blood lineage or by spiritual adoption, full salvation is not accessible to them. Israel is not a metaphor; it is literally the chosen people of God in the present-day world. The LDS church is one visible manifestation of that people. The other visible community of Israel is the Jewish people.[114]

Latter-day Saints believe that humans are admitted into Israel by coming to Christ through faith, repentance, and ordinances administered by individuals holding God's authorized priesthood. Through their patriarchal blessings administered by those with proper priesthood authority, Latter-day Saints learn which tribe they have been born or adopted into. In the past, most Latter-day Saints have been from either Ephraim or Manasseh, both sons of Joseph, but as the LDS church spreads, more and more of the tribes are represented in the blessings.[115]

Through the tribes of Israel, the promises to Abraham are being fulfilled, and his offspring are indeed blessing the nations. Israel is fulfilling her vocation, and in these latter days the vehicles of that fulfillment are

---

114. Doctrine and Covenants 133:34–35 reads, "Behold, this is the blessing of the everlasting God upon the tribes of Israel, and the richer blessing upon the head of Ephraim and his fellows. And they also of the tribe of Judah, after their pain, shall be sanctified in holiness before the Lord, to dwell in his presence day and night, forever and ever."

115. William James Mortimer, "Patriarchal Blessings," in *Encyclopedia of Mormonism,* 3:1066.

the tribes of Ephraim and Manasseh, represented primarily within the LDS church.

Doctrine of Creation

Creation and Covenant

As McKim notes, Barth holds that creation is the external basis of God's covenant of grace and that "creation sets the stage for the story of the covenant of grace."[116] The earlier discussion of the Latter-day Saint plan of salvation, a plan which was formed before the earth was physically created, demonstrates that Latter-day Saints also see creation as providing the arena in which the plan of salvation may be fulfilled. The Book of Mormon states, "Behold, the Lord hath created the earth that it should be inhabited; and he hath created his children that they should possess it" (1 Nephi 17:36). Thus, this earth and many others like it become the places where premortal spirits gain mortal bodies and rediscover the plan of salvation. They learn of their potential to dwell again with God through the Atonement of Jesus Christ.

Although Latter-day Saints agree with Barth that the earth is a place of human growth in relationship to God, they do not agree on the manner of creation (an issue that McKim does not raise). Barth asserts that the universe was created out of nothing (*creatio ex nihilo*); Latter-day Saints believe it was "organized" by God from preexisting material. In Latter-day Saint theology, matter, energy, and intelligence or intelligences are eternal.[117] God organized eternal, preexisting matter into an earth where human growth could occur and the plan of salvation could be worked out.

Jesus Christ—the Real Human Being

To Latter-day Saints, Jesus Christ is the perfect human. He is God, for he is the second member of the Godhead, but he is also fully human. He stands, as all humans should stand, in full harmony with and in obedience to God.

116. Karl Barth, *The Doctrine of Creation*, trans. J. W. Edwards, O. Bussey, and Harold Knight, vol. 3, bk. 1, *Church Dogmatics*, ed. G. W. Bromiley and T. F. Torrance (Edinburgh: T. and T. Clark, 1958), 44.

117. Joseph Smith taught:

Element had an existence from the time he [God] had. The pure principles of element are principles which can never be destroyed; they may be organized; and reorganized, but not destroyed. They had no beginning and can have no end. (Smith, *Teachings of the Prophet Joseph Smith*, 351–52)

"In the translation [referring to Gen. 1:1–2], 'Without form and void' it should read 'empty and desolate.' The word 'created' should be formed or organized." Ehat and Cook, *Words of Joseph Smith*, 60.

He is with God, and he hears the word of God, as well as being God's Word. He establishes a pattern for human obedience before God and leads us to show gratitude before the Father. Only he lived fully for others, giving his life that others might live. In a powerful affirmation of Christ's human perfection, the *Lectures on Faith* declare:

> The son, who was in the bosom of the Father, [is] a personage of tabernacle, made or fashioned like unto man, . . . being in the form and likeness of man, or rather man was formed after his likeness and in his image; he is also the express image and likeness of the personage of the Father, possessing all the fulness of the Father, or the same fulness with the Father; being begotten of him, and ordained from before the foundation of the world to be a propitiation for the sins of all those who should believe on his name, and is called the Son because of the flesh, and descended in suffering below that which man can suffer; or, in other words, suffered greater sufferings, and was exposed to more powerful contradictions than any man can be. But, notwithstanding all this, he kept the law of God, and remained without sin, showing thereby that it is in the power of man to keep the law and remain also without sin; and also, that by him a righteous judgment might come upon all flesh, . . . that all who walk not in the law of God may justly be condemned by the law, and have no excuse for their sins. And he being the Only Begotten of the Father, full of grace and truth, and having overcome, received a fulness of the glory of the Father, possessing the same mind with the Father, which mind is the Holy Spirit, that bears record of the Father and the Son.[118]

Because Christ is fully human and still perfect, he shows us that human beings may become like God. God wishes us to have eternal life as he does, and he wishes us to be joint heirs with Christ, receiving all that Christ has received. People will always worship the Father through the Son, but human beings may become gods, because those who have come to Christ as the Father has prescribed will live in God's presence and continue to fulfill the work of God.

Saviors

God expects humans to aid each other in gaining salvation. Barth stresses this communal nature of church and emphasizes the I-Thou encounters between people, as well as encounters between persons and God. Latter-day Saints also understand the Christian life to be one of community, beginning first with the family. Marriage in the temple for time and eternity creates this fundamental community, but marriage then becomes a symbol for

---

118. Joseph Smith, comp., *Lectures on Faith* (Salt Lake City: Deseret Book, 1985), 59–60.

the binding together of God's entire family—all who come to him through faith in the Lord Jesus Christ, repentance, baptism, and the other essential ordinances of the temple.[119]

The community of God's family is responsible to extend their fellowship to others. The missionary effort of the LDS church is a visible attempt to offer salvation and community to the world. But this program will not reach those who die, or have died, without a knowledge of the gospel and without saving ordinances. Are they condemned forever? No, say the Latter-day Saints, for God does not offer blessings to some that he withholds from others because of their time and place of birth. There is community between the living and the dead. The living can become "saviors" for these dead by providing, vicariously, in the temples of the LDS church, the necessary ordinances for salvation.[120] Just as Christ vicariously atones for human sin, he commissions and empowers humans to vicariously perform the saving ordinances for those who did not have the opportunity to perform ordinances for themselves while on earth. Hence, baptism and other ordinances are done for the dead, with the understanding that the dead may accept or reject the work done on their behalf.[121]

---

119. In 1995, the First Presidency and the Council of the Twelve Apostles of The Church of Jesus Christ of Latter-day Saints issued a statement on marriage: "We . . . solemnly proclaim that marriage between a man and a woman is ordained of God and that the family is central to the Creator's plan for the eternal destiny of His Children." "A Proclamation to the World," *Ensign* 25 (November 1995), 102.

120. Joseph Smith stated:

The main object [of gathering the people of God in any age] was to build unto the Lord a house whereby He could reveal unto His people the ordinances of His house and the glories of His kingdom, and teach the people the way of salvation; for there are certain ordinances and principles that, when they are taught and practiced, must be done in a place or house built for that purpose. . . . All men who become heirs of God and joint-heirs with Jesus Christ will have to receive the fulness of the ordinances of his kingdom; and those who will not receive all the ordinances will come short of the fullness of that glory, if they do not lose the whole. (*History of the Church*, 5:423–24)

121. Joseph Smith taught:

The Bible says, "I will send you Elijah the Prophet before the coming of the great and dreadful day of the Lord; and he shall turn the hearts of the fathers to the children, and the hearts of the children to the fathers, lest I come and smite the earth with a curse."

Now, the word turn here should be translated bind, or seal. But what is the object of this important mission? or how is it to be fulfilled? The keys are to be delivered, the spirit of Elijah is to come, the Gospel to be established,

Providing ordinances for the dead is essential to Latter-day Saints because salvation is not individual. It is corporate; there is no salvation for the living without their dead. Thus, Latter-day Saints see a whole dimension to the proclamation of the gospel that is not treated in Barth's theology at all.[122]

Doctrine of Reconciliation

McKim discusses the doctrine of reconciliation in different terms than Latter-day Saints would use in talking about the work of Christ. I will try to use the central ideas explicated by McKim while explaining Latter-day Saint perspectives under headings suggested by Barth's arrangement of ideas, but there may not be exact correlations in each instance.

Atonement

We have already seen that Christ is the center of the plan of salvation. A Book of Mormon prophet stated that "no flesh . . . can dwell in the presence of God, save it be through the merits, and mercy, and grace of the Holy

---

the Saints of God gathered, Zion built up, and the Saints to come up as saviors on Mount Zion.

But how are they to become saviors on Mount Zion? By building their temples, erecting their baptismal fonts, and going forth and receiving all the ordinances, baptisms, confirmations, washings, anointings, ordinations and sealing powers upon their heads, in behalf of all their progenitors who are dead, and redeem them that they may come forth in the first resurrection and be exalted to thrones of glory with them; and herein is the chain that binds the hearts of the fathers to the children, and the children to the fathers, which fulfills the mission of Elijah. (*History of the Church*, 6:183–84)

122. LDS church President Joseph F. Smith explained the preaching of the gospel among the dead:

And as I wondered, my eyes were opened, and my understanding quickened, and I perceived that the Lord went not in person among the wicked and the disobedient [dead] who had rejected the truth, to teach them; But behold, from among the righteous [dead], he organized his forces and appointed messengers, clothed with power and authority, and commissioned them to go forth and carry the light of the gospel to them that were in darkness, even to all the spirits of men; and thus was the gospel preached to the dead. . . . These were taught faith in God, repentance from sin, vicarious baptism for the remission of sins, the gift of the Holy Ghost by the laying on of hands, And all other principles of the gospel that were necessary for them to know in order to qualify themselves that they might be judged according to men in the flesh, but live according to God in the spirit. (D&C 138:29–30, 33–34)

Messiah, who layeth down his life according to the flesh, and taketh it again by the power of the Spirit, that he may bring to pass the resurrection of the dead, being the first that should rise" (2 Nephi 2:8).

As previously quoted, Joseph Smith said that "the fundamental principles of our religion are the testimony of the Apostles and Prophets, concerning Jesus Christ, that He died, was buried, and rose again the third day, and ascended into heaven; and all other things which pertain to our religion are only appendages to it."[123]

The atoning work of Christ, which includes the Resurrection, is the heart of the gospel. Christ made a substitutionary sacrifice, the mechanism of which we do not fully understand or know, through which he paid for the sins of all humankind. Because Christ was the perfect human, he could suffer and die for all humanity. Because he was the second member of the Godhead, he had the power to overcome death and, as a resurrected person, enter the precinct of his Father and open the way to the Father for those who would follow Christ. This is the good news of the gospel and God's answer to the Fall of Adam and Eve.[124]

Concerning the story of Adam and Eve, however, Barth and Latter-day Saints differ. Barth sees the account of their creation as a legend; Latter-day Saints understand the story literally. Adam and Eve really were the first parents of the human race, and they were literally created in the physical image of the Father and the Son.[125] Belief in God's physical nature is based on the appearance of the Father and the Son to Joseph Smith as two clearly identifiable embodied persons. Thus, while the work of God provides much common ground between Latter-day Saints and Barth, the physical nature of God is a principal point of difference. God is anthropomorphic (or, more accurately, man is theomorphic) as Adam and Eve were literally created in his bodily image (form) and possessed certain divine attributes, such as relationality, rationality, morality, and freedom.

---

123. *History of the Church*, 3:30.

124. Lehi, a Book of Mormon prophet, explained, "And the Messiah cometh in the fulness of time, that he may redeem the children of men from the fall. And because that they are redeemed from the fall they have become free forever, knowing good from evil; to act for themselves and not to be acted upon, save it be by the punishment of the law at the great and last day, according to the commandments which God hath given" (2 Nephi 2:26).

125. "Latter-day scriptures attest that Adam is a son of God, that his physical body was created by the Gods in their own image and placed in the Garden of Eden." Arthur A. Bailey, "Adam," in *Encyclopedia of Mormonism*, 1:15–16.

Appropriation of the Atonement

Barth stresses that the Atonement is appropriated through the Holy Spirit. Latter-day Saints would concur, but they would also stress some prerequisites. The first of these is faith in the Lord Jesus Christ as Savior, and in this they are in harmony with Barth and all other Christians. The encounter with the Lord in faith leads to a recognition of who and what one has become, thus necessitating repentance, the second prerequisite. Repentance entails a radical change in personal orientation and behavior. The truly repentant person is ready to receive the third prerequisite, which is baptism by immersion under the hands of one holding God's authoritative priesthood. This ordinance is so essential that baptisms are performed for the dead in temples. Finally, God validates a person's offering of faith, repentance, and baptism by giving him or her the gift of the Holy Ghost, which provides the power to live the Christian life and brings the Atonement into that person's daily life. Latter-day Saints believe that while works (including ordinances) are essential to salvation, they are not sufficient.[126] People's actions should reflect their professions of faith. The Holy Ghost enables both a change of heart and the ability to live as a new being.

Exaltation of Christ

McKim states, "In the exaltation of Jesus Christ, humanity is exalted" (McKim, 35). Statements like this lead some to suggest that Barth was a universalist. It sounds very much like Barth believed the effects of the Atonement to be unconditional for all. As stated earlier, Latter-day Saints believe the Atonement to be unconditional—removing the effects of Adam and Eve's transgression—and conditional—potentially removing the effects of personal sin. Exaltation, or dwelling in the presence of the Father and the Son, is conditional and is predicated on individual responses to the gospel.

---

126. The Latter-day Saints are often accused of believing that salvation comes by works, not grace. This is a false dichotomy. As noted earlier, it is only through the grace and merits of Christ that salvation is available to or can be appropriated by anyone (2 Nephi 2:8). However, the second principle of the gospel is repentance. No one can claim to love Christ, if he or she is not willing to obey the Lord and repent. ("If we say that we have fellowship with him, and walk in darkness, we lie, and do not the truth" [1 John 1:6]). Thus, Latter-day Saints expect to see Christians living lives that are Christlike. Works do matter because they reflect the state of a person's spirit. But even a faithful, Christian life is insufficient. God has also asked those who follow him to express their commitment through essential ordinances, without which there is no fulness of salvation. These works are required because God has required them, and these works or ordinances may be done for the dead by proxy in temples. The living are responsible for their own ordinance work. Thus, faith, a Christian life, and essential ordinances go hand in hand to bring about an individual's salvation.

Salvation outside of exaltation, however, is very broad, for most persons will receive some degree of glory—telestial, terrestrial, or celestial.[127] A few will be cast into outer darkness and completely separated from any divine light.[128] Exaltation is the highest degree of glory and is reserved for those who have appropriated the Atonement as the Lord has commanded, including receiving essential ordinances under the hands of authorized priesthood holders, who exist only within the LDS church. The telestial and terrestrial kingdoms are places of glory, but they are for those who have not appropriated the Atonement as God commanded and for those who have lived at variance with the light given them (D&C 76).

Responsible Discipleship

McKim defines "responsible discipleship" as being a "witness to God's love for the entire world" (McKim, 35). Latter-day Saints would be comfortable with that definition, but they would want to clarify it. First and foremost, responsible discipleship means preaching the fulness of the gospel of Jesus Christ to all who will listen.[129] Because Latter-day Saints believe that Christ's church was restored to the earth in its fulness in 1830, they preach to Christians and non-Christians alike. They see the missionary

---

127. "Paul ascended into the third heavens, and he could understand the three principal rounds of Jacob's ladder—the telestial, the terrestrial, and the celestial glories or kingdoms, where Paul saw and heard things which were not lawful for him to utter." *History of the Church,* 5:402.

128. Doctrine and Covenants 76:31–38 reads:

Thus saith the Lord concerning all those who know my power, and have been made partakers thereof, and suffered themselves through the power of the devil to be overcome, and to deny the truth and defy my power—They are they who are the sons of perdition, of whom I say that it had been better for them never to have been born; For they are vessels of wrath, doomed to suffer the wrath of God, with the devil and his angels in eternity; Concerning whom I have said there is no forgiveness in this world nor in the world to come—Having denied the Holy Spirit after having received it, and having denied the Only Begotten Son of the Father, having crucified him unto themselves and put him to an open shame. These are they who shall go away into the lake of fire and brimstone, with the devil and his angels—And the only ones on whom the second death shall have any power; Yea, verily, the only ones who shall not be redeemed in the due time of the Lord, after the sufferings of his wrath."

129. "We don't ask any people to throw away any good they have got; we only ask them to come and get more. What if all the world should embrace this Gospel? They would then see eye to eye, and the blessings of God would be poured out upon the people, which is the desire of my whole soul." *History of the Church,* 5:259.

Response: Roger R. Keller   55

effort, which has approximately sixty thousand missionaries in the field, as a clear manifestation of their witness for Christ and his love. Second, discipleship implies a life defined by the highest principles of morality and ethics. Persons seeking to enter the temple must answer questions relating to chastity, tithing, the Word of Wisdom (which asks Latter-day Saints to refrain from using tobacco, alcohol, tea, or coffee), treatment of family members, and attendance at church meetings. For Latter-day Saints, orthopraxy in daily living is every bit as important, if not more so, as orthodoxy is in theology.

Period of the Spirit

Barth asserts that the period between Jesus' Resurrection and the final victory is the time when the Holy Spirit creates the church and summons people to obedience. Latter-day Saints agree, for they seek to learn to live by the Spirit in their daily lives. The Spirit works both individually and corporately. Any individual may have guidance in his or her life and receive revelation from the Spirit.[130] Similarly, the LDS church is guided by the Spirit through the prophet who stands at its head,[131] and through priesthood and auxiliary leaders who receive revelation through the Spirit concerning their own areas of responsibility.[132]

Sacraments

McKim indicates that Barth changed his view of the sacraments over the years. Originally Barth held that sacraments were channels of grace, but he later came to understand them as symbols of human obedience before God. The Latter-day Saint would wonder why they cannot be both. There is no question, for example, that baptism combines grace with obedience. The Book of Mormon illustrates the role of obedience in baptism:

> And now, I would ask of you, my beloved brethren, wherein the Lamb of God did fulfil all righteousness in being baptized by water? Know ye not that he was holy? But notwithstanding he being holy, he showeth unto the children of men that, according to the flesh he humbleth

---

130. "It is the privilege of the Children of God to come to God & get Revelation." Ehat and Cook, *Words of Joseph Smith,* 13.

131. "But, behold, verily, verily, I say unto thee, no one shall be appointed to receive commandments and revelations in this church [for the whole church] excepting my servant Joseph Smith, Jun., for he receiveth them even as Moses. . . . For I have given him the keys of the mysteries, and the revelations which are sealed, until I shall appoint unto them another in his stead" (D&C 28:2, 7).

132. "It is also the privilege of any office in this Church to obtain revelations, so far as relates to his particular calling and duty in the Church." *History of the Church,* 2:477.

himself before the Father, and witnesseth unto the Father that he would be obedient unto him in keeping his commandments. . . . And again, it showeth unto the children of men the straitness of the path, and the narrowness of the gate, by which they should enter, he having set the example before them. (2 Nephi 31:6–7, 9)

While following Christ's example of obedience, Latter-day Saints also baptize for the remission of sins. Through the act of baptism, persons are spiritually washed clean. Thus, grace and ordinance both play roles in the salvation process. Latter-day Saints perform ordinances in obedience to God's commands, and in the process they are, through the grace imparted through participating in the ordinances, increasingly sanctified.

Conclusion

Because Barth's theology is so deeply rooted in scripture, and because he writes for the church, there is much common ground between him and Latter-day Saints. Terminology and frameworks for theology may differ, but the common emphasis on the Savior binds the two thought systems together. Barth addresses questions for which Latter-day Saint theology has plausible answers. Furthermore, because of this common emphasis, continued examination of both Barth's methodology and theology could be beneficial for Latter-day Saints. Although there are various points on which dialogue between the two camps could ensue, I will suggest two issues for continuous engagement: the Latter-day Saint notion of revelation and understanding of human nature.

As stated earlier, Latter-day Saints affirm that revelation is not limited to the manifestation of God's will and nature through the incarnation of Christ, nor is it limited to the testimonies recorded in scripture. As with prophets of old, God continues to instruct and guide modern-day prophets. Barth emphasizes that the ultimate expression of God's grace is the saving work of the Son of God (McKim, 32). Likewise Barth explains that God's willingness to provide saving grace through Jesus Christ and become a "covenant-partner" with men and women, illustrates that God has not and will not abandon the world (McKim, 33). Affirming God's willingness to enter a covenant relationship with his children through the Atonement of the Savior, Latter-day Saints also affirm that modern-day revelation heightens our understanding of God's grace and his willingness to continue to work with us both personally and communally as a covenant-partner, enabling each of us to establish a deeper relationship with the Father. Revelation, as it is understood by Latter-day Saints is the means by which God helps His children achieve their divine potential. As such, God will use whatever means possible to reveal to his children what they need to know for their own salvation and exaltation.

The Latter-day Saint understanding of the nature and purpose of human being could also serve as a stimulus for further dialogue between Latter-day Saints and other Christians. As explained by McKim, Barth claims that the Creation is the external basis of God's covenant of grace (McKim, 29). Latter-day Saints likewise assign a pivotal role to the Creation, asserting that the Creation is a fundamental step in humanity's eternal progression. Men and women, as children of God, have divine potential, and it is God's work and glory to see that his children fulfill this potential.[133] Affirmation of the divine potential of humanity can lead to a deeply meaningful relationship with God. For Latter-day Saints, God does not stand transcendent in the traditional sense: he works closely with humans to help them realize their ultimate potential. God is a covenant-partner concerned with our salvation; however, he is also a loving father whose glory it is to see that his children progress to become like him. Accordingly, this doctrine redirects and clarifies the traditional understanding of the purpose and goal of revelation, as stated above. It also brings a new level of meaning to the Atonement. By overcoming sin and death, Christ not only made it possible for human beings to become like his Father in Heaven, he also showed humans how to use this earthly existence to realize their divine potential. Thus Barth's assertions that through Christ people are reconstituted in authentic humanity and freedom (McKim, 33) and that Christ moves human nature upward (McKim, 35) are affirmed and expanded in Latter-day Saint theology. Likewise, as men and women are children of God with potential to become like God, Barth's assertion that "true self knowledge is in correlation with the knowledge of God" (McKim, 30) is especially meaningful for Latter-day Saints.

It is hoped that commonalities, as well as differences, are seen as these two theologies are compared. Similarly, it is hoped that future dialogue between Latter-day Saints and Protestant theologians will find fertile ground in the theology of Karl Barth. Though Latter-day Saints gain further insight through modern-day revelation, both theologies represent contemplation on the acts of God made manifest in Jesus Christ. Examinations of the teachings of Karl Barth and the doctrines of The Church of Jesus Christ of Latter-day Saints would benefit all Christians as Christian theology takes its first steps into the twenty-first century.

---

133. Moses 1:39 reads, "For this is my work and my glory—to bring to pass the immortality and eternal life of man."

Rejoinder

Donald K. McKim

Professor Keller's comparison of the theology of Karl Barth with that of the LDS church is a clear and forthright statement of places of commonality and difference between the two views. Keller well understands Barth's thought and helpfully organizes his response in relation to the categories where apparent affinities and differences appear. Thus we have a lucid look at the trajectories of both views.

As is often the case in comparing theological positions, the clearest points of divergence are with foundational matters. Sometimes identical or similar terms are used in two different systems yet with differing meanings or nuances that lead to significant divergences when the terms' implications are expanded. For example, no examination of the theologies of Barth and the LDS church can miss the basic category of "revelation" and its meaning. Keller notes that while for Barth, revelation finds its primary locus in Jesus Christ, LDS theology finds "knowledge about the nature of God and the Godhead is not derived solely from a knowledge of Jesus Christ. Rather, it comes also from the First Vision in which both the Father and the Son appeared to the fourteen-year-old Joseph Smith as fully embodied beings who were unified in purpose and love" (Keller, 39).

This difference seems most fundamental since it goes to the heart of the issue of authority. The sources of our theological understanding are starting points that guide what is construed as authoritative, or what has "warrant" for belief. For Barth, and for Protestant Christianity in particular, authority is found in God's revelation—supremely in Jesus Christ as he is attested in holy scripture. The Protestant Reformers, and Barth as well, were firm that the limits of God's revelation are found in the canonical scriptures alone. They would admit no extra-biblical sources from which valid knowledge of God could be derived. The insights of the Holy Spirit, given to the church, are understood as confirming what the scriptures say or teach and not, in themselves, as imparting new "sources" of revelation or authority.

This would seem to be the nub of the issue from which flow many of the other points of difference that Keller notes. The "extra-biblical scriptures" of the Latter-day Saints could not be recognized by Barth as providing valid sources of theological knowledge to be put on par with the church's canonical scriptures. Thus the gulf between Barth's view and the LDS view that "there are 'revelations,' not just of God himself but of other things" (Keller, 39–40) appears to be insurmountably wide.

Other differences between Barth and LDS theology appear in view of the Trinity. Barth adheres to the church teaching that the three persons of the Godhead—Father, Son, and Holy Spirit—are of one essence. The subordination of the Son and the Spirit to the Father, as Keller notes, is the LDS view (Keller, 40).

Another fundamental difference between Barth's theology and that of the Latter-day Saints arises when Keller indicates, "the gift of the Holy Ghost is God's response to certain human acts" (Keller, 42). He mentions this in the context of his treatment of the Holy Spirit as the "agent through which the Atonement is appropriated into individual lives." Barth would be allergic to language that would link the gift or work of the Holy Spirit to human activities of any sort; he always sought to maintain that the freedom of God is operative without regard to any "outside" or "external" forces. God is the one who chooses to "love in freedom." But the work of God—as Father, Son, or Holy Spirit—is always freely done and as "initiator" not as a respondent to what humans may do. Barth believed that a responding God could not truly be God because humans would be the ones who were, in a sense, prescribing what actions God would take—and thus limiting the divine freedom. This belief is related to Barth's later rejection of sacraments as "channels of grace." He was afraid that to say God "must" act through certain rituals or rites would make humans the ones who dictate what the divine activity must be.

Barth again differs from the Latter-day Saints on the doctrine of creation. This point was not raised in my initial section on Barth, but Keller perceptively points out the difference. Barth would hold to the traditional Christian view of creation ex nihilo (creation out of nothing), while the LDS view is that the universe was "'organized' by God from pre-existing materials . . . for they hold that matter, energy, and intelligence or intelligences are eternal" (Keller, 48). This difference in the "manner of creation" would be significant for Barth in seeking to maintain God's ultimacy and sovereignty. To admit any other "beings" or "principles" or "forms"—such as matter or energy—as being "eternal" alongside God would be, for Barth, a denial of God's primacy, sovereignty, and eternality. Since another entity sharing an eternal nature as well would be in effect a "rival god," God would not be the only reality to have existed "in the beginning" (Gen. 1:1).

Another example of what might be called an "exclusivity impulse" in Barth is his desire to preserve the uniqueness of Father, Son, and Holy Spirit as well as their primacy and power. In his section on "Saviors," Professor Keller points out that in LDS theology there is a community between the living and the dead so that "the living can become 'saviors' for those who cannot help themselves by providing vicariously the necessary ordinances for salvation in the temples of the Church." As Christ could atone vicariously for sin, "so humans can vicariously provide the saving ordinances for those who have not yet received them. Hence, baptism and other ordinances are done for the dead, with the understanding that the dead may accept or reject the work done on their behalf" (Keller, 50). Keller notes that Barth does not treat this dimension of the proclamation of the gospel among the dead. One reason for this is, perhaps, that Barth would reject any notion that salvation can come in any other way than through the death of Jesus Christ, and that would include rejecting the performance of "ordinances" on behalf of others. A personal appropriation of the message of the gospel— that God has reconciled the world in Jesus Christ—is important in Barth's thought, but his thought does not stretch beyond the present life and allow that others can act on behalf of those who have died. Barth's thought comes near the "brink of universalism" in that he stresses the universal nature of Christ's reconciling death. Yet he will not say that "all must be saved" for to do so—to say must—would limit God's sovereign freedom to act as God wills. Barth's refusal to speculate further—either concerning the ultimate fate of all those who have died or concerning any means for their salvation apart from their own earthly recognition of Jesus Christ as Savior and Lord—maintains the "exclusivity" of Jesus Christ as the only way, the truth, and the life (John 14:6).

In spite of all that has been said above about the theological differences between Barth and Latter-day Saints, Professor Keller's section on "Atonement" certainly sounds as though there are some ways of "speaking the same language" between Barth and the Latter-day Saints. After citing from Joseph Smith, Keller writes:

> The atoning work of Christ, which includes the Resurrection, is the heart of the gospel. Christ made a substitutionary sacrifice, the mechanism of which we do not fully understand or know, through which he paid for the sins of all humankind. Because Christ was the perfect human, he could suffer and die for all humanity. Because he was the second member of the Godhead, he had the power to overcome death and, as a resurrected person, enter the precincts of his Father and open the way to the Father for those who would follow Christ. This is the good news of the gospel and God's answer to the Fall of Adam and Eve. (Keller, 52)

These words, as they stand, sound as though they could have been written by Karl Barth! Barth too saw the Atonement and resurrection of Jesus Christ as the heart of the gospel. He believed that the sacrifice of Christ for human sin could never be fully understood and affirmed both the divinity and the humanity of Jesus who has opened the way to God by his resurrection from the dead. For Barth, God's "final word" was not the "no" of sin (the fall of Adam and Eve), but the resounding "Yes!" of Jesus' resurrection.

Keller concludes by indicating that despite terminological differences and variations in frameworks, the "common emphasis on the Savior binds the two thought systems together" (Keller, 56). The differences between the theologies of Barth and Latter-day Saints should be explored further, as they are real and significant. But common perceptions and similar emphases should be recognized as well. At some points, "surprising" convergences may emerge. Certainly the best path is the path of dialogue between the thought of Karl Barth and LDS theology. It is the way for exploration.

Reply to Professor McKim

Roger R. Keller

PROFESSOR MCKIM HAS CLEARLY IDENTIFIED POINTS OF DIFFERENCE between LDS thought and that of Karl Barth. McKim is absolutely correct that the concept of revelation is broadened among Latter-day Saints to include "information" in addition to the self-impartation of God in Jesus Christ. But even in the informational realm, God is still the revelator. Latter-day Saints are not dealing with natural theology or with what Barth called the *analogia entis*, the analogy of being. Only God makes himself or information about himself known. Such knowledge is not appropriated through reason or the natural world.

Secondly, McKim rightly notes that for Barth, God always operates without outside influences or forces. LDS thought disagrees. There are realities that are co-eternal with God. (McKim fails to make a compelling case against this conclusion.) But, for Latter-day Saints, God remains redemptively sovereign. He can and will fulfill all of his purposes and promises.

Among these outside influences is agentive freedom. For Latter-day Saints there is no concept of original sin that would make human response to the Word of God impossible. Humans can freely say both "yes" and "no" to God. To be unable to do both would mean that a human can do neither. Thus, there is a synergy between God and humanity. God offers, but the offer is contingent, by God's choice, on humanity's response, which is a free response to that offer.

In LDS theology, God offers humanity this same choice through sacraments or ordinances. God does not have to act through sacraments but graciously gives them to the church as special channels through which he and his Son may be accessed. Ordinances are offered to the human family by God. If used as they are offered, they then become, again by God's choice, "channels of grace" through which we encounter Christ's Atonement. In this light, God offers LDS church members the opportunity of participating with him in the salvation of the human family.

For Barth, the preached Word is virtually a sacrament. Humans participate in the saving process by proclaiming the one whom they know. Latter-day Saints extend that participation by asserting that God has given human beings not only the opportunity to participate in calling persons to Christ through the preached Word but also by enabling the dead to come to Christ through temple ordinances that God has given, so that worshipers may experience in a very small way what Christ did for the human family—he gave himself that humans might gain something they cannot do for themselves. Through temple attendance and performing the temple ordinances on behalf of someone an individual has never met, that individual learns the central tenet of Christian discipleship—life is giving self away in service to others with no thought of personal reward.

Finally, McKim notes that Barth does not "speculate" on the ultimate fate of those who have died. Latter-day Saints would claim that they do not speculate on an individual's ultimate fate either, but they would claim to have more knowledge of what occurs after death than would Barth because of their extended canon. Latter-day Saints believe that their knowledge of the relationship between the living and dead, preaching of the gospel to the dead, and temple ordinances for them are all rooted in scripture, albeit latter-day scriptures that contain some of the "things" God has revealed as part of the restoration in these latter days. But all these doctrines circle, as McKim has correctly pointed out, around the Atonement of Jesus Christ. The real question is how far does that Atonement reach by God's grace? Has he chosen to extend it to the living dead as well as to the living?

About the Authors

Donald K. McKim (Ph.D. University of Pittsburgh) is an ordained minister in the Presbyterian Church (USA), a member of the American Academy of Religion, the American Society of Church History, the Karl Barth Society of North America (charter member), and is past President and Vice-President of the Calvin Studies Society. He is the author of over twenty-five books, sixty articles, and four hundred book reviews. Formerly an Academic Dean and Professor of Theology at Memphis Theological Seminary, he now works with Westminster John Knox Press in Louisville, Kentucky.

Roger R. Keller (Ph.D. Duke University) received his M.Div. from Princeton Theological Seminary. His doctoral studies focused on twentieth-century Christian theology, and his dissertation focused on the theology of Karl Barth. He served as both a Presbyterian and Methodist minister previous to his joining The Church of Jesus Christ of Latter-day Saints. His areas of interest include the Book of Mormon and interfaith dialogue. He is a professor of Church History and Doctrine at Brigham Young University.

Appendix A

Church Dogmatics IV

Dogmatics	CD IV/1	CD IV/2	CD IV/3
Christology:			
Person	The Lord as Servant: *vere deus* (true God)	The Servant as Lord: *vere homo* (true man)	The true Witness
Office	The Judge judged in our place: The obedience of the Son of God = *munus sacerdotale* (priestly office)	The Royal Man: The exaltation of the Son of Man = *munus regale* (royal office)	Jesus is Victor: The glory of the Mediator = *munus propheticum* (prophetic office)
State/Way	The way of the Son of God into the far country = *status exinanitionis* (state of self-emptying)	The homecoming of the Son of Man = *status exaltationis* (state of exaltation)	The Light of life = the unity of both states
Doctrine of Sin:			
Sin as	Pride and Fall	Sloth and misery	Falsehood and condemnation
Soteriology:	The judgment of God as the justification of humanity	The direction of God as the sanctification of humanity	The promise of God as the vocation of humanity
Pneumatology:			
The work of the Holy Spirit			
In the community	Gathering the community	Upbuilding the community	Sending the community
In the individual	Faith	Love	Hope
Ethics CD IV/4			
The Christian life as an appeal to God	Baptism—with water—as the foundation of the Christian life in prayer for the Holy Spirit	The Lord's Prayer—Our Father—as (instruction in) the fulfillment of the Christian life	The Lord's Supper—Eucharist—as the renewal of the Christian life in thanksgiving

Taken from Eberhard Jüngel, *Karl Barth, a Theological Legacy,* trans. Garrett E. Paul (Philadelphia: Westminster, 1986), 48–49.

Appendix B

The Doctrine of Reconciliation in Karl Barth's Theology

Jesus Christ is one in being and action

Son of God	Goes into the far country	Humbles himself	Priestly	Salvation	Downward
[Humiliation]		[Death]	[Atonement]		
Son of Man	Homecoming	Exalted humanity	Kingly	Rule	Upward
[Exaltation]		[Resurrection]	[True Man]		
Lord Jesus Christ	Reconciliation of World	True Witness	Prophet	Light	Outward
[Present in world by power of Holy Spirit]		[Life]	[God-Man]		

Barth looks at the doctrine of Reconciliation in light of Jesus Christ and relates Christ to the parable of the Prodigal Son as an illustration. He sees the divine-human person, the two states of "humiliation" and "exaltation," and the traditional three offices of prophet, priest, and king as one in Jesus Christ. See *Church Dogmatics* IV/2, 21–25 and IV/1, 128–38.

Appendix C

The Doctrine of Reconciliation in Karl Barth's Theology

God moves

Downward	Sin as Pride God comes down but we exalt self	is overcome by	Justification	in calling of the Church	Faith
Upward	Sin as Sloth God lifts us up but we drag ourselves down by disobedience and sin	is overcome by	Sanctification	in building up the Church	Love
Outward	Sin as Falsehood God sends Jesus Christ as true witness to his own truth and humanity but we live a lie and act against the Truth	is overcome by	Knowing the Truth	in the missionary Church	Hope

See Karl Barth, *Church Dogmatics* IV/1, 358–513; IV/2, 378–498; IV/3 pt. 1, 368–480.

A Dialogue on the Theology of Reinhold Niebuhr

Reinhold Niebuhr:
A Case Study in Public Theology

Dennis P. McCann

How is it that a Roman Catholic thinker explores the work of Reinhold Niebuhr with a member of The Church of Jesus Christ of the Latter-day Saints? After all, Niebuhr was the foremost exponent of mainline Protestantism in his day, a tradition that in its worst moments has had little use for either Catholics or Latter-day Saints. Yet here we are, as they say, "Only in America." I believe that our marginal status, relative to mainline Protestantism, will allow Catholics and Latter-day Saints not only to bring different concerns to the study of Niebuhr's work, but also to help freshen the discussion of Niebuhr's Christian realism in ways that have eluded liberal Protestants for whom Niebuhr's thinking is quite familiar.

My own study of Niebuhr began before I had any idea who Niebuhr was or what his significance had been for American Christianity in the twentieth century. As a Ph.D. candidate at the University of Chicago Divinity School, I was interested in "political theology," a new form of socially engaged and politically transformative religious thought then emerging from German universities. Political theology appealed to me because it helped make sense of my own seminary experience in the 1960s as a social activist doing community organization work for a coalition of Catholic and Protestant churches in Columbus, Ohio, allied with the local chapter of the Congress of Racial Equality (C.O.R.E.). I regarded such work as an expression of my Christian commitment; however, I soon realized that I would need a robust theology of Christian social action if the religious basis of my commitment were to not wither away in the heat of the struggle for justice. That's what I hoped to find in political theology. But I also felt that this European cultural import would never get very far in the United States because it was embedded in a German context of social thought and praxis that was virtually impenetrable even for Catholic seminarians.

With these concerns in mind as we were brainstorming possible dissertation topics, David Tracy, my dissertation advisor, suggested I try reading Niebuhr. Could his work be the theological model I was looking for? Thus, I first read Niebuhr in search of a method that would make Christian social action publicly accountable. Later, as I continued to read him, I absorbed more and more of his substantive thinking about Christian faith and its relevance for interpreting contemporary American politics, history, and culture. Niebuhr's Christian realism also helped to shape my understanding of American Catholicism by forcing me to confront its marginal status outside the boundaries of mainline Protestantism.

Latter-day Saints, too, may wish to approach Niebuhr's work as outsiders. They may find him interesting for reasons similar to my own. His work may still offer some challenging insights into how a Christian theologian, committed to the ministries of an increasingly influential religious community, such as the LDS church, might help the faithful to understand and live up to their political and social responsibilities. Latter-day Saints may determine what worked and what did not and how compatible, if at all, his ideas are with the basic perspectives animating their own tradition of Christian faith.

Even if this is the Latter-day Saint agenda—as well as my own—there may still be formidable barriers to taking Niebuhr seriously today. Over and above his deep roots in mainline Protestantism and its liberal Social Gospel traditions, today's readers may find him hopelessly dated. His resistance to Henry Ford, Adolf Hitler, and Joseph Stalin may have been the defining moments of Niebuhr's own development as a Christian theologian, but what can these possibly mean to anyone whose experience of life has been shaped, not by life in the big industrial cities of the East, but by the distinctive history of the American West? My objective is to introduce Niebuhr's life and thought in a way that may help Latter-day Saints to determine its relevance for their own purposes. I will thus divide this presentation into two parts: first, a review of Niebuhr's life and the way his thought was shaped by the major social questions of his day; and second, an analysis of his mature theological position on Christian realism that seeks to expose its strengths and weaknesses as a theology. I'm wagering that the outsider status of Catholic and LDS theology may be a special advantage in reading Reinhold Niebuhr. With little at stake in the old quarrels and controversies that he carried on with his liberal Protestant colleagues, we may be able to read him, I hope, with an open mind.

Niebuhr's Life: The Context of a Public Theology

I'm told that members of the LDS community, for theological reasons, find genealogies unusually significant. Niebuhr's genealogy thus seems a good place to begin our inquiry, for his family history plays an unusually significant role in shaping his theology. Reinhold Niebuhr's father, Gustav, was born in 1863 in Lippe-Detmold, Prussia. Gustav was the second son of a yeoman farmer, Friedrich, whose ancestors had successfully held the farm since at least the thirteenth century. As the second son, Gustav had no hope of inheriting the farm, so as soon as he came of age, he immigrated to the United States, among other reasons, to avoid military service in the Kaiser's army. Shortly after his arrival in the United States, Gustav was ordained in the German Evangelical Synod in North America, the immigrant community spun from the Prussian state church and a merger of Lutheran and Calvinist traditions that had fostered the development of liberal Protestant theology beginning with the seminal work of Friedrich Schleiermacher. While working as a missionary in California, Gustav married Lydia Hosto, the daughter of another of the Synod's pastors. In quick succession, the Niebuhr children, Walter (1888), Hulda (1889), Herbert (1890, died 1891), Reinhold (1892), and Helmut Richard (1894), were born. Three of them were to achieve a significant place among liberal Protestant clergy in the twentieth century: Hulda as professor of Christian education at McCormick Theological Seminary in Chicago; Reinhold as professor of Applied Christianity at Union Theological Seminary in New York; and H. Richard as professor of Christian ethics at the Yale Divinity School. After Gustav's unexpected death in 1913, Reinhold's mother, Lydia, became the chief collaborator in Reinhold's pastoral ministry at Bethel Evangelical Church in Detroit, where his career as a public theologian would actually begin.

Niebuhr's genealogy tells us many things, one that Niebuhr himself came from an immigrant community, which shared an outsider's status relative to the nativist traditions of mainline Protestantism. We shall see that Niebuhr's public theology first emerged in the struggle his community waged over its future as a German immigrant church. But how far would it go in the direction of being Americanized as another Protestant denomination, and would the German language and culture be preserved through the church's ministries in Christian education? The family's decision to send the young Reinhold to Yale Divinity School in 1913 virtually ensured that he would become a leading light among the Americanizers. The church's struggle with its inherited German identity played itself out against the backdrops of World War I, mainline Protestantism's growing sympathy for the English and their allies, and nagging doubts about the patriotism of German immigrant communities. Though Niebuhr entered into these debates fully committed to the Americanist cause, after the Great War was over, he came to regret his uncritical enthusiasm for the Allied cause and adopted the Christian pacifism that would characterize his thinking until the eve of World War II.

Niebuhr's education was anything but leisurely. In 1913, Reinhold managed to graduate first in his class at Eden Theological Seminary in St. Louis, and he was then admitted to Yale. He quickly showed academic promise and was awarded the Divinity degree in June 1914 and the Master of Arts degree a year later. During his brief time at Yale, he was exposed to the intellectual traditions of American philosophy and the Protestant Social Gospel movement, and, judging by his correspondence to his teachers back home at Eden, he embraced these enthusiastically. When older brother Walter experienced a sudden reversal of financial fortune in 1915, Reinhold decided to terminate his formal education and go to work in his father's business. He later accepted a call to the ministry as pastor of Bethel Evangelical Church in Detroit.

Niebuhr labored in the Lord's vineyards in Detroit for thirteen years. During that time he attracted first local and, later, national attention for his Social Gospel preaching and journalism and for his political activism to empower blue-collar workers, improve race relations in America's burgeoning industrial cities, and foster peace and reconciliation in war-torn Europe. Sherwood Eddy, a prominent figure in the Young Men's Christian Association movement, became Niebuhr's patron and helped open the doors that would secure the growing influence that this immigrant's son was to exercise among mainline Protestants. As a result, in 1928 he was offered the professorship of Applied Christianity at Union Theological Seminary in New York, a position he held until his retirement in 1960. Shortly after he began teaching at Union, he and a newly arrived graduate student from Britain, Ursula Keppel Compton, fell in love with each other and were married in a Church of England ceremony at Winchester Cathedral in December 1931. As is evident from her own published writings, Ursula was probably the single biggest influence on Reinhold's development as a theologian and his growing appreciation for the traditions of classical Christianity, beyond the distinctively liberal German theology that he learned from his father.

The furious pace of Niebuhr's work as a teacher, prolific author, journalist, and social activist finally caught up with him, and in 1952, he suffered a debilitating stroke that left him with some brain damage, resulting in a long-term struggle with depression. Amazingly, Niebuhr continued to work at a frenzy that would have exhausted ordinary mortals, producing several more books in the 1950s and early 1960s. Nevertheless, in 1956, the Niebuhrs moved to Stockbridge, Massachusetts, so that Reinhold could avail himself of the therapy and personal friendship offered by psychologist Erik Erikson. In 1964, Niebuhr was awarded the Presidential Medal of Freedom by President Lyndon Baines Johnson, but this did not deter Niebuhr, in later years, from expressing his dissent against the conduct of the war in

Vietnam. On June 1, 1971, after a lengthy illness, Reinhold Niebuhr died at home in Stockbridge, Massachusetts.

The story of Reinhold Niebuhr's development as a Christian social activist and theologian is important because it establishes the context for understanding Niebuhr's theology as an expression of his work for the church in behalf of society as a whole. How his theology developed beyond this primary context is the question I hope to answer in the following section. I have identified five major issues that shaped Niebuhr's thought during his ministry in Detroit and his tenure as Professor of Applied Christianity at Union Seminary in New York. Each of these will be analyzed, not for their biographical interest, which is considerable, but for the light they cast on the development of Niebuhr's distinctive contribution to public theology— what admirers and critics have dubbed as Niebuhr's Christian realism.

The Issues That Shaped Niebuhr's Public Theology

In light of this brief sketch of Niebuhr's life, it should come as no surprise that Niebuhr's development as a public theologian is complex, unsystematic, and very much influenced by his reactions to the major events of his time. Five major issues shaped Niebuhr's public theology: (1) World War I and the crisis of German-Americanism (1915–23); (2) industrialization and the conditions of the working classes (1921–45); (3) fascism, communism, and U.S. participation in World War II (1934–44); (4) the postwar world: containment, the Cold War, and the nuclear stalemate (1946–71); and (5) civil rights (1931–71) and the war in Vietnam (1965–71). I will postpone the larger question of theological method implicit in Niebuhr's reactions until our discussion of the nature of Christian realism.

This list suggests that Niebuhr's involvement with these issues is not sequential. To a great extent the issues overlap, and lessons learned from one issue often impact the others. In analyzing these five issues, I will offer a brief sketch of each followed by Niebuhr's response to it. Implicit in all of them is a challenge to ourselves: "What can we learn from them?" While thinking about Niebuhr's development, we may want to ask ourselves the following questions: (1) Are these issues still our issues? (2) If not these, what issues should we be concerned about? and (3) Does Christian realism, as a model of public theology, offer resources for addressing our issues?

World War I and the Crisis of German-Americanism (1915–23)

What Niebuhr's church, the German Evangelical Synod in North America, experienced during World War I was, of course, not unusual. The Americanization of immigrant churches had been a matter of conscious policy for some. For example, the struggles among Roman Catholics in the United

States and the unconscious adaptation of other churches date back a full generation. One could argue that the changes in Latter-day Saint theology necessitated by Utah's application for statehood are other examples of Americanization—though hardly that of a recently arrived immigrant church.

The Evangelical Synod, however, was faced with serious controversy over whether the German language would continue to be used in church services, schools, and publications. Because American public opinion during the war was galvanized in support of the Allies and against Imperial Germany, the controversy was no longer confined to church policy but became a litmus for testing immigrant patriotism.

Niebuhr's posture on this issue seemed fully supportive of the Americanizers for characteristically German reasons. He invoked the traditions of German liberalism in support of greater openness to American cultural values and accused those who would resist Americanization of chauvinism. As pastor of the Synod's church in Detroit, Niebuhr sought to stimulate growth in church membership by opening the church to Christians from all ethnic groups.[1] He was unusually active in ecumenical affairs and worked closely with the coalition of religious groups supporting the United States's involvement in the war as an ally of France and the United Kingdom, a decision he was later to regret as he considered the extent of the reparations exacted from an exhausted Germany. Interestingly, like other Americanizers, he supported the temperance movement that eventually led to Prohibition. Niebuhr's posture is mostly biographical. His views guaranteed that when he did attract public attention in Detroit, he became known as a Social Gospel pacifist, seeking to make an impact on the larger society beyond the confines of his immigrant community. His response to the crisis of German-Americanism virtually assured that his social activism would be channeled in the direction of a public theology.[2]

Industrialization and the Conditions of the Working Classes (1921–45)

Before he began his ministry in Detroit, Niebuhr's life experience had not prepared him to deal with the problems that massive industrialization had created for working families struggling to survive in America's big cities. His lack of personal experience, however, was typical of Social Gospel Protestantism, which was primarily a movement of middle-class professionals bent on restoring the "Christian America" that still flourished in smaller

---

1. June Bingham, *Courage to Change: An Introduction to the Life and Thought of Reinhold Niebuhr* (New York: Charles Scribner's Sons, 1961), 111–12; Dennis P. McCann, *Christian Realism and Liberation Theology: Practical Theologies in Creative Conflict* (Maryknoll, N.Y.: Orbis, 1981), 8–9, 14.
2. McCann, *Christian Realism and Liberation Theology*, 14.

towns and rural areas.[3] Like other Social Gospel activists reacting to big city life, Niebuhr was forced to confront the realities of class conflict where labor was for sale like any other "commodity" and where workers were regarded as little more than just another "factor of production."[4] By the time Niebuhr was active in Detroit, the Social Gospel movement had helped build the coalition supporting the social reforms of the Progressive Era. But the new methods of mass production, pioneered locally by Henry Ford, eventually served only to intensify the crisis of industrialization. The postwar prosperity of the 1920s and Henry Ford's penchant for self-promotion at first led some to hope that the crisis had been resolved. His employees had received significant pay hikes and were often portrayed as the first beneficiaries of a new industrial system, but the illusion of progress was soon dispelled as Ford laid off most of his workers without compensation when the assembly lines were retooled for production of the new Model A.[5]

What had seemed to many in 1926 as merely the symptoms of growing pains soon appeared in another light as the Great Depression, which took hold in 1929–30. The conflict between labor and capital increasingly came to be seen as intractable, as not amenable to compromise, incremental reform, or moral suasion. Marxist ideology, which emphasized the historical inevitability of the class struggle, seemed particularly appealing as a general explanation for why the problems of industrialization could not be resolved apart from radical politics dedicated to full-scale social revolution. The workers would have to be organized to take what was rightfully theirs through any means necessary, including organized violence—or so it seemed.

Niebuhr's own stance on the crisis of industrialization was one of deepening pessimism and increasing openness to the program of Marxist social revolution. His ministry in Detroit had included serving on ecumenical task forces that sought to improve working conditions. Using his growing influence as a religious journalist for *The Christian Century,* he debunked Ford's "Utopia" and warned liberal Protestants against complacency in the struggle for social justice.[6] But in 1928, he, like many other Social Gospel activists, moved significantly to the political Left, supporting the Protestant-Socialist-Pacifist coalition and campaigning for Norman Thomas for president of the United States.[7] After Thomas was resoundingly defeated, Niebuhr concluded that the class struggle would not be resolved

---

3. Ibid.

4. Bingham, *Courage to Change,* 129.

5. Ibid., 131.

6. McCann, *Christian Realism and Liberation Theology,* 9; Bingham, *Courage to Change,* 139.

7. Bingham, *Courage to Change,* 157, 163.

through electoral politics or voluntary adjustments. He became increasingly disenchanted with the Social Gospel because of its religious optimism and political ineffectiveness, and he looked increasingly to Marxist-inspired organizations as allies in the struggle for social justice.[8] Though Niebuhr's views once more shifted dramatically against a Marxist social revolution as the 1930s wore on, the crisis of industrialization remained the crucible in which Niebuhr developed Christian realism as an alternative to the reigning theologies of the Social Gospel.[9]

Fascism, Communism, and U.S. Participation in World War II (1934–44)

Among the evils unleashed by the Great Depression, the rise of Nazism in Germany and the reinvigoration of fascism and communism were surely the worst. Desperate times seemed to require desperate measures, and each of these ideologies brought with it a deceptive appeal to the moral idealism of its adherents. These ideologies supported an unflinching resolve to achieve political goals using organized violence if necessary, a cynicism about democracy based on constitutional law and procedural justice, a new conception of the state as the exclusive organizing center for society as a whole, and above all, a wholesale rejection of the religious and moral traditions that had been honored—if only in lip service—throughout Western civilization until that time.

Nazism catered to the sense of grievance that understandably lingered in Germany thanks to the so-called Peace of Versailles that had ended World War I. But Hitler's rise to power, in the eyes of many, made a second world war virtually inevitable. The risk of war, however, was significantly compounded by the divergences between fascism and communism, for these ideologies were animated by moral visions that pointed in two very different directions. Nazism and fascism, on the one hand, were essentially two extreme forms of nationalism that saw the common good exclusively embodied in the blood and soil of a particular race of people. Communism, however, was animated by a militantly apocalyptic dream of universal solidarity and was transnational, utopian, and expansionist. Nazism as a form of fascism, though nationalistic, was also utopian and expansionistic. Both, eventually, were to be seen as a threat to the national security of the United States.

Based on his extensive involvement in post-WWI Germany, Niebuhr recognized early both the real problems that Nazism addressed and its fundamental immorality. As early as 1934, he predicted that Nazism would

---

8. McCann, *Christian Realism and Liberation Theology*, 11–12.
9. Ibid., 12.

once again put Germany on a collision course with the United States.[10] Niebuhr's realization of the true menace of communism, though decisive for the development of his mature theology of Christian realism, took longer to unfold. By 1934 he had become frustrated with American-Marxist politics, seeing that the revolutionary idealism offered by Marxism not only had its own cynical side but also was usually counterproductive politically.[11] He came to realize that it was not in the workers' interests to reject all compromises and incremental reforms in the hope of a utopian revolution. More to the point, however, events in Russia, particularly the so-called Moscow trials of the mid-1930s, confirmed that the weaknesses Niebuhr had detected in Marxist idealism were fatal and not amenable to gradual improvement.[12] The Hitler-Stalin pact of 1939, which paved the way for Hitler's march into Poland and the opening of World War II in eastern Europe, thus came as no surprise to Niebuhr.[13] He saw the clear danger to the United States and broke with his own previous support of Christian pacifism, arguing— against views then prevailing among liberal Protestants—that Christians had a moral duty to support U.S. involvement with Britain and France, once again, to save Western civilization.[14]

Niebuhr's much publicized decision to support Franklin D. Roosevelt's reelection to a third term in 1940 was not simply a result of his agreement with the President's foreign policy. By that time, Niebuhr had also begun to second guess his earlier rejection of Roosevelt's New Deal programs.[15] As the United States's slow progress out of the Great Depression accelerated (thanks to the Lend-Lease Act and other initiatives designed to make America "the Arsenal of Democracy"[16]), Niebuhr concluded that FDR's "piecemeal reformism"—an instinctive and not always coherent expression of the philosophy of American pragmatism—was morally preferable to the spurious revolutionary ideals held by Nazism and Soviet communism.[17] If social justice was to be realized, it would come through political pragmatism and not through any radical commitment to socialism. After WWII,

---

10. Ronald H. Stone, *Professor Reinhold Niebuhr: A Mentor to the Twentieth Century* (Nashville: Abingdon, 1972), 84–86; also Reinhold Niebuhr, *Reflections on the End of an Era* (New York: Charles Scribner's Sons, 1934).

11. Ronald H. Stone, *Reinhold Niebuhr: Prophet to Politicians* (Nashville: Abingdon, 1972), 69.

12. Bingham, *Courage to Change,* 213–14.

13. Richard Wightman Fox, *Reinhold Niebuhr: A Biography* (New York: Pantheon, 1985), 189, 190.

14. McCann, *Christian Realism and Liberation Theology,* 11.

15. Ibid.

16. See Stone, *Prophet to Politicians,* 89.

17. Ibid., 68–69.

Niebuhr institutionalized his commitment to New Deal reformism by becoming a founding member of Americans for Democratic Action—the quintessentially "liberal" postwar political action group.[18]

The Postwar World:
Containment, Cold War, and the Nuclear Stalemate (1946–71)

As 1944 was coming to a close, public attention began to shift from the exigencies of wartime mobilization to the practical and political challenges of ensuring a just and lasting peace. Goaded by the fear of a return to prewar isolationism that many felt had contributed to the outbreak of war, many people considered various schemes for world government. Something just less than world government did emerge in the form of the United Nations, dominated as it was by the victorious Allies. When these same Allies grew apart as the Cold War set in between the United States and the U.S.S.R., the United Nations became paralyzed, able to act only in those areas and on those issues where both the United States and the Soviet Union still had mutual interests. It soon became apparent, especially with the decline of Britain as a world power, that the United States no longer had the option of the "return to normalcy" such as it had exercised after World War I.

The challenge of global leadership was naturally compounded by the development of nuclear weapons. The United States had made the initial breakthrough with the Manhattan Project and had demonstrated at Hiroshima and Nagasaki the lethal potential of new technology of mass destruction. By 1949, however, the Soviet Union had developed nuclear weapons of its own, and the stage was set for the stalemate of "mutually assured destruction" as the world got used to living in the shadow of Armageddon.

Niebuhr was a major participant in the various policy debates that occurred in the United States in response to these issues. During the Truman administration he served as part of the brain trust assembled by George F. Kennan to help draft a new foreign policy for the postwar world.[19] Niebuhr's Christian realism came to share considerable common ground with the political realism cultivated by Kennan, Hans Morgenthau, and other Cold War intellectuals.[20] Niebuhr's own view had always maintained skepticism about the prospects of world government in the absence of global community.[21] Since the cultural and economic development of the

---

18. Fox, *Reinhold Niebuhr: A Biography*, 230–31; Stone, *Prophet to Politicians*, 158–59.

19. McCann, *Christian Realism and Liberation Theology*, 108; Bingham, *Courage to Change*, 388.

20. McCann, *Christian Realism and Liberation Theology*, 108.

21. Stone, *Prophet to Politicians*, 116–18.

planet had not yet progressed to the point where a political consensus was possible, no scheme of world government was likely to succeed. Niebuhr did, however, cautiously support the UN as an interim step, advocating a gradualist approach to creating the conditions that one day might usher in world government.[22] In its then present form, he believed the UN could be most effective as an ongoing attempt to stabilize the "balance of power" in international politics.[23] Still more useful and to the point, he believed, were the creation of NATO and its enforcement of Kennan's policy of "containment" against the U.S.S.R.[24]

As the Cold War heated up, Niebuhr asserted that international communism was a greater threat than Nazism, and he warned whoever would listen, particularly in the churches of mainline Protestantism, of the dangers of Soviet expansionism.[25] He was particularly worried about the attractions of what he termed "hard Utopianism,"[26] that is, the idealistic appeal that Soviet ideology possessed for third-world intellectuals and politicians. At the same time, he also warned against United States self-righteousness, particularly the idea that the Cold War was some kind of modern crusade.[27] He expected a protracted conflict and warned Americans against their characteristic impatience and dangerous longing for some sort of global showdown.

Niebuhr's views on nuclear weapons were similarly nuanced.[28] Though he initially defended the U.S. decision to drop atomic bombs on Japan, he later advocated a policy of "no first use" of nuclear weapons, which put him at some distance from strategic United States doctrine.[29] Even so, he opposed unilateral disarmament and consistently supported arms control negotiations.[30]

The challenges of the postwar world were not the crucible in which Niebuhr's Christian realism was forged, but they did provide the occasion in which his perspective gained its greatest following, especially by shaping public opinion beyond the mainline Protestant denominations. His analyses of the complexities of the postwar world won him a secular following, often

---

22. Ibid., 117–18.

23. McCann, *Christian Realism and Liberation Theology*, 98–99, 109; Stone, *Prophet to Politicians*, 187.

24. Fox, *Reinhold Niebuhr: A Biography*, 240.

25. Stone, *Prophet to Politicians*, 159.

26. Reinhold Niebuhr, *Faith and History: A Comparison of Christian and Modern Views of History* (New York: Charles Scribner's Sons, 1949), 208.

27. Stone, *Prophet to Politicians*, 172–73.

28. Ibid., 171–80; McCann, *Christian Realism and Liberation Theology*, 115.

29. Fox, *Reinhold Niebuhr: A Biography*, 240.

30. Ibid., 240–41.

self-designated as "Atheists for Niebuhr." After World War II, Niebuhr concentrated increasingly on foreign policy issues because he felt that "rough justice"[31] had been achieved by the New Deal reforms in the United States and that the groundwork had been well-laid for sustaining a generalized prosperity during the postwar period. American workers, in Niebuhr's view, now had a real stake in the system, and the system itself had become a model that could be exported to other developing nations.[32] Thus the focus of his own reflections appropriately shifted to the international arena and away from the questions of economic and social justice that had shaped the major tenets of Christian realism.

Civil Rights (1931–71) and the War in Vietnam (1965–71)

Although issues of civil rights and the war in Vietnam came to a head in the decade after Niebuhr's retirement from Union Seminary in 1960, they are important for understanding the controversies that have surrounded Christian realism since Niebuhr's death in 1971. The civil rights movement, of course, refers to the struggle to remove the vestiges of legal discrimination, or "Jim Crow" laws, enacted against African Americans. As the civil rights movement succeeded in establishing the legal and political rights of African Americans, its mandate was broadened by the Black Power movement to include efforts toward economic empowerment and cultural affirmation. The transformation of the civil rights movement coincided, of course, with the emergence of social movements protesting the United States's involvement in the Vietnamese civil war. In August 1967, Dr. Martin Luther King, generally regarded as the leader of the civil rights movement, acknowledged the convergence of these issues by accepting the presidential nomination of the National Conference for New Politics. Dr. King understood that the sacrifices being made in Vietnam fell disproportionately on African American and white youth whose poverty prevented them from qualifying for the education-based draft deferments enjoyed by children of the middle class. For the new generation of black and white youth who followed Dr. King, the "American dilemma" of race had now converged on the still unresolved problem of poverty and on-going uncertainty over the United States's dominant role in world affairs.

As far back as the 1920s, Niebuhr demonstrated concern over the racist discrimination suffered by African Americans.[33] Yet over the years, their cause did not receive his full attention probably because he tended to think

---

31. McCann, *Christian Realism and Liberation Theology*, 107.
32. Ibid., 116–18.
33. Stone, *Prophet to Politicians*, 31–34; Fox, *Reinhold Niebuhr: A Biography*, 90–94.

primarily in post-Marxist terms about social class, in effect minimizing the significance of race and culture while maximizing the significance of socio-economic status. When Niebuhr's students at Union seminary challenged him with their civil rights militancy, the views he expressed were moderate.[34] He supported Dr. King's Southern Christian Leadership Conference, which Niebuhr preferred over nonviolent political strategies tempered by a pessimistic view of just how fast inherited cultural prejudices may or may not be changed. Niebuhr's deep-seated suspicions against "utopianism" prevented him from fully endorsing the younger generation's call for Black Power.[35]

Niebuhr initially regarded Vietnam as another local conflict within the larger Cold War struggle. Like others Niebuhr was committed to the Kennan policy of containment; his understanding of changes then underway in the so-called third world pivoted on the global competition for influence between the U.S. and the U.S.S.R.[36] He initially supported U.S. military intervention in Vietnam, believing that Vietnam was another "domino" about to fall behind the Bamboo Curtain.[37] Challenged once more by his militant students, Niebuhr concluded by 1968 that the war was immoral because it could not be won without a disproportionate—and hence, unjust—use of military force.[38] The last articles that he published before his death in 1971 criticize further U.S. military involvement in Vietnam and actively encourage protesters in their efforts to end the war.

Despite this evidence of his changing views, Niebuhr's ambivalence toward what turned out to be the defining issues of the 1960s earned him the contempt of many younger theologians—Roman Catholic as well as Protestant—who regarded Christian realism as an "ideology of the Establishment."[39] In the 1970s and 1980s, they sought to develop versions of liberation theology.[40] Niebuhr did not live to see liberation theology, but had he done so, he probably would have understood it as a new version of the same Social Gospel idealism that he tried and found wanting in the 1920s.[41]

In recent years, especially with the collapse of communism in eastern Europe and the former Soviet Union, Niebuhr's thinking has once again attracted a following as many Christian social activists have come to

---

34. Fox, *Reinhold Niebuhr: A Biography*, 281–83.
35. Ibid., 282–83.
36. McCann, *Christian Realism and Liberation Theology*, 105–21.
37. Fox, *Reinhold Niebuhr: A Biography*, 284.
38. Stone, *Prophet to Politicians*, 194.
39. McCann, *Christian Realism and Liberation Theology*, 2, 19.
40. Ibid., 131–55.
41. Stone, *Prophet to Politicians*, 53–55; McCann, *Christian Realism and Liberation Theology*, 9–10.

recognize the wisdom of his anticommunism and the global significance of his defense—on religious grounds—of democracy as the precondition for economic and social justice. This is the context in which we make our own inquiry into the nature of Christian realism as a model of public theology. The crises that stimulated Niebuhr's theological development may have passed, but his theological achievement seems to have withstood the test of time.

Christian Realism: A Public Theology

There are essentially four questions that I wish to discuss in making a systematic analysis of Niebuhr's public theology: (1) Where is the realism in Christian realism? (2) What makes Christian realism Christian? (3) Why and how does Christian realism become explicitly theological? and (4) What makes Christian realism a public theology?

Where Is the Realism in Christian Realism?

Realism is a vexing term. It is often a thinly veiled form of self-congratulation: "I'm only being realistic. You, on the other hand, are a cynic, or worse, an idealist." Yet Niebuhr's mature theological perspective was first characterized as realism, not by himself, but by admirers like John C. Bennett.[42] There are, of course, many possible types of realism: political realism, moral realism, religious realism, and epistemological realism. The question is, which of these is Niebuhr's? We have seen so far that Niebuhr's experience as a Christian social activist left him increasingly disenchanted with the Social Gospel. He came to regard it as too idealistic to be an effective guide in the crises that, he believed, the United States was facing in the period after World War I.[43]

At stake here, I believe, was not simply Niebuhr's keen sensitivity to social conflict but also his intellectual commitment to philosophical pragmatism from his days at Yale. Though his early writings show the explicit influence of pragmatism, particularly that of William James, the pragmatic structure of Niebuhr's thought is usually implicit. His theological analyses, in particular, exhibit a Jamesian ethic of belief. Religious ideas are routinely judged by the assumptions of pragmatism's theory of meaning. Such ideas must "work"; otherwise they are meaningless. They should be regarded as practical hypotheses that must make a difference in how we think and act in the real world. In the absence of compelling scientific proof one way or another, religious ideas can be intellectually responsible and morally

---

42. McCann, *Christian Realism and Liberation Theology*, 2.
43. Stone, *Prophet to Politicians*, 49–53; Bingham, *Courage to Change*, 160.

appropriate, as James theorized, provided they can meet the pragmatic test of meaning.[44]

Niebuhr's pragmatism can be seen in the way he tested the practical efficacy of Social Gospel Christianity against what he considered the most attractive religious alternative at the time: revolutionary Marxism. He saw that Marxist social thought did make a difference, for it seemed superior to the Social Gospel in generating the moral passion necessary to mobilize workers for the social struggle.[45] He initially hoped to revitalize the Social Gospel by showing how its ideas could be made more efficacious.[46] When later he became disillusioned with Marxist politics, again, on practical grounds, he began to appreciate the political relevance of the "more conservative religious convictions" of classical Christianity.[47] Frustrated by the internecine quarrels among various sects of socialists and the ideological pretensions of virtually all political groups seeking to define the public agenda for social change, Niebuhr moderately observed that original sin is the only empirically verifiable doctrine of Christianity. As the political and intellectual climate of the 1930s continued to deteriorate, Niebuhr became convinced that all forms of modern idealism—including its mirror image, naturalism—fail the pragmatic test of meaning.[48] Their basic misunderstanding of human nature leads to serious errors in social analysis and political strategy that exacerbate the crises of contemporary society rather than mitigating them. Only "prophetic Christianity,"[49] in his view, meets the pragmatic test because it is the only perspective that is sufficiently paradoxical to understand the vicissitudes of human nature and thus provide useful insight and relevant proposals for overcoming the crises of contemporary society.[50]

This is the central argument animating Niebuhr's chief theological work, *The Nature and Destiny of Man*. The only adequate and sufficiently paradoxical perspective is that of "prophetic Christianity,"[51]—the biblically oriented, religious wisdom, whose efficacious power had been demonstrated through a pragmatic analysis provoked by the exigencies of the contemporary crises in Western civilization.[52] As the 1930s wore on, Niebuhr's religious

---

44. Stone, *Prophet to Politicians*, 145–51.

45. McCann, *Christian Realism and Liberation Theology*, 15–16.

46. Stone, *Prophet to Politicians*, 54–56.

47. Ibid., 125–29; McCann, *Christian Realism and Liberation Theology*, 18.

48. Stone, *Prophet to Politicians*, 95.

49. Reinhold Niebuhr, *The Nature and Destiny of Man*, 2 vols. (New York: Charles Scribner's Sons, 1948), 1:215.

50. Ibid., 1:219–227.

51. Ibid., 1:215.

52. Ibid., 1:69–70.

journalism clearly suggested that some biblical ideas could still be relevant; however, more extended and systematic argument was necessary to validate Niebuhr's perspective as genuinely theological. The opportunity to make his mark as a theologian came with the invitation to present the prestigious Gifford Lectures of 1939 in Edinburgh, Scotland.[53] To these we must now turn in order to consider the specifically Christian affirmations of Christian realism.

What Makes Christian Realism Christian?

"Prophetic Christianity" is a term that Niebuhr himself often used to describe his settled theological convictions.[54] It is also a term that could give rise to no end of confusion. In Niebuhr's view, prophecy is a discernment of the practical will of God that occurs at the intersection of faith and history.[55] It is not about making predictions or spotting trends but about constructing (construing or interpreting) reality as a manifestation of God's ongoing presence among us. Such acts of religious discernment do not necessarily give rise, in Niebuhr's view, to classical Christian doctrines of revelation.[56] A prophet is not necessarily a charismatic leader, or one through whom God has directly communicated a revelation. Nevertheless, to qualify as "prophetic" in Niebuhr's sense, religious discernments about God's ongoing activity in history—such as those formulated in a public theology—must be capable of persuading Christians to act in socially transformative ways.

Public theology is an attempt to formulate such discernments and to test them in a form of argumentation that validates them, both within the deeper contours of the religious traditions from which they spring and the wider concerns of the public at large. Many claim to be prophets, and there are many competing interpretations of prophetic Christianity. Public theology tries to expose the differences between true and false prophecy, adequate and inadequate theologies, effective and ineffective strategies for Christian social action. Some modern American theologians whose works fit this understanding of public theology, committed to critically testing the discernments of prophetic Christianity, include Walter Rauschenbusch, *Theology for the Social Gospel* (1917); Martin Luther King Jr., "Letter from the Birmingham Jail" (1957); John Courtney Murray, S. J., *We Hold These Truths* (1961); Gustavo Gutiérrez, *A Theology of Liberation* (1971);

---

53. Fox, *Reinhold Niebuhr: A Biography*, 178.
54. Niebuhr, *The Nature and Destiny of Man*, 1:214–16.
55. Ibid., 1:136–49.
56. Ibid., 1:125–31.

Mary Daly, *Beyond God the Father* (1973); and Michael Novak, *The Spirit of Democratic Capitalism* (1982).[57]

Niebuhr's Christian realism is but one example of public theology. As we have seen, his theology directly and explicitly seeks to differentiate itself from Rauschenbusch's Social Gospel, and the other writers just mentioned have all taken Niebuhr into account, one way or another.

Christian realism, then, is Christian in the minimal sense that it is a theological position that stands within the growing tradition of public theology. Of course, as the above list suggests, one may question whether public theology is authentically Christian, for all the theologians mentioned represent decidedly liberal and/or postmodernist perspectives and therefore are open to question regarding the authenticity of their Christian convictions. One conventional way to facilitate such questioning is to locate these perspectives against a map of the basic elements that are essential to any form of Christian theology. The map I'm using is taken from Max Stackhouse's *Public Theology and Political Economy: Christian Stewardship in Modern Society* (1987),[58] which derives a "Quadrilateral" of Christian theological authorities from the practices outlined in *The Book of Discipline of the United Methodist Church.*[59] I'm introducing it here because I'm convinced that it models, in suitably general terms, the tacit assumptions common to virtually all Christian theologians, past or present.

Figure 1 shows a schematic diagram of the Christian (or Wesleyan) Quadrilateral. The top of the Quadrilateral displays the interplay of scripture and tradition that occurs within all Christian communities regardless of their particular theological understanding of the relationship between the two or of the sole unsurpassable authority of scripture. The bottom side illustrates the role of reason (understood currently as the assured findings of the sciences and philosophy) and experience (understood as the personal and collective wisdom operative in Christian communities today) as they help define the questions that theologians and other members

---

57. Walter Rauschenbusch, *A Theology for the Social Gospel* (New York: Macmillan, 1917); Martin Luther King Jr., "Letter from the Birmingham Jail" (San Francisco: Harper, 1957); John Courtney Murray, S. J., *We Hold These Truths: Catholic Reflections on the American Proposition* (New York: Sheed and Ward, 1960); Gustavo Gutiérrez, *A Theology of Liberation: History, Politics and Salvation,* trans. and ed. Caridad Inda and John Eagleson (Maryknoll, N.Y.: Orbis, 1973); Mary Daly, *Beyond God the Father: Toward a Philosophy of Women's Liberation* (Boston: Beacon, 1973); Michael Novak, *The Spirit of Democratic Capitalism* (New York: Simon and Schuster, 1982).

58. Max Stackhouse, *Public Theology and Political Economy: Christian Stewardship in Modern Society* (Grand Rapids, Mich.: Eerdmans, 1987).

59. *The Book of Discipline of the United Methodist Church* (Nashville: United Methodist Publishing House, 1990).

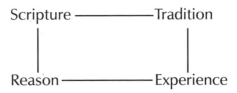

Scripture ——————Tradition

Reason ——————Experience

Figure 1. A schematic diagram of the Chrstian Quadrilateral

of the communities will ask of God through their continuous scrutiny of Scripture and Tradition.

Thus the Quadrilateral may help us trace the specifically Christian emphases of prophetic Christianity. Prophetic Christianity, in its various theological expressions, tends to emphasize the axes of Scripture and Experience. The insights generated in the interplay of the two, however, yield theological formulations that can be tested in relationship to the axes of Reason and Tradition. Thus, like all other forms of authentically Christian theology, Christian realism is formally accountable to all four authoritative sources, though its specific emphases may vary from other, equally authentic, theological perspectives. The Quadrilateral also maps the specific "hermeneutic circle" in which Niebuhr's theology unfolded[60] by locating the time-bound and culturally embedded aspects of his theological questions and answers. His perspective on prophetic Christianity is a response to questions that could only have been asked by Christians struggling to discern the will of God in a modern, rapidly industrializing democracy, such as the United States was in the middle third of the twentieth century. The Quadrilateral helps us to grasp the Christian intent, at least, of Niebuhr's Christian realism.

Why and How Does Christian Realism Become Explicitly "Theological"?

As we have already seen, Niebuhr's questioning of scripture and tradition was heavily influenced by his personal experience as a liberal Protestant pastor, religious journalist, and social activist. It was also shaped by what he thought reasonable, based on his critical reading of history, psychology, and the social sciences of the time. To render a theological account of one's Christian faith in terms of the norms embodied in all four points of the Quadrilateral may require an intellectual effort of considerable sophistication and complexity. Niebuhr put this forth in *The Nature and Destiny of Man,* a

---

60. McCann, *Christian Realism and Liberation Theology,* 202.

work considered by most of his students as his greatest theological achievement. In these two volumes Niebuhr argues for his particular interpretation of prophetic Christianity by formulating two conceptual structures for orienting Christian social action: theological anthropology and the theology of history. Both of these, as we will see, are meant to pass the pragmatic test for the meaning of religious ideas.

Theological anthropology is Christian realism's understanding of human nature: the human person before God is *simul justus et peccator* (Luther's existential paradox of the person who knows himself to be both sinner and saved through faith in Jesus Christ).[61] Christian realism's chief theological contribution is to spell out the practical consequences of this Reformation doctrine, particularly in a modern world dominated by competing ideologies of human progress.

According to Niebuhr, ideology, especially totalitarian ideologies that falsely promise utopia, is the modern expression of the perennial sin of idolatry and its derivatives: pride and sensuality.[62] As the rational expression of collective interests, ideology is "tainted," in that it can never be an unbiased, wholly disinterested, inclusive formulation of the common good. Religious ideologies are the most dangerous because the sinful "taint" in them is harder to detect and thus likely to inspire greater fanaticism than consistently secular ideologies.[63] Niebuhr's anthropology suggests that ideology can never be entirely eliminated—certainly not by reason even in the form of science, certainly not by "free-floating intellectuals," as Karl Mannheim hoped—but it can be partially overcome in "moments of prayerful transcendence,"[64] that is, through contrite self-criticism inspired by Christian faith. The intended consequence of Niebuhr's diagnosis of the problem of ideology is to lower the temperature on political and social conflict so that the threshold of violence might be lowered in them. A secondary consequence is to direct Christian social activists away from counterproductive and fanatical attempts to establish the kingdom of God on earth.[65]

Christian realism's theology of history is an attempt to formulate the general expectations for Christian social action in the world. It conveys, in short, Niebuhr's muted theology of Christian hope. For Niebuhr, the history of the world since the appearance of Jesus of Nazareth suggests that the

---

61. Martin Luther, "Vorrede auff die Epistel S. Paul an die Römer," in D. Martin Luthers Werke, *Deutsche Bibel,* vol. 7; E. T. Bachmann, trans. and ed., "Preface to the Epistle of St. Paul to the Romans," in *Luther's Works,* vol. 35, *Word and Sacrament I* (Philedelphia: Fortress, 1960), 370.

62. McCann, *Christian Realism and Liberation Theology,* 18, 58.

63. Ibid., 94–98.

64. Ibid., 96.

65. Ibid., 73.

transformation inaugurated by the Christ is only partially or ambiguously realized in history.[66] Niebuhr thus characterizes the gospel, the vision of a love transcending justice, embodied in the hope of the kingdom of God as an "impossible possibility."[67] The gospel thus acts as a lure that stimulates us to greater effort to create a society based on this vision, but it also acts as a goad by providing a standard against which to measure the inadequacies of our efforts. No society, no church even, can claim to embody the kingdom of God. All human institutions, in one way or another, betray the hope of the kingdom of God.[68] Niebuhr explicitly rejects Roman Catholic claims regarding the church and generally rails against the pretensions of "Christian perfectionism."[69]

Niebuhr's major pragmatic objective, however, is not to criticize the churches but to alert all Christians to the dangers of identifying the gospel with any secular ideology—such as Marxist socialism—that offers a counterfeit kingdom of God. Since the kingdom of God can, at best, only be approximated on earth, Christian social activists are warned against any total, all-or-nothing, once-and-for-all solutions to society's problems. His theology of history is thus an argument for a political strategy of "piecemeal reformism."[70] In international politics this translates into an acceptance of the principle of a "balance of power."[71] Christian perfectionism in its post–World War II political form—in Niebuhr's view, an unholy passion for a final Armageddon-like crusade against communism—thus stands repudiated, even though Niebuhr detests communism as deeply as any would-be crusader might. His theology of history also warrants his views on the political and moral superiority of Western-style democracy and its commitment to a social safety net for all citizens. The New Deal, in his view, is not the kingdom of God, but it has achieved a "rough justice"[72] that is preferable to the chaos, corruption, and sheer inhumanity spawned by communism and its evil twin, Nazism.

In order to make clear the relationship linking Niebuhr's theological anthropology and theology of history with the way in which the Quadrilateral is realized in his work as a whole, it may be useful to review the substantively biblical themes that are operative in both theological structures. These themes are Niebuhr's interpretations of the major

---

66. Ibid., 64–74.

67. Bingham, *Courage to Change,* 196; McCann, *Christian Realism and Liberation Theology,* 229.

68. McCann, *Christian Realism and Liberation Theology,* 50–51, n. 3.

69. Ibid., 59, 73.

70. Ibid., 105.

71. Ibid., 98–101.

72. Ibid., 107.

scriptural motifs, what he called "the truth in myths," namely the Creation, Fall, Redemption, and eschatology.[73] Each of these motifs Niebuhr is determined to "take seriously, but not literally."[74] That is, each is understood as a religious idea whose pragmatic efficacy is perennially demonstrated in the experience of those who live by them. To those who would question whether it is possible to take anything seriously that is not also taken literally, Niebuhr would respond with another "prophetic" warning against the specific forms of idolatry to which Christians typically are prone. Whether this response is persuasive to anyone not already committed to the basic presuppositions of liberal Protestantism, I will leave for your considered reflection.

Niebuhr's interest in the biblical account of the Creation is focused almost exclusively on its anthropological implications. Here Niebuhr shows little interest in using biblical narratives to develop a metaphysically coherent doctrine of God, particularly God's nature. The most likely explanation for his reticence here is not indifference to the reality of God as the ultimate mystery but his philosophical pragmatism which predisposes him to assume, rightly or wrongly, that doctrinal disputes about God's nature make no discernible difference in how Christians actually conduct themselves in the world. The anthropological implications of these same narratives, however, do make a difference, for they disclose the human person to be a paradoxical mix of finitude and freedom, which explains both "the heights and the depths" of human experience.[75] The characteristic sins of humanity—pride and sensuality—involve a refusal to faithfully live the paradox that is the image of God in us. All sins are ultimately forms of idolatry. One distinctive feature here is that though Niebuhr makes heavy use of the Pauline view of human nature outlined in the New Testament, he does not follow the usual inference from St. Paul's understanding of sin and death—namely, that death is essentially unnatural for humans and would not have happened save for the sin of our first parents. Death is intrinsically an expression of finitude and must be accepted as such. This may be the key to Niebuhr's refusal to understand redemption primarily in terms of resurrection in the afterlife.

Regarding the biblical account of humanity's fall from grace, Niebuhr defends the classical Christian idea of original sin as empirically verifiable doctrine. Nevertheless, its basis is symbolism rather than literal fact. The symbol of the Fall is particularly useful in emphasizing the universality of sin. No person, no institution, no society can claim to be exempt. Niebuhr believes that the confession, or awareness, of sin is essential in order to curb political violence based on the pretense of innocence and absolute justice.

73. Ibid., 37–49.
74. Ibid., 38.
75. Ibid., 46.

The universality of sin, in his view, is linked to modern analyses exploring the role of anxiety in human behavior (following Kierkegaard). Instead of accepting, in faith, the paradox of finitude and freedom as a gift from God, we regard it anxiously in ways that inevitably cause us to sin by overcompensating for our vulnerabilities.

Redemption, for Niebuhr, is the grace of Christian faith.[76] The gospel by which we are redeemed is a message, or religious vision, concretely embodied in the life and teachings of Jesus Christ. Though the gospel is an "impossible possibility," it does confer grace in two ways: as power and as wisdom. The power of the gospel, in Niebuhr's view, consists in its capacity to move us toward repentance, faith, and acceptance of God's justification of us.[77] The wisdom of the gospel is the existential truth appropriated from the message that prompts us to acknowledge our sin and place our trust in God.[78] The death of Jesus on the cross demonstrates the ultimate logic of this message. The hatred that Jesus received from his enemies testifies to the impossibility of his vision; the sacrificial love that Jesus modeled by personally transcending this hatred testifies to its enduring possibility. The natural bonds of love as mutual regard cannot be sustained apart from a willingness to embrace the sacrificial love of the Cross. This is as true of political community, for Niebuhr, as it is in personal relationships. Humanity will never achieve social justice without it.

For Niebuhr, eschatology—or the biblical accounts of the "the last things" that Christians hope for—provides a set of symbols that, like creation, define the limits of human understanding and human action in history.[79] True to his Social Gospel origins, Niebuhr regards the kingdom of God as the Christian faith's primary eschatological symbol.[80] What he says about the kingdom of God could be said about any of the other eschatological symbols: the Millennium, the Last Judgment, the general Resurrection, New Jerusalem, New Heaven, and New Earth. Niebuhr is agnostic about any literal fulfillment of the hopes conveyed in these symbols. He does not attempt to deny or debunk them. He will criticize them to the extent that pragmatic analysis shows them compounding our problems rather than solving them. Since, in Niebuhr's view, death is inevitable, not because of sin, but as the ultimate manifestation of our finitude, the hope of resurrection is not necessary to validate the redemption offered in Jesus Christ. The Resurrection, as Niebuhr characteristically if not cryptically avers, remains a symbol to be taken seriously but not literally. Later in life, he tended to

---

76. Ibid., 44, 60–61.
77. Ibid., 60–61.
78. Ibid.
79. Ibid., 50–51, n. 3, 72–74.
80. Ibid., 73.

hedge these rather minimalist views, possibly under the influence of his wife's Anglicanism and his growing sense of his own mortality. Those hoping to discover a more conservative reading of Christian eschatology from Niebuhr should consider his later and less highly regarded work *Faith and History* (1949).[81]

Judged by the standards of a Barth or a Tillich, or even more so, an Augustine or an Aquinas, Niebuhr's theological reflections, while often substantive, may seem exceedingly skimpy. Clearly, his ethical perspective and his political philosophy are shaped by his theological perspective, but even in *The Nature and Destiny of Man*, Niebuhr's theology may be regarded as tentative, more a work in progress than a definitive statement. But when Niebuhr's work is viewed against the achievements of the other models of public theology whom I mentioned earlier—Rauschenbusch, King, Murray, Gutiérrez, Daly, and Novak—Niebuhr's theology is as fully articulated as any of them. Why each of them should turn out to be so minimalist may be answered by considering our final question as to how Christian realism—such as it is—should be regarded as a public theology.

What Makes Christian Realism a "Public Theology"?

There are two senses in which Christian realism intends to be a public theology, both of which are already implicit in what has been said so far. The first sense of "public" refers to a theologian's accountability to the public at large. In other words, public theology is reflective of a philosophically articulated ethics of belief. The second sense of "public" refers to a theologian's accountability to the Christian community. In other words, public theology is reflective of the church's public mission in society. Distinctive of public theology is the realization that the church cannot be effective in carrying out its social mission without embodying a transparently adequate ethics of belief in its practices.

Niebuhr's ethic of belief, as we have seen, presupposes philosophical pragmatism, with its critical acceptance of the methods and assumptions of modern science, as the appropriate standard of cognitive responsibility. Niebuhr believes that it is imperative for Christianity, or any religious movement, to determine and to seek to live by an appropriate standard of cognitive responsibility. Everything he ever wrote suggests the usually tacit assumption that no religious movement in the modern world can be morally serious without also being intellectually serious. Given this assumption, public accountability sets the agenda for Christian apologetics.

---

81. Reinhold Niebuhr, *Faith and History: A Comparison of Christian and Modern Views of History* (New York: Charles Scribner's Sons, 1949).

Since philosophical pragmatism provides the best available account of a theologian's ethic of belief, its assumptions about meaning and truth will necessarily shape the limits and possibilities for Christian theological discourse. As Niebuhr's writings testify, some biblical narratives will continue to meet the pragmatic test of meaning and truth, while others will not. The ethic of belief does not necessarily require the theologian to explicitly repudiate those narratives that are pragmatically doubtful (unless silence regarding them risks perpetuating even greater evils), but neither does it encourage him or her to keep them alive artificially. For example, nowhere does Niebuhr repudiate the traditional Christian belief in the virgin birth of Jesus; this doctrine, along with other similar cases, finds no place in Niebuhr's perspective because he cannot see how its affirmation or denial might make any practical difference in the way Christians live their lives or how the churches conduct their mission in the world. The public theologian must concentrate on those elements of Christian faith, based as they are in Scripture and Tradition, that can and do make a practical difference. Any other course of action would be cognitively irresponsible.

The second sense of "public" focuses on the mission of the Christian churches in the world. Niebuhr's personal history guaranteed that he would be among those theologians who conceived of the church's mission in external rather than internal terms. Though he started out as a minister in an immigrant church, he became a Christian pundit who addressed the nation as a whole. In shifting his focus to the nation as a whole, Niebuhr, like all other public theologians, restructured his own thinking according to the logic of ecumenism or religious pluralism. The public theologian makes his arguments to a diverse audience, with whom he may or may not be able to achieve consensus about matters of faith, and he does so in order to make the church's mission more transparently effective in the world.

However, there is a hazard involved in public theology. How does a theologian make a contribution to public discourse regarding society's common concerns without betraying the faith of his own community? In making his theology relevant to a national audience, does the public theologian risk buying into plausibility structures that will unduly restrict the ways in which he interprets scripture and tradition in public? Public effectiveness or social relevance may come at too high a cost if it can be purchased only by remaining silent about certain affirmations usually considered central to Christian faith. One may question whether Christian realism's rather modest eschatology, for example, warrants no more than an equally modest public mission for the church, one which limits the socially transformative power of the gospel to the essentially negative function of critiquing the ideological pretensions of other public actors.

Conclusion:
Does "Prophetic Christianity" Need a Public Theology?

At the beginning of this essay, I argued that an outsider's perspective—such as that afforded by membership in The Church of Jesus Christ of Latter-day Saints—may be a significant advantage for interpreting Niebuhr's Christian realism. Latter-day Saints, I gather, have a very different understanding of prophetic Christianity than the one presupposed in Christian realism. In the LDS view, God still speaks through Christian prophecy—most dramatically in the founding of the LDS church through Joseph Smith, but even in our time through those officers whom the LDS church recognizes as possessing the gift of prophecy.

LDS faith and practice, it seems to me, raise important questions that can be addressed to Niebuhr and other public theologians. The chief of these is the question "Why?" Why develop a structure of theological inferences within a publicly validated ethic of belief if Christian prophets still receive revelations directly from God? As the LDS church continues to develop, public theology in Niebuhr's sense may thus be regarded as neither necessary nor inevitable. Nevertheless, understanding other forms of prophetic Christianity may be instructive for LDS theologians committed to the LDS church's own distinctive mission and ministry.

True to the ideal of prophetic Christianity honored by liberal Protestantism, Niebuhr recognizes no prophets beyond those commemorated in scripture: Niebuhr goes no further than canonical prophets like Amos and, of course, preeminently, Jesus. In this type of prophetic Christianity, theology is necessary to understand what the prophets of old have taught and to extend the lines of inference that might link their teachings to our present circumstances. Theology thus becomes an argument conducted in public, both inside and outside the church, that helps Christians to discern the path of faithfulness today. The church continually makes up its mind about itself and its responsibilities. However, theology is not the expression or defense of an infallible Magisterium any more than it is the communication of a prophet's revelations. This form of prophetic Christianity thus follows the Lutheran principle of *Sola Scriptura* (the authority of scripture alone).

If scripture is the ultimate authority to which theology is accountable, what is Niebuhr's approach to scripture? Niebuhr presupposes the vast body of German higher criticism propounded by figures such as Reimarus, David Friedrich Strauss, Wilhelm Hermann, and Albert Schweitzer. To recognize the authority of scripture is, for Niebuhr, to take it seriously but not literally. Taking scripture seriously means discerning the truth in its permanent "myths." Myth, for Niebuhr, is a powerful, religious story that confers identity on persons and communities. The truth in them is discerned pragmatically: for example, Niebuhr's reflections on the Genesis narratives and their anthropological significance. Scripture thus yields a coherent cycle of biblical themes, or myths, that form a world view that confers identity on Christians and their churches. These myths give us answers to the three central questions memorably formulated by Immanuel Kant: Who are we? What must we do? And what, if anything, may we hope for?

The theologian's task is to reconstruct the answers given to these questions in biblical myth in order to assist Christians in construing the world faithfully. The theologian may use the scientific study of religion in order to make comparisons between the Christian worldview and other worldviews. Niebuhr did exactly this throughout his career. But unlike other theologians, his reflections were circumscribed by his commitment to the pragmatic test for meaning. Thus, Christian realism is theology insofar as it carries out the traditional task of Christian theology, as defined by St. Anselm of Canterbury in *Fides Quarens Intellectum*.[82] Niebuhr's *fides* (faith) and his *intellectum* (understanding) are distinctively liberal Protestant and American pragmatist, but the *quaerens* (seeking) is classically Christian and robustly theological. Surely one could use St. Anselm's definition to map the work of theologians who share Niebuhr's Christian intent (his *Quarens,* if you will) and live in a very different understanding (*Intellectum*) of prophetic Christianity (*Fides*). What public theology might become within the form of prophetic Christianity represented by The Church of Jesus Christ of Latter-day Saints is a question that may be stimulated by considering Niebuhr's Christian realism. However, this is by no means the predetermined answer by either the strengths or the weaknesses of Christian realism as a model for public theology.

Response to Professor McCann

Richard Sherlock

Without question Reinhold Niebuhr was one of the most well known and widely quoted American theologians of the twentieth century. This was due in part to the gravity of the issues on which he spoke so forcefully: economic inequality, the need for strong action to combat fascism and communism, and the dangers of concentrated power in a democracy.

---

82. St. Anselm of Canterbury, "Fides Quarens Intellectum."

Not surprisingly, then, Reinhold Niebuhr's influence was not just on those students of his who labored behind the lectern or the pulpit. His theological influence was also felt on the battlefield, in the legislative chamber, at the negotiating table, and in the union hall.[83]

Ironically, Niebuhr did not, for the most part, create powerful new versions of theology or even ethics. Except for his crusade against pacifism in the late 1930s, he did not speak to the community of faith like Barth or even Bultmann.[84] He spoke from the community of faith to the wider world. In the broad sense, his students were as likely to be theorists of international relations like Hans Morgenthau, or political thinkers like Kenneth Thompson, as they were to be teachers in denominational seminaries.[85] Since Niebuhr spoke primarily to practical men who judged ideas on their relevance to lived experience, it is entirely appropriate to think carefully about his central insights and their relevance to such a supremely practical faith like Mormonism and its politically astute leaders, such as Brigham Young or Wilford Woodruff. That being said, in order to better identify the convergences and differences between Niebuhr's theology and LDS theology, I will first offer my own interpretations of Niebuhr's thought.

I. Sin and Grace

As Professor McCann notes, Niebuhr's most basic theological insight was surely his notion of the inadequacy of the liberal optimism that pervaded Protestant theology in *fin de siècle* Europe and America (McCann, 73–74, 79–80). Liberals like Harnack, Herrmann, and even, in an earlier phase of his work, Ernst Troeltsch had stressed the moral freedom and thus the

---

83. The secondary literature on Reinhold Niebuhr and his thought is vast. Only four titles will be mentioned here, each from different scholarly perspectives: Donald Meyer, *The Protestant Search for Political Realism, 1919–1941* (Berkeley: University of California Press, 1960); Charles Brown, *Niebuhr and His Age* (Philadelphia: Trinity, 1992); Fox, *Reinhold Niebuhr: A Biography*; and Robin W. Lovin, *Reinhold Niebuhr and Christian Realism* (New York: Cambridge University Press, 1995).

84. The best full account of Niebuhr's political thought and action is Stone, *Prophet to Politicians*.

85. In particular see Arthur Schlesinger Jr., "Reinhold Niebuhr's Role in American Political Thought and Life," in *Reinhold Niebuhr: His Religious, Social, and Political Thought,* ed. Charles W. Kegley and Robert W. Bretall (New York: Pilgrim, 1984), 189–222; also in the same volume, Kenneth Thompson, "The Political Philosophy of Reinhold Niebuhr," 223–51; Hans J. Morgenthau, "The Influence of Reinhold Niebuhr in American Political Life and Thought," in *Reinhold Niebuhr: A Prophetic Voice in Our Time,* ed. Harold R. Landon (Greenwich, Conn.: Seabury, 1962), 97–116.

capacity of human beings, either as individuals or as groups.[86] Though the American version of liberalism, the Social Gospel of the time, was not as naïve as it has been caricatured, the caricature is recognized precisely because it has a serious element of truth.[87]

In this respect the liberals were true disciples of Kant and Schleiermacher and eighteenth-century Pietism, which profoundly influenced both.[88] Further back, the liberals were influenced by the Puritan and Anabaptist traditions of personal righteousness and, in the case of the Puritans, social transformation. Seventeenth-century Calvinist treatises on the creation of a "holy commonwealth" in New England sound many of the same notes as the social gospel claims that the kingdom of God on earth was emerging in socialism or the labor movement.[89]

Niebuhr's critique of this sort of optimism reminds one less of any academic moral philosopher or theologian of recent vintage and more of most seminal thinkers before the twentieth century; it springs first from lived experience and only then is pressed to the written page.[90] Like the early Latter-day Saints and the American founders, Niebuhr was first a man of

---

86. The most comprehensive statement of the theological ethics of neo-Kantianism is Wilhelm Herrmann, *Ethik* (Tübingen and Leipzig: Mohr, 1901). See also Adolf von Harnack, *What Is Christianity?*, trans. Thomas Bailey Saunders (New York: Harper, 1957); Ernst Troeltsch, "Grundprobleme der Ethik," in *Gesammelte Schriften*, 4 vols. (Tübingen: J. C. B. Mohr, 1912–25), 2:552–672. For a concise review of these matters, see George Rupp, *Culture Protestantism: German Liberal Theology at the Turn of the Twentieth Century* (Missoula, Mont.: Scholars, 1977).

87. See especially C. Howard Hopkins, *The Rise of the Social Gospel in American Protestantism, 1865–1915* (New Haven: Yale University Press, 1940); Robert T. Handy, *The Social Gospel in America, 1870–1920* (New York: Oxford University Press, 1966). The greatest of the social gospel texts is Walter Rauschenbusch, *A Theology for the Social Gospel* (New York: Macmillan, 1917).

88. See Friedrich Schleiermacher, *On Religion: Speeches to Its Cultured Despisers*, trans. Richard Crouter (New York: Cambridge University Press, 1988); B. A. Gerrish, *A Prince of the Church: Schleiermacher and the Beginnings of Modern Theology* (Philadelphia: Fortress, 1984).

89. See Perry Miller, *The New England Mind: The Seventeenth Century* (New York: Macmillian, 1939).

90. This insight is, I believe, contained in James Gustafson's argument that, for Niebuhr, theology followed from ethics. What theology he developed was done to support a more primary ethical teaching. James Gustafson, "Theology in the Service of Ethics: An Interpretation of Reinhold Niebuhr's Theological Ethics," in *Reinhold Niebuhr and the Issues of Our Time*, ed. Richard Harries (Grand Rapids, Mich.: William B. Eerdmans, 1986), 24–45. Also see much the same point in Edward Le Roy Long, *A Survey of Christian Ethics* (New York: Oxford University Press, 1967).

action and only then a theological thinker. *The Federalist*, for example, is rooted less in an intensive study of theory and much more in a deep sense of history and practical experience.[91]

Niebuhr's first important book, *Moral Man and Immoral Society*, is in many ways based on personal experience more than ethico-religious theory.[92] What gives it force is the way in which a derivative theory is refined in the experience of a small, poor church in Detroit of the 1920s. Niebuhr found that preaching charity did not feed families. Turning the other cheek looked different when the result was a bullwhip from strike breakers hired by Ford.[93] Racial justice is not achieved by merely begging us all to "just get along." To use a more recent example, Martin Luther King's soaring rhetoric moved a nation. But real change took place when federal marshals enforced a right to vote. It is all to the good to treat your neighbor kindly, to let him see by the glow of your uncovered light. But if at the end of the day he is still jobless and hungry, something is lacking.[94]

Since we are not angels, argued Niebuhr, we should not delude ourselves that justice and liberty will survive by moral suasion and nonviolent witness. It will take force of the kind that we would be loath to apply to our spouses or close friends. Later he would remind us that Barth, Buber, and Tillich had to flee Germany and that Bonhoeffer was executed for his part in a plot on Hitler's life. In a world of human sinfulness, D-Day was a profoundly moral event, calculated to achieve only that modicum of justice of which real human communities are capable.[95]

Political life is a balance of competing interests, all of whom have dirty hands from dangerous and imperfect deeds. It is highly illuminating in this regard that in the late 1940s, Niebuhr did not feel out of place consulting with the State Department when the Cold War was developing in

---

91. It can also be noted that the greatest modern political theorists, Machiavelli, Hobbes, and Locke, were deeply engaged in the political activities of their own day. See for example Sebastian de Grazia's wonderful biography *Machiavelli in Hell* (Princeton: Princeton University Press, 1989); and Richard Ashcraft, *Revolutionary Politics and Locke's Two Treatises of Government* (Princeton: Princeton University Press, 1986).

92. Reinhold Niebuhr, *Moral Man and Immoral Society* (New York: Charles Scribner's Sons, 1932).

93. For this experience see Fox, *Reinhold Niebuhr: A Biography*, 62–110. See also Reinhold Niebuhr, *Leaves from the Notebook of a Tamed Cynic* (New York: Macmillan, 1929).

94. Niebuhr did write very approvingly of Martin Luther King and the civil rights movement of the 1960s. But the revolution succeeded because the rhetoric led to forceful action.

95. See Robin W. Lovin, *Christian Faith and Public Choices: The Social Ethics of Barth, Brunner, and Bonhoeffer* (Philadelphia: Fortress, 1984).

Berlin, Czechoslovakia, and China and was turning into real war in Korea.[96] Though it now appears that his actual influence on U.S. foreign policy was oversold, the fact that he and hardheaded practicals like George Kennan and Dean Acheson felt a commonality of perspective on international relations is a telling observation.

The second half of *Moral Man and Immoral Society* is a dated attempt to find a political, cum socialist, solution to the problem of economic exploitation and class antagonism.[97] Within a few short years, Niebuhr had admitted his error in thinking that there was any such "solution" to the human predicament in history. Socialism was simply another manifestation of the liberal optimism that Niebuhr had theologically rejected much earlier.

In his most fully worked out statements, *An Interpretation of Christian Ethics* and his Gifford Lectures, *The Nature and Destiny of Man*, Niebuhr staked out a careful view of sin and grace that would support the practical conclusions of *Moral Man*.[98] Drawn theologically from Augustine and the reformers, this view stressed the inherent limitations of the human enterprise in history and the concomitant necessity for saving grace in spite of our corruption.

Man is God's creature, with both freedom and reason as gifts from God.[99] Standing partially outside nature and thus enjoying freedom over nature, we are nonetheless bound inherently to nature. We are born "a little lower than the angels" (Psalm 8:5), and we deny either our divine destiny or our creaturely limits at our peril. Paradoxically for Niebuhr, the origin of sin lies not in our finitude, but in our capacity for self-transcendence. We can envision limitless possibilities for human achievement, and our sin derives from trying to seize heaven for earth.[100] Liberals erroneously sought to collapse the distinction between the moral relations appropriate in

---

96. Stone, *Prophet to Politicians*, 168–217.

97. Niebuhr, *Moral Man and Immoral Society*, 142–68. Niebuhr was never actually a Marxist, but up until the late 1930s, he was more enamored of socialism as a solution to the problems of economic disparity than he later would be.

98. Niebuhr later refused to support the formulation of certain problems in *An Interpretation of Christian Ethics* (1935; reprint, New York: Seabury, 1979). But I believe that crucial theoretical distinctions in *An Interpretation of Christian Ethics* are pervasive in his thought, and I have used *An Interpretation of Christian Ethics* in this regard. It is also true that some of the specific points made in *An Interpretation of Christian Ethics* are found in other essays from Niebuhr around the same time, and in such cases I believe it correct to cite *An Interpretation of Christian Ethics*.

99. Reinhold Niebuhr, *Nature and Destiny of Man: A Chrisitan Interpretation*, 2 vols. (New York: Charles Scribner's Sons, 1941, 1943), 1:17.

100. Niebuhr, *Nature and Destiny of Man*, 1:178–207.

public and private spheres because they first denied the gap between time and eternity.

Though Niebuhr pays obligatory homage to continental theorists of human finitude such as Heidegger, Niebuhr's most important intellectual ancestor is Augustine.[101] In fact, fourth-century apologists for the union of Christianity and Rome could sound very much like pre–World War I liberals with their easy rhetoric about the coming of the kingdom of God on earth via this ruler or that political scheme. *Pax Romana* and "Christian socialism" committed the same error. It was Augustine, writing in the shadow of the sack of Rome, who demolished this line of thinking. The city of God was not and never would be an earthly kingdom. It is the glory of humankind that they can envision heaven. It is our sin to pursue endlessly an ersatz kingdom of this world.[102]

In this respect, sin springs not from our epistemic limitations but from our willful attempt to transcend our limits. The knowledge of good and evil was not the corruption of Genesis—disobedience to divine limits was. Foreseeing the city of God, even longing for it, was acceptable, but seizing its mantle for the city of man was demonic. Viewed thus, it is precisely the *imago dei* that is the source of human corruption. Our freedom is our glory and our fate.[103] A doctrine of revelation may partially resolve the epistemic limitations of the human predicament as Niebuhr's teacher Macintosh argued.[104] Such a revelation does not, however, quiet the restless passions of the human soul. The longing for completeness and security, for which Christians ought to find an incarnational answer, they persist in trying to solve with the "arm of flesh."

Niebuhr's critique of liberalism is thus rooted in a Reformation doctrine of grace. The salvation offered by the cross reconciles humanity to God in spite of sin. We remain sinful, that is, full of or prone to sin, but God's love still reaches us without any reservation or reproach. Humanity stands justified before God, irrespective of anything we can do, because God himself

---

101. Niebuhr, *Nature and Destiny of Man,* 1:186–90. See also Reinhold Niebuhr, "Augustine's Political Realism," in *Christian Realism and Political Problems* (New York: Charles Scribner's Sons, 1953).

102. See Augustine, *The City of God,* trans. Marcus R. Dods (New York: Modern Library, 1950).

103. See especially Niebuhr, *Nature and Destiny of Man,* 1:70–85; and the selections in the section "Freedom," in Reinhold Niebuhr, *Faith and Politics: A Commentary on Religious, Social, and Political Thought in a Technological Age,* ed. Ronald H. Stone (New York: George Brazillier, 1968). See also the discussion in Lovin, *Christian Faith and Public Choices,* 119–57.

104. See D. C. Macintosh, "Experimental Realism in Religion," in *Religious Realism,* ed. D. C. Macintosh (New York: Macmillan, 1931).

redeemed us on the cross. In other words, Paul was transformed on the road to Damascus in spite of the fact that he was rounding up Christians to face the fate of Stephen.[105]

II. Morality in History

As stated before, Niebuhr's redemptive theology of grace entailed for him a rejection of perfectionist programs, Christian or otherwise. Like Augustine (who was converted to Christianity away from perfectionist sectarianism and later, as the Bishop of Hippo, waged a decisive struggle for a universal community of grace against the sectarianism of Pelagius and the Donatists[106]), Niebuhr saw the same sectarian error in the radical reformation with its chiliasm, its separatism, and its tendency to argue that Christians should not dirty their hands with matters of actual governance in the real world.

Professor McCann's fine book, *Christian Realism and Liberation Theology,* contrasts Niebuhr's thought with that of Latin American liberation theologians of the 1960s and 1970s and is an apt discussion of these reformation themes in Niebuhr's thought. Niebuhr would certainly agree with liberation theologians to the extent that they maintained that Christians, and even priests, should be engaged in a real-life struggle for political and economic justice, even if their clerical robes might get dirty. After all, the great practical influence for which Niebuhr is noted is his largely decisive argument against the pacifist and isolationist position of American Protestantism in the late 1930s. When people are starving and governments are hopelessly corrupt, he would certainly agree with the liberation theologians that the Christian church cannot remain a mere spectator.[107] To the extent, however, that liberation theologians preach that Christians should be "artisans of a new humanity" or that political and economic change, no matter how extensive, is to be equated with sanctification, such theologians

---

105. Niebuhr, *Nature and Destiny of Man,* 2:198–225.

106. For Augustine's debate with Pelagius, see Peter Brown, *Augustine of Hippo: A Biography* (Berkeley: University of California Press, 1967); and Paul Lehman, "The Anti-Pelagian Writings," in *A Companion to the Study of St. Augustine,* ed. Roy W. Battenhouse (New York: Oxford University Press, 1955), 203–34. For Pelagius himself, see Robert F. Evans, *Pelagius: Inquiries and Reappraisals* (New York: Seabury, 1967); and Robert F. Evans, *Four Letters of Pelagius* (New York: Seabury, 1968). On Donatism, see W. H. C. Frend, *The Donatist Church: A Movement of Protest in Roman North Africa* (Oxford: Clarendon, 1952).

107. For the story of his fight against pacifism see Fox, *Reinhold Niebuhr: A Biography,* chap. 8; and Dennis McCann, *Christian Realism and Liberation Theologies* (Maryknoll, N.Y.: Orbis, 1981).

preach theological nonsense. The delusions of grandeur and pride in such claims represent the essence of sin in Christian terms.[108]

Niebuhr's realism, in this way, approaches the moral teachings of the New Testament with greater reverence than his theological critics. He refuses to compromise the absolute moral standard of the Gospels as a measure of human imperfection.[109] He rejects any of the "halfway house" interpretations that have been so much a part of Christian theologians' attempts to reconcile the rigorous ethics of the Sermon on the Mount with the requirements of worldly governance.[110]

The moral demand of God is what it is: a pure standard of both thought and action. The standards thus established, however, are impossible for humanity to attain. Attempting to do so only leads to the enervation that Paul felt in trying to achieve salvation by strict obedience to the Mosaic covenant. Since Niebuhr rejected any of the compromises that appeared to let humanity off the moral hook, he is almost inevitably led to stress the same point as Paul did: the gracious salvation by God of those who fall woefully short.[111]

In crucial respects, this Christian moral standard of love is most relevant exactly because it is "impossible." The Gospels display in word and deed the moral truth that humanity outside the ambit of faith only perceives in the dimmest outline. In this way the absolute self-negating love of neighbor convicts all purely rationalistic forms of morality devised by philosophers. No degree of prudence or calculation can justify the goodness of the Samaritan or can obligate someone to give all his riches to the support of the poor.[112]

---

108. Juan Luis Segundo, *A Theology for Artisans of a New Humanity,* trans. John Drury, 5 vols. (Maryknoll, N.Y.: Orbis, 1973–74). Latin American liberation theologies are much too complicated to analyze here. For samples see the following titles: Gustavo Gutiérrez, *A Theology of Liberation: History, Politics, and Salvation,* trans. Sister Caridad Inda and John Eagleson (Maryknoll, N.Y.: Orbis, 1973); José Porfirio Miranda, *Marx and the Bible: A Critique of the Philosophy of Oppression,* trans. John Eagleson (Maryknoll, N.Y.: Orbis, 1974); Alfredo Fierro, *The Militant Gospel: A Critical Introduction to Political Theologies,* trans. John Drury (Maryknoll, N.Y.: Orbis, 1977).

109. Niebuhr, *Interpretation of Christian Ethics,* 104–23.

110. The best single brief review of the various approaches to the morality of the Sermon on the Mount is Harvey K. McArthur, *Understanding the Sermon on the Mount* (New York: Harper, 1960).

111. Niebuhr, *Nature and Destiny of Man,* 2:127–40.

112. Niebuhr, *Interpretation of Christian Ethics,* 97–119; Niebuhr, *Nature and Destiny of Man,* 1:244–47; Reinhold Niebuhr, *Beyond Tragedy: Essays of the Christian Interpretation of History* (New York: Charles Scribner's Sons, 1937), 271–86.

Once recognized in faith, however, the Samaritan displays in vivid relief the pretensions of any human claim to righteousness before God. Human beings always consider themselves in making moral decisions. Even if egoism is rejected as unable to account for the richness of the moral life, the needs and desires of the self reappear. Utility theory counsels us to consider one's own welfare along with and qualitatively equal to the welfare of others. However, it does not suggest that the agent should lose himself in the service of others irrespective of consequences.[113] Kantian formalism treats every agent as equally bound by a universal imperative. But Kant's examples of the working of this demand shows that it cannot justify absolute sacrifice of the self to others.[114] When the absolute moral demand of the life of *agape* is the standard, no one is secure. We are all beggars after the mercy of God.

Paradoxically, it is our capacity to recognize this moral failure that establishes the transcendence of humanity over nature. We can respond to the ideal of self-giving love because we are not completely enslaved to primal passions. It moves us because we intuit its goodness even if we cannot live up to its terms. Our capacity to respond to the pure love offered by God suggests the inadequacy of all purely human standards of righteousness, while our failures are seen sharply in the brilliant light of eternity.

Niebuhr's theology thus moves at two levels. First, given the moral standard of the New Testament, grace must suffice for salvation. The experience of grace then becomes one of redemption not transformation. It does not give us moral capabilities that we lacked before. Grace convicts us more strongly than nature, for we now see clearly the morality that we are incapable of exemplifying in our lives. Our righteousness before God is an imputed righteousness deriving fully from the Atonement and not from our efforts, however strenuous they may be.

---

113. The question of the relation of the New Testament concept of *agape* (love) to the standard categories of ethics is a rich topic to which much important work has been devoted. See, for example, Paul Ramsey, *Deeds and Rules in Christian Ethics* (New York: Charles Scribner's Sons, 1967); Paul Ramsey, *Basic Christian Ethics* (New York: Charles Scribner's Sons, 1954); Arthur J. Dyck, *Rethinking Rights and Responsibilities: The Moral Bonds of Community* (Cleveland: Pilgrim, 1994); George F. Thomas, *Christian Ethics and Moral Philosophy* (New York: Charles Scribner's Sons, 1955); and, especially, Gene H. Outka, *Agape: An Ethical Analysis* (New Haven: Yale University Press, 1972).

114. Alan Donagan's masterful *The Theory of Morality* (Chicago: University of Chicago Press, 1977), attempts to stretch Kantianism to include what he calls "Hebrew-Christian morality." As his most important critics noted, the problem is that to pull Kantian principles that far one must sneak Christian views into the beginning notion of a rational agent.

Nonetheless, Christians are freed by grace to engage more fully in the messy business of history. Since our righteousness is given by grace, Christians can act without guilt in imperfect situations—such as war, diplomacy, and politics. Keeping themselves safe from the world is of no effect on their eternal destiny. Hence, the morally enervating features of perfectionism can quite easily be rejected. Once perfectionism is rejected, the expression of love in history can be found in a search for justice. But this justice will be limited to the capacities of humankind as embodied in the rough realities of history. Market economics can be tamed by the government, but market economics cannot be replaced with the primitive communism of Acts. War to protect the innocent can be an expression of love of neighbor in the world. Forceful actions by energized groups like labor unions or the civil rights movement can demand respect for rights and freedoms that, while less than a city of God, are still an improvement over the historic lot of humanity.

Perhaps the most serious limitation of Niebuhr's moral teaching is the vagueness of his use of the substantive moral categories of "justice" and "love." For Niebuhr, these terms function as a dyad. One cannot be understood without the other. They are not, however, equivalent to either of the other great paired concepts in Christian moral thought: the Protestant "law and gospel" or the Catholic "natural and supernatural virtue." Niebuhr's dialectic of love and justice requires that to know one, a person must know the other. In crucial respects, Niebuhr understands justice as a shortened version of love. What justice requires, love will also, though to a richer and fuller extent.

Niebuhr's fundamental dilemma is one that he shares with contemporary "liberal critics" of liberalism. Like theorists such as Walzer, Taylor, and Galston, Niebuhr recognizes that any substantive notion of love as a form of human relation will require a pre-understanding of the good of the other as a human being. If, as Niebuhr repeatedly asserts, love is understood as selfless service on behalf of others, we must know what the good of the other is in order to recognize service. Love, and by extension in Niebuhr's view, justice, requires a rich view of the human good.[115]

The difficulty for any Christian thinker such as Niebuhr is that the view of the human good found in the New Testament is both richer than that required by, and fundamentally at odds with, the foundations of the liberal democratic order to which Niebuhr was increasingly committed. To see the point symbolically, one can point to the fact that the first book in the western world that bluntly argued that democracy is the best form of government, Spinoza's *Theological-Political Treatise*, also contained the most

---

115. See also William A. Galston, *Liberal Purposes: Goods, Virtues, and Diversity in the Liberal State* (New York: Cambridge University Press, 1991).

sustained criticism, published before the nineteenth century, of the Bible as anything other than the creation of corrupt and fallible human beings. Liberalism is committed to a political view of the human good as limited to the needs of the body. On the liberal view, the political order exists solely to provide a minimum of physical security necessary for individuals to pursue whatever vision of the human they find personally satisfying.[116]

On this view, justice as a political norm or virtue is divorced from the "commandment of love" in a most serious manner. Justice in liberal societies is found in a coordination of the activities of independent agents pursuing their own desires. What justice requires is a rule of law that allows these disparate desires to be pursued to their fullest extent possible. As the American framers called it, this was "self interest rightly understood." But the moral command of the New Testament was fundamentally different. Giving away your riches to follow Jesus or celebrating the submersion of one's desires in striving for God are not plausible versions of self interest except on a theological view of the ends of human existence. In theory, I would argue, Niebuhr's Christianity (and its attendant moral ideal) is deeply irreconcilable with his commitment to liberal democracy.

III. Mormonism and Morality

These observations now lead us to consider Mormonism and its own particular moral teachings. However, I consider it impossible to do a comparative survey of every aspect of LDS theology or ethics with any other theology available today. Nor can I write with the authority of a professional spokesman or leader. Therefore, my contribution is intended to suggest tensions within LDS theology and practice that provide a fruitful point of engagement with Niebuhr's mature theological and moral teachings.[117]

Having said this, the differences between these two theologies are easy to see. Though Niebuhr spoke approvingly of the "prophetic religion" of the Bible and of the need to recover this authentic faith from the erroneous accretions that had grown around it over nearly two millennia of history, the last thing he would have wanted or even comprehended was a real human being claiming a prophetic mantle and priestly authority supposedly restored by divine messengers. True, much of the Christian community had fallen under the influence of erroneous doctrine. But the solution

---

116. See Benedict Spinoza, *Theological-Political Treatise,* trans. R. H. M. Elwes (New York: Dover, 1951).

117. The primary LDS scriptural texts are cited as follows: Book of Mormon, cited by book, chapter, and verse; Doctrine and Covenants, cited by section and verse; Pearl of Great Price, cited by book, chapter, and verse. All are published officially by The Church of Jesus Christ of Latter-day Saints.

to this error was the preaching of biblical faith with renewed vigor, not actual new revelation from a divine source.[118]

Furthermore, Niebuhr continuously writes of "religious myths" in the Bible. These myths are not to be taken as literal events. Rather, they are stories which contain kernels of truth that pragmatic theological investigation must uncover. As Professor McCann states, "each [passage] is understood as a religious idea whose pragmatic efficacy is perennially demonstrated in the experience of those who live by them." In Niebuhr's own words:

> In this sense the myth alone is capable of picturing the world as a realm of coherence and meaning without denying the facts of incoherence. Its world is coherent because all facts in it are related to some central source of meaning; but it is not rationally coherent because the myth is not under the abortive necessity of relating all things to each other in terms of immediate rational unity. The God of mythical religion is, significantly, the Creator and not the First Cause. If He were a First Cause (a rational conception), He would be one of the many observable causes in the stream of things, in which case God and the world are one; or he would be the unmoved mover, in which case His relation to the world is not a vital or truly creative one.[119]

This statement has a degree of truth in it. It must be admitted, however, that Mormonism has not generally been sympathetic to such a "mythic" reading of key parts of scripture. Of course scripture has been written with moral or theological points in mind. But viewing scripture as history selected with a theological point is fundamentally different than viewing scripture as a mythic tale with a theological meaning. Furthermore, Mormonism has not been fertile soil for the growth of "high theology" such as Niebuhr's Gifford Lectures or any number of other texts. From the beginning, Mormonism has produced trenchant works of theological and philosophical analysis. But this relatively modest body of writing is the exception that proves the general rule. In general, Mormonism has regarded theological or philosophical analysis of faith and doctrine with a healthy degree of skepticism.[120]

---

118. Niebuhr, *Nature and Destiny of Man,* 2:23–34; Niebuhr, *Interpretation of Christian Ethics,* 13–62; Niebuhr, *Beyond Tragedy,* 89–111.

119. Niebuhr, *Interpretation of Christian Ethics,* 32. Also see Reinhold Niebuhr, "The Truth in Myths," in *The Nature of Religious Experience: Essays in Honor of Douglas Clyde Macintosh,* ed. Julius Seelye Bixler, et al. (New York: Harper and Brothers, 1937), 117–35.

120. The following are works written by LDS officials: B. H. Roberts, *The Mormon Doctrine of Deity* (Salt Lake City: Deseret News Press, 1903); Parley P. Pratt, *The Essential Parley P. Pratt,* ed. Peter Crawley (Salt Lake City: Signature, 1990); Orson Pratt, *The Seer* (Salt Lake City: Publishers, 1990); James E. Talmage,

Two broad reasons may be noted for this skepticism. First, a hierarchy claiming to receive continuous revelation from God would not seem to require theologians to advise on correct doctrine. In fact, it could be regarded as dangerous to promote an alternate source of specialized knowledge that could easily become an ersatz authority challenging the revelatory prerogatives of prophetic leadership.[121]

The second reason stems from the restorationist conviction that Mormonism was not a new religion or a new version of Christianity but was, rather, a restoration of the simple faith and organization that Christ taught to his disciples. Exactly when and how this simple faith was replaced by the abstruse speculations of theology and the machinations of uninspired religious leaders has remained vague and unspecified in LDS thought. At least one common view laid part of the blame on the early theologians who replaced the "plain and precious" truths of the gospel with the "philosophies of men,"[122] but in some ways this is a red herring.

Every reader uses the ideas of his own time to interpret scripture or any other text. In the 1930s, Shakespeare's *Richard III* was often read in light of Stalin's or Hitler's blood purges. In another example taken from scripture, modern readers do not now believe that the "sun stood still" as Ptolemaic astronomers would have said. Only the earth, the moving body, could literally stand still. A number of alternative interpretations can be read from the text, but the most literal one is simply ignored by the modern reader. Though these examples suggest that the complaint about human ideas detracting from the pure message of scripture is often overstated, the common LDS skepticism about the abstruse "philosophies of men" detracting from the plain gospel has been something of a barrier to any sort of theological analysis such as Niebuhr's, which would be premised on the

---

The Articles of Faith (Salt Lake City: The Church of Jesus Christ of Latter-day Saints, 1972).

121. For some examples and a brief discussion see Richard Sherlock, "Campus in Crisis: BYU, 1911," *Sunstone* 4 (January–February 1979): 11–15; and Richard Sherlock, "Darwinism and Mormonism: An Uncomfortable Interface," *Dialogue: A Journal of Mormon Thought* 13 (Fall 1980): 63–78.

122. There are numerous LDS treatments of "the apostasy." The most authoritative, though not the most scholarly, is James E. Talmage, *The Great Apostasy: Considered in the Light of Scriptural and Secular History* (Salt Lake City: Deseret News, 1909). See also B. H. Roberts, *Outlines of Ecclesiastical History* (Salt Lake City: George Q. Cannon and Sons, 1893). In the recent past, the most competent and prolific LDS writer on the apostasy was Professor Hugh Nibley of Brigham Young University, a well-trained student of the ancient world. See Hugh Nibley, *Mormonism and Early Christianity,* ed. Todd M. Compton and Stephen D. Ricks (Provo, Utah: Foundation for Ancient Research and Mormon Studies, 1987).

task of drawing out the hidden kernels of truth from an otherwise mytho-logical presentation in scripture.[123]

These surface disagreements would be readily evident to the committed LDS reader. But behind these obvious points of divergence lies the core of what might be called the theological difference between what Latter-day Saints would call the "restored gospel" and the position staked out by Niebuhr.

Niebuhr's theological heritage is that of the Magisterial Reformation. In fact, the denominational ties of his family were to the German Evangelical Church, which represents a merging of German Lutheranism and its Calvinist cousin inspired by nineteenth-century liberalism, which down-played theological differences, and the Prussian monarchy, which saw its interests furthered by a united, national church. For our purposes the Magisterial Reformation may be understood in distinction from both the hierarchical church orders of either Catholicism or Anglicanism and the voluntarist, separatist tendencies of what has come to be called the Radical Reformation.[124]

Niebuhr's criticism of Catholicism was the same as that of the reform-ers. Catholicism identified the church too closely with the kingdom of God. This identification allows a religious institution, involved in all of the relativ-ities of history, to claim unconditioned truth for its doctrines and, at times, inerrant authority for its magisterium. Thus it becomes one more vehicle for human pride. The Catholic doctrine of the church too easily offers a divine imprimatur for political and religious power and self-righteousness. The expansive capacity for sin to corrupt every act or judgment, even those of the "vicar of Christ" was a view that Niebuhr referred to constantly, espe-cially in his criticism of Catholicism.[125]

A different but complementary error was found in the Radical Reformation. If Catholicism too easily professed detailed moral norms for a complex world, the sectarians seemed too ready to avoid sin by sepa-rating from the world. They sought personal righteousness at the expense of worldly engagement. If the decisions required of statesmen or generals were too imperfect and the guidance of the Catholic moralists too formal-istic, one alternative is simple: don't be a statesman or a general. Leave the "sword" to others.[126]

This view of the Anabaptists inspired sectarians, whether Mennonite, Quaker, or Baptist, to hold that human beings were at least partially free and morally capable agents. The magisterial reformers attacked what

123. Talmage, *The Great Apostasy*, 24.
124. See Fox, *Reinhold Niebuhr: A Biography*, chap. 1.
125. *Nature and Destiny of Man*, 2:148–56.
126. Niebuhr, *Moral Man and Immoral Society*, 72–73; Niebuhr, *Interpretation of Christian Ethics*, 167–69; Niebuhr, *Nature and Destiny of Man*, 2:169–80.

they viewed as the semi-Pelagianism of late medieval Catholicism, but an even firmer view of human freedom and moral capacity can be found in Anabaptist literature of the Reformation.

These remarks are a prelude to a far-reaching claim I wish to make about Mormonism. Mormonism represents a hierarchical ecclesiastical order that holds special powers of priesthood and leadership combined with an emphasis on personal obedience and righteous works as having merit before God, which is at least Anabaptist in its flavor and background. In more traditional theological terms, Mormonism combines an authoritative magisterium with an emphasis on righteous works characteristic in Christian theology and history with its exact opposite.

If we consider just the classic understanding of the theological foundations of sectarianism as set forth in Ernst Troeltsch's *Social Teachings of the Christian Churches*, Mormonism's unique sacred texts can be read as a virtual *vade mecum* of sectarian theology. God is plainly presented most often as a lawgiver. The Atonement is viewed in legalistic, "debt repayment" terms after the fashion of Anselm. The Pelagian/Anabaptist emphasis on human freedom and the need for obedience to divine law is ever present.[127]

This emphasis on obedience to the commandments of God as the basis of personal righteousness is seen in vivid relief in the Book of Mormon and especially in the Doctrine and Covenants (which is a collection of authoritative revelations given almost wholly to Joseph Smith in the first decade and a half of the LDS church's existence). A detailed analysis of scriptural texts is not our purpose here.[128] One Book of Mormon text suffices to illustrate how Mormonism subtly transforms otherwise perfectly Protestant-sounding doctrines to emphasize the meritorious character of good works, a view that distinguished the radical reformation and that early Mormonism stressed:

> Do you exercise faith in the redemption of him who created you? Do you look forward with an eye of faith, and view this mortal body raised in immortality, and this corruption raised in incorruption, to stand before God to be judged according to the deeds which have been done in the mortal body? (Alma 5:15)

The rest of the extended teaching of Alma, a Book of Mormon prophet, continues in the same vein. He asks his listeners if, in the Day of Judgment, the Lord will invite them into his presence because their works have been

---

127. Ernst Troeltsch, *The Social Teachings of the Christian Churches*, trans. Olive Wyon, 2 vols. (New York: Harper, 1913), 993–1013.

128. In the Book of Mormon, see 1 Nephi 3:7, 4:18, 15:25, 17:3, 22:31; 2 Nephi 1:9, 9:27, 30:1, 33:15; Jacob 2:10, 7:27; Mosiah 2:22, 2:32, 2:41, 5:8, 23:14; Alma 3:26–27, 5:18, 12:19, 29:9, 37:35. On the legalistic interpretation of the Atonement see Alma 34.

"works of righteousness." Alma weaves in essential Christian themes such as having one's "garments . . . purified" through the blood of Christ, but then he returns to those phrases that Luther, in particular, would have condemned: "whosoever doeth not the works of righteousness" is condemned (Alma 5:16, 21, 36).

This is not the theology of the reformers of which Niebuhr was such a brilliant student. This aspiration of visible sainthood is the antithesis of Niebuhr's emphasis on the corrupting influence of the acquisitiveness and pride that undermines all human endeavors. A community of biblical love is not, for the Latter-day Saints, an impossible ideal with its relevance parsed out from its irrelevance to political and economic life. It is a living obligation for Latter-day Saints whose energies and capacities are not theirs alone. It is not just a standard that convicts us of our sin. It is a standard to which we are called by Christ and empowered to achieve by his grace.

The LDS theology of grace and free obedience to divine decree is a striking departure from Niebuhr. These differences are obvious to even the most casual student of Mormonism or the most superficial reader of Niebuhr's theological and moral works. I would like to suggest, however, that this easy contrast obscures as much as it clarifies.

First, we may consider the Book of Mormon passages that we examined earlier. These passages and others do not articulate a strong theology of grace as clearly as Luther or Calvin may have wished. There is a Pelagian (or semi-Pelagian) ring to a number of the passages, and individuals who have claimed that Mormonism is essentially a modern Pelagianism are not entirely mistaken in such an assessment.[129]

These texts do not, however, interpret themselves. They do not demand a purely Pelagian interpretation; nor do they require a belief that those who fall short of absolute obedience to divine command must be condemned. The Book of Mormon teaching on grace, obedience, and salvation can be read either from the standpoint of Paul's high theology of grace as set forth in Romans or from the standpoint of the commandments given to aspiring saints in the Doctrine and Covenants. If the largest part of the LDS theology of grace and salvation is read in terms of the early sections of the Doctrine and Covenants, then Mormonism does represent a sectarian theology that is the opposite of Niebuhr's. These sections lay out the notion that all other Christian creeds are false, that obedience to modern revelation is a key to salvation, that the Saints should gather out of the world into Zion, and finally that the Saints should practice the United Order.

But suppose that we read the Book of Mormon in light of Paul's more robust theology of grace as the precondition of successful obedience.

---

129. See Sterling M. McMurrin, *The Theological Foundations of the Mormon Religion* (Salt Lake City: University of Utah Press, 1965).

Salvation, on this account, is largely a gift. Only those who have freely accepted the gift can perform the mighty acts of righteousness to which latter-day revelation commands them.[130]

Suppose that the favorite LDS passage from James, "Faith without works is dead" (James 2:17), is read not to imply that works are meritorious but that failure to perform works of righteousness is simply the best evidence that one lacked saving grace in the first place.

The dialectical relationship between obedience and blessing, which is characteristic of the Doctrine and Covenants, is precisely what is fit for those who have had that transforming spiritual witness that most Christian faith communities know as grace. It is only because we are first accepted by God that we gain the strength to reach beyond ourselves to others. In a phrase from John that Niebuhr often quoted, "we love him, because he first loved us" (1 John 4:19).[131]

I believe, however, that there is a more profound connection between Niebuhr's political and moral theology and that of Mormonism than might be noticed even with a careful rereading of the Book of Mormon. To see this, let us begin by remembering the sources of Niebuhr's theology that we noted above. He did not find liberals erroneous in their reading of scripture or in their theological rigor. If anything, they were too wedded to a literal reading of the Sermon on the Mount as a blueprint for individuals and statesmen.

Niebuhr came to what was later called Christian realism via lived experience in a struggling community of faith. Niebuhr found that the harsh realities of time were not easily ruled by the morality of eternity. The elevated but relatively inflexible morality of pacifism and self-sacrifice did not solve the problems found in the messy world around us. Certainly Christian pacifism is a noble moral ideal. But what if turning the other cheek results in one's whole family and many fellow Christians being sent to the slaughter by tyrants? There is a vast and profound body of Christian thinking concerning the use of force in human affairs as the highest form of love of neighbor: a willingness to go to war to save him or her. This literature was informed not merely by the love commandment but also by the realities that any faith-community engaged in lived experience must confront.[132]

---

130. See James E. Faulconer, *Romans 1: Notes and Reflections* (Provo, Utah: Foundation for Ancient Research and Mormon Studies, 1999).

131. Niebuhr, *Interpretation of Christian Ethics,* 196.

132. See, especially, Paul Ramsey, *The Just War* (New Haven: Yale University Press, 1968); James T. Johnson, *Ideology, Reason and the Restraint of War* (Princeton: Princeton University Press, 1977); Michael Walzer, *Just and Unjust Wars* (New York: Basic, 1977); and William O'Brien, *The Conduct of Just and Limited War* (New York: Praeger, 1981).

The same point may be made in economic matters. The advice of the Savior to the rich man to sell all he has for his faith is a compelling ideal, as is the primitive community of Acts. In practice, however, forced equality never works. The force required for its practice only creates despotism. Moreover, giving away one's substance looks different if the result is the impoverishment of others. If Christians are called to relieve the miseries of the poor, the best way to do it seems to be economic growth in a market economy, not merely giving away wealth.

Let us then follow out the common theme of Niebuhr and the early Latter-day Saints—the origins of theology in lived experience—and consider Mormonism in this light. Closely examined in this way, we see a much more fruitful connection between Mormonism and Niebuhr's theology than we otherwise might recognize. Fundamentally, two sorts of challenges face any human community. First are those challenges that are grounded in the irreducible characteristics of human nature; for example, the plurality of our desires, the selfishness of our passions, and the limitations of our knowledge. These are natural limitations of our existence to which the great liberal theorists appealed in their defense of open societies and open markets. Since we have diverse passions and diverse interests, we must allow wide space for individual desire and initiative.

The second challenge is that contained in lived experience. Historical circumstance forces difficult choices that communities would rather not make. For example, the American regime has been profoundly influenced by the historical fact of slavery that predated its existence. Canada has been deeply and divisively affected by language divisions. Every regime has been influenced by its historical situation. But while none of these specific histories are inevitable, some history and, therefore, some historical limitation is inevitable. For example, Latter-day Saints hold that there are three fundamental missions for the LDS church: preach the gospel, perfect the saints, and redeem the dead through vicarious baptism and temple ordinances. Consider just the first two. Mormonism's isolation in the Great Basin for the better part of a century made the achievement of saintly righteousness much easier than it is in the age of mass media with what the Latter-day Saints will claim is the corrupting influence of sexual suggestiveness and violence that pervades it. But isolation in a world of their own is one of the least effective venues to preach the gospel to the world. One cannot possibly believe that sending over 50,000 missionaries around the world, as the Latter-day Saints now do, would be possible for a small, isolated sect in the Intermountain West. Without modern technology and media, one cannot possibly believe that the fundamental LDS scripture, the Book of Mormon, could be translated as it now is into more than 105 languages. The existential problem that contemporary Mormonism faces is finding the right balance between these two missions. In the last century, the balance was obviously struck one way. In this century, it is struck another. Every balance is open to question, none are perfect, and each is conditioned by historical experience.

In facing the twin challenges of nature and history, Mormonism found through harsh experience the need for moral, political, and economic compromise just as articulated by Niebuhr. Early LDS economic egalitarianism cut directly against the human desire for individual aspiration and achievement. The wealthy did not actually want to share fully with the less fortunate, and those of more ability and talent rebelled at the idea of those of lesser capacity eating their bounty. In LDS scripture, the Lord told the saints to stop practicing the complete communitarianism of the United Order and to practice instead the less strenuous principle of tithing that would prepare the faithful to one day live the complete law of consecration.

Theologically, we may say that the LDS prophetic leaders who reached this *modus vivendi* with the forms and limits of nature and history, Brigham Young and Wilford Woodruff, might properly be regarded together as Mormonism's closest analog to Reinhold Niebuhr. They engaged modernity fully so that the light of eternity could shine even in its darkest corners. They were, as Niebuhr, realists about the possibilities of nature and history. It is no denial of heaven or of the eschatological redemption of the earth, both of which Latter-day Saints affirm, to see that at present human nature is constituted by a duality of light and dark. We are a heavenly treasure in an earthly abode. As such, a Niebuhrian ethic that finds the deepest theological purpose in compromise precisely so that the good news of the gospel is made available in theory and practice to humanity is an ethic chosen freely, not a forced move dictated by demonic forces or prearranged decree.[133]

Paradoxically it is Mormonism's most fundamental and seemingly pre-modern conviction in continuing divine revelation that constitutes the essential ground of its engagement with modernity. Continuous revelation establishes God's presence in history as a source of wisdom and comfort to the community and its individual members. Somewhat like Niebuhr's reading of American history, Mormonism sees the footprints of God in the mundane history of peoples and empires from creation onward. Thus

---

133. Thus LDS prophet Wilford Woodruff did not claim to have been compelled by God to abandon the practice of plural marriage. Rather he very clearly stated that he was shown in a vision what terrible destruction the federal government would bring on the saints: imprisonment of leaders and confiscation of all Church property, including temples. He was then asked to choose which course to follow—to continue plural marriage as an isolated sect at the expense of spreading the gospel and redeeming the dead in temples, or moderating sectarianism on behalf of God's children living and dead around the world.

modernity, however much it may be at odds with the truth of the gospel and however destructive its moral forces, must be seen to have a divine purpose that continuing revelation engages.

In this sense, modern Mormonism both engages a sort of Niebuhrian realistic view of the political and economic possibilities of modernity and offers a richer sense of the transformative possibilities in history, not just above or past it. By the 1950s, Niebuhr had become a devout apologist for Cold War liberalism—the marriage of New Deal domestic policy and fierce anti-communist foreign and military policy found in the Americans for Democratic Action organization, which he helped to found.

But as his critics perceptively charged, this result seemed to make compromise itself a good, without a sustained analysis of the terms and results of such a compromise. It appeared to many that Niebuhr had concluded that since Christianity had no specific political or economic morality, compromise with the common opinions of the age was therefore both necessary and good. Common opinions' moral standing is derived from their benevolent commonality, while compromise with them is necessary because faith has nothing else to offer. It is one thing however to compromise with the zeitgeist on behalf of a compelling and noble end in history. It is quite another to hold that the opinions of the moment about political and economic morality must be adopted because faith has little else to offer.

Mormonism's compromises with political and economic liberalism are set within a context of transcendent ends that can be achieved in no other way. It supports the liberal consensus of modernity because eternity cannot be found in any other way. The LDS challenge is thus the opposite of that faced by Niebuhr and fellow Christian realists. Where Niebuhr's problem was to avoid letting the eternal end of humankind be engulfed in the supposed necessities of the historical moment, Latter-day Saints are more likely to see the deficiencies of any political position from the point of view of eternity and fail to pursue the good that is nevertheless possible. Whether this difficulty can be negotiated as Mormonism becomes a major world religion is yet to be determined, but the realism of Niebuhr and his associates might be a useful reading for Latter-day Saints as the millennium unfolds.

Rejoinder

Dennis P. McCann

RICHARD SHERLOCK'S REFLECTIONS ON Reinhold Niebuhr's Christian realism and the ways in which it both diverges from and converges with the LDS experience of Christian faith open up many rich possibilities for continuing theological conversation. I would like to highlight two of these for my own reflections. One is the relationship between faith and experience; the other is the theological significance of compromise, particularly, inasmuch as all Christians struggling with modernity, late modernity, or even, if you will, post-modernity, inevitably must come to terms with a dominant political culture that Sherlock rightly identifies as "liberalism." Sherlock tellingly underscores the stakes for all serious Christians in coming to a proper understanding of what, when, and how to compromise:

> It is one thing however to compromise with the zeitgeist on behalf of a
> compelling and noble end in history. It is quite another to hold that the
> opinions of the moment about political and economic morality must be
> adopted because faith has little else to offer. (Sherlock, 111)

Sherlock and I are in deep agreement that Reinhold Niebuhr's Christian realism offers a theological model of compromise that seeks to remain faithful to that "compelling and noble end in history" revealed to humanity through the mission and ministry of Jesus Christ. If Niebuhr's Christian realism were only a cleverly presented capitulation to modernity "because faith has little else to offer," there would be no point in continuing to discuss it, either for Latter-day Saints or Roman Catholics or any other serious Christians for whom it might serve as a model (Sherlock, 111).

Sherlock, I think, speaks for Niebuhr's disciples as well as Latter-day Saints when he observes that experience has taught us to support certain aspects of "the liberal consensus of modernity because eternity cannot be found in any other way" (Sherlock, 111). Christian faith, as Niebuhr insisted and Sherlock agrees, provides the perspective in which experience can be scrutinized and a critical "discernment of spirits" can unfold. Sherlock, like Niebuhr, does not therefore uncritically accept everything that can be regarded as characteristic of liberalism. What he means by this term is essentially modern democratic capitalism—the increasingly global regime of free markets operating within an effective and fair regulatory system, in which public accountability is guaranteed by the impartial rule of law based on universal human rights, the chief of which is religious liberty or freedom of conscience. His argument for why Latter-day Saints support the liberal consensus today—namely, that "eternity cannot be found in any other way" (Sherlock, 111)—roughly parallels Niebuhr's own belief, as captured in *The*

Children of Light and the Children of Darkness (1944): "Man's capacity for justice makes democracy possible; but man's inclination to injustice makes democracy necessary."[134] Experience, in short, has shown that the path of faithfulness—both for Latter-day Saints and all other Christians—is more securely traveled within an institutional order of liberalism than in any other viable alternative.

Nevertheless, as Sherlock rightly insists, Latter-day Saints and other Christians cannot help but experience their own support for the liberal consensus ambivalently, as some sort of compromise. The historic memories of the various Christian communities, as Sherlock shows in the case of Mormonism, suggest good reasons for this ambivalence. LDS faith is not only theocentric, it is also emphatically theocratic. Direct access to the will of God, according to LDS faith, was once more opened through the prophet Joseph Smith and continued with his successors in the prophetic office. Their spiritual, as well as political, authority within the community was based exclusively on their status as prophets. Sherlock insightfully recounts how the experience of Utah's protracted struggle toward statehood gradually clarified the terms of the compromise that Latter-day Saints made—and rightly made—with the dominant culture of political and economic liberalism. It was a compromise for the sake of faithfulness, for it allowed Latter-day Saints to overcome the threat of isolation and self-marginalization and focus on the LDS church's increasingly global mission, which surely must be acknowledged by all Christians for its fruitfulness and its positive and providential stimulus to evangelical reform and renewal.

The lesson that Sherlock draws from his reading of LDS experience, now supported by critical conversation with Niebuhr's Christian realism, is that all Christian communities will be faced with similar compromises, that they must negotiate for the sake of their own faithfulness as mission-driven movements and institutions. This is clearly the case in my own tradition of Roman Catholicism, which shares many characteristics with Mormonism, including a history of institutionalized theocracy. Just a generation ago, Vatican II, especially the Council's Decree on Religious Liberty, marked the climax of a process of accommodation to the liberal consensus that deserves careful scrutiny as another of these compromises. Catholic resistance to modernity throughout the nineteenth century reached its climax in Vatican I's official endorsement of papal infallibility, an historic development that itself has all the earmarks of compromise! And yet in the decades after Vatican I, Catholicism began a more constructive engagement with modernity that has produced fruits that most Catholics regard as both positive and providential, particularly, the church's support through the

---

134. Reinhold Niebuhr, *The Children of Light and the Children of Darkness* (New York: Charles Scribner's Sons, 1944), xi.

body of doctrine known as Catholic social teaching for a robust program of political and economic reform based on an intentionally Christian understanding of human rights.

An irreducible element of risk, however, is inherent in all such compromises. The history of Christianity is littered with examples—such as the Crusades, the seventeenth century's Wars of Religion, or, in a different venue, arguably, the adoption of organized monasticism as a model of Christian perfection—all examples of compromises that in retrospect have come to be regarded as dubious capitulations to the spirit of the times. These accommodations to what passed at the time for common sense and political necessity all had the support of the highest and most revered of religious authorities. How could anyone question the wisdom of the Crusades, for example, when they had the support of worthies such as St. Bernard of Clairvaux? Yet today any Catholic who would advocate religiously motivated violence would himself be regarded as a heretic. Can such risks be minimized, even as Christians continue to compromise for the sake of faithfulness?

How such risks are handled clearly differs from one Christian tradition to another. Niebuhr's Christian realism, at least indirectly, proposes one strategy for managing the inevitable risks of Christian engagement with the world, but it may not be appropriate for all Christians. Both Sherlock and I have suggested that there is something of an inverse correlation between theology and the gift of prophecy in the various communities—that the more a particular community cultivates a living tradition of prophetic authority, the less need there will be for highly developed public theologies such as Niebuhr's Christian realism. It is useful to recall that such theologies, until very recently, were identified almost exclusively with mainline Protestantism, whose theological heritage Sherlock tellingly identifies as "the magisterial reformation" (Sherlock, 105). Not until after Vatican II did Catholicism, for example, begin to stimulate similar forms of substantively theological reflection, first and somewhat hesitantly in European political theology, and then decisively in Latin American liberation theology. Niebuhr's Christian realism is substantively different from either of these, but it shares with them a tendency of deriving its theology from its ethical commitments and not the other way around. Beyond the obvious weaknesses revealed in such a tendency, there is an important strength: such theologies do tend to subject contemplated Christian compromises to a clear test of ethical justification. They are, of course, no guarantee that the communities will always avoid the monstrous evils unleashed by an excess of religious passion. But they can help set the terms for reasoned argument about the choices confronting Christian communities seeking the path of faithfulness.

Sherlock's reflections are most encouraging because they suggest that despite the differences among various Christian traditions, we are all faced with the common challenge of faithfulness in history, both personally and institutionally. The path of faithfulness is not always, maybe not even normally, obvious. Even in a community like that of the Latter-day Saints, who enjoy the gift of prophecy, there are struggles and controversies, if nowhere else at least in the hearts and minds of those possessed of this gift, who—as Vatican II's *Gaudium et Spes* so aptly described it—"have the duty of scrutinizing the signs of the times and interpreting them in light of the Gospel."[135] Sherlock is generous in his reading of Reinhold Niebuhr's theology, precisely because he can see beyond the historic differences between Niebuhr's heritage of magisterial Protestantism and his own LDS tradition and can identify certain points of convergence, not only in their basic understanding of Christian faith and experience, but also in the challenge of effective witness in the world, to which all Christians can and must respond. Those who still find merit in Niebuhr's Christian realism, as I do, are in Sherlock's debt; for coming to a better understanding of the LDS interpretation of "prophetic Christianity" may help us to see more clearly precisely what it means for public theology to be practical.

Reply to Professor McCann

Richard Sherlock

I GREATLY APPRECIATE DENNIS MCCANN'S insightful rejoinder to my essay on Reinhold Niebuhr. He has done me the honor of taking my essay seriously, even where we might disagree, for which I am grateful. I wish to make three short observations about his response.

McCann's original and important book *Christian Realism and Liberation Theology* compared and contrasted Niebuhr's theology of political engagement with that of the largely Latin American liberation theology—as seen in the works of Gutiérrez, Boff, Segundo, and others.[136] These

135. Dennis P. McCann, "Signs of the Times," in *The New Dictionary of Catholic Social Thought,* ed. Judith A. Dwyer (Collegeville, Minn.: The Liturgical Press / Michael Glazier, 1994), GS 4, cf. capitulations.

136. See Gustavo Gutiérrez, *A Theology of Liberation: History, Politics, and Salvation* (London: SCM, 1988); Leonardo Boff and Clodovis Boff, *Salvation*

thinkers were deeply affected by the injustice they saw around them and sought to develop a theology adequate to challenging and overcoming the systematic injustices of their homelands.[137]

McCann's comparison is relevant to Mormonism because it surely can be argued that the early LDS practice of the United Order (during the Ohio–Missouri period), as well as Brigham Young's later ideals, as seen in places such as Orderville,[138] presupposed a fundamentally new political, social, and economic order, where all things were held in common, patterned after examples in Acts and the Book of Mormon. In short, a new humanity was required.

Latter-day Saints tried implementing their form of large-scale Christian utopianism and failed, even when only hundreds were involved. Their failure makes the thought of drastically rearranging Brazil (which happens to be home to two leading liberation thinkers, Boff and Camera) after the pattern of Acts a mind-boggling proposal. McCann's work is, therefore, important for Latter-day Saints because he shows how Niebuhr both corrects this line of thinking in liberation theology and offers a realistic approach to Christian political engagement in the pursuit of earthly justice. I believe that an LDS engagement with Niebuhr will yield the same conclusion for Latter-day Saints: we can pursue an earthly justice even though we recognize from our own history that it will inevitably remain incomplete.

Secondly, I wish to call attention to McCann's observation that for Niebuhr theology is second to ethical commitments. In other words, theology is derived from ethics, not the other way around. This too seems to find a home in Mormonism. A perusal of the semi-authoritative *Encyclopedia of Mormonism* shows that Latter-day Saints hold a variety of views on many of the crucial theological issues of historic Christianity. For instance, Latter-day Saints are, broadly, social Trinitarians, as are many contemporary thinkers, like Cornelius Plantinga.[139] Nevertheless there is rarely complete agreement between members on the precise relation of the Father and the

---

and Liberation, trans. Robert R. Burr (Maryknoll, N.Y.: Orbis, 1984); and Juan Luis Segundo, *The Liberation of Theology,* trans. John Drury (Maryknoll, N.Y.: Orbis, 1976).

137. Juan Luis Segundo, for example, wrote the multivolume work *A Theology for Artisans of a New Humanity,* trans. John Drury, 5 vols. (Maryknoll, N.Y.: Orbis, 1973–75).

138. For more information about the United Order and its application in Orderville, see Leonard J. Arrington, *Great Basin Kingdom: An Economic History of the Latter-day Saints, 1830–1900* (Cambridge: Harvard University Press, 1958), 333–37.

139. Compare Paul E. Dahl, "Godhead," in *Encyclopedia of Mormonism,* ed. Daniel H. Ludlow, 4 vols. (New York: Macmillan, 1992), 2:552–53, to Cornelius Plantinga Jr., "Social Trinity and Tritheism," in *Trinity, Incarnation, and*

Son. Even more to the point is the question of divine knowledge of future contingencies—the so-called foreknowledge of God—and how it relates to human freedom. Latter-day Saints are firmly committed to human freedom and personal moral responsibility. But on the deeper questions there are a variety of views. Mormonism starts with what one Puritan writer referred to as a "call to a devout and holy life" and then works out enough provisional theology to ground such a call and its effects.

Finally, I wish to respond to McCann's idea that Mormonism is "theocratic." Actually, there is much less theocracy than outsiders might realize. McCann's own Catholic communion has a very rich tradition of precise thinking by theologians and the Magisterium about issues of life and death: care for the gravely ill or dying, just war theory, abortion, and so on. Mormonism has no such tradition and shows little inclination to establish one. Instead, on most of the great political and moral issues of our time, LDS church leaders most commonly advise individual members to pray for a personal spiritual witness as to what is right for them in a situation of decision. Therefore, although Latter-day Saint lives are certainly theocentric, the LDS church is theocratic only in very limited ways.[140]

This conclusion suggests a deeper dialogue with McCann and ultimately Niebuhr. If the essence of Mormonism is as I have described it, then Mormonism is profoundly anti-systematic in the sense of producing a systematic theology or a systematic moral theology. Latter-day Saints do not, for the most part, find tomes such as Tillich's *Systematic Theology* or Rahner's *Foundations of Christian Faith*, to name two important examples, congenial. This is not merely because Latter-day Saints differ on specific matters of doctrine, although such differences are important, but because, in the end, it is the very enterprise of systematics as seen in Niebuhr's *The Nature and Destiny of Man* that Latter-day Saints find uncongenial. Latter-day Saints seem to believe that enough common doctrine has been given to sustain the community; therefore, members must work the rest out individually through study and prayer.

For Latter-day Saints then, Niebuhr's work presents a quandary. He sought a Christian church that was vigorously engaged in the public order

---

Atonement: Philosophical and Theological Essays, ed. Ronald J. Feenstra and Cornelius Plantinga Jr. (Notre Dame: University of Notre Dame Press, 1989), 21–47.

140. "On most issues and in most elections, the [LDS] Church has remained neutral, admonishing its members to study the issues and vote according to their conscience." David B. Magleby, "Contemporary American Politics," in *Encyclopedia of Mormonism,* 3:1107. See also Roger M. Barrus, "Political History," in *Encyclopedia of Mormonism,* 3:1098–103; Gary C. Bryner, "Political Teachings," in *Encyclopedia of Mormonism,* 3:1103–5; and William Clayton Kimball, "Political Culture," in *Encyclopedia of Mormonism,* 3:1106–7.

on behalf of such earthly justice as was possible in mortality. On the eve of World War II he founded the late and lamented *Christianity and Crisis* as a vehicle for pushing the church to be more directly involved in the problems of the era, especially in war and peace. The optimism of the social gospel was gone. But that did not mean that the church should retreat from public life. It still had a duty to make decisions about war and peace, civil rights for African Americans, and other issues and to engage the public on behalf of what it saw as justice. Accordingly, in 1940, Niebuhr urged the Christian church to reject pacifism and support armed struggle against the forces of evil and later to support the civil rights movement and other struggles for equality.

Since the end of Utah's territorial period, Mormonism has simply refused to be politically engaged in the way that Niebuhr wanted churches to be engaged. There is very little serious LDS writing on the great moral issues of the twentieth century. During the Second World War many Latter-day Saints fought honorably on both sides, as general and local leaders counseled. But at least one of Mormonism's most important leaders, J. Reuben Clark, was an isolationist and a pacifist who would have thought that Niebuhr's service on the policy planning staff of the State Department after the war was wrong if not demonic. In short, on most of the great issues of our day, Mormonism embraces a chorus of voices, not a solo.

Additionally, the LDS emphasis on personal revelation cuts against the kind of vigorous political engagement that Niebuhr wanted. LDS church leaders did state that they were in favor of equal civil rights for minorities.[141] But LDS congregations were not recruiting grounds for the Freedom Summer of 1964 in the South. The LDS church generally opposes easy access to abortion, but it has never canonized the idea that human life begins at conception, but its "exceptions clauses," which permit an abortion in cases of rape, incest, fetal handicap, and situations where the mother's physical or mental health is endangered, allow so much room for personal inspiration that it is little wonder that Latter-day Saints have not worked with the National Right to Life Committee the way the Catholic bishops have. Mitt Romney, the Latter-day Saint contender for the 2008 Republican presidential nomination, endures sharp criticisms from political conservatives because of the pro-choice rhetoric he frequently employed while running for the U. S. Senate and the governorship of Massachusetts. Though Romney now claims a more conservative stance, the LDS exceptions for abortion seem to permit such divergent stances along the liberal-conservative continuum. In the same vein Utah is now thought of as one of the reddest of the red states. But from 1932 to 1950 devout Latter-day Saint and fervent New

---

141. Magleby, "Contemporary American Politics," 3:1107.

Dealer Elbert Thomas represented the state, only being defeated in a communist scare campaign in 1950. One recent issue on which the LDS church has officially been politically engaged is the question of gay marriage, which is an anomaly, not a harbinger.

Niebuhr wants the church to be engaged in a realistic struggle for earthly justice. But would Mormonism embrace such an engagement, or is it better to rely on the personal inspiration promised to members to make their own decisions for an imperfect justice in an imperfect world? Would Niebuhr's political sympathies be assuaged by the fact that the most numerous and most engaged communities are those much to the right of center? Niebuhr's challenge to Latter-day Saints is to avoid ignoring the world and hoping the problems will go away or at least stay away from their homes. The world will not go away, and I believe that Latter-day Saints should engage it decisively. However, I believe that Latter-day Saints have something to add to Niebuhr's call: a decisive emphasis on individual liberty and personal inspiration to work out the tentative, context-bound solutions in an imperfect setting.

About the Authors

Dennis McCann (Ph.D. University of Chicago Divinity School) received his S.T.L. in theology from the Gregorian University in Rome. McCann has had extensive academic experience in Hong Kong, China, and other countries in East Asia. Formerly a professor of religious studies at DePaul University and Executive Director of the Society of Christian Ethics, he is currently the Alston Professor of Bible and Religion at Anges Scott College in Decatur, Georgia. He has served on the Board of Directors of the Society of Christian Ethics and the editorial board of The Journal of Religious Ethics.

Richard Sherlock (Ph.D. Harvard University) graduated summa cum laude from the University of Utah before earning his M.T.S. and Ph.D. degrees from Harvard. He has taught medical ethics at the University of Tennessee Center for the Health Sciences and at the Faculty of Medicine at McGill University in Montreal Canada. He was also Professor of Moral Theology at Fordham University in New York City. He has published or has forthcoming over seventy articles, chapters, books, and reviews on bioethics, biotechnology, history of philosophy, political philosophy, philosophical theology, and Latter-day Saint history. He is currently a professor of philosophy at Utah State University.

Niebuhr Bibliography

Compiled by Dennis P. McCann

Reinhold Niebuhr's Major Works

Does Civilization Need Religion? New York: Macmillan, 1927.

Leaves from the Notebook of a Tamed Cynic. Chicago: Willett, Clark and Colby, 1929.

Moral Man and Immoral Society: A Study in Ethics and Politics. New York: Charles Scribner's Sons, 1932.

Reflections on the End of an Era. New York: Charles Scribner's Sons, 1934.

An Interpretation of Christian Ethics. New York: Harper and Brothers, 1935.

Beyond Tragedy: Essays on the Interpretation of History. New York: Charles Scribner's Sons, 1937.

Christianity and Power Politics. New York: Charles Scribner's Sons.

The Nature and Destiny of Man: A Christian Interpretation. 2 vols. New York: Charles Scribner's Sons, 1941–43.

Faith and History: A Comparison of Christian and Modern Views of History. New York: Charles Scribner's Sons, 1949.

The Irony of American History. New York: Charles Scribner's Sons, 1952.

The Self and the Dramas of History. New York: Charles Scribner's Sons, 1955.

Man's Nature and His Communities: Essays on the Dynamics and Enigmas of Man's Personal and Social Exsistence. New York: Charles Scribner's Sons, 1965.

The Essential Reinhold Niebuhr: Selected Essays and Addresses. Robert McAfee Brown, ed. New Haven: Yale University Press, 1986.

Works about Reinhold Niebuhr

Beckley, Harlan. *Passion for Justice: Retrieving the Legacies of Walter Rauschenbusch, John A. Ryan, and Reinhold Niebuhr.* Louisville, Ky.: Westminister/John Knox, 1992.

Benne, Robert. *The Ethic of Democratic Capitalism: A Moral Reassessment.* Philadelphia: Fortress, 1981.

Bingham, June. *Courage to Change: An Introduction to the Life and Thought of Reinhold Niebuhr.* New York: Charles Scribner's Sons, 1961.

Brown, Charles C. *Niebuhr and His Age: Reinhold Niebuhr's Prophetic Role in the Twentieth Century.* Philadelphia: Trinity Press International, 1992.

Clark, Henry B. *Serenity, Courage, and Wisdom: The Enduring Legacy of Reinhold Niebuhr.* Cleveland: Pilgrim, 1994.

Fackre, Gabriel. *The Promise of Reinhold Niebuhr.* Rev. ed. Lanham, Md.: University Press of America, 1994.

Fox, Richard Wightman. *Reinhold Niebuhr: A Biography.* New York: Pantheon, 1985.

Kegley, Charles W. and Robert W. Bretall, eds. *Reinhold Niebuhr: His Religious, Social, and Political Thought.* New York: Macmillan, 1956.

Lebacqz, Karen. *Six Theories of Justice: Perspectives from Philosophical and Theological Ethics.* Minneapolis: Augsburg, 1986.

Lovin, Robin W. *Reinhold Niebuhr and Christian Realism.* New York: Cambridge University Press, 1995.

McCann, Dennis P. *Christian Realism and Liberation Theology: Practical Theologies in Creative Conflict.* Maryknoll, N.Y.: Orbis, 1981.

Plaskow, Judith. *Sex, Sin and Grace: Women's Experience and the Theologies of Reinhold Niebuhr and Paul Tillich.* Washington, D.C.: University Press of America, 1980.

Stone, Ronald H. *Professor Reinhold Niebuhr: A Mentor to the Twentieth Century.* Louisville, Ky.: Westminster/John Knox, 1972.

———. *Reinhold Niebuhr: Prophet to Politicians.* Nashville: Abingdon, 1972.

West, Cornel. *The American Evasion of Philosophy: A Genealogy of Pragmatism.* Madison: University of Wisconsin Press, 1988.

A Dialogue on the Theology of Paul Tillich

Paul Tillich: Boundary Breaker

Joseph L. Price

In a very personal way I am indebted to the theological vision and pioneering spirit of Paul Tillich. He has served as boundary breaker for me, facilitating my confessional shift from a position of dogmatic legalism to one of theological tolerance and joy. As an undergraduate, I first encountered Tillich's thought in *Love, Power, and Justice*, and within a few weeks I began to explore his *Dynamics of Faith*, a work that I have read more often than any theological work outside of scripture. Although I had been a regular churchgoer for twenty years and had read countless devotional books and religious tracts, I cut my theological molars on Tillich and have continued to chew on his ideas for the past thirty years. I have taken courses on Tillich in three different graduate institutions and have taught his ideas to undergraduates and church lay groups as often as possible. It is with great enthusiasm, then, that I contribute an essay to this volume initiating a theological dialogue between the shapers of Christian theology at the dawn of the twenty-first century and Latter-day Saints, who may begin to sample portions of Tillich's thought.[1]

---

1. As a way to begin reading Tillich's works, I recommend that readers unfamiliar with existentialist thought start with samples of his sermons, many of which are collected in three volumes: Paul Tillich, *The Shaking of the Foundations* (New York: Charles Scribner's Sons, 1948); Paul Tillich, *The Eternal Now* (New York: Charles Scribner's Sons, 1963); and Paul Tillich, *The New Being* (New York: Charles Scribner's Sons, 1955).

In addition, there are several compilations of excerpts from his works, thematically arranged in order to provide a relatively quick sampling of his thought. Two of these volumes are F. Forrester Church, ed., *The Essential Tillich: An Anthology of the Writings of Paul Tillich* (New York: Macmillan, 1987), and Mark Kline Taylor, *Paul Tillich: Theologian of the Boundaries* (London: Collins, 1987). Of the books about Tillich, the comprehensive two-volume biography and historical analysis of his thought by Wilhelm and Marion Pauck stands out as most significant, and for

Because there have been hundreds of dissertations and books about Tillich and thousands of articles focusing on various aspects of his thought, my purpose is not to duplicate or reduce them, but to identify possible points of contact with the doctrine of The Church of Jesus Christ of Latter-day Saints where Tillich's theology might offer a distinct challenge.[2] From the expanse of Tillich's thought, I have selected three themes and issues that, from my non-Mormon perspective, seem to pose significant challenges to what I have learned about the spirituality and doctrine of Latter-day Saints. These are

1. the understanding of theology, especially as manifest in the development of his theological method of correlation;

2. the concept of God as being-itself, not a being, however superlative that being might be; and

3. the understanding of faith as the dynamic state of being ultimately concerned rather than as the acceptance and affirmation of dogmatic principles for which little if any empirical or logical evidence might exist.

For all Christians, there are other significant theological challenges advanced by Tillich, including his understanding of the nature of Christ, not as a supernatural incarnation of divine *being* (with a lower case *b*), but as a manifestation of New Being, of the overcoming of existential alienation with being-itself. Related to Tillich's existentialist Christology is his interpretation of salvation as relating to the depth of experience, the overcoming of alienation from others and from being-itself, an experience that is possible in the present temporal frame of existence. In other words, for Tillich, salvation has to do with the prospects for the "Eternal Now," not some unending form of post-mortem, personal existence. As important as these christological and soteriological challenges are, however, I will devote my primary attention to a brief introduction of Tillich's significance for contemporary theology, followed by an explication of his thought on the foundational concepts of theological method, God, and faith.

---

theological clarity and scope, the interpretation offered by his former student and colleague Langdon Gilkey is outstanding. Wilhelm and Marion Pauck, *Paul Tillich: His Life and Thought*, 2 vols. (New York: Harper and Row, 1976); Langdon Gilkey, *Gilkey on Tillich* (New York: Crossroad, 1990).

2. Among the essays that were published shortly following Tillich's death in 1965 was an essay by Louis Midgley, a political scientist at Brigham Young University, who praised Tillich for his influence on political science. The essay, "Religion and Ultimate Concern: An Encounter with Paul Tillich's Theology," initiated a series of essays on contemporary theologians in the then new journal *Dialogue: A Journal of Mormon Thought* 1 (Summer 1966), 55–71.

Tillich as a Boundary Breaker

Tillich was and is a boundary breaker, even now prompting shifting senses of where the lines form between the sacred and the secular, dissolving disruptions between objectives of theology and the perspectives of theologians, and relocating the direction of transcendence from one of beyond the horizons to the inner depths of one's own existence—the moment or place where being-itself might be touched in all its immediacy and particularity. As the pioneer for theologians of secularity in the last half of the twentieth century, Tillich initiated the extensive exploration of the spiritual dimension within nontraditional religious rituals and practices. "Such is the scope and tensive unity of his thought, that it has the capacity to make contact with, to 'touch,' and so to relate itself to almost every sort of position in almost every sort of diverse area," as his former student and interpreter Langdon Gilkey observes. "In this sense, he continually mediates in so many areas, and for this reason he interests and stimulates so many different sorts of thinkers." In the process of applying his method of correlation, especially as problems and prompts emerged within culture, Tillich assumed a mediating role "between almost all facets of cultural life and religion," Gilkey concludes, "that gives to his thought its uniqueness, its fascination, its near-universality of relevance, and its unceasing ability to illuminate the obscure corners of our existence."[3]

Rather than understanding religion as a special, spiritual facet of human experience, Tillich saw it as the dimension of the depth of human existence that prompts all human thought, informs all human feeling, and orients all human action. Religion is the dimension of depth in all human functions, endeavors, feelings, and being. Tillich's definition of religion as "that which concerns us ultimately" implies that what makes a statement religious is not that it focuses on transcendence or utilizes traditional ways of speaking about God, but that it asks ultimate questions about the meaning of existence. For Tillich, then, authentic spirituality, which plunges into the depths of a person's existence and explores the hidden recesses of a person's grounding in reality, gives rise to expressions about the depths. In turn, these expressions manifest the first words of theology, raising fundamental questions about the meaning of life, raising consciousness about limitations and possibilities of human experience, and probing concerns of ultimate significance about the nature of existence itself.

For Tillich, reflection upon and speculation about theological method do not precede the human experience of alienation, which itself prompts the question, "From what are persons alienated?" At its root this question is fundamentally theological, since the answer to the question is that the

---

3. Gilkey, *Gilkey on Tillich,* 57–58.

alienation of existence is from the power or source of being-itself that generates and germinates all existents. In fact, as he proclaims in one of his sermons, "God is nearer to us than we [are to] ourselves."[4]

Reflecting the mediating role that distinguished his intellectual career, Tillich often spoke of his life in terms of its being "on the boundary," even using that phrase as the title for a series of autobiographical essays.[5] Not only was his thought always pressing toward new intellectual horizons; his experience also manifested a pioneering spirit that, to a certain extent, aligns him with the early Mormon pioneers who moved beyond the boundary and settled in new territory, while maintaining connections with former relationships.

Most of the main events and transitions in Tillich's life can be traced fairly easily since several extensive biographical portraits and analyses have been published.[6] Yet because his life provides the context of human experience out of which and toward which his theology developed, a brief recapitulation of his primary accomplishments and movements is in order. The son of a Lutheran minister, Tillich was born in 1886 in a small German boundary town in Brandenburg that has been a part of Poland since World War II; during his teenage years, his family moved to Berlin. In 1910, he received a doctorate in philosophy from the University of Breslau before taking the licentiate in theology two years later at the University of Halle and being ordained in the Evangelical Church of the Prussian Union. He enlisted as a chaplain at the outbreak of World War I, and after witnessing the horror of war, lost his romantic fondness for the ease of German classical philosophy.

During the 1920s and early 1930s, he held academic appointments first at Berlin, then at Marburg (where he was a colleague with Martin Heidegger), Dresden, Leipzig, and Frankfurt, where he was suspended from professorial duties. As he recalled later, his publication of *The Socialist Decision* in 1933, which grew out of his leadership in developing German Religious Socialism, prompted the termination of his academic appointment.[7] He identified his suspension as an "honor," since he was the first non-Jewish professor dismissed from a German university during the rise of Nazism.[8] During his

---

4. Tillich, *Shaking of the Foundations,* 128.

5. Paul Tillich, *On the Boundary: An Autobiographical Sketch* (New York: Charles Scribner's Sons, 1966).

6. For biographical information, see Hannah Tillich, *From Time to Time* (New York: Stein and Day, 1973); the analytical tribute offered by Rollo May, *Paulus: Reminiscences of a Friendship* (New York: Harper and Row, 1973); and Pauck, *Paul Tillich.*

7. Paul Tillich, *Die Sozialistische Entscheidung* [The Socialist Decision] (Offenbach: Bollwerk-Verlag Karl Dott, 1933).

8. Pauck, *Paul Tillich,* 1:198, 288.

years on the philosophy faculty, Tillich attended to issues that broached the boundary between philosophy and theology, lecturing, for example, on "The Religious Content and the Historico-Religious Significance of Greek and Occidental Philosophy."[9] Tillich immigrated to New York and began working at the Union Theological Seminary in 1932. Although he continued to express interest in ancient philosophical roots, he turned his attention to more traditionally recognized theologians and theological issues. Remarkably, although he had held tenure at the time of his dismissal from Frankfurt, Tillich was not given tenure at the time of his appointment at Union. He earned it after four years and was promoted to the rank of professor seven years after his initial seminary appointment.[10]

Intellectually, Tillich began his career as a philosopher of religion, and he crossed a boundary in moving to a seminary home, becoming a theologian, or theologically obsessed philosopher. Yet "it would be wrong," Hans Schwarz warns, "to claim that Tillich had become more pious and more churchly in America." Although Tillich appreciated his new relationship with American churches, he reluctantly attended chapel services at Union, and later at Harvard he avoided church services altogether. "Neither a theologian of the church nor for the church," Schwarz concludes, Tillich "was never a church person but a theologian on the boundary to the world."[11] The shift from philosophical faculties in German universities to the theological faculty at Union Seminary, which was oriented at that time toward the training and cultivating of ministers, certainly affected his role in intellectual leadership. Although Columbia University was across the street from Union, few of Columbia's philosophers initially accepted Tillich, since they were not concerned with Schelling or with questions of ontology; they were excited instead by John Dewey and pragmatism.

At Union, Tillich "learned American theology 'primarily through dialogue,'" realizing that American theology had not shared the neo-orthodox enthusiasm of either Karl Barth or Rudolf Bultmann, but that it had become yoked to social ethics. As such, he felt that it reflected an overly optimistic character, despite the dregs of the Depression, which threatened social stability, and the onset of World War II. Toward the end of his life Tillich also admitted that he felt his shift from Germany to America had not merely been a shift in intellectual locus. He thought of himself, instead,

---

9. Hans Schwarz, "The Americanization of Paul Tillich," *Newsletter of the North American Paul Tillich Society* 22 (July 1996): 2.

10. Schwarz, "Americanization of Paul Tillich," 2–3; Pauck, *Paul Tillich,* 1:176–77, 197.

11. Schwarz, "Americanization of Paul Tillich," 4–5.

as a "migrant between two worlds," for he considered neither America nor Germany his homeland.[12]

Tillich's experience in traversing geographical and cultural boundaries is reflected in the specific ways that he worked with the territories of philosophy and theology. For Tillich, philosophy deals with the structure of being and theology with the meaning of being for us. "Philosophy asks the ultimate question that can be asked, namely, the question as to what being, simply being, means. . . . What is the meaning of being? Why is there being and not not-being? What is the structure in which every being participates?" By contrast, or better, by intensification, Tillich suggests, "Theology deals with what concerns us inescapably, ultimately, unconditionally [that is, being-itself]. It deals with it not as far as it *is* but as far as it is *for us.*" The existentialist character of his theology is underscored as Tillich insists that "in no theological statement can the relation *to us* be omitted." Yet the difference between existentialist philosophy, which conjectures about the structure of being and personal participation in existence, and theology is that theological deliberations include the element of "ultimate concern," without which, he concludes, "no assertion is a theological one."[13]

Depending upon what passage one reads, one is tempted to demand classification of Tillich as a philosopher of religion, as a philosophical theologian, as a theologically obsessed philosopher, or as a philosopher of theology. For Tillich, the thoroughgoing integration of philosophy and theology is rooted in their both being "being-obsessed." Furthermore, he adds:

> Both philosophy and theology become poor and distorted when they are separated from each other. Philosophy becomes logical positivism prohibiting philosophy from dealing with any problem which concerns us seriously—political, anthropological, religious—a very comfortable flight of philosophical thought from the tremendous realities of our period. Or it becomes mere epistemology, always sharpening the knife of thought but never cutting, because cutting toward a truth that concerns us demands venturing courage and passion. Or it becomes history of philosophy, enumerating one philosophical opinion of the past after the other, keeping itself at a noble distance, faithlessly and cynically—a philosophy without existential basis, without theological ground and power.[14]

The conceptual boundaries that Tillich perceived between various academic and professional disciplines were challenged by his integrative, holistic understanding of personal existence, especially as it is determined by

---

12. Ibid., 2, 4–5.

13. Paul Tillich, *The Protestant Era*, trans. James Luther Adams (Chicago: University of Chicago Press, 1948), 85, 87.

14. Ibid., 89.

the structure of being. It should not be too surprising, then, that Tillich rev-eled in and articulated alliances not only between existentialist philosophy and depth psychology, but also between religion and politics, theology and science, religion and society, and theology and art—to name several of the prominent scholarly boundaries that he traversed.

The Compass of Correlation

For Christians undertaking theology, the first of the significant challenges presented by Tillich's theology involves the method of the constructive process of "doing theology." In two particular ways, Tillich's method of correlation presses toward new horizons in the theological and cultural landscape. Using a self-application of the method through the "Protestant Principle," as he called it, he subjected his own theology and its sources to critiques of reason and justice, thereby engaging philosophy in correlation with—in response to and critique of—the revelation interpreted and elabo-rated in the theological answers to philosophical questions.

Prompted by, emergent out of, and reflective upon the human condi-tion, Tillich's method of correlation formulates existential questions. In response, theology must provide answers.[15] On repeated occasions, critics have attempted to reduce the method of correlation to a starkly drawn con-trast by saying that "philosophy and culture provide the questions by fram-ing concepts and categories, while theology provides the answers to the fundamental human questions." Focusing on this simple statement, critics have often misinterpreted Tillich's approach as a kind of neo-orthodox, supernatural "answer" to the questions posed by reason within a particular situation. "Tillich is *not* saying that philosophers are helplessly bewildered vacuities who go around only asking questions," Gilkey quips at this point, "and that theologians pass out answers to impoverished cultural theorists as John D. Rockefeller passed out dimes to impoverished small boys, though some of his [Tillich's] phrasings can sound that way."[16]

Rather, for Tillich, the task of philosophy is to pose questions of ulti-mate significance drawn from analysis of the human condition and experi-ence of finitude; and for theology, the challenge is to move beyond stodgy concepts that reiterate scriptures and dogma and to locate answers in the evocative character of revelatory symbols. Tillich's method of correlation involves more than the logical application of certain criteria to central sym-bols of Christian tradition. Mark Kline Taylor notes, "It [correlation] is an interpretive art requiring sensitive readings of both human situations and

---

15. See also Paul Tillich, *Systematic Theology,* 3 vols. (Chicago: University of Chicago Press, 1951), 1:60.

16. Gilkey, *Gilkey on Tillich,* 72.

also of Christian symbols in the tradition. It is a continual tacking back and forth between a situation and a Christian message that are always already in some kind of mutual interrelation."[17]

Addressing the questions articulated by philosophy and culture, theology must also wrestle with unanticipated moves by philosophy and cultural propositions, bracketing its anticipated answers to recurrent questions and re-envisioning responses in light of the new dimensions of the questions and situations themselves. Yet the answers proposed by Christian faith are "meaningful," Tillich avers, "only in so far as they are in correlation with questions concerning the whole of our existence, with existential questions."[18]

Tillich developed his method of correlation in a conscious attempt to avoid, as he put it, several "contradictory errors in theology"—the supranaturalistic, the naturalistic, and the dualistic. The supranaturalist tendency, he observes, "makes revelation a rock falling into history from above, to be accepted obediently without preparation or adequacy to human nature." By contrast, the naturalistic orientation "replaces revelation by a structure of rational thought derived from and judged by human nature." Avoiding the errors engendered by both of these perspectives, the method of correlation, as he puts it, "shows a way out of the blind alley in which the discussion between fundamentalism or neo-orthodoxy on the one hand, and theological humanism or liberalism on the other, is caught."[19] The third inadequate method that Tillich identifies is dualistic, which recognizes in a minimal way the problem that the method of correlation addresses. Building upon the naturalistic and supranaturalistic methods, the dualistic method seeks to explicate a positive relation between them "by positing a body of theological truth." Persons can reach this body of theological truth by exploring "natural revelation" (an oxymoron), especially as it might be formulated in the so-called proofs of the "existence of God"—a phrase that Tillich also regards as self-contradictory since God is being-itself, not bound by the structures and strictures of existence.[20]

Most analyses and commentaries on Tillich's method maintain focus on the process of correlation between the questions conceived and articulated by philosophy and culture and the theological responses offered out of the experience of faith in ultimate concern, particularly as faith draws upon the symbols and stories of Christian tradition. However, "the Protestant Principle," which involves an intense self-application of the process of correlation (or self-critique facilitated by that process), is often considered separately from Tillich's method. The Protestant Principle, which Tillich

---

17. Taylor, *Theologian of the Boundaries*, 126–27.
18. Tillich, *Systematic Theology*, 1:61–62.
19. Tillich, "Beyond Religious Socialism," *Christian Century* 66 (June 15, 1949): 733.
20. Tillich, *Systematic Theology*, 1:65.

develops in his essay by that title in *The Protestant Era,* recognizes that all human forms of reasoning and loving are imperfect and subject to ongoing, self-reflective critique (which will always prompt further self-critique) because they are human and arise out of the condition of alienation and estrangement from the ground of being. Because the expression of human freedom can be perverted, taking a direction of self-destruction, humans will always be in need of the self-directed application of critique known as the Protestant Principle. "The possibility of self-contradiction is rooted in the *self*-determination of [humans], the direction of which cannot be determined beforehand," Tillich writes. "This basic, underivable cleavage in human existence underlies all human history and makes history what it is."[21]

As suggested above, a crucial component in Tillich's method of correlation involves the identification and interpretation of symbols, which manifest the ideas of the revelation that theology works with as it unravels responses to the provocative philosophical questions of the correlative method. The very word "God" and the interpretive designation of "being-itself" are, Tillich contends, symbolic of the God beyond "God" to whom the word and explanation point.

For Tillich, the "stuff" with which the theologian works is a repository of symbols provided by revelation and experience. Even the word "God" is a symbol for the God beyond "God" who is the source of creation, the power of redemption, and the focus of Christian theology. In various essays throughout his career, Tillich elaborated his understanding of symbols.[22] For Tillich, symbols possess a disclosive power that exceeds the point of their reference. Symbols cannot be constrained to a denotative relationship. They are tensive, active, evocative, and potentially revelatory. The power of symbols enables them to open up, as Tillich says, "in two directions—in the direction of reality and in the direction of the mind," for they reveal hidden strata of reality and they facilitate new levels of awareness for the mind.[23]

Like signs, symbols point beyond themselves; but unlike signs, which are intentionally designed and thus arbitrary and consequently interchangeable, symbols participate in the power and meaning of that to which they refer. Because symbols cannot be intentionally crafted, their vitality emerges out of the situation that gives rise to their need. Symbols thus

---

21. Tillich, *Protestant Era,* 165–66.

22. Paul Tillich, *Dynamics of Faith* (New York: Harper and Brothers, 1957), 46. In chapter 3, "Symbols of Faith," Tillich presents a thorough explication of his theory of symbols. See also Tillich, *Systematic Theology,* vol. 1.

23. Paul Tillich, "Theology and Symbolism," in *Religious Symbolism,* ed. Frederick Ernest Johnson (New York: Institute for Religious and Social Studies, 1955), 109. See also Paul Tillich, "The Nature of Religious Language," in *Theology of Culture,* ed. Robert C. Kimball (London: Oxford University Press, 1959), 57.

emerge in the context of correlation, out of the response to a question or problem particular to a situation. The life of symbols is integrally connected to the correlative process, for symbols grow and die according to whether the generating and germinating conditions maintain their vitality and pertinence or whether they calcify or wither away. Not even scientific criticism can destroy symbols; it can only profane them, he concludes, by "exposing their symbolic character."[24]

The power of symbols and their social perception and significance can be illustrated well by the symbol of a nation's flag, which is designed for the functional purpose of identifying affiliation or possession. Beyond this functional role, the flag expresses a deeper sense of national values and identity, and is recognized by citizens as exemplifying distinct patriotic preferences, commitments, and hopes. In that regard, then, the flag becomes endowed with a symbolic power of the nation that cannot be transferred to another cloth representation, nor can it fully and accurately be transcribed in discursive language. The power is so thoroughly manifest in the symbol of the flag that attempts to desecrate the flag are often considered, by the citizens for whom the flag serves as a symbol, tantamount to critiques of the nation itself.

Symbols disclose levels of reality that otherwise would remain hidden in their particularity, complexity, and depth. They cannot be translated into literal discursive language and retain their revelatory or evocative power. They generate an excess of meaning, a surplus of significance. Not only do symbols express the power of their referent, they also provide access to undisclosed dimensions of the self in the interpretative act. While they disclose referential dimensions otherwise inaccessible, they also unlock dimensions of our own selves in the interpretive act, disclosing hidden dimensions of our own identities. In their referential capacity, symbols manifest their fundamental, communal character, for the meaning of symbols emerges from a shared perception of their communicative significance.

The importance of symbols for theologians is that through religious symbols truth is pursued and personal authenticity can be explored and expressed. Like other symbols, religious symbols disclose "the depth dimension of reality itself, the dimension of reality which is the ground of every other dimension and every other depth, and which therefore, is not one level beside the others but is the fundamental level, the level below all other levels, the level of being itself, or the ultimate power of being." Although religious symbols function as a compass in pointing persons to God, they

---

24. Paul Tillich, "The Religious Symbol," in *Myth and Symbol,* ed. F. W. Dillistone (London: SPCK, 1966), 32.

do not make God immanent, for as Tillich poetically puts it, "The wholly transcendent transcends every symbol of the Holy."[25]

The Horizon of God

Discussion of the nature of religious symbols and their relation to "being-itself" effectively introduces Tillich's second fundamental theological challenge to theistic Christians, a challenge that focuses on the nature of God. According to Tillich, "the idea of God has, by misuse through objectification, lost its symbolic power in such measure that it serves largely as a concealment of the unconditioned transcendent rather than as a symbol for it."[26] For Tillich, the word "God" is the symbol for God beyond the God of traditional theism. Lying on the boundary between the symbolic and non-symbolic realms of language, the word "God," Tillich asserts:

> connotes the unconditional transcendent, the ultimate, and also an object somehow endowed with qualities and actions. The first is not figurative or symbolic, but it is rather in the strictest sense what it is said to be. The second, however, is really symbolic, figurative. . . . God as an object is a representation of the reality ultimately referred to in the religious act, but in the word "God" this objectivity is negated and at the same time its representative character is asserted.[27]

Even the explanatory definition of God as "being-itself," Tillich contends, is symbolic, albeit the most nearly nonsymbolic statement that can be made about God.[28] Identifying the nature of God as "being-itself," however, we are still faced with the challenge of interpreting the symbol "God" in order to develop our understanding of self in relation to God.

For Tillich, the initial and fundamental theological question "is the question of God." All that exists is derived from God and sustained by God as Being. God is, as Tillich so often put it, the ground and power of being, and as such God is the answer to the fundamental question posed by existence. For "God is the answer to the question implied in being," and "'God' is the answer to the question implied in man's finitude[,] . . . the name for that which concerns man ultimately."[29] Throughout most of his theological

---

25. Tillich, "Nature of Religious Language," 58–59.

26. Tillich, "Religious Symbol," 32–33.

27. Ibid., 28.

28. At the time he wrote the first volume of his *Systematic Theology*, Tillich asserted that God as being-itself is the only *non*symbolic statement that one can make about God. Tillich, *Systematic Theology*, 1:238. However, by the time of the publication of his second volume in 1957, he had begun to realize that "everything we say about God is symbolic." Tillich, *Systematic Theology*, 2:9.

29. Tillich, *Systematic Theology*, 1:163, 211.

career, Tillich referred to God as the ground of being, the power of being, being-itself, or Being, using the upper case *B* and seeking to remove platonic associations of static abstraction from the empowering and creative force of Being. Toward the end of his life, however, and by the time he had written the third volume of his *Systemic Theology,* Tillich had begun to prefer the language of "Spirit" in order to emphasize the dynamic character of "Being,"[30] the self-designation by Yahweh in the revelation perceived by Moses in the burning bush. In this regard, then, God as Spirit or "Being" is the panentheistic source of existence, the active "verb from whom, in whom, and with whom all true movements move."[31]

In "The Depth of Existence," one of the sermons in his initial collection of homilies, Tillich attempts to explain this foundational concept to the Christians in attendance, not merely to theologians and philosophers: "The name of this infinite and inexhaustible depth and ground of all being is *God,*" Tillich proclaims:

> That depth is what the word *God* means. And if that word has not much meaning for you, translate it, and speak of the depths of your life, of the source of your being, of your ultimate concern, of what you take seriously without any reservation. Perhaps, in order to do so, you must forget everything traditional that you have learned about God, perhaps even that word itself. For if you know that God means depth, you know much about Him. You cannot then call yourself an atheist or unbeliever. For you cannot think or say: Life has no depth! Life itself is shallow. Being itself is surface only. If you could say this in complete seriousness, you would be an atheist; but otherwise you are not. He who knows about depth knows about God.[32]

For Tillich, the recognition that God is being-itself is crucial in order to conceive the distinction of the perfection of God as being beyond the substantive (that is, spatial) and temporal strictures of existence itself. For if God were existent, then God would represent only a distinction in degree from humans, albeit a degree *approaching* a difference in kind but not, metaphysically, constituting a difference in kind as such. For "a conditioned God," Tillich contends, "is no God,"[33] regardless of how minimal the conditions might seem to be, especially in comparison with impermanent and imperfect humans. In order to free the concept of God from the restrictions imposed by existence, Tillich calls for a return to a classical form

---

30. To emphasize the active dimension of the participial form "Being," Mary Daly offers the possibility of writing it as "Be-ing." Mary Daly, *Beyond God the Father: Toward a Philosophy of Women's Liberation* (Boston: Beacon, 1973).

31. Daly, *Beyond God the Father,* 198.

32. Tillich, *Shaking of the Foundations,* 57.

33. Tillich, *Systematic Theology,* 1:248.

of theology whose principal statement about God is *Deus est esse,* "Being as such." "Being in this sense," Tillich writes, "is not the most abstract category, as a mistaken nominalism asserts; it is the power of Being in everything that is, in everything that participates in Being."[34] Because the being of God is being-itself, Tillich avers that "God cannot be understood as the existence of a being alongside others or above others." For if God is actually *a* being as such, God would be "subject to the categories of finitude, especially to space and substance." Underscoring the interpretation that God is the symbol for the God beyond God, Tillich goes on to assert that "when applied to God, superlatives become diminutives" and locate God in the same categories as existents while trying to elevate God above them. "A theology which does not dare to identify God and the power of being as the first step toward a doctrine of God relapses into monarchic monotheism, for if God is not being-itself, [God] is subordinate to it." As being-itself, however, God is beyond both existence and essence, for being-itself exceeds, yet includes, spatiality, substantiality, and temporality, even being "beyond finitude and infinity."[35]

Because God is being-itself and includes all that is, as well as all threats to and protests of existence, God is the presupposition of and foundation for culture. Consequently, Tillich repeatedly affirmed his well-known dictum that "religion is the substance of culture, and culture the form of religion."[36] Without such a religious grounding of culture, the whole range of cultural life expressed through scientific experimentation and formulation, philosophical propositions and analyses, political policies and institutions, social structures and relations, as well as through artistic creations and artifacts, would be bereft of deep significance. They would become, as Langdon Gilkey has summarized, merely "empty, skeptical, undirected, and trivial" expressions.[37]

Although language about God as being-itself seems to be acutely abstract, Tillich emphasizes that the empowering and creative potential of Being render it as existentially significant, as vibrant and personal. Indeed, for Christians throughout history, attempts to understand God have often focused on the creative and loving character of God. In continuity with and refinement of this tradition, Tillich identifies the ontological grounding of the creative and loving character of God. Divine creativity is the same as the active character of being-itself. "God is creative because he is God."[38] Consequently, Tillich asserts, it is not meaningful to raise the typical

34. Tillich, *Protestant Era,* 63.
35. Tillich, *Systematic Theology,* 1:235–37.
36. Tillich, *Theology of Culture,* 47.
37. Gilkey, *Gilkey on Tillich,* 101.
38. Tillich, *Systematic Theology,* 1:252.

scholastic question about whether creativity is a necessary or contingent act of God because, as the empowering force of being-itself, God is not dependent on anything or anyone beyond the power of being-itself. For God, aseity is actual; it is self-generated and self-realized. In this sense then, Tillich concludes, creation is not contingent: "It does not 'happen' to God, for it is identical with his life. Creation is not only God's freedom but also his destiny."[39] Applying this idea, the conventional Christian narrative of creation ex nihilo—of the Creation as an original act that generated substance out of nothing—is not a historical or scientific account about the origin of the world. Rather, it is a dramatic story that underscores the relation between God and humans—that as existents, humans derive their very existence from the power of being-itself.

As Tillich locates the creative dimension of God in the very ground and power of being-itself, he also identifies love as an "ontological concept."[40] Love is "the reunion of the estranged," and *reunion* and *estrangement* presuppose an original union, which is being-itself.[41] Even the emotional character of love results from its ontological nature, for "the power of love is not something which is added to an otherwise finished process, but life has love in itself as one of its constitutive elements."[42] Although the emotional character of love emerges out of its ontological grounding, love should not be defined by focusing on its emotional manifestation. The identification of love with emotion, Tillich writes,

> leads necessarily to sentimental misinterpretations of the meaning of love and calls into question its symbolic application to the divine life. But God is love. And, since God is being-itself, one must say that being-itself is love. This, however, is understandable only because the actuality of being is life. The process of the divine life has the character of love.[43]

Love includes an emotional element, for the experience of reunion to which love aspires is characterized by full joy, a kind of "extreme happiness and the end of happiness."[44]

In providential creativity, the loving character and creative power of God become indistinguishable because God's creative activity "works toward the fulfillment of every creature and toward the bringing-together

---

39. Ibid., 1:252.

40. Ibid., 1:279.

41. Paul Tillich, *Love, Power, and Justice: Ontological Analyses and Ethical Applications* (New York: Oxford University Press, 1954), 25.

42. Ibid., 25–26. For the most comprehensive discussion of the ontological character of love and its relation to power and justice, see especially the section "An Ontology of Love," 24–34.

43. Tillich, *Systematic Theology*, 1:279.

44. Tillich, *Love, Power, and Justice*, 27.

into the unity of his life all who are separated and disrupted," which is the character of love. Because the language about God is finally symbolic, the fullness of God as creative, as love, as power, as wholly other, cannot be explicated. Finally, God remains a "mystery for finite understanding," a horizon always perceived and approached but never crossed nor fully delimited.[45]

The Frontier of Faith

A third major area of Tillich's theological challenges is the theological territory of faith, especially as it is surveyed in relation to the conceptual fields of dogma, truth, and doubt. The relation between faith and God does not require traditional Christian affirmation about the nature of God. For "whatever concerns a man ultimately becomes god for him, and, conversely, it means that a man can be concerned ultimately only about that which is god for him."[46] In his most succinct formulation Tillich defines faith as "the state of being ultimately concerned," and he identifies the ultimate concern of faith "with the desire of love: reunion with that to which one belongs and from which one is estranged."[47] Furthermore, "that" to which one belongs and toward which one seeks reconciliation or reunion is the very power of Being: God.

Faith does not require that one affirm revealed truths, contravene scientific conclusions, or deny reason. "There is no conflict," Tillich declares, "between faith in its true nature and reason in its true nature."[48] Faith requires more than mere assent to propositions, assertions, and revelations, which might be subject to a person's changing set of allegiances and preferences. Faith cannot be so casually or cursorily shifted from one concern to another. Rather, faith involves the whole person; it is experienced in the convergence of the volitional, intellectual, emotional, and physical aspects of one's identity. It is a spiritual experience of the whole person. Tillich associates faith, in fact, with the commandment in Deuteronomy that "You should love the Lord your God with all your heart, and with all your soul, and with all your might" (Deut. 6:5). As the condition of being ultimately concerned, faith is the experience of being grasped and possessed by the ultimate concern.

The inclusiveness and demands of faith are such that it can be known as faith only when it accepts the threat of its own demise. Faith must embrace the possibility of annihilation in doubt while it pursues truth, which is manifest in the character of love overcoming alienation. Truth can be

---

45. Tillich, *Systematic Theology*, 1:281, 280.
46. Ibid., 1:211.
47. Tillich, *Dynamics of Faith*, 112.
48. Ibid., 80.

experienced as liberating only in the context of concern with the ultimacy of being-itself, which must always recognize and include the threat of non-being. Doubt, in turn, should not suggest that it can be fully overcome in faithful pursuit of truth. For doubt is always necessarily present, in provocative as well as threatening ways, in all human pursuits of liberating truth and in all experiences of being grasped by the power of being-itself.

The need to examine the relation between faith and truth not only emerges from the orientation of faith toward truth as it pursues understanding of God (who commands faith's attention and allegiance as truly ultimate); it also becomes relevant for contemporary theological audiences as Tillich seeks to distinguish the truth of faith from its misperceived and mislabeled "conflict" with science.

In his discussion of truth in *Dynamics of Faith,* Tillich treats scientific, historical, and philosophical forms of truth in their relation to faith because, in part, the claims of science, the facts of history, and the propositions of philosophy are often portrayed as challenges to or conflicts with faith. This trinity of truths—scientific, historical, and philosophical—is not an exhaustive list of the forms of truth Tillich conceives, for elsewhere he alludes to and reflects upon poetic and mythic forms of truth. Each of these forms of truth evinces their distinct character when their sources are examined.

In general, Tillich recognizes the challenge of reason to the truth claims of Christian theology, particularly as scholarly pursuits locate the source of truth in science, history, and philosophy. Tillich enjoys the new ways through which truth becomes disclosed in academic study, and yet he is wary about the naïve or blind ways that students and scholars may restrict their pursuit of truth to academic study alone. "For them," he notes:

> scholarly truth is truth altogether. Poetry may give beauty, but it certainly does not give truth. Ethics may help us to a good life, but it cannot help us to truth. Religion may produce deep emotions, but it should not claim to have truth. Only science gives us truth. It gives us new insights into the way nature works, into the texture of human history, into the hidden things of the human mind. It gives a feeling of joy, inferior to no other joy. [The student] who has experienced this transition from darkness, or dimness, to the sharp light of knowledge will always praise scientific truth and understanding and say with some great medieval theologians, that the principles through which we know our world are the eternal divine light in our souls.[49]

Yet when the students and scholars are asked whether the truth that they have so discovered is "relevant to their lives," they often express a sense of loss or indifference to their newly perceived truths, while others indicate

---

49. Tillich, *New Being,* 66.

that non-scholarly pursuits and relations provide their daily lives with the deep sense of meaning (or the encounter with being-itself) that is associated with truth.[50]

The scholarly pursuit of scientific truth, as has been mentioned, is often conceived in contrast to, if not in conflict with, the pursuit of religious truth. But the truths of faith and the truths of science, Tillich boldly asserts, do not belong to the same realm of meaning. Their referents and their fora for discussion are distinct. "Science has no right and no power to interfere with faith," Tillich claims, "and faith has no power to interfere with science." The truth of a scientific statement or law is known by the adequacy of its description of the laws of nature or the structural principles of reality, and the truth of a scientific statement is verified by experimental repetition. Always subject to the scientific process of experimentation, the truths of science are consequently subject to revision, as evinced in the Copernican Revolution and the paradigm shift from Newton's Laws to Einstein's theories of relativity. As a result, the truths of science can only conflict with scientific principles since "science which remains science cannot conflict with faith which remains faith."[51] The political conflicts between evolutionary theorists and biblical literalists, however, are not struggles between science and faith; instead, they manifest a conflict between science's misappropriation of the human spirit and incorrect projections about the character of revelation and faith.

Even as the truths of science belong to a different realm of reference than those of faith, so, too, historical truths, or factual truths as Tillich considers them, operate in a frame that is not subject to certification by faith. "But faith," Tillich concludes, "can and must interpret the *meaning* of facts from the point of view of [a person's] ultimate concern. In doing so [faith] transfers historical truth into the dimension of the truth of faith."[52] Although it is possible for the facts of history to be assumed within the realm of faith, it is not possible for the truths of history to contest the truths of faith. Nevertheless, a problem that emerges for Christians involves the degree to which they desire that faith be built upon the certitude of historical facts. But Tillich avers, "the truth of faith cannot be made dependent on the historical truth of the stories and legends in which faith has expressed

---

50. At the beginning of his sermon "The Depth of Existence," Tillich poses a question that focuses on the importance of truth, especially as it is related to existence and being: "Why have [persons] always asked for truth? Is it because they have been disappointed with the surfaces, and have known that the truth which does *not* disappoint dwells below the surfaces in the depth?" Tillich, *Shaking of the Foundations*, 53.

51. Tillich, *Dynamics of Faith*, 81, 82.

52. Ibid., 86; emphasis added.

itself. It is a disastrous distortion of the meaning of faith to identify it with the belief in the historical validity of the Biblical stories."[53]

At this point in his treatment of how the truth of faith becomes entangled with expectations of historical truth, Tillich presents a litany of examples that show how scripturally oriented traditions have confused the kind of truth claims that their sacred texts make. Focusing initially on Islam and its affirmation of the absolute inerrancy of the Qur'an as revealed scripture, Tillich propounds that "it is not a matter of faith" for Muslims to decide if the existing, untranslated Arabic text of the Qur'an is "identical with the original text," to which the claims of inerrancy apply. Nor is it a project of faith for Jews and Christians to determine whether Mosaic passages of the Pentateuch are "sacred legend" rather than "actual history." Nor is it a function of faith for Christians to decide how much of the gospel narratives about the teachings of Jesus represent early Christian amalgamations of hopes about Jesus and fears about impending political persecution and retribution. Instead, Tillich argues, these questions must be addressed in terms of probability and in terms of historical research because they are questions about human history, about the human writing and transmission of texts.

In contrast to the issues raised in these questions about historical truths, "faith can say that something of ultimate concern has happened in history because the question of the ultimate in being and meaning is involved," Tillich asserts.

> Faith can ascertain its own foundation, the Mosaic law, or Jesus as the Christ, Mohammed the prophet, or Buddha the illuminated. But faith cannot ascertain the historical conditions which made it possible for these men to become matters of ultimate concern for large sections of humanity. Faith includes certitude about its own foundation—for example, an event in history which has transformed history—for the faithful. But faith does not include historical knowledge about the way in which this event took place.[54]

Consequently, the truth of faith cannot be jolted by criticism of historical events and traditions. "The independence of historical truth," as Tillich puts it, is one of the most liberating insights that one can develop from understanding faith as ultimate concern rather than as the affirmation of traditional creeds or stories as dogma.[55]

Tillich's discussion of the sacred (but not necessarily historically factual) character of scriptures leads him also to consider the contrast between

---

53. Ibid., 87.
54. Ibid., 88–89.
55. Ibid., 89.

the truth of faith and truth discovered, disclosed, or derived by philosophical sorts of reasoning. This contrast is often misunderstood as a conflict between revelation and reason. Such a conflict cannot arise when one understands faith in relation to its ultimate concern, for reason provides intellectual tools for interpreting reality while faith orients the application of those effective, intellectual tools for the analysis and interpretation of reality. "Reason is," Tillich asserts, "the precondition of faith." Reason provides tools for use in directing understanding. The relation of faith to reason is not one of blindness but one of reaching beyond the boundary. When reason, consciously bound by its own limits, reaches toward and beyond that over which reason exercises control, it is not completely bound by finitude and rises above it, engaging the infinite, the absolute, being-itself. When reason is thus "grasped by an ultimate concern" and "driven beyond itself," as Tillich claims, it does not void its rational character. Instead, reason becomes ecstatically fulfilled as it is driven beyond its finite limits and experiences the fullness of union with being-itself.[56]

For Tillich, the disjunction and perceived conflict between faith and reason grow out of a misunderstanding of the ways of knowing, a misunderstanding derived from the estrangement that humans experience in their own being. One challenge for theology in this instance is to focus on possibilities for rapprochement between faith and reason. Theology must ask, for instance, "whether the unity of faith and reason and the true nature of both of them must not be re-established by what religion calls 'revelation.'" Theology also must repeatedly question whether "reason in its distorted stage [is] not obliged to subject itself to revelation and . . . [whether] this subjection to the contents of revelation [is] the true sense of the term 'faith.'" Yet the concept and experience of revelation in such a reconciliatory way have been miscast by common perceptions of revelation as "divine information about divine matters, given to prophets and apostles and dictated by the divine Spirit to the writers of the Bible, or the Koran, or other sacred books." This misunderstanding of the nature of revelation also prompts an errant understanding of faith as the "acceptance of such divine informations, however absurd and irrational they may be." Tillich's understanding of revelation, however, is not developed in opposition to reason, which is the primary tool—estranged though it may be—of philosophy. Rightly comprehended, Tillich asserts:

> Revelation is first of all the experience in which an ultimate concern grasps the human mind and creates a community in which this concern expresses itself in symbols of action, imagination and thought. . . . Their internal and mutual conflicts are conquered, and estrangement

---

56. Ibid., 76–77.

is replaced by reconciliation. This is what revelation means, or should mean. It is an event in which the ultimate becomes manifest in an ultimate concern. . . . In such an experience no conflict between faith and reason is possible; for it is man's total structure as a rational being which is grasped and changed by the revelatory manifestation of an ultimate concern.[57]

Revelation, according to Tillich, is the occasion of discovery and disclosure when one finds that one's ultimate concern is judged as inadequate or idolatrous because it regards the symbols of faith, of God, as the object or goal of faith.[58] Revelation does not impart an ultimate concern where none existed previously. It, so to speak, purifies or refines or redirects one's ultimate concern by refocusing it on that which is "truly" ultimate: God as such, being-itself, the power of Being.

Although revelation generates an experience of ecstasy in its perception, and although it conquers the disruption or estrangement that separates the corrupted human experience of faith and reason, revelation does not dissolve or otherwise completely remove the disruption. But it does break the final hold of its grip. The corruption of faith and reason persists because finitude itself is the condition of our existence; and finitude is the condition for disruption and estrangement—for sin. The corruption of faith and reason "makes faith idolatrous, confusing the bearer and the manifestations of the ultimate with the ultimate itself. It deprives reason of its ecstatic power, of its tendency to transcend itself in the direction of the ultimate."[59] In the distorted relation between faith and reason, persons often consider reason as ultimate despite its finitude, and consequently they demean faith as being preliminary or, to one degree or another, uninformed.

Although traditional theological schemes often characterize doubt as a serious or significant distortion or corruption of faith, Tillich considers doubt to be an integral aspect of the condition of faith. "If faith is understood as belief that something is true, doubt is incompatible with the act of faith," Tillich writes. However, "if faith is understood as being ultimately concerned, doubt is a necessary element in it. It is a consequence of the risk of faith."[60] The risk of faith is endemic to the character of faith as ultimate concern, since that which is ultimate can be disclosed and known through symbols, which, in turn, cannot exactly specify their referent. Even ecstatic experiences of the holy contain within them the possibility that their origin or goal resides in self-delusion or self-gratification rather than in reconciliation with the ground of being. In every act of faith, in other words, the

---

57. Ibid., 77–79.
58. Ibid.
59. Ibid., 79.
60. Ibid., 18.

possibility of failure, corruption, or deception is possible. In contrast to traditional theological aspirations for certainty in faith, Tillich insists that certainty evinces idolatry, while doubt indicates true faith. As fervently as faith might be expressed, the element of *uncertainty* in faith cannot be removed or overcome. "Faith is certain in so far as it is an experience of the holy," Tillich acknowledges. "But faith is uncertain in so far as the infinite to which it is related is received by a finite being."[61] It is finally through courage, Tillich concludes, that faith exhibits its dynamic character, incorporating and transforming the destructive potential of doubt into serving as the creative prompt for faith itself.[62]

When persons proclaim their certainty as markers of the seriousness or significance of their faith, their arrogance suggests instead the absence of "the first condition of theological existence, which is the realization that one does *not* know whether he has experienced the Divine Spirit, or spirits which are not divine."[63] The insistence on being fully faithful belies one's claim because all persons, whether openly admitting their concerns or not, experience the "permanent threat" of despair in knowing truth. However, one's acknowledgment of doubt—one's awareness "of the element of insecurity in every existential truth"—manifests an inquisitive orientation that identifies the seriousness of one's faith because, Tillich reasons, in the depth of every serious doubt and every despair of truth, the passion for truth is still at work.[64] Consequently, serious doubt confirms the seriousness of faith.

Related to the issues of doubt and truth, Tillich identifies two "temptations" that confront all who ask questions about whether truth matters. One of these is the threat of indifference, of *not* caring about matters of truth. This challenge, Tillich suggests, is the way that the majority of modern and postmodern thinkers follow. In times of crisis, in the liminal and boundary situations of life involving tragic events (the loss of a job, a serious illness or injury, death, or the failure of a final exam), one finds that the tragic events often spur questions about experiences related to one's ultimate concern. Most persons, however, simply trudge through daily existence by distancing themselves from such serious questions, especially as they apply to oneself.

Distinct from indifference, the other "temptation" is to avoid asking challenging questions about whether truth matters by denying the possibility of articulating the concerns of existential doubt. Addressing dutiful and

---

61. Ibid., 16.

62. For Tillich's most expansive discussion of the role of courage in relation to faith and one's existence, see Paul Tillich, *The Courage to Be* (New Haven: Yale University Press, 1952); Tillich, *Dynamics of Faith*, 16.

63. Tillich, *Shaking of the Foundations*, 121.

64. Tillich, *Dynamics of Faith*, 20.

pious Christians, Tillich then challenges them to examine their own perceptions and pursuit of truth. Tillich warns that they are not exempt from the structures of doubt merely because they claim to possess the truths of Church. Countermanding the impulses of Christians to claim superiority for and exclusive rights to the truths of their institutions and traditions, Tillich argues that "there is not freedom but demonic bondage where one's own truth is called the ultimate truth. For this is an attempt to be like God, an attempt which is made in the name of God."[65] The nature of truth that frees the faithful in doubting is not the truth of reasonable propositions, creedal affirmations, or logical derivations. The truth that liberates is an ontological truth, an experience of reality, of being-itself. "If Jesus says, 'I am the truth,'" Tillich submits, "he indicates that in Him the true, the genuine, the ultimate reality is present; or, in other words, that God is present, unveiled, undistorted, in His infinite depth, in His unapproachable mystery." Clarifying the relation of truth to Jesus and his teachings, Tillich points out that "Jesus is not the truth because His teachings are true. But His teachings are true because they express the truth which He Himself is." They express the character of, and the reconciliation afforded by, the New Being that Jesus is as the Christ. The liberating function of truth, he continues, cannot be collapsed into the teaching of Jesus, despite mistaken efforts by pious Christian scholars and teachers throughout history, because "the words of Jesus, if taken as law, are not the truth which makes us free." Nor are the Church's doctrines about Jesus the truth that sets the faithful free. Regrettably, Tillich bemoans, these assertions about the truth of doctrines, claimed as truth itself, have become tools "to prevent the honest search for truth—weapons to split the souls of people between loyalty to the Church and sincerity to truth."[66]

An honest search for truth—the liberating truth revealed in the New Being of Jesus as the Christ—includes serious consideration and deliberation about whether one is of the truth. In other words, if doubt does not pertain in fundamental ways to one's experience in pursuit of truth, then truth cannot be perceived in reality, in truth. The person "who asks seriously the question of the truth that liberates is already on [the] way to liberation."[67] The liberation of truth emerges from the struggle in existence as one wrestles toward reconciliation with being-itself. Certainly, true seekers of truth, or "true doubters," will experience dimensions of the liberating power of truth, even if they do not initially perceive it as such. Liberating truth may be encountered suddenly, in spectacular fashion, as with blinding illumination like that experienced by Paul the Apostle on his journey to Damascus.

65. Tillich, "What Is Truth?" in *New Being,* 68.
66. Ibid., 69–70.
67. Ibid., 73.

Or, as Tillich indicates, the liberating truth may be encountered more gradually as "true reality appears like a landscape when the fog becomes thinner and thinner and finally disappears." One may even encounter liberating truth in the beauty and temporality of nature or in an intense or intimate relationship with a friend.[68] Because "the truth which liberates is the power of love, for God is love," and God is truth, Tillich cautions truth-pursuers to be suspicious of every claim for truth that manifests no evidence of love. When alienation is overcome in love, the truth and the reconciliatory power of Being (as revealed in the New Being of Christ) are not restricted to the recognition of revelation of New Being in Christ because the truth as love that liberates is ontological truth—the truth of being-itself that undergirds, informs, and includes all reality. Such truth, Tillich concludes, "liberates from illusions and false authorities, from enslaving anxieties, desires and hostilities, from a wrong self-rejection and a wrong self-affirmation."[69] And such truth in love liberates Christians to enjoy the ecstatic experience of reunion with being-itself in the frontier of faith.

Conclusion

In contemporary theological studies, the theology of Paul Tillich presents continuing theological challenges that distinguish his system and vision as pioneering. Pressing beyond the boundary characteristic of personal experience, Tillich uses his method of correlation as a compass to guide his thinking through the questions and concerns of philosophy and culture. Through the frontier of faith he explores the fields of truth, doubt, and freedom while diligently pursuing the ever-present, ever-alluring, but never fully graspable horizon of being-itself—of God. So comprehensive, so relevant, and so creative is Tillich's theology that Langdon Gilkey adjudges that it, almost alone among the theologies of the twentieth century, "represents *the* theological system with which almost everyone (at least in American theology) must wrestle, discovering themselves in encounter with him, perhaps in differentiation from him, perhaps in agreement with him, or, more usually, in a good measure of both."[70] As significant as Tillich's theology has been for the latter half of the twentieth century, his relevance as the theologian for the shift in centuries and millennia becomes all the more acute as his understanding of God and faith challenges Christians to combat dogmatism and contravene fundamentalism.

In several distinct and profound ways, the theology of Tillich presents challenges to Christians who have become accustomed to traditional

---

68. Ibid., 72.

69. Ibid., 73–74.

70. Gilkey, *Gilkey on Tillich*, 56; emphasis in original.

descriptions of a theistic character of God, who expect theology to pursue the clarification (and perhaps application) of dogma derived from scripture, and who conceive the goal of their faith to be the certainty that comes with full knowledge of God and complete obedience to divine commands. But Tillich inverts and challenges theistic expectations and projections by conceiving God in panentheistic ways, by removing the concept of God from being and existence to the ever-and-all-inclusive "category" of being-itself. He relocates the identity of theological method in its correlation with culture and reason, recognizing that the ultimate questions and issues of existence comprise the theological challenge to which the symbols of being-itself must relate. And moving beyond traditional associations of faith with affirmations of dogma, Tillich enlarges the understanding of faith to include the holistic, personal response that is required of persons seeking reunion with being-itself.

Response to Professor Price

Truman G. Madsen

PROFESSOR JOSEPH PRICE BEGINS HIS ARTICLE with personal debts to Paul Tillich. Let me respond with my own. While pursuing my doctorate at Harvard, I joined each graduate class that Tillich taught at Harvard, and also his course "Religion and Culture" for which one could receive credit in any department of the university. Further, I benefited from his comprehensive course on the history of Christian thought. Although his accounts were filtered through his own system, nevertheless, I gained an overview of the main philosophical and theological movements and trends in the western world. It is a tribute to Tillich's intellectual chivalry that he and his close associates approved, though he vehemently disagreed with, my dissertation. In my own seminars on Tillich, I have attempted to present the advantages for his notion of "Religion as Ultimate Concern" and to give unbiased expositions of his thought. In my writings, I have shown consistent appreciation for his probing the subjectivity of human, not just religious, awareness.[71] I

71. See Truman G. Madsen, "A Unique Mormon Aesthetic," keynote address, Fourth Annual Festival of Arts, Brigham Young University, Provo, Utah, March 7, 1972, private circulation.

have especially appreciated his providing clues on how religion may permeate all of culture, especially the realm of art.[72]

While appreciative of Tillich's contributions, from this point forward I will be approaching Tillich and Professor Price in a critical mode. Tillich once wrote that the kind of criticism which "merely insinuates" that he has undercut the biblical message could not be accepted as serious. That case could be made.[73] But LDS theology derives not just from biblical but a much more extensive collection of sources and a richer contemporary "repository of symbols" (Price, 131). The grid on which "challenges" might be framed is different, and as will appear in the LDS approach, radically different.

Price sees challenges to LDS theology in Tillich's method of correlation, his view of being-itself, and his view of faith (Price, 124). Limitations of space require that I deal only with being-itself, which indirectly relates to the other two issues. I will attempt to approach problems on Tillich's own ground and using his own premises.

I want to begin with what is for Tillich himself, in Price's word, "foundational": "The center of my theological doctrine of knowledge is the concept of symbol."[74] Price maintains, and I fully agree, that the concept of symbol is also the center of Tillich's theological system (Price, 131–33). Here Tillich, whom Price praises as a boundary-breaker, becomes a boundary-maker (Price, 125, 126, 127, 128). He attempts to establish an inviolate barrier between sign and symbol. Symbols, he insists, have meanings and powers and functions that signs do not and cannot have. For Tillich, as for Price, the most debilitating error in theologizing is to try to speak of God in "sharp propositions." Religious symbols, Price writes, cannot "accurately be transcribed in discursive [sign] language" (Price, 132), "they cannot be explicated" (Price, 137). So Tillich in theory, but not, as we shall see, in

---

72. My other relevant works include: Truman G. Madsen, "Paul Tillich and Religion as Ultimate Concern," delivered at Utah State, Weber College, the University of Utah, and Brigham Young University, 1958–59 (lithographed for private circulation); Truman G. Madsen, "The Contribution of Existentialism," *BYU Studies* 1, no. 1 (1959): 9–19; Truman G. Madsen, "Existentialism as a Philosophy," *Daily Universe* (BYU, Provo, Utah), April 20–24, 1964; Truman G. Madsen, "Three Theories of Religious Language," *BYU Studies* 2, no. 2 (1960): 227–40; and Truman G. Madsen, "The Role of Religious Symbolism: East and West," in *Mormonism: A Faith for All Cultures*, ed. F. LaMond Tullis (Provo, Utah: Brigham Young University Press, 1978), 207–26.

73. The case has been made by, among others, Nels F. Ferre, Reinhold Niebuhr, George Thomas, and Dorothy Emmet. See Charles W. Kegley, ed., *The Theology of Paul Tillich* (New York: Macmillan, 1952) for examples of Ferre (262, 264, 343), Niebuhr (chapter 9), Thomas (104), and Emmet (213). See also George H. Tavard, *Paul Tillich and the Christian Message* (New York: Scribners, 1962).

74. Kegley, *Theology of Paul Tillich*, 333.

practice, maintains that religious symbols cannot be transcribed or reduced to ordinary language at all.[75]

A primal question is how Tillich, given this untranslatability thesis, can emerge from symbolic solipsism; that is, from the subjective circle which he imposes on religious awareness. His writings identify existential and ultimate concern—mine, yours, or anyone else's—with Ultimate Concern (capitalized to show it is Divine) and with being-itself (Price, 133). He complicates the issues of reference and meaning by treating interchangeably the terms *being-itself, ground of being,* and *power of being* as if they were synonymous. He also compounds these problems further by deliberately using contradictory characterizations, which Price approves without demur. For example: "ground and abyss"; "transcendent and participating"; "beyond all beyonds" yet involved in the "negativities of finite existence"; "abstract in the extreme" yet "vibrant and personal"; "creating and sustaining" yet "threatening"; "incomprehensible mystery" yet "living."

One must have tolerance for paradox in all this. Tillich initially commits to the requirements of formal logic,[76] and he is critical of neo-orthodox and other theologians who "pile paradox on paradox." One may assume Tillich's undergirding thesis is that the pairings noted above are not paradoxes when understood as he intends them to be understood.

Furthermore, on top of his symbolic theory, or more precisely at its bottom, Tillich shakes his own foundations. He shifts and reshifts his position on how to articulate the status of his ontological assumption: being-itself.

His assurance of being-itself is not the outcome of argument or of appeals to revelatory knowledge. In Tillich's corpus "being-itself," "ground," and "power" function, as Price in various ways repeatedly affirms, as absolute presuppositions—not just for Tillich's theology but also for all culture (Price, 134–35). He does not use his symbolic apparatus to give these locutions a qualifying or self-negating gloss as he claims to do with other such formulations. Nor can he acknowledge, as critics say, that these terms, unless he defines them and validates his definitions, are without content or vacuous. Nor can he say they simply "point beyond" to what cannot be said. That would be a retreat into mystic ineffability that, typically, but not always, he rejects.

In facing this self-imposed dilemma, Tillich has gone through three stages that can be represented by the following statements.

---

75. Tillich's original article on symbols is titled "The Religious Symbol," republished as an appendix in *Religious Experience and Truth,* ed. Sidney Hook (New York: New York University Press, 1961), 301.

76. Paul Tillich, *Systematic Theology* (Chicago: Chicago University Press, 1955), 56–57, 150–53.

1. The sentence "God is being-itself" is a literal, proper, descriptive statement, but every other sentence about God is symbolic.[77]

2. The sentence "God is being-itself" is not literal but, like all other theological utterances, is itself symbolic (Price, 133 n. 28).

3. The one unsymbolic statement that can be made about God is that all statements about God must be symbolic.

Statement three is clearly not a statement about God but a statement about statements about God, a metastatement. It is an oblique and redundant way of saying what Tillich says in statement two.

For Tillich to conclude that being-itself is symbolic would be to defy his earlier agreement with his critics,[78] that if there were not a proper and descriptive statement for being-itself, his other symbolic derivations would be "meaningless."[79] The entire flotilla of symbols would be, as Ronald Hepburn quotes Tillich saying, "adrift unpiloted."[80]

If we take him at his latest position that "Being-itself" is itself symbolic and in no way representational or descriptive, three implications follow. Each raises questions about Tillich's account of religious symbols.

1. Religious symbols can only express ultimate concern for a group. They cannot be "coined" or intentionally crafted or introduced by anyone (Price, 131–33). Symbols must be "shared" and communal. But clearly, Tillich *did* coin the term "being-itself" and others like it. He introduced them to achieve what Price claims for him, a new and pioneering alternative to other "dead end" theologies (Price, 125, 133, 145–46).[81]

2. Religious symbols, according to Tillich, have an organic life of their own. They "grow, live and die." They cannot be refuted by independent scientific or philosophical criticism (Price, 131–33). But this view of symbol has never been alive for many groups, and it is not for the Latter-day Saints. In Tillich's view this may be lamentable but, given his symbolic theory, cannot be corrected by him or by

---

77. Ibid., 26.

78. For example, W. M. Urban.

79. Kegley, *Theology of Paul Tillich,* 334.

80. Ronald W. Hepburn, "Demythologizing and the Problem of Validity," in *New Essays in Philosophical Theology,* ed. Antony Flew and Alasdair MacIntyre (New York: MacMillian, 1955), 239.

81. Price says "being-itself" is a restoration of the *Esse ipsum* and the doctrine of analogy in medieval thought. But Catholic theologians, for example, Gustave Weigel, show "symbolic knowledge" in Tillich is not the same as analogical knowledge. See J. Heywood Thomas, *Paul Tillich: An Appraisal* (Philadelphia: Westminster, 1963), 198.

anyone. What, then, is the point of his entire theological enterprise, which itself "corrects" and modifies all Christian symbols?

3. If the symbol "being-itself" is alive only to those who have a "shared perception" of it (Price, 132), then those who find the symbol uncommunicative or illusory are excluded from the pursuit of truth in what Tillich calls the "depth dimension." The symbol fails to fulfill Tillich's claim that it and related symbols "open up," as nothing else can, the dimension of depth—even for the logician or ontologist who uses the word "is." For them, the realm of discovery and self-awareness and creativity is not in actuality "opened up" by this symbol (Price, 131).

In fact, the term "being-itself," both because of what it seems (albeit ambiguously) to affirm and to deny, leads Nels Ferre to conclude, "Tillich is not a Christian. He is a Hindu."[82] Sidney Hook concludes that Tillich is an atheist but "uses language to express the very superstitions he fears."[83] Brand Blanshard concludes that Tillich is a "reactionary irrationalist."[84] But these responses miss the major point that Tillich is determined to retain, namely his grasp on Christian symbolism.[85]

Let us then approach the question not as an ontological or even psychological issue but in a "holistic" personal way as Tillich admonishes (Price, 146).

This is my "holistic" concern: Does Ultimate Concern have ultimate concern for me? It does not help my existential quest to be told God is "nearer to me than I am to myself." Whether he is near or far, or beyond all beyonds, my intimate and ultimate care is whether he cares (Tillich continues to use the personal pronoun "he," even while denying that God is a person). If I am told that God is "the ground of all caring," that is no help. It is also no help at all to say, as Tillich often does, that my concern for such a Concern outside, or, for that matter, inside, myself, is idolatrous. Tillich says, "Theology must give answers" (Price, 129, 146). But, at root, my concern is not for an answer, it is for a response: a recognizable, experiential encounter. Tillich, at best, gives me a series of "therefores": God is love. Therefore being itself is love. Therefore the actuality of being is life.

82. Ferre made the comment on Hinduism to me personally. In a critique of Tillich's thought, Ferre also says, "Tillich's latest formulations in his *Systematic Theology* unfortunately show no indications of his accepting the classical Christian presuppositions." Nels F. S. Ferre, "Tillich's View of the Church," in Kegley, *Theology of Paul Tillich*, 299.

83. Tillich, *Religious Experience and Truth*, 63.

84. Ibid., 53.

85. See Paul Edwards, "Professor Tillich's Confusions," *Mind* 74 (April 1965): 192–214.

Therefore the process of the divine life has the character of love. Therefore love is the reunion of the separated (Price, 136). One may take these sayings to be informative. But they are not existential for me, as Tillich says they must be to be religious. These symbols may, as Price writes, "function as a compass" (Price, 132). But they "do not make God immanent." And love, immanent for me, is exactly what I seek. Without some touching reassurance, my concern remains projected but not reciprocated, hoped for amidst existential doubt. Tillich insists faith always involves doubt (Price, 142–43). So far as I can make out, my doubt here contains no element of faith, even though I am "grasped and shaken" by it (Price, 137).

So Tillich offers me only what Tillich disparages: a theoretical, detached, and therefore unmoving set of answers. What Price calls the "ecstatic experience of the fulness of reunion with being-itself" eludes me (Price, 145). Contrary to Tillich's assumption, understanding the meaning of this concept is not "inescapable" (Price, 128).

Let us now ask, whatever the obscurities and inconsistencies of Tillich's language, what are his intentions?

Price dwells on Tillich's, and his own, motivation to escape the limitations of particularism and dogma (Price, 145). In fact, he concludes that Tillich's total effort was to "combat dogmatism." This is achieved, as Price explains, by Tillich's removing religious discussion from historical, scientific, philosophical, and rationalistic approaches to religion.

About this I have two responses.

First, there is an alternative way to escape the divisive and closed effects of dogma and to make way for what Price apparently found in Tillich: "theological tolerance" (Price, 123). For Latter-day Saints it is to be open in three ways that Tillich's system forbids one to be.

1. One may be open upwardly to further clarifying and supplementing revelation, including revelation about revelation. The expectation is that this, as in the past, will be self-correcting and self-critiquing, but not as Tillich requires, self-negating. Further, one may, as Latter-day Saints do, refuse creedal formulations on the grounds that most such formulas will be supplemented and clarified by the growing content of experience.[86] But for Tillich this will not do. He defines revelation and the New Being in Christ as "final" and "the circle of the faith" (referring to the biblical constellation of symbols) as closed.[87] Moreover, for Tillich, revelation is not "divine information." It is a confrontation with Essential Mystery (Price, 141).

---

86. The ninth LDS Article of Faith affirms that there can be no final articles of faith, since more is yet to be revealed.

87. Tillich, *Systematic Theology*, 157–59.

2. One can be open inwardly to a self below the "depth self" that is construed by Tillich and Jung. For Latter-day Saints this is a substantial individual spirit. From it and through it come the deepest questions that for Tillich need correlating and also impressions from prior experience. But Tillich would dispose of "spirit beings" as a relic of supernaturalism. He would say of such spirit-entities what he says of biblical angels—"not beings but structures, archetypes of the collective unconscious."[88]

3. One may be open outwardly to the objectivities of religion. I once asked Tillich, "What would it do to your theology if it could be shown, per impossible, that Jesus never lived?" He replied, "Nothing." It is apparent that Tillich attempts to insulate and isolate historical researchers from theological presuppositions. But he himself completely takes for granted the general framework of the historical Jesus and the Christ of faith. In the final analysis, this illustrates on his own ground that (1) It does and will make a difference, an existential difference, whether Jesus lived, and (2) It does and will make an existential difference which of Jesus' reported sayings are authentic, and what these portend for the past, present, and future of religion.

Second, regarding Tillich's heroic attempt to exclude dogma from his system, it is crucial to observe that he himself does not and apparently cannot abide his own strictures. Throughout his system are many categorical, informational, and propositional assertions. They are put forward, whatever his hesitations about certainty, as certain, indeed, as self-evident axioms. They are not presented as if they needed further symbolic processing. And they are not subjected to the "balance" of self-negation. The result is that, what Price tells us Tillich set out to transcend, he actually re-invokes, namely, a body of theological dogma.

The eleven examples I present below are primary, not ancillary, theses in Tillich's writings. In each case the LDS alternative is not simply a qualification; it is a contrariety. If Latter-day Saints were pressed for the origins of their affirmations, the one-sentence answer would be that they are the outcome of what could be called theological empiricism.

1. *Tillich:* There is no other ground out of which existence springs than being-itself.

   LDS: There is more than one self-existent being, self-existent and co-existent with God.

---

88. Ibid., 260 fn. 8.

2. *Tillich:* God is not a person. "There is no evidence for his existence."[89]

   LDS: "God" is the proper name of a person. There is cumulative contemporary awareness of him as a revelatory person.

3. *Tillich:* A conditioned God is no God.

   LDS: God is conditioned by uncreated human freedom.

4. *Tillich:* Being-itself, and the symbols of being-itself, participate in the reality they symbolize.

   LDS: God participates in all that is, not by diffusion of "being," but by his emanating Spirit which is in and through all things.

5. *Tillich:* Nothing finite is similar to God.

   LDS: God is exactly what Tillich says He cannot be: a being different from those in his image in degree, but not in kind.

6. *Tillich:* God must be utterly transcendent, beyond all finitude.

   LDS: God is finite in some respects and infinite in others.

7. *Tillich:* There is no person-to-person relationship with God. "Reunion with God" means overcoming alienation from the Ground of Being.

   LDS: Religious experience is person-to-person, self-to-self, and subject-to-subject. "Reunion with God" is reunion with God.

8. *Tillich:* No one can escape the threat of nonbeing.

   LDS: The threat of nonbeing is fictional. There is only the threat of nonbecoming, falling short of human potential.

9. *Tillich:* "One does not know whether he has experienced the Divine Spirit or spirits which are not divine."[90]

   LDS: One can know by experience the holy from the profane, and the Divine from the demonic.

10. *Tillich:* There is no immortality, no "unending form of post-mortem personal existence" (Price, 124). Immortality for humans exists only in the memory of God.

    LDS: Immortality and eternal life are the continuation of individual, social, and family life in a transformed state.

---

89. Ibid., 245.

90. Paul Tillich, *The Shaking of the Foundations* (New York: Charles Scribner's Sons, 1955).

11. *Tillich:* There is no resurrection. Jesus did not have a "transmuted body." "Resurrection" is a symbol of "life beyond ambiguity" in an "eternal now" (Price, 124).

   LDS: There is bodily resurrection. Christ is the prototype. He was and will be seen, heard, and touched.

Conclusion

Tillich's symbolic theory leads to contradiction both on issues of linguistic reference and on issues of meaning. His sign-symbol distinction is an untenable dualism. For as we have shown, he himself processes propositions into symbols and then turns symbols back into propositions. And he makes truth-claims for them.

Overall, Price describes Tillich's project as a successful effort to provide an alternative position to naturalism, supernaturalism, and dualism (Price, 130).[91] We have shown that what he has instead proposed is a form of dualism and naturalism (a scientific or philosophical naturalist can agree with most of Tillich's negations above). But, Tillich's naturalism is presented in biblical vocabulary with an existential swerve.

Tillich's greatest contribution is also his greatest limitation. His is an elaborate phenomenology that leads to thoroughgoing introspection. But it is limited in that he himself, while claiming to hold on to it, neglects, sidesteps, and fails to take account of other crucial elements of the religious life, including what for him are anathema: objectivities. But then he reintroduces them. His ontology is, on close analysis, a set of conjectures. They need, as Tillich says of symbols, to be "broken" of their finality and certitude. Then they can be submitted to the disciplines from which he attempts to withdraw them. Otherwise he is vulnerable to the charge that he combines what cannot consistently be combined, and separates what cannot be consistently separated. His whole system needs to be re-examined in a closer tie with the totality of religious experience.

---

91. Kegley, *Theology of Paul Tillich*, 341.

Rejoinder

Joseph L. Price

TRUMAN MADSEN HAS ADVANCED THE DIALOGUE of Latter-day Saints with contemporary Christian theology in his considered response to my essay on challenges in Tillich's theology to LDS thought. I am honored to have the chance to reply to his response in brief measure. As I address some of the issues and themes that Professor Madsen himself has identified, I want to be careful to preserve the impetus that Tillich himself would have enjoyed in dialogue. For he thrived on dialogical experiences and exchanges, even making Christianity's encounter with other religions the subject of his final book.[92] He understood the purpose of theology itself to be one of articulating the human experience of the divine initiative in overcoming separation, of reconnecting humans with the divine itself. Recognizing this focus and function of theology, he engaged in dialogue with other Christians and persons of diverse faiths in order to understand better the human experience of reconciliation.

Provided this opportunity to supply a closing word on Tillich in this collection of essays and reflections, I want to avoid two seductive tendencies: One is to attempt to provide a final word on Tillich's thought, an attempt that would foreclose dialogue and prompt, at best, debate. The other is similar: to avoid the inclination to provide proof texts in Tillich's work, which showed cultural sensitivity by spanning two continents and ranging through almost a half-century and which was stimulated by several different, dominant cultural forces—the fighting of the *Bismarck* in World War I, the broken spirit of Germany following that war, the rise of Nazism, the war-time economy and spirit of the United States during World War II, and the initiatives of the Cold War. The very cultural forces whose dynamics he experienced and engaged shifted dramatically throughout his lifetime.

Although the shifts in cultural forces today make the current situation diffierent from those that Tillich himself encountered, there are distinct similarities at various junctures. Nonetheless, it would be inappropriate to try to locate the authoritative Tillichian concept or idea in a particular document, not only because of the difference in questions that have now arisen out of the cultural situation—in this case, the emergent dialogue with Latter-day Saints—but also because the attempt to objectify Tillich's work and to find in it an authoritative, final response would be to move it

---

92. Paul Tillich, *Christianity and the Encounter of the World Religions* (New York: Columbia University Press, 1963).

from its intended vehicular purpose—that of facilitating communication—to one of an artifact, that which is reified, objectified, and, perhaps, deified.

Certainly, I have not enjoyed the personal contact with Tillich in the way that Professor Madsen was enriched by his study with him at Harvard. Yet in talking and studying with several of Tillich's former students, I always find that I am able to understand various dimensions of his theology by listening to their stories, their perspectives, and their interpretations. My learning process, quite thankfully, continues as I read Professor Madsen's reasoned response to my initial essay. As I have engaged in this exchange, I have learned more about Tillich and about the beliefs and concerns of Latter-day Saints. I certainly appreciate the opportunity to have been involved in this new project.

At the beginning of his response, Professor Madsen identifies the LDS appreciation of correlation as a theological response to the existential questions posed by life's circumstances and concerns. I am not familiar with the theological perspective of Latter-day Saints about their understanding of revelation, so my response is tempered by my inability to probe LDS thought. But I am able to clarify, at least for readers unfamiliar with Tillich, some of his basic premises about revelation. As Professor Madsen notes, unlike Barth, who understood the revelation of God in Christ as being the special form of revelation from above, Tillich believed that revelation is on a continuum of intensity, with the divine revealed in all occasions and experiences when alienation and estrangement are overcome. Thus he understood that the foundation and focus of revelation are in the full revelation of God—of Being—in existence. And thus he called the full revelation of God in the Christ as New Being.[93] For Tillich, as Professor Madsen observes, the revelation of God in the Christ is final, not in the sense of its temporality or its sequence, but in the sense of its fullness. Being itself can be manifest, disclosed, and revealed in no way more thoroughly and extensively than as the New Being. And, for Tillich, the New Being indeed overcomes the fundamental alienation thrust upon us by the structure of existence itself—the strictures of temporality and the spatiality of finitude. By restoring the full potential of engagement between existentiells and Being, the Christ as New Being reconciles persons and God.

Because Tillich's concept of God is so closely tied to the symbols through which he knows God, it is advisable to clarify his thought on the

---

93. Although Tillich uses the title of *The New Being* for one of his collections of sermons (New York: Scribner, 1955), in that work he focuses on how persons of faith pursue the characteristics of New Being revealed in the Christ, rather than featuring the fullness of the revelation of "Being" as "New Being." For a thorough examination of the christological understanding of the New Being, see the second volume of Tillich's *Systematic Theology*.

names of God and the quality of symbols. Tillich does not want to get mired in the ontological/mythological conundrum about whether the naming of God gives the characteristics of the name to God. Rather, he understands that symbols possess an intrinsic power that relates to their signifier and the signified. Consequently, by the time of the publication of the third volume of his *Systematic Theology,* he moved beyond defining God as Being Itself and affirmed instead that "Being Itself" is the most nearly non-symbolic statement that can be made about God. As he had earlier identified in *The Courage to Be,* he writes his theology about "the God beyond God." The source, power, and destiny of all that is, Tillich affirms, is certainly a point of the divine reality to which humans can relate.

In the same way that Tillich avoids identifying God as a person, using language as literal references, so too he speaks of the demonic, as Professor Madsen points out. Tillich's recognition of the threats of non-being and the power of destructiveness is consistent with his use of language about the divine. He wants to avoid association of the demonic with projections of a personified devil in the same way that he wants to avoid the association of language about the divine with a personified projection of a superior being. In the same way that God is not a person but the source, power, and destiny of all that is, so too the devil is not a specific being, but the threat to all that is, not merely as chaotic reality but also as destructive possibility.

As I search for final words in this dialogue with Latter-day Saints and Professor Madsen, I want to express my appreciation for his section in a "comparative mode." As I had identified various points of challenge that Tillich poses to Latter-day Saints, it is quite constructive to have Professor Madsen identify a series of points of convergence between Tillich's thought and LDS beliefs. Such points certainly can provide a foundation for appreciation of a number of the insights and propositions that Tillich makes with regard to theology and the human experience.

In the spirit of appreciative dialogue, I turn to Tillich himself for concerns and hopes about the character of interreligious dialogue. Toward the end of his life, Tillich expanded his intellectual and spiritual engagement beyond the texts and traditions of Western Christianity, traveling to Japan and encountering there the piety and vitality of Asian religious traditions. Prompted by his Pacific journey and his dialogues with Asian monks and priests, as well as his Chicago colleague Mircea Eliade, he presented the Bampton Lectures at Columbia in 1961 and published them shortly thereafter as *Christianity and the Encounter of the World Religions.* His discernment about the character and function of dialogue provides a fitting frame with which to conclude my response to Professor Madsen and to continue dialogue with Latter-day Saints.

In the lectures, Tillich offers his perception of the particular challenges to Christianity posed by established religious traditions and emerging quasi-religions, and he remarks on the nature and challenge of dialogue itself. First of all, he notes, genuine dialogue requires self-judgment and honesty, moving away from polemical positions to ones that risk acknowledging points of vulnerability. In this risky process of honest self-reflection, not only will one learn afresh the experiences and insights of the partners in dialogue, one will also embark upon a process of self-discovery, learning hidden resources within one's own religious experiences and tradition. How can one begin this process of self-exploration and judgment that genuine dialogue demands? Tillich suggests that one begins by participating in the charter myths—the foundation events and their narrative transmission—of one's religious tradition. And how can one participate in such a historical event that occurred centuries earlier? Tillich avers that "participation in an event of the past is only possible if one is grasped by the spiritual power of this event and through it is enabled to evaluate the witnesses, the traditions and the authorities in which the same spiritual power was and is effective."[94]

Appealing to a second principle of interreligious dialogue, Tillich warns against the facile expectation that interreligious dialogue must move toward either a blended expression of common concern that the dialogical partners share or the conquest of one partner over others. Neither of these alternatives, Tillich asserts, provides the desired goal for genuine inter-religious dialogue. For "a mixture of religions destroys in each of them the concreteness which gives [each] its dynamic power," and "the victory of *one* religion would impose a particular religious answer on all other particular answers."[95] Writing specifically about the power of Christianity in its dialogue with Buddhism and religions of Asia, Tillich concludes that Christianity will bear the power of its revelatory tradition as its breaks through the particularity of its own expression. The way to achieve this self-liberation is through genuine inter-religious dialogue in which one is able "to penetrate into the depth of one's own religion, in devotion, thought, and action." And he concludes that "in the depth of every living religion there is a point at which the religion itself loses its importance, and that to which it points breaks through its particularity, elevating it to spiritual freedom and with it to a vision of the spiritual presence in other expressions of the ultimate meaning of man's existence."[96]

The opportunity to engage in a dialogue about the challenges of Paul Tillich's theology for Latter-day Saints presents stimulating possibilities

94. Tillich, *Christianity and the Encounter of the World Religions,* 80.
95. Ibid., 96.
96. Ibid., 97

for increased understanding of not only of Tillich's theology, but also of Christian theology and LDS thought.

About the Authors

Joseph L. Price (Ph.D. University of Chicago Divinity School) received his M.Div. from the Southern Baptist Theological Seminary, and an A.M. in Religion and Literature from the University of Chicago Divinity School before receiving his doctorate in theology from the same institution. He currently teaches religion at Whittier College, where he is the C. Milo Connick Professor of Religious Studies.

Truman G. Madsen (Ph.D. Harvard University) studied under Paul Tillich at Harvard University. He wrote his dissertation on Tillich's theory of symbols. Madsen has been guest professor at Northeastern University, Haifa University, and Graduate Theological Union. He is emeritus professor of philosophy at Brigham Young University, where he held the Richard L. Evans Chair of Religious Understanding and was Director of the Jerusalem Center for Near Eastern Studies in Jerusalem.

A Dialogue on Process Theology

Process Theology: What It Is and Is Not
David Ray Griffin

Process theology, understood as the type of theology based upon the process philosophies of Alfred North Whitehead and Charles Hartshorne, has become widely recognized as one of the major types of Christian theology, especially in the United States. Several books, including one that I co-authored with John Cobb,[1] offer introductions to what process theology is. To my knowledge, however, none of these introductions seeks clearly to distinguish what can be considered the core doctrines of process theology from other beliefs that have been held by various process theologians. That is, process theology can, on the one hand, be defined *historically* simply as a movement consisting of theologians who regard themselves as process theologians. Or, a little less relativistically, it can be defined as a movement comprised of Whitehead, Hartshorne, and theologians heavily influenced by the philosophical theology of one or both of them. On the other hand, not all the beliefs of all these theologians can be said to belong to the core of process theology understood *doctrinally* as a set of beliefs. This fact is most obvious with regard to doctrines about which there is disagreement among process theologians. For example, although some process theologians reject belief in life after death, others affirm it, which suggests that neither the affirmation nor the denial belongs to the core doctrines of process theology.

In distinguishing between what process theology is and is not, the title of this essay could suggest that my intention is to correct some false understandings of it based upon misinterpretations of statements by process theologians. There have certainly been numerous misunderstandings of this type. For example, one of Whitehead's doctrines is that all actualities—

---

1. John B. Cobb Jr. and David Ray Griffin, *Process Theology: An Introductory Exposition* (Philadelphia: Westminster, 1976).

from those in empty space through those comprising electrons, cells, and human minds to the divine actuality itself—belong to the same genus, that of actual entities. In expressing this point, Whitehead once wrote: "God is an actual entity, and so is the most trivial puff of existence in far-off empty space."[2] On the basis of this passage, one critic informed his readers that Whitehead's God is the most trivial puff of existence in far-off empty space!

In the present essay, however, my focus is on misunderstandings of a different type. In speaking of what process theology is, I am referring to a set of fundamental ontological and epistemological doctrines that are so fundamental and interrelated that acceptance of all of them is arguably a necessary (and probably sufficient) condition for someone's being considered a process theologian (of the Whiteheadian-Hartshornean type). In referring to what process theology is not, my focus is on other beliefs that have been held by process theologians but that, even if they are allowed by the core doctrines, are not entailed by them.

Belief in life after death can be used to illustrate the importance of what process theology is and is not. Several prominent process theologians, including Hartshorne and Schubert Ogden, have explicitly rejected this belief. This rejection has provided a basis for other theologians to reject process theology as such. For example, a lecture attacking process theology was written "in a rage" by the British theologian Austin Farrer after he read some books by Hartshorne and Ogden.[3] At the heart of Farrer's critique is the statement that Hartshorne's God is "human enough to have a natural need of his creatures" but not "divine enough to save their souls alive."[4] Reminiscent of Farrer's critique of process theology, which depends upon identifying the position of Hartshorne and Ogden on this issue with that of process theology as such, is a recent statement by John Polkinghorne. Responding to the suggestion that he should be considered a process theologian, Polkinghorne says: "The reason I decline the honour offered is that I do not find the God of process theology to be an adequate ground of hope . . . that there is a meaning to existence and a final fulfillment awaiting

2. Alfred North Whitehead, *Process and Reality: An Essay in Cosmology*, corrected ed., ed. David Ray Griffin and Donald W. Sherburne (New York: Free, 1978), 18.

3. Farrer's comment was made in a 1966 letter to Edward Henderson in relation to Farrer's lecture, "The Prior Actuality of God," which was to be given at Southern Methodist University, where Ogden was teaching, and then at Henderson's school, Louisiana State University. Farrer's comment is reported by Henderson in an unpublished ms., "Austin Farrer and Process Theology: Notes on 'The Prior Actuality of God.'" Farrer's lecture was later published in Austin Farrer, *Reflective Faith: Essays in Philosophical Theism*, ed. Charles C. Conti (London: SPCK, 1972), 178–91.

4. Austin Farrer, *Faith and Speculation: An Essay in Philosophical Theology* (New York: New York University Press, 1967), 170.

us."[5] In the same vein, Maurice Wiles, evidently on the basis primarily of Ogden's theology, writes of the "abandonment by process theology" of a future hope.[6] Even more explicitly, D. W. D. Shaw says that "Process theology . . . does not allow anything in the nature of active survival after death" and writes of its "monotonous, bleak account of the 'end.'"[7]

Although all of these theologians write sweepingly about process theology as such, they have, to use the old language of essence and accidents, mistakenly assumed one of process theology's accidents to belong to its essence. That this assumption is mistaken is shown by the fact that some process theologians, including John Cobb and myself, have affirmed life after death.[8] This affirmation would not say anything about process theology itself, of course, if it could be made only by ignoring or altering the basic philosophical position of Whitehead and Hartshorne. But this is not the case. Whitehead acknowledged in writing that his position on the mind-body relation allows for the possibility of life after death,[9] and Hartshorne has acknowledged this allowance in personal correspondence. No matter how many process theologians personally reject belief in life after death, accordingly, this rejection cannot be attributed to process theology as such. The same is true, of course, of the affirmation of life after death on the part of some process theologians: It does not belong to the core doctrines of process theology. What does belong to this core is the Whiteheadian-Hartshornean position on the mind-body relation, which is neutral on life after death, making it neither necessary nor impossible.

By generalizing this distinction with regard to life after death, we can answer the question as to the core doctrines of process theology understood

---

5. John Polkinghorne, *Science and Christian Belief: Theological Reflections of a Bottom-Up Thinker* (London: SPCK, 1994), 65–66.

6. Maurice Wiles, *God's Action in the World: The Bampton Lectures for 1986* (London: SCM, 1986), 51.

7. D. W. D. Shaw, "Process Thought and Creation," *Theology* 78 (July 1975): 345–55, at 351, 354.

8. See John B. Cobb Jr., *A Christian Natural Theology: Based on the Thought of Alfred North Whitehead* (Philadelphia: Westminster, 1965), 63–70; John B. Cobb Jr., "The Resurrection of the Soul," *Harvard Theological Review* 80 (April 1987): 213–27; David Ray Griffin, *God and Religion in the Postmodern World: Essays in Postmodern Theology* (Albany: State University of New York Press, 1989), ch. 6; David Ray Griffin, "Life after Death, Parapsychology, and Post-Modern Animism," in *Death and Afterlife*, ed. Stephen T. Davis (New York: St. Martin's, 1989), 88–107; David Ray Griffin, *Parapsychology, Philosophy, and Spirituality: A Postmodern Exploration* (Albany: State University of New York Press, 1997), 96–268.

9. Alfred North Whitehead, *Religion in the Making* (1926; reprint, New York: Macmillan, 1957); Alfred North Whitehead, *Adventures of Ideas* (1933; reprint, New York: Free, 1967), 208.

as a type of Christian theology. Christian process theologians are thinkers who seek to articulate Christian faith on the basis of the process philosophy of Whitehead and/or Hartshorne, employed as a "natural" or "philosophical" theology. Insofar as the core of Christian process theology can be specified, therefore, it exists at the level of the philosophical theology underlying the more specifically Christian doctrines and individual opinions of the various theologians.

It must be stressed, however, that the answer to the question of what process theology is, in distinction from what it is not, cannot be answered simply by reference to the beliefs of Whitehead and/or Hartshorne. The same distinction between core and peripheral beliefs must also be made with regard to them. The fact that "process theology" cannot simply be equated with everything that Whitehead and Hartshorne happened to believe is brought out most clearly by the fact that they disagree on several issues. Indeed, Hartshorne has specifically criticized Whitehead's views on several points on the grounds that Whitehead had affirmed positions on these points that were in tension with his more fundamental position, which Hartshorne shares.[10] Other process philosophers and theologians have made similar critiques of the views of Hartshorne as well as of Whitehead. To specify the core beliefs of process theology, accordingly, we cannot simply point to the philosophical theology of either Whitehead or Hartshorne. We would be closer if we pointed to all those doctrines on which they agree. But even that would mean including some peripheral elements in the core. For example, they probably both rejected belief in life after death, but this rejection, as we have seen, does not belong to the essential core of their position.

What does belong to this core, and thereby to the core of process theology, is a set of fundamental, interrelated ontological and epistemological doctrines. The viability of process theology should be judged in terms of these core doctrines, not in terms of the personal opinions about this or that topic of individual representatives of the movement, including Whitehead and Hartshorne themselves. After all, judged in terms of their theological helpfulness, what is important about philosophers is not their incidental beliefs but their core positions, which, when accepted, determine what else can and cannot be said in an intelligible, self-consistent way. Those of us who are process theologians are so not because we agree with everything that Whitehead and Hartshorne have written, but because we have found their core position to be philosophically more adequate and theologically more helpful than other available positions.

---

10. See David R. Griffin, "Hartshorne's Differences from Whitehead," in *Two Process Philosophers*, ed. Lewis S. Ford (Tallahassee: American Academy of Religion, 1973), 35–57.

In the remainder of this essay, I will articulate several of the doctrines of process theology that seem to me to belong to its core. Part of my motive in making this distinction, it should be evident, is to undermine some of the reasons for the wholesale rejection of process theology on the part of many theologians. As an advocate of process theology, I believe, of course, that it has much to contribute to the churches and to the world more generally, and I find it distressing to find these resources rejected out of hand because of a confusion of peripheral beliefs with core doctrines. Clearly distinguishing between these will not, to be sure, remove all the reasons for rejecting process theology, because most of its core doctrines are deeply controversial. This fact should not be surprising: Process theology would not have become a new, distinctive type of theology unless it involved challenges to more traditional ways of thinking. Because these challenges are to such widely held assumptions, the main achievement of my focus on the core beliefs of process theology may be, from the point of view of many thinkers, simply to provide them with even better reasons than they had before for rejecting it! Of course, I believe that all of these core doctrines can be shown to be more rational than their alternatives. Although I have argued these points elsewhere, I will be able to do very little of that in this essay, the title of which refers, after all, only to what process theology is—not to why it should be considered true, or at least less far from the truth than its alternatives.

I will characterize the essential core of process theology in terms of seven doctrines—one formal and six substantive. There is a degree of arbitrariness in settling on these seven: Some of them could easily have been divided into two or more doctrines or, contrariwise, some of them could be considered sub-points under other doctrines. Also, there are further doctrines, not discussed in this essay, that could well be included in the core of process theology. Nevertheless, the seven doctrines included here, being both distinctive of and essential to process theology, can serve to indicate and illustrate the difference between core and peripheral beliefs of process theologians. These seven doctrines are (1) hard-core commonsense presuppositions as the main test of adequacy, (2) panexperientialism with organizational duality, (3) nonsensory perception, (4) persons as personally ordered societies, (5) internal relatedness, (6) naturalistic theism, and (7) dipolar theism. I will discuss them in this order.

Hard-Core Common Sense

The central formal problem for theology is that of authority: On what basis, finally, do we claim some ideas to be true, others to be false? Process theology is based on the conviction that there are some notions that we all inevitably presuppose in practice, even if we deny them verbally, and that this set of notions should be accepted as the ultimate criterion for all systematic thinking, be it called science, philosophy, or theology. Referring to this principle as the "metaphysical rule of evidence," Whitehead says that "we must bow to those presumptions, which, in despite of criticism, we still employ for the regulation of our lives."[11] I have labeled this set of presumptions "hard-core commonsense notions." The term "common sense" indicates that these notions are common to us all, in spite of cultural differences. However, "common sense" is often used to point to parochial ideas, limited to a certain time and place. It is used derogatorily, for example, to refer to the prejudices that people inherit from their parents, or to ideas that science has now shown to be false. I differentiate, accordingly, between soft-core commonsense beliefs, which later discoveries can disconfirm, and hard-core commonsense beliefs, which later scientific discoveries cannot undermine because they are inevitably presupposed by all people in all their activities, including scientific activity.

For example, we all inevitably presuppose that we are in a world of other things and persons as real as we are. As Whitehead said, the notion that we directly perceive other actualities is "a presupposition of all common sense."[12] Accordingly, for me to accept the theory of solipsism, which says that for all I know I may be the only actual existent, would be to countenance a contradiction between my theory and one of the inevitable presuppositions involved in all my practices. The same is true of freedom. Many theories, both theological and scientific, have entailed determinism, according to which our present actions are totally determined by some power beyond our present experience itself, be it an all-determining God or all-determining molecules. These theories imply that our feeling of freedom, in the sense of self-determination in the moment, is an illusion. As Whitehead points out, however, our experience of partial self-determination, which lies behind our experiences of responsibility, self-approval, and self-reproach, "is too large to be put aside merely as misconstruction. It governs the whole tone of human life."[13] As Hartshorne says, everyone, including the philosopher who professes to be a determinist, is "busily engaged in trying to decide what the future is to be as though it were *not* yet wholly fixed."[14] There is nothing arbitrary in accepting the set of presuppositions constituting our hard-core commonsense notions as the ultimate criterion for our theories, because this acceptance follows from the first rule of reason, the

---

11. Whitehead, *Process and Reality*, 151.

12. Ibid., 52.

13. Ibid., 47.

14. Charles Hartshorne, *Beyond Humanism: Essays in the Philosophy of Nature* (1937; reprint, Lincoln: University of Nebraska Press, 1968), 137.

principle of noncontradiction: To deny explicitly a doctrine that one is affirming implicitly is to affirm self-contradictory doctrines.

Once we accept this criterion, we cannot rest content with doctrines, be they purportedly based on the authority of religious revelation or of the late modern scientific worldview, that involve "negations of what in practice is presupposed."[15] Acceptance of this criterion does not mean that all theological doctrines must be directly *based on* hard-core commonsense beliefs (which would be a form of foundationalism). It means only that no doctrines may *contradict* these beliefs. The implications, nevertheless, are not trivial. One implication is that the traditional doctrine of divine providence, according to which all events are fully determined by divine goodness, is ruled out. As already stated, we cannot help presupposing that the future is partly open, to be partly settled by our decisions. Also, another of our hard-core commonsense convictions is that things go wrong, that not everything that happens is ultimately for the best, that not all prima facie evil is merely apparent, but that genuinely evil events occur. Accepting hard-core common sense as the basic criterion of adequacy, however, does not count only against various beliefs of traditional theology but also against various doctrines of the late modern worldview, such as materialistic determinism and nihilistic relativism. According to materialistic determinism, all present events are fully determined by antecedent events, and according to nihilistic relativism, there are no criteria in the universe by which to judge some outcomes as better or worse than others. As Hartshorne says, no one can live in terms of these doctrines, so no one really believes them.[16]

Besides serving the negative role of eliminating many doctrines, acceptance of hard-core common sense as the fundamental formal criterion provides a positive goal for philosophical theology. After making the statement about the presumptions that we inevitably employ in practice in spite of criticism, Whitehead said: "Rationalism is the search for the coherence of such presumptions."[17] The task of philosophical theology, in other words, is twofold. It is, first, to try to discern all of these presumptions. As Hartshorne puts it, the basic task of philosophical theology is to discover, through cooperation, "what the bottom layer of our common human thought really is."[18] The second task is then to develop a position that shows how all of these presuppositions can fit together in a self-consistent way. How, for example,

---

15. Whitehead, *Process and Reality*, 13.

16. Charles Hartshorne, *The Logic of Perfection and Other Essays in Neoclassical Metaphysics* (LaSalle, Ill.: Open Court, 1962), 12; Charles Hartshorne, *Omnipotence and Other Theological Mistakes* (Albany: State University of New York Press, 1984), 19, 25.

17. Whitehead, *Process and Reality*, 151.

18. Charles Hartshorne, *Man's Vision of God and the Logic of Theism* (1941; reprint, Hamden, Conn.: Archon, 1964), 80.

is our conviction that all events have causes consistent with our conviction that some events, such as the decisions of human beings, involve a degree of freedom? In Whitehead's words, "One task of a sound metaphysics is to exhibit final and efficient causes in their proper relation to each other."[19]

Two final points: First, to describe the chief task of philosophical theology in terms of adequacy to our hard-core commonsense notions is not to say that it is restricted to them. Philosophical theology must also be adequate to well-established facts from the special sciences, such as the evidence that our world came about through a long evolutionary process. Second, any concrete theology is developed within the context of some living tradition, such as Christianity, Judaism, or Hinduism. As such it contains, beyond the beliefs reflecting the presuppositions of human beings as such, doctrines reflecting experiences that are more or less distinctive to that particular tradition. There is nothing in process theology that would rule out the belief that such experiences can be genuinely revelatory. Indeed, process theology implies that each tradition probably contains distinctive insights, based on such experiences, into the full nature of reality. Each tradition can enrich itself, accordingly, through genuine dialogue with other traditions.[20] Of course, process theology also implies—to reiterate the main point of this section—that a doctrinal formulation of such experiences, to be acceptable, must not violate any of our inescapable presuppositions.

Panexperientialism with Organizational Duality

One of those presuppositions, as already suggested, is freedom—the twofold assumption that our decisions involve a degree of self-determination and that these partially autonomous decisions guide our bodily behavior. Modern thought, being limited to a choice between dualism and materialism, has had difficulty doing justice to this twofold presupposition. Dualism has done justice to our free decisions: By saying that the mind is distinct from the body and not totally determined by it, dualism provides a locus for our free decisions. However, by saying that the mind is ontologically different— different in kind—from the matter of which the body is composed, dualists from the time of Descartes to the present have been unable to explain how mind and body can interact, as some contemporary dualists admit.[21] Largely to avoid this problem, materialism denies the distinction between mind and body, saying that the mind is somehow identical with the brain.

---

19. Whitehead, *Process and Reality*, 84.

20. See David Ray Griffin, ed., *Deep Religious Pluralism* (Louisville: Westminster John Knox, 2005).

21. See Geoffrey Madell, *Mind and Materialism* (Edinburgh: The University Press, 1988), 2, 140–41.

This equation, however, means that our feeling of freedom must be considered an illusion. Some materialists, recognizing that they in practice cannot help presupposing that they and other people make partially free decisions, admit that this inability to affirm genuine freedom is a serious problem.[22]

Process theology overcomes this standoff between dualism and materialism by rejecting the assumption shared in common by them—the view, articulated paradigmatically by Descartes, that nature is composed of bits of matter that are wholly devoid of both experience and spontaneity. This view, which implies that the mind as conceived by dualists has nothing in common with the stuff of which the body is composed, is what led to the insoluble problem as to how mind and body could interact and thereby to the collapse of dualism into materialism. Although this view of matter has been so widespread in the modern world that it is now generally assumed to be simply a matter of common sense, this view does *not* belong to our hard-core commonsense presuppositions but only to the soft-core common sense of our time, which means that it can be intelligibly rejected.

On the basis of a variety of reasons, which I discuss elsewhere,[23] process theology does reject this view of matter. That is, it rejects the notion of "vacuous actuality," which is the notion of something that is actual and yet devoid of experience. To reject the existence of vacuous actualities is to affirm panexperientialism, the doctrine that all actual entities have experience. In process theology's version of this doctrine, all experience has a degree of spontaneity, being partly self-determining. The panexperientialism of process theology, accordingly, holds that to be actual is to be a partially self-determining experience. To have experience is not necessarily to have consciousness, but it *is* to have feelings.

If all of the cells in the body, including the neurons composing the brain, have feelings, then the question of how mind and brain can interact can be answered. In Hartshorne's words, "cells can influence our human experiences because they have feelings that we can feel. To deal with the influences of human experiences upon cells, one turns this around. *We* have feelings that *cells* can feel."[24] On this basis, the numerical distinction between the mind and the brain, upon which dualists have insisted, can be maintained because this numerical distinction does not also involve an ontological dualism. Because of its panexperientialism, in other words,

---

22. See Thomas Nagel, *The View from Nowhere* (New York: Oxford University Press, 1986), 110–17; John Searle, *Minds, Brains, and Science* (London: British Broadcast Corporation, 1984), 86, 98.

23. See David Ray Griffin, *Unsnarling the World-Knot: Consciousness, Freedom, and the Mind-Body Problem* (Berkeley and Los Angeles: University of California Press, 1998).

24. Hartshorne, *Logic of Perfection*, 229.

process theology can affirm interactionism, which says that mind and body are distinct from each other and causally interact, because it is a *nondualistic* interactionism. Thanks to this nondualistic interactionism, which allows the mind to be a distinct actuality that makes real decisions that then influence the brain, process theology's solution to the mind-body problem affirms the freedom that we all presuppose in practice.

This nondualistic interactionism also provides a basis for affirming the possibility of life after death. The primary reason for doubting the reality of life after death in the late modern world has been the conviction that what we call the mind or the soul is simply the brain or certain aspects or functions thereof. Given this conviction, the idea that the mind or soul could survive the death of the body is nonsensical. By showing how the mind can intelligibly be said to be distinct from the body, process theology makes it possible to intelligibly affirm survival (that is, apart from a supernatural deity who could resurrect or re-create the physical body; process theology's rejection of such a deity is discussed below). As Whitehead said, because his philosophical position on the mind-body relation leaves the issue open, an affirmative answer to the life-after-death question can be given if there is good empirical evidence for it.[25]

Process theology's panexperientialism is also relevant to the question as to how God can influence the world. The idea of matter as devoid of experience created a God-world problem analogous to the mind-body problem, with the result that the God of modern theology has for the most part been directly related only to human experience. Modern theology has provided no way to understand how God could be creatively and providentially active in nature. This has been one of the main reasons for modern theology's widespread acquiescence in the Darwinian claim that the entire evolutionary process can be understood apart from divine guidance. Process theology, because of its panexperientialism, can understand God's influence on the world as analogous to the mind's influence on its body. At the same time, the idea that actual entities at every level embody an element of self-determination, which cannot be overridden, provides a basis for explaining how the idea that God is providentially active in nature is not contradicted by the vast amount of evil in nature (which bothered Darwin so greatly).[26]

---

25. Whitehead, *Religion in the Making*, 107.

26. On the problem of evil, see David Ray Griffin, *God, Power, and Evil: A Process Theodicy* (Philadelphia: Westminster, 1976; reprinted with a new preface, Lanham, Md.: University Press of America, 1991); David Ray Griffin, *Evil Revisited: Responses and Reconsiderations* (Albany: State University of New York Press, 1991); and reprinted with a new preface, Louisville: Westminster John Knox, 2004, Burton Z. Cooper, *Why, God?* (Atlanta: John Knox, 1988). On theism, evolution, and evil, see David Ray Griffin, "Evolution and Postmodern Theism," in *God and Religion*, 69–82.

Although panexperientialism clearly has many advantages, it has generally been scorned by both philosophers and theologians. It is often rejected as self-evidently absurd on the basis of the charge that it implies that things such as rocks and telephones have thoughts, or at least feelings.[27] The assumption behind this charge is that the "pan" in panexperientialism—or panpsychism, which has been the more common name—refers to *all things whatsoever*. There are, to be sure, forms of panpsychism that attribute experience to all identifiable objects, including rocks, telephones, and stars. The panexperientialism of process theology, however, says only that *all genuine individuals* have experience. Above the level of the most primitive individuals (such as, perhaps, quarks), it holds that there are two ways in which these primitive individuals can be organized. They can either form higher-level individuals, which have a unified experience, or merely aggregational societies, which do not. This organizational duality, which was articulated by Leibniz, has been affirmed by Whitehead and developed more completely and adequately in Hartshorne's doctrine of the "compound individual."[28]

This organizational duality allows panexperientialism, while avoiding an ontological dualism, to do justice to the obvious distinction between inert things, which provide no reason for supposing them to have experience, and things with the power for self-movement, which thereby suggest a unified experience. In a compound individual, such as a cat, the organization of the cells gives rise to a higher-level experience—that of the mind, anima, or soul—which can exert a dominating influence over the cells, thereby allowing the cat to make a unified response to its environment. In an aggregational society such as a rock, however, no higher-level, unifying experience emerges. So the rock itself is inert, even though the molecules, atoms, and subatomic particles of which it is composed are not: Because there is no higher power to coordinate their motions, the spontaneities simply cancel each other out. This is why mechanical laws work for

27. See Colin McGinn, *The Character of Mind* (Oxford: Oxford University Press, 1982), 32; Karl R. Popper and John C. Eccles, *The Self and Its Brain* (Berlin: Springer-Verlag, 1981), 55.

28. Alfred North Whitehead, *Science and the Modern World* (1925; reprint, New York: Free, 1967), 110; Alfred North Whitehead, *Modes of Thought* (1938; reprint, New York: Free, 1968), 21–24; Whitehead, *Adventures of Ideas*, 207–8; Charles Hartshorne, "Physics and Psychics: The Place of Mind in Nature," in *Mind in Nature: Essays on the Interface of Science and Philosophy*, ed. John B. Cobb Jr. and David Ray Griffin (Washington, D.C.: University Press of America, 1977), 89–96; Charles Hartshorne, "The Compound Individual," in *Philosophical Essays for Alfred North Whitehead*, ed. Otis T. Lee (New York: Longmans, Green, 1936), reprinted in Charles Hartshorne, *Whitehead's Philosophy: Selected Essays, 1935–1970* (Lincoln: University of Nebraska Press, 1972), 41–61.

aggregational objects, even though all individuals have some degree of freedom.[29] Because this distinction is so crucial to the plausibility of process theology, I include not simply "panexperientialism" but "panexperientialism with organizational duality" in its core doctrines.

Nonsensory Perception

Implicit in process theology's panexperientialism is another of its core doctrines, the reality of nonsensory perception. This doctrine is implicit in panexperientialism because by saying that all individuals perceive or feel other individuals, panexperientialism attributes a kind of perceptual experience to some things—such as cells, molecules, and electrons—that obviously do not have sensory organs. Whitehead coined the term "prehension" to refer to this more primitive, nonsensory form of perception. Besides occuring in organisms without sensory organs, prehension is, even in organisms with such organs, prior to sensory perception, being presupposed by it. For example, my visual perception of a tree is only possible because, after the information has been carried by photons to my eye and then by the neurons in my optic nerve to my brain, my mind prehends my brain cells, thereby receiving the information from them.

This acceptance of nonsensory perception is of utmost importance in process theology. It explains, for one thing, the origin of most of our hardcore commonsense notions. One problem with earlier forms of commonsense philosophy was that by accepting the modern equation of perception with sense-perception, their proponents had to attribute the common notions to a supernatural implantation in our minds or else simply leave them unexplained. Whitehead, however, shows how our direct prehension of the causal efficacy of prior events explains our knowledge not only of the reality of an actual world beyond ourselves, but also of three additional hard-core commonsense notions: the reality of causal influence; the reality of the past; and (thereby) the reality of time. Through our capacity for nonsensory perception, furthermore, we can explain our apparent awareness of those nonactual things called ideals or normative values—such as truth, beauty, and goodness—which we inevitably presuppose in our cognitive, aesthetic, and moral judgments, thereby making it impossible for anyone to be a complete relativist.

The acceptance of the reality of nonsensory perception also allows for the genuineness of theistic religious experience, in the sense of a direct awareness of God. Most modern thought, accepting the soft-core commonsense idea of modernity that we can perceive actualities beyond ourselves only by means of our physical sense organs, has assumed that no genuine religious

---

29. See Hartshorne, *Beyond Humanism*, 70, 315.

experience occurs, thereby making the universality of religion mysterious. Process theology holds that just as we directly prehend finite actualities in the vicinity of our minds, especially the cells in our brains, we also directly prehend the divine actuality, which as omnipresent is in the vicinity of all our minds. This direct prehension of God is also the basis for our experience of normative ideals, mentioned in the previous paragraph: Because ideals, as nonactual entities, can neither exist nor exert causal influence on their own, their objectivity and efficacy can be explained only by virtue of their subsistence in the experience of a universal actuality. In Whitehead's words: "There are experiences of ideals—of ideals entertained, of ideals aimed at, of ideals achieved, of ideals defaced. This is the experience of the deity of the universe."[30] This idea, that our experience of God explains the efficacy of ideals in our experience, underlies the generalization, to be discussed below, that God acts persuasively (not coercively) in the world.

This acceptance of nonsensory perception also opens the way for taking seriously the evidence for those forms of it commonly called "extrasensory" perception, such as telepathy. Whitehead, in fact, appealed to the evidence for telepathy to support his affirmation of the reality of a nonsensory mode of perception.[31] The evidence for telepathy and other forms of extrasensory perception, which has been studied by that branch of science known as psychical research or parapsychology, also provides the empirical evidence on the basis of which, Whitehead said, the question of life after death should be settled. Although Whitehead himself evidently did not affirm the reality of life after death—perhaps partly through inadequate knowledge of the evidence and partly because the evidence was not as convincing as it now is—some process theologians today do make this affirmation.[32]

Persons as Personally Ordered Societies

One more doctrine, both essential to and fairly distinctive of process theology, is that a person enduring through time is not a single actual entity but a personally ordered *society* of actual entities. The more general idea underlying this doctrine about persons is that actual entities, rather than enduring through time, are momentary events. Whitehead called them "actual occasions" and "occasions of experience" to emphasize this point. The enduring person, accordingly, is a temporally or personally ordered society of occasions of experience. As used here, the term "person" refers not to the human being as a psychophysical whole but only to the mind or

---

30. Whitehead, *Modes of Thought*, 103.

31. Whitehead, *Process and Reality*, 307.

32. I have done so on the basis of an evaluation of five types of empirical evidence in *Parapsychology, Philosophy, and Spirituality*, 150–268.

soul, as the dominant member of this compound individual. Whitehead, in fact, generalizes the term "person" to refer to any personally ordered society, so that electrons, atoms, molecules, and cells as well as animal souls can be considered persons. Although animal (including human) souls are not ontologically different in kind from inorganic enduring individuals such as molecules, the enormous difference in degree involved is brought out by calling them *living* persons. The point at hand, in any case, is that the human mind or soul is not a single, long-lasting actual entity—as the old word "substance" suggested—but a purely temporal society of momentary experiences.

This point, like the previous one about nonsensory perception, could simply be regarded as part of process theology's panexperientialism. Indeed, one reason for preferring this term to the older term "panpsychism" is that that older term, derivative from "psyche," suggests that the elementary units of nature are enduring individuals, whereas the term "panexperientialism" is more consonant with the idea that the ultimate units are momentary experiences. Nevertheless, it is best to treat this point separately both because it is distinctive of process theology's version of panexperientialism and because it has been the focus of special criticism. Austin Farrer, for example, said that "Whitehead sinned against the light, by saying that a personal existence in its continuity over time is a society of entities: for our standard example of an entity is a perduring person." Eric Mascall, to cite another example, said that Whitehead "does not seem to succeed in his attempt . . . to get 'persons' out of 'occasions.'"[33] Even some thinkers generally sympathetic to process theology have considered this aspect to be a problem, not a strength.[34]

What is lacking in these criticisms, however, is any reflection upon the reasons why Whitehead enunciated this view. He certainly knew that it went against soft-core common sense, at least in non-Buddhist cultures, and that any doctrine, to be credible, must do justice to our sense of personal identity through time.[35] But he decided that this sense of identity is not to

33. Austin Farrer to Ray Hart, December 14, 1965, quoted in Charles Conti, *Metaphysical Personalism: An Analysis of Austin Farrer's Metaphysics of Theism* (Oxford: Clarendon, 1995), 270–71; E. L. Mascall, *He Who Is: A Study in Traditional Theism* (New York: Longmans, Green, 1943), 152.

34. See, for example, David Pailin, *God and the Processes of Reality: Foundations of a Credible Theism* (London and New York: Routledge, 1989), 54.

35. Alfred North Whitehead, "Immortality," in *The Philosophy of Alfred North Whitehead*, ed. Paul Arthur Schilpp, 2d. ed., *The Library of Living Philosophers*, vol. 3 (1941; reprint, New York: Tudor, 1951), 682–700, especially 688–91; also in Alfred North Whitehead, *Essays in Science and Philosophy* (New York: Philosophical Library, 1947), 77–97, especially 84–86.

be explained by saying that the person is simply a single entity, numerically one through time. The fact that his alternative doctrine clashes with soft-core common sense is no more decisive than the fact that cell theory, atomic theory, and quantum theory have all clashed with the way things appear at first glance. To see whether Whitehead's doctrine should be accepted in spite of its clash with soft-core common sense, we need to see whether Whitehead had good reasons for affirming it.

One of his reasons was based on the development of quantum physics, which seemed to imply that the ultimate units of physics are not enduring particles but momentary events.[36] Whitehead was convinced that we need a monistic pluralism, according to which all actual entities are of the same metaphysical type. The idea that the "particles" of physics are really temporally ordered *societies* of momentary events, therefore, suggested to him the generalization that all enduring individuals are to be understood analogously. At the level of human experience, furthermore, this conclusion had support from phenomenological analysis. William James, famous for his phrase "stream of experience," came eventually to hold that this apparent stream actually consists of "buds or drops of perception."[37] Whitehead also evidently knew that Buddhists had long ago come to a similar conclusion.

The main reason for affirming this doctrine, however, was surely that it enabled him to overcome some otherwise insoluble problems. One of these is the old problem of reconciling the doctrine of enduring substances, understood to be strictly (numerically) self-identical through time, with the belief in real *relations* between these substances, which would constitute changing "accidents." The seriousness of this problem to acute metaphysical minds is illustrated by Leibniz, who was convinced that the strict self-identity of an actual entity is incompatible with changing relations. This conviction led to his notorious decision to make his monads "windowless," meaning that they had no openings to receive influences from other monads.

Although Whitehead accepted Leibniz's insight that the strict self-identity of an actual entity is incompatible with changing relations, he also recognized the inescapable assumption that we and other enduring things enter into real relations with each other. He reconciled these two beliefs by thinking of an individual in the strictest sense—a fully *actual* entity—as an experiential event that "becomes" but does not "change," so that "no subject experiences twice."[38] With regard to "the notion of an actual entity which is characterized by essential qualities, and remains numerically one amidst the changes of accidental relations and of accidental qualities," Whitehead

36. Whitehead, *Science and the Modern World*, 34–36.

37. William James, *Some Problems in Philosophy*, ed. Henry James Jr. (New York: Longmans, Green, 1911), ch. 10; quoted by Whitehead, *Process and Reality*, 68.

38. Whitehead, *Process and Reality*, 29, 35, 80, 147.

says that although it can be useful for many purposes, "in metaphysics the concept is sheer error."[39] A Whiteheadian actual entity, therefore, has no changing relations. But this fact does not mean that an enduring individual, such as an electron, a cell, or a mind, does not have changing relations. Unlike the Leibnizian monad, the Whiteheadian enduring individual is full of windows: Each occasion of experience begins as an open window to past events. Once it has prehended those past events, the experience's window is closed, as it were, so that it enters into no relations with subsequent events while it decides how to respond to the influences upon it. That occasion of experience then "perishes," being succeeded by a subsequent occasion of experience, which begins with relations to that previous event and other completed events in its environment. Accordingly, the enduring individual, with its changing relations to other things, retains only relative self-identity through time. Self-identity in the strictest sense is true only of the momentary actual occasions. In this way, our conviction that we are truly related to the world, with its incessant change, is reconciled with the insight that the self-identity of an individual, considered in the strictest sense, is incompatible with changing relations.

Closely related to self-identity is a feature of the problem of freedom not yet discussed. Earlier I dealt with one of the necessary conditions for intelligibly affirming freedom: That the mind be held to be distinct from the brain, with its billions of cells, so that the mind can be considered a unitary actuality capable of exerting self-determination. Another problem, however, is how the mind's self-determination or final causation can be conceived to be related to efficient causation, both that which is exerted on the mind by the brain cells and that which the mind exerts back upon those cells. This has been a problem not only for dualists but even for panpsychists, insofar as they conceived of the mind and a brain cell as each numerically self-identical through time. Not seeing how efficient causation from the brain cells could influence the mind while the mind is exercising self-determination or how the mind while it is exercising self-determination could also exert efficient causation upon the brain cells, many thinkers have affirmed parallelism, according to which mind and brain run along "in sync" with each other without really interacting. One problem with this view is explaining how they remain "in sync" if they do not influence each other; Leibniz spoke of a divinely pre-established harmony, but most later parallelists, eschewing this supernaturalist solution, have left it a mystery. Equally serious is the fact that parallelism does not do justice to our inescapable assumption that our bodies influence our conscious experience, or to our inescapable

---

39. Ibid., 79.

assumption that we not only make real decisions but that these decisions, once made, then influence our bodily activities.

Whitehead's doctrine of enduring individuals as personally ordered societies of occasions of experience is designed to show how efficient causation and self-determination are interrelated. The occasion begins by receiving efficient causation from prior events. This reception of influences from past events constitutes the occasion's "physical pole." Then the occasion, allowing in no further influences, decides precisely how to create itself out of these efficient causes, thereby exercising final causation in the sense of self-determination. This self-determination is the occasion's "mental pole." Once this self-determination is completed, the occasion's moment of subjectivity comes to an end, and it becomes an object for future subjects, exerting efficient causation upon them. Given this view, we do not have to wonder how an event can exercise final causation at the same time that it is receiving efficient causation from others; it does not. Nor do we have to wonder how, while an event is exercising final causation and thereby determining what exactly it is to be, the event can exert efficient causation on others. Whitehead's doctrine of temporal atomicity allows for a *perpetual oscillation between subjectivity and objectivity and thereby between final and efficient causation.* After an actual entity in its mode of subjectivity receives efficient causation from prior occasions, it exercises final causation or self-determination. Then, in its mode of objectivity, it exercises efficient causation upon subsequent occasions.

In these ways, the idea that persons are personally ordered societies of momentary occasions of experience helps us make sense of several of our hard-core commonsense presuppositions. Process theologians believe that these benefits more than compensate for the fact that this doctrine runs contrary to the soft-core commonsense belief that the enduring individual is a single, actual entity, numerically one through time. Another benefit emphasized by Hartshorne depends upon the doctrine, not yet mentioned, that the "physical pole" of an occasion of experience is also called its "conformal pole." To explain: A prior actual entity, being an occasion of experience entirely constituted of feelings of various types and grades, is prehended in terms of one of its feelings. That prior feeling is the "objective datum" of the present feeling. But because that "objective datum" was itself a feeling of a prior feeling, it had its own "subjective form," which is *how* it felt that prior feeling, which involved some form of emotion. In feeling that prior feeling, the present occasion of experience will initially, in the physical pole of its experience, conform to the emotional tone of the prior feeling. In Whitehead's words:

> The primitive form of physical experience is emotional—blind emotion—received as felt elsewhere in another occasion and conformally

appropriated as a subjective passion. In the language appropriate to the higher stages of experience, the primitive element is *sympathy,* that is, feeling the feeling *in* another and feeling conformally *with* another.[40]

Hartshorne, combining this doctrine with the doctrine that one's self-identity through time is based upon one's (social) appropriation of one's own prior experiences rather than consisting in "mere numerical oneness," says that this twofold doctrine supports the religious view that "the participation of experiences in other experiences, i.e., 'sympathy' or, in terms of its higher and happier forms, 'love,'" is "the foundation of all other relations."[41]

Internal Relatedness

Process theology's fifth core doctrine, the reality of internal relatedness, has already been suggested in previous points. In contrast with sensory perception, which is generally understood in terms of a sensory datum that merely "represents" some outer object, the doctrine of the priority of a nonsensory "prehension" says that we actually take aspects of other things into ourselves, so that they are constitutive of us. The doctrine that a person is a temporal society of brief occasions of experience, with perhaps a dozen such occasions occurring in a second of human experience, says that other things are entering into us, and we into them, many times per second. Indeed, the doctrine that the soul is a society of occasions of experience means that the person's self-identity through time is constituted by social relations, being based on the fact that one's present experience is largely constituted by the internal appropriation of one's prior experiences. Process theology is, thereby, a radically social, relational theology. To emphasize this feature of it, many advocates use the name "process-relational theology."

This doctrine of internal relatedness does not, however, rule out the reality of external relations. An occasion of experience prehends only *prior* occasions of experience. It does not prehend future occasions because such occasions do not yet exist to exert causal efficacy and thereby to be prehended. Nor does it prehend contemporary occasions, because such occasions, being in "unison of becoming" with itself, are also not yet fully determinate, and so cannot exert causal efficacy. Any two occasions are defined as contemporaries, in fact, if neither influences the other. Any occasion of experience, accordingly, is externally related to contemporary and future occasions. It is not externally related to the fact that *there will be* future occasions: An occasion's "anticipation" of the future, meaning its

40. Ibid., 162.

41. Hartshorne, *Logic of Perfection,* 120; Charles Hartshorne, *Creative Synthesis and Philosophic Method* (LaSalle, Ill.: Open Court, 1970), xvii; Hartshorne, *Beyond Humanism,* 26.

anticipation *that,* and to some extent *how,* it will influence future occasions belongs to its essence. But it is externally related to the occasions that will actually occur in the future in all their determinateness. This external relatedness is part and parcel of the ontological realism of process theology: Things are what they are prior to, and therefore independently of, their being perceived by others. External relatedness in this sense, accordingly, is not contrary to, or a limitation on, process theology's doctrine of internal relations, but an essential aspect of it: The "other" can enter into our experience only if it has its individuality independently of our experience.

This doctrine of internal relatedness is important in many ways. As Hartshorne has stressed, this social view of self-identity, in which each moment begins with the appropriation of feelings from others, provides a basis for taking literally the New Testament idea that we are "members one of another," which means that our relations to our "own" past and future are not different in kind from our relations to the pasts and futures of other people. The idea that we can "love others as we love ourselves" is, accordingly, not ruled out as metaphysical nonsense, as it is by the doctrine that our relation to our own future and past is one of sheer identity while our relation to the past and future of other individuals is one of sheer non-identity.[42] This idea has constituted one of the appeals of process theology to feminist theologians.[43] In conjunction with the idea that all individuals have experience and thereby intrinsic value, this idea of internal relatedness also provides the basis for a strongly ecological theology, which has been another of the major appeals of process theology in recent decades.[44] Of importance to more traditional concerns as well as to an ecological theology is the fact that this doctrine provides the basis for a vision of mutual immanence between God and the world. According to this vision, God is not only incarnate to some degree in all individuals, but also the world enters into the divine experience—a notion that is suggested by "panentheism," one of the terms for process theism. Using this notion as a transitional point, we will now turn to process theology's doctrine of God.

---

42. Hartshorne, *Logic of Perfection,* 16–18; Hartshorne, *Creative Synthesis,* 191.

43. See, for example, Sheila Greeve Devaney, ed., *Feminism and Process Thought,* The Harvard Divinity School/Claremont Center for Process Studies Symposium Papers (New York: Edwin Mellen, 1981); Catherine Keller, *From a Broken Web: Separation, Sexism, and Self* (Boston: Beacon, 1986); Rita Nakashima Brock, *Journeys by Heart: A Christology of Erotic Power* (New York: Crossroad, 1988).

44. See, for example, Jay B. McDaniel, *Of God and Pelicans: A Theology of Reverence for Life* (Louisville: Westminster / sJohn Knox, 1989); Charles Birch, *Regaining Compassion for Humanity and Nature* (Kensington, Australia: New South Wales University Press, 1993); and Frederick Ferré, *Hellfire and Lightning Rods: Liberating Science, Technology, and Religion* (Maryknoll, N.Y.: Orbis, 1993).

180 A Dialogue on Process Theology

Naturalistic Theism

Perhaps the best-known doctrine of process theology is its insistence that divine power is persuasive, not coercive. By itself, however, this statement is ambiguous. It might be understood to mean that although God *could* act coercively, so as totally to determine events in the world, God has voluntarily relinquished complete divine control over the world in order to allow the world's causal processes to have a degree of autonomy, even to allow some creatures to exert a degree of self-determination. For example, David Pailin says that process theology endorses "the notion that God deliberately chooses to respect our personal freedom by having limited influence over what happens."[45] If this were the position of process theology, it would simply be a form of supernaturalism, according to which God could interrupt particular causal processes now and then in order to guarantee a particular outcome, or could even at some point decide to take complete control of the world as a whole—as some supernaturalists believe that God will do if nuclear holocaust or some other form of ecocide becomes imminent. (Given Pailin's misconstrual of process theology on this all-important point, it is not surprising that he concludes that its theodicy offers no improvement over the standard free-will defense.[46]) Process theology, however, is a form of *naturalistic* theism, according to which this kind of supernatural intervention or takeover is not possible. The hypothesis of process theism, furthermore, is that this impossibility is not simply moral, based upon a divine judgment that it is better not to intervene, but *metaphysical,* based upon the very nature of things. It lies in the nature of things, process theology suggests, that creativity—the twofold power to exert self-determination and then to exert causal influence upon others—is inherent in the world as well as in God.

Traditional theism was based on the opposite hypothesis—the speculation that this twofold creative power inherently belongs only to God, because God was said to be the only necessarily existent actuality. The existence of a world was said to be wholly contingent, dependent upon the divine will. The result was *extreme* voluntarism, according to which God not only had the freedom to make decisions in relation to the world (which would constitute a *moderate* voluntarism), but even the freedom to decide whether to have a world at all and thereby the freedom to interrupt any of the world's causal processes. This idea was undergirded by the (nonbiblical) doctrine of creation ex nihilo, according to which our world was not formed out of any previously existing finite material. The implication of this doctrine was that

---

45. Pailin, *God and the Processes*, 168.
46. Ibid., 145, 168.

the inherent structure and power of the creation was wholly subject to the divine will.

Whitehead rejected this traditional "theory of a wholly transcendent God creating out of nothing an accidental universe." In its place he enunciated a new version of the doctrine that "the creation of the world is the incoming of a type of order establishing a cosmic epoch . . . not the beginning of matter of fact."[47] The naturalistic character of Whitehead's theism, meaning its rejection of extreme voluntarism, consists in the fact that his position "exhibits the World as requiring its union with God, and God as requiring his union with the World," which reflects Whitehead's insistence that "the relationships of God to the World should lie beyond the accidents of will, and that they be founded upon the necessities of the nature of God and the nature of the World."[48]

This position does not mean that *our* world, with its form of order involving electrons, protons, neutrons, and so on, has existed forever. This world, being a particular "cosmic epoch," does exist contingently, being a product of divine volition (as well as of its own creativity, which is to be discussed below). Process theism affirms divine voluntarism in this moderate sense and thereby the doctrine that God's existence is transcendent to, in the sense of wholly independent of, our particular world. By saying in the above quotation that God's existence requires that of the World (capitalized), Whitehead means that God always exists in relation to a world, in the sense of a plurality of finite actualities (which might at times be in a state of chaos). Hartshorne has expressed this idea by speaking of God as "the soul of the universe." The point is that if it belongs to the very nature of God to be the soul of the universe, it would be nonsense to think of God's existing apart from a universe of finite actualities. This position does not, however, make God's existence contingent, because the existence of a multiplicity of finite actualities is not contingent. We can say, indeed, that such a realm exists because the existence of God, which is necessary, entails it. What exists necessarily, in other words, is not simply God, as traditional theism holds, or simply a world, as some forms of atheism hold, but God-with-a-world.

Whitehead's reference to the "necessities of the nature . . . of the World" means that this realm of finite actualities embodies various principles that are metaphysical or necessary in character, not being derivative from a contingent divine decision. These metaphysical principles, being common to all possible worlds that God could create, lie deeper than the "laws of nature" of our particular cosmic epoch (such as Planck's constant and the inverse square law of gravitational attraction), which exist only contingently. Because

47. Whitehead, *Process and Reality*, 95, 96.
48. Whitehead, *Adventures of Ideas*, 168.

these metaphysical principles have not been freely imposed, they cannot be freely canceled or interrupted. To speak of them as necessary, however, does not mean that they constitute an *alien* limitation on the divine freedom. Rather, as Hartshorne has stressed, the metaphysical principles are best understood as part and parcel of the divine essence; God is, in Whitehead's phrase, their "chief exemplification."[49] That God cannot violate them is no more a limitation on God than that God cannot act contrary to other dimensions of the divine essence—that God cannot, for example, be ignorant or unloving or go out of existence.

Because these metaphysical principles are the basic causal principles of the world, to say that they cannot be violated is to say that God cannot interrupt the world's basic causal powers—the twofold power of actualities to exert self-determination and efficient causation. This point brings us back to the main implication of naturalistic theism, which is that the word *God* does not name a being that, existing outside the basic causal nexus of the universe, can interrupt it. This doctrine allows theism to be reconciled with both evil and science. With regard to evil, process theologians need not try to explain why God does not occasionally intervene in the world to prevent especially horrendous suffering; nor need they try to dismiss this question by an appeal to "inscrutable mystery." With regard to the implication of this view for the relation between science and religion, process theism insists on the same fundamental point as does scientific naturalism, which is precisely the assumption that the world's basic cause-effect structure could never be interrupted.[50] This insistence does not mean that God exerts no causal influence in the universe. God can exert influence without interrupting the world's basic causal nexus because divine causation is everlastingly a natural part of this nexus.

The naturalism of process theism involves, as we have seen, a distinction between God and creativity. Whereas traditional theism said that creative power essentially belongs to God alone, process theism holds that it belongs both to God and a multiplicity of finite actualities. Because creativity is that which is embodied in all actualities, both divine and finite, Whitehead referred to creativity as the ultimate reality.[51] Also, because of the way in which his theism developed—out of a somewhat Spinozistic position, in which all events were embodiments of an underlying "substantial activity," which later became Whitehead's "creativity"—Whitehead sometimes used language suggesting that God is subordinate to, in the sense of derivative

---

49. Whitehead, *Process and Reality*, 343.

50. I discuss this issue at great length in *Religion and Scientific Naturalism: Overcoming the Conflicts* (Albany: State University of New York Press, 2000).

51. Whitehead, *Process and Reality*, 7, 20, 21.

from, creativity. For example, he referred to God as creativity's "primordial, non-temporal accident" and its "primordial creature."[52]

The fact that process theology is not to be simply equated with everything that Whitehead happened to say is especially important at this point. These passages, which are problematic from most theistic perspectives, have led many theologians to reject Whiteheadian-Hartshornean philosophical theology. The subordination of God to creativity suggested by these passages, however, in no way belongs to the essential core of process theology. In the first place, other passages in Whitehead's writings say that creativity exists only by virtue of its embodiment in God and other actualities and that, in fact, there is no meaning to "creativity" apart from "God."[53] In the second place, Whitehead's subordinationist language has been criticized by other process theologians. Speaking of Whitehead's "defective" exposition of his own natural theology, Hartshorne says: "One is forced to suppose him mistaken, or at least ill-advised in his choice of words, in some passages."[54] And John Cobb, besides arguing that the implication of Whitehead's philosophical theology is that the role of God as creator must be more drastic than Whitehead himself recognized,[55] has said that this system implies that there are two ultimates—creativity, the metaphysical ultimate or the ultimate *reality,* and God, the religious ultimate or the ultimate *actuality*—with only God being worthy of worship.[56] Again, what is important about process theology—what it *is*—is what its core doctrines say and imply, as distinct from other things that its members, including its founders, may have thought and said.

Dipolar Theism

Process theology's doctrine of God can be best characterized as naturalistic dipolar theism. Having treated the naturalism in the previous section, I will now discuss the dipolarity—or, I should say, the dipolarities, as process theology involves a *double* divine dipolarity. Because of various factors revolving around the ambiguity as to the meaning of its dipolar theism, this aspect of process theology has probably provided the greatest source of confusion. Much of this confusion derives from Whitehead's own ideas about

52. Ibid., 7, 31, 349.

53. Ibid., 7, 25.

54. Charles Hartshorne, "Whitehead and Contemporary Philosophy," in *The Relevance of Whitehead: Philosophical Essays in Commemoration of the Centenary of the Birth of Alfred North Whitehead*, ed. Ivor Leclerc (New York: Macmillan, 1961), 25–26.

55. Cobb, *Christian Natural Theology,* 206–14.

56. See John B. Cobb Jr., "Buddhist Emptiness and the Christian God," *Journal of the American Academy of Religion* 45 (March 1977): 11–25; and Cobb, *Beyond Dialogue,* 42–43, 86–90.

God, which he himself, according to Hartshorne, characterized as "very vague."[57] Some of the confusion has been due to the fact that Hartshorne has endorsed a different divine dipolarity without always making clear that he is doing so.

Most fundamentally, the affirmation that there are two "poles" in God means that God, besides influencing the world, is also influenced by it, which implies that God is not unchanging in all respects. In what Hartshorne calls "monopolar theism," by contrast, the idea that God was unchanging in some respect implied that God was unchanging in all respects, a conclusion that created several problems. For example, God was said to be omniscient, but the idea that the unchanging divine consciousness knows the changing world created a mystery. God was said to be compassionate, but how, as Anselm put it, could God be both compassionate and impassible? Our basic purpose was said to be to serve God, but how could we make any contribution to a wholly immutable, impassible deity? Contrariwise, if God is said to change in some respect, the monopolar idea of God would imply that God changes in *all* respects, which would lead to the question of how God retains self-identity. Given a dipolar theism, these problems need no longer exist.

In his version of dipolar theism, Whitehead distinguished between two natures of God: the primordial and the consequent. The "primordial nature" of God is God as envisaging the primordial possibilities (which Whitehead called "eternal objects") with appetition for them to be realized in the world. The "consequent nature" of God, by contrast, is God as being influenced by the world, receiving the experiences of the worldly actual entities into the divine experience. The distinction between the primordial and consequent natures, therefore, did double duty, distinguishing not only (1) between God as unchanging and changing, but also (2) between God as influencing the world and being influenced by it. Problems were created, however, because Whitehead tried to use the same distinction to serve these quite different purposes. One resulting problem is that by attributing God's causal influence in the world solely to the primordial nature, which is eternal in the sense of timeless and unchanging, Whitehead fails to explain how God can provide ideal aims to the world that are relevant to its present condition. Whitehead affirmed that God provides "particular providence for particular occasions."[58] But he did not explain how such providence could be provided by the eternal side of God's reality alone. Indeed, in the passage in which he affirmed this particular providence, he attributed it to God's *consequent* nature, thereby implying that his doctrine requires revision.

---

57. Hartshorne, "Whitehead and Contemporary Philosophy," 26.
58. Whitehead, *Process and Reality*, 351.

This implied need for revision is shown even more clearly by the multiple ways in which Whitehead's doctrine of God violates one of his own most famous declarations, namely, that "God is not to be treated as an exception to all metaphysical principles," but as "their chief exemplification."[59] One way in which he violates this is based on the fact that the primordial nature of God is, precisely as a "nature," a mere abstraction from God, not a full-fledged actuality. Whitehead himself points this out, saying that God "in this abstraction" is "deficiently actual."[60] And yet Whitehead attributes causal efficacy to this nature, thereby violating his own "ontological principle," according to which only full-fledged actualities, not mere abstractions, can exert causation. Likewise, Whitehead attributes God's conscious knowledge of the world to God's "consequent nature," which violates his own principle that a nature, being an abstraction, cannot have experience.

The two problems discussed above, plus some more to be discussed below, are all rooted in a doctrine that makes Whitehead's God violate metaphysical principles in a second way. That is, Whitehead referred to God as a single, everlasting actual entity (rather than as an everlasting personally ordered society of divine occasions of experience). As we saw above, however, the idea of an actual entity that "remains numerically one amidst the changes of accidental relations" is said to be a *metaphysical* error.[61] In describing God as such an actual entity, therefore, Whitehead clearly violated his own dictum that God should not be treated as an exception to metaphysical principles.

The fact that Whitehead thought of God as a single, everlasting actual entity, furthermore, led him to think of the divine dipolarity as an instance of the distinction between the physical and mental poles of an actual entity. He thereby spoke of the primordial nature as God's mental (or conceptual) pole and of the consequent nature as God's physical pole.[62] These identifications meant, however, that he had to speak of a reversal of poles: If the mental pole is "primordial" and the physical pole is "consequent," then the mental pole must be said to be prior to the physical pole.[63] This reversal arguably involves making God an exception to a third metaphysical principle, because it would seem to be a metaphysical principle that an actual entity's mental pole arises out of its physical pole. Whitehead's definition of God as an everlasting actual entity results, furthermore, in a fourth violation. On the one hand, it seems to be a metaphysical principle that contemporary actual entities are causally independent of each other. On the

59. Ibid., 343.
60. Ibid.
61. Ibid., 79.
62. Ibid., 88, 345.
63. Ibid., 348.

other hand, God, as an everlasting actual entity, said to be contemporary (in unison of becoming) with all worldly actual entities, is also said both to influence the world and to be influenced by it, neither of which should be possible. (A. H. Johnson reports that when he asked Whitehead about this problem in 1936, Whitehead replied: "This is a genuine problem. I have not attempted to solve it."[64])

For all the suggestiveness of Whitehead's discussion of God, then, it is riddled with problems. As serious as these problems are, however, they do not imply inconsistency in process theology as such, because these problems do not follow from any of the core principles. Indeed, other process theologians, especially Hartshorne and Cobb, have developed revised doctrines that, besides avoiding the various problems in Whitehead's own doctrine, are more consistent with his basic principles.

In Hartshorne's doctrine, God is conceived by analogy not to a single actual occasion but to a living person, so that God is a personally ordered society of divine occasions of experience. The divine dipolarity is not, therefore, based on the distinction between the physical and mental poles of a single actual entity. Defined as the distinction between God's "abstract essence" and "concrete states," it is analogous to the distinction between, on the one hand, a person's general character and, on the other hand, his or her concrete experiences, each of which instantiates that general character. Analogously to the way in which a person's character remains (virtually) the same over considerable periods of time, even though his or her concrete states involve constant changes from moment to moment, God's abstract essence remains (absolutely) the same, even though God's concrete states, which involve God's responses to the (changing) world, involve changes from moment to moment.

Hartshorne's dipolarity, then, is aimed at showing how God can be both unchanging and changing, both eternal and temporal. The most important distinction to Whitehead—that between God as influencing the world and being influenced by it—is not rejected in Hartshorne's writings, but it is also not emphasized. This one-sidedness is overcome in Cobb's 1965 book, *A Christian Natural Theology,* in which a chapter on "Whitehead's Doctrine of God" is followed by one called "A Whiteheadian Doctrine of God." Cobb develops a doctrine that, by combining the strengths of both Whitehead's and Hartshorne's treatments, overcomes the exceptions to metaphysical principles involved in Whitehead's doctrine and gives equal emphasis to the two dipolarities. Although it took some time for a coherent doctrine expressing it in an intelligible way to be formulated, naturalistic theism with

---

64. A. H. Johnson, "Some Conversations with Whitehead Concerning God and Creativity," in *Explorations in Whitehead's Philosophy*, ed. Lewis S. Ford and George L. Kline (New York: Fordham University Press, 1983), 3–13, especially 10.

this double dipolarity—distinguishing both between God as influencing the world and being influenced by it and between God as changing and unchanging—should be included among the core doctrines of process theology.

Summary and Conclusion

Process theology should not be identified with all the beliefs of any of its representatives, even those of its founders, but with a few interrelated doctrines at its core, which determine what else can be coherently said. Assessments of the adequacy and helpfulness of process theology should be made primarily in the light of these core doctrines, which have allowed and even encouraged various Christian process theologians, in the light of new concerns and new evidence, to formulate positions that go beyond those of the founders of the movement. This creative development can be expected to continue as theologians from other religious traditions appropriate the core doctrines of process theology to help articulate the distinctive experiences and insights of their traditions. These new positions will equally be examples of process theology, as long as the core doctrines are retained. Members of other traditions, of course, may have new suggestions as to the identification of the core doctrines of process theology, or at least as to which core doctrines to emphasize.[65]

Response to Professor Griffin

James McLachlan

OF THE MANY THEOLOGICAL POSITIONS IN CHRISTIANITY, process theology may be one of the most attractive to members of The Church of Jesus Christ of Latter-day Saints who willingly engage in theological dialogue with Christians and members of other world faiths. Process theologians have repudiated the doctrine of creation ex nihilo and reinterpreted the nature of God along lines radically different from traditional Christian theology. Moreover, process theologians believe in what David Ray Griffin calls "theological freedom," that the individual has the power

---

65. Since writing this essay in 1996, I have written and published *Reenchantment without Supernaturalism: A Process Philosophy of Religion* (Ithaca: Cornell University Press, 2001), in which I use much of the material in this essay. In that later discussion, however, I expand the number of core doctrines to ten.

of self-determination even in relation to God. They speak of a plurality of essential, self-caused beings who come together in the unity of the divine life and consider time to be ultimately real. Latter-day Saints should find some of process theology's concepts familiar, compatible, and attractive. Some LDS writers have already appealed to or collaborated with process theologians. For instance, Alfred North Whitehead and Charles Hartshorne, the founders of process theology, have been cited in the writings of several Church authorities and scholars,[66] and Mormon philosopher Truman Madsen and process theologian John Cobb Jr. coauthored the entry on theodicy in the *Encyclopedia of Mormonism*.[67]

However, the seeming rejection of personal life after death by such well-known process thinkers as Whitehead, Hartshorne, and Schubert Ogden has led some Christian theologians to reject process theology. Professor Griffin cites, as an example, Austin Farrer's objections to process theology.[68] Farrer claims that Hartshorne's God is "human enough

---

66. See Victor L. Brown in *132nd Semi-annual Conference of The Church of Jesus Christ of Latter-day Saints* (Salt Lake City: The Church of Jesus Christ of Latter-day Saints, 1962), 27; Delbert Stapley in *Official Report of the 139th Annual Conference of The Church of Jesus Christ of Latter-day Saints* (Salt Lake City: The Church of Jesus Christ of Latter-day Saints, 1969), 44; Hugh W. Nibley, *Approaching Zion* (Salt Lake City: Deseret, and Provo, Utah: Foundation for Ancient Research and Mormon Studies, 1989) 533, 542; Hugh W. Nibley, *Enoch the Prophet* (Salt Lake City: Deseret, and Provo, Utah: Foundation for Ancient Research and Mormon Studies, 1986), 83–84; Hugh W. Nibley, *The Ancient State* (Salt Lake City: Deseret, and Provo, Utah: Foundation for Ancient Research and Mormon Studies, 1991), 314, 391–92, 426–27, 436; Hugh W. Nibley, *The World and the Prophets* (Salt Lake City: Deseret, and Provo, Utah: Foundation for Ancient Research and Mormon Studies, 1987), 288–89, 297–98, 309; Garland E. Tickemyer, "Joseph Smith and Process Theology," *Dialogue: A Journal of Mormon Thought* 17 (Autumn 1984), 75–85; David L. Paulsen, "Reassessing Joseph Smith's Theology in His Bicentennial," *BYU Studies* 45, no. 1 (2006): 112–17; Blake T. Ostler, *Exploring Mormon Thought: The Attributes of God*, 2 vols. (Salt Lake City: Kofford, 2001), 1, 28, 43–64, 474–75; Blake T. Ostler, *Exploring Mormon Thought: The Problems of Theism and the Love of God*, 2 vols. (Salt Lake City: Kofford, 2006), 2, 72.

67. John Cobb and Truman G. Madsen, "Theodicy," in *Encyclopedia of Mormonism*, ed. Daniel H. Ludlow, 4 vols. (New York: Macmillan, 1992), 4:1473–74. Truman Madsen wrote a very favorable review of John Cobb's A *Christian Natural Theology* in *BYU Studies* 6, no. 3 (1965): 186. In addition, Madsen cites significant agreement between Latter-day Saints and process theologians; i.e., that God must include becoming as well as being. He refers to a personal correspondence with Charles Hartshorne. Truman G. Madsen, "Are Christians Mormon?" *BYU Studies* 15, no. 1 (1974): 75.

68. See also Austin Farrer, "Prior Actuality of God," in *Reflective Faith*.

to have a natural need of his creatures" but not "divine enough to save their souls alive" (Griffin, 162).[69]

Latter-day Saint beliefs in personal immortality and a universal resurrection are also inconsonant with an eschatology limited to the Whiteheadian/Hartshornean doctrine of objective immortality where the creature persists only as a memory in the mind of God. Indeed, this doctrine is much further from LDS understanding than the traditional Christian notions of heaven for the blessed and an eternal hell for the damned that Latter-day Saints have repudiated. At the heart of the LDS doctrine of everlasting life is the belief that "[God's] work and [God's] glory [is] to bring to pass the immortality and eternal life of man" (Moses 1:39).

In "Process Theology: What It Is and What It Is Not," Professor Griffin offers a defense of process theology by distinguishing its core doctrines from conflicting beliefs held by various process theologians. For example, Griffin classifies critiques like Farrer's as misunderstandings of process theology's core doctrines. Griffin himself and his Claremont colleague, John Cobb, both affirm life after death. Both Whitehead and Hartshorne, process founders, reject it, at the same time admitting its possibility. Thus, according to Professor Griffin, the rejection of life after death is not among the core doctrines of process theology. This fact should make process theology potentially more attractive to Latter-day Saints. In a way similar to some Latter-day Saints, some process thinkers see the person as a progressing string of *actual occasions* moving through the everlasting reality of time. This is similar to the LDS belief in life after death as eternal progression.[70]

Griffin is certainly right when he claims that for the purposes of understanding process theology we need to clarify and distinguish core process doctrines from those that may be held by individual process thinkers. Process theology may be based on the thought of Whitehead and Hartshorne, but it cannot be reduced to everything they said. In his essay, Professor Griffin has outlined seven core doctrines of process theology: (1) hard-core commonsense presuppositions as the main test of adequacy; (2) panexperientialism with organizational duality; (3) nonsensory perception; (4) persons as personally ordered societies; (5) internal relatedness; (6) naturalistic theism; and (7) dipolar theism. Each of these

---

69. Austin Farrer, *Faith and Speculation*, 170.

70. This idea of continued life beyond the death of the body makes process thought appealing to Buddhists also, as it resonates with Buddhist ideas of rebirth. Also, the individual may cease to exist as an individual when the drive toward perfection is satisfied as is the case in some interpretations of Buddhist enlightenment. Cobb and Griffin, *Process Theology*, 124–25. See also Griffin, *God and Religion*, 25–27.

could be fruitfully compared with LDS doctrines, but I have chosen to focus my response on the three core doctrines of process theology that seem most closely related to LDS thought: (1) hard-core common sense in relation to process theology's doctrines of freedom and creativity; (2) naturalistic theism; and (3) dipolar theism.

Hard-Core Common Sense and Core Doctrines of Freedom and Agency

Hard-core common sense "is based on the conviction that there are some notions that we all inevitably presuppose in practice, even if we deny them verbally" (Griffin, 166). Under this heading Griffin discusses the existence of other persons and things besides ourselves and the fact that things really do sometimes go wrong. Accepting such practical realities means that process theologians rule out solipsism from the beginning and reject any claims that evil is only apparent and not actual. Key among elements of hard-core common sense is the doctrine of freedom. Process theology rejects determinism, in part because determinism can only be affirmed theoretically. A person cannot practically live as a determinist, for each individual inevitably lives as if she makes choices that will affect her future.

In *God and Religion in the Postmodern World*, Griffin discusses three ways that freedom has been thought of in the Western theological tradition. He designates these: cosmological, theological, and axiological freedom.[71] Cosmological freedom is freedom in relation to other finite things in the cosmos. It is accepted by traditional theists, like Augustine, who locate human freedom in relation to the created realm, though not in relation to God's power or knowledge. This type of freedom is compatible with predestination or with strong doctrines of God's foreknowledge and omnipotence. Creatures are free within time and space, but God, who is in eternity, knows the actions and choices of each creature. Thus, Augustine and Calvin's doctrines of predestination enjoy vindication under the banner of cosmological freedom.

Process theology goes beyond cosmological freedom to affirm theological freedom, or freedom in relation to God. Theological freedom assumes a given creature has a degree of self-determination in relation to divine power and, at least, some axiological freedom, the freedom to actualize ideals according to that creature's individual goals, desires, and aspirations. Griffin says that to believe in axiological freedom is to believe that one can consciously decide "to live more fully in accord with the divine

---

71. Griffin, *God and Religion*, 113–15.

will."[72] This emphasis on theological and axiological freedom stems from the key assertion in process theology that creativity is not reserved to God but is an essential element of every entity in the universe,[73] which might appeal to Latter-day Saints, who also maintain conviction in theological and axiological freedom.

Theological and axiological freedom are related to Whitehead's basic principle of process thought: creativity. Creativity involves the bringing into being of new realities from pre-existing events or materials. Creativity is, thus, not reserved to God alone but is an essential characteristic of all reality. This is related to other hard-core commonsense doctrines, such as the real existence of others who are as free as I am and have an actual ability to resist God's purposes and frequently do. The centrality of freedom and creativity informs process thought's core doctrines concerning the character of God: naturalistic theism and dipolar theism.

Naturalistic Theism and Dipolar Theism

In naturalistic theism, God and the world presuppose each other. Creativity is a central idea that extends from subatomic particles to living cells to minds and souls. God does not create unilaterally, but inspires the creatures to create themselves and in turn God is created in relation to them. Thus, God is dipolar, being both eternal and temporal. The eternal cosmic ideal entails His reciprocal relation to creatures, and thus God is capable of change and growth. God is the ultimate example of a relational being, drawing persons toward self-creation. This creativity is the *imago dei*. God is the great artist creating beauty out of the chaotic world, the cosmic adventurer drawing the creation to higher and higher states of order, and a part of the universe not ontologically different from His creatures with whom He is mutually interdependent.

For Whitehead and process theologians, God's creativity and dipolar nature necessarily mean that God is not the metaphysical ultimate.[74] In *Science and the Modern World*, Whitehead argues that if God were the metaphysical ultimate, the ground of all being, God would also be the source of evil: "If this conception be adhered to, there can be no alternative except to discern in Him the origin of all evil as well as of all good. He is then the supreme author of the play, and to Him must be ascribed its shortcomings, as well as, its success."[75] Whitehead contends that creativity

---

72. Ibid., 113–15.

73. Whitehead, *Process and Reality*, 7.

74. Cobb, *Christian Natural Theology*, 142.

75. Whitehead, *Science and the Modern World*, 161.

is the metaphysical ultimate.[76] God engages in a *mutually creative action* with creatures, thereby bringing the creation from chaos to cosmos. For this reason, process theology rejects creation ex nihilo.

For Whitehead, the history of Christianity constitutes a tragic failure precisely because it has tried to make God the sole ground of all being. The failure consists in seeing God as the divine despot imposing laws on the world. Christian theology, as valuable as it is and has been for the growth of Western civilization, has conceived God as a coercive power in the form of a Roman emperor or Byzantine *Basileus*. In *Adventures of Ideas*, Whitehead calls for a return to the original intuitions of Christianity, which are much nearer to persuasion and the aims of civilization.[77] Christianity failed when it cut the finite off from God and created an infinite gulf between God and the world. God became Caesar. God became eminently real, but the world was derivative; God was necessary to the world, but the world was not necessary to God. Mysticism, which existed on the fringe of theology, became the only way to bridge the gulf and the only way to experience God in the world.[78] For Whitehead, religion prevails only when it can render clear to the popular understanding "*the eternal greatness of the passing of a temporal fact.*"[79] What must be achieved by religion is emphasis on the intimate relation between God and the world, the eternal and the finite. The goal of theology, as it is the aim of civilization, must be "a reconciliation of [these] seeming incompatibilities."[80]

---

76. In *A Christian Natural Theology*, John Cobb points out that Whitehead never argues that creativity "exists," rather, it is a characteristic of actual entities:

> Creativity is specifically described as one of the ultimate notions that along with "many" and "one" are "involved in the meaning of the synonymous terms 'thing' 'being,' and 'entity.'" We cannot think of an entity except as a unity of self-creativity in which the many factors of the universe become one individual thing which then becomes a part of the many for creative synthesis into a new one. (206)

In the same sense no Latter-day Saint would think that agency "exists" but would not think of intelligences except as agents.

77. In *Adventures of Ideas*, Whitehead writes, "The nature of God was exempted from all the metaphysical categories, which apply to the individual things in this temporal world. The concept of him was a sublimation from its barbaric origin. He stood in the same relation to the whole World as early Egyptian or Mesopotamian kings stood to their subject populations. Also the moral characters were very analogous." Whitehead, *Adventures of Ideas*, 169.

78. Ibid., 173.

79. Ibid., 40; emphasis added.

80. Ibid., 173.

Charles Hartshorne claims that the failure of traditional Christian theology is based, in part, on a monopolar idea of deity that sees God only in terms of attributes like eternity, simplicity, impassivity, and omnipotence. These beliefs led theologians like St. Anselm to reject compassion as inherent in God's nature because if God is moved by our suffering, and thus changes in some respects, God would have to change in all respects. So, if God's perfection is defined as changelessness, God cannot be compassionate—for to be compassionate is to be moved by another's misery. Hartshorne argues that the tradition has only emphasized one aspect of perfection (changelessness, self-sufficiency, etc.), ascribing these to deity while granting only derivative reality to aspects like temporality and relation. He argues that God must be seen as the preeminent example of both aspects. Hartshorne's division of the poles is as follows:

Classical Divinity	Creaturely Being
(Perfect Being)	(Deficient Being)
Being Itself, Infinite	Finite
Necessary	Contingent
Independent	Dependent
Absolute	Relative
Pure Act	Potentiality
Impassible	Passive
Changeless	Changing
Eternal *(Nunc Stans)*	Temporal *(Nunc Fluens)*

Process theology is concerned with the religious sense of perfection. Hartshorne accepts from Anselm the idea that God (Perfection) is that which is supremely worshipful, estimable, and unsurpassably great: that being which none is greater than and which none can surpass. However, Anselm's traditional notion of perfection eliminates the second column of attributes from the divine nature. But the process theologian asks, are dependence, relatedness, potentiality, change, and temporality *always* deficient attributes? For the traditional theologian, change cannot be allowed in our conception of the perfect being. Assuming God is presently perfect, he reasons as follows: If God changes, then God changes either for the worse or for the better. If for the worse, we cannot admire God without exception for God is no longer what God was. If God changes for the better, we must say God lacked something. Therefore, change cannot be allowed in God.

Hartshorne argues that there is really no reason to suppose that God cannot change. Is not divinity supremely worthy of worship and admiration if it undergoes increasing change for the better? Do we admire someone less because we know he/she would be happier tomorrow because his/her daughter would be cured of a present affliction? Certainly not. Therefore, if God rejoices less today than he/she would tomorrow if the world were better, would we admire God less? Or, is such independence admirable? If God is dependent in any way, do we admire God less? Hartshorne's point is that in almost every way we conceive of perfection in relation to creatures, dependence and relatedness are valued as perfections. In the world as we know it, do we not believe that the higher the being, the greater the dependence, indebtedness, sensitivity, and perturbability?

> Imagine someone to read aloud an eloquent poem in the presence of: (A) a glass of water, (B) an ant, (C) a dog, (D) a human being unacquainted with the language of the poem, (E) a human being knowing the language but insensitive to poetry, or (F) a person sensitive to poetry and familiar with the language.[81]

In the preceding example, it is the beings that are the most open to influence that we normally regard as the most perfect. Process theology notes that the greater the power we ascribe to creatures, the greater is our concept of God as the author of creatures.

Thus, the point at issue is not whether God is perfect, but rather whether one's *conception* of God's perfection is *correct, practical,* and *reasonable*. Process theologians, like Mormons, are not modern critics of the nature of God. They are modern critics of a specific *model* for the nature of God.

Can we worship a God who does not have profound sympathy for our misery? Can we worship a God who does not rejoice in our joys and is not moved by the tragedies of the world? The ontological presuppositions of nonrelativity and impassivity (pure act, etc.) in God *preclude* a personal relationship between God and the world. Process theology, therefore, assigns to divinity a dipolar nature; i.e., necessary *and* contingent aspects comprise divinity and, through the latter, God is necessarily related to the world.

These distinctions have and will prove fundamental in distinguishing LDS conceptions of God from traditional Christian conceptions. Joseph Smith rejected the traditional conception of God. The Latter-day Saint doctrine of the relation of God and persons concerns the literal humanity of God and the potential divinity of human beings. Joseph Smith set out this doctrine most clearly in his 1844 funeral sermon for King Follet:

> God himself was once as we are now, and is an exalted man, and sits enthroned in yonder heavens! That is the great secret. If the veil were rent today, and the great God who holds this world in its orbit, and who

---

81. Charles Hartshorne, *The Divine Relativity: A Social Conception of God* (New Haven: Yale University Press, 1948), 49.

upholds all worlds and all things by his power, was to make himself visible,—I say, if you were to see him today, you would see him like a man in form—*like yourselves in all the person, image, and very form as a man.*[82]

He continued:

> I am dwelling on the immortality of the spirit of man. Is it logical to say that the intelligence of spirits is immortal, and yet that it had a beginning? The intelligence of spirits had not beginning, neither will it have an end. That is good logic. That which has a beginning may have an end. There never was a time when there were not spirits; for they are co-equal [co-eternal] with our Father in heaven.
>
> Intelligence is eternal and exists upon a self-existent principle. It is a spirit from age to age, and there is no creation about it. All the minds and spirits that God ever sent into the world are susceptible of enlargement. . . .
>
> The first principles of man are self-existent with God. God himself, finding he was in the midst of spirits of glory, because he was more intelligent, saw proper to institute laws *whereby the rest could have a privilege to advance like himself.*[83]

While God is conceived to be a literal Father of spirits, the logical corollary, attributed to Joseph Smith and developed by the LDS poet Eliza R. Snow, was that there is also a literal mother in heaven. As early as 1839, the Prophet Joseph Smith taught the concept of an eternal mother, as reported in several accounts from that period.[84] Out of this teaching came a poem penned by Eliza R. Snow, "O My Father":

> In the heavens are parents single?
> No, the thought makes reason stare!
> Truth is reason; truth eternal
> Tells me *I've a mother there.*
>
> When I leave this frail existence,
> When I lay this mortal by,
> Father, *Mother,* may I meet you
> In your royal courts on high?[85]

---

82. Joseph Smith Jr., "The King Follet Discourse," in *History of The Church of Jesus Christ of Latter-day Saints*, ed. B. H. Roberts, 2d ed., rev., 7 vols. (Salt Lake City: Deseret, 1978), 6:305; emphasis added.

83. Smith, "King Follet Discourse," 311–12.

84. Jill Mulvay Derr, "The Significance of 'O My Father' in the Personal Journey of Eliza R. Snow," *BYU Studies* 36, no. 1 (1996–97): 98.

85. *Hymns of The Church of Jesus Christ of Latter-Day Saints* (Salt Lake City: Church of Jesus Christ of Latter-day Saints, 1985) no. 292; emphasis added.

This poem was set to music and has become a popular Mormon hymn. In the October 1893 General Conference, President Wilford Woodruff declared it a revelation.[86] This doctrine was formalized in 1909 when the First Presidency of the Church, under Joseph F. Smith, issued the statement "On the Origin of Man," which teaches that humanity is the literal offspring of a Father and Mother in Heaven:

> The Father of Jesus is our Father also. Jesus Himself taught this truth, when He instructed His disciples how to pray: "Our Father which art in heaven," etc. Jesus, however, is the firstborn among all the sons of God—the first begotten in the spirit, and the only begotten in the flesh. He is our elder brother, and we, like Him, are in the image of God. All men and women are in the similitude of the universal Father and Mother, and are literally the sons and daughters of Deity.[87]

LDS church leader B. H. Roberts was among the first to really attempt a systematic apology for the LDS idea of God, asserting that Joseph Smith's doctrine of the co-eternality of God and persons is not polytheism.[88] Roberts develops an idea of the oneness of God through what he calls the "generic idea of God" in which humanity participates in the Divine Nature. In this sense, God is defined as human beings who have arrived at an identification with basic reality—beings who have become morally perfect. The Divine Nature, to which all divine beings attain, is One:

> Man being by the very nature of him a son of God, and a participant in the Divine Nature—he is properly a part of God; that is, when God is conceived of in the generic sense, as made up of the *whole assemblage* of divine Intelligences that exist in all heavens and all earths.[89]

Elsewhere, Roberts notes the interrelationship between God, the supreme intelligence, and other intelligences, God's children. This relation is mutually interdependent: God cannot be perfect without us nor we without God.

> To this Supreme Intelligence are the other intelligences necessary? He without them cannot be perfect, nor they without him. There is community of interest between them; also of love and brotherhood; and hence community of effort for mutual good, for progress, or attainment

---

86. Derr, "Significance of 'O My Father,'" 98.

87. James R. Clark, ed., *Messages of the First Presidency of The Church of Jesus Christ of Latter-day Saints* [1833–1951], 6 vols. (Salt Lake City: Bookcraft, 1965–1975), 4:203.

88. B. H. Roberts, *The Mormon Doctrine of Deity* (Salt Lake City: Deseret News Press, 1903), 163. Quoting Mormon scripture, Roberts affirms that "Man was also in the beginning with God. Intelligence . . . was not created or made, neither indeed can be" (D&C 93: 29).

89. Roberts, *Mormon Doctrine of Deity*, 166.

of the highest possible. Therefore are these eternal, Divine Intelligences drawn together in oneness of mind and purpose—in moral and spiritual unity.[90]

Thus, LDS doctrine asserts the importance of community in order for God to be God.

There is a good deal of the Latter-day Saint doctrine of God that is amenable to interpretation via process theology, which includes a dipolar conception of God as both infinite and finite because God and creation are mutually interdependent, temporal, and related genetically and in the "generic" ideal of perfection, which arises out the fact of their mutual relationship. The ideal, unlike Platonic forms or Whitehead's eternal objects, exists only in the being of actual beings. There is an element in humanity, "intelligence," that is self-existent and free in the strong sense of that term, meaning free in relation to God. In LDS scriptures, these self-existent beings participate in the creation of the world from the beginning (see Abraham 3–4). This sense of freedom and creativity in LDS doctrine is shared with process theology.

Latter-day Saints, who, like process thinkers, reject creation ex nihilo on the grounds that it is not compatible with freedom and creativity, also accept that God is not the metaphysical ultimate and sole ground of being. Joseph Smith indicated that both God and "man" are "self-existing" beings.[91] There are a variety of ways that Latter-day Saints can talk about this doctrine theologically other than via process theology, but they cannot return to traditional theism. This does not mean that Latter-day Saints and process theologians have to abandon theism. This would be the case only if we regarded theism as the sole province of Christians in the Platonic/Aristotelian tradition that goes back to the early church fathers; well intentioned as theism was, for Latter-day Saints it has often been seen as one of the sources of the "Apostasy."[92]

In *God and Religion in the Postmodern World*, Griffin puts forward a generic idea of God. "God is (1) the Supreme Power, (2) the personal, purposive creator of our world, who is (3) perfectly good, (4) the source of moral norms, (5) the ultimate guarantee for the meaningfulness of human life, (6) ground for the hope in the ultimate victory over evil, (7) alone worthy of

---

90. B. H. Roberts, *A Comprehensive History of The Church of Jesus Christ of Latter-day Saints, Century One*, 6 vols. (Provo, Utah: Corporation of the President, The Church of Jesus Christ of Latter-day Saints, 1965), 2:399.

91. Smith, "King Follet Discourse," 307–9.

92. James E. Talmage, *The Great Apostasy* (Salt Lake City: The Church of Jesus Christ of Latter-day Saints, 1968). Talmage describes the "Apostasy" as a falling away from the true doctrine as taught by Christ and the loss of the Church as organized by the Savior.

worship."[93] Latter-day Saints could agree with Griffin on this conception of God, which does not require creation ex nihilo as a guarantee of divine omnipotence. This also places God with us, within the universe. The idea is quite different from what Griffin characterizes as the supernaturalistic idea of the relation of God and world that became normative for traditional Christian theology. In the "extreme voluntarism" of Western theology, the only reason anything and everything (including evil) exists is solely due to the omnipotent will of God.[94]

Griffin argues that many contemporary problems of nuclear weapons and imperialism are related to worship and imitation of raw power because human beings try to imitate what they regard as ultimately real. Latter-day Saints should find Griffin's analysis appealing because it is so similar to the rejection of Satan, the father of lies. The power of evil is coercive. In section 121 of the Doctrine and Covenants, coercion is ruled out as a possible righteous activity of either human beings or God (see Doctrine and Covenants [D&C] 12:39–42). In The Pearl of Great Price, Satan advocates the use of coercive force to guarantee the moral submission of humanity (Moses 4:4). God and Christ reject Satan's proposal in favor of divine persuasion and agency for all. There is a strong sense in LDS doctrine that Satan's coercive plan is a lie from the beginning, because it is rejection of reality itself, which is founded in the agency, creativity, and co-eternality of intelligences. The idea of God as a non-coercive Father is such an important part of LDS doctrine that in the Book of Mormon the prophet Alma states that were God to coerce our repentance, mercy would rob justice and "God would cease to be God" (Alma 42:13, 22, 25). For Latter-day Saints, like Whitehead, freedom or creativity is the metaphysical ultimate, and, like Whitehead, creativity/freedom does not "exist" but is a property of persons (intelligences). This is the significance of Roberts's generic idea of God.

Some LDS Reservations about Process Theology

Latter-day Saints place main emphasis on the moral element of our relation with God, each other, and the world. Griffin and Cobb have asserted that process theology rejects any view of God as "cosmic moralist." They assert that process theology rejects the idea that "God's most fundamental concern is the development of moral attitudes. This makes primary for God what is secondary for humane people, and limits the scope of intrinsic importance to human beings as the only beings capable of moral attitudes. Process theology denies the existence of this God."[95] This emphasis on the richness

---

93. Griffin, God and Religion, 77.

94. Ibid., 132.

95. Cobb and Griffin, Process Theology: An Introductory Exposition, 8.

of experience seems to equate love primarily with emotion and desire. But for Latter-day Saints, love has a moral element that is seen as respect and mutual relation that encloses and transcends emotion and desire.

With respect to life after death, the LDS church is a universalist religion. All beings have immortality through the atonement of Christ. Joseph Smith claimed that not only humans but animals and planets have eternal spirits (Moses 3:5, 19; 7:48–49; Abraham 3:18–19). Every creature is immortal, having everlasting life, but *"eternal life"* is interpreted as deification. Deification is almost always viewed in terms of developing the moral attitudes that lead to perfection and, consequently, an infinite task. The centrality of moral perfection in the universe elevates those humans who achieve moral perfection. This moral perfection is close to Martin Buber's I-Thou relation, where each person values the other in her uniqueness.[96] Thus, all will attain immortality, but only those who learn to love perfectly will attain godhood, eternal life. Eternal life is the life of a community whose love for each other is at the basis of reality itself. In the Doctrine and Covenants this eternal community is clearly stated:

> When the Savior shall appear we shall see him as he is. We shall see that he is a man like ourselves. And that same sociality which exists among us here will exist among us there, only it will be coupled with eternal glory, which glory we do not now enjoy. (D&C 130:1–2)

In the process theologian's vision, God loves creatures naturally: there is no choice, no moral decision, and no temptation toward egoism.[97] Here it seems that in the process view, God is open to the same attack that Hegel lodged against Kant's god. God's holy will actually prohibits God from being moral, for God has no experience of the temptation and choice experienced by human beings.

In LDS doctrine, God, like the God of process theology, is the "fellow sufferer who understands," but God cares, in part, because God, as a once finite and human person, developed compassion through the experience of temptation and suffering in human existence. God thus fully realizes how significant temptation and suffering are for human beings. In the Book of Mormon, Alma explains that it is only through the experience of the temptations and suffering of human existence that Christ becomes fully compassionate, fully loving, and fully moral:

> And he will take upon him death, that he may loose the bands of death which bind his people; and he will take upon him their infirmities, that his bowels may be filled with mercy, according to the flesh, that he may

---

96. See Martin Buber, *I and Thou* (New York: Scribner/Macmillan, 1988).
97. Griffin, *God and Religion*, 148.

> know according to the flesh how to succor his people according to their infirmities. (Alma 7:12)

Christ could not fully understand the suffering of this world until his immortal spirit-body became mortally embodied and fully human. Joseph Smith and B. H. Roberts describe God as a person, morally perfected in love, who is fully related to other persons. A part of this perfection has been the experience of life as a finite individual with all its temptations and imperfections. So, morality plays a fundamental role in the LDS universe.

Considering the nature of the universe, Griffin provides a beautiful summary of God as the *telos* of the activity of all creatures:

> In this sense, Whitehead says, truth, beauty and goodness provide "the final contentment for the [Divine] Eros of the universe." What we do in this regard, even in the inner recesses of our souls, is also important again, for it is known by the appreciative consciousness of the universe. The contribution we, thereby, make to the everlasting life of God is in fact the basis for the ultimate importance of our lives. Even if our lives do not continue beyond bodily death, they are of ultimate importance.[98]

He agrees with Whitehead and Hartshorne that God is the lure that pulls us beyond our natural egoism, but he also agrees that individual lives have ultimate importance, even if they are not eternal, because of their contribution to God. At this point, Latter-day Saints must part with process theologians, because for Latter-day Saints, individual persons are by their eternal nature of "ultimate importance" to themselves and not only God. From an LDS perspective, God's purpose and significance is the nurture and development of eternal life in and for us. All beings are eternal and free. Though process theology allows the possibility of life after death, Professor Griffin asserts that the "ultimate meaning" for the creature's existence is its *contribution to God, the enrichment of God's experience:*

> It is *not* my intention to develop and defend a conception of life after death in this chapter, and certainly not with any hint of certainty. Here, more than with most issues, we see in a glass darkly, if at all. But it is important to see that a meaningful idea of life after death does not necessarily include the problematic notion that life after death would be literally unending. By making this distinction, we retain the insight of Whitehead and Hartshorne that the *ultimate meaning of life consists in our contribution to God.*[99]

Process theologians have claimed that anthropocentrism, the idea that God created the universe for humanity alone, is a weakness of traditional Christian theology. This antipathy to anthropocentrism is understandable,

---

98. Ibid., 25.
99. Ibid., 107; emphasis added.

for certain interpretations of theism have lent themselves to the rape of the environment, which is seen as existing only for human consumption.[100] Anthropocentrism easily becomes arrogant about the place of humans in the universe.

Ultimately, in process theology there is a "theocentrism" in which the universe exists primarily for its contribution to God. For process theology, the emphasis is on wider and richer experiences for all individuals and ultimately God, who feels all their experiences. God needs and enjoys the experiences of all the beings of the universe. The experiences of complex beings, like humans, add more to God's experience because of their greater breadth and depth. Latter-day Saints view humanity not only as made in the "image," but as literally the offspring of God and, as previously stated, God's work and glory is the deification of humanity. From an LDS perspective even Griffin, Cobb, and Hartshorne have retained too much of traditional Christian theology. The process theologian criticizes traditional theism because the creature added nothing to God, but in process theology the creature exists primarily for her contribution to God. What then of the eternal importance of the creature's love for another creature independent of how this affects God?

Conclusion

There are many potentially fruitful points of contact between Mormonism and process thought. Both share a rejection of the doctrine of creation ex nihilo in favor of a strong doctrine of theological and axiological freedom. Both speak of a plurality of essential, self-caused beings who come together in the unity of the divine life. And both see creativity and freedom as essential characteristics of God, humanity, and all creation.

Latter-day Saint scholars interested in theology have already begun an interchange with process thinkers, and it is evident that process theology offers much to LDS scholars interested in explicating the theological implications of LDS teachings. In process theology's core doctrines, as outlined by Griffin, it seems evident that there are few, if any, theological options offered by the Western tradition as inviting to LDS thinkers as those that are offered by the tradition following Whitehead and Hartshorne.

---

100. Latter-day Saints and process theologians could agree on this, though it is impossible for both to avoid a certain anthropocentrism. Process theologians have argued against deep ecologists that humans have greater intrinsic value than other earthly creatures because humans have richer experiences of value. See Frederick Ferré, *Being and Value: Toward a Constructive Postmodern Metaphysics* (Albany: State University of New York Press, 1996), 297–304. Latter-day Saints see the earth itself as possessing a soul (Moses 7:56–58).

Nevertheless, Mormonism possesses unique doctrines of God and persons that are radically different from traditional theologies, even doctrines as radically different from the tradition as process theology.

Rejoinder

David Ray Griffin

I THANK JAMES MCLACHLAN FOR HIS THOUGHTFUL and irenic response to my essay, in which he carefully notes both similarities and divergences between LDS and process theologies. In this reply, I will discuss three matters. In the first section, I discuss a few misimpressions about process theology that some of McLachlan's comments might create. In the second section, I mention what I consider two especially strong points in LDS theology that McLachlan brings out. In the final section, I point to a possible self-contradiction in LDS theology suggested by McLachlan's essay.

Some Possible Misimpressions about Process Theology

Although McLachlan is fair and generally careful in his portrayal of process theology, a few of his comments could give some false impressions about process theology, in particular about its views on God, morality, and life after death.

Naturalistic and Dipolar Theism

McLachlan says that the God of process theism calls others to create themselves and "in turn God is created in relation to them" (McLachlan, 191). He also suggests that the divinity of God "undergoes increasing change for the better" (McLachlan, 193). These statements could give the impression that God's very deity or divinity has been self-created through interaction with the universe. According to process theology's dipolar theism, however, God has an abstract essence that is strictly immutable and impassible (thereby having characteristics attributed by classical theism to God as a whole, which is why Hartshorne likes to call this position neoclassical theism). For example, although God's concrete knowledge is always growing, because there are always new things to know, God's omniscience, understood as the abstract characteristic of always knowing whatever is (then) knowable, does not increase, because it is already maximal. Likewise, God does not become more loving, although God's concrete love is always growing, because there are always new creatures to love. So, although the full, concrete reality of God changes for the better, in the sense of being constantly enriched, God does not become more loving, intelligent, or divine. Process theists, accordingly, could not affirm the statement of Joseph Smith, quoted by McLachlan, that "God himself was once as we are now" (McLachlan, 194).

Similar qualifications would have to be made with regard to some of McLachlan's statements regarding dependence. Although it is true that, for process theology, "God and creatures are mutually dependent" (McLachlan, 191), this statement might be wrongly taken to imply that God is dependent on the creatures in exactly the same way as they are dependent on God. Creatures are dependent on God for their very existence (as well as for part of the actual content of their experience), whereas the divine existence is not dependent upon that of any particular creature. A related misimpression could be created by McLachlan's discussion of dependence and perfection (McLachlan, 193–94). He is certainly correct to emphasize Hartshorne's rejection of classical theism's implied contention that all independence is admirable, so that all dependence would betoken imperfection. But Hartshorne also points out that *some* forms of independence *are* admirable, such as ethical independence, in the sense of continuing to will and do the good no matter what happens.

These points can be brought out more clearly in terms of McLachlan's observation that the divine dipolarity means that God is both contingent and necessary. The present divine actuality, meaning God's present concrete experience, is contingent, being dependent upon the partially self-determining events that have occurred and continue to occur in our universe. But the bare fact that God exists as an omniscient, all-loving being is necessary, being independent of this or any other particular universe. Process theology does, to be sure, say that the universe of creatures is also necessary as well as contingent, in that *some* such universe exists just as necessarily as does God; this hypothesis is part and parcel of process thought's naturalistic theism. It remains the case, however, that God is the only *individual* who exists necessarily; the existence of the rest of us is purely contingent.

Also potentially misleading is McLachlan's statement that, for process theism, "God is a part of the universe." This statement is true in the sense that God is not wholly outside of "the universe," as if God could have existed without any universe at all. But it is potentially misleading insofar as it could be taken to mean that God's existence requires this particular universe, or that God is one more finite being among others within the all-embracing universe. As McLachlan points out later, process theism says that God is both finite *and* infinite (McLachlan, 197). As infinite, God is not limited temporally, having always existed, or spatially, being all-inclusively omnipresent—which means that instead of saying that God is part of the universe, one should say that the universe is in God (which is the meaning of pan-en-theism).

In sum, although I appreciate McLachlan's irenic effort to bring out the similarities between LDS and process theisms in their opposition to classical theism, it is also important not to suggest that process theism is closer to LDS theism, and thereby more remote from classical theism, than it really is.

God and Morality

In discussing the relation between God and morality, McLachlan finds problematic process theism's contention that God naturally and hence necessarily loves all creatures. The implication is, contends McLachlan, that the holiness of process theism's God "prohibits God from being moral" (McLachlan, 199). The issue here revolves around what we *mean* by being *ethically good*. As I had pointed out in the passage to which McLachlan refers, Hartshorne says that if it necessarily involved the idea of resisting temptation, then we could not say that God is ethically good. But, Hartshorne suggests, we have a broader notion of moral goodness, according to which it "means being motivated by concern for the interests of others," and this idea *does* apply to God. Indeed, Hartshorne says, in this sense "God alone is absolutely ethical."[101]

McLachlan also suggests that Mormonism lays far more emphasis on "the moral element of our relation with God, each other, and the world" than does process theology (McLachlan, 198). His basis for this claim is the statement, made by John Cobb and me, that process theology rejects the idea of God as "cosmic moralist" and thereby the idea that "God's most fundamental concern is the development of moral attitudes."[102] Like many others, however, McLachlan has evidently misunderstood the import of this statement. God's most fundamental concern, by hypothesis, is the increase of intrinsically satisfying experiences. But this notion, far from making morality less important, gives it divine support. Whether one describes the most general moral maxim in terms of working for the greatest happiness of experiencing creatures, treating them as ends in themselves, or respecting and promoting their rights, this theology says that, insofar as we do this, we are serving as agents of, and even imitating, God's own deepest purpose. If God is moral in the Hartshornean sense of "being motivated by concern for the interests of [all] others," then we can fulfill our desire to imitate deity only by cultivating such motivation. McLachlan says that process theology

101. Griffin, *God and Religion*, 143–44.

102. Cobb and Griffin, *Process Theology: An Introductory Exposition*, 8.

"seems to equate love primarily with emotion and desire" (McLachlan, 199). That is true if "emotion" is understood to mean "compassion" or "sympathy," both of which literally mean feeling the feelings of others as one's own, and if "desire" is understood to mean desiring the good of others. Love thus understood constitutes (by hypothesis) the two sides of the divine love.

Life after Death

With regard to the issue of life after death, McLachlan says that Mormons would agree with Austin Farrer that Hartshorne's God is not divine enough to save God's creatures' souls alive (McLachlan, 189). However, as I tried to make clear by distinguishing Hartshorne's personal views from process theology as such, the fact that Hartshorne personally does not believe in life after death does not mean that Hartshorne's God lacks the power to enable our souls to survive bodily death (a point that Hartshorne himself has granted in personal correspondence). This issue, however, leads to one of the especially strong features of LDS theology.

Two Especially Helpful Doctrines of LDS Theology

Limiting myself in this section to points somewhat distinctive of LDS theology that are raised by McLachlan's paper, I will discuss two doctrines of LDS theology through which it may have an especially helpful contribution to make to theology more broadly, and to process theology in particular.

The Importance of the Creatures' Love for Each Other

Having said that "in process theology the creature exists primarily for her contribution to God," McLachlan asks: "But what about the eternal importance of a creature's love for another creature independent of how this affects God?" (McLachlan, 201). Because life after death (as distinct from its possibility) is not included among the core doctrines of process theology and was not discussed by Whitehead and Hartshorne, there has been little discussion by process theologians of life after death and therefore of the issue McLachlan raises. Because I, with Whitehead and Hartshorne, use the term *eternal* to refer to the strictly nontemporal, I would revise his question to ask about the *everlasting* importance of our love for one another. Also, because I not only agree with them that importance for the finite ultimately implies importance for the infinite but also consider only God to be infinite, I would not think we could properly consider our love for each other to be ultimately independent of its importance for God. But I agree that process theology's attempt to account for our sense that life is ultimately meaningful could be enriched by considering the importance of our mutual love in a life that continues far beyond this present one.

Deification

Another feature of Mormon thought not usually included in process theology is the understanding of salvation as a process of deification. Although this idea has been central to Eastern Orthodoxy, it has had little place in Western (Augustinian) theology, out of which process theology grew. It would, however, be a good term to describe the process through which God creates and saves us, in that God becomes incarnate in each moment of experience in such a way that the divine forms that are possibilities for our existence enter into us, literally transforming us. Process theists, to be sure, could *not* understand our deification to mean that we would literally become divine in the sense of acquiring the metaphysical attributes that uniquely characterize the divine essence. We could, however, use the term to illuminate not only the nature but also the goal of God's constant efficacy in us—a goal that is easier to take seriously if we think of our journey with God as continuing far beyond the present life, so that there is time for the divine persuasion to overcome the tremendous gap that now exists, at least in most of us, between what we are and the best that we could be.

A Possible Self-Contradiction in LDS Theology

From my perspective as a process theologian, it appears that there is a contradiction between LDS doctrine of divine persuasion, on which it and process theology agree, and its appeal to a type of revelation that process theology could not support. On the one hand, says McLachlan, LDS theology appeals to the extrinsic authority of a particular revelation. As I use "extrinsic authority," it means that certain doctrines can be taken to be true solely or at least primarily because of the mode through which they allegedly came to us: namely, through a (relatively) infallible revelation from God. On the other hand, says McLachlan, Mormonism accepts the "idea of God as non-coercive" (McLachlan, 198), which means that the insistence by process theologians that "the creature has a degree of self-determination in relation to divine power" (McLachlan, 190) is endorsed by LDS theology (McLachlan, 197).

The question is: How can both of these doctrines be held? As I understand the idea that God's power is persuasive, as distinct from coercive, it implies that God cannot override either our own power of self-determination, through which we can resist and distort the direct divine influence on us, or the power of other creatures to influence us, thereby infecting us with ideas that are false, whether because of sinful distortion or simply the ignorance that is an inevitable aspect of finitude. There is no basis, therefore, for assuming that any human being, whether Jesus, Paul, or Joseph Smith, was protected from the cultural conditioning and other sources of fallibility that infect the thinking of the rest of us. Unless McLachlan is understanding either extrinsic authority or divine noncoercion in a different way, accordingly, I do not see how he (and other Latter-day Saints) can consistently affirm both ideas.

In any case, I thank McLachlan for his thought-provoking response, and wish him and Mormonism well.

Reply to Professor Griffin

James McLachlan

PROFESSOR GRIFFIN'S CLEAR DELINEATION OF SEVEN CORE BELIEFS of process theology challenges Latter-day Saints who wish to reflect theologically to similarly articulate the content of their core doctrines. Yet LDS theological reflection and formulation is still in its infancy; much is needed for Latter-day Saints to make their beliefs clear not only to outsiders but to their own faith community. One of the ironies inculcated by this situation is that some Latter-day Saints might find themselves in closer agreement with some of Griffin's criticisms of my presentation of LDS beliefs than with my presentation.

I appreciate Professor Griffin's corrections to the possible misimpressions of process theology that could be engendered by my discussion of naturalistic and dipolar theism. His clarifications have not only enhanced my understanding of these process core beliefs, but they have also helped me understand my own beliefs better. These increased understandings are among the fruits of dialogical conversations undertaken in good faith.

I think that one way that LDS theologians appropriate the process model to illuminate their own theological understanding would be via B. H. Roberts's "generic idea of God." In process terms, this idea of God can be equated with God's primordial nature or essence—that is, the set of properties (or attributes) severally necessary and jointly sufficient for divinity. As such, the divine nature is singular, impersonal, and changeless. The consequent nature of God, a moniker loaned from process thought, would be personal and changing in relation to the world and its creatures.

For an example of extreme consequent change, we read in Alma 42 that if God were to coerce us, even out of love and mercy, he (the consequent God) would cease to be God (the "generic" God). On this model, while the divine nature is necessarily changeless, the personal being who is God, through action or possibly inaction (allowing "mercy to rob justice") could cease to be God. As has been seen, the process distinction between God's primordial and consequent natures can illuminate LDS thinking on this issue.

I find a tension between LDS thought and process theology in the idea that God always needs a universe, though not this particular one. Once again I think that Latter-day Saints could accept this process conclusion if they understood "God" to refer to the divine nature or essence. However, as a Latter-day Saint, I believe the concrete personal Being who is historical is tied to the particular beings of this universe.

On the question of God and morality, I suspect many Latter-day Saints might actually side with Professor Griffin against me, for I think many Latter-day Saints would agree that God is determinately or necessarily good by nature. What I find problematic in process theism is the metaphysical guarantee of God's goodness, that God necessarily loves all creatures. This is an old objection against conventional theism that is found in Hegel's objection to Kant's doctrine of the holy will; is found in Camus' rejection of God, for moral reasons, as other than humanity in "The Myth of Sisyphus" and *The Rebel*; and is wonderfully stated by Ivan Karamazov's Grand Inquisitor in Dostoevsky's *The Brothers Karamazov*. In the latter instance, the Inquisitor asks Christ how a God who is necessarily immune to temptation can demand the free response from humans who are not powerful enough to resist the temptations of bread, security, and power. If one is naturally good and has no understanding, beyond an abstract one, of alienation, fear, and the temptation to despair, can we say that he or she really understands the other person and can demand moral goodness of them?

I agree with Professor Griffin that the issue here revolves around what we mean by being *morally good*. And I recognize the power of Hartshorne's position that God's goodness "means being motivated by concern for the interests of others," but I think this is a question of will and not simply natural necessity. Hartshorne's objection that a being who is always undergoing temptation is not really morally good is important here. It might be disturbing, for example, to think in relation to God's goodness that God is constantly being tempted by the desire to coerce us into being good. We could ask if such a being really is good. But I think that in this very quandary lies the strength of Joseph Smith's suggestion that even God was once human. On the basis of his firsthand experience, God remembers what it was like to be tempted. In becoming God, God has overcome temptation—but his godhood is a result of the exercise of will, not of metaphysical necessity. When Alma says that were God to coerce our repentance, even though acting out of his mercy, mercy would rob justice and "God would cease to be God" (Alma 42:13, 22, 25), it seems that it must be possible for God to do it. That is, it is metaphysically possible that God *could coerce* our response, but God *will* not do it. I suspect that Latter-day Saints accepting my objection about the goodness of God might still be able to appropriate even this aspect of process thought through the interpretation of Roberts's "generic Idea of God" that I suggested above. Generically or abstractly considered, God is necessarily good, whereas God as a person is God because of free acts of will.

A Possible Self-Contradiction in LDS Theology

I believe Professor Griffin sees a possible contradiction in LDS theology because I did not in my essay adequately explain what I take to be the LDS understanding of revelation as a continuing process. If I understand his objection correctly, Professor Griffin uses "extrinsic authority" in the sense of God's revelation of the timelessly eternal reality. Although Latter-day Saints often use the word "eternal," they understand it to refer to everlasting, not timeless, being. Latter-day Saints do not attribute infallibility to the scriptures because the scriptures are filtered through human understanding—whether by the prophets who received and wrote the message or we who are attempting to understand it. Even here the "external authority" of the revelation comes from the "call" of God. In seeing God as another person, Latter-day Saints understand God's revelation as "one person speaking to another"—whether this is "face to face" as in Joseph Smith's First Vision, through a messenger as in the visitation of the Angel Moroni, or, what is much more common, through the inspiration of the Holy Spirit. But Joseph Smith, or Paul, or anyone receiving inspiration, is not understood as completely free from their environment.

I think Latter-day Saints understand God's revelation as a call from another person who is awaiting our creative response. God is an infinitely wise and compassionate being who indicates through servants or directly through inspiration the basic guidelines that should govern our existence. But the message always comes through the filter of human understanding, and God asks for a creative, loving response on our part, not mere compliance. I would liken it to the call I see in the face of a loved one. In a sense they present me with an "external authority," a demand for a response. Whether and how I will respond is up to me. In this sense I don't see an essential difference between the LDS understanding of revelation and the process understanding of God as lure.

About the Authors

David Ray Griffin (Ph.D. Claremont Graduate University) did graduate work at the Claremont School of Theology, Johannes Gutenberg University in Mainz, Germany, and Claremont Graduate University. He is a founding co-director of the Center for Process Studies and the author of over thirty books and one hundred seventy-five essays. He is emeritus professor of philosophy and theology at the Claremont School of Theology and Claremont Graduate University.

James McLachlan (Ph.D. University of Toronto) did graduate work at the Université de Paris/Sorbonne, Indiana University, and Pennsylvania State University before beginning his doctorate program in religious studies at the University of Toronto. He has taught philosophy at Brigham Young University, was a visiting scholar at Claremont School of Theology, and is professor of philosophy and chair of the Department of Philosophy and Religion at Western Carolina University.

A Dialogue on Liberation Theology

Liberation as a Faith Option

Robert McAfee Brown

It has been my fate—or more accurately my privilege—to write many words about liberation theology since that moment in 1971 when a reading of the galley proofs of Gustavo Gutiérrez's *A Theology of Liberation* inverted my theological world.[1] Nevertheless, I cannot, a quarter of a century later, reduce the insights of liberation theology to a systematic treatise, with all the familiar headings and subheadings that mark out such a work.

For one thing, liberation theology is still in its infancy, when measured against other theologies treated in this volume. For another, it is the product of engagement with the poor, much more than an intellectual dialogue between the rich. And it is more a new *method* than a new *content*, which the following pages will try to advance. It is volatile and new enough so that much of its inherited vocabulary has already been rendered time bound.

But the arena of discussion must really be the locales of injustice and corrupt social structures more than creating comparative doctrines of, say, atonement or soteriology. Liberation theologians have not sold out to ethicists concerning their basic subject matter, but have proposed a new ethic, theological to the core and challenging to those who have not yet been confronted by it.

A final caveat to keep the record clear: the true creators of liberation theology are the poor. I am not poor, and there is a certain presumption in trying to speak on behalf of those who are. I will do my best to be a faithful transmitter, but I will not claim more than is appropriate for my effort. Where matters remain unclear, that must be chalked up against the interpreter, rather than against the material being interpreted.

---

1. Gustavo Gutiérrez, *A Theology of Liberation: History, Politics, and Salvation*, trans. and ed. Caridad Inda and John Eagleson, rev. ed. (Maryknoll, N.Y.: Orbis, 1988).

Imagine a short man in front of a tall blackboard, lecturing in fully understandable English that is slightly charged with a Spanish accent. Invariably he makes three points in his presentation. Whether this is a subconscious tribute to trinitarian theology, an example of Hegel's philosophical method, or simply a recognition that three points are about all an audience can absorb, this is all that those who are already writing Ph.D. theses about the short man in front of the tall blackboard have left to ponder.

The man we are describing is one of the most eminent—and most humble—Christian thinkers on the scene today, Gustavo Gutiérrez, a Peruvian Roman Catholic priest, who serves a parish in a poor barrio of Lima, Peru, and still finds time to write books that have permanently altered the theological landscape of both Catholicism and Protestantism.

He writes theology as one of "the people"—which in Latin America means the *poor* people—instead of as a scholar, though he is at home in the company of scholars. The theology is usually called "liberation theology," and to increasing numbers of Christians it has a more authentic ring than a theology of the well-to-do, or even a theology of the white, male, middle class.

It is not so much something "new" that Gustavo Gutiérrez has articulated, as it is a recovery of something "old," old as the Hebrew and Christian Scriptures—a belief that God has a special concern for the poor, and that God seeks to empower the poor so they can work for liberation from the grinding oppression that has beaten them down for centuries.

Three Levels of Liberation

But to say only that would be to perpetuate a serious misinterpretation often leveled at Gutiérrez and those who share his concerns. For while it is true that the "liberation" he writes about and lives out is a liberation from the socioeconomic structures that devastate and destroy the poor, it is much more than that, and those who try to write him off as someone concerned only with a political revolution camouflaged by a dubious ideological veneer, do a disservice not only to him but to the truth.

Since the Christian church has usually been very short on dealing with the *sinful structures* of corporate life, it is appropriate that a significant part of Gutiérrez's concern has to do with overcoming and replacing structures that demean human life rather than ennoble it. But that is only the first level of the liberation struggle, and there are two other levels that are equally important. In fact, Gutiérrez insists that if one is not dealing simultaneously with all three levels, one is not dealing responsibly with any of them.

So the second liberation offered by the Christian gospel is liberation from an attitude that says, "We can't really make a difference, the cards are stacked against us and the most we can do is accept our lot and hope for a reward in heaven." In some cultures, the word *fate* would be employed to describe this position, meaning, "whatever happens was intended" or fated to happen, and "there is nothing we can do about it."

Gutiérrez rejects this position, claiming that it is in opposition to the Christian gospel, which is a message of empowering people precisely to "make a difference," to realize that God intends better things for them, and that they must be God's instruments in creating a world based on justice rather than injustice and on life rather than death. Where there is evil, God intends good and calls the members of the human family—God's family— to prepare the way for the coming of God's kingdom, a kingdom that will be God's *gift*, but makes use of all human effort. So liberation is liberation from a sense of impotence, a feeling that nothing can be done, and a warped notion that God wants things to remain as they are.

There is a third level of liberation as well. For God not only offers a vision of a new world, a new society, but also a vision of new individuals, new persons, who have been liberated from the power of sin and guilt and death over their own lives, by the redemptive activity of Jesus Christ. This has been the chief (and often exclusive) message of Christianity in the past: "God has reached out to us in love and mercy. Our sins are forgiven, and we are empowered to make a fresh start and live as God intended us to live."

It is only when these three levels can be recognized as *one* level, that we discover a new possibility for us: God offers liberation from evil structures, from fate, and from individual sin and guilt.

The Life and Times of Gustavo Gutiérrez

Who is this Gustavo Gutiérrez, the short man in front of the tall blackboard, who brings us such news? Gustavo Gutiérrez was born in 1928 in a poor section of Lima, Peru. He is a *mestizo*, a "half-breed," and came not from the elite of Lima's society, but from among its poor. At the age of twelve he suffered a severe case of osteomyelitis and spent almost all of his teenage years in bed or in a wheel chair.

Partly because of his illness, he decided first of all to become a doctor, perhaps even a psychiatrist. But while he was a university student, his vocational orientation shifted, and he decided to become a priest. Since he already had an outstanding scholastic record, he was chosen by the church to receive advanced theological training in Europe, where he spent a decade as a student at Louvain, Lyons, and Rome. Having received the very best of continental Catholic training in the 1950s, he returned to Peru and began working with students and with the poor. He soon discovered that his classical training had not fitted him to work in the midst of poverty.

And so, in the course of a few years, he had to "relearn" the Catholic faith, seeing it "from below," from the perspective of those at the bottom of the heap, or, as he often says "from the underside of history." He discovered that this was the perspective of the Hebrew prophets as well, and of Jesus and Paul, and, indeed a whole strata of subsequent Catholic teaching to which theologians in privileged positions had paid insufficient attention. As a result, Gutiérrez's writings are saturated with biblical material, along with statements by popes and Councils that offer a new perspective on the gospel and its message to the oppressed—a message that carries with it the ring of liberation.

There was another factor—or more accurately, another person—who helped Gutiérrez in this transition, a Spanish Dominican priest, Bartolomé de Las Casas (1474–1566). In the early years of the Spanish subjugation of the continent, he was sent to Latin America as a bishop. Las Casas (who is really the first Latin American "liberation theologian") sided with the Native Americans, the poor and oppressed of his day, and, in the face of heavy opposition, confronted the Spaniards who came to the "new world" to exploit it and kill any Native Americans who stood in their way.

Some things became very clear to Las Casas: (1) there is such a close connection between salvation and social justice that those who practice injustice cannot expect to be saved; (2) the Native Americans are not "infidels" (as the *conquistadores* considered them), but "the poor" about whom the gospel speaks so centrally; (3) theology has political consequences, so that a theology that leads to murder and enslavement is a false theology; (4) one's own position is validated only if one is involved in the struggle, not if one is a detached spectator; (5) when the Indians are scourged and afflicted, Christ himself is suffering in them, so that the one who scourges and kills an Indian is scourging and killing Christ.

Gutiérrez saw all these concerns, relevant in Las Casas's day, to be equally relevant in his own day, and his ongoing exposure to this brave precursor has been a lasting influence on him. So important is the message of Las Casas that Gutiérrez has recently published a 650-page history of his life and times, the first part of which sets out his basic thesis: our fundamental choice is between *God* and *gold,* and to choose gold is to make gold into God—the ultimate idolatry.[2]

While all this was going on in Gutiérrez's own life, Pope John XXIII had convened the Second Vatican Council of the Roman Catholic bishops from all over the world to help bring the Catholic Church into the twentieth century. After the Council, which opened many new doors to contemporary Catholics, the Latin American bishops convened a council of their own at Medellín, Colombia, in 1968 to look at their world through the eyes of the

---

2. Gustavo Gutiérrez, *Las Casas: In Search of the Poor Jesus Christ,* trans. Robert R. Barr (Maryknoll, N.Y.: Orbis, 1993).

newly promulgated concerns of the Vatican Council—the Second General Conference of the Latin American Episcopate.

Gutiérrez was present at the meetings of these bishops in Medellín as a *peritus,* or theological consultant, and played a significant role in the creation of the documents issued at Medellín, particularly those titled "Peace" and "Justice."[3] They remain noteworthy decades later not only because they opened up new perspectives on the world, but also because they ushered in a whole new way of doing theology. Instead of starting with "timeless truths" that are to be applied to the present order, the bishops began each of their sixteen documents with an analysis of the modern world—what was going on, what was wrong, what needed changing. After this, they looked at the nature of the Christian faith in the light of their sociological analysis and tried to understand its message in relation to the modern world. Finally, they proposed "pastoral considerations" that outlined programs of social action to transform the present world into a better place for all.

Just a few weeks prior to the Medellín Conference, Gutiérrez had given a lecture on "a theology of liberation" that likewise employed this pastoral consideration. Three years after Medellín he published a book called *A Theology of Liberation* that achieved almost instant recognition and transformed him from a relatively unknown parish priest into a world-renowned figure. His is still the best introduction to liberation theology.

However much the perspectives of the book gave new hope to the poor and oppressed, the book did not please the church authorities, who saw in it dangerous tendencies that could implicate the Roman Catholic Church too much in the political arena. They thought they detected within its concern for "change" a taint of Marxism, and feared that the socially and economically privileged position of the church in Latin American society would be threatened if so much attention was given the plight of the poor, the church's collusion with the rich, and alliances with a presumed atheist philosopher. Along with this new attention to "theology from the underside of history" came new efforts by those who occupied the underside, focused in what came to be called "Christian base communities," a new phenomenon within the heretofore rigidly structured hierarchical church.

The "base communities" were groups of fifteen to twenty people, meeting with or without a priest, who engaged in Bible study, liturgical expression, and application of both activities to their own situation. Such application might range from challenging local police brutality to contesting unfair exactions by the wealthy landowners of revenues from the poor

---

3. "Peace," in *The Church in the Present-Day Transformation of Latin America in the Light of the Council,* 2 vols., 2d ed., proceedings of Second General Conference of Latin American Bishops (Washington, D.C.: Division for Latin America—USCC, 1968), 2:53–65; "Justice," in *The Church in the Present-Day,* 40–51.

who were tenant-farmers with no legal rights on the huge estates. There was no stopping the proliferation of the base communities. Soon there were at least one hundred thousand of them, functioning all over Latin America, and making the Bible relevant, beyond anyone's imagining, to the immediate and pressing concerns of "the poorest of the poor."

These two events—the gradual emergence of "liberation theology" and the rapid emergence of the base communities—were unexpected results of the Medellín documents, and each provided undergirding for the other. Gutiérrez gave a personal accounting of what had happened to him during these years, particularly in his understanding of the reality of poverty, in a meeting with other theologians at El Escorial in Spain in 1972.[4] There were three transforming insights to be recorded:

1. He discovered that *poverty is destructive,* something against which one must always fight. This went counter to much popular Catholic thought that claimed "poverty" as a virtue, and taught that in instances of dire necessity a handout from the rich to the poor was a sufficient response. After all, Jesus had said, "The poor you have always with you" (Mark 14:7), and it could be expected that if the poor remained meek and uncomplaining in this life, it would work to their favor in the life to come.[5]

2. He also discovered that *poverty is not accidental but structural,* which is why handouts won't suffice. The poor are poor not because they are shiftless or lacking in ambition. They are poor because of a society that barely tolerates their presence, and needs them only as a constant labor pool, to be used as a threat and resource by those with power. It goes like this: "You don't want to work for thirty cents a day? Then get out of the way because there are a dozen people in the line outside who will be glad to take your place." If this is a true reading of reality, handouts emphatically won't change the situation. Only a restructuring of the social order, doing away with the excessive distance between rich and poor, will suffice.

3. He discovered that *the poor are a social class.* They belong to a strata of society not acknowledged by the rest. They are the marginalized, the insignificant, and if one is going to opt for the poor, one will discover the stern barriers of social class that militate against doing so. What is going on in reality is what, in Marx's famous phrase, is called "class struggle." To affirm the existence of "class struggle" is not necessarily to be enmeshed in a specific ideology, such as Marxism, but simply to acknowledge what is actually happening.[6] Marx did not invent class struggle; he only observed it.

---

4. Robert McAfee Brown, *Gustavo Gutiérrez: An Introduction to Liberation Theology* (Maryknoll, N.Y.: Orbis, 1990), 32.

5. Ibid.

6. James B. Nickoloff, ed., *Gustavo Gutiérrez: Essential Writings* (Minneapolis: Fortress, 1996), 118.

When Gutiérrez put these three discoveries together, he concluded that to serve the poor one must engage in political action. Such a conclusion does not dictate exactly what form the political struggle must take, or which political party one must join. These are issues with which Christians in *any* situation must struggle. A recognition that the actual state of the world demands commitment and involvement on the part of Christians is vital.

The conservative bishops were alarmed by these developments, as Gutiérrez became a symbol of possible change within the church and the world. It frightened them. As a result, he began to be attacked in articles, conferences, and books. The most conservative of the bishops hoped that a follow-up conference to the Medellín meetings finally held in Puebla, Mexico, in 1979 would provide an occasion to destroy both liberation theology and the base communities, not to mention Gutiérrez himself.[7]

To make a long story short, they did not succeed. All the targets of their wrath emerged from the Puebla meetings stronger than before. The result was that the personal attacks on Gutiérrez as the cause of all the trouble were intensified. But to make an even longer story short, the effort to pin a "Marxist" label on him was unsuccessful, for the very appropriate reason that there was no substance to the charge. Two "Instructions" from Rome about liberation theology, while containing a good deal of criticism, left the impression, when the smoke had cleared, that much of what liberation theology stood for could be embraced within a Catholic framework.[8]

A Sampling of Other Writings

When not moving around on the global scene, Gutiérrez is at home doing what he considers his major job, acting as a parish priest for a Catholic community in Lima and living out the things about which he talks and writes. Brief reference to some of his subsequent writings will characterize him more clearly.

The Power of the Poor in History (1983) is a collection of essays on themes centrally related to the Puebla conference.[9] The essays are biblically oriented and historical treatments of Christian faith when seen from the "underside." They demonstrate how central is his commitment to, and use of, the scriptures.

We Drink from Our Own Wells (1984) is particularly significant since it appeared during the time the author was charged with being a

---

7. John Eagleson and Philip Scharper, eds., *Puebla and Beyond: Documentation and Commentary,* trans. John Drury (Maryknoll, N.Y.: Orbis, 1979).

8. Brown, *Introduction to Liberation Theology,* 141–48.

9. Gustavo Gutiérrez, *The Power of the Poor in History: Selected Writings of Gustavo Gutiérrez,* trans. Robert R. Barr (Maryknoll, N.Y.: Orbis, 1983).

"horizontalist," that is, one who looks only at human ethical issues and neglects the "vertical" dimension of God's relationship to human life.[10] Gutiérrez, however, expanding on material published a decade earlier in *A Theology of Liberation,* describes beautifully what he calls "the spiritual journey of a people," and further develops his "spirituality of liberation," in a way that has already made the book one of the most penetrating devotional writings of our time.[11] He further shows in this book how our "theological" and our "political" concerns are inseparable, demonstrating that concern for the here and now must be firmly anchored in our faith in the eternal God who has appeared in the here and now in the person of Jesus of Nazareth.

On Job: God-Talk and the Suffering of the Innocent (1987) is a book combining careful biblical exegesis and pastoral considerations.[12] It is a full-length commentary on the Book of Job, asking how we can talk about God in the world of suffering, particularly unjust suffering, and affirming that we must combine "prophetic" speech and mystical or "contemplative" speech, since neither is sufficient without the other.

A more recent book, *The God of Life* (1991), is a series of Bible studies stressing the fact that, even in the midst of death and destruction, God is still the God of *life.*[13] This is yet another expression of the hope and power that the liberating message of the Bible can bring. All of the chapters originated in conferences with lay groups. If *On Job* appeals particularly to the "educated," *The God of Life* is for those without much formal education.

Anyone who reads these and other books by Gutiérrez will realize how wide of the mark the conventional accusations against him are—that he is "really a Marxist," that he "espouses" violence, that he does not take belief in God "seriously," that his use of the Bible is "too selective," and so on. Since not even the powers of the Church in Rome have been able to make such charges stick, the best way to honor Gutiérrez is not to keep rehashing discredited charges, but to take him on his own terms, as one whose integrity can be trusted. Our task, therefore, is to listen to his message and then ponder what kinds of changes in our own lives are necessary on the basis of what he tells us. That this task is not always taken seriously by "academic theologians" only suggests the even greater credibility of his theology. What,

---

10. Gustavo Gutiérrez, *We Drink from Our Own Wells: The Spiritual Journey of a People,* trans. Matthew J. O'Connell (Maryknoll, N.Y.: Orbis, 1984).

11. Gutiérrez, *Theology of Liberation,* 22–24.

12. Gustavo Gutiérrez, *On Job: God-Talk and the Suffering of the Innocent,* trans. Matthew J. O'Connell (Maryknoll, N.Y.: Orbis, 1987).

13. Gustavo Gutiérrez, *The God of Life,* trans. Matthew J. O'Connell (Maryknoll, N.Y.: Orbis, 1991).

then, are some of the recurring positive emphases that stand out even in a brief summary?

Five Basic Themes

1. Surely the basic theme is the gospel's central *concern for the poor* and the need for the church to become "the church of the poor." As Gutiérrez points out, this theme is not original with him; its inspiration for our day comes both from statements by Pope John XXIII and from an important intervention by Cardinal Lercaro at the first session of Vatican II, pleading with the church to become "the church of the poor," and thus make Pope John's dream for the Council a reality.[14] That the Council did not, on the whole, respond to this proposal is all the more reason to try to make it a central concern in the subsequent life of the church.

The concern has been given flesh and blood in the phrase "a preferential option for the poor," a theme anticipated at the conference of the Catholic bishops of Latin America at Medellín, in 1968, just three years after Vatican II, and concretized at their next meeting in Puebla, Mexico, in 1979.[15] As Gutiérrez makes clear, this does not mean that God does not love all people, but it does mean that if God's children are to express love toward all people, they must begin with the poor.

In treating the plight of the poor, Gutiérrez talks not only about lack of money, but also *lack of power.* Perhaps the most recurrent theme in this and his other writings is that to be poor is to be *insignificant,* that is, not to count, to be ignored, to be deemed unworthy of attention.[16] Part of the way society expresses this lack of concern for the poor is by economic deprivation. But society is so structured that as long as the needs of the insignificant can be ignored, there will be a cancer at the heart of society. Salvation (meaning wholeness or "health") for the poor is a condition of salvation for everyone else as well.

2. In a world where the poor predominate, the message of good news is the message of *gratuitousness,* a key word in all Gutiérrez writings.[17] While it is a somewhat awkward word in English, the reality to which it points is crucial in any language. It is a way of talking about *grace,* the freely given gift of love that God offers all, whether deserving or not. This is the heart

---

14. Gustavo Gutiérrez, *The Truth Shall Make You Free,* trans. Matthew J. O'Connell (Maryknoll, N.Y.: Orbis, 1990), 167–68.

15. Nickoloff, *Essential Writings,* 78. See pages 78–148 for more discussion on this topic.

16. Ibid., 143–45.

17. Gutiérrez, *We Drink from Our Own Wells,* 107. See pages 107–13 for more discussion.

not only of the biblical message but of the whole Christian tradition at its best, and it is the "atmosphere" (as Gutiérrez likes to say) in which human endeavor (or "efficacy," as he also likes to say) is nurtured. To receive the grace-filled gift of love involves a willingness on our part to share that love, to be a conduit through which grace flows to the otherwise despairing and disempowered.

3. But it is not the job of the powerful to "do things" for the disempowered, even through gratuitous acts. The demand on the powerful is, quite simply, to *share power,* so that the previously powerless are empowered to take control of their own lives—to live lives, in other words, that are fully human. This is part of what it means to recognize "the right of the poor to think," rather than having their thinking done for them by others.[18]

Here Gutiérrez clearly issues important reminders to all of us. Christian life is not just thought; it is action as well. Conversely, it is not just action; it is thought as well. The Christian life is a constant attempt to keep those realities in creative tension with each other. Neither is adequate alone. Just what kinds of thought and what kinds of action are demanded will, of course, vary in different contexts in response to different questions.

And here an important division occurs. The "non-believer" (or at least the one for whom belief is difficult) represents those of us who inhabit modernity, who may ask a question, such as, "How can I believe in God in an age of science?" But the "non-person" (or at least the one whom the world treats as a non-person), will ask a different question, such as, "In a world that treats me as a 'nothing,' how can I believe there is a God who loves me?"

On several occasions, Gutiérrez wrestles with the latter question, answering it by frequent reference to the book of Job, as previously mentioned, and the way in which Job discovers that there must be a joining of two kinds of speech. One kind asks questions *about* God and those who try intellectually to "justify" God's reality in the midst of evil. The other is communication *with* God (sometimes called "mystical language") in which the discovery of God's "gratuitousness" empowers one to enter the struggle for justice.

4. In situations of death—the perennial situation of those who live in places like Latin America—the great gift of Christianity is its commitment to *a God of life.* This is a message Gutiérrez has increasingly employed in the last decade, as the high incidence of martyrdoms has come close to the lives of all Latin Americans committed to the struggle for peace and justice. As we have seen, Gutiérrez's book on *The God of Life* stresses the liberating message of God entering into and struggling against the situation of

---

18. Gutiérrez, *A Theory of Liberation,* xxi.

the imperiled, enacting a conviction that resurrection and life, rather than crucifixion and death, are the final realities. Death not only comes from the noisy power of the death squads, but from the silent power of poverty, endemic to the economic system that is itself a cause of death. So combating death in the name of the God of life means entering the political and economic arenas to work for change.

5. All this is focused in a life of *Christian spirituality*, a theme present in Gutiérrez's writings from the earliest essays. Spirituality, which according to Gutiérrez means to follow Jesus Christ, is not a retreat to some other world, but more committed involvement in this world, after the pattern of Jesus, who, whenever he goes apart to pray in the desert or on a mountain top, returns to the world of injustice and epilepsy, and lives his life, and dies his death, and rises from the dead, in defiance of all the destructive forces of the here and now.[19] The gospel story frees us, Gutiérrez insists, to love, even in the midst of the unlovely.

An earlier theme returns in this connection: "gratuitousness" can render us effective in bringing about change. The body is important in this endeavor; any so-called "spirituality" that denies the body is disqualified from serious consideration. As Rutilio Grande, a Salvadoran priest, whose body was riddled by the bullets of assassins said, "Our people are hungry for the true God, and they are hungry for bread." That is a both/and for Gutiérrez, never an either/or.[20]

The Man, Once More

We must keep returning to Gutiérrez's life, so that our theology will not become too ethereal or cerebral. He is, we find, committed not only to the centrality and validity of the Christian revelation, but also committed to discerning ways in which that revelation can be embodied in the lives of those who likewise affirm it. He is a man of international renown who nevertheless prefers to be described as a parish priest in his own country. He is a man not impressed by honors, and even a little disturbed when they are showered on him. His recognition that he is no longer really one of "the poor" because of his education and reputation, and the problems this poses, is disarmingly honest.

And also, lest we fail to notice it throughout the printed pages, he is a person with a sense of humor, a gift one wishes God would establish more lavishly on all theologians. For example, after addressing the Anglican bishops at their Lambeth Conference in the summer of 1988, he later informally commented, "In the Roman Catholic Church there are many rules; is very

---

19. Brown, *Introduction to Liberation Theology*, 98–101.
20. Gutiérrez, *We Drink from Our Own Wells*, 103.

difficult. In the Anglican Church, it seems to me, there are many customs; is more difficult."[21] While having many rules is difficult, having many customs is even more difficult. His own church, relying on rules, has given him many problems, and it is to his credit that he remains loyally within it, recognizing that Christian faith is always a communal commitment, not only of the mind, but of heart, soul, and strength as well. In all of these areas he remains one from who we have much to learn.

Theology, Again

The appropriate engagement with liberation theology should come into focus when we are no longer trying so hard to learn a system of thought, but when we begin a new engagement with life. Juan Luis Segundo, a Jesuit priest from Uruguay, who had his own problems with the Roman Curia, used to caution those seeking exposure to liberation theology. The starting point, he insisted, is a presupposition open to anyone—whether Christian or not. It is the assumption that *"the world should not be the way it is."* If you are satisfied with the world as it is, you will never understand what we are about.[22] Liberation theology is not a mere rearrangement of our theological furniture, it is a starting all over again. It is a theological adventure that is never completed, and yet which can always be shedding new light on who we are and what is demanded of us. There are a few ways available for building this new structure:

1. *"Theology,"* Gutiérrez suggests, *"is a love letter to the church."*[23] A love letter is never simply an itemization of information. It is the declaration of a mystery: "He says he loves me! How can that be? And yet it *is!*" The more we come to know one another, the deeper the love can become, in spite of the realization that the other now has further excellent reasons to break off the relationship—and does not do so.

This is mystery of a high order, and something for which there can never be sufficient gratitude to "explain" what is going on. A love letter written twenty years ago will have a different tone from one written last week. The relationship is deeper and the reality being pointed to is more fixed and sure—with surprise all along the way. It is not primarily a piece of information, but an outburst of joy.

2. We learn something more about the relationship typified in the love letter. It is that *theology, per se, is never the first thing.* We experience love and

---

21. Gustavo Gutiérrez, conversation with author, at Gustavo's sixtieth birthday party, 1988.

22. Brown, *Introduction to Liberation Theology,* 51.

23. Gustavo Gutiérrez, in conversation, quoted in Brown, *Introduction to Liberation Theology,* 102.

we try to talk about it or write about it, and the attempts never get close to the real thing. It is what Gutiérrez calls "the second act."[24] The first act is commitment, a dedication to the other, and out of that engagement we can begin to think about the commitment we have made, test it, take risks on its behalf, and discover in the midst of living out the commitment, that its truth or falsity will emerge.[25] It is not—to make a parallel Gutiérrez likes to make—so different from what Anselm had in mind when he uttered the words "I believe in order that I may understand."[26] This is what is offered to us—the possibility of belief and commitment as something on which to build. We take a risk, and our belief is either vindicated in living it out, or it is not. We will never know for sure, unless there is a genuineness in our testing, or experimenting.

3. And this leads us into a new situation where we begin to discover a methodology that, while difficult, is helpful. It is, to employ Gutiérrez's full definition of theology, "critical reflection on Christian praxis in the light of the Word of God."[27] It is reflection, drawing together all that we have on hand so far, and testing the waters, that is, critical reflection, not just little forays. It is reflection on praxis, a technical word that means more than just "practice." Praxis is the experience of thinking and doing, doing and thinking, learning by an excursion of faith that something seems to hold and to cohere, and empowers us to take the next step—a step from thinking to believing, a believing that helps us take risks. But not just any praxis, since the whole exercise involves trying to do all this "in the light of the Word of God."

The Word of God, Jesus Christ—as found in scripture, as expressed in the example and promises of Jesus, the living expression of God, and as the increasing assurance we can gradually accumulate—is finally to be trusted, honored, and followed in life and in death.

The process is never completed, but will be the situation in which the believer dwells as long as life lasts. As John Robinson pointed out centuries ago in describing the Christian scriptures, "God has yet more light to break forth from His Holy Word."[28]

This is not simply the same old material slightly brightened up and polished, but rather a new way of looking at the world and looking at our faith. We begin to see things differently. Some of our own assurances are called into question. We begin to reexamine some of the values we had held

---

24. Brown, *Introduction to Liberation Theology*, 102.

25. Nickoloff, *Essential Writings*, 55-56.

26. Gutiérrez, *Power of the Poor in History*, 55-56.

27. Gutiérrez, *A Theology of Liberation*, 11; Brown, *Introduction to Liberation Theology*, 102.

28. John A. T. Robinson, *Honest to God*, 2d ed. (London: SCM, 2001).

onto so tightly. Without developing the point in detail, I close by suggesting two areas in which we can engage in reevaluations that are helpful in other areas as well.

One of these is our understanding of Marxism, which some liberation theologians have used as an interpretive tool, quite apart from any commitment to the structure of Marxist thought as a whole.

If a descriptive category like "class struggle" describes what is going on in the world, it must be taken seriously, even if Karl Marx said it. If a descriptive category like "human perfectibility" does not accurately describe what is happening in the world, it need not be taken seriously, even if a theologian said it.

The presence of an idea in the Bible like "liberty for the oppressed" is not invalidated simply because Karl Marx affirmed it eighteen hundred years later.

Certain parts of Marxist analysis can be affirmed without affirming the whole Marxist philosophy. (This is perhaps the greatest single point of difference between liberation theologians in the third world and academic theologians in the Sacred Congregation in Rome.)

"A social mortgage has been placed on all private property" was not said by Karl Marx, but by Pope John Paul II.[29]

Another reevaluation is called for to establish distinctions in looking at violence with twentieth-century eyes that are also Christian. The issue of violence in relation to liberation theology is usually imposed from the outside. It is not at the center of Latin American debates, for it is not a realistic option for most oppressed (and unarmed) people.

The human situation is already violent, not only because of repression and terrorism, but because of injustice, unemployment, malnutrition, and starvation—all of them "violent" realities.

Gutiérrez distinguishes three kinds of violence as (1) the institutionalized violence of the present order, (2) the repressive violence that defends institutionalized violence, and (3) the counter-violence to which Christians may sometimes feel forced in the face of massive injustice.

Appeals to counter-violence are morally appropriate only when all other means of bringing about social change have failed.

All of these items, of course, demand extended debate and discussion but they assume much more credibility when examined through the lenses that liberation theology furnishes, rather than examined frivolously by those seeking merely to score a debating point.

At the end of our mutual self-examinations, it seems clear that a new kind of theology emerges and that, for those who are open, all pathways of

---

29. Brown, *Introduction to Liberation Theology*, 154.

Dominant Theology	Liberation Theology
1. Responds to the nonbeliever whose faith is threatened by modernity	1. Responds to the *nonperson* whose faith is threatened by forces of destruction
2. Begins with the world of modernity and remains thought-oriented	2. Begins with the world of oppression and becomes action-oriented
3. Is developed "from above": the position of the privileged, the affluent, the bourgeois	3. Is developed "from below": from the "underside of history," the position of the oppressed, the marginalized, the exploited
4. Is largely written by "those with white hands," the "winners"	4. Is only beginning to be written; must be articulated by those with dark-skinned, gnarled hands, the "losers"
5. Focuses attention on a "religious" world that needs to be reinforced	5. Focuses attention on a political world that needs to be replaced
6. Is linked to Western culture, the white race, the male sex, the bourgeois class	6. Is linked to "the wretched of the earth," the marginalized races, despised cultures and sex, the exploited class
7. Affirms the achievements of culture: individualism, rationalism, capitalism, the bourgeois spirit	7. Insists that the "achievements" of culture have been used to exploit the poor
8. Wants to work gradually, reforming existing structures by "supervision"	8. Demands to work rapidly through liberation from existing structures by "subversion"

mutual exploration can be not only exciting but enlightening. The accompanying chart is offered as a means of beginning exploration.

A Personal Word from the Author

There are some inherent difficulties in writing from one perspective to another. The greatest difficulty, of which I have never been so conscious before, was illustrated for me by my initial difficulty in constructing a form for this paper. *There was no neutral stance* I could occupy and hope to do justice to a series of comparisons between two very different theologies. No matter where I started, I found myself making judgments that were ill-founded. I could not, as already indicated, preserve neutrality. Nor could I make significant comparisons between liberation theology and Mormon theology; for although I think I know liberation theology fairly well, I could make no such claim about Mormonism without getting very close to caricature, which is hardly a vehicle for initiating exchange. I hoped to avoid appealing to stereotype, and not to skew my remarks in ways that would leave us finally further apart than at the beginning.

My way out of this double impasse has been, for me at least, refreshing. For I have made no claims about my understanding of Mormon theology, and I limit myself to as clear an exploration as possible of liberation theology. I do not yet search for agreements that may or may not be there. That comes later. A building of understanding will come only gradually and must not be forced. So I am not yet searching for analogies or comparisons. They may or may not emerge. What I hope will emerge will be the beginnings of an exchange that will proceed at its own tempo and gradually draw us closer together.

Response to Professor Brown

Warner Woodworth

In "LIBERATION AS A FAITH OPTION," Robert McAfee Brown offers an insightful and personal essay regarding the origins and current thrust of liberation theology, grounded in the substantive work of Gustavo Gutiérrez. I admire Brown's candid, honest expression regarding the difficulty of carrying out a systematic analysis that compares the theology of the poor with that of The Church of Jesus Christ of Latter-day Saints.

So I too choose to write from the heart, not merely from my intellectual reasoning. Hence, the personal becomes the political, a premise that is consistent with both liberation and Latter-day Saint theologies. Neither system offers a neutral perspective; nor do they focus on religion as metaphysics or an arena for formal debate and deliberation. Rather, they are both a call for change and repentance, and a push for action. One's faith is a force of motivation to transform the world, not merely a reason to study and theorize about the human condition.

Like Brown, I too hope that by describing and analyzing Latter-day Saint and liberation theologies a deeper understanding and appreciation for the legitimacy of both sets of belief will gradually appear. Although arenas of difference and sharp contrasts may also emerge, it just may be that the commonalities between the two theologies outweigh the differences.

My exposure to liberation theology began during my doctoral work at Michigan and continued through the 1970s and 1980s. My encounters with the poor in Latin America have continually reinforced the importance of liberation as a method for change among various disadvantaged groups. I've labored among oppressed urban dwellers in the shanty-town favelas of Rio de Janeiro, Brazil; among exploited workers in the copper mines of Chile and the tin mines of Bolivia; among marginalized peasants in the fields; and among urbanized squatters in several Mexican cities. I've also worked with indigenous guerillas in the highlands of Guatemala, where entire villages have been rounded up and shot by the military junta; with Marxist revolutionaries in the Sandinista era of Nicaragua; and with impoverished women in the informal economy of Peru who battle not only class struggle, but also sexism and gender-related exploitation.

During more recent experience of the 1990s, I've seen the applicability of liberation theology to the crushing poverty of people in other parts of the globe. As I have worked with black Christian groups in Africa, I have seen their growing attraction to Black Liberation Theology as they attempt to move social structures toward greater equality and justice and reverse the oppression of the African poor. Likewise, for the past decade, I have labored with Filipino groups in Manila, Cebu, and Davao as they struggle to create a more democratic Philippines. The theology of liberation exploded as a successful tool for change, a path toward "People Power," through the revolt that overthrew dictator Ferdinand Marcos in 1986. The subsequent elected presidents, Cory Aquino and then Fidel Ramos, each achieved a degree of reform and peace. Yet most Filipinos still suffer greatly from unemployment, lack of access to land, and increasing struggles to survive. As I have worked with the oppressed of the Philippines to establish community worker-owned cooperatives, microenterprises, and access to credit among the poorest of the poor, I have continually heard them discussing the teachings of liberation theology as they seek to diagnose the causes of their poverty and develop alternative paths for exiting their wretched condition.

With this summary of my LDS background and cross-cultural experience in theologies of liberation and change, let me turn to the central themes of this essay. Essentially, I hope to explicate LDS teachings regarding the plight of the poor and the role of religion in countering oppression and injustice. After highlighting key LDS doctrinal insights that seem in harmony with liberation theology, the essay will conclude with an assessment of the two belief systems, as well as a listing of major writings on LDS social and economic features.

Temporal Teachings of Joseph Smith and Brigham Young

Imagine the two early leaders of The Church of Jesus Christ of Latter-day Saints: the prophet Joseph Smith, tall and imposing, a natural leader with great capacity to rally new believers in the cause; and Brigham Young, a short, stocky LDS apostle who learned of Joseph's vision and then, when the prophet was persecuted and finally killed by a violent mob, humbly took the mantle of leadership of the westward march to build Zion. Their views of Jesus and his gospel were at odds with the religious establishment of their day and its elitist assumptions. Instead of embracing the theology of scholars, they held a revolutionary, even radical, view that attacked the premises of traditional belief. The result was severe criticism, persecution, and ultimate rejection by leading religionists and politicians of the United States in the 1830s and after.

Similar to Gutiérrez, the early leaders of the Church did not claim that they had something "new," but that they were preaching the "old" religion of Jesus and his Apostles. In their view the American establishment's form of Christianity had become distorted and corrupt. What was needed was a "restoration" that would bless and lift those in need. Declared Joseph Smith, "I calculate to be one of the instruments of setting up the Kingdom of Daniel, by the word of the Lord, and I intend to lay a foundation that will revolutionize the whole world."[30] The new believers who embraced the LDS faith consisted largely of society's underdogs—the poor, the underclass, the jobless, the farmers, the laborers, the squatters, the immigrants, and the downtrodden.

LDS Teachings on Poverty

Established Christianity assumes that suffering poverty in this life is a natural and necessary evil and that the toil and degradation of one's daily struggles will eventually be overcome, but only in the afterlife. Seeking for adequate jobs, food, and shelter is the travail of mortal existence and supposedly has little to do with heavenly things.

LDS theology rejects such a dichotomy. To the Latter-day Saints, the spiritual and temporal are one. As President Brigham Young put it, "In the mind of God there is no such a thing as dividing spiritual from temporal, or temporal from spiritual; for they are one in the Lord."[31] Modern LDS scriptures affirm this view: "That which is spiritual being in the likeness of that which is temporal" (Doctrine and Covenants [D&C] 77:2; see also

---

30. Joseph Smith Jr., *Teachings of the Prophet Joseph Smith*, comp. Joseph Fielding Smith (Salt Lake City: Deseret, 1959), 366.

31. Brigham Young, in *Journal of Discourses*, 26 vols. (Liverpool: F. D. Richards, 1855–86), 11:18, December 11, 1864.

D&C 14:11; 29:34–35). Thus, gospel living ought to be a two-way street in which the spiritual flows toward the temporal, and vice versa. According to another early LDS church prophet and president, Joseph F. Smith:

> It was the doctrine of Joseph Smith, the original revelator of "Mormonism," that the spirit and the body constitute the soul of man. It has always been a cardinal teaching with the Latter-day Saints, that a religion which has not the power to save people temporally and make them prosperous and happy here, cannot be depended upon to save them spiritually, to exalt them in the life to come.[32]

Such radical views as these contradicted those of traditional Christendom. As Brown suggests, the traditional view of Christianity was that fate caused poverty, and human beings ought to simply accept their lot and make do. But Gutiérrez, like Joseph and Brigham, offers a liberating alternative: humankind does not have to accept injustice and oppression passively, but people can act, make changes, and become empowered citizens of this world, here and now, as well as of heaven in the future.

LDS theology is quick to emphasize that true religion must include the temporal, not just the spiritual. Indeed, seven of the Bible's Ten Commandments relate in some way to economic activity. Of 112 revelations Joseph Smith received and recorded as the Doctrine and Covenants, 88 deal at least partially with financial or economic matters. Another early LDS prophet and president, Wilford Woodruff, declared at a general church conference in 1873:

> Strangers and the Christian world marvel at the "Mormons" talking about temporal things. Bless your souls, two-thirds of all the revelations given in this world rest upon the accomplishment of this temporal work.... This is the great dispensation in which the Zion of God must be built up, and we as Latter-day Saints have it to build.... We have it to do, we can't build up Zion sitting on a hemlock slab singing ourselves away to everlasting bliss.... We are obliged to build cities, towns and villages.[33]

In agreement with liberation theology, President Woodruff calls for the creation of new systems of righteousness and the overthrow of the structures of sin and injustice. Gutiérrez's concern likewise focuses on the "overcoming and replacing of structures that demean human life rather than ennoble it" (Brown, 212).

---

32. Joseph F. Smith, "The Truth about Mormonism," *Out West* 23 (1905): 242.
33. Wilford Woodruff, in *Journal of Discourses*, 16:268–69, October 8, 1873.

LDS Scriptural Teachings on Poverty

Ample examples from the Bible and modern LDS scripture reflect LDS views of poverty. In the Old Testament, for example, Exodus 22 stresses that God's people serve those in need, not oppressing the stranger, not exploiting the poor, not afflicting the very poorest of the poor—widows and orphans. Through his ancient prophets, God commands that we not persecute the poor (Ps. 10:2), but rather that we share our goods with them (Deut. 15:7), have mercy on them (Prov. 14:21), and bring them into our homes (Isa. 58:7). In the New Testament, Jesus declares that his preaching is to the poor (Matt. 11:5) and that true Christians can receive treasure in heaven by giving to the poor (Luke 18:22). Similarly, the Apostle Paul preaches that Christ's disciples are to always remember the poor (Gal. 2:10). Of course, many other biblical citations compare to liberation theology and refer to our mission as followers of Jesus to labor in behalf of the poor and marginalized.

But Mormonism offers even more. In the Book of Mormon, for example, numerous references could be interpreted as a "theology of the poor": people are all "beggars," indebted to God (Mosiah 4:19); true saints are to "succor those that stand in need," to give of their substance and to not judge or condemn the needy (4:14–18), "that ye may walk guiltless before God" (4:26). One prophet likewise explains that righteous societies are those that do not turn away the needy but labor to eliminate poverty (Alma 1:27; 4:13; 5:55; 34:28). Ungodly societies are those puffed up in their pride (Helaman 4:12; 3 Nephi 6:10–18; 4 Nephi 1:24–29; Mormon 8:37).

Finally, the Doctrine and Covenants contains similar concerns about the pride that comes with great riches, the wearing of costly apparel and jewelry to distinguish Haves from Have-Nots, and the evils of emerging social classes. In fact, Christ's gospel is designed to be directed specifically toward the poor (D&C 35:15; 42:30; 52:40). Modern revelations explain that righteous Christians consecrate their riches unto the poor (D&C 42:39) and that those who will not impart of their substance to the needy are not genuine saints (D&C 56:16). The widows and orphans are to be provided for (D&C 83:6), and a feast of "fat things" should be prepared for those in poverty (D&C 58:8). Finally, the poor will eventually inherit the earth (D&C 88:17), and "the poor shall be exalted, in that the rich are made low" (D&C 104:16).

According to LDS theology, as with liberation theology, inequality is a major cause of sin. Book of Mormon prophets consistently condemned those societies characterized by great economic inequality (Mosiah 29:32; Alma 4:12–15; 28:13; 3 Nephi 6:14). On the other hand, good societies were characterized by social systems of justice and equality (Alma 16:16; 4 Nephi 1:18). Zion has always been defined as a community in which there are no rich or poor, as illustrated by the people of 4 Nephi, of whom it was written, "Surely there could not be a happier people among all the people who had been created by the hand of God" (4 Nephi 1:16). Likewise, the account of Enoch and his righteous people described in the Book of Moses portrays a true social utopia: "And the Lord called his people Zion, because they were of one heart and one mind, and dwelt in righteousness; and there was no poor among them" (Moses 7:18).

Such an ideal social structure is a far cry from today's global inequities. LDS and liberation theologies are both clearly concerned with today's injustices and social evils. Approximately 30 million Americans, some 13 percent of the total population, live in official poverty. Roughly a fourth of all children are at risk because of poor economic conditions. Corporate downsizing, and therefore unemployment and homelessness, are on the rise. Real wages, adjusted for inflation, are not as high currently as they were in the 1970s. Meanwhile, the ratio of CEO pay to the average worker's salary is now over 200:1, a stark contrast from that of two decades ago, when it was 29:1.[34] Unfortunately, in the third world, inequality is even worse. According to the World Bank and other sources, roughly 1.4 billion people, 23 percent of earth's total population, are estimated to be living in absolute poverty. They suffer from hunger and malnutrition, lack of education, and vulnerability to disease and death.[35]

LDS theology has always expressed concern regarding the problems of inequality and poverty. It takes literally God's words to Joseph Smith: "But it is not given that one man should possess that which is above another, wherefore the world lieth in sin" (D&C 49:20). The following signed statement by the LDS church's First Presidency and the Quorum of the Twelve Apostles suggests the degree to which LDS theology parallels the theology of liberation:

> One of the great evils with which our own nation is menaced at the present time is the wonderful growth of wealth in the hands of a comparatively few individuals. The very liberties for which our fathers contended so steadfastly and courageously, and which they bequeathed to us as a priceless legacy, are endangered by the monstrous power which this accumulation of wealth gives to a few individuals and a few powerful corporations. . . . If this evil should not be checked, and measures not taken to prevent the continued enormous growth of riches among the class already rich, and the painful increase of destitution and want among the poor, the nation is likely to be overtaken by disaster; for,

---

34. James W. Lucas and Warner P. Woodworth, *Working Toward Zion: Principles of the United Order for the Modern World* (Salt Lake City: Aspen, 1996), 23–30.

35. Ibid., 31–39.

according to history, such a tendency among nations once powerful was the sure precursor of ruin.[36]

Perhaps the clearest LDS advocate of socio-economic equality is Orson Pratt, an early LDS apostle. He cites God's revelation to Joseph Smith, "Be one, and if ye are not one, ye are not mine," a commandment given in 1831 before the Church was even a year old. "In what respects are the Saints required to be one? We answer: They are required to be one in things temporal and spiritual, in earthly and heavenly things. . . . The command to 'be one' embraces all other commands." Later in this great discourse, Pratt observes that "an inequality in property is the root and foundation of innumerable evils; it tends to division, and to keep asunder the social feelings that should exist among the people of God. . . . It is the root of all evil."[37]

LDS Economic Trends

The origins of The Church of Jesus Christ of Latter-day Saints were set in the context of the political and economic struggles experienced by the American working class and European converts—laborers, woodworkers, boilermakers, tailors, and so on. These groups were similar to the social classes of early Christian converts in Jesus' day—carpenters, fishermen, and the like. After LDS pioneers successfully colonized the West, however, they began to overcome their earlier poverty, and during the first half of the twentieth century most Latter-day Saints had become middle-class Utahns.

However, in the more recent past, members of the LDS faith in industrialized nations have become increasingly more like the early founders of the LDS church—blue-collar workers. Far from being merely a Utah-based church or a white, middle-class American institution, today's LDS church consists of people from a wide range of locations and socio-economic backgrounds. For instance, over half of the church's members today are non-U.S. citizens and all growth projections for the future suggest that it will increasingly be a third-world church, consisting of mostly Latin Americans, Asians, and Africans. Crushing poverty and struggles against social injustice will be the primary characteristics of future converts.

Consider, for instance, LDS growth in Latin America. In 1960 there were only 22,503 Latter-day Saints throughout all of Latin America, a mere 1.3 percent of the total church membership. By 1970 there were 160,355, or 5.5 percent. By 1980 the numbers shot up to 11.2 percent, a total of 519,626 Latinos. That total more than quadrupled by 1990 to 2,229,000, almost 29

---

36. Edward J. Allen, *The Second United Order among the Mormons* (New York: AMS, 1967), 129–30.

37. Orson Pratt, *Masterful Discourses and Writings of Orson Pratt*, comp. N. B. Lundwall (Salt Lake City: Bookcraft, 1962), 624–25, 633.

percent of all Latter-day Saints. Church membership growth in Colombia doubles every three years. The number of Latter-day Saints in Brazil, which stands at over a million today, doubles every four years. Membership in Mexico doubles every eight years.

What all of this suggests is that at the turn of the century, over half of the worldwide LDS church consisted of people from a Latin American cultural background. They would not speak English, they would be brown-skinned, and they would be extremely poor.[38] Another 300,000 were projected to consist of poverty-stricken Filipinos with their cultural and ethnic mix of Spanish and Chinese.[39]

Trends such as these have had far-reaching effects on LDS church functions. Many congregations may appear increasingly like the *communidad de base* of liberation theology. LDS traditions have long emphasized the power of small groups, such as local wards or governing councils. Also, because there is no professional clergy in the church, local congregations operate at the grassroots by continually changing leaders who are drawn from the local membership and must be sustained by the group. This gives people a real sense of empowerment and the ability to address local problems most relevant to present needs and conditions.

As third-world societies experience greater poverty and turbulent economic conditions, Latter-day Saint communities or "wards" within these societies will become much more pragmatic. Hyperinflation will shift the worship agenda to meet member needs—unemployment, hunger, and health care. In recent years under unusual circumstances, I have personally witnessed Latin American groups gathered in LDS chapels on the Sabbath to trade beans for rice, corn for meat, and so on. Those with jobs and a paycheck share their financial resources with their poor neighbors through a practice known as "fast offerings." They go without meals one Sunday a month and donate the money they would have spent on food to be allocated to the jobless or hungry in the congregation.

While most such groups do not use Marxist terms that define themselves as the proletariat locked in a power struggle with the bourgeoisie, many LDS converts in Latin America and Africa have been political leftists to some degree. They come from the "underside" of history, and although many abandon Marxist rhetoric, they see their lives as Latter-day Saints to be a struggle against oppression. They tend to perceive themselves as marginalized, not only because they are poor, but also because they are Latter-day Saints.

---

38. Lucas and Woodworth, *Working Toward Zion*, 3–5.
39. Ibid., 7–9.

LDS Theology Regarding Indigenous People

Perhaps a final interesting aspect that unites the perspective of both liberation theology and LDS theology is the brief reference in Brown's writings
to the Spanish priest of the 1500s, Bartolome de Las Casas. He, more than
any other Catholic leader during the era of the conquistadores, felt the pain
of oppressed and exploited indigenous tribes caused by the European inva-
sion of the Western Hemisphere. Rather than view native peoples as lower
life-forms or infidels to be brutalized by white, educated Christians who
enjoyed superior status because of their well-deserved privilege and lofty
understanding of the gospel, de Las Casas viewed natives as the very poor
that Christ intended to bless. Rather than become enslaved, they were to be
lifted up.

Beyond the summary Brown gives, the writings of Gutiérrez elsewhere
amplify this issue in poignant ways. Gutiérrez points out that de Las
Casas argued

> that social justice was one of the demands of the gospel. Justice for de
> Las Casas was closely bound to salvation. The covetousness and thirst
> for gold of the conquerors and colonizers led them to exploit the Indians
> iniquitously. . . . If they did not stop robbing, plundering, and exploiting
> the Indians, without doubt they were condemned because no one can be
> saved without observing justice.[40]

To the emperor in Spain, Bartolome de Las Casas eventually wrote of the
conquistadores:

> It is not true that they want to save and convert the Indians, rather they
> want to protect themselves in this in order to rob, despoil, oppress and
> enslave their neighbors. They do not want to save the Indians, nor preach
> the faith, nor do any other good.[41]

This perspective of de Las Casas, whom Brown describes as the very
first proponent of liberation theology, seems to be strikingly parallel to LDS
theology. For instance, Joseph Smith perceived the Native Americans to
be rightful heirs of the Book of Mormon promises because their ancestors
were among the original people of ancient Book of Mormon times. When
they had the gospel preached to them, they were zealous in their faith and
raised their families in peace and righteousness.

Instead of the racist views most white Americans held of "savage natives"
in the 1830s, Joseph Smith and his associates viewed Native Americans as
people of promise, the once-oppressed who would eventually "blossom

---

40. Gustavo Gutierrez and M. Richard Shaull, *Liberation and Change: Freedom
and Salvation—A Political Problem* (Atlanta: John Knox, 1977), 62.

41. Quoted in Gutierrez and Shaull, *Liberation and Change*, 62.

as the rose" (D&C 49:24). Surprisingly, the Book of Mormon champions the Indians' place in world history, assigning them a more glorious future than modern American whites.[42] Thus, Joseph Smith sent several LDS missionaries to Native American tribes just a few months after the church was organized in April 1830. They did not go out as military conquerors or seekers of gold but as humble servants of the people. The LDS elders declared to indigenous groups in the American frontier that the Book of Mormon was their book, the words and revelations of God to their American ancestors. Through this understanding, Native Americans would come to know of their forefathers and learn that they were of the ancient house of Israel, a remnant of the Jews (D&C 3:18–20; 10:48; 19:27; 28:8; 32:2).

Ultimately, early Latter-day Saints were commanded to "flee" from the mainstream United States and find refuge among the lands of the peaceable indigenous people in the wilderness. Upon the expulsion of pioneer Latter-day Saints from Illinois and Missouri to the Rocky Mountains, Brigham Young counseled his people to make peace, not war, with the natives. Typical Westerners abused and exploited Native Americans, even taking random rifle shots at them, just for sport. But Latter-day Saints operated from a different ethic—they fed and educated the natives. Brigham Young held to a policy of peaceful coexistence, and he continually searched for ways to succor and uplift indigenous peoples.

According to Book of Mormon prophecy, the Lord will "commence his work among all nations . . . to bring about the restoration of his people upon the earth. And with righteousness shall the Lord God judge the poor, and reprove with equity for the meek of the earth" (2 Nephi 30:8–9). God declares that the sorrow, suffering, and destruction of the Indians shall end in the last days, that they will gain access to a sacred record "hid up unto the Lord," and that this record—the Book of Mormon—will come forth from the Lord "in his own due time" as a blessing to indigenous people (Mormon 5:12).[43]

These teachings and practices are consistent with the tenets of Bartolome de Las Casas's liberation theology regarding God's concern for the indigenous poor and his great assurance that true Christianity is a theology that blesses and lifts native peoples, not one that exploits and oppresses them.

---

42. See Richard Lyman Bushman, *Joseph Smith: Rough Stone Rolling* (New York: Alfred A. Knopf, 2005), 98ff.

43. Armand L. Mauss, *All Abraham's Children: Changing Mormon Conceptions of Race and Lineage* (Urbana, Ill.: University of Illinois, 2003).

Conclusion

Theology for the "poorest of the poor," as articulated by Gutiérrez, Brown, and others, consists of concern for the Have-Nots and the ways in which they may become empowered. The ultimate objective of true Christianity is not that of accepting the world as it is, but of changing it. Liberation theology is a gospel of action to change the current system—praxis, thinking and doing, doing and thinking.

My sense is that in a number of fundamental doctrines, liberation theology and LDS theology have much in common. Like Karl Marx, early LDS church leaders recoiled at the dehumanizing elements of the Industrial Revolution. As an early LDS missionary in England, Elder Heber C. Kimball recorded his visceral reactions to the growing gap between rich and poor: "Wealth and luxury abounded, side by side with penury and want . . . the rich attired in the most costly dresses, and the next minute was saluted with the cries of the poor."[44] Likewise John Taylor, later to become the president of the LDS church, described the painful shock of seeing shopfloor conditions of exploited British workers:

> Thousands of them are immured in immense factories, little less than prisons, groaning under a wearisome, sickening, unhealthy labour; deprived of free, wholesome air; weak and emaciated, not having a sufficiency of the necessaries of life.[45]

These early leaders and their successors continually preached gospel values with the objective of lifting the poor. Declared Elder Parley P. Pratt:

> I expect the saints also to give money for the support of the poor among them, and this to the extent of all they have to spare; and I shall teach them so to do, and if they do not do it, their religion is vain. . . .
>
> We preach a religion which very materially affects men's purses; and a religion which does not affect men's purses is worse than none.[46]

A church, according to LDS theology, should first become aware of the plight of poverty and then, through empathy with those who suffer, design programs and strategies to lift the poor. Mere empathy will not suffice. Care for the poor must be pragmatic and lead to concrete outcomes. It consists of assisting the poor to obtain self-sustaining jobs in order to support themselves and their families. President John Taylor, for one, told LDS church

---

44. Quoted in Lucas and Woodworth, *Working Toward Zion*, 91.

45. John Taylor, *The Government of God* (Liverpool: S. W. Richards, and London: Latter-day Saint Book Depot, 1852), 12.

46. Parley P. Pratt, *Writings of Parley Parker Pratt*, ed. Parker Pratt Robison (Salt Lake City: Deseret News Press, 1952), 184.

leaders that they ought to find "employment for every man and woman and child . . . that wants to labor."[47]

A "handout" or other almsgiving may be helpful in the short term, when emergencies such as an illness, accident, or natural disaster arise. But the religion of Jesus Christ must go beyond mere giving in order to significantly change the world. Economic policies must be developed, and practical strategies must be devised that alter the structures of power and enable the poor to move up. LDS theology utilizes a variety of mechanisms beyond simple handouts to empower poor people. For instance, throughout LDS history, United-Order systems of productivity have been created, worker-owned cooperatives have been formed, and, more recently, microenterprise and microcredit systems for self-reliance have been designed and implemented around the world for poverty-stricken Latter-day Saints and their non-LDS neighbors. In 2000 LDS church president Gordon B. Hinkley announced the implementation of the "Perpetual Education Fund." Designed after the Perpetual Emigration Fund of the mid-1800s, the Perpetual Education Fund allows LDS youth in third-world circumstances to borrow money in order to pursue higher education, to be paid back only when employment is secured. Such efforts are based on a hand-up, rather than a hand-out. They generate self-determination and control of one's future rather than dependency. Perhaps the principles elucidated by former church president Joseph F. Smith best capture the essence of LDS theology toward the poor:

> The [LDS] Church has always sought to place its members in a way to help themselves, rather than adopting the method of so many charitable institutions of providing for only present needs. When the help is withdrawn or used up, more must be provided from the same sources, thus making paupers of the poor, and teaching them the incorrect principle of relying on others' help, instead of depending upon their own exertions. . . . Our idea of charity, therefore, is to relieve present wants and then to put the poor in a way to help themselves, so that in turn they may help others.[48]

While some adherents to LDS theology might downplay the parallels between LDS religion and liberation theology, there is much in common between the two paradigms. A primary purpose of The Church of Jesus Christ of Latter-day Saints is "to transform society so that the world may be a better and more peaceful place in which to live," according to David O. McKay, the Church's prophet in the 1950s.[49]

---

47. John Taylor, in *Journal of Discourses*, 20:165, March 2, 1879.

48. Joseph F. Smith, "The Message of the Latter-day Saints on Relief for the Poor," *Improvement Era* 10 (August 1907): 832.

49. David O. McKay, in *111th Annual Conference of The Church of Jesus Christ of Latter-day Saints* (Salt Lake City: The Church of Jesus Christ of Latter-day Saints,

While acknowledging that there may also be divergent views regarding certain aspects of theology and action with respect to the world's poor, this essay attempts to emphasize areas of integration. The attitude I bring to the task of comparing and contrasting LDS theology with the theology of liberation reflects the spirit of LDS church official and scholar B. H. Roberts, who injoined the following Christian saying on doctrinal issues at the general conference of the church in 1912: "In essentials, let there be unity; in non-essentials, liberty; and in all things, charity."[50]

This seems consistent with Joseph Smith's embrace of much that is good in other religions and philosophies: "In reality and essence we do not differ so far in our religious views, but that we could all drink into one principle of love. One of the grand fundamental principles of 'Mormonism' is to receive truth, let it come from whence it may."[51]

As Spencer W. Kimball, president of the church in the 1970s, put it, "The gospel of Jesus Christ is a gospel for all the world and for all people. . . . You will find so-called Mormonism to be a growing, vibrant, dynamic, and challenging church, indeed a way of life, touching upon every avenue of living, every facet of life."[52] Both LDS and liberation theologies share a number of commonalities within the broad arena of lifting the poor and transforming the world as it now is and as it has been over past centuries of deprivation and suffering. As one who shares much of the same faith with Gutiérrez and Brown, I salute my fellow travelers as we walk the road of the "poorest of the poor" together. Perhaps President John Taylor's words most clearly give the sense of a common mission we share—Catholic theologians pushing for human liberation through their powerful voices in behalf of the poor, and I, a Latter-day Saint elder, a global pilgrim trying to serve the poor. The congruence between our two theological disciplines seems to fit President Taylor's counsel:

> We are engaged in a work that God has set his hand to accomplish . . . to introduce correct principles of every kind—principles of morality, social principles, good political principles; principles relative to the government of the earth we live in . . . with all our weaknesses and foibles clinging to us the Lord has called us from the nations of the

1941), 106, as quoted in David O. McKay, *Gospel Ideals: Selections from the Discourses of David O. McKay* (Salt Lake City: Improvement Era, 1953), 104.

50. B. H. Roberts, in *83rd Annual Conference of The Church of Jesus Christ of Latter-day Saints* (Salt Lake City: The Church of Jesus Christ of Latter-day Saints, 1912), 30.

51. Joseph Fielding Smith, comp., *Teachings of the Prophet Joseph Smith* (Salt Lake City: Deseret, 1977), 313.

52. Spencer W. Kimball, "The Stone Cut without Hands," *Ensign* 6 (May 1976): 7.

earth to be his co-adjutors and co-laborers, his fellow-workmen and assistants, in rolling forth his purposes.[53]

When we see the gospel from the underside, from the wretched struggles of the global poor, the very mission and ministry of both liberation theology and LDS theology fit together in many ways. May we continue to walk this path as God's co-laborers in the years to come.

Rejoinder

Robert McAfee Brown

THIS PAPER CANNOT HOPE TO MATCH THE CLARITY and compassion of Professor Woodworth's contribution. This is not a statement of gratuitous praise but a genuine cry of gratitude. The most I can do is offer a few introductory remarks in response and see if they can provide us with material for initiating further dialogue.

The Importance and Unimportance of Starting Points and Conclusions

The starting point of a theological exercise is often arrived at with meticulous care, whether it be in christology, ecclesiology, philosophy, or the like. As it develops, its various parts are seen to be converging on a creative synthesis. A liberation theology has its own contribution to this exercise. As we will presently note, liberation theology's contributions bear the hallmark of their places of origin, but I want particularly to offer the most distinctive contribution to our present endeavor. Its origin is with Juan Luis Segundo, who says there is a starting point *anyone* can adopt. It goes, very simply, *"The world should not be the way it is."* There is also an ethical dimension to this starting point, for Segundo goes on to remark, "If we believe that the world is all right the way it is . . . we will never understand what liberation theology is all about."[54]

Let this starting point, and its ethical corollary, provide a basis for further discussion. Segundo's starting point can lead in innumerable directions.

53. John Taylor, in *Journal of Discourses*, 15:169, May 26, 1872.
54. Brown, *Introduction to Liberation Theology*, 51.

Let us accept and develop the largesse that such a starting point implies. It is but an excellent beginning on which to build.

Theology as the Work of the Poor

Professor Woodworth develops this point in great and helpful detail, and I return to it in order to make sure we continue to give him his due. Gutiérrez, as earlier suggested, speaks of "doing theology from the underside of history." We have to hear this as more than a romantic possibility. It means often being hungry, lacking the minimal sufficiencies for sheer physical survival. It means being unable to buy books or to procure travel allowances to go to international conferences and living also with an ongoing anger at the unfair allocations of food, drink, education, hospital services, and all the things those of us in the northern hemisphere often take for granted. It means never being secure about the morrow and having almost no possibility for such things as academic tenure or endowed chairs in universities.

The above catalogue may seem far distanced from the situation of theologians, as we know them elsewhere, but it is just that distance that must be acknowledged and seen as part of the ongoing situation and issue of liberation theologians.

A Conference: An Experiment

Suppose a group of North American theologians were to decide that they must enter into dialogue with a parallel group from Latin America, or any part of the third world. Much good could be done if, for example, instead of reading learned papers to one another, each member of the group had a half day to share his or her own life story. No doubt there would be expressions of guilt over extravagant living standards coming from the North American component, possibly a healthy aspect of the dialogue. But, at the least, we would need to draw out of such an experience a recognition that the harsh disparities between the two groups in terms of sustainable living standards were finally not just theological, but also social, political, and economic, and that we must learn about such disciplines in order to get to the root causes of the disparities.

This is not necessarily an agenda that will attract theologians from the north or the south. But those who ignore these realities will finally have to acknowledge that we live in the midst of a "sinful nation" in the most profound and deep sense of the words. At the very least, those from the north would have to acknowledge that themes from the south will not go away or be forgotten. They will fester and become more deeply-rooted.

The question becomes, to those in the north, *How can the rich learn from the poor*? Is it even possible for that to happen in any significant way? I do not pretend to have an answer to that question. I know, at least, that such an endeavor will have to be undertaken communally rather than individually and that those who engage in the struggle will have to be prepared for hard sailing until some trust is built up on both sides. In any such situation, there are redemptive possibilities that can resist the most firm attempts to take the poor off the agenda.

An Extra Proposal: Existential Reading of Scripture

An attempt to create situations where the dialogue can continue would appear more and more necessary. I think the ingredient needed, if we are to recognize the necessity of doing theology from the underside, would be comprehension of another phrase of Gutiérrez's, theology is always "the second act."[55] His point is that the first act is always commitment—engaging oneself with what is going on. Only when a fundamental act of commitment to the cause of the poor has been made will new things begin to happen. Here I propose to enter again into the situation as participant rather than as a mere reporter.

There are at least three parts of the life of faith that can be called "scripture," as we discover them in times of trouble. We are called upon, I believe, to read these different kinds of scripture existentially. This is a word that has gotten rather tired from overuse and needs to be reclaimed. To read existentially is to read with passion, with engagement out of the collection of writings that comprise what we call Holy Scripture. I learn from the liberation theologians that the writings of the prophets are a collection from which we must not stray too far. This is true of all our traditions and yet we continue to need such reminders.

We must accord almost the same veneration to the tradition that has grown up around certain writings that carry on the story that the Bible will never let us finish. I believe that within this grouping are the stories of the people often a little more like us. These people have a special capacity for revealing truths that we often lose at great cost to them and us. At all events, they are ones who have put themselves on the line and who are always on the edge of what may appear close to heresy, but they in so doing help us to refine our own faith.

In addition we are to keep looking at and (sometimes) following the "scriptures" as *our inner selves.* These scriptures remind us that we are a motley crew standing always in need of help. Their great gift to us will be to remind us that God's greatest problems surely come from the moderates. "Better a live heresy than a dead orthodoxy," P. T. Forsyth used to say, and

---

55. Ibid., 102.

if we take him with a grain of salt the poor can communicate new courage to us.

It is easy to say or write such things and utter them from the safety of ecclesiastical structures that, sadly, have taken the place of the "tents" of our forebearers. In all the matters this paper has discussed we are driven back finally to alternative kinds of "scriptures." The rediscovery of the Bible is perhaps the greatest gift we have received from liberation theologians. Let us not be disdainful to the wonder of that gift.

Reply to "Brother" Brown

Warner Woodworth

I AM GRATEFUL FOR THE LOVING WORDS of Robert McAfee Brown. If I may be so bold, I want to now refer to him in the LDS vernacular as "Brother Brown."

Changes over Time: Starting and Concluding Points

Much has changed since we drafted our earliest manuscripts in the late 1990s. Sadly, Brother Brown has passed on to his heavenly reward. Because of his lifetime of devotion to the "least of these," God's poor, I'm confident the reward will be great. As Christ taught, "Inasmuch as ye have done it unto one of the least of these my brethren, ye have done it unto me" (Matt. 25:40).

Another change we must inexorably face is the ongoing reality of poverty around the globe. In the past several years, millions more children have been born into lives of wretched poverty. And millions of them have already died because of that global reality. Globalization expands the gap between rich and poor. Events such as genocide and drought in Africa and wars in Iraq and Afghanistan have pushed millions more into the ugly reality of poverty.

As a consequence of these changes, over 842 million people in the world today are continually hungry. "Five billion people live in the developing world" (125 countries) while only about 50 nations (0.9 billion people) make up the developed global economy, according to Bread for the World Institute.[56] As I reflect on this incongruity, the words of Mother Teresa come to mind: "It is a very great poverty to decide that a child must die that you might live as you wish."[57] This wonderful nun of Calcutta, "Saint to the Poor," moved out from the safety and seclusion of her convent precisely because, as Brother Brown quoted Juan Luis Segundo as saying, "the world should not be as it is."[58]

Theology and the Poor

I was pleased to learn from Brother Brown of Gutiérrez's notion about "doing theology from the underside of history." It fits so well with a favorite quotation that I use in my Brigham Young University courses. The words are those of Dietrich Bonhoeffer, a Protestant pastor and a victim of the Holocaust in Nazi Germany who was hanged in the Flossenburg Concentration Camp in 1945.

> It is an experience of incomparable value to have learned to see the great events of the history of the world from beneath; from the viewpoint of the useless, the suspect, the powerless, the oppressed, and the despised— in a word, from the viewpoint of those who suffer.[59]

Seeing history and/or doing theology from the "underside" opens one's eyes to the suffering of others. It helps us understand the plight of the jobless man, the malnourished child, and the mother who is severely ill but who lacks access to healthcare. It develops empathy in us that drives remedial action. Without such empathy, the gap between Haves and Have-Nots may never be reduced.

56. Bread for the World Institute, "World Hunger and Poverty: How They Fit Together," http://www.bread.org/hungerbasics/international.html#text1 (accessed April 26, 2005).

57. This quote is generally attributed to Mother Teresa, see http://www.ad2000.com.au/. Mother Teresa also said, "I feel that the poorest country is the country that has to kill the unborn child to be able to have extra things and extra pleasures." Mother Teresa, *My Life for the Poor*, ed. José Luis Gonzáles-Balado and Janet N. Playfoot (San Francisco: Harper and Row, 1985), 61.

58. Brown, *Introduction to Liberation Theology*, 51.

59. Dietrich Bonhoeffer, *Letters and Papers from Prison*, trans. R. H. Fullen, et al. (New York: Macmillan, 1971), 17. For a concise biographical note on Bonhoeffer, see Geffrey B. Kelly, "Dietrich Bonhoeffer," in *A New Handbook of Christian Theologians*, ed. Donald W. Musser and Joseph L. Price (Nashville: Abingdon, 1996), 85–97.

An Experiment

I love Brother Brown's proposal for a conference on liberation theology that would bring together priests of Northern countries with their counterparts from Southern countries. Instead of formal papers and academic debates, each participant would simply tell his or her personal story in terms of faith, economics, and social justice. This process would move those of us from the industrialized nations to really listen and learn. Such a dialogue would build new global awareness, as well as perhaps life-changing guilt and a commitment to action.

Existential Scripture Reading/Scripture Living

Translating the truths of the scriptures into our personal lives is a great challenge. Brother Brown recommends that we read the prophets existentially and with passion, that we accept traditions that have emerged down through history, and that we also listen to the living "scriptures" written in our minds and hearts. To my mind, this is the bottom line of liberation theology. It is a process of internalizing, not simply adhering to, the Ten Commandments written on external stone tablets or the pages of Exodus.

As I conclude, let me mention that in 1999 I went to Central America where some four dozen BYU students spent the summer doing "theology for the poor." They taught indigenous communities appropriate technology such as new square-foot gardening techniques that will triple the amount of fruit and vegetables produced in small family gardens. They cared for babies in the huge Hospital Hermano Pedro, a facility bearing the name of a priest who dedicated his life to nurturing sick and abandoned Mayan children in Antigua, Guatemala. They set up computer labs with donated equipment in rural villages to help overcome the digital divide and offered micro-enterprise training to help Latino families become self-sufficient through tiny family-run businesses. Another team labored to rebuild houses in El Salvador that were damaged or destroyed by the terrible 7.6 magnitude earthquakes in 2001. The horrendous toll of the quakes included 1,200 dead; 8,000 injured; 150,000 homes destroyed; and another 186,000 homes badly damaged.[60]

These young BYU social entrepreneurs know very little about liberation theology. In training them for three to four months of voluntary service

---

60. For more information on this earthquake, see Jake Spence, Mike Lanchin, and Geoff Thale, *From Elections to Earthquakes: Reform and Participation in Post-War El Salvador* (Cambridge: Hemisphere Initiatives, 2001), 3; and "The El Salvador Earthquakes of January and February 2001: Context, Characteristics, and Implications for Seismic Risk," http://www.geologie.ens.fr/~madariag/Papers/ElSalvadorEarthquakes.pdf.

prior to our departure for Central America, we spent most of our time emphasizing teamwork, management, the effectiveness of non-governmental organizations, project planning, and other skills. When I went down to El Salvador to assess results with a group of donors and organizational consultants, we went to a place called "Habitat," a squatter community of victims of a huge quake in the 1970s. Families there are still waiting for government aid and promised help from the United Nations and the Red Cross.

I was struck during our visit with the power of one to make a difference. Thousands of families were suffering, and here was a group of young middle-class, American volunteers who were dedicating their time and energy to alleviating the anguish these families were experiencing. These were just average kids, quite unsophisticated, but they were making a real difference.

On the wall of the run-down, tin-roofed shelter in Habitat where we met with barrio leaders for an assessment was a huge photo of one of my heroes, Archbishop Oscar Romero, who spent his life in service to the needy. The words "el profeta" were scrawled in handwritten graffiti on the wall immediately above Romero's photo. He championed the poor, and because of that he was accused of being a leftist, a communist, and labeled with other derogatory names. In 1980, he was gunned down in the Chapel of Divine Providence at his San Salvador cathedral, a martyr to the cause of the poor. The evidence over the years since has pointed to right-wing paramilitaries known as "death squads" as the perpetrators of his murder. To make matters worse, when crowds of poor Salvadorans gathered to pay homage on the outside steps and plaza of the cathedral during Father Romero's funeral, government troops fired on the masses, killing forty and wounding hundreds more.

In my own LDS tradition, Joseph Smith suffered a similar fate. He too, in the minds of many, was a radical prophet for the downtrodden. Like Romero, he railed against oppressors of the poor and preached against the wicked—those who were both rich and proud and who did not share their material blessings. Smith declared that he was out to "revolutionize the whole world," to "lift up the hands which hang down, and strengthen the feeble knees" of those who are weak and impoverished (D&C 81:5). And like Romero, the Prophet Joseph was gunned down for his ideas.

Both Joseph Smith and Oscar Romero died because of their reformist ideas for changing the world. They hated injustice, fought for equality, and were killed by assailants who got away with their crimes.

At BYU, where I have my office, a picture of each of these martyrs hangs on my wall, side by side. They never knew each other, but they shared a common mission—that of serving the marginalized and teaching a gospel for liberating the poor. Separated by 140 years of history, they are now united in death. Their (and our) causes are very much alive and will be better advanced as Latter-day Saints and liberation theologians achieve mutual understanding and engage in cooperative work.

About the Authors

Robert McAfee Brown (Ph.D. Columbia University) earned a bachelor of divinity degree from Union Theological Seminary in New York and served as a Navy chaplain from 1945–46. He was a Presbyterian minister and pacifist, a writer and public speaker, an ecumenist and radical thinker, a political activist and from time to time a jailed man of conscience. He was a teacher at Amherst College, Stanford University, Union Theological Seminary and the Pacific School of Religion. He died in 2001.

Warner Woodworth (Ph.D. University of Michigan) has been a visiting scholar at the University of Rio de Janeiro, Brazil; the International Institute of Labour Studies in Geneva, Switzerland; the University of Hawaii; Vilnius University, Lithuania; and a return to the Michigan Business School. While working on his doctoral degree at the University of Michigan, he established an LDS Institute of Religion in Ann Arbor, where he taught several institute classes. He has co-founded fifteeen NGOs that provide microfinancing and humanitarian service to poor communities. He is author or co-author of ten books, over 150 articles, and hundreds of conference papers presented around the globe. He is a professor of organizational leadership and strategy at the Marriott School of Management, Brigham Young University.

Liberation Theologies:
The Global Pursuit of Justice

Robert McAfee Brown

Bibliography A

Thus far, it would appear that liberation theology is of intense interest to a few people spread across the globe but concentrated in Central and South America, with increasing spillover into our own hemisphere.

Bibliography A recognizes that there is much to learn from the theological strands pointed to in the text itself. There will be some, at least, who may find exploration in this area challenging and rewarding. Bibliography A includes a few further resources that will enable such research to continue. Many books listed in the section below are substantial, and will provide much food for theological thought. Most of them have bibliographies of their own, encouraging even further study.

Some of Gutiérrez's Own Writings

Essential Writings of Gustavo Gutiérrez. Ed. James B. Nickoloff. Maryknoll, N.Y.: Orbis, 1969. An invaluable collection of source readings.

The God of Life. Maryknoll, N.Y.: Orbis, 1991. Biblical resources for social transformation.

Las Casas, In Search of the Poor of Jesus Christ. Maryknoll, N.Y.: Orbis, 1993. The definitive work.

On Job: God-Talk and the Suffering of the Innocent. Maryknoll, N.Y.: Orbis, 1987.

The Power of the Poor in History. Maryknoll, N.Y.: Orbis, 1983. Essays on theology and politics.

A Theology of Liberation: History, Politics and Salvation. Rev. ed. Maryknoll, N.Y.: Orbis, 1998. Still the basic work.

We Drink from Our Own Wells. Maryknoll, N.Y.: Orbis, 1994. A "spirituality of liberation."

Books about Gutiérrez and other Latin Americans

Brown, Robert McAfee. *Gustavo Gutiérrez: An Introduction to Liberation Theology.* Maryknoll, N.Y.: Orbis, 1990. Treatment of his life and thought.

Ellis, Marc H., and Otto Maduro, eds. *Expanding the View: Gustavo Gutiérrez and the Future of Liberation Theology.* Maryknoll, N.Y.: Orbis, 1990. A condensed edition.

————. *The Future of Liberation Theology: Essays in Honor of Gustavo Gutiérrez.*
    Maryknoll, N.Y.: Orbis, 1989. A large *Festschrift* with many contributors.
Hennelly, Alfred T. *Liberation Theologies: The Global Pursuit of Justice.*
    Mystic, Conn.: Twenty Third Publications, 1995. A comprehensive "global
    pursuit."
————. *Liberation Theology, A Documentary History.* Maryknoll, N.Y.: Orbis,
    1990. A treasure-trove of primary sources.
Sobrino, Jon, and Ignacio Ellacuria, eds. *Mysterium Liberationis.* Maryknoll,
    N.Y.: Orbis, 1993. A large symposium of mature reflections.

Bibliography B

Leaving the impression that liberation theology is a concern only of the
Latin American world misses the mark. What one discovers is that even
though books about liberation theology have almost become a cottage
industry, they represent only the tip of the iceberg in relation to total productivity. The above essay may have contributed to misunderstanding, limiting itself (for reasons of time and space) largely to Hispanic sources. But
the materials touched upon, however briefly, are only one part of the ongoing impact of this very young theology. No one has begun to do justice to
it, until such an one realizes that liberation theologies do not begin where
there are theologians and libraries and printing presses, but whenever and
wherever there are such realities as injustice, oppression, hunger, torture,
and anything else that impedes the possibility for a new humanity.

The theology takes different forms in different indigenous situations
with different vocabularies and different customs out of which new theologies are forged. These new theologies deserve examination before the quest
is over. Bibliography B will note briefly the broader spectrum of liberation
theology writings, lest a one-sided view of it from this article result. One
book listed above, Hennelly's *Liberation Theologies: The Global Pursuit of
Justice*, is an excellent transition from one area of concern to many more.

Aquino, María Pilar. *Our Cry for Life: Feminist Theology from Latin America.*
    Maryknoll, N.Y.: Orbis, 1993. Latin American women raising their voices.
Cone, James H. *God of the Oppressed.* New York: Seabury, 1975. An early but
    still relevant, ground-breaking book. See also Cone, James H. *Martin and
    Malcolm and America.* Maryknoll, N.Y.: Orbis, 1991. Liberation issues in
    the black community of the United States.
Fernandez, Eleazar S. *Toward a Theology of Struggle.* Maryknoll, N.Y.: Orbis,
    1993. A liberation theology for the Philippines.
Moody, Linda A. *Women Encounter God: Theology Across the Boundaries of
    Difference.* Maryknoll, N.Y.: Orbis, 1996. A map of the topography and
    the trials.

Park, Andrew Sung. *The Wounded Heart of God: The Asian Concept of Han and the Christian Doctrine of Sin.* Nashville: Abingdon, 1993. A sensitive cross-cultural treatment.

Pieris, Aloysius. *An Asian Theology of Liberation.* Maryknoll, N.Y.: Orbis, 1988.

Song, Choan-Seng. *Theology from the Womb of Asia.* Maryknoll, N.Y.: Orbis, 1986. Building new bridges.

Thistlethwaite, Susan Brooks, and Mary Potter Engel, eds. *Lift Every Voice: Constructing Christian Theologies from the Underside.* San Francisco: Harper and Row, 1990. Connecting with liberation groups throughout the world.

West, Gerald O., ed. *Biblical Hermeneutics of Liberation: Modes of Reading the Bible in the South African Context.* Maryknoll, N.Y.: Orbis, 1995. Just what the title describes.

Williams, Delores S. *Sisters in the Wilderness: The Challenge of Womanist God-Talk.* Maryknoll, N.Y.: Orbis, 1993. Powerful challenges from biblical resources and elsewhere.

Liberation Bibliography

Warner Woodworth

The selections below highlight a number of LDS-related works that focus on the church and the poor. While Latter-day Saint scholars have much to learn from liberation theology, those whose theological interests focus on the poor may want to learn more about the economic and temporal teachings of LDS theology as well. The following is a brief list of suggested readings on these topics:

Alexander, Thomas G. *Mormonism in Transition: A History of the Latter-day Saints, 1890–1930.* Urbana: University of Illinois Press, 1986.

Arrington, Leonard J. *Great Basin Kingdom: An Economic History of the Latter-day Saints, 1830–1900.* Cambridge: Harvard University Press, 1958.

Arrington, Leonard J., Feramorz Y. Fox, and Dean L. May. *Building the City of God: Community and Cooperation among the Mormons.* Salt Lake City: Deseret, 1976.

Bushman, Richard L. *Joseph Smith and the Beginnings of Mormonism.* Urbana: University of Illinois Press, 1984.

Cook, Lyndon. *Joseph Smith and the Law of Consecration.* Provo, Utah: Grandin, 1985.

Flanders, Robert Bruce. *Nauvoo: Kingdom on the Mississippi.* Urbana: University of Illinois Press, 1965.

Geddes, Joseph A. *The United Order among the Mormons: An Unfinished Experiment in Economic Organization.* Salt Lake City: Deseret News Press, 1924.

Gottlieb, Robert and Peter Wiley. *America's Saints: The Rise of Mormon Power.* New York: Putnam's, 1984.

Heinerman, John, and Anson Shupe. *The Mormon Corporate Empire.* Boston: Beacon, 1985.

Huff, Kent W. *Joseph Smith's United Order: A Non-Communalistic Interpretation.* Orem, Utah: Cedar Fort, 1988.

Kauffman, Ruth, and Reginald Wright Kauffman. *The Latter-day Saints: A Study of the Mormons in the Light of Economic Conditions.* Urbana: University of Illinois Press, 1912; reprinted in 1994.

Encyclopedia of Mormonism. Ed. Daniel H. Ludlow. 4 vols. New York: Macmillan, 1992.

Lucas, James W. and Warner P. Woodworth. *Working toward Zion: Principles of the United Order for the Modern World.* Salt Lake City: Aspen, 1996.

McNiff, William J. *Heaven on Earth: A Planned Mormon Society.* Oxford, Ohio: Mississippi Valley, 1940.

Mangum, Garth L., and Bruce D. Blumell. *The Mormons' War on Poverty.* Salt Lake City: University of Utah Press, 1993.

Nibley, Hugh W. *Approaching Zion.* Ed. Don Norton. Salt Lake City: Deseret, 1986.

Robison, Lindon. *Becoming a Zion People.* Salt Lake City: Hawkes, 1992.

Rudd, Glen L. *Pure Religion: The Story of Church Welfare Since 1930.* Salt Lake City: The Church of Jesus Christ of Latter-day Saints, 1995.

Wagner, Gordon E. "Consecration and Stewardship: A Socially Efficient System of Justice." Ph.D. diss, Cornell University, 1977.

A Dialogue on Feminist Theology

Can a Male Savior Save Women?
Liberating Christology from Patriarchy

Rosemary Radford Ruether

In Vatican and Roman Catholic Episcopal statements, Christology has been the keystone argument against women's ordination. It is said that women, by nature, cannot image Christ. Therefore they cannot be priests, since priests represent Christ.[1] This argument has been echoed in other Anglican, Lutheran, and Eastern Orthodox high church statements. What is the meaning of this use of Christology against women's full participation in the Christian church? If women cannot represent Christ, in what sense can Christ represent women? Does this mean that Christ does not redeem women but reinforces women's bondage in a patriarchal social system? If this is the case, shouldn't women who seek liberation from patriarchy reject Christianity?

A traditional claim is that Christ is the redeemer and representative of all humanity. He overcame bondage to sin, the universal human dilemma. Thus, it would seem that the symbols that the Christian church uses to express Christology should manifest a like universality and inclusivity. These symbols should embrace the authentic humanness and fulfilled hopes of all persons. How is it possible that more than half of humanity, more than half of the members of Christian churches themselves, find themselves inferiorized and excluded by Christology?

---

1. This argument that women can't be ordained because they don't image Christ is found in the "Vatican Declaration on the Question of the Admission of Women to the Ministerial Priesthood" (1976), sec. 27. The argument was repeated in the pastoral letter by Pope John Paul II, "The Dignity and Vocation of Women," September 31, 1988, sec. 26; and in the pastoral on women by the American Catholic bishops, "One in Christ: A Pastoral Response to the Concerns of Women for Church and Society" (second draft: Origins, April 5, 1990, sec. 115, 730).

In this article I will examine the development of the Christological symbols and how they have been shaped by an androcentric ideology that explicitly excludes women from representing Christ. I will then ask whether Christology can be liberated from this androcentric bias and become genuinely inclusive of all women.

Early Christianity used the word *Logos* to define the presence of God made incarnate in Jesus Christ. This term drew on a long tradition of religious philosophy. In Greek and Hellenistic Jewish philosophy, the divine Logos was the means by which the transcendent God came forth in the beginning to shape the visible cosmos. The Logos was simultaneously the immanence of God and the ground of this visible cosmos. In Hellenistic Jewish terms, the Logos, or *Sophia* (Wisdom), was God's self-manifestation by which God created the world, providentially guided it, and was revealed to it. It was also through the Logos that the world was reconciled to God.

The Logos was particularly identified with the rational principle in each human soul. By linking the term *Christ* (Messiah), through whom God redeemed the world, to the Logos, as the creational principle, early Christianity prevented a split between redemption and creation that was threatened by Gnosticism. Christians affirmed that the God revealed in Jesus Christ was the same God who created the world in the beginning. Christ was the authentic ground of creation, manifest in fulfilled form. This concept of the Logos as the divine identity of Christ would seem to be inclusive of women, pointing all humans, male and female, to the foundation of their true humanness.[2]

But this Hellenistic philosophical tradition was also shaped in a patriarchal culture that gave the terms *Logos* and *Christ* an androcentric bias. Since divinity, sovereign power, rationality, and normative humanity were assumed to be masculine traits, the theological points of reference for defining Christ were specified in male terms. Normative humanity, the image of God in "man," and the divine Logos became interlocking androcentric concepts in the theological definition of Christ, reinforcing the assumption that God is male and that the human Christ must also be male in order to reveal the male God.

Mainstream Christianity has never said that God is literally male, but it has assumed that God represents preeminently the qualities of rationality and sovereign power. Since men were assumed to be more rational than women and exercised the public power denied to women, the male metaphor

---

2. For the development of Logos Christology in the New Testament, especially in the Gospel of John, see C. H. Dodd, *The Interpretation of the Fourth Gospel* (London: Cambridge University Press, 1953), 263-85. For its development in the second century, see Erwin R. Goodenough, *The Theology of Justin Martyr* (Amsterdam: Philo, 1968), 139-75.

was seen as appropriate for God, while female metaphors for God came to be regarded as inappropriate and even pagan. The Logos who reveals the "Father" was presumed to be properly imaged as male, even though the Jewish Wisdom tradition had used the female metaphor, Sophia, for this same idea. The maleness of the historical Jesus reinforced this preference for male-identified metaphors, such as Logos and Son of God, over the female metaphor of Sophia.

In Trinitarian theology, the use of the word *Son* for the Logos or second person of the Trinity is misleading since it suggests a subordinate and derivative status of the Logos, such that the male child is "begotten" by and under the power of his Father. This "Son-Father" metaphor is used to represent the immanence of God as derived from divine transcendence. Taken literally, these metaphors reinforce the maleness of God and establish a patriarchal relationship between the two male persons of God.

These notions of God's maleness also affect the interpretation of the concept of *imago dei*. Genesis 1:27–28 explains, "So God created man [Adam] in his own image, in the image of God he created him, male and female he [they] created them." This formula, with its plural, collective term for God, leaves open the possibility that the human thus created is to be understood generically. Genesis 1:27 teaches that the image of God is possessed by both men and women. This would mean that woman shares in the stewardship over creation referred to in Genesis 1:26.[3]

However, most patristic and medieval tradition rejected the possibility that women were equally theomorphic.[4] In most interpretations the concept of *imago dei* was distinguished from gender difference. One way to interpret this distinction was to make the *imago dei* asexually spiritual—neither male nor female. Gender difference would then refer to the bodily characteristics that humans share with animals but not with God. Following Philo, some church fathers saw gender as appearing only in the fallen state of "man." For example, Gregory Nyssa read the text in this way.[5]

St. Augustine also claimed that women possess the image of God in a sex-neutral way, but as females they do not actually image God. Men possess

---

3. For a critical exegesis of this passage, see Phyllis A. Bird, "'Male and Female He Created Them': Gen. 1:27b in the Context of the Priestly Account of Creation," *Harvard Theological Review* 74, no. 2 (1981): 129-59.

4. For essays on the historical development of the exclusion and gradual inclusion of women as *imago dei*, see Kari Elisabeth Borresen, ed., *Image of God: Gender Models in Judaeo-Christian Tradition* (Minneapolis: Fortress, 1995).

5. Gregory Nyssa, *De Hominis Opificio* [On the Creation of Man] 16.7; see Rosemary Radford Ruether, "Misogynism and Virginal Feminism in the Fathers of the Church," in *Religion and Sexism: Images of Women in the Jewish and Christian Traditions,* ed. Rosemary Radford Ruether (New York: Simon and Schuster, 1974), 153-55.

the image of God, while women are included in it only under the male. Femaleness does not image God but images the bodily creation that the human male is given to rule over.[6] Such an interpretation of the image of God reflects the patriarchal legal and social order in which the *pater familias,* or male head of the family, is the corporate head and representative of the whole *familia*—women, children, slaves, animals, and land under his control. He alone possesses personhood juridically in the public order.

This concept of women as lacking full personhood, in the image of God only derivatively, was reinforced by the scholastic appropriation of Aristotelian biology. This (false) biology asserted that the male alone provides the seed or form of the offspring, while the female contributes only the material substratum that is formed.[7] If this process is fully carried out and the male seed fully forms the female matter, males will always be born.

According to Aristotelian biology, females are the result of a defect in gestation in which the maternal matter fails to be fully formed by the male seed. In this construct of male to female as form to matter (that denies the existence of the female ovum), the female is defined as a defective human, lacking in full humanity and inferior in bodily strength, adequate rationality, and moral self-control. These defects preclude both autonomy and rule over others for females and demand that women be subject to men.

The female is defined by medieval theologians such as Thomas Aquinas (who appropriates this Aristotelian view) as a non-normative human who lacks the fullness of human nature. The male is the perfect or complete expression of the human species. Aquinas concludes from this anthropology that the maleness of the historical Jesus was an ontological necessity, not a historical accident. In order for Jesus (as the Christ) to represent humanity as a whole, he must be male, because only the male possesses the fullness of human nature. The female cannot represent the human, either for herself or generically.[8]

This interlocking set of ideas about the maleness of God, the Logos of God, the *imago dei,* and Christ threaten to undermine the basic Christian belief that women are included in the redemption of "man" won by Jesus Christ. The church fathers assumed women were included, while being humanly non-normative and nontheomorphic, because they assumed a patriarchal ideology in which women are included under an ontological male theology, just as they were included under and represented by the male head of the family juridically in patriarchal society and law.

---

6. Saint Augustine, *De Trinitate* (Trunhoiti: Typographi Brepols Editores Pontificii, 1968), 7.7.10.

7. Aristotle, *De Generatione Animalium,* 729b, 737-38.

8. Saint Thomas Aquinas, *Summa Theologica* (Chicago: Encylopedia Britannica, 1990).

Today women have won the rights of citizens or "civil persons" in the political-juridical order. Higher education, opened to women, has disproved the notion of women's inferior intelligence. Aristotelian biology has been proven false. Indeed the actual gestation of the child proceeds in the opposite way, with the female ovum and uterus shaping a female generic fetus from which a differentiation process must take place in order for a male to develop.[9] All the androcentric assumptions on which the Christological symbols were based have been called into question.

Today a Christology that elevates Jesus' human maleness to ontological necessity makes the Christ symbol noninclusive of women. In order to reaffirm the basic Christian belief that women are included in redemption in Christ, all the symbolic underpinnings of Christology must be reinterpreted. Is this possible? What might this mean? In order to reassess the relationship of Christology and gender, we might start by examining the more gender inclusive possibilities of the basic symbols of God and the image of God, Christ, and the Logos of God on which Christology was built. We should also consider Jesus' own teaching and praxis.

Jewish tradition sees God beyond gender. God is thought of as both a ruler and a parent. This divine ruler-parent sometimes exercises power in wrathful and judgmental ways, but, at other times, is merciful, forgiving, compassionate, patient, and long-suffering. In terms of gender stereotypes, God is androgynous. Sometimes female metaphors are explicitly used for these maternal aspects of God.[10] However, since the male pronoun is used for God, this might suggest that God is an androgynous male.

But Judaism also rejects literalism about verbal or visual images used for God. God is beyond all such creaturely images, and to take any image literally is idolatry. In order to combine these two insights, God's androgynous nature and transcendence of all anthropomorphic literalism, we must be clearer about the metaphorical character of such gender images. In God's self, God is neither male nor female (nor humanly gendered at all). But our metaphors for God must be both male and female. This cannot be done simply by combining patriarchal masculine and feminine gender stereotypes or even by giving a male God a feminine side, for this still leaves women without full humanity.

We might use gender symbols in a way that affirms that God both transcends and yet includes the fullness of the humanity of both men and women. Women are rational agents who reflect these qualities of God, while men have caring, nurturing capacities. Only then can we say that both men

---

9. Mary Jane Sherfey, *The Nature and Evolution of Female Sexuality* (New York: Random House, 1972).

10. For example, see Isaiah 42:13-14 and 49:14-15. Also Leonard Swidler, *Biblical Affirmations of Women* (Philadelphia: Westminister, 1979).

and women possess the image of God, in mutuality, and yet also as full persons in their own right. Women are not simply included under a male head, or thought of as a complementary part of a whole found only in the heterosexual couple.

Another way the Hebrew tradition brought androgyny into God was to picture the immanences of God in female metaphors. The most notable of these is the Wisdom metaphor. Wisdom caring for the cosmos is pictured as a woman caring for her household (see Wisdom of Solomon 6–9). This Wisdom idea is of particular significance for Christians because, theologically, Wisdom plays the same role as the Logos (and was the original version of this idea). She is the presence of God as means of creation, revelation, and redemption. Jesus' divinity is sometimes identified as the Wisdom of God (Luke 11:49; Matt. 11:18–19).[11]

Recognition of the Wisdom version of this concept deliteralizes the metaphor "Son of God" for the second person of the Trinity. The idea that the immanence of God is like a "son," or male offspring, in relation to a genitor, or "father," cannot be taken literally. God as Logos-Sophia is neither male nor female, and can be imaged in both genders. We must also ask whether the parent-child metaphor for imaging the relation of divine transcendence and immanence needs to be discarded as more misleading than revealing.

But surely, one might say, the Jewish notion of the Messiah was always and only male. The Messiah idea originated as a title for the kings of Israel and, later, as the ideal and future King of Israel.[12] Although rulers, representing divine sovereignty, were generally thought of as male, female rulers were not unknown in the ancient Middle East. Jesus' own preferred title for the Coming One (whom he probably did not identify with himself) was "ben Adam," usually translated "Son of Man." This term, drawn from the Book of Daniel and other apocalyptic literature, sees the Messiah as the collective expression of Israel—itself the representative of corporate humanity.

In Jewish liturgy "ben Adam" refers to females as well as males, despite its androcentric form. Since generic humanity cannot be seen today as normatively male, a more accurate translation of this term would be "The Human One." This is the way the *Inclusive Language Lectionary,* prepared

---

11. See James M. Robinson, "Jesus as Sophos and Sophia: Wisdom Tradition and the Gospels," in *Aspects of Wisdom in Judaism and Early Christianity,* ed. Robert L. Wilkin (London: University of Notre Dame Press, 1975), 1–16; and Elisabeth Schüssler Fiorenza, "Wisdom Mythology and the Christological Hymns of the New Testament," in Wilkin, *Aspects of Wisdom in Judaism,* 17–42.

12. See S. Mowinckel, *He That Cometh* (New York: Abingdon, 1954).

by the National Council of Churches of Christ of the U.S.A., chose to translate this term for liturgical reading of scripture.[13]

From an examination of the symbols used for Christ, we turn to the praxis of the historical Jesus as interpreted in the gospels. Here we see the figure of an iconoclastic prophet of God who stands in judgment of social and religious systems that exclude subordinated and marginalized people from divine favor. Jesus' mission is seen as one of bringing good news to the poor and hope to the despised whom the priestly and clerical classes regarded as unworthy of redemption. Jesus' prophetic praxis confronts these male leaders for their pretenses of special privilege with God and their exclusion of the unlearned and "unclean."

Among the despised groups, women are often examples of those who are able to hear God's prophetic word and be converted, while the male elites close their hearts. Because women were at the bottom of those systems of privilege decried in the gospel stories, they become the representatives of the "last who shall be first in the Kingdom of God." Luke, in the Magnificat, makes Jesus' mother, Mary, potentially despised as one whose child is not her husband's, the exemplar of the messianic community. She is the servant of God who will be lifted up as the mighty of the world are put down from their thrones (Luke 1:45–55).[14]

All four Gospels tell the Jesus story as a drama of mounting conflict in which the messianic prophet is rejected, first by his family and hometown folk, then by religious leaders and the crowd of his popular followers, and finally by his own male disciples. It is the core group of his female followers who remain faithful at the cross and are first at the tomb, first witnesses of the resurrection, and commissioned by the Risen Lord to take the good news back to the male disciples huddled in the upper room.[15]

---

13. See "Human One (RSV Son of Man)," in *An Inclusive Language Lectionary: Readings for Year A* (Philadelphia: Westminster, 1983), appendix.

14. See Jane Schaberg, *The Illegitimacy of Jesus: A Feminist Theological Interpretation* (San Francisco: Harper and Row, 1987), 92-110, for the view that Luke believed Mary's son to be illegitimate, and framed the Magnificat as a statement that God vindicates the most despised of society, the "fallen" woman.

15. In the synoptic Gospels it is Mary Magdalene who is central to the group of female disciples who are "last at the cross and first at the tomb." Although John puts Mary, Jesus' mother, and the disciple John as central figures at the cross, he has the most extended narrative of Mary Magdalene's key role as first witness of the resurrection. Mary Magdalene plays the key role in gnostic claims for women's apostolic authority: see George W. MacRae and R. McL. Wilson, trans., "The Gospel of Mary," in *The Nag Hammadi Library in English*, ed. John Robinson (San Francisco: HarperSanFrancisco, 1988), 523-27.

Some scholars have rejected the story of the empty tomb as secondary and unhistorical.[16] But they have failed to ask why all four Gospels tell the story in this way. Is it not to make dramatically clear that despised women, last in the present social and religious order, are the faithful remnant who are first in the redeemed order?

Luke also includes women in his account of Pentecost. He uses the text of the prophet Joel to buttress his story of the restoration of the prophetic Spirit to the messianic community, in which the Spirit is given to the "men servants and the maid servants," such that "[their] sons and [their] daughters shall prophesy" (Joel 2:28; Acts 2:17–21). This mention of women indicates that women were included in the prophetic office in Hebrew scripture and in early Christianity.[17] The late second century church order, the Didache, shows that there were still Christians in that period who saw the prophet as the normative church leader.[18]

Yet the ministry of women was quickly suppressed by an insurgent patriarchal concept of the church.[19] One clue to this repression lies in the ambivalent understanding of the church as a messianic community. One group of early Christians understood this apocalyptically, as an impending end of this present world, terminating its mortality and need for reproductive renewal. For them, women have been liberated from traditional gender roles by Christ, since both male and female Christians belonged to a transcendent, heavenly order where marriage and reproduction would no longer be necessary.[20]

The patriarchal churchmen who rejected women's ministry saw the church as part of the existing creational social order. For them, the patriarchal, slave-holding social order is still normative for Christian society. The new freedom of women to travel as itinerant preachers, freed by Christ from marriage, was repressed in favor of a Christianity that declared that women were second in the Creation and first in sin. They are thus to be

---

16. See Edward Schillebeeckx, *Jesus: An Experiment in Christology* (New York: Seabury, 1979).

17. Elisabeth Schüssler Fiorenza, "Word, Spirit, and Power: Women in Early Christian Communities," in *Women of Spirit: Female Leadership in the Jewish and Christian Traditions,* ed. Rosemary Ruether and Eleanor McLaughlin (New York: Simon and Schuster, 1979).

18. Didache, trans. James A. Kleist (New York: Newman, 1948).

19. Elisabeth Schüssler Fiorenza, *In Memory of Her: A Feminist Theological Reconstruction of Christian Origins* (New York: Crossroad, 1983).

20. The alternative Pauline tradition that sees woman as liberated from marriage into itinerant ministry through chastity is expressed in the non-canonical "Acts of Paul and Thecla." For interpretations of this conflict between eschatological and patriarchal Paulinisms, see Dennis Ronald MacDonald, *The Legend and the Apostle: The Battle for Paul in Story and Canon* (Philadephia: Westminister, 1983).

silent in church and can be saved by suffering the pains of childbearing (1 Tim. 2:11–15).

The conflict between egalitarian, eschatological Christianity and patriarchal, historical Christianity continued in the second and third centuries in the Gnostic and Montanist struggles.[21] It was resolved in the late fourth to sixth centuries in a new synthesis of the two. In this synthesis the eschatological ideal of chastity was shorn of its egalitarianism and began to incorporate the patriarchal, clerical leadership class.[22] Marriage was reaffirmed as the lifestyle of most Christians, but only as a second class, lay stratum of the church.[23]

Celibate women were gradually shorn of the remnants of pastoral ministry and segregated into convents under male episcopal control.[24] The patriarchal, hierarchical church leaders could then be incorporated into the Roman empire as new agents of its rule. This fourth century synthesis of patriarchal, imperial church organization, together with a clericalized monastic counterculture, was passed on as normative Christianity for the next thousand years. Yet a resistance to it from both celibate women and married clerics continued through the Middle Ages.[25]

---

21. Montanist women prophets were accused of abandoning their husbands, which suggests that they shared the view of the Acts of Paul and Thecla that women converts to Christ transcend their marital obligations. Gnostics believed that spiritual rebirth enabled women and men to transcend sex and procreation and enter a state of spiritual androgyny. Both groups supported women in ministry. See Fiorenza, "Word, Spirit, and Power," 42; and Elaine Pagels, *The Gnostic Gospels* (New York: Random House, 1979), 48–69.

22. The Council of Elvira, AD 400, was the first to mandate clerical continence. The council documents show the connection between clerical sexual continence and obsession with control over female sexuality. See Samuel Laeuchli, *Power and Sexuality: The Emergence of Canon Law at the Synod of Elvira* (Philadelphia: Temple University Press, 1972).

23. It became formulaic for fourth century advocates of asceticism, such as Jerome and Athanasius, to affirm three levels of blessing on female states of life: one-hundred-fold for virginity, sixty-fold for continent widowhood, and only thirty-fold for marriage. See William E. Phipps, *Was Jesus Married? The Distortion of Sexuality in the Christian Tradition* (New York: Harper and Row, 1970), 142–75.

24. See Susan Fonay Wemple, *Women in Frankish Society: Marriage and the Cloister, 500–900* (Philadelphia: University of Pennsylvania Press, 1981).

25. The period between AD 500 and 1500 saw a continuous struggle of celibate women to retain autonomy and ministry, as well as the resistance of the lower clergy to the imposition of clerical celibacy. See Lina Eckerstein, *Women under Monasticism: Chapters on Saint-lore and Convent Life between AD 500 and 1500* (New York: Russell and Russell, 1963). See John Boswell, *Christianity, Social Tolerance, and Homosexuality: Gay People in Western Europe from the Beginning of the Christian Era to the Fourteenth Century* (Chicago: Chicago University Press, 1980), for the eleventh-century movement

The Reformation represented a revolt against clerical celibacy. It restored the married clergy, and later abolished monasteries for both men and women.[26] It rooted itself all the more exclusively in the Christianity that saw the patriarchal family as the nucleus of the church, modeled by the married pastor and his obedient wife and children. The household codes became the norm for a Christian society with new force.[27]

But the eschatological counterculture did not disappear with the suppression of Monasticism. Rather it returned in its more radical form, in mystical and millennialist sects such as the Shakers, who saw the church as a messianic community living in the last days of world history, departing from the evil structures of a worldly society and its church. Freed from gender roles, men and women "saints" became equal in a new redemptive society. Women were again mandated to preach and prophecy "in the Spirit," reflecting the new dispensation of the feminine side of God.[28]

We have here two different Christologies and views of the church. Patriarchal Christianity equates the Lordship of Christ with the lordship of Caesar. Christ as divine Logos is the apex of a hierarchical sociopolitical order baptized as Christendom. As a delegate for Heavenly Father, Christ rules over the cosmos and is, in turn, the source of the ecclesiastical, political, and social hierarchies of church, state, and family—clergy over laity, king over subjects, and husbands over wives.[29] Women represent the bodily realm that is to be ruled over by the male Christological principle in each system of dominance and subjugation.

In the mystical and millennialist Christologies, by contrast, Christ is the transcendent ground of being for the redeemed, who have departed from this fallen world and its corrupt social systems and now await and anticipate a redeemed order beyond this world. Christ restores the redeemed to

---

to enforce clerical celibacy, seen by the married clergy as a monastic, homosexual movement.

26. There was some notable resistance to Protestant closing of monasteries by nuns. See Jane Douglass, "Women and the Continental Reformation," in Ruether, *Religion and Sexism*, 309-14.

27. The Puritan leaders place major emphasis on the household for defining marriage. See M. W. Perkins, *Christian Oeconomie: Or, a Short Survey of the Right Manner of Erecting and Ordering a Familie, According to the Scriptures* (London: Felis Kyngston, 1609); and William Gouge, *Of Domesticall Duties* (Norwood, N.J.: W. S. Johnson, 1976).

28. See Joyce L. Irwin, *Womanhood in Radical Protestantism, 1525-1675* (New York: Edwin Mellen, 1979). Also Rosemary Radford Ruether, "Women in Utopian Movements," in *Women and Religion in America*, ed. Rosemary Radford Ruether and Rosemary Skinner Keller (San Francisco: Harper and Row, 1981), 46-100.

29. Averil Cameron and Stuart G. Hall, trans., *Eusebius' Life of Constantine* (Oxford: Clarendon, 1999), 10.7.

prelapsarian unity and grounds their entrance into heavenly life in Christ by putting aside sexual activity and reproduction. Thereby they recover the sinless and spiritually androgynous mode of being before the fall into sin and death, which necessitated gender and reproduction. Since sex and family relations are no longer necessary, gender hierarchy can also be abolished. As spiritual peers of men, women can participate equally in church leadership.[30]

These two Christologies appear opposite. Yet they are both based on a common presupposition: patriarchy is the order of creation. They assume that patriarchy can be left behind only by leaving the created order. To change this pattern, creation itself must be defined as egalitarian in its original nature. This original egalitarianism must be seen, not as a heavenly state before embodiment, but as our true nature as embodied, historical persons. Only then can patriarchy be placed under judgment as an unjust distortion of our human capacities and social ordering of relationships. Equality between men and women can then be envisioned as a social reform within history that restores our original nature, rather than something possible only by an ahistorical departure from the past and embodied existence.

The basis of this egalitarian anthropology was laid in the Society of Friends, but it only became politically effective by its marriage to liberalism with the declaration that "all men are created equal." Originally this included only white propertied males, leaving intact patriarchal dominance over women, servants, and slaves.[31] Gradually it was applied to subjugated groups: propertyless men, slaves, and women.

Today, egalitarian anthropology is taken for granted in Western society in theory, however much it may be contradicted in practice. Even the Pope and the Catholic bishops now feel compelled to affirm that women are not inferior in human capacities and are equal sharers in the image of God. But they cling to a Christology based on a patriarchal anthropology, attempting to use this to exclude women from equality of leadership in the church, while abandoning the more basic exclusion of women from political rights in secular society.[32]

---

30. The nineteenth-century Shakers most fully develop this sexual egalitarianism of the mystical-millennialist tradition. *The Testimony of Christ's First and Second Appearing*, 4th ed. (Albany, N.Y.: United Society, 1856).

31. The reply of John Adams to his wife's exhortation to "remember the Ladies" in the civil rights of the American Constitution clearly reveals the exclusion, not only of women, but also slaves, Indians and propertyless white servants, from Adams concept of those persons with civil rights. In *Feminism: The Essential Historical Writings*, ed. Miriam Schneir (New York: Random House, 1972), 3-4.

32. This claim to affirm women's secular equality through the concept of *imago dei* is found in both the pastoral letter on women by John Paul II, "The Dignity and

This contradiction between egalitarian anthropology for secular society and patriarchal Christology for church hierarchy reflects a new church-world split. Patriarchy, no longer defensible for secular society, is sacralized as a special order of the church. The result is that Christology loses its basic integration with creation. Christ no longer restores and redeems creation, but now stands as a sacred patriarchal order of the church that is unconnected with creation. This new creation-redemption split reverses the dilemma of classical Christianity, in which creation was assumed to be patriarchal, while redemption in Christ overcame female inferiority (at least spiritually).

In order to recover the integration of Christ and creation essential to a coherent theology, Christology must be recast by integrating it with egalitarian anthropology. Once we have discarded patriarchal anthropology with its false biological underpinnings that regard women as less complete expressions of human nature than men, we must affirm women as equally theomorphic. If women share equally in the image of God, then they also share equally in the care of creation. This care cannot be limited to a dependent, domestic sphere.

If women are equally theomorphic, then God must be imaged as female as well as male; thus, the ground of that fullness of personhood is present in both women and men. This means that the maleness of the historical Jesus has nothing to do with the manifestation of a divine "Son" from a divine "Father." Both the gender and the parent-child characteristics of these symbols must be deliteralized. God transcendent is the depths of being that we encounter in redemptive experiences, but is nonetheless one and the same God.

In Jesus we encounter, paradigmatically, the Logos-Sophia of that one God who is both mother and father. But how do Christians then deal with the maleness of the historical Jesus if it is no longer seen as ontologically necessary to manifest a male immanence of a male God? Doesn't the very fact that Jesus is a male continue the assumption that women receive redemption from men but cannot represent God as redemptive actors?

Christian feminists cannot resolve this problem by suggesting that Jesus' non-patriarchal sensitivity to women and his vulnerability in suffering somehow makes him "feminine" and thus inclusive of women. All this does is make Jesus a model for an androgynous male, presumably for the holistic capacities that every male should develop. But this does nothing to affirm a like holistic humanity for women. Rather, I believe Christians must affirm the particularity of Jesus, not only in gender, but also in ethnicity and culture, and the limitations of any single individual to be universally paradigmatic.

Vocation of Women," and the American Catholic Bishops pastoral letter on women, "One in Christ."

What we find in classical Christology is a dissolution of all other aspects of Jesus' historical particularity, his Jewishness, his first century cultural setting, and a corresponding elevation of his gender to universal ontological significance. In contrast, I believe we should encounter Jesus not only as male, but in all his particularity as a first century Galilean Jew. We must then ask how we can see him as paradigmatic of universal human redemption in a way that can apply to females as well as males and to people of all ethnicities and cultures.

This investigation must take us through several stages of revisionist thought about Christology. First, we must see that what is paradigmatic about Jesus is not his biological ontology, but rather his life and practice. Jesus becomes paradigmatic by embodying a certain message. That message is good news to the poor, the confrontation with systems of religion and society that incarnate oppressive privilege, and affirmation of the despised as loved and liberated by God. Jesus did not just speak this message; he gave his life to embody this presence of God and was crucified by those in power who rejected it.

Second, we must cease to isolate the work of Christ from the ongoing Christian community. This Jesus we find as a historical figure exemplifies a way of life that is still critical in a world where religion still sacralizes false and oppressive privileges. As Christians we follow Christ's Way. While Jesus is the foundational representative of the Way of the cross and liberation, he is not its exclusive possibility. Each Christian must also take up this same way and, in so doing, become "other Christs" to one another. The church becomes a redemptive community, not by passively receiving a redemption won by Christ alone, but rather by collectively embodying this path of liberation in a way that transforms people and social systems.

If we are clear that the redemption signified by Christ is both carried on and communicated through redemptive community, Christ can take on the face of every person and group and their diverse liberation struggles. We must be able to encounter Christ as Black, Asian, Aboriginal, or as woman. This also means that the coming Christ, the incompleted future of redemption, is not the historical Jesus returned, but rather the fullness of human diversity gathered in a redemptive community. This is the "Human One" who is to come, who bears the face of all suffering creatures longing for liberation.

Finally, this Way of Christ need not and should not be seen as excluding other Ways. The creating, inspiriting, and liberating presence of God is available to all humans in all times and places. It has been expressed in many religious cultures, some that parallel the Christ-way, and some that complement it with other spiritualities. The challenge of Christology today may be to try not to extend the Christ symbol to every possible spirituality and culture, but to accept its limitations. Then we can allow other ways and peoples to flourish in dialogues that can reveal God's many words to us.

Feminist Critique and the Re-visioning of God-Language

Rosemary Radford Ruether

FEMINIST THEOLOGY ENGAGES IN A CRITIQUE of patriarchal images and concepts of God and also in a re-visioning of God-language inclusive of women and men. I will begin by expressing my view of the problem of patriarchal God-language. What I am not saying is that the traditional patriarchal language for God has been fine for men but has excluded women, so we need some additional feminine language for God to relate God to women as well as to men. I am not interested in simply adding feminine God-language to complement and round out our inherited masculine God-language. I commence with the assumption that language for God that subordinates women is detrimental to men as well. Although such patriarchal God-language may appear to give men a God who is "for men," it does so in the sinful ways that powerful men have wished to be "for themselves." This distorts and limits the humanity of men as much as it does the humanity of women. A God who is alienating and dehumanizing to women is harmful to everyone, and even to the well-being of the planet earth itself. Therefore, the task of feminist critique and the re-visioning of God-language must go beyond adding mother-nurturer images to father-ruler images and must rethink the root metaphors of our relation to God in terms of their ethical effects.

What then has been the problem with the images of God we have inherited? Feminist critique has focused on the idea that God is imaged as male, and so only men can represent God.[33] Even if the maleness of God is not taken in a literal, biological sense, nevertheless godlikeness is expressed in activities that men can do but women cannot. The Episcopal bishop of San Francisco put this crudely a few years ago in explaining his opposition to the ordination of women. God, he said, creates by begetting

---

33. See Daphne Hampson, "The Challenge of Feminism to Christianity," *Theology* 88, no. 725 (September 1985): 341–50.

the Word of God. Since only men can beget, only men can represent God.[34] Early Christian tradition would have stressed ideas such as God's sovereign power or rule and would have assumed that men could exercise such rule, but women could not. In the era of Margaret Thatcher that assumption was less convincing, hence the bishop's flight to the exclusively male biological act. But one suspects that his idea of the male sexual act of begetting is strongly mixed up with power that dominates and rules over the bodies of others, namely, the bodies of women.

The notion that men are godlike and women are not is thus linked with the fundamental model of God's relation to the world as ruler to ruled. Men represent the mind and power that rule over others as a body; women represent the bodily, creaturely being that is ruled over. It was on the basis of this metaphor of male to female, as ruling mind to dominated body, that Augustine, in his treatise on the Trinity, denied that women possess the image of God "in themselves." Women stand in relation to God only through the male "who is their head." Not only is Augustine saying that women image the body, but also that women's bodies are simply an extension of men's bodies, jointly ruled over by one head, namely, the man's head. This thoroughly denies women's autonomous personhood. It also makes clear that when a theology rejects the appropriateness of imaging God as female, at the same time it denies that women are in the image of God.[35]

The God-language we have been discussing does not actually image God in terms of male persons as a whole, but in terms of a particular role played by some males, namely, the exercise of power over others by ruling-class males. Thus the image of God as Father in this tradition is based on a patriarchal concept of the paterfamilias in which the father is lord or master of not only his wife, but of his children and servants as well. It is useful to remember that in this Roman legal definition of the father of the family, the father is not a member of the family himself. He is outside of it as one who possesses and rules over it. The *familia* in Roman law did not include the father, but referred to those persons and things owned and ruled over by him: his wife, children, servants, chattel, lands, and properties. It is not accidental that the three images we have for the relationship of the church to Christ, or humans to God, are those of sons, spouse, and servants. These represent the three categories of persons ruled over by the paterfamilias, whose essential relationship to wife, children, and servants is that of Lord. Servants, however, might be emancipated, and sons might grow up to be

---

34. The statement was made by the Episcopal Bishop of San Francisco, C. Kilmer Myers, in 1978, as part of a challenge to the ordination of women at the 1978 Biennial Convention of the American Episcopal Church.

35. Augustine, *The Trinity*, ed. Father Charles Dollen (Boston: Daughters of St. Paul, 1965).

householders in their own right. This leaves women to become the prime representatives of the dominated body, of those whose essential nature it is to be ruled over by others, never to govern themselves or others.[36]

These images of God as paterfamilias, or Lord, foster many ethical problems in our construction of relationships, not only between men and women, but also between all groups of people divided by class or race into dominant and subservient relations. It also raises problems about how we understand our relationships to our own bodies and the relationship of humans to nature. The God who is a disembodied, sovereign mind outside of the cosmos both leaves creation itself without the presence of God and suggests that we come to God by turning away from the world and rejecting our bodies. This notion also suggests that God rules the world as an emperor, with a combination of force and mercy. In this context, sin is to be understood as rebellious behavior against divine sovereignty. Such insubordination brings down divine wrath upon us, reducing us again to subjugation. Since such insubordination of subjects against God is unforgivable, the only way we can be restored to divine favor, as good children or loyal subjects, is through the mercy and forgiveness of God.

Such a notion of divine mercy fosters an essentially passive relation to God. Since divine will and human will are seen as over, against, and mutually exclusive of each other, we proclaim that God is all only by declaring ourselves to be nothing. Such a model of divine-human relations fosters the same relationship between human rulers and those ruled. On one hand, annihilating wrath and violence is appropriate for "bad woes" who dare to rebel against our righteous rule. On the other hand, obedient subjects are those who carry out the orders of their masters without taking any responsibility for their own actions. I suggest that Ronald Reagan's construction of his role in the world in the early 1980s corresponds closely to this model of righteous divine sovereignty. He only imitated God when he punished rebellious sinners in Libya and Nicaragua with righteous wrath, while beaming benignly at tyrants who enriched themselves by obediently doing his will. Reagan's violence and his type of Christian piety were not contradictions, but were of one piece. This, I hope, suggests why such a notion of God is not only hurtful to women, but dangerous for all life on earth.

In recent years there has emerged in Western culture a post-Christian or neopagan feminist spirituality that sees this model of the violent, militaristic male God as essential to the biblical Jewish and Christian traditions. These feminists believe that this kind of patriarchal God overthrew an earlier understanding of the divine as Goddess. They believe that there were earlier cultures and peoples, repressed and conquered by patriarchal cultures,

---

36. David Herlihy, *Medieval Households* (Cambridge: Harvard University Press, 1985), 1–4.

who not only saw the divine as Goddess (as female), but who understood the divine-world relation differently. Instead of remaining outside of and ruling over the world, the Goddess is seen as pervading the world from within, nurturing the world as an expression of her own body. Such a Goddess not only affirmed the female as goddesslike, but fostered peaceful, cooperative relations among human beings and between humans and non-human nature.

The era of the Goddess was one of peaceful mutuality and shared abundance for all. This contrasts the patriarchal God, who fosters competition and hierarchical social systems with poverty and exploitation at the bottom and leisured wealth at the top, and who keeps this unjust system intact through military might. For these neopagan feminists, this earlier happy era was overthrown by violence either by the Jews, the creators of the patriarchal understanding of God who taught us to view all pagans as evil idolaters, or by some earlier patriarchal coup that began with civilization or early urban society in Sumaria. The goddesses of the ancient Near East and other cultures that retain such female deities are vestiges of this earlier Goddess, while Judaism, Christianity, and Islam represent successive efforts to purge from their views all traces of the Goddess in favor of the patriarchal God.[37]

Before Christians (and other patriarchal monotheists) rush to protest the unhistoricity of this picture, the lack of evidence of such a link between goddesses and peaceful egalitarian societies within ancient Near Eastern societies, or the existence of such societies before the rise of written history, it is important to recognize what these post-Christian feminists are saying. They describe a God-language that alienates and horrifies them and imagine the kind of understanding of the divine that would indeed be salvific for all living things. In other words, we must read their story, not as an accurate account of what happened in one thousand or four thousand B.C., but as a powerful myth whose cultural locus is nineteenth and twentieth century Western Europe and America, particularly after Hiroshima, when male military power indeed threatened to annihilate all life on earth. We need to take this story seriously as a *cri de coeur* of those who accurately see the dangerous effects of one kind of God-language and who try to project an alternative model of spirituality that could foster a different ethic towards one another and the beautiful planet that is our threatened home. It is only when biblical monotheists take with equal seriousness the

---

37. For example, Carol P. Christ, "Why Women Need the Goddess: Phenomenological, Psychological, and Political Reflections," in *Womanspirit Rising: A Feminist Reader in Religion*, ed. Carol P. Christ and Judith Plaskow (San Francisco: HarperCollins, 1979), 273–87; Starhawk, *The Spiral Dance: A Rebirth of the Ancient Religion of the Great Goddess* (San Francisco: HarperCollins, 1979); Elizabeth Gould Davis, *The First Sex* (Baltimore, Md.: Penguin, 1971); and Merlin Stone, *When God Was a Woman* (New York: Dial, 1976).

threat of nuclear madness to global survival, and the way one type of God-language has either promoted or made us indifferent to such violence and oppression, that we can look back at our tradition and see whether it is an accurate expression of the origins of biblical monotheism in relation to the earlier polytheistic religious culture.

The post-Christian feminist picture of the era of the Goddess is a contemporary Garden of Eden myth. It does not refer to some actual historical time in prehistory, but it does capture a powerful mythical memory of how earth might be fair in contrast to the violence and injustice of history. The question is, to what extent has biblical monotheism promoted the very history of violence and oppression that it has protested with its stories of original goodness and future redemption? To answer this I would like to take another look at the essential characteristics that separate the biblical understanding of God from the ancient Near Eastern world.

First, ancient Near Eastern views of deity do not consist of a single Goddess, but of many gods and goddesses. Divinity is manifest in a plurality of deities, which, like humans, come not only in two genders, male and female, but also in successive generations. The gods and goddesses are one big, multigenerational, sometimes loving, more often quarrelsome, family. Second, the successive generations of the gods and goddesses are seen as evolving within the evolution of the cosmos itself. Thus, for ancient mythology, the story of cosmogony, the generation of the cosmos, is told through theogony, the generation of the gods from the inchoate, monstrous forms of the beginning to the bright, beautiful human forms of the deities who rule over the settled world of city-states.[38]

Third, this present heavenly world of gods and goddesses is modeled after a ruling and leisured aristocracy. The essential metaphor of ancient mythology, which dates as far back as written records in Sumeria, is relating gods and humans to aristocrats and servile classes. In the literary traditions of antiquity, goddesses as well as gods are pictured in a leisured ruling class. Contrary to our post-Christian mythology, goddesses like Inanna, Ishtar, or Anath are not primarily fertility figures. They do relate to the promotion of fertility, but no more than do male deities. Moreover, although they have offspring, goddesses have little correspondence to our romantic notion of nurturing motherhood. The essential image of an ancient goddess is that of a queen, not a "Queen Mum" or a consort of a king, but a queen ruling in her own right. The social world in which she is queen is one of feudal aristocracy, not absolute monarchy. It has a multiplicity of rulers, male and female.

---

38. See the Babylonian Creation Epic in Isaac Mendelsohn, ed., *Religions of the Ancient Near East: Sumero-Akkadian Religious Texts and Ugaritic Epics* (New York: The Liberal Arts, 1955), 17–46; *Hesiod's Theogony* (New York: The Liberal Arts, 1953), 56–78.

This feudal aristocracy, however, unites as one class vis-à-vis the world of mortals below them. The essential differences between humans and gods are that humans must work and die, while gods neither work nor die. As the Babylonian creation story explains, after the slaying of Tiamat to fashion the cosmos out of her body, human beings were created by the gods in order to work, allowing the gods to be at leisure. Thus, the basic analogy of divine to human as ruler to ruled, as king to servant, and as leisured class to working class, was not invented by patriarchal monotheism. It is found in the earlier world of ancient polytheism.[39]

What, then, is essentially different about biblical God-language from the ideas of the Babylonians and Canaanites? First of all, there is much continuity between the two, so we should think of the ancient Hebrews not as rejecting one religious world for a completely new one (although this is the way they saw themselves and how we have been taught to see them), but as making creative revisions in a common stock of religious ideas. What were those creative revisions? First of all, there is monotheism—an idea that grew gradually from asserting that their God was the only God for Israel to the far-reaching belief that this God actually created and sustained all reality and history.

Does monotheism automatically mean that the one God is seen as male and hence that the male is the normative bearer of the image of God, while polytheism is necessary to allow for parallel gender personifications of deity? Insofar as that God is construed as male, monotheism greatly enhances male domination. The master-servant model of divine-human relations is connected with the male over female model in a way that makes God the ultimate sanction of gender hierarchy. Male-female hierarchy now finds its root model in divine-human hierarchy. This leads to the kind of patriarchal theology that I discussed at the outset.

However, there are critical elements in Hebrew monotheism that should have mitigated and can now mitigate against the identification of monotheism with only the male gender. God is thought of as beyond all literal anthropomorphic images. So concerned were the Hebrews that people should not take either pictorial or even verbal images literally that all visual pictures were forbidden and the holiest name for God was not allowed to be pronounced. This understanding of the distance between God's nature and our human experience leads to the apophatic tradition in Christian theology. This has been restated by Sallie McFague in her book *Metaphorical Theology: Models of God in Religious Language*.[40] In it, she declares that since all of our language for God is necessarily drawn from human experience,

---

39. Mendelsohn, *Religions of the Ancient Near East,* 37.

40. Sallie McFague, *Metaphorical Theology: Models of God in Religious Language* (Philadelphia: Fortress, 1982).

its application to God can only be analogical or metaphorical, not literal. To take male imagery for God literally, to imply that God is male and not female, is idolatry.

Although the Hebrew scriptures use predominately male images and gender grammar for God, they do at times use female images. This occurs when God is given both male and female roles; for example, in one passage he is compared to a warrior and in another to a birthing mother. The Wisdom tradition sees the immanence of God as Wisdom in female personification. This line of thought continues in the Jewish mystical tradition that sees the divine *Shekhina* or Holy Presence of God with Israel in female personification.[41] There are also expressions of this view in Syriac Christian imagery of the Holy Spirit as female.[42] Yet this does not fully free us of gender stereotypes. To see God transcendent as male, God immanent as female, to relate the two as husband and wife, is obviously built on social role complementarity. This assumes a very powerful role of the wife as ruler of her household and teacher of her children and imagines divine Wisdom operating in a similar way in the household of the world. This also clearly explains that biblical thought did not literally pronounce God as male. God, who is beyond gender, can be imagined in metaphors drawn from the social roles of both males and females.

A second important aspect of biblical theology is divine transcendence. God is both detached from and a forerunner of the cosmos. God does not evolve within it in the manner of polytheist theogonies. Yet the Hebrew sense of God does not easily fit into the Greek philosophical concept of an immutable, transcendent being, although Christian theology united the two. The Hebrew anthropomorphic sense of God combines the qualities of a good ruler and an anxious parent. This God is concerned with punishing wickedness and establishing righteousness and also with educating and directing Israel. Such a God exhibits a whole range of human emotions; God is even a being capable of repentance or a change of mind. Thus when the people of Nineveh repented and turned from their evil ways, God responded by "repenting" of the punishment that God had intended to mete out to them (Jonah 3:10).

The picture of God as an immutable, disembodied spirit, outside of and ruling over the world, lends itself to a one-sided, authoritarian concept of the divine-world relationship. We relate to God by turning away from embodied reality. We obey God by negating ourselves. But this picture fits less well with other elements of Jewish and Christian theology. The idea that God brings forth God's Wisdom or begets the divine Logos, becoming

---

41. Raphael Patai, *The Hebrew Goddess* (New York: KTAV, 1967).
42. James Hamilton Charlesworth, ed. and trans., *The Odes of Solomon* (Oxford: Clarendon, 1973).

immanent as Creator, Revealer, and Redeemer of creation, reintroduces an element of divine "theogony" or process within God as an expression of God's relationship with the creative process. The Christian belief that God becomes incarnate and even suffers and dies on the cross disputed the Greek sense of immutable transcendence and was the source of early Christian conflicts over patripassianism. This conflict was partly resolved by allowing the divine Logos to suffer, but not the "Father."

But what does this mean if the Logos is of one being with the "Father"? Greek theology tried to bridge God and body by suggesting that this change-able aspect of God, the Logos, was not only an intellectual blueprint for the cosmos but also the ground of its being. The Christian sacramentality of writers such as Irenaeus is rooted in the sense of the cosmos as the bodying forth of the Word and Spirit of God.[43] The incarnation of God in Christ then is not unique, but rather exemplary, as it paradigms the bodying forth or incarnation of God, not only in all humans, but in the whole cosmos. Feminist theology, along with process theology and ecological theology, seeks to correct the authoritarian, antimaterial concept of God's transcendence with incarnational and interactive views of divine-world relations.

Finally, the Hebrew God is one who liberates captives, who intervenes on behalf of the poor and the oppressed. Even God's primordial work of creating the cosmos is remembered in the context of that essential historical act that establishes God's relation to Israel; God chose a people who were considered nonhuman slaves. God liberated this people from bondage to Pharoah, the great embodiment of imperial rule. Although biblical religion continues the basic Near Eastern analogy of human to God as servant to king, a new element is introduced into the idea of serving God. Israel serves God as a people liberated from the servitude of wordly power. In the creation story of the first chapter of Genesis, written in all likelihood in conscious correction of the Babylonian creation story, God creates humanity, not to be God's slaves, but to put God at ease. God exemplified both creative work and rest by laboring six days in creation and then resting, commanding humans to do the same.

Humans are created in the image of God; that is, they share the divine sovereignty in caring for the earth. We are divine stewards, not slaves. Since the role of exercising divine care over the earth is given to humanity generically, male and female, this leaves open the possibility of a radical egalitarianism among human beings. Feminist and abolitionist writers, commenting on this text in the nineteenth century, were quick to note that no like dominion is established between one group of humans and another,

---

43. Irenaeus, *Adversus Haereses*, in *Early Christian Fathers*, ed. Cyril C. Richardson (Philadelphia: Westminster, 1953), 358–97.

either by class, race, or gender.[44] Yet it took people shaped by the democratic ideas of liberalism to draw out this possibility from the text. Patristic and medieval Christian theology, as we have seen, justified the subordination of women in the original order of creation by denying that women autonomously possessed the image of God.

The idea of God as liberator reflected a common stock of ancient Near Eastern ideas of kingship. The righteous king established justice by correcting wrongs done to the most disadvantaged in society—widows and orphans. Kings also exercised benevolence and mercy by liberating captives and forgiving debts. But biblical language at times goes beyond this general idea of justice and mercy within established relations of power. It suggests that God not only justly deals with individuals, but also overturns systems of unjust powers, puts the mighty down from their thrones and lifts up the lowly, and establishes a new world order where every household has its own land, its own vine and fig trees, where none need fear violence. This more radical idea of God as liberator has been a key source of Western movements for social justice, political democracy, socialism, anti-racism, anticolonialism, and feminism. These movements have generally seen themselves as secular or anti-Christian because they have identified religion with the sanctification of social hierarchy. Liberation theologies represent a Christian reappropriation of God as liberator as the essential message of the Bible.

These biblical shifts in God-language suggest two radically different directions that our understanding of God might go. One direction takes the emphasis on transcendence and monotheism into modeling God as a distant male with absolute power over subjects who are to be kept in submission by threats of punishment and promises of mercy. This God establishes social hierarchies of men over women, masters over slaves, and kings over subjects as the expression of the ultimate hierarchy of God over creation. Other aspects of the biblical God suggest a very different direction, a God who establishes no social hierarchy among human groups, where all are made in God's image and exercise joint care over the earth as representatives of God. This God enters human struggle and suffering to overcome systems of unjust domination to create a new earth of peace and justice where God's will is supreme.

Feminist theology develops this second direction of biblical faith by re-envisioning it in the context of women's equal personhood with men. To conclude this essay, I will explore several aspects of this feminist re-visioning of the liberationist tradition of biblical faith. Some contemporary

---

44. Sarah M. Grimke, "Letters on the Equality of the Sexes and the Condition of Women," in *Feminism: The Essential Historical Writings*, ed. Miriam Schneir (New York: Random House, 1972), 36–48.

post-Christian feminists have argued that it is necessary to return to poly-theism in order to fully affirm women as autonomous beings.[45] I disagree with this view. I feel that humanness is more fundamental than differences of gender, as well as other differences between humans, such as race and culture. The unity of God is an essential presupposition of the underlying unity of all humanity and creation. Plurality needs to be affirmed within a unity that underlies and upholds all elements. This means that one element of particularity, such as maleness, the white race, Western culture, or the Christian religion, cannot be made the norm of unity. Even human beings cannot be the sole norm of the preciousness of life. The one God who upholds us all, both in our authentic differences and relationships, cannot be modeled exclusively on white, ruling-class, Christian, male human beings. God transcends all these differences and cannot be literally identified with any of them. God upholds everything, not only through impersonal power, but through personal love. God is the heart of all things in a community, allowing us to enter into communion with each other. God, therefore, can be imaged metaphorically in terms of all aspects of our entrance into loving and life-giving relationships. God can be imaged as male and female, with the face and dress of all cultures. God is the bird and the lamb, wind, fire, and water, as well as all human persons.

The solution to the white, ruling-class, male monopoly on God-language is not to move to abstract, generic, impersonal language. This solution to the problem of inclusive language, that translates God as Lord and King into God as sovereign, fails to recognize the metaphorical, analogical, and poetic nature of religious language. It also fails to address the question of how we envision divine power in relation to our own. God-language, which recognizes the inclusive and metaphorical nature of religious language, should move towards a pluralism of images, male and female, and include images drawn from nature as well as from human society.

But is God equally imageable in terms of all the plurality of experience? Is there no principle of discrimination between more or less appropriate images? I think that images of God can be drawn from all the plurality of natural goodness, which includes both genders, many races, and all of nature. But it does not equally include the social roles, both dominant and subservient, that have been created by human sin. Therefore, the languages of kings and subjects, masters and slaves, fatherhood in patriarchal domination and motherhood in submissive nurturing, need to be eschewed as social stereotypes that enshrine unjust social relations. To use them uncritically of God and God-human relations is to give divine sanction to human

---

45. Carol P. Christ, "Symbols of Goddess and God in Feminist Theology," in *The Book of the Goddess, Past and Present: An Introduction to Her Religion*, ed. Carl Olson (New York: Crossroad, 1983), 231–51.

evil. Thus, while we need to image God in terms of female and male persons, we also need to reach for creative images that shatter conventional patriarchal stereotypes and point us to a vision of full and liberated persons, male and female, able to enter into mutual relations with each other. The image of Wisdom as a strong woman, ruler of her own household, who invites others to a banquet that she prepares, is one such image. Surprising, paradoxical language, such as that found in the parables of Jesus, where women often illustrate the roles of the divine, is particularly appropriate for the kind of transformative imagination that we need to overcome gender stereotypes in religious language.

The stereotype of God as Father as the primary image of modern Christianity thus comes into question. The objection to this image is not simply that it is male, but rather that it is based on a certain construction of fatherhood or male parenting, as the paterfamilias, an all-powerful ruler that keeps women, children, and servants in a state of permanent dependency. To seek to escape such a relationship with authority figures is then construed as rebellion against divine patriarchy. We need a different model of divine parenting, based not on domination and dependency, but on wise nurture that guides those who are dependent, as weak or wounded persons, into graduate adulthood where they are able to enter into reciprocal and responsible relationships with each other. Neither our images of father as paterfamilias nor our images of mother as infantilising nurturer are models of good parenting. Applied to God such neurotic images of fathering or mothering make for bad ethics in human relations.

God as parent remains an important image of God. It is a root image for relation to persons to whom we owe our life and growth. But we need to model God after what we know to be good parenting, not neurotic parenting, the guidance of the young toward responsible adulthood, rather than servile obedience or infantilising dependency. Both mother and father need to be coparents in the joint exercise of nurturing authority. Authority without nurture cannot be assigned to men, and nurture without authority cannot be forced upon women. It is in this context of good parenting that God is both mother and father, affirming not only the nurturing aspect of divine parenting, but the nurturing aspect of fathering as well.

I suggest that Jesus' language for God as *Abba* expresses this re-envisioned idea of God as parent. *Abba* was the baby's affectionate and trusting name for the father. Such a name for God overthrows God as paterfamilias. God is like a parent in whose love one can unconditionally trust. Yet God is not a parent who infantilises or creates master-slave relations between people. In the words of Matthew, "call no man your father on earth, for you have one *Abba,* who is in heaven" (Matt. 23:9). Relation to God as parent makes us all brothers and sisters; it does not establish some as lords and others as servants. The notion of God as parent, mother and father, should be supplemented by other models of human relationship—God as tutor (in the sense of one who teaches us how to learn), God as lover, God as friend. These relationships draw us toward responsible adulthood and into loving and reciprocal relations with each other.

This re-envisioning of God, in terms of liberating, loving, and mutual human relationships, also suggests a need to rethink divine transcendence in relation to creation. Instead of seeing divine transcendence as disembodied and absolute power, God ruling over the world by remote control, one might think of it as the divine matrix of being and new being. God is that "still more" of transcendent being, from which we ourselves and all things emerged from nothingness, and that "still more" that opens up potential for transformation and newness of life beyond our sinful deformations of our creative possibilities.

God does not create in a way that crushes our freedom. God grounds our finite freedom and presents to us free choices of good possibilities. God strengthens us against our own failures to live up to this potential. God also suffers and is wounded by human evil; God is hung on the cross of human misery and violence. Both humans and God are reciprocal partners in building a redeemed earth. God cannot redeem the world apart from our free and loving response to God, which is, simultaneously, a choice to love and support one another.

Response to Professor Ruether

Camille S. Williams

Rosemary Radford Ruether's published works on women and religion span three decades[46] and incorporate aspects of many disciplines into a feminist liberation process theology. Her writings reflect psychoanalytic, anthropological, and linguistic theories expressed in narrative, analysis, argument, poetry, and prayer. Ruether describes her approach as dialectical self-criticism of distortions of self and community and her work as finding the "healing and liberating word" that "emerges from the Christian tradition,

---

46. For a partial list of her works, see Mary Hembrow Snyder's essay "Rosemary Radford Ruether" in Donald W. Musser and Joseph L. Price, eds., *A New Handbook of Christian Theologians* (Nashville: Abingdon, 1996).

once freed of its distorted consciousness."[47] Her studies of the alternative history for women in religion focused her work on two major questions: "What is the vision of social reconstruction adequate to the liberation of women? and What is the new theology or worldview that would express liberation from sexism?"[48] Reaction to her work hinges on the reader's acceptance of both her modes of analysis and her styles of argument.

There are in her writings some notions that parallel LDS beliefs.[49] For example, Ruether's critique of the unembodied, transcendent God of Hellenistic Christianity will sound familiar to those who believe LDS scriptural teachings that God is embodied. Her pleas that we feed the hungry and that we protect and preserve the earth and all life forms resonate with King Benjamin's teachings that we are all beggars who should not turn away the poor (Mosiah 4:16–19) and that the earth herself mourns her pollutions (Moses 7:48–49), longing for the day she will be cleansed and renewed. In addition, Ruether's condemnation of the view that evil resulted from Eve's misdeeds is not incompatible with the LDS doctrine that we are punished for our own sins and not for the transgressions of Adam or Eve and that mortality is a positive good, rather than a penalty we bear.

Responding personally to Ruether is easy: she is straightforward about what she will not believe, witty, and not ungentle. She is most engaging when moved upon by her passion for doing right by her sisters and brothers. One can hardly dissent with her view that "God cannot redeem the world apart from our free and loving response to God which is, at the same time, a choice to love and support one another" ("Feminist Critique," 275). As one who participated in the civil rights movement, who has a successful forty-plus-year marriage, and who has raised three children, her commitment demonstrated to justice and to her own family is in itself commendable. However, significant portions of her feminist cultural critique of the Judeo-Christian tradition contrast sharply with LDS doctrine and practice. Her support for elective abortion and acceptance of homosexuality, for example, are inconsistent with the value LDS doctrine places on the husband-wife, parent-child relationships. In her sociological approach to religious symbols, she considers women demeaned by "God-talk," which represents God as *Father* and Christ as *Son*. She judges the traditional family as oppressive

47. Rosemary Radford Ruether, *Disputed Questions: On Being a Christian* (Maryknoll, N. Y.: Orbis, 1989), 141.

48. Ruether, *Disputed Questions*, 126.

49. Members of The Church of Jesus Christ of Latter-day Saints refer to themselves as *Latter-day Saints* (LDS) and are often called *Mormons* because of their belief in The Book of Mormon: Another Testament of Jesus Christ. I do not speak for the LDS church or its members, but I believe that my comments in this paper are in keeping with the doctrines, policies, and practices of the LDS church.

to women[50] and rejects Christian soteriology in any but a nonexclusive, metaphorical sense ("Male Savior," 252–64).

In contrast, the LDS church teaches that each of us is literally the spirit daughter or son of an Eternal Father and Mother[51] with the capacity to become like them and that the family is an eternal, God-ordained structure, originating before this life (D&C 76:24) and continuing beyond this life (D&C 132:19). In LDS doctrine, Christ is the only name under heaven whereby we can be saved (2 Nephi 25:20; Acts 4:12). A literal atonement culminates in physical resurrection and in the promise of receiving exaltation, or eternal life with our Father in Heaven. Apart from contrasting points of theology, however, two major differences between Ruether's feminist "re-visioning" and that of the LDS "restoration" are the authority and outcome claimed by each. By setting forth in some detail how Latter-day Saints generally think and believe about God and family, I hope to add to this dialogue by laying a foundation upon which further discussions can proceed with sensitivity especially toward those two differences.

LDS "God-Talk": The Father and the Son

The LDS church has no official theologians;[52] its three books of scripture in addition to the Bible are considered to be the word of God.[53]

---

50. Ruether, like many 1970s feminists, saw woman's traditional role in the family—particularly the doing of housework—as disadvantaging women socially, economically, and psychologically. As Ruether wrote in the 1970s: "It is in this arena that women are not only exhausted physically and rendered unfit for the more demanding and more mobile work of the leadership group. Here also the basic model of woman as the 'shitworker' of society is created and daily reinforced. Even the jobs she is given in the work force will tend to belong primarily to the same category of shitwork." Rosemary Radford Ruether, *New Woman, New Earth: Sexist Ideologies and Human Liberation* (New York: Seabury, 1975), 181.

51. God the Father is referenced numerous times throughout scripture; God the Mother is inferred from Doctrine and Covenants 132 and from "O My Father," a hymn written by Eliza R. Snow and approvingly quoted numerous times by LDS church presidents and apostles. Actually, very little is known about either the Father or the Mother, relative to what is known about Christ. We pray to the Father in the name of the Son; by the Son, under the direction of the Father, the world was created; the Son is Jehovah of the Old Testament and the Christ of the New Testament.

52. Though without official theologians, members of The Church of Jesus Christ of Latter-day Saints believe the doctrines of their faith were known anciently, lost to an apostate world, then restored beginning with a farm boy's prayer and vision in which God revealed that all of the churches extant in 1820 were flawed.

53. The three LDS books of scripture are the Book of Mormon: Another Testament of Jesus Christ, the Doctrine and Covenants of the Church of Jesus Christ of Latter-day Saints, and the Pearl of Great Price.

Latter-day Saints believe their church is led by prophets[54] who receive revelation, which is neither ahistorical nor merely contingent.[55] Members, therefore, believe that the language they use to describe God reflects reality, rather than mere human projections. The LDS church is based on foundational events central to the faith and the belief that events such as Christ's birth, atonement, death, and resurrection and Joseph Smith's First Vision are quite literal.[56] The LDS church claims that authority from God through continuing revelation to Joseph Smith and his successor prophets "restored" Christ's church after a general apostasy.

Ruether's claim, not uncommon among Christians, "that all of our images of God are human projections," is not supported by LDS doctrine, nor is the view that we are at liberty to reconstruct the "images of God" to better suit contemporary sensibilities.[57] Joseph Smith saw two separate *embodied* personages: God the Father and his Son, Jesus Christ. LDS scripture teaches that God and Jesus Christ have bodies "of flesh and bones as tangible as man's."[58] God, Christ, and Satan are all real, individual persons,

---

54. The president of the LDS church is considered to have all priesthood authority to receive revelation for the church. The president's two counselors and the twelve apostles are also sustained by the membership of the LDS church as prophets, seers, and revelators (D&C 107:21–24, 91–92).

55. In LDS thought, revelation is contextual but not merely contingent. For example, Joseph Smith's First Vision (of the Father and the Son) was contextual in that Joseph was praying to know which church he should join, and the vision was in answer to that prayer (Joseph Smith—History 1:9–20). That Joseph saw two "personages" of the Godhead was not, apparently, contingent upon what he already knew about God, for the sects he studied and considered joining—the Methodist, the Presbyterian, and the Baptist churches—all are Trinitarian. Had the vision been filtered through Joseph's social conditioning, we might have expected him to have envisioned something that did not contradict Trinitarian notions or to have been told which of the churches he should join. What he received was neither part of the socio-religious belief system in which he lived, nor was it a synthesis of competing images or theories extant in the religious thinking of the time. It was a repudiation of the religions of the day, and the religion which was to be restored was not given at that time but only over the course of the next several decades.

56. If those events never happened, there are no grounds for belief. There is no tradition of a "higher" or metaphorical interpretation of scripture that derives spiritual meaning from stories of persons who never existed or of events that never occurred.

57. Rosemary Radford Ruether, "Imago Dei: Christian Tradition and Feminist Hermeneutics," in *The Image of God: Gender Models in Judaeo-Christian Tradition*, ed. Kari Elisabeth Børresen (Minneapolis: Fortress, 1991).

58. LDS scripture continues that "the Holy Ghost has not a body of flesh and bones, but is a personage of Spirit. Were it not so, the Holy Ghost could not dwell in us" (D&C 130:22; see also 1 Nephi 11:11); the devil does not have a body detectable to touch by the human hand (D&C 129:8).

not abstractions, not forces, not ideas, not symbols. This belief affects both LDS epistemology and ontology.[59]

The embodiment of God and humankind is central to what we know of God's plan for us and for himself. The fatherhood of God is judged a straightforward truth rather than a species of primitive anthropomorphism. Christ, our elder spirit brother and the Only Begotten of the Father in the flesh, is like the Father in purpose but is not one in substance with the Father. In keeping with LDS belief that correct religion is based on the realities of existent things and beings, LDS faithful hope to enter into God's discourse rather than establish their own discourse.[60] That the veil between God and humankind is permeable is taken as a given: God can and does make himself understood; God the Father is not an uncommunicative or deadbeat dad.

For Latter-day Saints, the maleness of God the Father and Christ the Son is part of their eternal identity, not the outgrowth of misogynist or any other imagery. Just as gender is an essential characteristic of who God is, "[g]ender is an essential characteristic of [each] individual['s] premortal, mortal, and eternal identity and purpose"; each person "is a beloved spirit son or daughter of heavenly parents, and, as such, each has a divine nature and destiny."[61] In LDS thought, biological sex is not, as Ruether asserts, relevant only to reproduction in this life. Sexual intimacy within the bounds of marriage for other than reproductive purposes is also honorable and bonding and contributes to the joy and fulfillment that God intends for husbands and wives.

In LDS soteriology, the prospect of gaining a mortal body—becoming more like the Father and the Mother—caused God's spirit children to shout with joy (Job 38:7), and though "Father Adam, the Ancient of Days and father of all, and our glorious mother Eve" (D&C 138:38–39) transgressed

59. God gave his spirit children moral agency both in the premortal life and in mortality. He also gave them commandments and light, or knowledge, to use in the exercise of their agency. Even premortally, some chose to follow God and Christ, and some chose to follow the devil (Abraham 3:24–28).

60. What is important is what God means to tell us in scripture and what he wants us to understand. It is anticipated that even those born into the LDS church, "cultural Mormons," must, like anyone else, be converted to the restored gospel of Jesus Christ. It is a commonplace in LDS thought that each individual must actively seek spiritual knowledge and use that knowledge to evaluate all things.

61. "The Family: A Proclamation to the World," Ensign 25 (November 1995). The proclamation on the family has not yet been canonized, but I believe it soon will be. That maleness or femaleness is an eternal aspect of the individual may be derived from Doctrine and Covenants 132:19–22 and from the much quoted hymn by Eliza R. Snow, "O, My Father," which affirms the reality of both a Heavenly Father and Heavenly Mother.

God's commandment, they blessed us by bringing all humankind into mortality, the next step in eternal progression. To Latter-day Saints, Eve's exercise of agency enabled each of us to gain a physical body.[62] Rather than viewing her as spiritually weaker than Adam, LDS scripture sees her decision as reflecting the limited understanding she and Adam had prior to their knowing "good and evil" (Moses 6:11). Because the heavy burden of childbearing was to be hers in the mortal state, it was appropriate that she, rather than her husband, choose to accept her calling as "Eve . . . the mother of all living," whose God-given name was recognized by Adam (Moses 4:26). Had Adam made that choice for Eve—obligating her to bear children—he would have locked her into a role that she may not have chosen.[63] Her decision, followed by Adam's decision to remain with her, allowed each of them to choose the path to mortality, to assent to their respective callings. She—like Adam, like Christ, like each of us—chose her mortal challenge, though she did not and could not fully understand the import of her choices. The first couple learned wisdom while in the mortal state, where, Eve explained, we come to know "the joy of our redemption, and the eternal life which God giveth unto all the obedient" (Moses 5:11). Or in the words of a Book of Mormon prophet, "Adam fell that man might be; men are, that they might have joy" (2 Nephi 2:25). Our creation, mortal existence, Christ's atonement, and the resurrection are not the mysteries of God's good pleasure but are part of God's eternal work "to bring to pass the immortality and eternal life of man" (Moses 1:39).[64]

---

62. See, for example, Elder Richard G. Scott, "To Live the Great Plan of Happiness," http://www.deseretnews.com/confer/96fall/eg1okylz.htm; also "The Joy of Living the Great Plan of Happiness," *Ensign* 26 (November 1996): 73–75.

63. This is reflected in current LDS church practice:

> Bringing children into a loving home is considered a sacred privilege and responsibility of husbands and wives. Given that context, birth control is a matter left to the prayerful, mutual decisions of a righteous couple, with the counsel that husbands must be considerate of their wives, who experience the greater physical and emotional demands in bearing children. A woman's health and strength are to be preserved in childbearing; thus, wisdom should govern how a husband and wife carry out the responsibility to become parents and to care for their offspring. (Terrance D. Olsen, "Sexuality," in *Encyclopedia of Mormonism*, 3:1306)

64. As "The Family: A Proclamation to the World" states, "In the premortal realm, spirit sons and daughters knew and worshipped God as their Eternal Father and accepted His plan by which His children could obtain a physical body and gain earthly experience to progress toward perfection and ultimately realize his or her divine destiny as an heir of eternal life."

In LDS doctrine, because Satan and a third of the hosts of heaven rebelled (seeking God's power, rather than his will) (D&C 29:36) they did not and will not receive mortal bodies, their progression is damned or stopped, and they cannot become like God. The unembodied Satan "seeketh that all men might be miserable like unto himself" (2 Nephi 2:27). Whatever destroys or demeans the body or spirit, including attitudes and practices that discourage childbearing or that make parents unwilling to care for their young, are all considered part of Satan's efforts to disrupt mortal existence and the eternal progress of those who chose premortally to follow God's plan (Abraham 3:26). Women, as mothers, make it possible for others to enter mortality—not a small task. Like Eve, women are the mothers of "all living" and are "saved in childbearing, if they [the husband and wife] continue in faith and charity and holiness with sobriety [prudence]" (1 Tim. 2:15) just as Eve was saved by her own "seed" (Gen. 3:15; Moses 4:21), the child borne of Mary. Christ worked the atonement in the flesh, taking upon him humankind's "infirmities, that his bowels may be filled with mercy, according to the flesh, that he may *know according to the flesh* how to succor his people according to their infirmities" (Alma 7:12; emphasis added).

Christ bore in the flesh an infinite weight of suffering. Shortly before his death he compared the coming grief of the disciples to the experience of childbirth (John 16:21). Birth, baptism, and Christ's atonement are linked by their material similarities:

> Inasmuch as ye were born into the world by water, and blood, and the spirit, which I have made, and so became of dust a living soul, even so ye must be born again into the kingdom of heaven, of water, and of the Spirit, and be cleansed by blood, even the blood of mine Only Begotten. (Moses 6:59)

Our mortal embodiment—and Christ's—was not possible without an embodied woman; without Christ's incarnation and atonement, the resurrection of our souls (our bodies and spirits, eternally joined, D&C 88:15) and eternal life are not possible. This is not recycled Republican motherhood. It is the recognition that just as Christ's service to us all involves embodiment and teaching and sacrifice, so does the service of women and men in mortality. Women's bodies are not demeaned in LDS theology but are central to the plan of salvation, God's "great plan of happiness" (Alma 42:8). A religion that fails to account for the affirmative good of the mortal body and life on earth is unlikely to appeal to an LDS audience, and any perspective that discounts the important role of mothers undervalues women.

LDS theology affirms the literal resurrection of the physical body. Those, such as Ruether, who deny a bodily resurrection but object to a gnosticism that demeans embodiment must wrestle with several problems: The problem of the entire loss of the body at death. Or, if there be a spiritual but no literal physical resurrection, the problem of the loss of the most salient features of the human body—sexual dimorphism. Or, if there be a resurrection of body and spirit (in LDS terms, the "soul," D&C 88:15) but no continuation of the relationships of husband and wife or parent and child, then the perfected resurrected body without the power to give life would be, in some sense, less whole than the body in mortality. Efforts to transcend the body, either by freeing the spirit from it or subduing the body by spiritual means, suggest that the body is in some sense unworthy of the spirit encased within it. In contrast, LDS scripture teaches that spirit is "finer" matter than flesh but is not immaterial (D&C 131:7) and that the dead awaiting Christ's resurrection and their own "had looked upon the long absence of their spirits from their bodies as a bondage" (D&C 138:50). In LDS doctrine, embodiment is a kind of freedom and does not present the body/spirit problems of traditional Christian theologies.

Ruether's feminist theology seeks to correct the "anti-material concept of God's transcendence with incarnational and interactive views of divine-world relations" ("Feminist Critique," 271) but succeeds only in the disincarnation of the individual body and the dissolution altogether of individual consciousness. The negative traditions associated with the dualisms[65] of matter/spirit, body/mind, immanence/transcendence, are replaced by an appreciative eco-ephemeralism, in which materiality churns us up, and transcendence collapses into material process itself. So what of the meaning of our lives? Ruether professes not to know: "It is in the [metaphorical] hands of Holy Wisdom to forge out of our finite struggle truth and being for everlasting life. Our agnosticism about what this means is then the expression of our faith, our trust that Holy Wisdom will give transcendent meaning to our work, which is bounded by space and time."[66] This solution, however, comes up short. If there is one thing each of us must and can do, and which feminists surely claim to do, it is to make meaning of our bodies and our lives. A feminist theology that appeals finally to ignorance fails on its own terms.

The Family of God

Ruether suggests that having a "permanent parent-child relationship to God" portrays God as a "neurotic parent who does not want us to grow up. To become autonomous and responsible for our own lives is the gravest sin against God," and, according to Ruether, "prolong[s] spiritual infantilism

---

65. Rosemary Radford Ruether, *Sexism and God-Talk: Toward a Feminist Theology* (Boston: Beacon, 1983), 37, 160.

66. Ibid., 258.

as virtue and . . . make[s] autonomy and assertion of free will a sin."[67] This seems to be a misreading of the Christian view that it is spiritually important to want what God wants, to have unrighteous desires replaced by the desire to do the will of God. Using moral agency—making choices—however, does not destroy the parent-child relationship we have with God any more than marrying severs the parent-child tie with our mortal parents. Neither our wanting what is best for our children nor God's wanting what is best for us hampers a child's development or marks the parent unfit. The rationale for saying "Not my will, but thine, be done" (Luke 22:42) is the knowledge that Father really does know best and that God does not want anything that is not good. Such faith, of course, relies on the existence of an actual teleological being with, at least, the powers of cognition.

Ruether objects to giving one's will to God on several grounds. One is that what has been taken to be God's will was actually the will of fallible and sometimes wicked men. This resulted, in her view, in hierarchies that keep some people poor and powerless, in servitude of one kind or another to rich, powerful men.[68] A second ground for her objection is that the neurotic, infantilizing parent-child relationship with the divine has justified a view of the family that is a "way of enculturating us to the stereotypic male and female roles. The family becomes the nucleus and model of patriarchal [hierarchal] relations in society . . . reinforc[ing] patriarchal power rather than liberating us from it."[69] Her third objection is that the pattern of Christian eschatology, "a view that believes in the possibility of human transcendence of mortality,"[70] has resulted in seeking "an ultimate future at or beyond the end of history and the escape of the soul from the body to Heaven."[71] The effort to do God's will in order to overcome the earthly and the here and now (that is, resurrection and immortality and eternal life in heaven), has, in Ruether's view, resulted in a callous degradation of the environment and of women (the most earthy of humans) in the name of a future good. Recognizing our finitude, she believes, will help us focus on living better now so that we may bequeath to our children a better society and a less-ravaged earth.

In considering the first ground, we can readily grant that Christians, and others, have sinned against the earth and against women. Admittedly, some may have appealed to Christian belief to cover their sins. But that is not proof that Christian belief itself is the cause of sin. Some will use their belief in human finitude to justify their bad acts: "Eat and drink; for

---

67. Ibid., 69.
68. Ibid., 28–29.
69. Ibid., 70.
70. Ibid., 240.
71. Ibid., 250.

tomorrow we die" (1 Cor. 15:32) and if "we are guilty, God will beat us with a few stripes, and at last we shall be saved in the kingdom of God" (2 Nephi 28:7–8). But others, such as seventeenth- and eighteenth-century revolutionaries and nineteenth- and twentieth-century communists, sin, too. This Ruether admits, adding that some founders of revolutionary movements have relied too heavily on technology and had become almost deified and have wielded corrupt authority. They, too, are willing to justify the means they use today with the promise of a better future. Stalin focused on improving the here and now and the future of future generations through massive cultural changes—thirty million people were killed and the pollution of the former Soviet states' environment exceeds that of the West. Even a glance at the repression of women in ancient and contemporary mainland China or India or Africa presents numerous counterexamples. Christianity has no corner on bad men or bad decision-making.

Her second objection to giving will to God (treated at length below) characterizes the traditional family as an extension and source of corrupt culture: "One must look at all the hierarchies of exploitation and control that emanate out of the family pattern of female mothering and domestic labor."[72] It is not that Ruether is anti-family or hostile to males; she is arguing that even well-intentioned people in a male-dominated society participate in what is sometimes called "structural sin," the unreflective acceptance of patterns of dominance and submission in a specific cultural context.

Her third reason, that looking to the future encourages living badly in the present, is problematic, too. Careless choices can also come from atheism or the belief that "when a man [is] dead that [is] the end thereof" (Alma 30:18). If it be true that there is no reckoning with God in this or in a future life, then some humans will be tempted to believe that "every man fare[s] in this life according to the management of the creature; therefore every man prosper[s] according to his genius, and . . . every man conquer[s] according to his strength; and whatsoever a man [does is] no crime" (Alma 30:17).

Ruether relies on an ecofeminist ethic to prevent belief in the God(dess) of evolution from retaining the Social Darwinism that has also been used to justify the subjugation of indigenous people and the subordination of women. But concern for the environment has actually replicated, to some extent, the fight against women's bodies by targeting female fertility as a negative force for individuals and for nations. The good feminist woman

---

72. Rosemary Radford Ruether, *Gaia and God: An Ecofeminist Theology of Earth Healing* (San Francisco: HarperSanFrancisco, 1992). 171–72. A feminist commonplace, her analysis, like Marxism, privileges paid labor and the power it brings and posits the distortion of human relationships according to the alienation resulting from the materialist culture, of which Christianity in general is a part.

"manages" her fertility so that it does not impinge upon her education or career or cause concern about overtaxing earth's resources. Abortion allows her to refuse life-support to the unwanted or ill-timed child.[73] Concern about overpopulation and the desire to improve the status of women has resulted in the deaths of at least thirty million unborn children in this nation since Roe's legalization of abortion in 1973 and has encouraged the manipulation of women's bodies to perfect technologies that would make women barren. Concern for the world's poor is the impetus for sending unsafe IUDs (intrauterine devices) to third-world women, those least likely to be able to use them safely. Contemporary ecopolitics problematizes the female body as the means of overpopulation and must advocate female sterility as a means to insure earth's fecundity.

The LDS church has never encouraged careless procreation but has taken the Lord at his word that all things in the earth are the Lord's and that "the earth is full, and there is enough and to spare" (D&C 104:14, 17).[74] The greedy misuse and abuse of resources is the primary cause of poverty, rather than a simple equation of population growth with environmental degradation.

Ruether sees possibilities for improvement in an ecological ethic that fights against corrupt authority and seeks harmony rather than domination with nature and with other people.[75] That hope is not contradicted by LDS belief. God pronounced all his creations good, the implication being that humans have no right to destroy the good—his creations. One of the problems with any belief or philosophy is that those who seek to do evil—or even the well-intentioned—may misuse whatever is at hand, and proposed solutions may have unintended negative consequences. In LDS thought, the earth itself will "die," but because it "filleth the measure of its creation, and transgresseth not the law . . . it shall be sanctified . . . quickened again . . . and the righteous shall inherit it" (D&C 88:25–26). Humans have no right to kill it, however. In fact, Latter-day Saints believe humans are stewards over the earth and agree with Ruether, as presumably would most Christians, that we must not abuse the environment.[76] Scripture repeatedly condemns

73. For further discussion, see Camille S. Williams, "Thoughts of a Pro-Life Feminist," *World and I* 6 (October 1991): 569–85.

74. LDS efforts to care for the poor include periods of living what was called the United Order, a system of contribution, stewardship, and sharing. Today, members volunteer in the LDS church's welfare system and contribute fast offerings to assist the poor.

75. Ruether, *Sexism and God-Talk*, 88–92.

76. I am not contending that Latter-day Saints or Christians in general necessarily have a better ecological track record than others, merely that they cannot use their religion effectively to justify ecological depredations.

those who use their authority or religious teachings to cover their own sins or to encourage others to sin. The elders of the early church were counseled to care for those in the church not "as being lords over God's heritage, but being ensamples to the flock" (1 Pet. 5:3). LDS scripture recognizes that "we have learned by sad experience that it is the nature and disposition of almost all men, as soon as they get a little authority, as they suppose, they will immediately begin to exercise unrighteous dominion" (D&C 121:39).

Christ's redemption should not breed pride in us but humble us and make us amenable to the virtues of patience, kindness, and charity (2 Peter 1:2–9). Christian faithful have generally been aware that power and authority can be abused; no foolproof or devilproof method of preventing misuse of power has emerged. The ethic of the ecologist struggles with similar tensions: does one use legislation, education, litigation, protest, or terrorist tactics to stop the commercialization or destruction of ecosystems? All such methods exist among professed environmentalists; many other ways of living or failing to live as Christians do, too.

The Traditional Family

Ruether's environmental awareness takes little account of the "ecology" of the family, perhaps because she sees the family in its present form as an unnatural distortion of what might be. Her view of enculturated sex roles is grim: "Sexism as sin centers on distorted relationality. . . . Women . . . are denied those capacities for autonomous selfhood, decision making, and critical intelligence monopolized by males."[77] While she also condemns the roles given males as restricting male development in part, some of her statements about men border on stereotypic male bashing. Of male-female relations she writes, "He reduces her to the body that services his domestic and sexual needs but with whom he does not communicate. She experiences the slow soul-starvation of communication denial."[78] One could hardly make a broader generalization. Ruether further contends that "in fact there are few women, even today, who have not experienced at least one or two beatings from husbands or boyfriends."[79] That astonishing claim simply is not supported by available data, at least not in U.S. data. There is far too much violence in many relationships, for any violence is too much, but no reputable researcher has contended that almost every woman has been beaten at least once or twice.

The intimacy of marriage and family life allows opportunity for greatest service or for grossest exploitation. Every human trust entails the pos-

77. Ruether, *Sexism and God-Talk*, 174.
78. Ibid., 174.
79. Ibid., 175.

sibility of betrayal. The family need not be painted worse than it was or now is. Patricia Smith notes that "the value of living in families is indisputable in general. It may be disputable in particular cases in which basic family obligations of cooperation and support are not met, but bad families are not counterexamples to the value of good families."[80] The LDS claim that good families are central to individual happiness and social stability is not an assertion that family life in general is what it should be. It is asserted that the family, imperfect as it now is, is the only institution in this life that is capable of perfection in the next life. The recommended division of labor within the family recognizes that children are worthy of our best care. Pregnancy, birth, lactation, and child care are both important and taxing, so women should, where possible, be relieved of the necessity of wage-earning during childbearing and child-rearing years. Giving birth and caring for children is considered a part of mortality and ultimately more important than the activities that will end with this life, such as professions or careers.[81] Both men and women are counseled to put family before career or any other interest. In 1935, LDS apostle David O. McKay, later president of the LDS church, cautioned men to put home first in their lives, warning that "No other success can compensate for failure in the home." McKay declared that God "ordained man and woman for the home. . . . If anyone makes a loving home with all his heart, he can never miss heaven."[82]

In contrast to Ruether's view that Christianity can encourage passivity, infantalization, or a spirit of domination, LDS theology encourages individuals to take care of God's creations and to treat others well, especially in the family. That family roles are enculturated, for better or worse, at least allows each generation to evaluate what has worked and what has not.[83]

---

80. Patricia Smith, "Family Responsibility and the Nature of Obligation," in *Kindred Matters: Rethinking the Philosophy of the Family*, ed. Diana Tietjens Meyers, Kenneth Kipnis, and Cornelius F. Murphy Jr. (Ithaca, N.Y.: Cornell University Press, 1993), 54.

81. See, for example, Elder Boyd K. Packer's explanation that service in the home and family takes priority over service for the church, in "Parents in Zion," *Ensign* 28 (November 1998): 22–24.

82. David O. McKay, "Home Building Paramount," in *150th Annual Conference of The Church of Jesus Christ of Latter-day Saints* (Salt Lake City: The Church of Jesus Christ of Latter-day Saints, 1935): 115–16.

83. LDS people distinguish some enculturated family roles from eternally important family roles and attempt not to confuse ends with means or substance with form. "Disability, death, or other circumstances may necessitate individual adaptation" in terms of work inside and outside the home. What is fundamentally important is that both husband and wife, father and mother view their marriage and family as more important than their own pride, their respective careers, their hobbies, or their social status. "The Family: A Proclamation to the World," 102.

Freedom from gender roles within the family is most aptly demonstrated in our time by the non-husband, anti-father: the male who engenders a child but does not marry the mother and supports neither in any way. He plays the role of lover and leaves a generation of children to grow up not knowing what a father is. Likewise, with the high rate of divorce in the United States, many children grow up with little idea of husband and wife roles, though they are very familiar with the single parent role.

Gordon B. Hinckley, president of the LDS church, maintains that families need "the leadership of a good and devoted father who stands at the side of an able and kindly mother"; a father who will pray with and for his family. He notes that young boys need to see a father functioning in the home to motivate them to be good fathers themselves. "I do not believe that women resent the strong leadership of a man in the home," Hinckley continued. "He becomes the provider, the defender, the counselor, the breadwinner and lends and gives support when needed."[84]

Recent research has documented that "faith-oriented fathering" can produce positive, nonexploitive relationships in religious families in which husbands and fathers view themselves as servants.[85] An ideology that seeks a roleless world may not be achievable nor desirable. Freedom is built upon the successes and mistakes of others—the history of a discipline, an institution, a religion, a family structure. Which of us would contend that each individual must create his or her own language in order to be free and explore all of his or her innate human possibilities?

Nor is it obvious that we need to eliminate gender roles in the family and in Christianity in general by integrating women into male roles and men into female roles. The minimal necessary, least invasive, most ecologically sound change would be to value equally the female and the male roles in the family and in the church. That is the crux of the difficulty for many feminists: they do not value the traditional roles of women and assume that men and society have not and do not value those roles either. Or, if feminists grant the importance of mothering, they are likely to object to that as a career because the male and female realms "are not at all comparable in power. Without access to public power and skills, woman cannot survive alone, whereas man's control of power and resources means that woman's services are more readily replaceable."[86] Nor can men survive alone without access to public power and skills—witness the plight of many inner-city males. Survival is important. A good deal of LDS discussion about the family,

---

84. Gordon B. Hinckley, as quoted in Kristen Moulton, "Fathers Urged to Lead Their Families," *Daily Herald* (Provo, Utah), April 25, 1998, A1–A2.

85. David Dollahite, "Fathering, Faith, and Spirituality," *Journal of Men's Studies* 7 (Fall 1998): 3–15.

86. Ruether, *Sexism and God-Talk*, 174.

however, is not focused on what it takes for each individual family member to survive but on the ways that mutual reliance in the family can benefit the family as a whole. The focus is frequently on those even less prepared to fend for themselves than are women: children. The traditional role-division emphasizes care of our children, a worthy ethic even when carried out by flawed humanity.

The Feminist Case against Religion and Family

It is the admission that women suffer followed by the assertion that men are called or ordained to protect women that wears away feminist patience. If men were divinely appointed to protect women but exploit and harm women instead, then either God is a bad judge of human character, or men have usurped the "protector's" role, declared it to be the will of God, and used that role for their own selfish ends. Yet, concluding that men have poorly protected women does not prove that they were not called to do so. In feminist interpretation, however, religions that have assigned males leadership and protective roles in the family and in the church have, in the end, assisted in the exploitation of women. Certainly some men exploit some women; some men do not exploit women but are charged by feminists with benefiting from the general exploitation of women. It is this extended argument that discomfits some religious women.

Feminists have recounted the suffering of women as a means of seeking change, emphasizing that it is the *structure* of society, home, and church that allows harm to women to continue. But for women like me, whose fathers, brothers, husbands, and sons have treated us well (sometimes better than we have treated them), the structure of the society, church, and home has not resulted in exploitation.[87] For the woman sexually abused by a male relative or physically abused by a lover or a son, the structure of church, home, and society may, indeed, be part of the oppression she experiences. Shall we conclude on the basis of *my* experience that social structures do not oppress women? Or conclude on the basis of the abused woman's experience that social structures *do* oppress women?[88] A reasonable conclusion

87. Superson, and some other feminists, would probably argue that I simply have not recognized that I am exploited by the males in my life.

88. This, of course, is the point to factor in knowledge that there is violence in same-sex relationships, too, despite the feminist response that it is "heterosexism"—the insistence on gender roles based on biological sex that contributes both to violence against women and, via internalized self-hatred, to violence in same-sex relationships. For a discussion of the links posited between male dominance and "heterosexism" and homophobia, see Rosemary Radford Ruether, "Homophobia, Heterosexism, and Pastoral Practice," in *Homosexuality in the Priesthood and the Religious Life*, ed. Jeannine Gramick (New York: Crossroad, 1989), 21–35.

is that our lives illustrate a range of human capacity and experience within those social structures: the males who acted in their "roles" chose either to help and care for or to exploit but were not *caused* by the structure to do either. To have women's safety dependent upon the good intentions of men, is for feminists unsatisfactory. The truth of the matter is, however, that all people are dependent, always, on the good intentions of others.

The simplest structural change feminists have proposed to reduce women's vulnerability is separatism of one kind or another, at least in the short term. Mary Daly is the feminist theologian most associated with feminist religious separatism, and, while Ruether sees Daly's work as a valuable excursus on what the plight of women really has been,[89] Ruether and most other feminists advocate a subtler separatism.

Ruether's goal of working from women's religious experience illustrates the view that women must turn away or be liberated from religious tradition adjudged as saturated with male experience. Feminists physically or emotionally or academically or religiously or politically separate themselves from males—from fathers, brothers, husbands, and sons—and must do so if they are to be the political "advocate[s] for female subjectivity," as Grant phrases it.[90] So at least in the short term, like the kulak farmer or the Cambodian college professor, men are individually and collectively class criminals. Most feminists are separatists in theory only, but feminist ideology certainly forms the basis for a more long-lived emotional estrangement. Tactics of separation range from the incessant invective of Daly, Dworkin, and MacKinnon, to the stereotyping or essentializing of men as sometimes exhibited by Ruether (though she recognizes the need for men and women to work together), to the opportunistic male-bashing of greeting cards and males-just-don't-get-it jokes. Such separatism is deadly to marriages, family life, and communities.

If every structure exploitable by men against women—or one person against another—were restructured to give women more power, it is argued, then women would not suffer so much. This has been the impetus for change in the legal status of women in this country during the past two hundred years. But because logically every human structure is exploitable by those who intend to exploit, the restructuring will never be enough, will never be finished. In fact, the feminist position, since the legal disabilities of women in the U.S. were virtually erased, is that there are *invisible* structures that yet allow men to exploit women or that only through women's equal participation—not just equal opportunity to participate—in all aspects of all social institutions will new structures and new attitudes toward women

---

89. Ruether, *Sexism and God-Talk*, 187.

90. Judith Grant, *Fundamental Feminism: Contesting the Core Concepts of Feminist Theology* (New York: Routledge, 1983), 103.

emerge. What results is the constant need to measure, negotiate, broker, and assert women's power relative to men's. This strategy, like religion or democracy, does not guarantee equality or change of heart; however, it does insure that women's focus will be on power relations vis-à-vis men and that an estrangement of trust and purpose will insinuate itself in all male-female relationships. This is no recommendation.

The woman who guards against exploitation from her husband has already branded him exploitive. Henry B. Eyring, of the LDS church's Quorum of the Twelve Apostles, notes that "there are important ways in which planning for failure can make failure more likely." The examples he gives are the husband who takes work he knows will not allow him to be home enough to be an "equal partner" and the woman who trains for a career that is "incompatible with being primarily responsible for the nurture of her children."[91] Each has prepared to make it alone, and, because each has prepared to be alone, it may be harder for them to cooperate in what might be best for their family, especially for their dependent children. We have raised a generation of professionals, many of whom expect their primary source of growth or fulfillment to come from their careers. They intend to be unalienated, or at least well-paid professionals, not merely workers with a way to sustain life. Knowing God and living a good life, whatever one's workaday activities, is the way of fulfillment for many religious people. LDS doctrine further identifies marriage and family as an essential part of the way toward living more as God lives. In LDS belief, salvation and exaltation are not individual, both require the building of relationships with deity and with other people. Thus, the work done in the family of God and individual families is the most important work for both women and men.

Psychologist Emily Reynolds argues that "traditional" women are as interested in changing the world as their careerist sisters. But those working in the home full time have dedicated themselves "to changing the world one child at a time."[92] Such an appeal to the importance of women's role within the family has long been derided by feminists as a ruse to control women, to keep them in the home and out of the workforce. Ruether, for example, charges that emphasizing the importance of the mother-child relationship has been "a cultural means of forcing upon women a job that men have both idealized and, at the same time, have shunned as dirty, tedious, and beneath their dignity." Characterizing work within the home as fundamentally valuable—though lacking in status and pay—obscures, according to Ruether's analysis, the fact that men "enforce on women . . . the tedious and rote roles of domestic labor: the cooking, the housecleaning, the washing of

---

91. Henry B. Eyring, "The Family," *Ensign* 28 (February 1998): 16.
92. Emily Reynolds, conversation with Camille S. Williams.

garments, the repetitive servicing of daily needs. Sexism means that women are the servant class for these tasks."[93]

To dismiss homemaking as the grunt work of the species is inaccurate and demeaning. Any labor paid or unpaid may be reduced to its least or most attractive feature in the mind of the analyst. Grading student papers is inherently no more nor less tedious than writing essays for publication, than drafting pleadings, than traveling from one city to another for yet another professional conference, than bathing an infant, than sorting laundry, than washing dishes. It is inconsistent for feminists to insist that embodiment is good, even enjoyable, but to dismiss the labor of sustaining and comforting our material bodies—feeding, clothing, washing, and housing them—as inevitably repetitive and tedious. Even Ruether's image of "Wisdom as a strong woman, ruler of her own household, who invites others to a banquet that she prepares" (Ruether, 274) argues against stereotyping homemakers generally. Ruether's analysis of women's work in capitalism—similar to the Marxist-socialist analysis—privileges work outside the home because that work gives women more economic and social power. She opines, though, that because females are more in touch with "real relations and the processes of life" they may be more victimized but less dehumanized than men.[94] This implicitly affirms that some women, rather than surviving as powerless, dependent creatures, have actively resisted the dehumanization of the modern workplace through their work in the family.[95]

Family hierarchies—family roles—may also be less rigid than some analysts propose. Any male (or female) at the "apex" of the family hierarchy sees his or her position shift over time. The good of family members converge across the developmental span despite the fact that relationships are frequently asymmetrical. Infants require intensive care; the infant that reaches adulthood because of the parents' efforts may in turn offer intensive, extensive care to aged or infirm parents. The spouse who early in marriage supports the family may later be supported by the other spouse. The non-wage earner who runs errands for the wage earner may receive reciprocal service during his or her own periods of employment. A son or daughter gives loving support to the surviving parent grieving the lost husband or wife. In families and in society, the good of women, men, and children converges over time.

---

93. Ruether, *Sexism and God-Talk*, 177.

94. Ibid., 179–80.

95. For a discussion of the importance of work in the home, see Kathleen Slaugh Bahr and Cheri A. Loveless, "Family Work—in the Twenty-First Century: While Our Culture Pursues Eden, We Must Work to Bring Zion," in *Charting a New Millennium: The Latter-day Saints in the Coming Century*, ed. Maurine Proctor and Scot Proctor (Salt Lake City: Aspen, 1998).

Feminism, like any ideology it criticizes, both "reveals" some social practices as hypocritical but also hides and distorts some actions of some feminist ideologues. Insofar as women label others sexist in order to hide their own sins, the tactic can be useful for eviscerating or silencing those we do not want to argue with or those we choose not to the take the time and effort to persuade.

Ruether seeks to change not just the expectations and behaviors of women but also those of men. And, Ruether warns, male conversion from sexism is risky for the male ego. A man has to overcome not only "'pride' in masculinity that oppresses women but also their fear of loss of male status by which they oppress themselves and each other."[96] Apparently then, men's humanity, like women's, will never be known until sexism is vanquished. The struggle "against sexism is basically a struggle to humanize the world, to humanize ourselves, to salvage the planet, to be in right relation to God/ess." When males are ready to recognize this, "without co-opt[ing] or pander[ing] to women," they will be ready to "join hands [with women] in a common struggle."[97] There is a predictable circularity to this argument or, alternatively, a kind of "we'll know humanity when we see it" faith in the future. This seems an example of theory degenerating into wishful slogans.

Feminist theory is not modest in its claims. Ruether paints an extraordinary view of history and male-female relations:

> Sexism creates a vast pollution of the channel of human communication. The biasing not only of language and symbols, verbal and visual, but the organization of space, the nonverbal language of dress and body signals, keeps all this intact, as both law and custom, so that neither male nor female is capable of imagining, much less acting upon, an alternative [except feminists, of course]. Culturally, sexism defines the whole system of reality, from "matter" to 'God.' One cannot challenge sexism without the dethronement of the cultural universe as an authentic and good model of life.[98]

The term *sexism* is used to refer to everything from sex roles in an intact family to prostitution to female genital mutilation to wearing aftershave to serving as a priest or a nun. That flexible pejorative seems to cover quite a lot that is bad, quite a lot that might be indifferent, and even some that is good. Sexism is condemnable for its proven and potential negative effects but apparently irredeemable for any good it encompasses. Ruether sees sexism as "also the distortion of male humanity," and that distortion is an endemic disease in which there is "a ravaging of relationships and an

96. Ruether, *Sexism and God-Talk*, 191.
97. Ibid., 191–92.
98. Ibid., 178.

insensitivity to this ravaging."[99] She describes "the normal male mode of relationship is one of conquer or be conquered, dominate or be dominated." This hierarchicalism leads to abstractionism that enables violence, rather than "real contact and shared feeling with existing human reality."[100] These generalizations about men are no more accurate than are generalizations about women, no less totalizing.

In like manner, Ruether's analysis of domination and power relations in religious imagery, for the most part, ignores scriptural images and examples of fathers as protective providers (Job 29:12–16; Luke 2:48), as tutors (Prov. 1:8; 3:12; 4:1–5), as loving (Mark 14:36, which Ruether mentions), as compassionate (Ps. 103:1–14; Luke 11:11; 15:12–22), and as nurturing (Job 29:16; John 15:1).[101] Those emotions and actions of love were not drained of meaning in the setting of the paterfamilias, nor do they appear to be merely calculated to consolidate power. Ruether's highly selective use of male imagery in scripture, coupled with her dismissal of much of the female imagery as too often reinforcing cultural hierarchies and stereotypes, does little to elucidate scriptural imagery.

Conclusion

Ruether's respect for the natural world and her skepticism about Gnosticism are likely to ring true for LDS readers. Many would also find her commitment to ending poverty extremely appealing and could envision a companionable afternoon working with her at a LDS church welfare farm or cannery. Unless her reader were already converted to feminism, however, her critique of religious teachings and practices might remain less than appealing.

Given the disparity between LDS doctrine and Ruether's feminist treatment of the respective natures of God, human beings, and families; of the origin, nature, and interpretation of knowledge, scripture, and ecclesial history; and of the ends and purposes of life, much of Ruether's feminist critique cannot be applied to LDS belief and practices.[102] In fact, the usual feminist critique of the Judeo-Christian tradition, of which Ruether's work is a part, does not touch or worry many women—LDS or not—because the feminist critique seems too often partial or a misreading of scripture, practice, or tradition. Some women are more troubled by what they perceive to be the level of unhappiness in the lives of the feminists they know than they

---

99. Ibid., 177.

100. Ibid., 179.

101. This short list is given as a reminder and does not exhaust the scriptural examples.

102. Ruether's critique cannot apply even to the issues that discomfit LDS feminists: plural marriage, priesthood ordination, and the patriarchal order.

are about feminist allegations. This is not a naïve judgment made in ignorance of the suffering of women but a spiritual judgment. Christ promised a "Comforter" to teach and to give a peace not of this world, a peace that removes trouble and fear from the heart (John 14:26–27). Many find no peace in feminist theology, which they perceive as condemning the family.

To some extent feminists and nonfeminists disagree about what is good and what is evil. Religious women whose faith and experience tell them family is good are wary of ideologies that call the family evil (Isaiah 5:20–21).

A strong commonality of experience exists among LDS and other religious people who see the purpose of life as found primarily within family relationships. In bad family relationships everyone *feels* exploited, and each may be. In good family relationships each family member feels free to give him- or herself wholly to the family without fear of exploitation and to accept others' giving without fear of exploiting them. Feminist views of the housewife as parasite or children as burdens or men as oppressors are antithetical to the most important means of love and support most people have: marriage and family. To say women's lives have been wasted or their abilities undeveloped because they have chosen childbearing and child rearing—those beloved activities for which women have given their lives across time—is a misogynistic mistake, whether committed by males or females. That kind of misogyny can exist only where childbearing and child rearing have already been dismissed as unimportant or injurious to women.[103]

Family relationships and relations to God and to the religious community are relations of trust. Not minimal, but maximal trust makes both faith and family life possible. Family relations are unavoidably undercut by the belief that men are exploiters or that they are third-party beneficiaries of the exploitation of women. The belief that female autonomy is unalterably compromised by childbearing and that the care of children is tedium dressed up as nobility will not strengthen the mother-child bond. Any philosophy or ideology that is so potentially destructive to these fundamentally important relationships is unlikely to be widely accepted by an LDS community.

---

103. See, for example, Eileen L. McDonagh, "My Body, My Consent: Securing the Constitutional Right to Abortion Funding," *Albany Law Review* 62, no. 3 (1999): 1057–1118. McDonagh contends that women have the right to government-funded abortions, arguing that pregnancy harms women and that the government is required to alleviate that harm.

Rejoinder

Rosemary Radford Ruether

A RELIGIOUS COMMUNITY SHOWS ITSELF resilient and creative when it can intentionally open itself to conversation with points of view sometimes seen as alien to itself. This conversation undertaken between LDS thought and the cutting edge of modern theologies, including feminist theology, is such a demonstration of the promise of the LDS tradition.

Camille S. Williams's paper is a carefully crafted, primarily negative challenge to my paper on feminist theology that shows a wide reading of my work and addresses both substantive ethical and theological issues. I will respond to both her remarks on family and gender roles and on her delineation of theological differences.

I find her arguments somewhat different in these two areas. On family and gender roles she sometimes resorts to caricature of a feminism that represents neither my position, nor that of mainstream feminism. On theological themes she provides a straightforward affirmation of differences between LDS views and mine and, in some cases, mainstream Christian views.

A major example of her distortion of feminism is her effort to characterize it as overtly or covertly separatist. I believe that some feminists have been guilty of rhetorical excess that does not sufficiently distinguish between the distortions of patriarchy they seek to criticize and the good potential of men as well as women for healthy relationships. The goal of the feminist movement generally has not been separatism, but a changed relationship of men and women that promotes genuine egalitarian partnership. Separatism is a very marginal view among feminists, although the media has typically emphasized it in order to discredit feminism. Williams follows this same strategy in seeking to define feminism as separatism.

My own theological anthropology has explicitly rejected an essentialist view of maleness and femaleness that views one side as good and the other as bad, in favor of the full humanness of men and women (which means both men and women are capable of good and evil). I believe in family planning for the sake of responsible and committed partnership by both men and women, and also for the sake of good, caring child raising. I also think the smaller family is indicated by the current population crisis. I am pro-partnership of women and men in families and in society. I am against social structures and ideologies that distort the full humanity of both women and men, forcing men into work roles that give them little time for parenting and women in domestic roles that prevent their larger social development.

Williams bases her arguments on an assumption that gender natures and roles of men and women and the structure of the family are fixed and God-given from eternity. In contrast, I regard the notions that men are more rational and suited to leadership and women more nurturing, emotive, and suited to dependency as social constructs that arise in the context of particular social and economic arrangements in which men were assigned work outside the home and women were assigned the full-time care of children, making women economically dependent upon men.

The family pattern Williams assumes to be normative itself is very time bound. It was created with industrialization when the family household economy was changed for an economy based on separation of work and household, assigning men to paid work and women to unpaid household work. Before the Industrial Revolution, both men and women worked and parented together within a household economy. Furthermore, this kind of split between home and work as a gender division of roles was never accessible except to a mostly white middle class in the mid-nineteenth to mid-twentieth century. The economic state for the working class and blacks always required both parents to work. Dual-income households are now normative for the white middle class as well, for reasons that have more to do with economics than feminism.

Indeed most middle-class professionals today find themselves in a work trap that requires a ten- or twelve- rather than an eight-hour day, making it even more difficult for men and women to combine parenting and income-producing work. What is needed is not an effort to return to a nineteenth-century model of the full-time housewife dependent on one male income, but to create social supports for both men and women that will allow both to share parenting and both to participate in the larger work world. Instead of lengthening the workday, we should shorten it to a thirty-hour workweek with flexible work hours, making real partnership of men and women as both workers and parents possible.

The real crux of the difference between my views and those of Camille Williams is her rejection of social analysis and ideology critique. Basically she wishes to reduce the problem of abuse of women in family and society to exceptional individuals, men or women, who fail in their responsibilities. But she rejects both the possibility of distorted historical social structures that are inherently unjust and false ideologies designed to justify and sanctify unjust social structures. Most particularly she rejects any possibility of social or ideological critique of the LDS tradition and its family and social patterns, seeing these as divinely revealed and hence infallible.

Claims of inerrancy of revealed tradition are ways of cutting off the very question of ideology critique before it can even be asked. I do not intend to engage in ideology critique of Mormonism because I regard this as the job of Latter-day Saints, not that of persons outside the LDS tradition. The purpose of ideology critique of a religious tradition is for the sake of pruning away its distortions in order to reclaim its liberating core and potential. This work can be done only by those within and committed to particular communities and traditions, not those outside and against them.

I regard the critique of patriarchy in the Christian tradition as liberating that tradition's core vision of "good news to the poor, the liberation of the oppressed," which is the heart of Jesus' message. But in order to understand this message, one also has to be able to denounce those forces that produce poverty and oppression and falsely justify them as the "order of nature" and the "will of God." Jesus himself and indeed the biblical prophetic tradition as a whole engaged in such social analysis and ideology critique when they denounced those who "grind the faces of the poor" and "oppressed widows and orphans," and who simultaneously claim that their abuse is a mandate from heaven.

Indeed Jesus did not spare the family in his critique, and the Gospels are full of statements that set discipleship of Jesus against the family. Luke 14:26–27 states, "If anyone comes to me and does not hate his own father and mother and wife and children and brothers and sisters he cannot be my disciple." The early church saw itself as a new counter-cultural community, set against family and social patterns of their day. Christian feminist theology is rooted in the biblical prophetic tradition that questions existing social patterns, including those of the family, in order to envision redemptive possibilities.

The subordination of women in the family, violence toward women, and women's exclusion from larger development cannot be put down as simply the failing of individuals. These are expressions of a millennial old legal, economic, and social structure, which, until the early twentieth century, denied women civil personhood, forbade their entry into higher education and professions, and made wife beating legal. While kindly individual men may have forsworn abuse, and bad men taken full advantage of the law to abuse women, the abuse is structural and demands structural reform, just as slavery had to be abolished as a legal institution of property relations between whites and blacks in order to make blacks equal civil persons with whites. It was not enough simply to exhort slave masters to be kind to their slaves.

Ideologies are cultural patterns that justify abusive social structures and make them appear to be normal, natural, and the will of God. Since religion was, until recently, the primary way that social structures were justified, it is not surprising that religious mandates have often been used to justify such sinful patterns as sexism, racism, and war. Feminist theology is about the critique of such ideological patterns that justify sexism; the goal of such critique is to reclaim the full humanity of women and men in mutual partnership as the true promise of the "good news."

Williams also challenges my critique of patriarchal God-language by assuming that God as father and mother mirrors an eternally fixed gender role and family pattern. She also is clear that this gender division in God that founds that division among humans is to be taken literally. God really is a flesh and bone male human being writ large, divine, and immortal. This view diverges not only from mine as a feminist theologian, but also from the mainstream Christian tradition. Although the mainline Christian tradition has used mostly male names for God, it has understood these as metaphors, not as literal references to a flesh and bone male. Indeed the Jewish and Christian traditions as a whole would have to regard such literalism as idolatry, a failure to recognize that God is beyond our words and images, not literally identical with our names and images. All our words and images are taken from our finite experience with creaturely particularity, while God as source of all life infinitely transcends such creaturely particularity.

More appealing to me are those who are trying to reclaim Mormonism's liberating promise for women. They see particularly positive promise in its view of the divine embodied in both male and female form as such a liberating tradition. They want to free the female embodiment of the divine from her "shadows" behind the male God so that both can stand together as partners and as models for the partnership of men and women in church, family, and society, growing together into their divine and immortal promise.

While I applaud the effort of some LDS interpreters to overcome the spirit-flesh dualism in God by seeing God as enfleshed, I think this cannot be done by taking God as a male (and female) literal human. By regarding God the Father and Mother as literally embodied in human male and female bodies, one enhances the divine human, but severs God from the larger creation. In what way can and must we also say that God is embodied in the whole creation, as "God's body," to quote Sally McFague's phrase?

Contemporary earth science sees the cosmos as eighteen billion years old and the earth as five billion years old, while the human species has only existed for a tiny fraction of that time, around half a million years, becoming a dominant species even more recently. How can God be embodied only in the human species, if the human species is a latecomer to the planet? For God to be creator of the universe, one needs a bigger God than one who is embodied only in human and perhaps only in the bodies of "white" or Euro-American humans.

Perhaps even more challenging to Mormonism will be the consideration of ecofeminist theology. How does LDS thought respond to the contemporary ecological challenge, not only in terms of population issues, but also in terms of a cosmology that is more than anthropomorphic? How do we take seriously that God is really transcendently immanent in the whole universe, not just in human beings?

In this paper a dialogue has begun. Let us hope that it continues and deepens. We can all profit by the enrichment of the best of each other's traditions.

Reply to Professor Ruether

Camille S. Williams

SINCE THE NINETEENTH-CENTURY SUFFRAGE MOVEMENT, if not since the founding of the Relief Society, the LDS community has seen itself as offering opportunities for women to grow, to serve, and to lead. Since Elizabeth Cady Stanton's day, those outside the LDS faith have been puzzled by that characterization that has seemed self-evident to the LDS community. The conversation within this book between the tenets of feminism and the tenets of the LDS faith is, in some sense, a continuation of that mutual puzzlement, but perhaps also, a step toward a better understanding of both feminist religious thought and LDS thought.

Conversing about religious belief and practice, social justice and the methods used to achieve it, affords opportunity for self-examination by both individuals and communities. Certainly Ruether's critique of the Judeo-Christian tradition and her observations about LDS practice and belief will provoke examination for years to come.

Ruether rightly condemns inherently exploitive social structures. Slavery, for example, and the legal disabilities under which women did and do live are condemnable. It is not at all obvious, however, that gender roles within the family in contemporary U.S. society constitute a social structure as pervasive or as harmful, or even in the same category, as legal slavery, or coverture. I don't deny historical facts of exploitation or discrimination but ask whether a feminist ideology has the ability to cure the problem. A particular social structure, say the traditional family, is neither a necessary nor a sufficient condition for the exploitation of women. Nor is the widespread use of part-time or flextime work a necessary nor a sufficient condition for the real partnership of men and women as workers and parents that Ruether envisions. I do agree that some social structures and practices may be more likely to support good family life than others. Nevertheless, I question whether the roles of husband and wife, mother and father, as presently constituted in the United States, may be accurately categorized as oppressive to either women or men, especially when compared to practices such as slavery.

Social analysis and ideological critique can be useful, but there is no neutral ground upon which to stand to make the critique. I believe that feminist theology could benefit from a greater willingness to examine its own philosophical bases as rigorously as it examines ecclesiastical, social, and familial practices.

LDS doctrine differs from Christian tradition and from feminist thought in important ways. There is a different ontology: LDS doctrine characterizes human beings as being fundamentally pre-existent and eternal, like the God who begat them, and as having the potential to become like him. An embodied God is not conceptualized as hampered by that glorified body. LDS thought supposes that God should not be constrained by the limits of human logic, either as embodied in creeds or in the ephemeral knowledge bases of sociology, science, or feminism.

LDS epistemology posits both revelation through prophets and apostles with authority from God, as well as personal revelation for each individual. From an LDS perspective, revelation does not shut down conversation. On the contrary, continuing revelation opens up possibilities by opening up open-ended conversations with God for prophets, for communities, and for individuals. Individual revelation is exercised as the primary way of discerning good from evil. Prophetic revelation, open to verification by individuals through personal revelation, is also a means of judging the relative merit of competing truth claims, including competing individual revelations. Such a revelation-based epistemology prevents conversation from being mere conversation; rather it preserves and supports the centrality of truth as essential to meaningful conversations—particular conversations about important things, such as the family and the role of women. Such prophetic guidance may prevent a conversation from going awry. That our exchange in this book partakes of our own failings is a given; that it, nevertheless, produces greater insight and provides a forum for meaningful conversation is an impetus to continue.

About the Authors

Rosemary Radford Ruether (Ph.D. Claremont Graduate School) received a B.A. in Religion and Philosophy at Scripps College, Claremont University California, and her M.A. and Ph.D. degrees from Claremont Graduate School in Ancient History and Classics and Patristics, respectively. She is the author of 28 books, 12 book collections, 105 encyclopedia essays, and approximately 500 articles in journals and magazines. She is an emeritus professor at Garrett-Evangelical Theological Seminary, where she held the Georgia Harkness Professor of Applied Theology, and is the Carpenter Professor of Feminist Theology at the Graduate Theological Union in Berkeley, California.

Camille S. Williams (J.D. Brigham Young University) is the Administrative Director of the Marriage and Family Law Grant at the J. Reuben Clark Law School at Brigham Young University. She has taught family law for undergraduates and has participated in professional seminars on law and topics related to the family. She has also taught courses at Brigham Young University in Shakespeare; in reading, reasoning, and writing; in ethics and rhetoric; and in the philosophical roots of American feminisms. Her research and writings are on family and women's issues, with an emphasis on the mother-child relationship.

A Dialogue on Womanist Theology

Womanist Theology

Dwight N. Hopkins and Linda E. Thomas[1]

WOMANIST THEOLOGY IS THE NAME CHOSEN BY BLACK WOMEN in various fields of religion who wish to claim two things: first, black female religious scholars, pastors, and laywomen emphasize the positive experiences of African American women as a basis for studying theology and ethics; second, the title *womanist theology* separates black women from the racism of white feminist theologians and the sexism of black male theologians. Womanist theology grows out of black theology and therefore differentiates its theological claims from white feminist theologians who ignore racism. And, in this instance, African American female scholars join with their black brothers in the struggle against white supremacy in the church, society, and educational institutions. The reality of being black in America unites womanist and black theologies. At the same time, their female experiences in patriarchal America lay a basis for black women's coalition with white feminists. African American female religious scholars have to live out their dual status of race and gender before God. In sum, womanist theology answers the claim for a unique encounter between God and black women on the one hand, and struggles against white supremacy and discrimination by black men on the other.

Womanist theology, moreover, takes its theological guidelines from the definition of womanism given by Alice Walker in her 1983 book *In Search of Our Mothers' Gardens: Womanist Prose:*

> Womanist 1. From womanish. (Opp. of "girlish," i.e., frivolous, irresponsible, not serious.) A black feminist or feminist of color. From the black folk expression of mothers to female children, "You acting womanish," i.e., like a woman. Usually referring to outrageous, audacious,

---

1. This introduction to womanist theology previously appeared in Dwight Nathaniel Hopkins, *Introducing Black Theology of Liberation* (Maryknoll, N. Y.: Orbis, 1999), chapter 4.

courageous or willful behavior. Wanting to know more and in greater depth than is considered "good" for one. Interested in grown-up doings. Acting grown up. Being grown up. Interchangeable with another black folk expression: "You trying to be grown." Responsible. In charge. Serious. 2. Also: A woman who loves other women, sexually and/or nonsexually. Appreciates and prefers women's culture, women's emotional flexibility (values tears as natural counterbalance of laughter), and women's strength. Sometimes loves individual men, sexually and/or nonsexually. Committed to the survival and wholeness of entire people, male and female. Not a separatist, except periodically, for health. Traditionally universalist, as in: "Mama, why are we brown, pink, and yellow, and our cousins are white, beige, and black?" Ans.: "Well, you know the colored race is just like a flower garden, with every color flower represented." Traditionally capable, as in: "Mama, I'm walking to Canada and I'm taking you and a bunch of other slaves with me." Reply: "It wouldn't be the first time." 3. Loves music. Loves dance. Loves the moon. Loves the Spirit. Loves love and food and roundness. Loves struggle. Loves the Folk. Loves herself. Regardless. 4. Womanist is to feminist as purple is to lavender.[2]

Walker's four-part definition contains aspects of (1) tradition, (2) community, (3) self, and (4) criticism of white feminism.

Its History

Womanist theology has a history which emerges out of both the 1970s white feminist movement and the 1950s and 1960s black civil rights and black power movements. As the civil rights struggle picked up momentum, pressure, and limited victories, the Equal Rights Amendment in the late 1960s and 1970s brought dramatic attention to the feminist movement. The results of the feminist movement, from the perspective of womanists, indicated at least two things: (1) the increased presence of white women in various jobs and in seminaries, and (2) the realization by black women that racism still persisted in the feminist movement. Though black women were female, they still encountered racial hierarchy among their white female colleagues.

Similarly, in the civil rights and black power movements, black women experienced discrimination from black men. The following classic story describes a meeting between Stokely Carmichael, then chairperson of the Student Nonviolent Coordinating Committee (SNCC), and some black female members of SNCC during the late 1960s. In this conversation, the black women raised questions about the fair treatment and recognition of women in the student organization. Carmichael's response was that the

2. Alice Walker, *In Search of Our Mothers' Gardens: Womanist Prose* (New York: Harcourt Brace Jovanovich, 1983), xi–xii.

only position for black women in the movement was a "prone" position. It was this type of oppressive attitude and exploitative practice that black men carried into seminaries. Just as white women were increasing their numbers in graduate schools of religion, black men were making inroads. When black women began slowly to enter seminaries, they were faced with black men's resistance to them receiving ordination and with denial of their calling by God.

The history of the term *womanist theology* begins after a 1979 article (written by Jacquelyn Grant) that spoke more about a black feminist theology. The article, "Black Theology and the Black Woman," called into question the most fundamental belief of black theology as a theology of liberation. It challenged this liberation assertion by showing how black theology contradicted its own claims, evidence, warrants, qualifications, and criteria. Grant argued that if black theology described itself as a theology of liberation—meaning that Jesus Christ was with the most oppressed and God was working for the liberation of the least in society—then why was it that black theology was at best silent about black women and at worst oppressing them? In this article, Grant also draws lines of theological difference with white feminist theologians but asserts that the primary focus of her article is the development of a black woman's voice in black theology.

In searching for black women in black theology, Grant concluded that black women are invisible. This is true because either (1) black women have no place in the practice of God-talk and God-walk, or (2) black men are capable of speaking for black women. Similar conclusions can be drawn about black women in the black church and the larger society:

> If the liberation of women is not proclaimed, the church's proclamation cannot be about divine liberation. If the church does not share in the liberation struggle of black women, its liberation struggle is not authentic. If women are oppressed, the church cannot be "a visible manifestation that the gospel is a reality."[3]

In her 1985 article "The Emergence of Black Feminist Consciousness," Katie G. Cannon produced the first written text to use the term *womanist*. There she writes:

> Black feminist consciousness may be more accurately identified as Black womanist consciousness, to use Alice Walker's concept and definition. As an interpretive principle, the Black womanist tradition provides the incentive to chip away at oppressive structures, bit by bit. It identifies those texts that help Black womanists to celebrate and to rename the

---

3. Jacquelyn Grant, "Black Theology and the Black Woman," in *Black Theology: A Documentary History, 1966–1979*, eds. Gayraud S. Wilmore and James H. Cone (Maryknoll, N.Y.: Orbis, 1979), 423.

innumerable incidents of unpredictability in empowering ways. The Black womanist identifies with those biblical characters who hold on to life in the face of formidable oppression. Often compelled to act or to refrain from acting in accordance with the powers and principalities of the external world, Black womanists search the Scriptures to learn how to dispel the threat of death in order to seize the present life.[4]

Cannon's scholarship introduced womanism as an innovative category for all black women's religious work. However, the first text using the specific phrase *womanist theology* was written by Delores Williams in "Womanist Theology: Black Women's Voices," which appeared in the March 2, 1987, edition of *Christianity and Crisis*.[5] In that piece, Williams used Alice Walker's definition of womanism as a theoretical framework to equate black women's theology with the womanist definition.

Further defining the quiltlike configuration of womanist diversity in harmony and solidarity, I have written the following about the complementing threads and rainbow mixtures in womanist theology:

> We are university, seminary and divinity school professors. We are ordained and lay women in all the Christian denominations. Some of us are full time pastors; some are both pastor and professor. We are preachers and prayer warriors. We are mothers, partners, lovers, wives, sisters, daughters, aunts, nieces and we comprise two thirds of the black church in America. We are the black church. The church would be bankrupt without us and the church would shut down without us. We are from working class as well as middle class backgrounds. We are charcoal black to high yellow women. We love our bodies; we touch our bodies; we like to be touched; we claim our created beauty. And we know that what our minds forget our bodies remember. The body is central to our being. The history of the African American ordeal of pain and pleasure is inscribed in our bodies.[6]

Theological Method

In the development of theology and ethics, womanists write about a holistic relation to the divine; they argue for positive, sacred, human connections at the locations of gender, race, class, sexual orientation, and, to a certain degree, ecology. In fact a holistic methodology and a holistic worldview

---

4. Katie G. Cannon, "The Emergence of Black Feminist Consciousness," in *Feminist Interpretation of The Bible,* ed. Letty N. Russell (Philadelphia: Westminster Press, 1985), 40.

5. Delores Williams, "Womanist Theology: Black Women's Voices," *Christianity and Crisis* 47 (March 2, 1987): 66–70.

6. Linda E. Thomas, "Womanist Theology, Epistemology, and a New Anthropological Paradigm," *Journal of Constructive Theology* 2 (December 1996): 19–31.

constitute what it means to practice womanist theology. Womanist theology is holistic in terms of (1) the many theological ways black women face oppression and struggle for liberation, (2) the use of many disciplines of analyses, and (3) the diverse dimensions of what it means to be a human being, including the spiritual, cultural, political, economic, linguistic, and aesthetic aspects of life. Furthermore, from the perspective of Delores Williams, womanist theological method is informed by at least four elements: a multidialogical intent, a liturgical intent, a didactic intent, and a commitment both to reason and to the validity of female imagery and metaphorical language in the construction of theological statements.[7]

Multidialogical intent allows Christian womanists to engage in many conversations with different people from various religious, political, and social communities. The desire of womanists in these exchanges is to focus on the "slow genocide" by exploitative systems of poor African American women, children, and men. Liturgical intent means that black female religious scholars will develop a theology relevant to the black church, especially its worship, action, and thought. At the same time, womanist theology challenges the black church with the prophetic and critical messages coming from the practice of black women. In a word, black church liturgy has to be defined by justice. Didactic intent points to the teaching moment in theology as it deals with a moral life determined by justice, survival and quality-of-life ethics. All of these concerns can yield a language which is both rich in imagination and reason, and filled with female story, metaphor, and imagery.

Part of the methodology of womanist theology comprises both epistemology and practice—how one obtains knowledge and how one witnesses in ethics. How do womanists get their knowledge, and how does knowledge relate to their practice? First, in the analysis of Kelly Brown Douglas, womanist theology is accountable to ordinary women—poor and working-class black women.[8] This means that womanists must teach beyond the seminaries and divinity schools and in churches and community-based organizations. Put differently, "it will be church and community-based women who will teach womanist theologians how to make theology more accessible."[9] Also, if womanist theology is accountable to church- and community-based women, then womanist conversations must take place beyond the academy. It must have as its primary talking partners and primary location poor and working-class women and their realities in churches and community organizations. In addition, womanist theology must work with church women

---

7. Jacquelyn Grant, "Womanist Theology: Black Women's Voices," in *Black Theology*, 269.

8. Kelly Brown Douglas, *The Black Christ* (Maryknoll, N.Y.: Orbis, 1994), 114.

9. Ibid.

to help empower them and to help them speak their voice so that church leadership will respond or change. Black women comprise about 70 percent of the membership of black churches and are the financial supporters and workers of the church.

Moreover, for me the method of womanist methodology "validates the past lives of enslaved African women by remembering, affirming and glorifying their contributions." After reflecting critically on these foundational foremothers' stories, the methodology then constructs a new model:

> We who are womanists concoct something new that makes sense for how we are living in complex gender, racial, and class configurations. We learn from the rituals and techniques which our foremothers originated to survive in hostile environments and from how they launched new perspectives, reconstructing knowledge of a liberative approach for black women's lives. This self-constituting dynamic is a polyvalent, multi-vocal weaving of the folk culture of African American women.[10]

Furthermore, womanist methodology uses ethnographic approaches which allow black women scholars to enter the actual communities of poor black women "in order to discover pieces to create a narrative for the present and the future."[11] Summing up the holistic dimension of the varied sources in womanist theology, Emilie M. Townes states:

> Yet the anchor for womanist thought is the African-American church and its people. The history of the Black church is not only religious, it is social. The social conditions and worldviews of its people have had an intricate connection. Womanist thought reflects some of this intimacy. Examples of this can be found in the deeply spiritual and moral aspects [of sacred and secular black writers and singers]. West African religions, vodun, and folktales are mediums. Life in the church—from preacher's admonitions to choir crescendos to board meeting and power struggles— all are resources and guardians of communal memory and accountability. Academic theological discourse is also a part of womanist reflection and thought. Such are the touchstones for womanist reflection.[12]

One of the most creative models for practicing the womanist theological method was initiated by Teresa L. Fry.[13] Over a period of six years, Fry

---

10. Thomas, "Womanist Theology," 22.

11. Ibid.

12. Emilie M. Townes, "Introduction," in *A Troubling in My Soul: Womanist Perspectives on Evil and Suffering,* ed. Emilie M. Townes (Maryknoll, N.Y.: Orbis, 1993), 2.

13. Teresa L. Fry Brown, "Avoiding Asphyxiation: A Womanist Perspective on Intrapersonal and Interpersonal Transformation," in *Embracing the Spirit: Womanist Perspectives on Hope, Salvation, and Transformation,* ed. Emilie M. Townes (Maryknoll, N.Y.: Orbis, 1997), 79–92.

worked with black women in churches, individual interest groups, and various other organizations with membership ranging from five hundred to six hundred. Fry states that the women created S.W.E.E.T. (Sisters Working Encouraging Empowering Together), which was an intentional womanist effort to support black women's attempts at both spiritual and social liberation. The project was truly holistic: ages covered 7 to 78; educational levels started at grade school and reached graduate levels; women were married, widowed, single, and divorced; they included heterosexual, lesbian, and bisexual members; their religious affiliations were ecumenical, interfaith, or none at all; some "had been incarcerated or on the way to jail, or knew someone there." There were "Deltas, Alphas, Zetas, Sigmas, and Links sitting along side Granny, MaDear, Mama, Big Momma, and Auntie."[14]

S.W.E.E.T. organized

> annual seminars, inclusive sermons, intensive women-centered Bible studies, monthly workshops, relationship-building exercises, small group discussions, potluck dinners, informal and formal luncheons, community action projects, intergenerational mentoring groups, individual and group counseling sessions, guest speakers and in-group speakers, panel discussions, role-playing, ethnographies, health support groups, and African American women's literature study and discussion groups. Alice Walker's definition of womanist was used as the point of departure for each discussion.[15]

The following addition was added to Walker's definition: a womanist also "'believes in Somebody bigger than you and me'" and "'possesses a radical faith in a higher power.'"[16] Throughout the various sessions, women were encouraged to think for themselves and form their own opinions and models of life by starting with their own stories; each person had a chance to lead meetings. One rule governed all of S.W.E.E.T.'s activities: "We will respect our sister's space, speech, issues, voice, pain and sensitivities."[17] They used titles such as Sister, Girlfriend, or first names, and elders were respected with the names of Miss or Mother (for the spiritual anchors of the group). From Fry's report, the spirituality of the organization was itself holistic, entailing organized Christian beliefs to personalized feelings of the spiritual:

> Women were not pressured to be a member of a church, but there was an understanding that the group was spiritually based. Each sister determined and articulated her own sense of spirituality. African American spirituality is the conscious awareness of God, self, and others in the

---

14. Brown, "Avoiding Asphyxiation," 80.

15. Ibid.

16. Ibid, 85–86.

17. Ibid., 80–81.

total response to Black life and culture. It is an expressive style, a mode of contemplating God, a prayer life, and that which nourishes, strengthens, and sustains the whole person. We coupled prayer, testimony, tears, laughter, or silence with embracing each other.[18]

Further components of S.W.E.E.T. included ethnographies about members' mothers, grandmothers, and other mothers; investigations of black women leaders in different fields and in history; discussions on how to change and save the black family based on African family values; black clergywomen in the pulpit, revisioning inclusive liturgies, and seeing women's roles in the Bible; "Back to the Kitchen Table" programs held on Saturday mornings in different homes; an intergenerational group, "It Takes an Entire Village to Raise a Child"; and "Loving and Care for Yourself" gatherings (for example, concerning hysterectomy, breast cancer, divorce, new Christians, single mothers, exercising, and self-affirmation).

Intellectual Developments

The writing of books on womanist theology is slowly gaining momentum. Katie G. Cannon's *Black Womanist Ethics* is the first womanist text to be published. In this work, she sets out to establish womanist liberation ethics. Cannon shows that

> Black women live out a moral wisdom in their real-life context that does not appeal to the fixed rules or absolute principles of the white-oriented, male structured society. Black women's analysis and appraisal of what is right or wrong and good or bad develops out of the various coping mechanisms related to the conditions of their own cultural circumstances. In the face of this, Black women have justly regarded survival against tyrannical systems of triple oppression as a true sphere of moral life.[19]

However, this moral wisdom does not completely save African American women from institutionalized social evils, but uncovers whatever negative ethics might undermine or attack their womanhood. Cannon seeks to educate black women about their own moral struggle by using the experience of common people as well as the oral tradition. For specific sources, she draws on her own family stories, slave narratives, black folk culture, biblical interpretations, black church history, and the African American women's literary tradition, which, she argues, is "the best available literary repository

---

18. Ibid., 81.
19. Katie G. Cannon, *Black Womanist Ethics* (Atlanta: Scholars, 1988), 4.

for understanding the ethical values Black women have created and cultivated in their participation in this society."[20]

From a liberation perspective, Cannon wants to increase the literature on ethics that shows poor, working, African American women as moral agents. She uses the disciplines of ethics, history, political economy, and literary studies in a systemic analysis of sex, race, and class. Her aim is to map out survival strategies and call for action.[21] The essentials of her ethical goal lie in the following: (1) Cannon creates womanist educational styles as a new way of rigorous investigations for teaching a critical consciousness; (2) distinct, investigative methodologies arise from her work, which unmask race, class, and gender oppressions embodied in hierarchical structures requiring transformation; (3) she criticizes mainstream Eurocentric male-normative ethics exemplified in traditionally accepted debates, doctrines, and theories; and (4) with womanist experiences as the judge, Cannon creates "fresh ethical controversies relevant to [black women's] particular existential realities as they are recorded in the writings of African American women."[22]

In the field of ethics, Cannon works with the established structures but not uncritically. Indeed, these structures are approached with new questions from poor black women's lives. With the discipline of history, she unearths the historical context in which black woman have found themselves as moral agents; this history exhibits patterns of moral wisdom and ethical behavior. With the study of political economy, she takes the following stand: Once "chattel slavery and White supremacy have become interstructured through capitalist political economy only the elimination of a capitalist mode of production can open the way to making racism dysfunctional."[23] And literary criticism helps black women's writings (once subjected to critical, theo-ethical lenses) supply the expressions of black women's issues, feelings, and conduct that the literature attempts to reflect.

In 1989, one year after Katie G. Cannon published the first womanist book, *Black Womanist Ethics*, Jacquelyn Grant wrote *White Women's Christ and Black Women's Jesus: Feminist Christology and Womanist Response* to explore the key idea of Jesus the Anointed One in the black church.[24] Although both graduated from Union Theological Seminary in New York City, Cannon trained in ethics and Grant in systematic theology. For Grant, black women experience a three-dimensional reality of racism, sexism, and

---

20. Katie G. Cannon, *Katie's Canon: Womanism and the Soul of the Black Community* (New York: Continuum, 1995), 61.

21. Ibid., 25.

22. Ibid., 70.

23. Ibid., 146.

24. Jacquelyn Grant, *White Women's Christ and Black Women's Jesus: Feminist Christology and Womanist Response* (Atlanta: Scholars, 1989).

classism. One therefore must apply a holistic approach to Christian theology because black women face several levels of sin. The oppression of racism and the subjugation of sexism have created a disproportionate number of black women within the ranks of poor and working-class people. Consequently, the everyday survival attempts and resistance struggles of poor black women should anchor and judge the truth of any womanist claims.

As a systematic theologian, Grant poses the question of where God and humanity meet. For her, it is a question of divine revelation to poor black women at two central locations: first, God makes God's self known by direct communication to poor African American women; and second, God's revelations are manifest in the Bible as black women experience this text in their own context. As a Christian systematic theologian, Grant seriously considers the decisive revelatory appearance of God in the black woman's Jesus.

Poor black women, in their everyday lives, have affirmed Jesus in several ways. First, Jesus has been a divine co-sufferer who has empowered them in times of intense oppression. A dynamic of mutual identification took place where both Jesus and poor African American women shared in each other's suffering.

Second, poor black women called on the name of Jesus as a way to condemn the demonic, earthly, authoritative claims of white racists. Thus for these women, since Jesus is actually God, no earthly human or race could assert any claim of divine authority and supremacy. The literal sacredness of Jesus meant that black women did not need to obey or submit to white people.

Third, both Jesus and poor African American women represent the particular and the universal. Black women (due to their three-part condition of gender, race, and class) relate to the racial suffering of black men, the gender discrimination of all women, and the economic exploitation endured by all working-class and poor people. As a result, the tridimensional aspect of black women applies not only to their particular situation, it also covers the universal experiences of all oppressed people. "Likewise," Grant argues,

> with Jesus Christ, there was an implied universality which made him identify with others—the poor, the woman, the stranger. . . . [F]irst he identifies with the "little people," Black women, where they are; secondly, he affirms the basic humanity of these, "the least"; and thirdly, he inspires active hope in the struggle for resurrected, liberated existence.[25]

Fourth, Grant describes the idea of Jesus as a theological symbol for poor black women. Symbols do not take a mere secondary and, consequently,

---

25. Ibid., 217.

unimportant status in Grant's theology. On the contrary, there exists a direct connection between theological symbolism and the oppression of women especially concerning the use of Jesus' maleness to oppress women. Yet, Grant does not pursue the road of changing Jesus from a man to a woman. Her claim is elsewhere: "I would argue," she states, "that the significance of Christ is not his maleness, but his humanity. . . . [F]or me, it means today, this Christ, found in the experiences of Black women, is a Black woman."[26]

Summarizing her approach to the Jesus and black woman connection, one can detect at least five attributes of Jesus which held poor black women together and encouraged them daily to keep going. Jesus acted as co-sufferer (for example, God through Jesus came to suffer with the poor), equalizer (for example, because Jesus came for all, Jesus thus equalizes all), freedom-giver (for example, the issue is not just to become equal to an oppressor but to be free), sustainer (for example, Jesus functioned as family), and liberator (for example, Jesus' liberation activities give power to poor black women in their struggle for their own liberation).

Yet, continues Grant, there have been evil forces who have opposed the faith stance and truth claim of poor African American women by imprisoning Jesus in patriarchy, white supremacy, and the privileged class.[27] Male oppressors have intentionally used Jesus' male gender to maintain their hierarchy and dominance over women in the church and society. This fact, for Grant, stands out in the entire course of Christian history. In this history, the argument states that because Jesus was a male, men are entitled to dominance and control over females. Still African American women face more than sexism. Racism, observes Grant, has often been seen as the defining characteristic of the black American women's position. Especially in the church, one finds white supremacy lodged systematically in the ongoing use of a European white male model to portray Jesus in pictures both in white and black churches. Consequently, Grant proclaims that the Christian church in North America has been a bastion of the sin of racism.

Jesus has been imprisoned not only by sexism and racism, but also by the privileged classes in their manipulation of the notion of servanthood. For the elite, the idea of servanthood has reinforced the subservience, obedience, and docility of politically oppressed classes and people. They deny the existence of Jesus' real servanthood by changing his poor status into a royal one. Jesus' birth in a stable, his being a Jew, and his death among common

26. Ibid., 220.
27. See Jacquelyn Grant, "Womanist Jesus and the Mutual Struggle for Liberation," in *The Recovery of Black Presence: An Interdisciplinary Exploration,* ed. Randall C. Bailey and Jacquelyn Grant (Nashville: Abingdon, 1995), 129–42.

criminals disappear in the theology of the ruling elite. Grant summed up her view on Jesus and poor black women with the statement:

> I am arguing that our servanthood language existentially functions as a deceptive tactic for keeping complacent non-dominant culture peoples and the non-privileged of the dominant culture. Thus, the White Jesus, the Jesus of the dominant culture, escapes the real tragedy of servant-hood, but oppressed peoples do not.[28]

A year before the appearance of Grant's *White Women's Christ and Black Women's Jesus*, Renita J. Weems published her *Just a Sister Away: A Womanist Vision of Women's Relationships in the Bible* (1988).[29] Weems, trained in the Hebrew Bible at Princeton Theological Seminary, uses this work to look beneath the obvious in the Bible to discover a place for women, especially black women, in God's new community. For her, an important way of understanding how women see themselves is by investigating how they treat other women. Female relations, understandably, occupy a central role in this text. Furthermore, part of her biblical method is to examine bib-lical stories and create what might have been the feelings and concerns of ancient women. Weems admits that her creative reconstructions make no claim to fact, yet they suggest realistic scriptural testimonies. Her womanist imagination and personal commentary shed new light on women in scrip-ture, uniting biblical times with women's struggles today.

Using the story of the Egyptian Hagar and Hebrew Sarai, Weems inter-weaves themes of social rivalry, sexual abuse, economic exploitation, slav-ery, and ethnic prejudice. This story serves as a discussion point for North American black and white women's relations during slavery and even today. Despite the various levels of difference between Hagar (the slave) and Sarai (the slave mistress), Weems concludes that

> At some time in all our lives, whether we are black or white, we are all Hagar's daughters. When our backs are up against a wall; when we feel abandoned, abused, betrayed, and banished; when we find ourselves in need of another woman's help (a friend, neighbor, colleague, relative, stranger, another man's wife); we, like Hagar, are in need of a woman who will "sister" us, not exploit us.[30]

The Hebrew scripture tale about Ruth and Naomi becomes, for Weems, a model expression of profound friendship between a widow and her griev-ing mother-in-law. Such a special and unique female bond, furthermore, details a precious friendship which goes beyond nationality, religion, and

---

28. Ibid., 137.

29. Renita J. Weems, *Just a Sister Away: A Womanist Vision of Woman's Relationships in the Bible* (San Diego: LuraMedia, 1988).

30. Ibid., 17.

age differences. Here too the reader discovers the binding commitment between two women who pursue a very rough life without being attached to, or defined by, males. This is a depiction of stubborn loyalty and lasting love. As Weems notes, "This is the first commandment of friendship: to be a sister to a friend even when she is neither in a position nor disposition to reciprocate the sisterhood."[31]

In the story of Queen Esther, Weems imagines the responsibilities and pressures of women married to public figures—that is, the delicate balance between obedience under the public eye and the self convictions of independent women. In another biblical story concerning the friction between Miriam (Moses' sister) and Zipporah (Moses' wife, who may have been Ethopian), Weems investigates the difficult challenge of rivalry against one's sister-in-law and the harmful effects of insecurity and jealousy, both obstacles to women pooling resources for the mutual benefit of women.

In her book *Battered Love: Marriage, Sex, and Violence in the Hebrew Prophets,* Weems focuses on the theme of "sexual violence as a poetic portrayal of divine retribution."[32] She explores the question of how sexuality is imagined and used in biblical language—for instance, the recurring image of comparing Israel's social and political situation with the experiences of promiscuous women. Furthermore Weems writes:

> Commentators frequently note the ways in which elaborate descriptions of naked, battered women's bodies function in the prophecies of Hosea, Jeremiah, and Ezekiel as a poetic device for discussing divine punishment and social anarchy. Inveighing, as prophets normally did, against the official practices of the religious and political establishments, all three used imagery associated with bodily functions, particularly those related to female sexuality, to denounce public policies they thought profane.[33]

Accordingly, Weems explores why the male prophets used such symbols as the promiscuous wife, the mutilated lover, and the aggressive whore for their male audiences. Weems concludes that by associating the issues of marriage and sex with violence, the prophets increased the public's emotions of shame, terror, disgust, and dread. In a related manner, prophetic language united romance and violence, thus causing feelings of fascination and repulsion. In a word, the authenticity of a prophet depended on his ability to link female sexual behavior to God's demands against Israel.

Trained in theology at Union Theological Seminary in New York City, Delores S. Williams published her first book, *Sisters in the Wilderness: The*

---

31. Ibid., 30.

32. Renita J. Weems, *Battered Love: Marriage, Sex, and Violence in the Hebrew Prophets* (Minneapolis: Augsburg Fortress, 1995), xiii.

33. Ibid., 1–2.

Challenge of Womanist God-Talk, in 1993.[34] Instead of the exodus model supported by black theologians and most womanist religious scholars, Williams provocatively inserts the wilderness imagery as most representative of black American women's reality. Therefore, instead of believing in liberation as the key, Williams states that survival and a productive quality of life represent the central thread in womanist theology and ethics (for example, areas of study and practices which focus on the well-being of all black people, including women, men, and children). The Hagar and wilderness concepts gave Williams a biblically based Christian model which de-emphasized the authority of males and lifted the roles of women. Williams found the Hagar story deeply entrenched in African American traditions and, simultaneously, paralleling black women's experiences today. And instead of God being a liberating divinity, God operated as a supreme being offering survival and hope for a productive quality of life for the African slave Hagar and her son Ishmael. Williams declares:

> I concluded, then, that the female-centered tradition of African-American biblical appropriation could be named the survival/quality-of-life tradition of African-American biblical appropriation. . . . In black consciousness, God's response of survival and quality of life to Hagar is God's response of survival and quality of life to African-American women and mothers of slave descent struggling to sustain their families with God's help.[35]

Equipped with her new model, in contrast to the central claims of black theology of liberation, Williams's rereading of the Hagar passage unveils the following key social, personal, and religious concerns relevant to the survival and quality of life of black women: motherhood (a problem within the black community's self-understanding); surrogacy (found both in the ante- and post-bellum periods); ethnicity (centered on skin color consequences); and wilderness (African American women's parallel to Hagar's life in the wild). A theological exploration of these notions inevitably leads to a critical conversation with black liberation theology—over method, doctrine, and ethics—and feminist theologies—accenting commonalties and differences among all women of color and white women.

It is in conversation with black theology of liberation that Williams suggests that there is nothing divine in the blood of the cross and Jesus' death. On the contrary, what happened to Jesus on the cross represents human defilement and attack on the divine. Black women should avoid such ideas like surrogacy and, instead, cling to the ministerial vision which

---

34. Delores S. Williams, *Sisters in the Wilderness: The Challenge of Womanist God-Talk* (Maryknoll, N.Y.: Orbis, 1993).

35. Ibid., 6.

God gave Jesus when the latter was alive. Such a ministerial vision of life entails correct relationships on earth brought about through words, touch, compassion, faith, love, and kicking out earthly examples of evil and by replacing them with prayer.

Finally, Williams concludes her argument with an exposure of the sins African American denominational churches have committed against black women. The remainder of her book poses a hopeful example of a womanist church shown in the Universal Hagar's Spiritual Churches. Though there persists strong, male-centered strands within this nationwide church, Williams, nonetheless, sees positive counter trends highlighting the role of women in theology, ritual, and church administration.

Emilie M. Townes's first book, *Womanist Justice, Womanist Hope*, was likewise published in 1993.[36] Receiving her Ph.D. in Religion and Society and Personality from Garrett-Evangelical Theological Seminary at Northwestern University, Townes uses Ida B. Wells-Barnett (a late nineteenth-century activist intellectual) for what Townes envisions "as a substantial scholarly historical and ethical inquiry into the social and moral lives of African-American women in the contemporary church."[37] Wells-Barnett serves as an adequate role model for the recovery of black women's tradition because of her strong commitments to both the church and justice. Especially appealing for Townes is Wells-Barnett's social and moral viewpoints, which, for Townes, provide foundational planks for a womanist ethic of justice.

Specifically, Wells-Barnett's social and moral perspectives give us the ingredients for several aspects of a womanist, Christian, social ethic today. First, the ethic of authority is divided into two types of moral practices. One thrives on subjugation and domination while the other more healthy model "reflects community, partnership, and justice." Second, obedience, as an additional ethic, should avoid the power imbalance between the self over the other or the other over the self—relationships of blind submission. A person living an appropriately obedient life discerns the will of God and links justice to transforming the world. Third, an ethic of suffering includes the goal to fight against the reality of suffering. This womanist practice flows from viewing suffering as contrary to God's plan for redemption and placing the victim in a reactive mode which obstructs the need for proactive personal and systemic measures against the causes of suffering. Fourth, a liberation ethic from a womanist stance sees the spiritual dimension of liberation including pride and self-worth. The spiritual part relates to the social aspect of liberation. When we have both, then each individual can participate in the world as a proactive, social agent. Fifth, a reconciliation

---

36. Emilie M. Townes, *Womanist Justice, Womanist Hope* (Atlanta: Scholars, 1993).
37. Ibid., 1–2.

ethic acknowledges an objective side where God, through love and grace, has forged new social interactions among human beings. The subjective realm becomes real when human beings act to reconcile among themselves in a harmonious fashion.

In her second text, *In A Blaze of Glory: Womanist Spirituality as Social Witness,* Townes sees womanist spirituality emerging out of the writings of three black women novelists. Toni Morrison's *Beloved* speaks to black people's very being and the characteristics of their survival. Alice Walker's *The Color Purple* contextualizes cultural images by discovering the dimensions of creation and a resulting necessary social witness. Paule Marshall's *Praise Song for the Widow* reveals a spirituality linked to self-worth, images of blackness, and self-esteem issues. In sum, womanist spirituality is "embodied, personal, communal" and it is "the working out of what it means for each of us to seek compassion, justice, worship, and devotion in our witness."[38]

The Black Christ, by Kelly Brown Douglas, explores the historical and contemporary issues surrounding the black community's gravitation to a black Christ, and then offers a theological response to the color of Christ debate. Brown Douglas, a systematic theologian also trained at Union Theological Seminary, asks black churches why focusing on the black Christ has empowered them to fight against racism but has left them on the sidelines in the struggle against sexual, class, and gender oppression. The churches, Brown Douglas claims, have failed to keep in balance both Christ's prophetic actions (for example, commitment to the poor) and the color appearance (for example, skin pigmentation). Fundamentally, the answer to the question of Christ's color is found in a theological response, and Brown Douglas presents one womanist interpretation.

To give evidence for her argument, Brown Douglas explores a historical context surrounding the perception of the black Christ in the African American community. The roots of the black Christ, for her, spring from enslaved black people's portrayal of this deity, black nationalists' usage of this symbol, and black literature's creation of the Christ picture. The American slavery period indicates two perspectives on Christ: the slave owners preached a spiritualized white Christ in order to justify white skin privileges over black, and blacks, in turn, underscored the prophetic and liberating activities of Christ's daily ministry with the poor and marginalized. Here with the least in slave society, Christ became "a fellow sufferer, a

---

38. Emilie M. Townes, *In A Blaze of Glory: Womanist Spirituality as Social Witness* (Nashville: Abingdon, 1995), 11, 13; Toni Morrison, *Beloved* (New York: Knopf, 1987); Alice Walker, *The Color Purple* (New York: Washington Square, 1983); Paule Marshall, *Praise Song for the Widow* (New York: Putnam's, 1983).

confidant, a provider, and a liberator,"[39] all aspects of a black focus on Jesus' ministry and not on Jesus' abstract spirit. Relatedly, Jesus' ministry helped the enslaved black Christians to wage resistance against white Christian supremacy, in the material and the spiritual world, on earth and in heaven. The presence of Jesus meant the divine gift of God's freedom to enslaved black people, and, hence, the poor and the enchained accepted such a gift by organizing for liberation. It is the enslaved black Christian's focus on Jesus' earthly ministry, a prophetic proclamation and a transformative witness, which defines the black Christ during slavery.

If African American Christian slaves supported the critical importance of Jesus' earthly ministry, black nationalists have identified radically with the black skin color of Christ. At stake is the self-esteem of blacks and the literal interpretation of God's image. That is to say, if blacks are made in God's image and African Americans are black, then God's real color is also ebony. Similarly, early twentieth-century black fiction and short stories written by such notables as Langston Hughes, Countee Cullen, and John Henrik Clark, linked Christ with actual black skin color. But, from Brown Douglas's reading, in each moment of this historical context (of slavery, nationalism, and literature), no one consistently tied blackness and Christ's liberating activity in a comprehensive manner. The womanist approach to Christ moves closer in this direction.

Such a womanist voice, for Brown Douglas, interweaves around two main threads—a sociopolitical and a religio-cultural. A sociopolitical strand speaks of wholeness for the black community:

> Black women have been traditionally concerned, not just for their welfare, but for the welfare of their entire community and families—sons and daughters, husbands and brothers. . . . As a result of their consistent commitment to their families and their community, Black women have searched for a "politics" of wholeness as they have evaluated their participation in various freedom movements, such as the contemporary woman's movement and the 1960s Black freedom struggle.[40]

This sociopolitical analysis of wholeness, moreover, highlights race, gender, class, and sexual oppression as dangers to the well-being of the entire black community, but especially black women. This analysis has two sides because it looks both inside and outside the black community to see how these harmful practices prevent the full humanity of African American women and the whole black community and family. The other part of the womanist theological voice, for Brown Douglas, is a religio-cultural analysis which embraces the liberating aspects of black religion and culture rather

---

39. Douglas, *Black Christ,* 24.
40. Ibid., 98.

than the negative parts. She argues that not everything black or African is healthy for the black community.

Finally, Brown Douglas claims, Christ is black because Christ does have black skin and black features. Yet more than the color characteristics, Christ is black because we meet God as a sustainer, liberator, and, very important for her, prophet engaging and challenging the African American community. And, with her specific womanist contribution, Brown Douglas states that Christ is found in the faces of the poorest black women in the African American family and community. She confesses:

> I affirm that Christ is found where Black people, men as well as women, are struggling to bring the entire Black community to wholeness. While my womanist perspective highlights the significance of Christ found in the faces of Black women in struggle, especially poor Black women, it does not eliminate the possibility of Christ being seen in the faces of Black men who struggle for Black women's and men's lives and wholeness.[41]

Living with the poorest of the poor and focused on a goal of full life and wholeness, the black Christ is a black woman, but not exclusively.

Karen Baker-Fletcher, with a doctorate in theology from Harvard University, uses Anna Julia Cooper (a late-nineteenth-century activist intellectual) as a primary source for developing contemporary womanist reflections. Baker-Fletcher's *A Singing Something: Womanist Reflections on Anna Julia Cooper* (1994) uses the symbol of voice to discover womanist lessons for today. She writes:

> The theme of voice is central to my discussion. I examine Cooper's argument for women's movement from silence and subjugation to a model of bold vocalization and independence to consider how her concept of woman's voice provides a resource for a contemporary theological concept of women's embodiment and prophetic message of freedom and equality. Today, as womanists both build on and move beyond Cooper's thought, we will find it necessary to consider a diversity of women's voices among Black women.[42]

To bring black women's voice to fruition, in Baker-Fletcher's opinion, womanists must take seriously the importance of story, inclusive of women's sociological studies, fiction, autobiography, scholarly essays, discussion with friends, poetry, and song. Out of the story style and the instructive lessons from the life and writings of Cooper, Baker-Fletcher concludes five theological themes for womanist theology: the power of voice, the power of making do, the power of memory, the power of holding things together, and

---

41. Ibid., 109–10.
42. Karen Baker-Fletcher, *A Singing Something: Womanist Reflections on Anna Julia Cooper* (New York: Crossroad, 1994), 15.

the power of generation. These are all God-given gifts found in, but not limited to, African American women who by using them have survived and produced an abundant life for black women and their families and communities.

Marcia Y. Riggs, who received her doctorate in ethics from Vanderbilt University, explores the late-nineteenth- and early-twentieth-century black women's club movement (in which Ida Wells-Barnett and Anna Julia Cooper were leaders) to determine some distinct socioreligious models for the contemporary womanist ethical resolution of the moral dilemma. Her first text, *Awake, Arise and Act: A Womanist Call for Black Liberation,* "analyzes the moral dilemma that social stratification in the black community poses for black liberation and the ethical praxis needed to address that dilemma." And Riggs traces "the development of competitive individualism versus intragroup social responsibility in the black community—a dilemma at the center of social stratification and black oppression today."[43]

Riggs offers a theoretical framework to help move her ethical investigations toward her final goal of black liberation from white racism, patriarchy, and capitalism. For her, social stratification within the African American community comes from black oppression and therefore needs an intellectual analysis to achieve black liberation. "Parallel structures," the first plank in her theoretical outline, teaches us how stratifications internal to the black community are parallel to the larger society. "Internal colonialism" helps one to understand black existence as similar to an oppressed colonial status where differences within the black community can be controlled by colonial influences outside of the community. Internal colonialism means nonblack people can increase conflict among African Americans (for example, similar to a divide and rule strategy). Third, her theoretical framework includes the interaction of a race-gender-class consciousness. In a word, Riggs summarizes, "the dilemma of competitive individualism versus intragroup social responsibility has its basis in both socioeconomic realities and a race-class consciousness that has evolved throughout black history. The race-gender-class consciousness of black women offers an alternative perspective for analyzing this dilemma."[44]

Furthermore, Riggs claims that the justice of God and justice for blacks are God's commands, and their coming together creates socioreligious responsibility. Therefore justice (for example, socioreligious responsibility replacing competitive individualism) affirms both black self-help and racial solidarity, on the one hand, and advocates self-determination within the larger American society on the other. Restated, justice as an ethic of socioreligious responsibility holds "in tension the specific aims of racial

---

43. Marcia Y. Riggs, *Awake, Arise, and Act: A Womanist Call for Black Liberation* (Cleveland: The Pilgrim, 1994), 1.

44. Ibid., 10–11.

elevation, amelioration of gender and class oppression, and comprehensive reform of society for the good of all citizens."[45] With God's justice as the center of value in the African American community, a "mediating ethic," as Riggs coined, provides a positive alternative "whereby accommodative and aggressive social activism, religious radicalism for societal change, and progress for individual Blacks and Blacks as a group could be maintained."[46]

Riggs also states that the black women's club movement offers a three-part moral vision for the twenty-first century. The first element deals with the virtue of giving up one's privilege of difference, whether racial, gender, or class. The second component involves the value and obligation of inclusivity, which can translate to all black women coming together across class lines. Ultimately, inclusivity connects work on behalf of black women to supporting the health of all black people, as well as struggling for justice for all. The third dimension of the moral vision is religious responsibility—the perspective and practice of linking racial uplift with God's justice. A womanist call for black liberation, consequently, will yield fruit when black women and the black community act as moral agents toward their final aim. Riggs illustrates:

> Black liberation, therefore, refers to collective advancement of Blacks with the goal of transforming the economic and political structure of American society. The goal is ideologically nationalistic in that it emphasizes the need for black people to engender and sustain a communal identity. Black communal consciousness is critical to an ethic for black liberation. The contention here is that the social stratification of Blacks is a factor that undermines black communal consciousness, and consequently, black liberation.[47]

Conclusion

Womanist theologians and ethicists have impacted and advanced black theology by their consistent call for recognition of the holistic realities of oppressions affecting the black community and for various approaches to resolve these theological and ethical problems. Black women's unique contribution is that their very lives make up an identity of gender, race, and class strands within one body, mind, and spirit—the black woman. Womanists, moreover, have persistently plowed the diverse fields of black women's and the black community's experiences to give us lessons for today. Sources range from talking with friends to reading obscure scholarly texts. God

---

45. Ibid., 80.
46. Ibid., 82.
47. Ibid., 12.

appears and offers the grace of liberation and wholeness wherever God so chooses. Finally, womanists have taken old religious language and symbols and given them new meaning. Womanists have called for a new witness in contrast to traditional theological categories and dominant moral agency assertions. Perhaps womanists will expand their holistic method, sources, and claims to produce extended treatments on a host of other topics, such as the black body, ecology, and music. Wholeness, a compassionate intellect and an intellectual passion, the willingness to be led by the spirit wherever it goes, the interweaving of concern both for black women's realities and the black community's predicament and possibilities, the bridging of feminist and black liberation theologies, among other things—all these show us the practice and potential of womanist religious thought.

Response to Professor Thomas

Valerie M. Hudson with Alma Don Sorensen

We HAVE LEARNED MUCH from reading "Womanist Theology" by Hopkins and Thomas. Womanist theology, in contrast to feminist theology, speaks to the religious experiences of persons suffering from the triple oppression of poverty, racism, and sexism: in particular, it speaks to the religious experiences of black women. In this essay, we will seek to find common ground between womanist theology and LDS theology as a basis for future engagement between the two. For this reason, we have chosen the LDS concept of Zion as a means of opening dialogue with womanist theologians.

For Latter-day Saints, Zion is no fictional utopia meant only to inspire our actions, nor is it simply a future post-mortal state to be enjoyed by perfect beings. Zion is real and obtainable, and we are enjoined by God to be actively engaged in building it.[48] Zion is the ultimate social organization God desires for us, his children, in mortality. Furthermore, Zion is to be

---

48. Discourses from LDS prophets in the early days of the LDS church emphasized this interpretation of Zion, as evidenced by an address given by LDS church president Lorenzo Snow: "Let us try to build up Zion. Zion is the pure in heart. Zion cannot be built up except on the principles of union required by the celestial law. It is high time for us to enter into these things. It is more pleasant and agreeable for the Latter-day Saints to enter into this work and build up Zion, than to build up ourselves and have this great competition which is destroying us." Clyde J. Williams, comp., *Teachings of Lorenzo Snow* (Salt Lake City: Bookcraft, 1984), 181.

built upon the principles that order the celestial kingdom, where God, the Lamb, and the worthy live (D&C 78:7; 105:5), and it is only through full obedience to these celestial principles and laws that Zion can be established. In historical cases where Zion has been built, it has been formed by a deep understanding of the love of God for all his children and a knowledge of our infinite indebtedness to him for all that we have, including our very lives.

An illustrative example of this process is found in the Book of Mormon story of King Benjamin's people. These people had been "diligent" in keeping the commandments, but there was something lacking (Mosiah 1:11). Just before his death, King Benjamin preaches a mighty sermon in which he declares that even if the people served God with all their might, they would be unprofitable servants, for God has given them everything: "Can ye say aught of yourselves? I answer you, Nay. Ye cannot say that ye are even as much as the dust of the earth; yet ye were created of the dust of the earth; but behold, it belongeth to him who created you. And I, even I, whom ye call your king, am no better than ye yourselves are" (Mosiah 2:25–26). After preaching to them the significance and power of the atonement of Jesus Christ (who had not yet been born on the earth at the time of the sermon), he declares:

> Are we not all beggars? Do we not all depend upon the same Being, even God, for all the substance which we have? . . . And behold, even at this time ye have been calling on his name, and begging for a remission of your sins. And has he suffered that ye have begged in vain? Nay; he has poured out his Spirit upon you, and has caused that your hearts should be filled with joy. (Mosiah 4:19–20)

This new understanding causes a mighty change in the hearts of the people and elicits two great transformations in them. First, they unite. When King Benjamin asks if they are ready to covenant with the Lord to obey his commands, they "cried with one voice, saying: Yea, we believe all the words which thou [Benjamin] hast spoken unto us; and also, we know of their surety and truth, because of the Spirit of the Lord Omnipotent, which has wrought a mighty change in us, or in our hearts, that we have no more disposition to do evil, but to do good continually" (Mosiah 5:2). This unity is a hallmark of Zion, for scripture tells us that the Lord calls his people Zion when they are of one heart and one mind and dwell in righteousness (Moses 7:18).

However, it is the second transformation that King Benjamin's people underwent that speaks specifically to the oppression central to womanist theological analysis. In this particular historical episode, it is the oppression of poverty that is the focus, as we shall now see.

Poverty

The second transformation King Benjamin's people undertook was to create a society of equality. They realized that each individual is equally loved and valuable to God and that because God loves each person equally, everyone has a sacred responsibility to love every other person as an equal.[49] A second hallmark of Zion, then, is that "there [is] no poor among them" (Moses 7:18). This feature is essential to Zion because the Lord has said that "if ye are not equal in earthly things ye cannot be equal in obtaining heavenly things" (D&C 78:6). In the celestial kingdom, all are equals, which means that if we do not live as equals on earth, we are unprepared to live in the highest level of the celestial kingdom.[50] As an earlier Book of Mormon prophet proclaimed, "Think of your brethren like unto yourselves, and be familiar with all and free with your substance, that they may be rich like unto you" (Jacob 2:17). No people unified in heart and mind and having been moved "to do good continually" would be willing to allow suffering caused by economic or social inequality. In his own discourse, King Benjamin teaches,

> And now, if God, who has created you, on whom you are dependent for your lives and for all that ye have and are, doth grant unto you whatsoever ye ask that is right, in faith, believing that ye shall receive, O then, how ye ought to impart of the substance that ye have one to another. And if ye judge the man who putteth up his petition to you for your substance that he perish not, and condemn him, how much more just will be your condemnation for withholding your substance, which doth not belong to you but to God, to whom also your life belongeth; and yet ye put up no petition, nor repent of the thing which thou hast done. (Mosiah 4:21–22; see also vs. 23–28)

A spiritual change of heart within an individual brings about a striving for unity and equality, and all who love the Lord will strive to build such a social order. Thus, the theme of antipoverty found in womanist theology is at the very heart of the Zion-building activities of the LDS community. Its tangible manifestation at the current time is found in the welfare program of the LDS church, its recently instituted education program for LDS church members in underdeveloped countries, and its worldwide system of storehouses for the needy, all of which are maintained by member offerings, volunteering of members' time, and repayment by those who benefit, either

---

49. Compare 4 Nephi 1:15.

50. Indeed, LDS theology is also unusual in that it posits that those who are worthy to live in the celestial kingdom live there as gods and are "made equal with him [Christ]" (D&C 88:107). Thus, the equality in the celestial kingdom even cuts across the divine/mortal dividing line.

in currency or time. Temple-endowed Latter-day Saints covenant to live the law of consecration and expect, at some point, to live the law in its fullness.

Racism

The ideal of Zion also speaks to the second oppression, that of racism. Given this emphasis on unity and equality, it follows that racism of any kind cannot exist in a community striving to establish Zion. Our duty as followers of Jesus Christ is not to maintain or encourage but to overcome any such divisions by the purification of our hearts. This purification comes through his Atonement as we repent of our sins, and when we are purified, we will come to know what King Benjamin and his people knew: that we are *all* equal and *all* valuable to God, regardless of race.

Indeed, when the ancient Nephites established a Zion-like community after the coming of the Savior to the American hemisphere, lineage-based or race-based distinctions *disappeared*. The record states, "there was no contention in the land, because of the love of God which did dwell in the hearts of the people. . . . There were no robbers, nor murderers, neither were there Lamanites [a lineage or race distinction], nor any manner of -ites; but they were in one, the children of Christ, and heirs to the kingdom of God" (4 Nephi 1:15, 17).

It is important to note that the disappearance of race-based and lineage-based distinctions was not a physical occurrence—whole races of people were not destroyed. There was no "manner of -ites" among the people because they had resolved to abandon these distinctions. They considered themselves one people.

In this time of social equality, this Zion-like community "had all things common among them; therefore there were not rich and poor, bond and free, but they were all made free, and partakers of the heavenly gift" (4 Nephi 1:3). However, when the perfect social order began to break down, the first consequence of spiritual decay was that "they did have their goods and their substance no more common among them" (4 Nephi 1:25). Additionally, class-based distinctions began arising again (4 Nephi 1:26), as did lineage- or race-based distinctions (4 Nephi 1:36–38). The culmination of this fall from grace was the destruction of the entire Nephite society.

In sum, LDS scripture plainly teaches that there cannot be any lineage- or race-based distinctions that would undermine the unity and equality of Zion. The theme of antiracism found in womanist theology is also reflected in LDS theology.

Sexism

LDS theology's opposition to sexism is framed by three unique assumptions: (1) gender is a permanent part of an individual's spiritual makeup; it existed before mortality and will exist after death;[51] (2) God has a physical body of flesh and bone, and one of our rewards for faithfulness in the premortal existence is to receive the great privilege of obtaining a material body and experience mortal life; and (3) the primary work of God is to have children and nurture them into full godhood.[52] Therefore, from an LDS perspective, gender, bodies, and sexual reproduction are goods of eternal significance.

These three assumptions imply a doctrinal conclusion: We have both a Mother and Father in Heaven. In their union through the holy ordinance of eternal marriage, they serve as partners in their divine work, and we are literally their children. Thus, marriage is designed to be the foundation for eternal family relationships. Given these very unique starting assumptions, LDS theology consequently approaches the "woman question" in ways that are at odds with standard Western feminism.

The contrast with standard Western feminism becomes clearer when we think of what an LDS woman typically aspires to be and do: she aspires to remain a woman forever; she aspires to have the body of a woman forever; she aspires to be married to a man forever; and she aspires to have children with this man forever. It is possible that some feminist scholars might view this wish list as starkly antifeminist. This is one of the areas in which the womanist theology of black women seems closer to LDS theology than standard Western feminism. In Thomas's review, it is apparent that

---

51. "Gender is an essential characteristic of individual premortal, mortal, and eternal identity and purpose." The First Presidency and Council of the Twelve Apostles of The Church of Jesus Christ of Latter-day Saints, "The Family: A Proclamation to the World," *Ensign* 25 (November 1995): 102.

52. Actually, *have* is not the right word here. In LDS theology, God does not create intelligence; rather, God *organizes* intelligences to the point where they can be called God's children, a process that is known as "spirit birth." In 1914 before the general assembly of the LDS church, Elder Charles W. Penrose taught the following about spirit birth: "For man in spirit form, in his spirit nature, is an independent entity. It is an organized being, a son of God or a daughter of God, as the case may be, and in the spirit birth he obtained not only an eternal organization, but power and intelligence by which he can determine and understand light from darkness, truth from error, and choose between that which is right and that which is wrong." Charles W. Penrose, in *84th Semi-annual Conference of The Church of Jesus Christ of Latter-day Saints* [Salt Lake City: The Church of Jesus Christ of Latter-day Saint, 1914], 40. More recently, the First Presidency and Quorum of the Twelve Apostles have affirmed this belief in the document "The Family: A Proclamation to the World," in which they declared that "all human beings—male and female—are created in the image of God. Each is a beloved spirit son or daughter of *Heavenly Parents*" (emphasis added).

black women who have helped create womanist theology rejoice in being women. They do not seek to become men nor do they seek to abolish gender as a precursor to closeness to God. They seek to find reasons to rejoice in being women and having womanly experiences. They are "womanish." These themes would find great resonance in the LDS community.

The Example of Adam and Eve

With womanist theologians, Latter-day Saints see the story of Adam and Eve, our first parents, as the exemplar for gender relations.[53] A standard critique of Western secular feminism is that it applies to the women of the world desiderata and cultural assumptions rooted in Western culture. Given the high Western divorce rates and the fact that women and children make up the bulk of the West's poor, the claim that the women of the world would be better off if they lived, thought, and acted like Western women is suspect at best. Instead, in sustaining and encouraging human life, Latter-day Saints feel it best to turn to Adam and Eve as true role models. This story, concerning as it does the first parents of all who have ever lived, is applicable to all men and women and thus does not represent the imposition of any one particular culture. Indeed, to the contrary, this story is given to us by the Lord as a corrective to fallen traditions—if we understand it correctly.

The story of Adam and Eve begins with their creation in the image of God: "male and female" (Moses 2:27; 6:9; Abraham 4:27). The title "God" has a plural meaning here and seems to refer to both Heavenly Mother and Father.[54] As noted earlier, the primary work of bringing about the eternal life and continuation of humankind is always done by an exalted woman and man united in the everlasting covenant of marriage (D&C 131:1–4; 132:6, 16–24). Together, they are "God." Heavenly Father does not live "separately

---

53. Elder Russell M. Nelson of the Quorum of the Twelve Apostles taught that many lessons can be learned from studying the lives of Adam and Eve, the first of which is that Adam and Eve labored side by side and that "Eve served in matriarchal partnership with the patriarchal priesthood." In speaking further about how we can learn from their example, he added that "the complete contribution of one partner to the other is essential to exaltation. . . . Any sense of competition for place or position is not appropriate for either partner." "Lessons from Eve," *Ensign* 17 (November 1987): 87.

54. The Hebrew word for *God* in the singular is *El* or *Elowahh*. The plural or honorific form takes the ending "im," as in "Elohim," a term commonly used in the Hebrew Bible that means "divine ones" or "gods" (male and female inclusive) in the plural form, or "god," "goddess," and "the true god" in the honorific form. Francis Brown, *A Hebrew and English Lexicon of the Old Testament with an Appendix Containing the Biblical Aramaic, Based on the Lexicon of William Gesenius as Translated by Edward Robinson* (Cambridge, Mass.: Riverside, 1977), 43.

and singly" as do the beings who "are not gods" and who experience only the lower degrees of immortal life (D&C 132: 17). When Adam and Eve were made in God's likeness, Adam was formed in the likeness of God the Father and Eve in the likeness of Heavenly Mother.[55]

The creation of Adam and Eve in God's image, male and female, reveals a full-fledged equality between them. They were created equally in that image (Moses 2:26–27), each needs the other,[56] and one does not fulfill a lesser part than the other in the realization of that whole (2 Nephi 26:28, 33). As the ultimate symbol of equal partnership, God brought together Adam and Eve in the Garden of Eden—a union with the promise that one day they themselves would be like their Heavenly Father and Mother.[57]

One of the lessons we learn from the story of Adam and Eve is that proper gender relations are at the heart of life. God created only two beings at the dawn of human history: a man named Adam and a woman named Eve. We infer that no male-male or female-female relationship can substitute for the critical importance of male-female relations. In the eyes of God—our Father and Mother in Heaven—the most important choices being made in any society are between men and women.

Unfortunately, the story of the Garden of Eden has been perverted in many faiths to justify the belittling and demeaning of women. However, for Latter-day Saints, the story of the Garden of Eden takes on a very different cast. The story is used to teach that the first woman and man served together as equals in Christ, in preparation for becoming joint heirs with him in the world to come. Their lives and labors together, both in the Fall and afterward, provide the example for men and women of God of all ages

---

55. In an address to women, LDS church president Spencer W. Kimball told them that they were "made in the image of our heavenly Mother." Edward L. Kimball, ed., *Teachings of Spencer W. Kimball* (Salt Lake City: Bookcraft, 1982), 25. President Kimball further stated that both God "and our mother in heaven value us beyond any measure. They gave our eternal intelligences spirit form, just as our earthly mothers and fathers have given us mortal bodies." Spencer W. Kimball, *My Beloved Sisters* (Salt Lake City: Deseret, 1979), 25.

56. "Neither is the man without the woman, neither the woman without the man, in the Lord" (1 Cor. 11:11).

57. LDS prophets have taught that God married Adam and Eve and that their marriage was for all eternity. LDS church president Joseph Fielding Smith stated, "Here is a clear statement that the marriage covenant, when properly performed, is eternal. It is not to be annulled and come to an end at death. The first marriage performed on earth was the marriage of Eve to Adam, and this was before there was any death, therefore it was intended to be forever." Joseph Fielding Smith, *Answers to Gospel Questions*, 5 vols. (Salt Lake City: Deseret, 1960), 3:23. President Spencer W. Kimball also taught that "Adam and Eve were married for eternity by the Lord." Kimball, *Teachings of Spencer W. Kimball*, 292.

to emulate. The story of the Garden of Eden is a celebration of Eve, not a condemnation of her.

In the garden, Eve and Adam were not yet mortal and were "in a state of innocence, having no joy, for they knew no misery; doing no good, for they knew no sin" (2 Nephi 2:23). They could not do good or have joy because they did not yet know good from evil. Only by coming to know good from evil and choosing the good can men and women become gods and enjoy the fullness of celestial life (Moses 4:28; Jacob 1:7).

Eve played the leading role in this transformation by being the first to partake of the fruit—thereby becoming the first agent—and by persuading Adam to do the same. Though her act is formally a transgression, it is an act celebrated by both God and mankind.[58] LDS prophets teach that Eve is to be honored for partaking of the fruit of the tree of the knowledge of good and evil; Eve provided the way for the spiritual growth and progression of all humanity by making it possible to obtain a knowledge of good and evil. Without such an act, none of God's children would be able to exercise their own agency or fulfill their divine potential. By persuading Adam to do what she had done and become what she had become, she acted as his "help meet," as she was foreordained to do (Moses 3:18).[59] By being help meets to

---

58. That Eve's transgression was not a sin is a teaching of LDS authorities. For instance, Elder Dallin H. Oaks of the Quorum of the Twelve Apostles stated in a conference address, "[Eve's] act, whatever its nature, was formally a transgression but eternally a glorious necessity to open the doorway toward eternal life." He further revealed that "Joseph Smith taught that it was not a 'sin,' because God had decreed it." Latter-day Saints also reject the notion that Eve or her daughters were cursed for her transgression in the garden. Elder Oaks further explained, "Some Christians condemn Eve for her act, concluding that she and her daughters are somehow flawed by it. Not the Latter-day Saints! Informed by revelation, we celebrate Eve's act and honor her wisdom and courage in the great episode called the Fall." Dallin H. Oaks, "The Great Plan of Happiness," *Ensign* 23 (November 1993): 73.

59. It is, in fact, incorrect to associate the expression "help meet" with a subordinate relationship. The Hebrew word used in this scripture (Gen. 2:18) is *ezer*, which is a masculine noun meaning "help," "succor," or "one who helps" (see Brown, *A Hebrew and English Lexicon*, 740). Although it is translated as "help meet" only in Genesis 2:18 and 2:20 in the English King James version of the Bible, the word *ezer* occurs numerous times throughout the Hebrew Bible. In other instances the word is translated simply as "help," but it is significant to note that it is often used to refer to God as "help," as in Deuteronomy 33:7, in which Moses gives a blessing to Judah and asks the Lord to be "an help" to Judah from his enemies (see also Ps. 33:20; 70:5; 115:9–11; and 121:1–2, in which the Lord is referred to as our "help"). "Meet" here is *neged* (with the form in Gen. 2:20 being *cenegddo*), most often translated as "in front of" but only when used in relation to God. It is significant that when Adam identifies all creation by giving individual names to all, he could not find anything *cenegddo*, equal, or corresponding to him—hence the need to bring forth Eve. As Elder Boyd K. Packer of the Quorum

each other and serving together, Adam and Eve could fulfill the purpose of the everlasting covenant of marriage they entered into in the Garden—and personally become as the gods (Moses 5:10–11; D&C 131:2; 132:6, 19–20).

It also may be said that Adam, as a mortal agent, was born of Eve by hearkening to her and partaking of the fruit as well. This "birth" enabled him to pass from a state of innocence to moral agency (2 Nephi 2:13, 22, 25). As we see it, Eve could also be said to have given birth to herself, as a mortal agent, by yielding to her divinely inspired desire to become as the gods. Thus, in this sense, man is not only born of woman, but woman is also born of woman. Thus Eve became "the mother of all living" in a double sense: she introduced mortality and knowledge, or agency, to all humankind by being the first to partake of the fruit. We owe, in part, our existence and agency to Eve and her transgression, which transgression was foreordained by and in accordance with the will of God.[60]

The work of women as mothers and the work of women as lovers of men continue to this day. The righteous daughters of Eve continue to bring forth new souls into humanity, and by loving and nurturing them, the love of mothers awakens in their children the power to distinguish good from evil and the desire to lay hold upon good. In general, mothers prepare their children in such a way that these new souls will have "the work of the law written in their hearts" (Rom. 2:15). Women also, in general, continue to love men and to desire a committed and faithful union with them. In a sense, the daughters of Eve must get the sons of Adam to partake, must turn them toward that ideal union that is the foundation of the plan of salvation and exaltation for God's children. This is as much a part of the divine stewardship of woman as motherhood.

Lastly, the story of Adam and Eve illustrates important insights regarding the nature of the patriarchal order. In the highest degree of the celestial kingdom, exalted women and exalted men are joint heirs and equals with each other (D&C 76:94–95; 88:107; 132:19–20; Rom. 8:17). The order of family government with a husband and a wife standing together as equals is called the patriarchal order. The use of the word *patriarchal* to describe the rule of heaven may be somewhat misleading because some wrongly interpret the term to mean that men rule over women. But this is not so, as we have

---

of the Twelve Apostles points out, "The word *meet* means equal. Man and woman, together, were not to be alone. Together they constituted a fountain of life. While neither can generate life without the other, the mystery of life unfolds when these two become one." Boyd K. Packer, "A Tribute to Women," *Ensign* 19 (July 1989): 73. We are indebted to Becky Schulthies and Professor Richard Draper for their transliteration assistance in this matter.

60. For an excellent treatment of the LDS viewpoint concerning the Fall, see Beverly Campbell, *Eve and the Choice Made in Eden* (Salt Lake City: Bookcraft, 2003).

seen. The patriarchal order is better described in the terms that LDS church president Ezra Taft Benson used:

> The order of priesthood spoken of in the scriptures is sometimes referred to as the patriarchal order because it came down from father to son. But this order is otherwise described in modern revelation as an order of family government where a man and woman enter into a covenant with God—just as did Adam and Eve—to be sealed for eternity, to have posterity, and to do the will and work of God throughout their mortality.[61]

In the relationship between Adam and Eve, all powers and keys were used in a system of equal partnership: the patriarchal order of the priesthood. United by the celestial law of marriage, they lived as equal partners in mortality, in preparation to live as equal partners in eternity. Indeed, some LDS scholars believe that God did not proclaim that Adam should "rule over" Eve, but rather, that Adam should "rule with" Eve.[62] They labored together as the Lord taught them to do so they could become as the "gods," who serve together as "joint heirs," and share "all power" as equals (D&C 76:94–95; 78:5–7, 21–22; 105:4–5; 132:19–20, 32; Rom. 8:17). Thus, Heavenly Father and Mother have given us Adam and Eve as exemplars of how we, regardless of culture or era, are to have gender equality and respect.

---

61. Ezra Taft Benson, "What I Hope You Will Teach Your Children about the Temple," *Ensign* 15 (August 1985): 9. The concept of the family order was also expressed by Joseph Fielding Smith in the following statement: "All may enter the grand circle of the family in the celestial kingdom, if they will.... Few find the strait and narrow way which leadeth to the exaltation and *eternal lives*, which is the *family order,* because their minds are set upon the things of this world, and they refuse to accept the things which pertain to the celestial world." Joseph Fielding Smith, *The Way to Perfection* (Salt Lake City: Deseret, 1984), 255. Robert L. Millet teaches that the patriarchal order is an order of the Melchizedek Priesthood presided over by both the husband and wife: "The patriarchal order, established in the days of Adam (see D&C 107:40–42), was and is an order of the Melchizedek Priesthood. It is, in fact, what we know as the new and everlasting covenant of marriage." He also said that "God established the patriarchal order, a system of family government presided over by a father and mother, patterned after what exists in heaven." Robert L. Millet, "The Ancient Covenant Restored," *Ensign* 28 (March 1998): 38.

62. When the Hebrew word *msh'l* (usually translated as "rule") is used in conjunction with *bet* (in most cases translated as "with," "by," "in," or "at") the better translation is "rule with" rather than "rule over." We are indebted to Professor Donald Parry of the Department of Ancient and Near Eastern Languages at Brigham Young University for this translation. See *The New Brown-Driver-Briggs-Gesenius Hebrew and English Lexicon: With an Appendix Containing the Biblical Aramaic* (Peabody, Mass.: Hendrickson, 1979), 89–90.

Applications of the Adam and Eve Story

LDS men and women who have internalized God's plan for an equal partnership between men and women in marriage and in society are less vulnerable to false teachings of this fallen world concerning women. They understand that men are not to control or dominate the lives of women, especially the lives of their wives.[63] Love, respect, and equality are the heart of the restored gospel of Christ. As LDS church president Gordon B. Hinckley has said:

> It is commonplace with us to say that we are sons and daughters of God. There is no basis in the gospel for inferiority or superiority as between the husband and wife. Do you think that God our Eternal Father loves his daughters less than he loves his sons? No man can demean or belittle his wife as a daughter of God without giving offense to her Father in Heaven.[64]

Furthermore, men are not entitled to the "final say" in a marriage relationship simply because they are men. Household decisions should be made in unanimity, as all collective decisions are made in the councils of Zion (D&C 107:27–29). As LDS church president Howard W. Hunter explained:

> A man who holds the priesthood accepts his wife as a partner in the leadership of the home and family with full knowledge of and full participation in all decisions relating thereto. . . . The Lord intended that the wife be a helpmeet for man . . . equal and necessary in full partnership. . . . For a man to operate independent of or without regard to the feelings and counsel of his wife in governing the family is to exercise unrighteous dominion.[65]

Elder L. Tom Perry of the Quorum of the Twelve Apostles has been equally straightforward:

---

63. President Spencer W. Kimball emphasized the need for sisters to direct their own lives and stewardships in the following statement: "Each of our sisters has the right and the responsibility to direct her own life. But be not deceived; each of us must also be responsible for our choices. This is an eternal principle." Kimball, *My Beloved Sisters*, 23.

64. Gordon B. Hinckley, *Cornerstones of a Happy Home* (Salt Lake City: The Church of Jesus Christ of Latter-day Saints, 1984), 6.

65. Howard W. Hunter, "Being a Righteous Husband and Father," *Ensign* 24 (November 1994): 50–51. President Spencer W. Kimball stated the same thought in this manner: "When we speak of marriage as a partnership, let us speak of marriage as a *full* partnership. We do not want our LDS women to be *silent* partners or *limited* partners in that eternal assignment! Please be a *contributing* and *full* partner." Spencer Kimball, *My Beloved Sisters*, 31.

Remember, brethren, that in your role as leader of your family, your wife
is your companion. . . . There is not a president and vice-president in a
family. We have co-presidents working together eternally for the good
of their family. They are united in word, in deed, and in action, as they
lead, guide, and direct their family unit. They are on equal footing. They
plan and organize the affairs of the family jointly and unanimously as
they move forward.[66]

Similarly, sex roles within a society should be scrutinized to determine
whether they pertain to sex-specific powers and keys. Since the work of
exalted men and exalted women is unified, there is plenty of opportunity
for men to assist women and women to assist men. LDS leaders have taught
that LDS men should be actively engaged in child care and care of the house.
Elder Boyd K. Packer of the Quorum of the Twelve Apostles stated this in
unequivocal fashion:

There is no task, however menial, connected with the care of babies, the
nurturing of children, or with the maintenance of the home that is not
[the husband's] equal obligation. The tasks which come with parenthood,
which many consider to be below other tasks, are simply above them.[67]

---

66. L. Tom Perry, "Fathers' Role is Anchoring Families," *LDS Church News*, published by *Deseret News,* April 10, 2004, 15.

67. Boyd K. Packer, *Things of the Soul* (Salt Lake City: Bookcraft, 1996), 174. In the April 1998 general conference, Elder Boyd K. Packer also taught that although women and men can and often do similar work within and without the home, there are distinct male and female natures that must be recognized:

Be careful lest you unknowingly foster influences and activities which
tend to erase the masculine and feminine differences nature has established.
A man, a father, can do much of what is usually assumed to be woman's
work. In turn, a wife and a mother can do much—and in time of need, most
things—usually considered the responsibility of the man, without jeopardizing their distinct roles. Even so, leaders, and especially parents, should
recognize that there is a distinct masculine nature and a distinct feminine
nature essential to the foundation of the home and the family. Whatever
disturbs or weakens or tends to erase that difference erodes the family and
reduces the probability of happiness for all concerned. (Boyd K. Packer,
"The Relief Society," *Ensign* 28 [May 1998]: 73)

In a similar vein, President Gordon B. Hinckley has advised that legislation
should provide equality of opportunity, equality of compensation, and equality of
political privilege. But any legislation that is designed to create neuter gender of that
which God created male and female will bring more problems than benefits: "I wish
with all my heart we would spend less of our time talking about rights and more talking about responsibilities. God has given the women of this church a work to do in
building his kingdom." Gordon B. Hinckley, *Teachings of Gordon B. Hinckley* (Salt
Lake City: Deseret, 1997), 690.

Likewise, general stereotypes regarding occupations should be carefully examined; women can excel at activities considered the traditional purview of men and vice versa. The *Encyclopedia of Mormonism* states that "LDS principles argue unequivocally for the development of the full potential of each person, regardless of gender."[68] President Gordon B. Hinckley said,

> There must be respect for the interests of one another. There must be opportunities and encouragement for the development and expression of individual talent. Any man who denies his wife the time and the encouragement to develop her talents, denies himself and his children a blessing which could grace their home and bless their posterity.[69]

The restored gospel of Christ is cause for celebration concerning women's issues. In no other place are women regarded so equally and with so much respect.

As noted previously, "patriarchy" and "patriarchal order" do not mean that men may rule over women. No hierarchy or coercive power could result from the true exercise of these divine principles. The purpose of the patriarchal order is to establish a space where the full equality of men and women can flourish and eternal life can be enjoyed. Outside the context of gospel principles, differentiation inevitably leads to hierarchy and inequality. But one of the most revolutionary aspects of the restored gospel is its ability to differentiate, not with hierarchy but with *equality*. This message is one of profound import for all women. The strongest and most progressive force for women in the world is the gospel of Jesus Christ.

Gender equality is the final and ultimate question of any society. If it is a lesser thing to be a woman, then, according to LDS theology, couples will never obtain eternal life and communities will never become Zion. The debate over the equality of women is no fringe issue but rather the issue at the very heart of our future possibilities. If a man spurns a woman or treats her as an inferior, then godhood is beyond his grasp. To live gender equality is to live as a man and a woman who are worthy to be exalted together to godhood. If godhood is our highest possibility, then those who cannot treat the other sex as equals deny themselves the fullness of life.

Concluding Reflections

In conclusion, we see that temporal equality, racial equality, and gender equality are not side issues when it comes to discussing Zion: all three equalities are integral to its establishment. Becoming a Latter-day Saint includes making our best efforts to overcome the bonds of classism, racism,

68. Mary Stoval Richards, "Feminism," in *Encyclopedia of Mormonism,* ed. Daniel H. Ludlow, 4 vols. (New York: Macmillan, 1992), 2:507.

69. Hinckley, *Cornerstones of a Happy Home,* 6.

and sexism, and, insofar as the overthrow of this "triple oppression" is at the heart of womanist theology, womanist theology and LDS theology share a great deal of common ground.

The analysis put forward in this essay has been thus far oriented toward intellectual understanding of LDS doctrine concerning these issues. But that analysis is incomplete. There is a knowledge of the heart that is arguably even more powerful than the knowledge of the mind. I (Valerie Hudson) would like to share with you the journey that my heart had to make to reach a full peace, particularly concerning gender issues.

Early on as my heart was converted to the restored gospel of Jesus Christ, the horrors of the world seemed to press in on me, closer and closer, demanding to be heard and recognized. It was as if the unbearable pain of these stories—vicarious though it was—left me speechless before the throne of God. One story in particular affected me very deeply: the story of Margaret, a slave woman in the antebellum South, who fled with her mother, her man, and her children to the North.[70] Before reaching freedom, the family was caught. Margaret slit the throats of her little children with her own hand rather than let them go back into slavery. Perhaps only a mother could understand the horror and despair of that act. Her case was much discussed in Abolitionist circles of the time. One man was speaking eloquently in behalf of Margaret's action when a former slave woman stood up and asked him, "Is God dead, then?" It takes great courage to receive the wisdom of that question, which is: even in the best of lives there would be deadly despair without hope in Christ; and if Christ does live, then there cannot be deadly despair even in the worst of lives, even in the worst lives of women, black women, poor women, all men and women.

The Book of Mormon also contains the same message. In the final Nephite-Lamanite wars, Mormon described how Nephite women and children were forced by their Lamanite captors to feed on the flesh of their husbands and fathers and how Lamanite women were raped, tortured, and killed and their flesh eaten by their Nephite captors as a token of bravery (Moroni 9:7–19). But Mormon goes on to say to his son, to whom he is writing,

> My son, be faithful in Christ; and may not the things which I have written grieve thee, to weigh thee down unto death; but may Christ lift thee up, and may his sufferings and death, and the showing his body unto our fathers, and his mercy and long-suffering, and the hope of his glory and of eternal life, rest in your mind forever. (Moroni 9:25)

Christ's victory is our victory: the gospel of Jesus Christ is the only plan that will overcome the Fall and all of its tragic consequences, including those

---

70. Cynthia Griffin Wolff, "Margaret Garner: A Cincinnati Story," *The Massachusetts Review* 32, no. 3 (1991): 417–40.

that directly and negatively affect the lives of women oppressed by dis-crimination. The gospel is the strongest, most progressive force for women, the poor, the oppressed. In the Garden of Gethsemane, Christ felt all our pain—he felt rape, he felt death in childbirth, he felt sex slavery. If Christ is real, then his victory is ours and we can claim it for ourselves. If he con-quered, he will succor to the extent of the wound. All sad things will come untrue for his faithful ones; all that was lost will be returned; all who were taken will embrace us again. "[Women] are that they might have joy" (2 Nephi 2:25)!

On my reading of the scriptures, there will be something like a great Truth and Reconciliation Commission in Heaven. No loss can be made up unless the loss is fully voiced, is heard and felt and acknowledged by all in the family of man, and is recompensed through justice and mercy. The Book of Mormon cites Isaiah's claim that "all things shall be revealed unto the children of men which have ever been among the children of men, and which ever will be even unto the end of the earth" (2 Nephi 27:11). The Book of Mormon further states, "There is nothing which is secret save it shall be revealed; there is no work of darkness save it shall be made manifest in the light" (2 Nephi 30:17) and "revealed upon the house-tops" (Mormon 5:8; see also D&C 88:108–110). In the Doctrine and Covenants, God him-self proclaims, "The rebellious shall be pierced with much sorrow; for their iniquities shall be spoken upon the housetops, and their secret acts shall be revealed" (D&C 1:3). We will build Zion only as we "mourn with those that mourn; yea, and comfort those that stand in need of comfort" (see Mosiah 18:9). The tribulations of all nations, all peoples, all groups, all indi-viduals will be felt, understood, mourned, and atoned.

Joseph Smith taught very plainly, and there is no more comforting doc-trine, that "All your losses will be made up to you in the resurrection, pro-vided you continue faithful. By the vision of the Almighty God, I have seen it."[71] How could there be a good, or a God, if this were not truth?

There is a work that must be performed in this regard, which work womanist theology undertakes. We Latter-day Saints are enjoined to "waste and wear out our lives in bringing to light all the hidden things of darkness, wherein we know them; and they are truly manifested from heaven—These should then be attended to with great earnestness. Let no man count them as small things" (D&C 123:13–15). Womanist theology brings to our hearts and minds the experiences and reflections of the triple oppressed. This is blessed work, which helps build the Kingdom of God on earth—Zion. In our theology, Zion is no mysterious locale of some future existence. We build—or fail to build—Zion every day in our homes, communities, and

---

71. Joseph Smith Jr., *History of The Church of Jesus Christ of Latter-day Saints*, ed. B. H. Roberts, 2d ed., rev., 7 vols. (Salt Lake City: Deseret, 1971), 5:362.

nations. We have tried in our own small way to confront head-on any such discrimination in our own community[72] and also in an international context.[73] There is plenty of work for all, and we are delighted to plough those fields with womanists such as Linda Thomas. In a way, womanist theology leads us to understand that Zion is only really Zion if black women find peace there.

Though we all struggle every day to be our best selves and not our worst selves—which struggle is reflected in miscommunication and regretful acts and bruised feelings—finding the Christ who took upon him the pains of the most oppressed can free us, oppressed and oppressors, to fall into each other's arms with new hearts. He is the rock, he is the foundation upon which a new world, Zion, can be anchored and raised among us today.

Let us not wait a moment longer! Linda, did you and I not join in this song as we left our premortal existence?

> Sisters, now our meeting is over,
> Sisters, we must part.
> And if I never see you any more,
> I will love you in my heart.
> And we'll land on the shore, yes, we'll land on the shore,
> Oh, we'll land on the shore, and be safe forevermore[74]

Come toward me, my sister, as I come towards you. Let us weep and smile together as we share our lives freely. Let us remember who we were to each other before this mortal existence. And then let the Son rise in our hearts and make us sisters indeed!

About the Authors

Dwight N. Hopkins (Ph.D. Union Theological Seminary; Ph.D. University of Cape Town, South Africa) received a M.Div. and M.Phil from Union Theological Seminary. Hopkins is a constructive theologian working in the areas of contemporary models of theology, black theology, and liberation theologies. He has authored and edited fourteen books on black theology and is coeditor, with Linda E. Thomas, of the Black Religion/Womanist Thought/Social Justice Book Series from MacMillan. His latest book is *Being Human: Race, Culture, and Religion* (Augsburg, 2005). He is a professor of theology at the University of Chicago Divinity School and is an ordained American Baptist Minister.

---

72. Valerie Hudson, with Alma Don Sorensen, *Women in Eternity, Women of Zion* (Springville, Utah: Cedar Fort, 2004).

73. Valerie Hudson, with Andrea M. Den Boer, *Bare Branches: The Security Implications of Asia's Surplus Male Population* (Cambridge, Mass.: MIT Press, 2004).

74. Libana, from the album *A Circle is Cast*, 1986.

Linda E. Thomas (Ph.D. American University in Washington D.C.) received her M.Div. from Union Seminary. A cultural anthropologist and constructive theologian, Thomas has published dozens of articles and essays in academic publications. Her books include *Under the Canopy: Ritual Process and Spiritual Resilience in South Africa* (University of South Carolina, 1999), which explores the everyday lives of black South Africans trapped by systems of structural poverty and the ways religion and culture fueled their resilience during Apartheid; and *Living Stones in the Household of God* (Fortress, 2004), a collection of essays about black theology in the new millennium. She is currently professor of theology and anthropology at the Lutheran School of Theology at Chicago.

Valerie Hudson (Ph.D. Ohio State University) is a professor of political science at Brigham Young University. Her areas of expertise are foreign policy analysis, national security policy, international politics, and women and the developing world. Hudson is a nationally recognized scholar in foreign policy analysis. Her coauthored book *Bare Branches: The Security Implications of Asia's Surplus Male Population* (The MIT Press, 2004) was named best book in political science in 2004 by the Association of American Publishers.

Alma Don Sorensen (Ph.D. University of Illinois) taught political science at Indiana University before joining the faculty at Brigham Young University. He specializes in moral and political philosophy and in public ethics and public policy. He coauthored, with Valerie Hudson, *Women in Eternity, Women of Zion* (Cedar Fort, 2004).

A Dialogue on Black Theology

Black Theology of Liberation
Dwight N. Hopkins

BLACK THEOLOGY IS THE FAITH OF AFRICAN AMERICANS in a God of liberation who affirms the positive cultural and political experiences of poor black people as foundational sources in their quest for full humanity. In addition, black theology is the belief that, in their witness for a full humanity on earth, this God of liberation dwells among them. Essentially, the message of the gospel is liberation of poor and oppressed communities. Therefore, the task of theology is to investigate the nature of Jesus Christ's work of liberation with the silenced of society and to help those silenced to feel that their search for a comprehensive freedom is found in the Good News of Jesus Christ.

The Origin of Black Theology

Black theology, as a twentieth-century Christian theology, arose from three main sources: (a) the critique of Joseph R. Washington Jr.'s *Black Religion;* (b) the Civil Rights movement of the 1950s and 1960s; and (c) the Black Power movement of the 1960s.

Joseph R. Washington Jr.'s Black Religion

In 1964, Joseph R. Washington Jr., an African American religious scholar, published his *Black Religion,* in which he argued several points. First, he asserted specific definitional presuppositions. Religion, for him, denoted a belief in various dimensions of the human experience. As such, it was only a partial reflection of faith.

> Faith demands a fundamental change in the individual. Its direction is shaped and tested by a community of believers instructed by tradition and history. Faith must always be a response to God. Religion may be a response to whatever the individual desires. Faith stands in judgment on all religion, and is the critic of every religion. It is the concern with the Ultimate above every limited or limiting concern. Thus, faith is not

concerned solely with one aspect of a man's life but with the whole of life. It is out of faith that one makes every decision and wills to be loyal to God in every moment. But in religion a man may place his value on some goal or god which he confuses with God.[1]

For example, one could have belief in a political party or a justice movement or direct mass action. Faith, in contrast, meant a specific belief in God through Jesus Christ. According to Washington, "Faith begins with the cross and resurrection of Jesus Christ, not with the man from Nazareth or with the Sermon on the Mount. The Christian is one who has faith in Jesus Christ as Lord."[2] Since it required a specific belief, faith could be found only in a tradition, especially the historic Protestant Christian tradition from Europe, and could be manifested only in the institutional church. In other words, the true church is the one that has specific faith (as opposed to religion) in the God of the Hebrew and Christian scriptures. Even a belief in the religion of Jesus did not stand as an authentic mark of the true church. Furthermore, only with faith, tradition, and an ecclesiastical institution could one have and develop a theology. In short, theology arises from a church grounded in a firm faith handed down through tradition.

Second, Washington claimed that black people in the United States were religious people who had developed religious institutions. This part of the argument affirmed positively the historic struggle for justice, freedom, and equality of these religious institutions, something from which white churches could learn. In fact, Washington detected the belief in the struggle for justice for the oppressed in society as far back as the slave church. If there was a problem regarding the genealogy of contemporary black religious organizations, it was their deviation from their strong justice heritage throughout the decades since the pre–Civil War days.

However, Washington continued, a belief in the religion of justice or even a religion of the justice of Jesus did not qualify for faith. Faith can only be in God manifested in Jesus Christ, passed down from European Christian succession, housed in European and white American churches, and anchored in theology—a rational investigation of European and white American Christianity. As a result,

> Negroes have failed to make real contributions to Protestantism, the Christian faith, or the Christian Church, or to suggest any ecclesiastical change in the white organizations after which they are modeled. The reason for this failure is not inherent inability; it is primarily because of the fact that Negro institutions were not established to propound

---

1. Joseph R. Washington Jr., *Black Religion: The Negro and Christianity in the United States* (Lanham, Md.: University Press of America, 1984), 22. Washington's book was originally published in 1964 by Beacon Press.

2. Ibid., 23.

theology or liturgical matters. . . . Black religion perverted the historic Christian faith.[3]

The force of Washington's argument hinged on the deleterious impact of Christian white supremacy and the evils of segregation perpetrated on the part of white Americans. Only white churches had a faith (not just religion) and were the heirs of European tradition. Meanwhile, the sin of racism had forcefully kept black people out of the Christian church, its faith, and, consequently, its theology. As Washington put it, "The central theological questions of faith, particularly the teachings of the Church on social issues, have not entered the religious realm of the Negro."[4] If theology can arise only out of white churches—the true defenders of the faith—then black religious organizations were at best institutions for justice and at worst mere organizations of infantile clowning. The solution, for Washington, was for black religious organizations to go out of business and join white American churches in order to have access to theology. Once these religious organizations finally had access to faith, their positive contribution to white churches would be the emphasis on and experience of justice work.

Many prominent white religious scholars and clergymen hailed *Black Religion* because it was an intellectual articulation of the authenticity of white American ecclesiastical formations and a bold critique of the nature of the black church. The book was not merely an esoteric academic treatise. On the contrary, its publication arrived full force in the midst of the black church's leadership of the Civil Rights movement. Thus the text repositioned the white church as the center of Christian faith and witness in America. And its anti-black religion thrust summoned African American believers to forsake their independent status and assimilate into their church's white counterpart.

In contrast to the white clerical community's warm reception of *Black Religion,* African American religious leaders condemned the book because of its uncompromising assertion that black religious gatherings did not include faith, lacked a theology, and failed as churches. In order to become a church and possess a theology, Washington's program called for black people to merge with whites and adopt the latter's theology. Consequently, black theology arose, in part, as a systematic investigation, development, and enunciation of a Christian theology for black people moving toward liberation.

The Civil Rights Movement

If Washington's academic publication proved an albeit negative incentive for the emergence of a black theology of liberation, the Civil Rights and Black

---

3. Ibid., 38–39.
4. Ibid., 255.

Power movements provided positive intellectual energy from the grass roots. The contemporary Civil Rights movement began on December 1, 1955. On that day, a black female worker, Rosa Parks, sat down in a Montgomery bus and refused to give her seat to a demanding white man. Her act of radical defiance against the evils of Southern segregation laws sparked a new generation of civil rights protest. Because she was tired from a day's work and because she felt mistreated, Mrs. Parks—a black Christian woman—began a movement that propelled Reverend Martin Luther King Jr., the black church, and the North American black struggle for justice into the national and international arenas. For 382 days, King and the Montgomery blacks based in African American churches successfully boycotted city buses to protest segregation, walking for freedom. An elderly Christian black woman captured the determined spirit of protest: when asked about the weariness of walking to and from work, she replied, "My feets is tired, but my soul is rested." It was these tired "feets" marching for freedom in the streets that symbolized the historic religious resistance of black Americans since slavery.

The black church of the 1950s and 1960s, under King's leadership, played a vanguard role in breaking down legal segregation, primarily in the South. The black church knew that the Christian gospel contradicted the discriminating laws of white supremacy. By meeting, organizing, worshipping, and singing in the church, the Southern black community was empowered by the spirit of freedom.

The Civil Rights movement was a radical and militant chapter in the history of the African American struggle for liberation and the practice of freedom. It positioned many African American churches into direct mass action that broke laws. The movement emptied the pews of many churches and enabled members to shut down the normal functions of local governments by disrupting the business-as-usual attitudes and practices of whites with power. Building on the persistent legal battles of the National Association for the Advancement of Colored People (NAACP) in the 1940s and early 1950s, the Civil Rights movement, through the African American church, added a new form of protest. Blacks moved out from the court chambers dominated by the NAACP and into the streets and backwoods of the Southern states.

The major innovation that the eventual founders of black theology of liberation took from the Civil Rights movement entailed a redefinition of what it meant to be a church. That is to say, the movement redefined the church as a militant, revolutionary manifestation of Jesus Christ in the streets on behalf of the poor and marginalized. A true African American church must witness outside of buildings and on behalf of the least in society. The church had to follow the way of Jesus Christ, who came, died, and was resurrected for the pain and captivity of the oppressed, and through them, therefore, bless all humanity.

The Black Power Movement

The Black Power movement, the third source for the rise of a black theology of liberation, commenced with the call for Black Power during a civil rights march on June 16, 1966, in Greenwood, Mississippi. The march was headed by Dr. King and Stokely Carmichael, the chair of the Student Nonviolent Coordinating Committee (the youth wing of the Civil Rights movement). Given the national and international focus on Southern efforts at justice, Carmichael specifically chose this march to launch his summons. Therefore, Black Power resistance literally grew out of the Civil Rights movement.

The struggle for Black Power resulted from (a) the failure of the federal government to implement the 1954 Supreme Court decision against segregation; (b) the widened gap between African Americans during the so-called "decade of Negro progress" between 1955 and 1965; (c) the impatience of young black civil rights organizers who categorized white liberals as hypocrites wanting to lead black people's freedom struggle while, at the same time, slowing it down; (d) the intensified terrorism of white segregationists; and (e) the undying spirit of Malcolm X (assassinated in February 1965). With sobering, insightful clarity, Malcolm had declared: "The worst crime the white man has committed has been to teach us to hate ourselves."[5] That is why black people burned their hair to make it straight or curly. And for similar reasons, they bleached their skin and tried to make their noses and lips thinner. In addition to denying their natural and beautiful self-identity, with which God had blessed them, African Americans did not equitably share in the resources of the nation. White men controlled the major institutional resources of America. To love oneself, then, involved both the right of self-identity (for example, the slogan "black is beautiful") and the right of self-determination (for example, control of the means of producing and distributing the nation's resources).

In the midst of the 1966 cry for Black Power, urban rebellions, and political and cultural demands in the African American community, black theology was born. African American pastors, church administrators, and laypersons found themselves at a crossroads. On the one hand, many of them had been staunch participants in the Civil Rights movement. On the other, the radical shift of the freedom movement to Black Power and the involvement of many of their own community in this new thrust presented a dilemma for pastors of black churches. In July 1966, the ad hoc National Committee of Negro Churchmen (NCNC) was formed to reply to the new

---

5. Malcolm X, *The Autobiography of Malcolm X* (New York: Grove, 1966).

Black Power movement. They chose to publish a full-page statement on the movement, which presented a favorable theological interpretation, in the July 31, 1966, edition of the *New York Times*. From the Black Power movement, these originators of black liberation theology concluded that theology (for example, faith in and witness with a God of freedom) had something to do with power. The history of black and white relations had followed a skewed dynamic. White Christians had monopolized power without conscience while blacks had had conscience but no power.

The voices and protests of black people forced the issue of the role of Christianity in the black community. Thus, black theology arose for the affirmation of African American humanity and as an answer to the reality of black liberation moving against white racism. Where were God and Jesus Christ in the urban areas of rebellion? Was the African American church simply serving an Uncle Tom, otherworldly role, or was it aiding in black control of the community and black people's destiny? Could blacks continue to uphold the theology of integration and liberalism? When stripped of its "whiteness," what did Christianity say to black Americans? Could black identity, culture, history, and language become authentic sources for developing theology? If not, could one be black and Christian? Furthermore, in the growing African American revolt, what did a blue-eyed, blond-haired, "hippie-looking" Jesus have to do with Black Power and black liberation?

As a twentieth-century Christian theology, black liberation theology arose from a group of pastors and church leaders, rather than emerging from an academy or academic scholars. As previously mentioned, the ad hoc NCNC included African American pastors and church executives, the majority of which predominantly belonged to white denominations. These pastors and executives united to respond favorably to the June 1966 Black Power call. By favoring black liberation over integration, the committee, at that time, broke with Reverend King and the Civil Rights movement.

One of the NCNC founders stated that a group of black church people "found ourselves in a vacuum" and thus formed the committee. The turbulence in the black community had caused more and more black church people to choose between the "vacuum" of integrationism and the relevancy of black liberation. He continued, "We had gotten to the point where we had to hear God speaking through what we [the black church and the black community] were going through."[6] And where did the committee hear the word of God? Previously the white church power structure had supported and given money to only the formally educated and "reasonable" Negro church leaders such as Martin Luther King Jr. No matter how many marches the civil rights churches and organizations undertook against racism, the white

---

6. Calvin B. Marshall, interview by author, March 17, 1987.

church thought that it shared the same "theology" with the black church, since it believed it could draw on a common theological framework and speak a common theological language.

In complete contradiction to this integrationist, white, liberal theological construct, the NCNC began to hear the word of God elsewhere. Another early figure in the NCNC recounted how the committee

> began to talk about what would be the response of the black church, not simply to what Martin Luther King, Jr. was doing, because many people were participating in [the Civil Rights movement] as churches, but also to take some account of the more militant groups such as the Black Muslims, . . . Black Panthers, Ron Karenga's group, . . . [and] Stokely Carmichael.[7]

The seeds of black theology in the United States sprouted with the formation of NCNC in 1966.[8] However, not until the spring of 1969 would these first attempts at new life grow into fruition, when James H. Cone's book *Black Theology and Black Power* appeared in March 1969.[9] NCNC and the African American church had finally acquired a scholarly work that sharply presented the black religious experience not merely as a challenge to the sociological practice of the white church, but as a devastating criticism of the traditional white theology dominant in both white and black churches. Cone argued, in brief, that Black Power was the gospel of Jesus Christ.

The Intellectual Leadership of Black Theology

Cone's first book marked the birth of a unique Christian trend in the United States—a critical, intellectual investigation of black theology of liberation. Below we examine the intellectual contributions of James H. Cone, J. Deotis Roberts, Gayraud S. Wilmore, and Charles H. Long—four key scholars whose diverse emphases and creative tensions were crucial to the foundation of black theology of liberation as a twentieth-century Christian theology.

James H. Cone

James H. Cone is considered the founder of black theology of liberation. Cone, a distinguished professor of systematic theology at Union Theological Seminary in New York City, developed his black theology upon the gospel

---

7. Leon W. Watts, interview by author, March 23, 1987. Both Marshall (in the previous footnote) and Watts are members of the African Methodist Episcopal Zion Church, one of the historic black denominations.

8. Later the National Committee of Negro Churchmen changed its name to the National Conference of Black Churches.

9. James H. Cone, *Black Theology and Black Power* (San Francisco: Harper Collins, 1969).

of Jesus Christ as it related to the African American church and the Civil Rights and Black Power movements of the 1960s. He began his theology by interpreting the African American freedom struggle through the systematic doctrines of classical theology. In this comparative sense, Cone remained in the mainstream of classical theology.[10]

Cone's unique emphasis was to introduce liberation of the poor, specifically the African American poor, as the controlling key of all systematic theology. Cone wrote his first text, *Black Theology and Black Power,* during the upheaval of 1968. In April of that year, a white assassin's bullet had ended the life of Martin Luther King Jr. With that bullet, the movement for peace, nonviolence, and racial fellowship ground to a halt. Within a week of King's murder, 130 cities erupted in flames. National Guard and army troops descended upon the African American ghettoes. Forty-six civilians died; over three thousand were injured; and twenty-seven thousand were arrested. Those whites who held structural power had intensified their war on black America. Consequently, Cone perceived Black Power and black theology as co-laborers in the field of African American liberation: "Black Power and Black theology work on two separate but similar fronts. Both believe that Blackness is the primary datum of human experience which must be reckoned with, for it is the reason for our oppression and the only tool for our liberation."[11]

Cone, an African Methodist Episcopal clergy person, advocated a black theology that sought power for oppressed black people, a rearrangement of power to eliminate racist oppression and to enhance African American freedom. Similar to Malcolm X's faith claim, Cone called for a religion whose primary theological cornerstone demanded the political eradication of racial discrimination.

I characterize the theological writings of Cone as a Black Christian Theology of Liberation. It is *black* because he believes the African American experience to be the primary location of black theology. It is *Christian* because the basic question for his theology remains, "What does the Christian gospel have to say to powerless black [people] whose existence is threatened daily by the insidious tentacles of white power?" It is *theology* because he reflects on the very presence of God, "actively involved in the

---

10. Albert Cleage, an African American pastor and black church leader during this time, labels his "very good friend Dr. James H. Cone" black people's "apostle to the Gentiles" because Cone drags "white Christians as far as they are able to go (and then some) in interpreting Black Theology within the established framework which they can accept and understand." Albert Cleage Jr., *Black Christian Nationalism: New Directions for the Black Church* (New York: William Morrow, 1972), xvii, note.

11. James H. Cone, "Black Power, Black Theology, and the Study of Theology and Ethics," *Theological Education* 4 (spring 1970): 209.

present-day affairs of [black people]." And it is about *liberation* because he describes liberation as the "central idea for articulating the gospel of Jesus."[12]

In fact, the Christian gospel of liberation and the liberation of the poor form the heart of Cone's systematic theology. The target of liberation for Cone centers on the destruction of the structure of American white racism. This demonic system has crushed the African American person to the status of a nonperson. "The white structure of this American society," Cone elaborates, "personified in every racist, must be at least part of what the New Testament meant by the demonic forces."[13] Though he later broadens the target to include women's oppression, capitalism, and imperialism, Cone's entry point in the development of his black theology hinges on African American people's struggle against racism.

For Cone, the human procession toward black liberation against this demonic structure begins in divine freedom, for the freedom of God "is the source and content of human freedom." Grounded in divine freedom (meaning God's own free choice to create humans in freedom and to be with them in the realization of freedom and liberation in history), black liberation, or black freedom, stresses the divine will to execute human emancipation. The image of God, who is freedom in being, will, and function, determines humanity's created state and long-term goal in life. At the same time, one cannot have divine freedom—and human freedom—without divine justice. Freedom, or liberation, goes along with justice. And divine justice makes black liberation more than a human effort and goal; it makes liberation a divine intent. God's righteousness changes God's freedom into a practical realization of human liberation in history.[14]

In addition to anchoring the concepts of divine freedom and divine righteousness, black liberation also links up with salvation and "God's Kingdom" in Cone's theology. Salvation is no longer a supposedly inward calmness or invisible cure in the afterworld, a belief which acts like a sedative in support of racism. On the contrary, God, through Christ, enters the depths of oppression and liberates humanity from all human evil, including racism. Cone sounds another universal note of liberation in his doctrine of God's kingdom. The kingdom stands for all the world's poor because they

---

12. Cone, *Black Theology and Black Power*, 32, 38; James H. Cone, *My Soul Looks Back* (Nashville: Abingdon, 1982), 53; James H. Cone, "Christianity and Black Power," in *Is Anybody Listening to Black America?*, ed. C. Eric Lincoln (New York: Seabury, 1968), 3.

13. Regarding the "nonperson" comment, see Cone, *Black Theology and Black Power*, 11, 40–41, for Cone's view on "white structure of this American society."

14. See James H. Cone, "Freedom, History, and Hope," *The Journal of the Interdenominational Theological Center* 1 (fall 1963): 56; and Cone, *Black Theology and Black Power*, 43.

have nothing in this world. Cemented in historical liberation, the kingdom embodies the poor's hope and organizes them for practical liberation.[15]

God's liberation of black people through Christ's cross and resurrection marks the centrality of Cone's Christology. For Cone, the Christian scripture reveals Jesus' person as the Oppressed One. The Bible tells the story of Jesus' oppression; the contemporary story tells of African American people's oppression. Because African American people have suffocated under extreme affliction, the center of Jesus' work is a black Christ identified with liberation from black suffering. In a word, the Oppressed One in black suffering expresses divine identity and divine activity: Christ is black because of how Christ was revealed and because of where Christ seeks to be. Having fused the liberation of the oppressed with the identity and work of Christ and having situated that liberation in the African American community,[16] Cone boldly asserts, "Christianity is not alien to Black Power, it is Black Power."[17]

Cone cites a distinction between the literal and symbolic nature of Christological blackness. In explaining the contrast, Cone offers a warning for the possible short-term nature of a black Christology: "I realize," he confesses, "that 'blackness' as a christological title may not be appropriate in the distant future or even in every human context in our present." But today the literalness of Christ's blackness arises from Christ entering and converging literally with black oppression and black struggle. Furthermore, Cone continues, Christ's symbolic status of blackness appears in Christ's "transcendent affirmation" that God has never left the universal oppressed alone.[18]

Cone's political doctrine of Jesus adds a new dimension in his fight against white theology. He brings together the Jesus of history with the Christ of faith to complement the liberation theme. Cone does argue that we know what and where Jesus is today based on what Jesus did while on earth. But at the same time, Cone creates new political meaning in the crucifixion and resurrection by focusing on the theme of liberation. Calvary and the empty tomb prove to be central in Cone's Christology;[19] Jesus' death and resurrection reveal "that God is present in all dimensions of human liberation."[20]

---

15. James H. Cone, "Black Theology and Black Liberation," *Christian Century* 87 (September 16, 1970): 1086–87; Cone, *Black Theology and Black Power*, 36–37.

16. Cone, *Black Theology and Black Power*, 34, 38, 120; also see James H. Cone, *A Black Theology of Liberation*, 2d ed. (Maryknoll, N.Y.: Orbis, 1986), 120–21.

17. Cone, *Black Theology and Black Power*, 38.

18. James H. Cone, *God of the Oppressed* (New York: Seabury, 1975), 135–37.

19. Cone, *A Black Theology of Liberation*, 110–24.

20. Ibid., 118.

Finally, Cone's black theology focuses on the poor. Christ died on the cross and rose from the dead to liberate the poor and the oppressed, in direct opposition to the mission of the satanic on earth. Christ rescues the downtrodden from the material bondage of "principalities and powers," though in this liberation process the oppressors also gain their freedom because the object of their oppression—the now freed poor—no longer occupies an oppressed status.[21] The dynamic effect of Jesus Christ bringing deliverance for both the oppressed and the oppressor raises the question of the importance of reconciliation in Cone's black theology.

Even though *Black Theology and Black Power* expresses the thundering challenge of a manifesto against white people and their racism, Cone never excludes the possibility of reconciliation: "I do not rule out the possibility of creative changes, even in the lives of oppressors. It is illegitimate to sit in judgment on another man, deciding how he will or must respond. That is another form of oppression."[22]

The white oppressor might change and become reconciled with the black oppressed in the latter's liberation movement. For Cone, the essence of the gospel is the practice of freedom for the black poor, and it is this Christian context that defines relations with whites.

Cone developed his doctrine of reconciliation primarily and consistently with concern for the liberation of oppressed blacks. Therefore, in order to yield meaningful and productive reconciliation, only the black community can set the conditions for reconciliation. On the other hand, the "white oppressor" suffers from an enslavement to racism and gives up any capability to offer suitable reconciliation terms. The oppressed lay down "the rules of the game." The rules established by oppressed African Americans aim at the heart of white racist power. In fact, Cone writes, "There will be no more talk about reconciliation until a redistribution of power has taken place. And until then, it would be advisable for whites to leave blacks alone."[23]

Cone describes two types of reconciliation—objective and subjective. Because Jesus Christ died on the cross and rose from the dead, the devil and satanic forces experienced defeat. The cross-resurrection triumph brought about the objective reconciliation—divine victory at Calvary and the tomb

---

21. Cone, *Black Theology and Black Power*, 35, 42–43; see also Cone, *A Black Theology of Liberation*, 6.

22. Cone, *Black Theology and Black Power*, 4.

23. Ibid., 145; James H. Cone, "Toward a Black Theology," *Ebony* 25 (August 1970): 114. In his reconciliation position, Cone combats (a) white people's seemingly inevitable practice of setting the terms in black-white encounters. By redistributing power, white inclination to abusive authority over blacks lacks the potency to implement itself; and (b) he fights for the right of the oppressed community to self-determination when dealing with oppressors.

objectively shattered the walls of hostility between white and black. Now that God has objectively liberated the oppressed from the finality of demonic clutches such as white racism, oppressed humanity (African American people) must assume its responsibility to fight consciously along with God in Christ against injustice. The oppressed must act as if they are truly emancipated in a subjective sense; they must fight with total effort against white racism and for freedom. This is subjective liberation. Therefore Cone maintains the consistency of his liberation theme in both objective and subjective reconciliation.[24]

For blacks to bring about reconciliation, their task is to fight white oppression. For whites, reconciliation can mean only one thing—coming to God through black people, through whom Jesus is leading a movement for freedom.[25]

J. Deotis Roberts

J. Deotis Roberts, an ordained Baptist minister and the second person to write a book on black theology, started his intellectual ministry before Black Power and the late 1960s freedom struggle by black America gave rise to Cone's theology. Roberts studied Christian Platonism during the 1950s at Edinburgh and Cambridge Universities in England. He became interested in questions concerning philosophy and faith, which he examined in his first two books, *Faith and Reason* (1962) and *From Puritanism to Platonism in Seventeenth Century England* (1968). Roberts's conversational partner was classical European-American philosophical theology. However, with urban rebellions flooding Dr. Martin Luther King's movement, Roberts began to respond theologically to the radical change in black people's political scenery.

To understand Roberts's black theology, one has to see him as the product of two larger political developments: civil rights (from the mid-1950s to the mid-1960s) and Black Power (from the late 1960s to the mid-1970s). He and Dr. King finished their doctoral degrees around the same time in the 1950s. Both came out of a Baptist environment in the American South, which suggested that African Americans could improve their social status through hard work, impeccable educational credentials, and a reliance on Christian nonviolence. Eventually, a successful black could achieve the reward of integration with white people. Hence, Roberts matured in the King–Civil Rights ethos. But while he was a professor at Howard University, the political

---

24. James H. Cone, "Theological Reflections on Reconciliation," *Christianity and Crisis* (January 22, 1973): 307–8.

25. See Cone, *God of the Oppressed,* 245; and Cone, *Black Theology and Black Power,* 150–51.

turmoil and violence of Black Power also directly affected him. In fact, he taught there while Stokely Carmichael (the founder of Black Power) was a student. Consequently, Roberts tried to stay within the Black Power movement and bring his insights from the King–Civil Rights era.

Later, as a distinguished professor at the Eastern Baptist Theological Seminary, Roberts set out to develop a black political theology. Underscoring the importance of politics and theology, he published his first black theology book in 1971, *Liberation and Reconciliation*. Further situating himself with a political theology, he named his second black theology book *A Black Political Theology* (1974). But even in his controversial first work, one finds his explanation of black political theology: "The reason why Black Theology is 'political' is that the one-to-one approach is inadequate and unattractive to any black who is aware of the serious or insidious character of racism."[26]

Within this theology, Roberts establishes a clear intent which guides his entire theological system. "What I am seeking," he writes, "is a Christian theological approach to race relations that will lead us beyond a hypocritical tokenism to liberation as a genuine reconciliation between equals."[27] He intends to combine liberation and reconciliation, to build on and go beyond Cone's unbalanced (in Roberts's view) liberation-of-the-poor contribution.

Roberts's thinking is a Black Christian Theology of Balance. He explains his *black* theology as "inner city" theology reflecting upon black awareness and Black Power. It is *Christian* because he makes it equal with a "constructive restatement of the Christian faith," and he finds the "raw material" for black theology in the African American church. It is *theology* because Roberts describes his activity as "reasoning about God," and he uses a theological methodology of *balance*. Referring to this theological outlook, Roberts summarizes: "I tried to bridge the two generations of Dr. King and the one of the new Black Power and black consciousness movement. . . . My whole methodology and whole outlook would mean that I would almost have an equal balance. . . . I'm on both sides of the fence."

Roberts's most noted, and controversial, issue deals with his balanced handling of the Christian liberation–reconciliation doctrine. Roberts stakes out his fundamental claim here. "Thus I have spoken of . . . liberation and reconciliation. . . . A worthy Black Theology has to be balanced in this way."[28]

---

26. J. Deotis Roberts, *Liberation and Reconciliation* (Philadelphia: Westminster, 1971), 34; J. Deotis Roberts, *A Black Political Theology* (Philadelphia: Westminster, 1974), 26.

27. Roberts, *Liberation and Reconciliation*, 27–28.

28. Roberts, *Liberation and Reconciliation*, 43; his "on both sides of the fence" comments are from my March 19, 1987, interview with him; for other references to his "balance" approach, see Roberts, *Liberation and Reconciliation*, 13. For his definition of theology, see J. Deotis Roberts, "Black Theology in the Making," *Review and*

Whereas James H. Cone encourages genuine reconciliation after a redistribution of white political power, Roberts stands for black liberation against white racism and, simultaneously, for reconciliation with white people. Because of Roberts's theology of balance, I will treat liberation and reconciliation together. He targets both liberation and reconciliation as the "twin goals" and "two main poles" of black theology.[29] Liberation implies black people's freedom from the bondage of white racism; reconciliation suggests that black freedom does not deny white humanity but meets whites on equal ground. Roberts seeks to develop both aims in a balanced way, that is, in terms of (a) always explaining one in relation to the other, and (b) utilizing them as the core around which he weaves his systematic theology.

Roberts seeks to place Cone's Christology in proper perspective. Cone believes Christ was not literally white and that the divinity assumes blackness by his presence among the oppressed African American community. In *Liberation and Reconciliation,* Roberts also writes of his belief in a black Messiah, though not in the literal, historical sense. For him, the black Messiah speaks to a psychocultural crisis engendered by white American religion's notion that only a white Christ could be worthy of adoration. In Roberts's opinion, one must not limit Christianity merely to the white Christ's worthiness. The black experience also has to be a major source for contemporary Christology. A psychological need materializes to make Christ and the gospel address the black person directly. As a black image, Christ becomes one among black people, and the black person retrieves his or her own dignity and pride.

Furthermore, Roberts does not wish to challenge white Americans to worship a black Christ, thus demanding a vengeful repentance from them for worshipping a white Christ. This type of "revenge" would dehumanize whites as they have done to African Americans. Besides, affirmation of a

---

Expositor 70 (summer 1973): 321. On his interpretation of "Christian," review J. Deotis Roberts, "Black Theology in Faith and Ethics," in *Black Theology Today: Liberation and Contextualization* (New York: Mellen, 1983), 58; J. Deotis Roberts, "Black Liberation Theism," *Journal of Religious Thought* 33 (spring-summer 1976):33; and J. Deotis Roberts, "The Roots of Black Theology: An Historic Perspective," in *Black Theology Today,* 83. For black theology as "inner city" theology, examine Roberts, *A Black Political Theology,* 115.

29. Roberts, "Black Theology in Faith and Ethics," 65; Roberts, *Liberation and Reconciliation,* 26. He also writes: "I stand somewhere between the generations—that is, on the boundary between the black militants and the old-fashioned civil rights integrationists, and also between the 'by whatever means necessary' ethicists and the view that ends and means are organically one. It is my view that liberation and reconciliation must be considered at the same time and in relation to each other." Roberts, *Liberation and Reconciliation,* 13.

black Christ, for Roberts, includes room for a white Christ. But, applying his balanced methodology, if whites could overcome their superior-inferior state of mind and their color-consciousness and could worship a black Messiah, then reconciliation would be nearer. Still, Roberts claims, real reconciliation through black and white equality would allow American blacks and whites to transcend the skin color of Christ and reach out to a "universal Christ" without color.[30] At this point, Roberts clarifies the black Messiah–colorless Messiah relation in his liberation-reconciliation model in which the black Messiah functions in a symbolic and mythic capacity. In the black experience, the black Messiah liberates blacks; at the same time, the universal Christ reconciles both black and white Americans. Jesus Christ the Liberator offers liberation from white oppression and forgiveness from sin and exploitation within the African American community; Jesus Christ the Reconciler brings black people together and black and white people together in "multi-racial fellowship."[31]

Roberts's *A Black Political Theology* further elaborates his Christology. In this text, Christ operates above culture and in culture while liberating the whole person and speaking to the need for peoplehood. Christ is the focus of a theology of social change and political action. And he is the Liberator who casts his lot with the oppressed. Along with "mainstream Protestantism," Roberts agrees that the *essence* or *substance* of Christology lies in the universal Word—the lordship of Christ over each person. Black Christology takes for granted this universal definition and puts it in the *form* of the black experience. The existential and personal Christ liberates and the universal Christ reconciles all Americans, black and white.[32]

Gayraud S. Wilmore

As one of the founders of black theology, Gayraud S. Wilmore has had a major impact on contemporary black theology. Wilmore, an ordained Presbyterian minister (now retired from the Interdenominational Theological Center in Atlanta, Georgia), participated in the very early meetings of the ad hoc National Committee of Negro Churchmen. He first chaired the committee's theological commission and crafted its pioneering black theological direction. Though trained in social ethics, Wilmore shifted his emphasis to black history and black theology. His *Black Religion and Black Radicalism* (1972) filled a major gap in the early black theological movement—the need

---

30. Roberts, *Liberation and Reconciliation*, 139–40.

31. Ibid., 80.

32. For an account of his Christological claims, that is, black Messiah, colorless Christ, liberation and reconciliation, see Roberts, "The Black Messiah," in *Liberation and Reconciliation*, 130–35; and J. Deotis Roberts, "Jesus Means Freedom," in *A Black Political Theology*, 117–38.

for a fresh account of the many streams of resistance in black religious history. The two volumes of *Black Theology: A Documentary History* (1966–79; 1980–92), which he coedited with James Cone, are the classic textbooks on black theology.[33]

I refer to Wilmore's theology as black theology of religious thought. The phrase *religious thought* comes directly from a self-description of his work. With this new phrase, Wilmore wants to ground any discussion of black theology in a time long before the polemics against white theology of the 1960s. Furthermore, he evaluates theology within the general perspective of "black religious thought."

> If we are going to talk about black theology, we really need to go back to the beginning and not assume that black theology began with the publication of Dr. Cone's book in 1969. But when we do that, we have to agree that we are not using theology in the strictly academic and technical sense. What we really might use better is the term ... black religious thought.[34]

Wilmore argues for this designation of black people's religious experience—black religious thought—because he believes that from it grows black Christian theology. He wants to dig deeper, for he discovers something broader beneath academic theology, which, in his opinion, reflects the confessions of the Christian church, the apostolic faith, the Old and New Testaments, and church disciplines. Given his preference for the term "black religious thought," how does Wilmore define theology?

Black theology, Wilmore states, is not the mere opposite of the dominant Christian theology, a black version of white classical theology. On the contrary, black theology gains its importance by getting the meaning of black freedom from specifically black theological resources. Wilmore asks this question: In what ways do black Christian, non-Christian, and secular groups comprehend, feel, and practice liberation as their ultimate concern? Unraveling this ultimate concern is the theological work of black theology. When it does this, continues Wilmore, black theology fulfills its proper task by pointing the way toward emancipation for the entire black community. Furthermore, the key to black theology is freedom for black people and, in that process, freedom for all God's humanity.[35] Thus Wilmore works on a black theology that leans more toward the liberation strands in non-Christian black movements.

---

33. Gayraud S. Wilmore, *Black Religion and Black Radicalism* (Maryknoll, N.Y.: Orbis, 1972); Gayraud S. Wilmore, *Black Theology: A Documentary History* (Maryknoll, N.Y.: Orbis, 1993).

34. Gayraud S. Wilmore, interview with author, February 19, 1987.

35. See Wilmore, *Black Religion and Black Radicalism*, 218–19.

Even when one supports the importance of black theology, one still has to look at the beginning of this theology, which predates the black church. In that sense, Wilmore does not view theology as merely a church discipline. "The seminal Black Theology of the African slaves on the plantations of the New World existed prior to the existence of the black church as such. Its first theologians were not theologically trained professors, but preacher-conjurers."[36]

Although theology goes back to the period before and during the historic African American church's resistance against slavery and racism, the thought of the black religious experience embraced the attempts of all black secular and non-Christian groups to express the meaning and values of the black reality in the United States, Africa, and the Caribbean. Even today, theology extends beyond the black church as a religious institution. It includes aspects of black life and culture, contends Wilmore, that white scholars would call secular, non-Christian, and sometimes anti-Christian.

Wilmore writes in order to "create a new set of interpretive tools," a new pair of "eyes" for the African American community. How does the overall black community bring forth its ultimate concerns and solutions in a situation of racist exploitation? For Wilmore, the area of probing is neither European-American theology nor simply black-church documents. He searches black oral tradition and literature, sifting through mythology, ethical norms, and folklore. There, he discovers black religious thought.[37]

Black religious thought serves as the umbrella to and background ingredient for a black theology. Black thought gives rise to, and includes, black theology. Offering a much broader perspective, black religious thought allows Wilmore to move from the confines of a systematic church theology to the unbounded religious experience nourished by the masses of African American people. For the entire community, black religious thought is held together by a basic glue: an indestructible belief in freedom, a freedom born in the African environment. The informal, uncategorized religious thought of black folk, therefore, opens up a whole new world of sources with which to sharpen a new black interpretation for liberation. As long as belief in freedom regulates the sources, following Wilmore's line of reasoning, the possibilities of black cultural, theological creativity seem endless.

In *Black Religion and Black Radicalism*, Wilmore uncovers three locations for theological sources.[38] In his three-source division, he does not directly include scripture and early church tradition. The presuppositional status of the Bible and apostolic faith leads to their de-emphasis in the

---

36. Gayraud S. Wilmore, "Black Theology: Its Significance for Christian Mission Today," *International Review of Mission* 63, no. 250 (April 1974): 214.

37. Wilmore, *Black Religion and Black Radicalism*, 237.

38. Ibid., 234–41.

development of his black religious thought. Wilmore wishes to promote non-Christian resources. First, he highlights the lower-class black community's folk religion. In his judgment, black faith as folk religion has been the motor for all major revolutionary and nationalist, mass-based movements of blacks, and it has also kept alive some parts of Africa's cultural importance for black America. Sometimes folk religion overlaps the black Christian church; other times it unfolds in movements like the Nation of Islam, Marcus Garvey's efforts, black Islam, black Judaism, the Azusa Street Revival, and that of Daddy Grace.

The second source is the "writings, sermons, and addresses of the black preachers and public men and women of the past."[39] Wilmore agrees that not all historical black heroines and heroes were members of the clergy. But he claims that almost all experienced religious conditioning from the black community. They reflected the unique spirituality of African American life and culture built on black faith. Both the black clergy and the black cultural artists have drawn on the religious and theological themes of suffering, struggle, hope, justice, faith, survival, and liberation of African American people. Therefore, one must also seek theological implications in the essays of Alice Walker, the poetry of Countee Cullen, the novels of Richard Wright, and the tales of Langston Hughes. For Wilmore, black theology is not developed in white seminaries; it is found "in the streets, in taverns and pool halls, as well as in churches."[40]

The traditional religions of Africa make up the third source of black theology. Wilmore instructs us to remember the long history of African Americans; black people are an *African* people. Consequently, the religious and theological connections to ancient and modern Africa bear heavily on contemporary black knowledge of God. The particular way God revealed God's self in precolonial Africa contributes to the survival and liberation of black people on both sides of the Atlantic. A modification of African traditional religious beliefs, values, and practices could very well bring about a rebirth of African American religion in North America. Here Wilmore also calls for a cooperative venture between black Americans and Africans to rediscover and uncover common "belief structures and worship practices" in black religious norms and traditions.[41]

Wilmore believes that any future work on black theology has to go back to the period of African American slave life. I include this as his fourth and final source. During slavery, various theological and religious themes came together to make up the basis of black religious thought. The following

---

39. Ibid., 236.
40. Ibid., 238.
41. Ibid., 238–40.

shows Wilmore's position on the black cultural elements in slavery-based black religion.

> In the formation of a new common language, in the telling of animal tales and proverbs, in the leisure-time practice of remembered handicrafts, in the preparation of foods, homemade medicines, and magical potions and charms, in the standardization of rituals of birth, marriage, and death, in the creation of modes of play and parody, in the expression of favorite styles of singing, instrumental music, and the dance . . . the slaves wove for themselves the tapestry of a new African American culture.[42]

These unified cultural aspects were integrated into a basic religious conception of life and reality. To find out why and how black Christians and the entire black community look at the world in a religious way, one has to go back to these cultural elements. In the unique ways in which African American culture formed itself, one discovers the plain theology of black religious thought, cut from the survival of the African spirit in the slavery of the New World—for example, Africanisms (a partial conscious or unconscious memory of Africa).

Wilmore asserts that Africanisms occupy a prominent role in black religion and, therefore, in the construction of an authentic black theology of liberation. He advocates giving more attention to the religious implications of the remains of African values and the African worldview. Wilmore points out several religious themes that he believes survive from Africa in the black community.

a. In black life, there exists no sharp separation between the secular and the sacred, or religion and life.

b. Religion is practical. It relates directly to food, shelter, economic life, child rearing, and recreation. Religion must work in everyday life.

c. Like Africa, the overall black community places a premium on family and solidarity in communalism as opposed to excessive individualism.

d. Black folk worship God with the fullness of their bodies, minds, and spirits. This devotion links to liberation because the Spirit descends and unbinds both the soul and the body. "The same Spirit which calls us out of the rigidity of our psychosomatic entity, calls us out of the tyranny of our political bondage." For Wilmore, the doctrine of the Spirit includes the freeing of the body and the soul.

---

42. Ibid., 222.

e. When the black community speaks of the presence of God and the Spirit in its midst, it speaks of the spirit of black ancestors' lives.[43]

With these religious Africanisms, Wilmore wishes to carry out a correction of the "whitenization of black religion." Africanisms mean that God, the Lord of all people and cultures, created Africanness in black Americans. Since they are created by God, Africanisms inherently contain creative, positive theological value for black people and all humanity. In brief, they contain possibilities for liberation.

To understand Wilmore's theological conception of liberation or freedom, one has to keep in mind his attraction to African culture. He describes how the black masses' religious move toward freedom grew out of their past African environment. In this earlier African situation, freedom pointed to real deliverance on earth, liberation from all powers that inhibited the holistic release of mind, body, and spirit. Any power that tried to stop the full advancement of the individual in community would be defeated. At this point, Wilmore emphasizes that liberation stands for more than politics and economics. It means

> freedom of the person as a child of God, the freedom to be himself and herself most fully, to realize the most creative potential of his or her psychophysical nature. . . . The freedom that black religion celebrates and black theology seeks to explicate is simply the freedom to be a human being.[44]

For Wilmore, freedom in the theological sense is each individual of the community reaching the height of his or her God-given possibilities. One achieves divinely initiated liberation once one reaches the fullest potential of one's mind and body. Divine freedom results in full human creativity; therefore, blocking human wholeness attacks divine purpose.

Wilmore sees a necessity to use theological language when writing about black people's ultimate concern for liberation because of the origin of black folk's yearning for liberation. Liberation comes from blacks' natural consciousness of a transcendent reality. In that reality, freedom intertwines inseparably with the essence of humanity created in *the image of God*.[45] Thus, in addition to being a *child* of God and reaching full *wholeness,* an African American person undergoes a liberated experience with the complete realization of God's *image* in herself or himself. In fact, attaining

---

43. Wilmore's views and quotes on Africanisms come from Wilmore, interview; Wilmore, *Black Religion and Black Radicalism,* 239; and Gayraud S. Wilmore, "Reinterpretation in Black Church History," *Chicago Theological Seminary Register* 72 (winter 1983): 29.

44. Wilmore, *Black Religion and Black Radicalism,* 219.

45. Wilmore, "Significance for Christian Mission Today," 215.

maximum human potential mirrors the *divine image*. God created humanity to be human in the fullest sense of the word. To be human is to succeed in
all that is humanly possible. For black Americans, then, there is an African
religious and cultural sense that human creativity contains God's image.

Furthermore, liberation shows us God's command, a mandated theological ethic. The black Christian community, Wilmore writes, needs
to regain "a sense of cultural vocation that relates to their experience of
struggle in terms of both spiritual formation and social transformation."[46]
Wilmore, in using the phrase "cultural vocation," pinpoints at least two
things. First, liberation does not come from a whimsical human decision
about what to do in life. On the contrary, the Divine calls and bestows upon
humanity the vocation—a lifelong pursuit in response to God's word—to
be free. Second, spiritual formation and social change come together in a
vocation of culture. Culture acts as the umbrella for the holistic liberation
and mixture of the spirit and body. Wilmore's preference for culture as the
context for politics becomes clear in this instance. For him, to see liberation primarily in political terms would narrow black people's religious way
of life to a political liberation in reaction to whites. Whereas culture, as he
uses it, expresses a total mind-body-spirit religious way of believing and
doing, a cultural perspective seems to imply a proactive black religious style
of being.[47]

Though he gives preference to culture, Wilmore does indeed recognize the inseparability of political and cultural liberation. Yet, he avoids
a one-sided goal of political liberation because he believes that it gives an
incomplete result and produces a deformed goal. In Wilmore's view, one
cannot reach the fullest measure of human liberation while remaining captive to the oppressor's culture. People have to "appreciate and value their
own traditions in art and music and literature and family life and chil-
drearing habits and recreation and all the multiplex aspects of human life."[48]

---

46. Gayraud S. Wilmore, "Spirituality and Social Transformation as the Vocation
of the Black Church," in *Churches in Struggle: Liberation Theologies and Social
Transformation in North America*, ed. William Tabb (New York: Monthly Review,
1986), 240–41.

47. Wilmore, "Spirituality and Social Transformation," 240–53.

48. Wilmore, interview. Previously, Wilmore had written:

To speak of the mission and strategy of the black church as the cultural
rather than political is not to deny the political, but to subsume it in a
larger context; and it is precisely in such a context that we can see how the
spiritual dimension of life impinges upon the problems and possibilities of
social transformation. This means that we intend to encompass the entire
scale of perceptions, meanings, values, behavioral patterns, etc., all integrated in that system of symbols we call culture . . . and take passionate

The African American community does not engage in these cultural activities as an idle pastime. Again, for Wilmore, in these cultural activities one identifies sources of religious and theological values held over from Africa. Until black folks appreciate the cultural way, and thus the religious way, political liberation is only half a victory: African American people would win the political battle but lose the overall cultural (religious and theological) war to their white oppressors. Thus only with success in the cultural sphere will black liberation give us a thoroughgoing victory over demonic principalities and powers on earth.

Charles H. Long

Throughout the 1970s, Charles H. Long waged a vehement struggle against attempts at creating a black theology and against neglecting the primacy of culture in African American life and religion. Past president of the American Academy of Religion and retired from the University of California at Santa Barbara, Long does not count himself as a black theologian, since he obtained his formal studies in the history of religions. Indeed, his discipline affects directly his interpretation of black theology. Therefore a look at his definitions of history and religion will aid this study.

> By "history" I mean the particular temporal-spatial cultural situation in which man responds to that which is sacred and by "religion" I mean the structure of the myth, symbol, or religious response through which man apprehends the sacred. The historian of religions is interested in understanding the enduring structure of these responses.[49]

History operates as cultural location for humanity's response to the sacred. Put differently, the place of human activity and its connection with the holy is culture. Culture gives birth to religion. And religion provides structures through which humanity understands the holy. Here Long hopes to avoid the common error of simply accepting white people's religious structures and then having blacks adopt it—a mistake of African Americans who mimic white religious structures. Rather, he targets the white religious structure itself and attempts its deconstruction and subsequent reconstruction from something religiously new.

Long agrees with Wilmore's de-emphasis of strictly Christian sources and broadening of black religious thought and his accent on non-Christian and secular elements. Long complements Wilmore's work

---

actions on the basis of such conception. (Wilmore, "Spirituality and Social Transformation," 248)

49. Charles H. Long, "The West African High God: History and Religious Experience," *History of Religions* 3 (winter 1964): 331.

by using a unique definition of religious language. In fact, I label Long's perspective a Black Religious Language. He characterizes religion as the fountainhead out of which all other important realities, including theology, emerge. "For my purposes," he writes, "religion will mean orientation—orientation in the ultimate sense, that is, how one comes to terms with the ultimate significance of one's place in the world."[50] Religion, then, deals with how a people decides on its own ultimate significance in a cultural time and space. Thus, the *entire* African American community is religious because it confronts the question of ultimate significance. As a result, for Long, all languages—languages about God, salvation, and creation—extend out of religion.

Language has an exact meaning for Long. In this sense, language does not mirror reality; language is reality. "All you have is language," comments Long:

> There is nothing behind, before, underneath, overarching or whatever. So whatever reality you want to talk about is in the language. . . . So that language has its own materiality. It is not so much that there is a reality there and I'm using these words just to say what I want to say about it. I am saying that in language is the reality that I am expressing. . . . I do not think language is just something that represents something else.[51]

Here one can better grasp the fundamental problem Long has with the meaning and origin of language, especially religious language. He does not view religious language as a flimsy shadow of some other real religious substance. Religious language *is* religious substance. In his perspective, languages express power when they support the way of life and the structures of the people for whom languages speak. Therefore genuine black religious language is the actual and material expression of what takes place within African American culture and life.

With his definitions of religion and language, Long submits both theology and Christianity to a deconstructive criticism. Instead of reinterpreting theological categories, Long dismisses the notion of black theology altogether because theology as theology represents a language or "power discourse" of those (white) people who have the power to define cultural categories. African American people and poor people, argues Long, have not had the privilege of establishing cultural categories. Then why should

---

50. Charles H. Long, *Significations: Signs, Symbols and Images in the Interpretation of Religion* (Philadelphia: Fortress, 1986), 7. In a personal interview, Long commented that out of religion "all the other languages come . . . all of it comes from this attempt to orient yourself in your time and space. . . . Religion is produced out of the culture. . . . Given all that, and for black theology to come along and then narrow [religious language] all down again." Charles H. Long, interview with author, February 21, 1987.

51. Long, interview.

black people adopt the existing dominant culture and thus enter the "imitative game" of saying they will attain their liberation by virtue of acting like those who have oppressed them? Again, theology is white people's power language.

Relatedly, and similar to Wilmore, Long has a major problem with black theology because, in his words, "it is church theology." Yet in Long's assessment, churches incorporate only that segment of black religion and culture that has self-consciously separated itself as Christian. In fact, the African American community also includes a great deal of other religious life that boasts Ultimate Concern. By naming themselves advocates of black theology, African American religious intellectuals miss the non-Christian types of religion in black culture. As a result, theology, black theology in particular, narrows the categories of religious language in the African American community.[52]

Using the same reasoning, Long cautions against accepting Christianity as an authentic religion for the liberation of black religious language. He states that Christianity is probably the only religion that has a theology, partly because "Christianity is not a grassroots religion . . . that grows up out of the ground of the people."[53] Even when Christianity spread across Europe, one has to remember that some other type of religious language existed before Christianity arrived. In Long's opinion, even before Christianity came to different shores throughout the world, people were practicing a vibrant cultural and religious life. Briefly, both theology and Christianity operate as dominating power languages. And so, one needs other sources for black religious language.

Long approaches other sources in order to answer this question: What are the religious elements in the cultural experience of black folk? He contrasts his approach to that of James H. Cone. Cone and other theologians, for Long, function essentially as "apologetic [theologians] working implicitly and explicitly from the Christian theological tradition." Cone has accepted the theological structure of the Christian religious language. Long then raises the theological, methodological shortcomings in apologetic theology. "This limitation of methodological perspectives" on the part of Cone, Long contends, has resulted in a narrow understanding and the exclusion of certain creative possibilities among African American people.[54]

Long turns his eye toward the more vitally important expressions forthcoming from the black community itself. There one begins with the

52. Long, interview; Charles H. Long, "Freedom, Otherness and Religion: Theologies Opaque," *Chicago Theological Seminary Register* 73 (winter 1983): 20–22.

53. Long, interview.

54. Long, "Perspectives for a Study of Afro-American Religion in the United States," *History of Religions* 11 (August 1971): 55.

raw data of black religious language that includes Christians and non-Christians. For example, Long says he "would spend as much time with Count Bassie, Jimmy Lungford, and Cab Calloway, and black poets, and all these kind of folks as I would with ministers." He includes other such notables as Carter G. Woodson, W. E. B. Du Bois, George Washington Carver, and Jelly Roll Morton.[55] Both ministers and nonministers struggle to give religious significance to black life and experience. To Long, the nonministers occupy a position in black religious language just as creative and just as powerful as the ministers.

Long's religious and theological sources fall into four groups.[56] Agreeing with Wilmore, he first points out the involuntary presence of Africa's descendants in America. When the first Africans arrived in the New World, the process of creating black Americans commenced. Involuntary presence proved and continues to prove key to that creation. In other words, slavery, and today's oppression of the black community, had to have affected in a unique way how enslaved Africans viewed their Ultimate Concern (that is, that which was holy for them). Therefore, involuntary presence and orientation communicate deep-seated religious meaning. The slave experienced negativity in bondage and, at the same time, created a different reality from a unique perception of Ultimate Concern. Within the context of slavery, the enslaved African and African American changed and created their experience of the holy on the level of religious consciousness.

Like Wilmore, Long also looks to the black community's engagement with the holy in tradition, a second source. The oral tradition of black folklore offers a gold mine of creative religious possibilities. What does a combing of slave narratives, black sermons, the words and music of the spirituals and the blues, the cycle of Br'er Rabbit, and High John the Conqueror stories tell us about religious consciousness? "These materials reveal," Long writes, "a range of religious meanings extending from trickster-transformer hero to High God."[57]

In addition, slaves adopted and put new meaning in the imagery of the Bible, a third source. They interpreted God's deliverance of Israel from Egyptian bondage, Long states, as a sign of hope. Furthermore, the slaves saw God as the omnipotent, moral deity, who held power to set things right. And the slaves never, or hardly ever, accused God in situations of suffering. For example, to maintain their humanity in the face of the majority population's acts of white supremacy, slaves experienced the biblical God as a "transformer of their consciousness." In particular, Long examines the slaves'

---

55. Long, interview.

56. Long, "Perspectives for a Study," 59–62. From his three sections I deduce four sources. Unless indicated otherwise, quotations in this section come from this article.

57. Ibid., 61–62.

stories about their coversion experiences and discovers a combination of a practical "God acting in history" and a concern for "mystification of consciousness." Here in these conversion stories, the appearance of God overwhelms the slaves in the black religious experience, not in the Trinitarian dogma. Accordingly, these theological structures (of how God acts in ordinary events and transforms religious consciousness) can give clues about black religious consciousness for the entire African American community. In other words, in the slaves' interpretation, the God who acts and transforms in the Christian conversion experience is also found in the religious consciousness of non-Christian movements like the Black Muslims and the Black Jews.[58]

The slaves also did see some difference between God and Jesus Christ. Consequently, Long admits that to the extent blacks have believed in Christianity, language about the Trinity has appeared. However, for African Americans, the Trinity became real not in dogma and doctrine, but in their practice of religion on a daily basis. The slaves simply experienced Jesus as another form of God and not as the abstract second person of the Trinity. Particularly in biblical stories, Christ acted in various ways which helped the slaves to survive. For them, the Christ of the Bible became a "fellow sufferer," a "little child," a "companion," and a "[person] who understands." Long cites the essence of Jesus' religious structure in Jesus' role of companion and creator, "a deity related more to the human condition than deities of the sky, and the subjection of this deity to death at the hands of men."[59]

Also reflecting Wilmore's concern, the image and historical reality of Africa make up Long's final source. Admittedly, the slave masters' brutal actions during slavery did splinter and thus affect adversely whatever cultural forms Africans brought with them from their home continent. Yet, Long states, one cannot overlook the ebbing and flowing of the image and historical reality of Africa within the religious consciousness of black America since its creation. More specifically, the image and the reality have manifested themselves in black dance, music, and political theory. Thus, part of black folk's Ultimate Concern is the feeling of not having a real home. On the one hand, African American existence is an American existence, suggests Long. On the other hand, being black in the world (in America) means being forced from one's original home in Africa and then trying to set up a new home in the United States. This produces an instinctive yearning for a connectedness to the continent of Africa.

Long defines an Africanism as a kind of orientation toward and way of looking at reality. He claims that this method of grasping and looking at reality has probably carried over from Africa to black America. Africans

---

58. Ibid., 63–64.
59. Ibid., 64 n. 15.

touched the New World shores with religious beliefs and rituals. They were not empty heads, or without imagination. Despite white acts of cruelty in breaking up families and forbidding the speaking of African languages—all aimed at cultural domination—the structure of viewing the world, on which African languages thrived, continued to exist. Since Long describes religion as orientation toward one's Ultimate Concern in life, black people's African understanding of the world implies religious importance. For example, though West Africa includes different peoples and languages, underneath this difference lies a structural unity revealed in religious and language forms. Because a great majority of American slaves originated in West Africa, the attempt to stop them from talking in their own African languages and cultural styles did not necessarily mean they lost the religious structural unity they brought with them from Africa. Long mentions the example of shout songs on the part of slaves, their secret "conjuring" meetings, and the continued presence of African rhythm and dance in American culture.[60]

However, the major area of Africanism study, for Long, appears to be the religious implications of the image of Africa in the minds of slaves. Even if the slave could not directly remember Africa, the imprint of Africa's image stuck as a place of historical departure. Brutally removed from their homeland, Africans still maintained an unconscious or conscious memory of Africa, which stood for their beginning, like a form of creation. Theologically, the image of Africa presents these questions for Long: Does the forced removal of black folk from their homeland indicate a peculiar divine intent with strategic implications? This question is somewhat similar to the Hebrews' traveling in the wilderness on the way to Canaan. Are African Americans on the way to a land of milk and honey? Are they to reconnect to their sisters and brothers on the Continent to share their God-ordained freedom? Or perhaps, as a typification of God's purpose on earth, are they to bear the burden of taking the lead and changing American society into what God has created all humankind to become—that is, to overcome the tower of Babel cultural wars and establish the harmonious unity of diverse American cultures "speaking in tongues" about the same God? Long's exploration of the image and history of Africa opens up further religious avenues filled with theological possibilities.

Long's religious and historical image structure of Africa in black religious consciousness also touches on "eschatological hope" for black Americans (that is, the future and long-term hope). The religious value of Africa is such that it is unnecessary to actually return to beginnings, in the sense of massive pan-African migration. Yet, a clear imprint of Africa in the

---

60. Ibid., 56–58.

religious consciousness could provide a foundation for the future of African American freedom. The knowledge that God created a black lineage from a definite land could imply that the movement toward independence and wholeness in Africa has a direct link to black America. Just as God moves in mysterious ways in African liberation, cannot and will not God move in a similar manner by giving freedom to the same blood and flesh of Africans in America? Africa might be the model for African American liberation.[61]

Understanding what Long sees as the target of liberation helps us appreciate his goal of liberation. Long charges European Americans with executing a second creation in the case of black communities in America. "The oppressed must deal with . . . the fictive truth of their status as expressed by the oppressors, that is, their second creation."[62] The West forged black America out of the West's own history and language. To begin with, Africa's descendants would not be in the United States, asserts Long, if Europeans had not brought them here. Since Africans' arrival, whites have continued defining what it means to be black in white America. The dominant America, then, used its cultural language, its way of looking at reality, and its practice of religion to make blacks invisible. Referencing European conquest of African slaves (and Native Americans), Long asserts, "The economic and military conquest was accomplished, but another conquest more subtle and with even longer-lasting effects had taken place. This was the linguistic conquest."[63]

Within the conquest of language, theology is an oppressive system that prevents black people from having authentic cultural meaning. Usually, theology functions like an imperialistic language system. Along with Christianity, it superimposes itself upon preexisting religious structures. When it arrives in a country or community for the first time, it smothers other religions that were already in place before the arrival of Christianity.

The artificial, second creation by European cultural practices comes after the first creation, the work of God. Thus the African American people's struggle for liberation has been to reaffirm its truth and autonomy given in the first creation. In a sense, black liberation resides in black people renaming themselves in accord with the first creation. Admittedly, they cannot literally return to the beginnings. Therefore liberation, in the

---

61. For his views and suggestions on Africanism, see Charles H. Long, "A New Look at American Religion," *Anglican Theological Review Supplementary Series 1* (July 1973): 122; and Long, "Perspectives for a Study," 57–59.

62. Long, *Significations*, 170. Long also elaborated similar points in my interview with him.

63. Ibid., 106.

long term, should bring about a third creation—God's new creation of a new humanity.[64]

Liberation will come with a new language, Long reasons, not merely in regard to its content and semantics, but in the essence of its structure, rhythm, and texture. A liberative language helps humanity to become human in the world. For instance, because of the physical restrictions of slavery, Africans had to imagine and carry out actions of change mainly in the religious consciousness. Thus, the location of new language has to be situated in the religious consciousness, which is the orientation toward Ultimate Concern.

In addition to liberation in new language and the religious consciousness, African Americans' fight for their God-created humanity takes the form of validating cultural identity. Long asserts, "A great deal of the fight for human rights [by African Americans] is not only economic but a fight for the legitimation of Black cultural forms—those that have survived from Africa and those created in America."[65]

Long indicates that Christ plays a role in this move toward legitimation. Denied cultural forms of identity, the black theologian has heard the voice of Christ speaking to the cultural and psychological identity issue. Thus Christ's identity with the black reality provides a way out of cultural chaos.

Part of correcting the cultural identity chaos entails a return to the African American past, a need for an intellectual and cultural investigation. Long calls for a project to clarify the meanings of "those strange, profound, comical and sober deposits of [black folk's] past." This effort has major implications. If we fail to interpret those parts of black history, then it means perpetual slavery. Therefore, those deposits "must be vindicated or we shall never be free."[66]

Pursuing his liberation in cultural identity, Long has proposed that a study be undertaken of the interrelatedness of different religious traditions in the United States. In the dialogue, each tradition would hold equal status with no one assuming "the normative structure of discourse." Culture would be the focal topic of the investigation, and the participants would use a "hermeneutic of deciphering." The result of such an equal give-and-take might reveal a new, genuine structure of religious meaning for America.[67]

---

64. Charles H. Long, "The Black Reality: Toward a Theology of Freedom," *Criterion* 8 (spring–summer 1969): 6. Long points out the possibility of liberation for the larger humanity coming through the "otherness" in the black community.

65. Charles H. Long, "Structural Similarities and Dissimilarities in Black and African Theologies," *Journal of Religious Thought* 32 (fall–winter 1975): 16–17.

66. Ibid., 24.

67. Charles H. Long, "New Space, New Time: Disjunctions and Context for New World Religions," *Criterion* 24 (winter 1985): 7.

Remembering Long's description of language possessing its own materiality, one can see how an important conversation created from equality and
liberation affects and effects a new religious relation among America's cultural distinctions. Because language is real, then different people sharing
their languages equally means we are moving closer to equal social relations among all peoples.

Conclusion

Black theology of liberation began between 1966 and 1969. One can argue
that one of its greatest contributions to all theologies is that it initiated
a systematic investigation of the gospel as liberation for the oppressed.
However, within this common-faith agenda, disparate voices have sought to
live out nuanced vocational perspectives. James H. Cone, J. Deotis Roberts,
Gayraud S. Wilmore, and Charles H. Long exemplify the founders or first
generation of black theologians. Since 1966, their message has continued
to reverberate and deepen. Today, in addition to the intellectual presences
of these founders and their peer group, a second generation of black male
scholars and an entirely new, but related, vocational movement has arisen
with womanist theology—the Christian writings and witness of black
women. With the ongoing dynamic of black theology, fostered by its scholarly and church work, black theology of liberation appears to be not only a
twentieth-century Christian theology, but one that will continue well into
the new millennium.

Response to Professor Hopkins

Eugene England

I BELIEVE THAT MORMON THOUGHT AND black theology confirm each other
in important ways and can contribute significantly to each other through
dialogue, but black theology also seems to me to *rebuke* Mormon popular
theology and behavior in three major ways—all indirectly, of course. First,
it can remind Mormons that our religion, if we include the large mass of
unofficial sermons, writings, jokes, folk-tales, actions, opinions, and other
expressions of Mormon people, has been at best self-contradictory about
race and at worst openly racist. Mormons at various times have excused and
even contributed directly to the oppression of black people and the poor

in America that eventually gave rise to the Civil Rights and Black Power movements and to black theology. And black theology can remind us that, despite the ending of all official discrimination in 1978, Mormons have not yet, either officially or unofficially, clearly repudiated the racist theology and popular beliefs that grew up as rationales for that discrimination.

We have celebrated the twentieth anniversary of the remarkable revelation ending the official denial of priesthood and temple privileges to blacks, which was announced by President Spencer W. Kimball on June 9, 1978, and which most of us received with such jubilation that we can remember exactly what we were doing when we got the joyful news. This is a good time to remind ourselves that many Mormons are still in denial about that ban, unwilling to talk in Church settings about it, and that some Mormons still believe that blacks, as well as other colored people, come color-coded into the world, their lineage and even their class a direct indication of failures in a previous life.

The Book of Mormon, published in 1830 when the Church was organized, announced unequivocally that "all are alike unto God . . . black and white" (2 Nephi 26:33) and that "every man that is cursed bring(s) upon *himself* his own condemnation" (Alma 3:19; emphasis added). At that time, very few American whites, if any, believed those claims, but Joseph Smith spoke and acted consistently with them until his assassination in 1844. Evidence clearly indicates that Joseph anticipated sending missionaries to Africa and welcoming blacks into the Kirtland and Nauvoo temples, that he took a strong stand against slavery from early 1842, especially in his 1844 campaign for the U.S. presidency (where he proposed compensating all slave-owners over a period of six years), and that he consistently advocated "equal Rights" for all Americans, specifically what he called "national equalization" for freed slaves.[68]

However, Mormon publications equivocated when the Church came under threat of violence as being "Abolitionist" in Missouri in the early 1830s.[69] Many Mormon converts from the South kept their slaves and indeed took them West with them (where Utah became the only Western territory that allowed slavery). By 1852 at the latest blacks were specifically denied the priesthood and temple blessings. The slaveholders' theology that claimed blacks were descended from Cain through Ham and were subject to "natural

68. See Lester E. Bush, "Mormonism's Negro Doctrine: An Historical Overview," *Dialogue: A Journal of Mormon Thought* 8 (summer 1973): 13, 16–20, 22.

69. See Joseph Smith Jr., *History of the Church of Jesus Christ of Latter-day Saints*, ed. B. H. Roberts, 2d ed., rev., 7 vols. (Salt Lake City: Deseret, 1971), 3:xxii–xxvii (hereafter cited as *History of the Church*).

servitude"[70] was expressed by Mormon leaders and publications, and indeed from then on Mormons were generally in line with predominant American attitudes and practices concerning race.[71] In the twentieth century speculation by Mormons that blacks were being punished for some sin committed before they came to earth gradually gained in popularity and was extended to other races. When I was growing up in the 1940s and 50s in Utah, I was a racist in what appeared to be a thoroughly racist society. In the 1960s, as the forces that produced black theology—the Civil Rights and Black Power movements—gained in strength, there was criticism, both from without and within the Church, of the priesthood ban and racist Mormon teachings, criticism that produced its own apologetic theological response by white Mormon writers. In 1960 John J. Stewart published *Mormonism and the Negro*[72] and in 1967 John Lewis Lund published *The Church and the Negro*.[73] Both books approvingly reviewed the Cain and Ham theology. They also asserted unequivocally that "the Priesthood . . . is denied to the Negroes because of their behavior in the pre-mortal existence"[74] and not only that but *all* races and conditions of birth are determined by "conduct in a life before this"—using an analogy with our being "punished" in the life after this according to our conduct now.[75] These books were so popular as to be reprinted, especially Stewart's, which was reissued in 1964 and 1967 and even published again in 1978, *after* the priesthood ban was lifted.

Thus, in a tragic case of the tail wagging the dog, a Church *practice* was made on the basis of a racist popular *theology*—even though many thought the practice to be historical and sociological in origin and therefore temporary, as it in fact proved ultimately to be. President Kimball told the press after the 1978 revelation that the revelation came at this time because conditions and people have changed. "It's a different world than it was twenty or

70. See David M. Goldberg, *The Curse of Ham: Race and Slavery in Early Judaism, Christianity, and Islam* (Princeton: Princeton University Press, 2003), and Stephen R. Haynes, *Noah's Curse: The Biblical Justifications of American Slavery* (Oxford: Oxford University Press, 2002), both reviewed in a review essay by Stirling Adams in *BYU Studies* 44, no. 1 (2005): 157–69.

71. See Brigham Young, in *Journal of Discourses*, 26 vols. (Liverpool: F. D. Richards, 1855–86), 2:184–85; 7:290–91; and 10:110–11. See also Bush, "Mormonism's Negro Doctrine," 22–39. See generally Armand L. Mauss, *All Abraham's Children: Changing Mormon Conceptions of Race and Lineage* (Urbana: University of Illinois Press, 2003), reviewed by Cardell K. Jacobson in *BYU Studies* 45, no. 2 (2006): 163–66.

72. John J. Stewart, *Mormonism and the Negro* (Orem, Utah: Bookmark, 1960).

73. John Lewis Lund, *The Church and the Negro* (n.p., 1967). In the preface, Lund states, "It is not the author's privilege, prerogative or intention to speak for The Church of Jesus Christ of Latter-day Saints, often referred to as the Mormon Church."

74. Lund, *Church and the Negro*, 108–9.

75. Stewart, *Mormonism and the Negro*, 28,

twenty-five years ago. The world is ready for it."[76] But, as is too often the case, we Mormons didn't all follow the prophet and continued to believe the racist theology, even though the practice that gave rise to it had ended—and even though it contradicted central Mormon doctrinal principles.

For instance, the scriptures and common sense suggest clearly that each of us is punished solely for our own sins, not through lineage, that no one is punished for a sin he does not know about and have opportunity to repent of, and that the analogy of being judged as we come into this life just as we will into the next is false because, in fact, as we move from here into the next life we are *not* punished or rewarded by God but simply continue to *be* what we *are* (celestial, telestial, or whatever) and can act and associate accordingly. In other words, the best way to judge what any person was like in a previous life is, to paraphrase Martin Luther King, by the nature of their character, not the color of their skin. However, that racist theology became a basis for perverting more important principles like free agency, even for imagining *God* as a racist—partial, a respecter of persons, punishing his children for lagging in a "lap" of the eternal race with extra handicaps of skin color and poverty in the next.

Of course, there was opposition to that influential popular theology that denied agency and made God into a racist—a sort of Mormon theology of liberation if you will. In 1970, Stephen Taggart published *Mormonism's Negro Policy: Social and Historical Origins*, which thoroughly discredited the Cain-Ham theology and attempted to show that "God did not place a curse on the Negro . . . his white children did."[77] In 1973, *Dialogue: A Journal of Mormon Thought* published Lester E. Bush's more thorough and reliable study, "Mormonism's Negro Doctrine: An Historical Overview,"[78] with responses by Hugh Nibley and myself. Nibley recommended much more thorough study and discussion of the issues as a "prelude" to revelation,[79] and I argued, using the evidence Bush had uncovered, that the ban was indeed a "practice," with no scriptural or doctrinal support (that is, neither provided a basis for believing in some kind of ontological difference between races).[80]

---

76. "Not for Women," *Deseret News*, June 13, 1978, quoted in John J. Stewart, *Mormonism and the Negro*, 4th ed. (Bountiful, Utah: Horizon, 1978). For a most insightful, personal history of the 1978 revelation on the priesthood, see Edward L. Kimball, *Lengthen Your Stride: The Presidency of Spencer W. Kimball* (Salt Lake City: Deseret, 2005), 195–245.

77. Stephen Taggart, *Mormonism's Negro Policy: Social and Historical Origins* (Salt Lake City: University of Utah Press, 1970), 81.

78. Bush, "Mormonism's Negro Doctrine," 11–68.

79. Hugh Nibley, "The Best Possible Test," *Dialogue* 8 (summer 1973): 73–77.

80. Eugene England, "The Mormon Cross," *Dialogue* 8 (summer 1973): 78–86.

I wrote that the practice, even if were "inspired" or at least "allowed" by God, was not because God was a racist but because *we* are, especially in America and as an inheritance of slavery. We were, I concluded, like the children of Israel in the desert, living, by God's sufferance but to his sorrow, a lower law. I pointed out that the policy did not apply to Asian and Pacific Island blacks, that it was already changing as we became less racist (with light-skinned blacks of unproven ancestry in Africa and Brazil receiving the priesthood), and predicted that it would be ended when we were ready to *accept* God's will in a way that would bless all his children, including us whites, whom I saw as being terribly harmed *ourselves*, both morally and spiritually, by the priesthood denial.[81] The most comprehensive effort towards such a Mormon theology of liberation so far is *Neither White nor Black: Mormon Scholars Confront the Race Issue in a Universal Church*,[82] edited by Armand Mauss and Lester Bush.

But there have been other resources, of the kind black theologians, following the lead of Gayraud S. Wilmore and Charles H. Long, have found in non-traditional sources like slave narratives, folklore and practices and preaching, black oral and written literature, etc. Black voices have been speaking to Mormons as well. The first were Alan Gerald Cherry's *It's You and Me Lord: My Experience as a Black Mormon*[83] and Mary Frances Sturlaugson's *A Soul So Rebellious*.[84] Both were converts before the priesthood revelation and talk frankly about their resistance to joining what they saw as a white racist Church and the problems they encountered in the Church, but they also express the mature, even heroic, ability of black Mormons from that period to separate the truth of the Gospel, which they were convinced of by the Holy Spirit, from the deficiencies in Mormon culture. In 1988 I collected narratives by blacks from Africa for my book *Converted to Christ through the Book of Mormon*, which showed that, in addition to the explosive growth in black converts in Africa, similar to that in early Mormonism, these converts were having spiritual experiences and visions very similar in power and in content to those of early Latter-day Saints.[85] In the early 1990s Dale LeBaron collected more of such narratives, all from Africa, in *All Are Alike Unto God*[86] and Jessie Embry reported on

81. England, "Mormon Cross," 78–86.

82. Lester E. Bush and Armand Mauss, eds., *Neither White nor Black: Mormon Scholars Confront the Race Issue in a Universal Church* (Midvale, Utah: Signature, 1984).

83. Alan Gerald Cherry, *It's You and Me Lord: My Experience as a Black Mormon* (Provo, Utah: Trilogy Arts, 1970).

84. Mary Frances Sturlaugson, *A Soul So Rebellious* (Salt Lake City: Deseret, 1980).

85. Eugene England, *Converted to Christ through the Book of Mormon* (Salt Lake City: Deseret, 1989).

86. Dale LeBaron, *All are Alike unto God* (Salt Lake City: Bookcraft, 1990).

the extensive LDS Afro-American Oral History Project in *Black Saints in a White Church*. There, through both interviews and analysis, she explored in more complexity the black American Mormon experience, from those who joined before the revelation and were embittered by persecution to those who stayed faithful through spiritual conviction to those who joined after the revelation and have stayed faithful but feel they are not being used in Church leadership because of prejudice.[87]

The same year as Embry's book appeared, Elder Helvecio Martins published his autobiography, giving us in moving detail the life of the black Brazilian who joined the Church in 1972, became a leader without priesthood and friend of President Kimball and eventually a General Authority—and is perhaps the one human being most directly responsible for the yearning prayers of President Kimball that led to the priesthood revelation.[88] Fictional literature about the black experience has been very scant, but in 1995 Scott Livingston's play, *Free at Last!*, which deals very honestly with the experience of a black coming into the Church and meeting racist Mormons just before the priesthood revelation, was performed at BYU, in the Margetts Theater. The largely black cast decided to have open discussions with the audience after each performance, and those turned into a remarkable form of guerrilla theater, where Mormons talked openly about racism, racist theology, and black experience in the Church. These resources need to be studied more carefully by Mormon thinkers, who could use the insights of black theologians on related issues to help develop their own theology of liberation.

Dwight Hopkins makes clear that the "father" of black theology, James H. Cone, not only focuses on the poor and on Christ's work in liberating the victims of oppression and racism, but that "in this liberation process the oppressors also gain their freedom because the object of their oppression—the now freed poor—no longer occupies an oppressed status."[89] It is clear in scripture that a central quality of God is that he is impartial— "no respecter of persons"—and that a chief evidence that one has truly come to Christ (even a *requirement* for fully experiencing the Atonement and being saved, as I will discuss more fully later) is that all economic, class, and racial distinctions are done away. In other words, oppression, including racism, is a major *sin*, from which we must be saved.

---

87. Jessie Embry, *Black Saints in a White Church* (Salt Lake City: Signature, 1994), reviewed by Marcus Helvecio T. Martins in *BYU Studies* 36, no. 2 (1997): 255–60.

88. Helvecio Martins with Mark Grover, *The Autobiography of Elder Helvecio Martins* (Salt Lake City: Aspen, 1994).

89. Dwight N. Hopkins, *Black Theology USA and South Africa: Politics, Culture, and Liberation* (Maryknoll, N.Y.: Orbis, 1989), 45.

The majority of Mormons were clearly still racists in the 1960s. One of the most humorous if not heart-breaking indications of this was the widespread elation felt by Mormon intellectuals when Mormon scholar Armand Mauss, in 1966, published in the *Pacific Sociological Review*, a comparative study of attitudes toward race in a variety of Mormon and other Christian congregations. His results showed that, despite all the publicity that had alleged, on the evidence of the priesthood ban, that Mormons were unusually racist, they were actually no more racist than other American Christians! Mauss himself took no comfort in his findings and spoke out strongly against the false racist theology.[90]

In the thirty years since then, much progress has been made and some reconciliation has been achieved—and it has occurred for white Mormons in much the way James H. Cone insisted any reconciliation must—by "coming to God through black people, the place where Jesus is leading a movement for freedom" (Hopkins, 352). Let me try to be so clear on this matter I cannot be misunderstood. We Mormons owe an enormous and as yet unexpressed debt of gratitude to black people for helping liberate us from false and destructive ideas about race, for saving our souls from the sins of racism and oppression, and for making possible the world-wide expansion and growth of the Church that we prize so much. The work of Martin Luther King and Malcolm X, as Hopkins explains in a chapter of his book, *Shoes That Fit Our Feet: Sources for a Constructive Black Theology*, though the two men seemed quite different, achieved a unified effect in the civil rights and Black Power movements that changed the world and provided the impetus and vision for continual future change.[91] Those movements, I believe, saved America from a violent revolution, gave political and cultural direction to African Americans of the kind black theology now describes and promotes, and permanently aroused the conscience of many American Christians, including Mormons.

That change in Mormons made possible the revelation of 1978 and that in turn made possible the explosive growth of Mormonism since, especially in nations of color. It made possible, in February 1998, the first visit of a Mormon prophet to black people in Africa and the announcement of a temple to be built in Accra, Ghana.[92] Mormonism recently passed the ten million mark and the point where half its members live outside the United States. In not many years, if present trends continue, over half the Church will be nonwhite and then, in a few more years, over half from the oppressed

90. Armand L. Mauss, "Mormonism and Secular Attitudes toward Negroes," *Pacific Sociological Review* 9 (fall 1966): 91–99.

91. Dwight N. Hopkins, *Shoes That Fit Our Feet: Sources for a Constructive Black Theology* (Maryknoll, N.Y.: Orbis, 1993), 170–206.

92. Editor's note: The temple in Accra, Ghana, was dedicated in January 2004.

classes throughout the world. If the predictions of non-Mormon scholars that the Church will reach 200 million of such mainly colored, oppressed peoples by the middle of the next century is fulfilled,[93] and if the Church is not just *big* but the true Zion community Joseph Smith envisioned, it will lead people not only to better private morality (freed from drugs and abuse and sexual sin) but also to greater social morality (freed from racism and sexism and economic oppression). If that happens, it will have made possible in good part by Martin and Malcolm and, yes, black theologians like Dwight Hopkins and Linda Thomas—as well as black Mormon heroes like Alan Cherry and Helvecio Martins.

However, work still needs to be done—perhaps in a "Mormon theology of liberation," because, though behavior has changed dramatically, the false ideas that were invented to rationalize racist practices are still with us. In his book *Tolerance*, published in 1993, Elder John K. Carmack, one of the Church's General Authorities, felt it necessary to say, "We do not believe that any nation, race, or culture is a lesser breed or inferior in God's eyes. Those who believe or teach such doctrine have no authority from either the Lord or his authorized servants."[94] Yet the 1997 reprinting of a popular theology reference book for Mormons continues to state, under "Races of Man," that all racial variation from the original race of Adam comes through "racial degeneration, resulting in differences in appearance and spiritual aptitude," invokes the Cain–Ham lineage to explain the black race, and asserts that the Lamanites, whom Mormons believe are among the ancestors of American Indians "received a dark skin and a degenerate status."[95] No wonder Elder Boyd K. Packer, speaking in 1987 concerning the Church's entry into third-world nations, exclaimed, "We can't move *there* with all the baggage we produce and carry *here*! We can't move with a 1947 Utah Church!"[96]

Now, let's turn to ways black theology *confirms* fundamental Mormon teachings and ideals. When I heard Dwight Hopkins speak, I first thought black theology sounded somewhat narrow—in both its subject matter (oppression) and its main audience (the oppressed). But as I listened and reflected I was convinced that Christ indeed came chiefly to liberate the

---

93. Rodney Stark, "So Far, So Good: A Brief Assessment of Mormon Membership Projections," *Review of Religious Research* 38 (December 1996): 179.

94. John K. Carmack, *Tolerance* (Salt Lake City: Bookcraft, 1993), 64.

95. Bruce R. McConkie, *Mormon Doctrine* (Salt Lake City: Bookcraft, 1997).

96. Boyd K. Packer, "Address to the Church Coordinating Committee Meeting," September 8, 1987, copy in library, Historical Department. Church of Jesus Christ of Latter-day Saints, Salt Lake City, UT; cited in Lee Copeland, "From Calcutta to Kaysville: Is Righteousness Color-coded?" *Dialogue: A Journal of Mormon Thought* 21 (fall 1988): 97.

oppressed and that that message is the chief one for us all, in our double roles as oppressed and oppressors. Black theology of liberation begins with Christ's very first announcement, in Nazareth, of his mission: "to preach the gospel to the poor . . . to preach deliverance to the captives, to set at liberty them that are bruised" (Luke 4:18). Mormon scriptures record that whenever a new dispensation of Christ's gospel opens, the response is a desire by the people who have faith to do away with economic, racial, and class distinctions. In the New Testament the newly converted faithful "sold their possessions and goods, and parted them to all men, as every man had need" (Acts 2:44) and learned that after genuine conversion "there is neither Jew nor Greek . . . bond nor free . . . male nor female: for ye are all one in Christ Jesus" (Gal. 3:28). Modern scriptures tell us that the ancient city of Enoch became righteous enough to be taken up into heaven "because they were of one heart and one mind . . . and there was no poor among them" (Moses 7:18) and when Jesus Christ appeared in America after his crucifixion and taught his Gospel there, the newly converted "had all things common among them; therefore there were not rich and poor, bond and free, but they were all made free" (4 Nephi 1:3).

Exactly the same impulse for liberation and equality moved the new converts to what Joseph Smith called restored Christianity in the 1830s: They learned right away that "black and white, bond and free, male and female . . . all are alike unto God" (2 Nephi 26:33) and that "it is not given that one man should possess that which is above another, wherefore the world lieth in sin" (D & C 49:20). The newly converted faithful yearned and tried mightily to live these ideals in the midst of a violently racist and exploitatively capitalistic American society. They practiced the Law of Consecration in Missouri, holding all things in common, covenanted to share all they had with the poor so they could make the trek West with them, and established fully communitarian United Orders throughout Utah territory. As Mormon historian Davis Bitton has shown, Mormon leaders "denounced exploitation of workers, profiteering by merchants, putting property and private interests before the public welfare, and expansionist warfare motivated by greed . . . [They] showed some sympathy for revolutions, preached something very close to the labor theory of value, and called for economic planning to further the common good."[97] In response to such ideals, the U.S. government nearly destroyed the Church, and it was forced to submit to federal power and moved into the accommodation to American political and economic practices that began in 1890.

However, that Zion ideal remains strong, not only ready to be put into literal large-scale practice in a *Church-directed economy* of equality when the

---

97. Davis Bitton, "Anti-intellectualism in Mormon History," *Dialogue: A Journal of Mormon Thought* 1 (fall 1966): 118, n. 20.

Lord so directs, but constantly reaffirmed as a temple covenant to be practiced *individually* right now. I've known Mormons, at all levels of income, who have lived modestly, with consciously restrained consumption, and, as their temple covenant of consecration requires, used *all* the resulting surplus to help others. They understand the clear (and never rescinded) command of the Lord, "In your temporal things you shall be equal, and this not grudgingly, otherwise the abundance of the manifestations of the Spirit will be withheld" (D&C 70:14; see 78:6), and they believe the assurance of the Lord that "the earth is full, and there is enough and to spare," that *force* by him or earthly governments will not bring equality because his children are "agents unto themselves" (D&C 104:17), so it must be done "in [his] own way." But these Mormons also accept the way the Lord says he has "decreed to provide" for equal distribution and an end to oppression: "the poor shall be exalted, in that the rich are made low . . . Therefore, if any man shall take of the abundance which I have made, and impart not his portion . . . unto the poor and needy, he shall, with the wicked, lift up his eyes in hell, being in torment" (D&C 104:17–18).

In describing the work of black theologian Charles H. Long, Hopkins tells of Long's ideal of genuine dialogue between different religious traditions in the United States, in which "different people sharing their languages equally means we are moving close to equal social relations among all peoples" (Hopkins, 370). I have been trying here to engage in such a dialogue, learning from the perspective and language and methods of black theology. Let me now attempt a couple of Mormon contributions, critical responses if you will. Black theologians speak of the need to reject "dominant white theology" and its language—both because of its historical errors and its tendency to support status quo oppression, but it seems to me a central error of traditional Christianity (white theology) was to assume that God created the world and his children out of nothing and is himself omnipotent, omnipresent, and omniscient. Those ideas and that language are not genuinely biblical but came into Christianity from Greek philosophy and were preserved in the creeds and became "traditional," with John Calvin providing the powerful arguments that such a God is wholly sovereign, that is, absolutely in control of history, social movements, and personal salvation. No matter how much liberal Protestants try to equivocate, the consequences seem to me to undermine our ability to fully trust God, to understand evil, and to have hope that human agents can truly do away with such things as oppression and racism. I see black theologians asking questions such as what God may have had in mind in allowing slavery—or allowing the continuing oppression of blacks, or what he may be planning for them to achieve as part of the future salvation of all the world, all apparently without questioning God's omnipotent sovereignty.

Mormonism teaches that God is genuinely related to us. Indeed, God is, in fact, a Divine Couple, a literal Father and Mother of our spirits, the same *kind* of beings we are—personal, with bodies, capable of genuine emotion, including weeping over us in our oppression and oppressiveness. We believe that we have existed coeternally with God in embryonic form and that all of us, whatever our race or condition, have the potential of eventually becoming like our divine Parents. This means that we have genuine agency, ability to choose, even *against* God's will, and that God *cannot* override our choices and simply do away with evil. He has knowledge and power beyond our imagining, including the power to save every one of us *if* we will let him, but not the power to prevent evils like slavery or to *use* us in inscrutable ways. Such a God, it seems to me, is able to attract our complete trust and hope. It is, I believe, the God that black folk and white folk intuitively tend to believe in—and that black theologians, attentive to the ideas and language of the oppressed, might well investigate more thoroughly in dialogue with Mormons.

We also might talk constructively about the danger of what still seems to me a rather narrow focus in "black theology" on victimage, especially *one's own* rights and *other people's* sins. One danger was revealed in the historical experience that led black women toward "womanist theology"—the discovery that white feminists, in their fight for liberation, could still be racist and that black men, in their right for liberation, could still be sexist. Christ seems to call us to a more universal sense of sin in everyone, *starting* with ourselves. He asks that we "resist not evil"—which I'm sure doesn't mean ignore social evil but perhaps that we fight it with careful attention to the danger of multiplying cycles of evil with revenge or any other form of evil, however "justified." We must find creative ways, as Paul writes, to "Be not overcome with evil, but overcome evil with good" (Rom. 12:21), because a quest for liberation can easily turn self-righteous, have its own blind spots, and even perpetuate oppression in new forms.

Now let me close with a more positive "contribution" for all of our thinking about oppression and our human tendency to reject the "other"—whether by class, race, or gender. Jesus not only began his ministry by announcing he was called "to the poor"; he ended it by asserting that when he comes to judge the world, to divide the "sheep form the goats," his *only* criterion will be whether we have actually done to the "least" of his brethren what we *think* we would do for him: "I was an hungered, and ye gave me meat . . . I was a stranger and ye took me in . . . in prison, and ye came unto me" (Matt. 25:35–36). Joseph Smith builds on this crucial understanding, which seems to me central to the project of "black theology," by teaching the *reasons* that overcoming classism and racism—any discrimination or failure to aid and free the oppressed—is not only a sinful denial of Christ's announced mission and damaging to society, but also interferes directly with the salvation of souls, both of the victims and the victimizers. The *Lectures on Faith* teach that "it is . . . necessary [to see] that [God] is no respecter of persons, for . . . [otherwise] men could not exercise faith in him . . . they could not tell what their privileges were, nor how far they were authorized to exercise faith in him, or whether they were authorized to do it at all, but all must be confusion."[98] This describes exactly how it must feel to be an oppressed person in a racist or sexist culture, supposedly being punished or limited in some way for something inherent in our nature or resulting from our conduct in a now forgotten pre-existent life with no way to repent of that "something" and no certainty about its effects on our future. By persisting in oppressive teachings and practices we are denying others—and ourselves—full access to Christ and his plan of redemption.

The Book of Mormon explains most fully *why* judgment and partiality to others rejects the process of salvation from sin through the Atonement of Christ and denies *ourselves* access to it (see Moroni 7, for example). The Atonement is an expression of unconditional love from God powerful enough move us, if we *accept* that love, to repent and be saved. If we are caught up in what the Book of Mormon calls "the bands of justice" in our relations with others—refusing unconditional love for others because they do not "deserve" it—we will refuse that love for ourselves, whom we know in our hearts are *also* not deserving. Even if we focus only on "justice" for the oppressed, we will lose sight of the mercy that makes Atonement possible—for others and ourselves. The Book of Mormon teaches us that in order to "retain a remission of [our] sins from day to day" (Mosiah 4:26) we must be focused on mercy and forgiveness—for others and ourselves. Specifically, we must be constantly engaged in imparting "our substance to the poor . . . such as feeding the hungry, clothing the naked, visiting the sick and administering to their relief, both spiritually and temporally, according to their wants" (Mosiah 4:26)—which is precisely what black theology tells us.

---

98. Joseph Smith Jr., comp., *Lectures on Faith* (Salt Lake City: Deseret, 1985), lecture 3.

Rejoinder

Dwight N. Hopkins

Eugene England has written a theologically thoughtful and faith-filled essay on the dialogue between Latter-day Saints and black theologians. It reflects a theology and a faith that makes a difference and has something at stake. Because of its nuance and complexity, I cannot respond to all of his claims, each of which is very important on its own. However, I will touch on some topics that may lead to further conversations.

First, I am struck by the depth of Eugene England's self-critique, offered both of the Latter-day Saints and for himself. It is rare to admit publicly previous white supremacist thought and practice that, to my knowledge, no other white or predominantly white institution, religious or otherwise, has undertaken in such a thorough and revealing manner. What it underscores is the character of the Latter-day Saints, at least as enunciated by Eugene England. The character of a group or of an individual more often than not says more about the person or organization than a thousand books could ever unveil. What strikes me is the character of self-critique and honesty. What does this self-interrogation as public theology say regarding honesty? The honesty of this particular self-critique reveals the ability to look at the facts about oneself, affirm the best of one's religious tradition, and embrace the evil in order to transform it. It is the ability to undergo vigorous public self-scrutiny, the ability to be open and release the toxicity of the past. In a word, it is the ability to progress beyond a self-interested concern for possible embarrassment and to speak the truth freely to the power of evil. This type of honesty is the substance and depth of liberation. Black theology is also about divine-human liberation; therefore, it encourages this dimension of the dialogue.

Black theology, in addition, shares other parallels with the Latter-day Saints. Both are minority religious communities in the United States. Both have been vilified (historically and currently) as sects, aberrations, heresies, affronts to the gospel of Jesus Christ, and/or provincial religious groups. Yet, the Latter-day Saints are one of the fastest growing religions in the United States. Black churches are also spreading in numbers and influence. This includes not only the historic black churches, but also individual black congregations in white denominations. Indeed, most of the dying churches in the United States are associated with the traditional white churches and their derivatives, brought to this continent by the Christian colonizers from Europe. Perhaps what will save these churches is yielding to the leadership of black, Latino, Asian American, and other minority congregations within their different denominations. Likewise, perhaps learning from the Latter-day

Saints could help in the salvation of these churches. Jesus came not for the status quo that aids a business-as-usual of privilege for certain races, even if this privileged group calls itself Christian. Jesus came from and to be with the margins and cursed of this earth. Black theology and Latter-day Saints have been "condemned" by the powers of the mainstream.

I was also struck by the occurrence of liberation themes in LDS tradition, especially when Eugene England cites the unique LDS testaments. And it is in the revelations and words found in such books as Moses and Nephi that we encounter texts that could be lifted directly from some of the standard black theology essays from 1966 to the present. Mainstream theologies and churches in the United States use all types of bodies of knowledge, a host of concerns, complex books and sermons, powerful and persuasive discourse that have the net effect of obscuring the basic fact that in America there is a small group of white families with wealth who control and set the direction for this country and the basic fact that Jesus came to participate in the liberation of the majority who lack wealth, racial, and gender privileges. It is my hope, just as in black theology, that scholars of the LDS church, in the spirit of Professor England's words, will continue to mine the shafts of LDS sources to discover more liberation witnesses in the Bible, sacred LDS texts, LDS church tradition, autobiographies, speeches, and folklore.

The texts utilized by Eugene England exhibit a forthright move to confront racism. In this move, liberation surfaces as a critical component. I think if we follow this line of argument and witness, we have to push further into the realm of gender relations for both black theology and LDS society. Not all black theologians are firm on the equality of women. I suspect that the case is similar in LDS circles. In other words, we must continue this vocation of racial equality with a vocation of gender equality. I can safely say that those black theologians who embrace the liberation of Jesus as the norm of all God-talk and God-walk wish to see the full creativity of God's gifts to women manifest in all levels of black theology and the Christian church. One cannot be against racism and, at the same time, not share wealth, resources, decision-making, and responsibilities with women. To be against anti-black racism and to be a sexist is contradictory. The wealth and resources of this earth belong to God, and we—black and white, female and male—are mere stewards in the divine "vineyard" of creation. Nothing belongs to us in the ultimate sense. So when a pattern continues to exist where some possess divine resources based on their race and gender and others are excluded because of their race and gender, one has to ask whether this is the spirit of God at play or some other spirit.

Again, let me push a little further. I want to know why there was a discrepancy in Joseph Smith's courageous belief and practice regarding black equality with white, on the one hand, and the wretched borrowing of pro-slavery theology by Latter-day Saints, on the other? I think there needs to be more investigation of this discrepancy. My own read of white power and negative affirmation action enjoyed by whites since the 1607 arrival of Anglicans in Jamestown, Virginia, and the 1620 arrival of Pilgrims in Massachusetts attests to the following. Perhaps the discrepancy is due to the power, wealth, resources, leadership, feelings of superiority, and white skin privileges enjoyed by white Latter-day Saints, both the slave owners and non–slave holders. Someone benefits from racism; and, it seems to me, that is why, in general terms, it is so difficult for white liberals and conservatives, of all faiths and persuasions, to overthrow the structure and system of white supremacy and privileges. Of course, all of us can point to instances of progress. But it is progress within the framework of a negative affirmative action for whites. It reminds me of how men point to "all the progress" women are making while these same men hold steady to the system and structure of male supremacy. I think that each man in the United States, if he honestly looked in his heart, knows that he benefits by virtue of his male gender. Likewise, I suspect the same for white Americans.

What is immediately and ultimately at stake in the dialogue between black theology and Latter-day Saints is to pursue the Way on earth of the New Commonwealth of a full and free divinely given humanity that God is ushering in. We both want to be faithful in that process. And I think the example of England's essay, beginning from his profound self-criticism to his biblical account of the final judgment, provides a forum for ongoing conversation. And black theology welcomes it.

About the Authors

Dwight N. Hopkins (Ph.D. Union Theological Seminary; Ph.D. University of Cape Town, South Africa) received a M.Div. and M.Phil from Union Theological Seminary. Hopkins is a constructive theologian working in the areas of contemporary models of theology, black theology, and liberation theologies. He has authored fourteen books on black theology and is coeditor, with Linda E. Thomas, of the Black Religion/Womanist Thought/Social Justice Book Series from MacMillan. He is a professor of theology at the University of Chicago Divinity School and is an ordained American Baptist Minister.

G. Eugene England (Ph.D. Stanford) did graduate work at MIT and received a M.A. from Stanford University. He founded *Dialogue: A Journal of Mormon Thought* and has shaped both the past and future of LDS writing through the Association for Mormon Letters, which he co-founded and has actively promoted. He taught Mormon Literature at Brigham Young University from 1977 to 1998 and was Writer in Residence at Utah Valley State College until his untimely passing in 2001.

A Dialogue on Myth Theology

Langdon Gilkey's Myth-Creative Liberal Theology: Synthesizing Tillich, Niebuhr, Schleiermacher, Ricoeur, Eliade, and Whitehead

Gary Dorrien

THE ABRUPT ENDING OF THE NEOORTHODOX ERA took an emerging generation of Protestant theologians by surprise. In the case of Langdon Gilkey, the downfall of a once-powerful neoorthodox establishment in the early 1960s became an occasion of creative dislocation. It drove him back, methodologically, to the experience-oriented theological liberalism of Friedrich Schleiermacher. It moved him to elaborate a considerably more expansive and synthetic theological vision than he originally sought, appropriating not only the theologies of his teachers, Paul Tillich and Reinhold Niebuhr, but also the religious thinking of Schleiermacher, Mircea Eliade, Paul Ricoeur, and Alfred North Whitehead. It also caused him to develop a myth-creative liberal theology that appropriated mythographic arguments from the history of religions and phenomenological and neoorthodox traditions, against the grain of the entire liberal tradition.

Theological Upheavals and Secular Consciousness

For more than forty years following World War I, twentieth-century Protestant theology was dominated by a small group of theologians that included, most notably, Karl Barth, Paul Tillich, Emil Brunner, Rudolf Bultmann, Reinhold Niebuhr, and Dietrich Bonhoeffer. Together they effected one of the most dramatic transformations of an inherited theological landscape in Christian history. Though all of them had good reasons for disputing the propriety of the labels that their critics and followers applied to them (especially the name "neoorthodoxy"), all of them except the martyred Bonhoeffer sought to extend the legacies of their work through their younger followers. In the early 1960s, a sizable generation of young theologians appeared to be well prepared to carry out this assignment.

Protestant theologians such as Gilkey, Jürgen Moltmann, Eberhard Jüngel, Schubert Ogden, John Macquarrie, Hermann Diem, Heinrich Ott, and William Hordern saw themselves as interpreters and refiners of the great theological systems of the past generation. Gilkey proposed to carry on the work of Tillich and Niebuhr. Moltmann's early impression was that Barth had already said everything worth saying. Jüngel was a straightforward Barthian, while Ogden and Macquarrie made cases for Bultmannian demythologizing and existential interpretation. Various others sought to mediate the differences between major figures. Diem proposed to mediate between Barth and Bultmann, while Ott sought a way-station between Barth and Bonhoeffer. Hordern defended a blended American-style neoorthodoxy that drew from Barth, Brunner, Niebuhr, and Tillich. A dominant school of Christian realists proposed to carry on Niebuhr's style of theological ethics. In 1965 Gilkey spoke for many of them in describing their generational self-understanding: "We saw ourselves a generation of 'scholastics' whose function would be to work out in greater detail the firm theological principles already forged for us." "We knew from our teachers what theology was, what its principles and starting point were, how to go about it."[1] Theology in the last third of the twentieth century would presumably synthesize and refine the Barth-to-Niebuhr theologies.

But this is not what happened. The neoorthodox/Christian realist continuum that Gilkey took for granted in his early career was blown apart in the 1960s by an explosion of liberation theologies that took little instruction from the dominant theologies of the previous generation. In his own way, and with mixed feelings, Gilkey contributed significantly to the downfall of American-style neoorthodoxy. Having established his early reputation as a celebrant of what he called "the unusual grace of neo-orthodox Christianity," in the early 1960s Gilkey increasingly doubted that so-called "neoorthodoxy" actually offered a coherent alternative to theological liberalism.[2] He asked the leaders of the neoorthodox Biblical Theology movement to explain what God had actually done in the "mighty historical acts"

---

1. Langdon Gilkey, "Dissolution and Reconstruction in Theology," *Christian Century* 82 (February 3, 1965): 135.

2. "Unusual grace" quote in Langdon Gilkey, "Neo-Orthodoxy," in *A Handbook of Christian Theology: Definition Essays on Concepts and Movements of Thought in Contemporary Protestantism*, ed. Marvin Halverson and Arthur A. Cohen (Cleveland: World, 1958), 259. For an example of Gilkey's early neo-orthodox theology, see Langdon Gilkey, *Maker of Heaven and Earth: A Study of the Christian Doctrine of Creation* (Garden City, N.Y.: Doubleday, 1959).

on which Biblical Theology was purportedly founded. This simple question had a stunningly deflating effect on the rhetoric and self-confidence of the neoorthodox biblical studies establishment. Gilkey judged that Biblical Theology was not biblical and not even intelligible as an alternative to liberal scholarship. Shortly afterward, James Barr demonstrated that Biblical Theology interpretations of Scripture were based on false semantic arguments and a contrived nonbiblical concept of history.[3]

Together, these critiques ended the Biblical Theology movement. An imposing intellectual and institutional superstructure collapsed virtually overnight. Gilkey later confessed that this turn of events was confusing, frightening, and embarrassing to him all at once. He had begun his theological career under the assumption that neoorthodox theology contained "universal value and truth." He had expected to spend his career refining the right blend of arguments from Brunner, Tillich, and Niebuhr. He had believed that these theological giants and the scripture scholarship of the Biblical Theology movement had already established the "solid ground" on which his own theological thinking could move forward. But this presumably solid ground had turned out to be shifting ice, he reported, and "as the weather has grown steadily warmer some of us have in horror found ourselves staring down into rushing depths of dark water." Gilkey later recalled that while he was certain that Niebuhr, in his prime, would have known how to respond to the post-neoorthodox theological situation, "I could find no handle with which to begin."[4]

Gilkey judged that the most telling symptom of this new theological situation was the existence of something that he called "God-is-Dead theology." It was he who announced the emergence of this rather novel theological movement in 1963. Though its leaders had never heard of each other until he drew attention to them, their writings did represent something worth naming. Theologians such as Paul van Buren, William Hamilton, Thomas J. J. Altizer, Richard Rubenstein, and others were calling for a secular theology that rejected every existing form of Christian or Jewish theism. They argued that religious thinkers were obliged to radically rethink the fundamental categories of Jewish and Christian faith in a "world come

---

3. Langdon Gilkey, "Cosmology, Ontology, and the Travail of Biblical Language," *Journal of Religion* 41 (July 1961): 194–205; James Barr, "The Multiplex Nature of the Old Testament Tradition," reprinted in James Barr, *Old and New in Interpretation: A Study of the Two Testaments* (New York: Harper and Row, 1966), 17–19; James Barr, "Revelation through History in the Old Testament and in Modern Theology," *Princeton Seminary Bulletin* 56 (1963): 4–14; and James Barr, *The Semantics of Biblical Language* (London: Oxford University Press, 1961).

4. Gilkey, "Dissolution and Reconstruction in Theology," 135; closing quote in Langdon Gilkey, *Gilkey on Tillich* (New York: Crossroad, 1990), xiii.

of age" that had outgrown its need for religion. Gilkey's announcement set off an explosion of position-taking in the mass media as well as hundreds of sermons by defensive clerics. If theologians didn't believe in God, how could Christianity survive? Did the spectacle of atheist theologians prefigure the disintegration of American religion and culture?

At the height of a prolonged media controversy over the question of God's demise, the secular theologians began to realize that they had little in common. The differences between Hamilton's Feuerbachian humanism, van Buren's commitment to verificationist language analysis, Altizer's ecstatic Nietzschean romanticism, and Rubenstein's post-Holocaust Jewish paganism were too great to sustain Gilkey's claim that they were leaders of any kind of movement. Some of the polemics against them must have made some of them regret Gilkey's role in instigating their Warholian fifteen minutes.

Gilkey's Response to Secularism

Long after the controversy over God-is-Dead theology subsided, Gilkey persisted in taking it seriously. In different ways, the radical theologians insisted that there is no credible basis for affirming the existence of the God of Judeo-Christian theism. Some of them drew inspiration from the later writings of Dietrich Bonhoeffer, who, from his Nazi prison cell in the closing years of World War II, proclaimed that only a religionless Christianity could have any meaning in a world come of age. As Gilkey remarked, the challenge of the secular theologians was to call into question "the reality of God, and so the possibility of meaningful talk about him." Gilkey's major work of this period addressed the challenge of contemporary anti-theistic theology and set the stage for Gilkey's theological alternative.[5]

Naming the Whirlwind: The Renewal of God-Language was Gilkey's prolegomena to any future theology. It was not a work of constructive theology, but a prolegomenal work that sought to demonstrate the meaningfulness of religious language under the conditions of what he called the reigning "secular mood." In Gilkey's view, the secular mood was not a philosophy, but the prerational disposition and cultural background out of which all modern philosophies have arisen. It was characterized by distinctively modern ways of thinking about contingency, relativity, temporality, and autonomy. To the secularized consciousness, he observed, such religious

---

5. See Dietrich Bonhoeffer, *Letters and Papers from Prison,* ed. Eberhard Bethge (New York: Macmillan, 1971), 277–82; Langdon B. Gilkey, "A New Linguistic Madness," in *New Theology No. 2,* ed. Martin E. Marty and Dean G. Peerman (New York: Macmillan, 1965), 39–49; and Langdon Gilkey, *Naming the Whirlwind: The Renewal of God-Language* (Indianapolis: Bobbs-Merrill, 1969), 5.

notions as transcendence, providence, and divine order are simply unreal; secular "reality" is grounded in the immediate dictates of experience and the institutional social constructions produced by experience.

To take the triumph of secular consciousness seriously is to rule out the option of basing theology on any appeal to revelation or any metaphysical system, Gilkey asserted. The needed theology takes Schleiermacher's option of disclosing the meaning of religious language through an analysis of ordinary life experience, this time by developing a hermeneutical phenomenology of experience.[6] In the manner of the early Heidegger, he proposed that the hidden religious dimension of human existence can be uncovered by pursuing a phenomenological interpretation of ordinary (secular) experience. Unlike Husserl's phenomenology, it did not claim to uncover the eternal necessary forms apparent to consciousness, but only the latent meanings or implicit structures of ordinary experience. Unlike Heidegger, on the other hand, Gilkey's work was not concerned with uncovering the ontological structures of human existence, but only with disclosing experiences of ultimacy as aspects of ordinary existence.[7] Put differently, it conducted an "ontic" rather than an ontological analysis. Building on the distinction in analytical philosophy between meaning (meaning as use value) and validity (verification through experience), *Naming the Whirlwind* generally excluded the question of validity or truth in theology.[8] Gilkey's concern was to demonstrate that, whatever the status of its truth claims may be, religious language is (or can be) meaningful. His opening section argued that the defining secular experiences of contingency, relativity, temporality, and autonomy cannot be adequately conceptualized or comprehended on purely secular grounds.

The point was to clear a space for theological reflection, but Gilkey cautioned that only a new kind of theology could meet the challenge of modern secularism. *Naming the Whirlwind* reviewed the past century of liberal and neoorthodox responses to the "secular thesis," arguing that the recent spate

---

6. Gilkey, *Naming the Whirlwind*, 20, 234.

7. See Edmund Husserl, *Ideas: General Introduction to Pure Phenomenology*, trans. W. R. Boyce Gibson (New York: Humanities, 1969); Martin Heidegger, *Being and Time*, trans. John Macquarrie and Edward Robinson (New York: Harper and Row, 1962); Martin Heidegger, *An Introduction to Metaphysics*, trans. Ralph Manheim (New Haven: Yale University Press, 1961); and Marvin Farber, *The Foundation of Phenomenology: Edmund Husserl and the Quest for a Rigorous Science of Philosophy* (Albany: State University of New York Press, 1943).

8. See Alice Ambrose, "Linguistic Approaches to Philosophical Problems," in *The Linguistic Turn: Recent Essays in Philosophical Method,* ed. Richard Rorty (Chicago: University of Chicago Press, 1967), 147–55; and A. J. Ayer, *Language, Truth and Logic* (London: Gollancz, 1946).

of death-of-God theologies was a product of the failure of modern theology to take the modern secular mood seriously enough. For all of their internal disagreements, he observed, theological liberalism and neoorthodoxy both assumed that human fulfillment is attainable only in relation to a total environment symbolized as "God." But the secular consciousness has no experience or conception of a divine ground. The only reality known to secular reason is that human life is left on its own to create whatever meaning it may find in a radically contingent cosmos. "The heart of modern secularity is that human experience, secular or religious, is devoid of relation beyond itself to any ground or order, and that there is no form of human thought that can by speculation come to know of such a ground or order," he remarked.[9] Having reached an apparently terminal stage in the process of secularization, the modernized consciousness is far more totalizing in its negation of the sacred than Schleiermacher imagined.

Liberal and neoorthodox theologies typically challenged the secular understanding of secular experience on either theological or metaphysical grounds, but Gilkey proposed to take secularity more seriously. He proposed to follow the lead of the death-of-God theologians without accepting their conclusions. Some of the radical theologians rejected God-language while trying to save Jesus as an object of religious discourse; others projected their personal experiences of nothingness onto the cosmos; all of them endorsed the secular understanding of secularity.[10] Gilkey countered that "Jesus without God" makes no sense as the basis for a credible theology and that most of the radical theologians overgeneralized their own experience. His alternative focused on the question of how secular experience should be understood.

A Phenomenological Approach to Ultimacy

The problem with the secular understanding of secular experience was that it could not provide the symbolic forms that are necessary to understand

9. Gilkey, *Naming the Whirlwind*, 188–90. See Langdon Gilkey, "Social and Intellectual Sources of Contemporary Protestant Theology in America," *Daedalus* 96 (winter 1967): 69–98.

10. See Thomas J. J. Altizer and William Hamilton, eds., *Radical Theology and the Death of God* (Indianapolis: Bobbs-Merrill, 1966); Thomas J. J. Altizer, *The Gospel of Christian Atheism* (Philadelphia: Westminster, 1966); William Hamilton, *The New Essence of Christianity* (New York: Association, 1961); Paul van Buren, *The Secular Meaning of the Gospel* (New York: Macmillan, 1963); Gabriel Vahanian, *The Death of God* (New York: G. Braziller, 1961); and Langdon Gilkey, "Secularism's Impact on Contemporary Theology," *Christianity and Crisis* (April 5, 1965), reprinted in C. W. Christian and Glenn R. Wittig, eds., *Radical Theology: Phase Two* (New York: Lippincott, 1967), 17–23.

its actual character. The death-of-God theologians were right to take the modern secular mood seriously, but wrong to endorse the secular understanding of modernity. Gilkey observed that secularism has interpreted human life as though it should be understood solely in terms of biology, chemistry, social environment, and other measurable finite forces. It has emphasized the contingency of human existence and dismissed all symbolic religious language as unintelligible. But there is a generative dimension of secular existence that is explicable only through the use of symbolic or mythological religious language, he argued. This is the dimension of ultimacy, the presence of unconditionedness in human life through which a self faces mortality and embraces its relative meanings. Built into every person's experience and world is a human-making dimension that transcends both selfhood and environment.[11] Paul Ricoeur maintained that religious symbols reveal an otherwise hidden dimension of human existence. If this claim is true, Gilkey proposed, it should be possible for a hermeneutical phenomenology to disclose the latent sacral elements of experience.

This project would not be merely an elaboration of Ricoeur's hermeneutical analysis. For Ricoeur, the work of hermeneutics was to uncover the meanings that religious symbols disclose about experience.[12] Gilkey rejected Ricoeur's Wittgensteinian assumption that language precedes experience. He observed that language is impossible without being, process, relatedness and experience. Because these ontological categories lie behind the possibility of language, he argued, a hermeneutic of "actual experience" is also possible. Gilkey did not claim that a phenomenological analysis can prove the existence of a dimension of ultimacy, because analysis can only disclose something and point to it, "it cannot prove that it is there." The establishment of a dimension of ultimacy by means of a phenomenology of experience thus "rests solely on our 'seeing' for ourselves that we do experience this dimension, that it does in fact appear in its strange way in the experience of all of us."

This dimension of ultimacy in human experience is the ground and limit of human being, he argued; it is the presupposition of all relative human thinking and acting. It is not what is seen "but the basis of seeing; not what is known as an object so much as the basis of knowing; not an

---

11. Gilkey, *Naming the Whirlwind*, 251–54; see Langdon Gilkey, "Unbelief and the Secular Spirit," in *The Presence and Absence of God*, ed. C. F. Mooney (New York: Fordham University Press, 1969), 50–68.

12. See Paul Ricoeur, *The Symbolism of Evil*, trans. Emerson Buchanan (New York: Harper and Row, 1967), especially 165: "What is myth if it is not gnosis? Once more we are brought back to the function of the symbol. The symbol, we have said, opens up and discloses a dimension of experience that, without it, would remain closed and hidden."

object of value, but the ground of valuing; not the thing before us, but the source of things; not the particular meanings that generate our life in the world, but the ultimate context within which these meanings necessarily subsist."[13] It is the reality of this dimension of human life that makes religious language meaningful and necessary.

Restricting himself to an ontic phenomenological description of human experience rather than an ontological analysis of the structures of being, he argued that the dimension of ultimacy manifests itself as the source or ground of being and as a recognition of fundamental human *limits*. As the ground or horizon of the given, it appears as the source of being; negatively, as the limit of the given it appears as the ultimate negation of being, the nihilating power of the Void. The dimension of ultimacy is also disclosed in the activity of knowing and as the source and basis of values; without it we have nothing. Since the loss of this dimension of unconditioned transcendence would eradicate all value, meaning and being, Gilkey observed, religious language appropriately refers to it as the realm of the sacred. The essential element of mystery within the sacred compels us to use religious language in talking about it. In every moment human beings depend upon and are threatened by the dimension of ultimacy within them. The experience of ultimacy is part of ordinary life, yet requires a different use of language than the discourse about measurable things spoken by science. In this crucial way, he argued, the language of modern secularity is too spiritually impoverished to account for the realities of secular experience.[14]

Naming the Whirlwind compiled ample phenomenological evidence for this thesis. Gilkey showed that some trace of ultimacy is perceptible in every experience of human creativity, thought, desire, and fear. He argued that it is disclosed in the experience of contingency as a nihilating unconditioned threat, as explicated in existentialism, modern literature, and psychology. It is disclosed in the desperate drive for unconditioned power or status acted out by achievers who want to guarantee their security. It is disclosed in the innumerable ways that people seek to achieve immortality or divert their attention from their awareness of mortality. In every conscious and unconscious effort to find an unconditioned answer to the nihilating power of the Void, human beings disclose the reality of ultimacy in their lives. Gilkey argued that religious language is meaningful as a "thematizing answer" to the question of how one might find love, meaning, and courage in the face of an otherwise coldly indifferent universe. Religious language is not rooted in any special experience or realm of history, but in ordinary human experiences that are interpreted "religiously" by one's primary spiritual community.

---

13. Gilkey, *Naming the Whirlwind*, 282, 296.
14. Ibid., 306–14.

"The mythical language of a community discloses to us the structures of ultimacy in which our community lives, and through these symbols the face of ultimacy manifests itself to us," Gilkey explained. "Thus particular symbolic forms, carried by a community and a tradition, are the essential media of each human apprehension of ultimacy and so of our creative answers to ultimate issues."[15] In each religious community or tradition, the manifestation of the community's experience of the sacred is symbolized in ways that distinctively define its identity. The way that each community or tradition interprets the appearance of the sacred is shaped by the character and structure of its symbols. But in each case, including Christianity, Gilkey cautioned, the *what* that is disclosed through the community's religious symbols is never the sacred by itself, but always the manifestation of the sacred in and through the finite. The *what* is never an unmediated object, but always relational to a given pattern of experiences and symbols.

Gilkey and Theological Liberalism

Schleiermacher had argued that any attempt to speak truthfully about God or God's self-disclosure "can only express God in his relation to us." It followed for him that any attributes that theology may ascribe to God "are to be taken as denoting not something special in God, but only something special in the manner in which the feeling of absolute dependence is to be related to him."[16] Gilkey adopted this approach in every respect, excepting its romanticism. Schleiermacher believed that religious symbols can be drawn out of feelings, but for Gilkey, even "feelings" or "experiences" were relational phenomena resulting from the interaction of symbols and life. Theological liberalism after Schleiermacher typically assumed that symbols are produced by experience, but Gilkey's perspective was informed by sociological and social-psychological theories that view "experience" as being shaped by the language, customs, and symbols of a given community.[17] In his view, Christian experience combined the forms of awareness that derive from our existential situation with the symbolic patterns or myths through which this situation is apprehended.

In *The Symbolism of Evil*, Ricoeur maintained that the key achievement of history of religions scholarship, especially as exemplified by Mircea

---

15. Ibid., 419.

16. Friedrich Schleiermacher, *The Christian Faith*, trans. H. R. Mackintosh and J. S. Stewart (Edinburgh: T. and T. Clark, 1928), 44–52, 194–200.

17. For example, Clifford Geertz, *The Interpretation of Cultures* (New York: Basic, 1973); George Herbert Mead, *Selected Writings* (Indianapolis: Bobbs-Merrill, 1964); Herbert Blumer, *Symbolic Interactionism: Perspective and Method* (Berkeley: University of California Press, 1986).

Eliade, is that it has uncovered the explanatory significance of myth through the process of dispensing with its explanatory pretensions. "For us, moderns, a myth is *only* a myth because we can no longer connect that time with the time of history as we write it, employing the critical method, nor can we connect mythical places with our geographical space," Ricoeur observed. By getting rid of the expectation that myths should convey factual information, however, history of religions scholarship has unveiled the explanatory significance of myth, which Ricoeur called its "symbolic function." The function of myth is to disclose with emotive power the bond between human beings and the sacred. The irony of modern religious studies is that in the process of demythologizing myth, Ricoeur noted, modern historical consciousness has uncovered the truth of myth and thus made myth "a dimension of modern thought."[18]

This argument informed all of Gilkey's work on the mythic dimensions of religious language from *Naming the Whirlwind* onward. He contended that the conventional modern understanding of myth as untrue fable makes the secular mind not only unable to understand religion, but also blind to its own mythic elements. For Gilkey, as for Ricoeur and Eliade, myth was a certain mode of language "whose elements are multivalent symbols, whose referent in some strange way is the transcendent or the sacred, and whose meanings concern the ultimate or existential issues of actual life and the questions of human and historical destiny." Understood in this way, religious language is essentially mythical, and the work of theology is to present "involved yet disciplined reflection" upon the mythical symbols of particular religious traditions.[19]

With all of its differences on other issues, the liberal tradition spoke with one voice in taking an essentially pejorative approach to myth. Those who first took seriously the problem of Christian myth took it for granted that myth belongs to a primitive stage of consciousness. Theological liberalism offered various strategies to adapt Christianity to an Enlightened myth-negating consciousness. This was what it meant for theology to be modern and progressive. Gilkey's approach to myth was closer to the myth-creative theorizing of his teachers, Tillich and Niebuhr, but both of them wrote as opponents of the liberal tradition.[20] Gilkey's novel blend of liberal and myth-affirming sources raised the possibility of a new kind of liberal theology. He

---

18. Ricoeur, *Symbolism of Evil*, 5.

19. Langdon Gilkey, "Modern Myth-Making and the Possibilities of Twentieth-Century Theology," in *Theology of Renewal*, ed. L. K. Shook, 2 vols. (Montreal: Palm, 1968), 1:283.

20. See especially Reinhold Niebuhr, "The Truth in Myths," in *The Nature of Religious Experience*, ed. J. S. Bixler (New York: Harper and Brothers, 1937), 117–35; Paul Tillich, *Dynamics of Faith* (New York: Harper and Brothers, 1957), 48–54; and

conceded that the prescientific cosmology and neo-Aristotelian metaphysics of traditional Christian theism present serious problems for modern theology, but he argued that the liberal and Bultmannian demythologizing strategies failed to address a deeper problem. The fundamental problem for modern theology is that the secular mind, while not recognizing its own mythical elements, is highly attuned to the mythic elements in *every form* of religious language and therefore rejects all religious beliefs as mythical. To the secular mind, Bultmann's kerygmatic existentialism sounds as strange and unreal as the Bible's prescientific cosmology. None of the various strategies to overcome or demythologize the mythic elements of Christianity make Christianity credible to the modern secular mind addressed by modern theology. In this situation, Gilkey judged, theologians must present a keener and more sympathetic interpretation of the explanatory significance of myth.

Historical, Linguistic, and Referential Implications of Ultimacy

Drawing upon Eliade's analysis of "primitive" and ancient forms of mythical language, Gilkey noted that the language of all premodern religious traditions expresses a particular mode of human self-understanding, "namely, one achieved through an experienced relation to the fundamental sacral structures of man's cosmic environment."[21] Unbroken myth proposes that a special quality of intimacy with sacral structures of space, time, nature, and history can be found and continually reexperienced by opening one's self to the reality of the sacred as disclosed through sacred symbols. These mythical forms offer a guide to the mysteries of life and death and provide models for the follower's personal and social life.[22] Myths shape the horizon of human experience by providing a conceptual structure for formative natural and social experience; they legitimate a community's relation to nature and its social structures; they help community members deal with pain and tragedy and give them grounds for hope that evil will be overcome; and they provide sources for moral reflection and judgment.[23]

Rudolf Bultmann, *New Testament and Mythology and Other Basic Writings,* trans. Schubert M. Ogden (Philadelphia: Fortress, 1984), 1–44.

21. Gilkey, "Modern Myth-Making," 286; reworked discussion in Langdon Gilkey, *Religion and the Scientific Future* (New York: Harper and Row, 1970), 66–67.

22. See Mircea Eliade, *A History of Religious Ideas,* vol. 1 of *From the Stone Age to the Eleusinian Mysteries,* trans. Willard R. Trask (Chicago: University of Chicago Press, 1978); Mircea Eliade, *The Sacred and the Profane: The Nature of Religion,* trans. Willard R. Trask (San Diego: Harcourt Brace, 1987); and Mircea Eliade, *Myth and Reality,* trans. Willard R. Trask (New York: Harper and Row, 1963).

23. Langdon Gilkey, *Catholicism Confronts Modernity: A Protestant View* (New York: Seabury, 1975), 86. See Langdon Gilkey, *Nature, Reality, and the Sacred: The Nexus of Science and Religion* (Minneapolis: Fortress, 1993), 17–33.

Multivalence is central to Gilkey's conception of myth. Mythical symbols do not refer only to finite objects, but also to the transcendent and unconditioned manifestations of the sacred in and through sacred symbols. Most ancient mythical forms are cosmogonic; they connect the sacred to the originating divine powers that created the world, and thus these mythical forms offer to reconcile or restore human beings to their original creation. Most of them also posit some notion of eternal return; they seek salvation from damnation, alienation, dissolution, or chaos through ritual re-enactment of the founding symbolic forms.[24] Gilkey observed that ancient myth is therefore invariably backward-looking. It presupposes a cyclical view of time and assumes that freedom is not fulfilled through creativity, but through one's participation in the ritual re-enactment of original forms given by the gods.[25]

Hebrew religion and Christianity embrace only parts of this ancient mythical structure. Gilkey noted that the Christian emphasis on linear history, historical revelation, the liberating power of the "new" in history, and the openness of the future to an eschatological end of history make Christianity very different from religions that sacralize a myth of eternal return. Early Christianity was strongly future-oriented and historical by comparison to backward-looking cosmogonic religions that presuppose a cyclical view of the structure of time.

But even in the forms that predated its later development of a sacramental cultus, early Christianity shared other mythical elements with ancient religion, especially the notion of divine reality as transcendent, creative, providential, and ordering. Gilkey cautioned that it is precisely these traditional mythic elements in Christianity that modern secular reason finds meaningless. The secular mind disbelieves in any transcendent or sacred reality within or beyond the physical world known to science. It has no sacral home in the cosmos, but "knows" that it has been thrown into a purposeless world in which human subjects are on their own to create their own meanings. It therefore celebrates the creative possibilities of human autonomy and disparages the repressive, communal, backward-looking spirit of the mythic imagination. The modern spirit is insistently anti-mythical, Gilkey explained: "It is of the essence of modernity to believe that myth is part of the infancy of man, to be outgrown in the scientific and autonomous age of modernity."[26]

The revealing and ironic contradiction in the secular mind's account of the world is that it invariably resorts to mythical language in expressing

---

24. Mircea Eliade, *The Myth of the Eternal Return: Or, Cosmos and History*, trans. Willard R. Trask (Princeton: Princeton University Press, 1974).

25. Gilkey, "Modern Myth-Making," 287.

26. Ibid., 290–91.

its "anti-mythical" worldview. The ideals of the self promoted by modern secular culture provide instructive examples. The rationalist image of the critical, scientific "man of reason" is a mythical construct, as is the "authentic" self of existential philosophy, the unrepressed and loving self of humanistic psychology, the liberal democratic self of civic humanism, and the pragmatic manager of business culture. These images of the ideal self are clearly different from each other, Gilkey noted, yet all of them are distinctively *modern* ideal-types with common mythical features. All of them assume that to understand something is to have power over it, since knowledge requires control over the objects of knowledge. Secular reason simply assumes that consciousness and knowledge should be used to transmute the (previously) blind determining force of consciousness into means by which human power over nature may be obtained.

Freedom and Morality

Modern secularists further assume that the realization of freedom is always a moral good, however differently this "good" is pictured among the various images of the ideal self. Gilkey observed that the secular mind always conceives freedom as being freedom *from* evil, not freedom *for* evil. In every modern secular mythology, the ideal self finds emancipation from its particular form of bondage through some transformation of consciousness. It is increased *awareness* of the dynamics that determine the self against its will that liberate the self to find its "true" identity. Secular reason resolves the problem of evil in the self's behavior through its various mythologies of awareness, for which evil is always located "outside of freedom." To the extent that the modern self has been liberated to become truly rational or authentic or loving or democratic or pragmatic or whatever, it is liberated from its former evil. "Fate and sin arise from beyond the inward center of man: in ignorance, in repression, in the false objectification of things, in prejudice and false ideals," Gilkey explained. Secular reason therefore trusts in faith that greater knowledge and awareness will make the world a better place. Evil in the world will decrease as people become more rational and gain greater control over nature and history.[27]

This is precisely the myth that Niebuhr demolished in *Moral Man and Immoral Society*. Following Niebuhr, Gilkey observed that the prospect of increased human control over nature is just as likely to imperil human freedom as to advance it. The modern secular predisposition is to view evil as a problem to be solved; secular reason therefore typically adopts an engineering or medical model of analysis in which the putative causes of evil are identified, isolated, controlled, and extinguished. To understand the factors

---

27. Ibid., 301–2.

that cause evil is to be able to extinguish it. "We really believe that if we know or are aware of everything, if we understand all relevant causes and factors, we can control everything," Gilkey remarked.[28] As Niebuhr repeatedly cautioned, however, this faith in the redemptive power of rationality ignores the immense possibilities for evil that the attainment of knowledge and power always holds.[29]

Because it problematizes the mystery of evil, secular reason typically embraces a false myth. Gilkey countered that the phenomenon of evil is a mystery of existence that infects human freedom, including the efforts of all who strive to gain power to eliminate evil. This truth of human experience is explicable only in the language of myth and symbol. Secular existence raises ultimate questions that only mythical language can thematize. Even the pursuit of scientific truth discloses traces of ultimacy, he noted, "in the eros or passion that supports its individual and social embodiments, in the role of global visions and of the theoretical structures that follow from them, and finally in the self-affirmation of the rational consciousness as knowing veridically in proximate judgments." These *human* aspects of science disclose a dimension of ultimate concern, "a relation to an unconditioned value, order, certainty, and being beyond our own making."[30] But when science is turned into scientism or positivist philosophy, its mythic elements must be shunned. Having set out to eliminate mythical reasoning, the secular mind tries to rationalize the mysteries of life and creates poor myths in the process.

Gilkey argued that the mythical discourse that is needed would be temporal, multivalent, and cognizant of its limitations. Theologically, it should emphasize process, history, and the dynamic character of divine reality as a corrective to the backward-looking static cosmogonic myths of ancient religion. It must be multivalent in its language, referring to the finite and to that which transcends the finite. As a mode of language that explicates concrete human experience, myth must speak to both the mystery of existence and the concrete life forms of historical existence. Gilkey frequently invoked Ricoeur's argument that while mythical language may refer to factual propositions, it does not properly assert, entail, or contain information.[31] As a multivalent mode of language, myth refers to both the finite and the transcendent, but its references to the finite must be understood to have no normative meaning as historical or scientific information.

28. Gilkey, *Religion and the Scientific Future*, 78.

29. See Reinhold Niebuhr, *Moral Man and Immoral Society: A Study in Ethics and Politics* (New York: Charles Scribner's Sons, 1947); Reinhold Niebuhr, *The Self and the Dramas of History* (New York: Charles Scribner's Sons, 1955).

30. Gilkey, *Religion and the Scientific Future*, 62.

31. Gilkey, *Catholicism Confronts Modernity*, 100.

In other words, mythical language necessarily refers to the finite as its medium of transcendence, but it does not provide information about the nature or character of the finite. "Revelation tells us of the God who manifests himself in nature and in the events of history, but not of the character of nature and what must have happened and when in that history," Gilkey explained.[32] The language forms of myth are always phenomenal, historical, and personal, but mythical meaning always points beyond these forms to a realm of transcendence.

The desire to understand is not the deepest need in human life. For this reason, Gilkey acknowledged that myth is not the first or even the most important element of religious experience. The origins of religion lie "in deep prereflective levels of awareness, 'prehensions' of the sacral forces on which man depends," he explained. Religion is the product of the interaction between these "prehensions" and humankind's deepest subjective responses to the world, "responses both of joy, gratitude, celebration, and confidence or hope on the one hand, and of anxiety, terror, despair, and guilt or remorse on the other."[33] The purpose of myth is to organize the totality of one's desires, environment, and social situation into a reflective form that makes sense of the world.

Modernity, Temporality, and Historical Transcendence

It follows that the purpose of theology is to explore reflectively the meaning and validity of mythical discourse. What makes modern theology distinctive in religious history is the fact that modern theologians know that their myths are myths. Theology no longer claims to be able to make indicative statements about matters of fact. It is only as broken myth that Christianity's mythical inheritance can be appropriated. Gilkey's reflections on this theme were singularly determinative for his post-neoorthodox thinking. More than any particular problem in theological method or interpretation, it was his deepening awareness of the novelty of modern theology that moved him to rethink his theological perspective. Contemporary theology must not content itself with using old categories and doctrines in modern ways, he insisted. It is not enough to claim some kind of continuity with classical Christianity, even if one uses the words of classical theology, because in the modern situation we understand these words differently. Modern people understand Christian myths to be mythical. What is therefore needed in theology, Gilkey urged, is a religious discourse that bridges the gap between religious experience and secular experience.

---

32. Gilkey, "Modern Myth-Making," 310. See Gilkey, *Nature, Reality, and the Sacred*, 150–53.

33. Gilkey, *Religion and the Scientific Future*, 103–4.

This is what Tillich and Bultmann sought to do. Gilkey judged that their preeminent influence in the 1940s and 1950s was attributable to this feature of their work. Tillich, Bultmann, and Niebuhr all sought to bridge the gap between Christian faith and modern secular experience.[34] Gilkey sought to build on their mediating work. Like his teachers, especially Tillich, he asserted that if theological language is to be made intelligible to the modern secular mind, it must look for the basis of its discourse in secular experience. *Naming the Whirlwind* (1969) uncovered the dimensions of ultimacy in personal, existential experience; *Religion and the Scientific Future* (1970) and *Nature, Reality, and the Sacred* (1993) looked for dimensions of ultimacy in cognitive experience, especially scientific inquiry; *Shantung Compound* (1966) and *Reaping the Whirlwind* (1976) found dimensions of ultimacy in social and historical existence; *Catholicism Confronts Modernity* (1975) and *Message and Existence* (1979) used the disclosure of ultimacy method to explicate Gilkey's constructive theology; *Society and the Sacred* (1981) and *Through the Tempest* (1991) looked for sacral dimensions in various aspects of modern culture.[35] As Gilkey explained in *Catholicism Confronts Modernity*, the burden of modern theology was to synthesize the myths, stories, and symbols of Christian experience with modern scientific and philosophical reason.[36] The influence of Niebuhr and Tillich over his pursuit of this project marked nearly every page of his work, but as Gilkey developed his constructive theology of history in the 1970s, he acquired a nearly equal debt to Whiteheadian process thought.

His prolonged effort to rethink the Christian doctrine of providence was crucial to this theological turn. For many years, Gilkey reflected on the religious meaning of his experience as a prisoner of war in a Japanese-controlled internment camp in China during World War II. For nearly as many years, he puzzled over the fact that modern theology had so little to say about providence. *Shantung Compound* described his wartime imprisonment and, especially, the insights about human nature, consciousness, and evil that he drew from this experience. The impact of his wartime experience upon his developing thought informed all of his theological work, especially his writing about the sacral dimensions of politics, destiny, and fate. In an early section of his dense, symphonic theology of history,

34. See especially Paul Tillich, *Theology of Culture* (New York: Oxford University Press, 1959); Reinhold Niebuhr, *Faith and History: A Comparison of Christian and Modern Views of History* (New York: Charles Scribner's Sons, 1949); and Rudolf Bultmann, *Jesus Christ and Mythology* (New York: Charles Scribner's Sons, 1958).

35. For a more comprehensive and detailed analysis of Gilkey's theological work, see Gary Dorrien, *The Word as True Myth: Interpreting Modern Theology* (Louisville: Westminster John Knox, 1997), 128–86.

36. Gilkey, *Catholicism Confronts Modernity*, 85.

Reaping the Whirlwind, he remarked that those who scorn the guardians of social order reveal that they have never been hungry or faced the prospect of anarchy. He admonished that because it is good to continue to live, the work of politics is good work; human life cannot flourish in the absence of stable social structures. At the same time, the anxieties that human beings rightfully hold about their security can easily become demonic, "and this concern for our being generates the peculiar intensity of political and economic conflict, as well as the dominance of these areas over other values of life."[37] Gilkey's major work of constructive theology offered a religious interpretation of the human historical struggle for survival and freedom. *Reaping the Whirlwind* reinterpreted the Christian understanding of divine providence in the light of modern historical consciousness and the ambiguities of modern social existence.

Tillich's theology of providence began with an ontology of history that posited the polarity of self and world as the basic structure of existence. His theological system interpreted the polarity of destiny and freedom as an element of the self/world structure.[38] Gilkey embraced Tillich's claim that an adequate theology of providence requires a grounding theory of historical being, but he believed that Tillich's categories of self and world were too static to account for the dynamism of history. The opening sentence of *Reaping the Whirlwind* declared that "change is basic in human experience and in the world that is experienced." Gilkey's theology of history sought to explicate the religious meaning of this truism by adopting the Whiteheadian dialectic of freedom and destiny. He proposed that the primary ontological structure of historical existence is not self and world, but actuality and possibility. History moves and is experienced in the interplay of freedom and destiny, bringing together the historical given with the actualization of new possibilities. The process dialectic of destiny-freedom not only provides a more dynamic understanding of the ontological structure of historical being, he explained, but also shows how this fundamental structure "entails its own deepest grounds."[39]

His implicit thesis was that history cannot be interpreted adequately by secular reason alone. A theological interpretation of the ultimate dimensions of historical existence is possible and necessary. Moreover, because

37. Langdon Gilkey, *Reaping the Whirlwind: A Christian Interpretation of History* (New York: Seabury, 1976), 48.

38. See Paul Tillich, *Systematic Theology,* 3 vols. (Chicago: University of Chicago Press, 1951), 1:79–81, 235–89.

39. Gilkey, *Reaping the Whirlwind,* 370. See Alfred North Whitehead, *Process and Reality: An Essay in Cosmology* (New York: Macmillan, 1929); Alfred North Whitehead, *Modes of Thought* (New York: Free, 1966); and Charles Hartshorne, *The Divine Relativity: A Social Conception of God* (New Haven: Yale University Press, 1976).

the inevitability of change raises deep existential and religious problems for human beings, this theological perspective must hold structure and process together, interpreting history through the dialectic of freedom and destiny. "It is in temporal man's movement into the new future, not in some frozen eternal moment, that the 'shock of non-being' largely occurs, and the questions of courage, wisdom, and justice are posed," Gilkey observed. The religious dimension of each future-entering person causes him or her to experience history as ultimate threat or ultimate promise. It is because of the dimension of ultimacy in historical experience that political existence "is at once filled with deep violence, cruelty and destruction, that it searches for ultimate meanings, that it is directed by ultimate moral judgments and buoyed up with ultimate hopes."[40] To be human is to be immersed in temporal change, he noted, yet it is also at the same time to transcend passage so that we may be aware of our temporality, know it, fear it, judge it, and shape its future.[41]

We make history by transcending the historical temporality in which we are immersed. This struggle for freedom and life has an inherently religious character. Gilkey argued that the crucial question for a theology of history is not whether the historical dialectic of destiny and freedom has a religious dimension, since this dimension of ultimacy is readily demonstrated. The crucial question is whether history has a unifying transcendent ground: "Is there such a principle or factor uniting past actuality and not-yet possibility, destiny and freedom in their widest scope, an ultimate creativity and sovereignty in history that makes intelligible the ultimate dimension or horizon of history and the quest for an ultimate order and a sacred norm?"[42]

Reaping the Whirlwind amplified Gilkey's theory of myth by laying the groundwork for his response to this question. Every theology or philosophy of history has a mythical character, he observed. Every interpretation of history as a whole tells a story about the relation of determining forces or destiny to freedom in a way that seeks to make sense of the known world. Moreover, every religious or philosophical attempt to account for the whole of history takes up questions about meaning, historical good and evil, and prospects for the future, as well as questions about the norms that should govern human existence. Orthodox Christianity, Enlightenment humanism,

---

40. Gilkey, *Reaping the Whirlwind,* 118-21.

41. This is also a major theme of transcendental Thomist theology, especially in the work of Karl Rahner. See Karl Rahner, *Spirit in the World,* trans. William Dych (New York: Herder and Herder, 1968); and Karl Rahner, *Foundations of Christian Faith: An Introduction to the Idea of Christianity,* trans. William Dych (New York: Seabury, 1978).

42. Gilkey, *Reaping the Whirlwind,* 122.

modern Progressivism, and Marxism are four prominent examples of myths that have provided the symbols that represent, in Tillichian terms, the "religious substance" of presently competing interpretations of history. "When we ask why the form of language we have called myths is not only appropriate to the interpretation of history but inevitably basic to all interpretations of history, cultural or theological, we encounter the dialectic of mystery and meaning in historical existence," Gilkey wrote, invoking a Niebuhrian theme.[43]

For Niebuhr, the fundamental task of a theology of history was to sort out and dialectically interrelate the ambiguous, paradoxical tangents of mystery and meaning that are constitutive of all historical experience. To regard meaning either as undialectically transcendent to historical passage or as totally immanent within it is to depart from what Niebuhr called the "biblical approach to history." Meaning is always constitutive of historical experience without being identical with or exhausted by experience.[44] Following Niebuhr, Gilkey affirmed that the biblical understanding of history is "based on a theologically formulated myth: a cluster of religious symbols concerned with the evident mystery—both transcendent and immanent, both of God and of man's freedom—in historical life in relation to its elusive and yet real meanings."[45]

Gilkey's normative response to the question of a unifying transcendent ground wedded the traditional Christian understanding of God as the source of all being to the process dialectic of destiny and freedom. He proposed that God should be understood as the source of being but that God's being should be conceptualized in terms of the process dialectic of achieved actuality and future possibility. Whitehead conceived divine reality as distinct from the more basic reality of creativity, but Gilkey argued that creativity should be understood as constitutive in the power of being that is God's being. "It is God as the power of being that carries forward the total destiny of the past into the present where it is actualized by freedom," he explained. "Creativity, the flux or élan of existence out of which in process thought each new occasion arises becomes, in other words, the power of being of God, the providential creativity of God that originates and sustains our continuing existence."[46]

43. Ibid., 151. See Tillich, *Theology of Culture*, 40–51.

44. See Reinhold Niebuhr, *Beyond Tragedy: Essays on the Christian Interpretation of History* (New York: Charles Scribner's Sons, 1951), 1–24; and Niebuhr, *Faith and History*, 103–37.

45. Gilkey, *Reaping the Whirlwind*, 151–53. See Niebuhr, *Faith and History*, 118–19; and Niebuhr, "The Truth in Myths," 133.

46. Gilkey, *Reaping the Whirlwind*, 249. See Langdon Gilkey, *Nature, Reality, and the Sacred*, 202–4.

As the creative power of being and source of our total existence, the divine being influences, through secondary causes, all self-actualizations of the present as well as the causal efficacy of the past upon the present. God does not ordain the form or content of destiny; the inheritance from the past which appears in the present as "the given" is always the product of human freedom and natural causation. "But the efficacy and so the continuing being of that achieved actuality, its power after having actualized itself to continue in being in order to become the presented destiny (the 'data') effective within the next event, and so a living aspect of that present actuality, this is the work of a power that transcends contingency and passage," Gilkey wrote. God is the power that makes the process of becoming possible. As the dynamic power that transcends contingency and temporality, God is the ground of the possibility of process and is therefore also the ground of the possibility of causation, order, and cognition. Gilkey argued that Christian theology should take from process thought the notion that God is in dynamic process, but he asserted that it must reject the Whiteheadian doctrine that God is therefore subject to process: "For process, if taken seriously, means the passing out of existence of what has been."[47] If the reality of the given world is to be affirmed, there must be a divine being whose power transcends the finite temporality of destiny and freedom. But if God is such a power, and thus the worthy object of Christian devotion, God must not be subject to passage.

Providence and Possibility

The core of Gilkey's understanding of divine providence derives from this argument that God "acts" in and through the secondary causes of destiny and freedom. He observed that the ontological dialectic of destiny, self-actualization, and undetermined possibility yields (and requires) the notion of God as the source and ground of becoming, actuality, and possibility. As the ground of the movement from the actual into the possible, God is the limiting and ordering source for future possibility. It followed that divine providence is "the sustaining and creating work of God within the ambiguity of historical life that leads to the divine eschatological fulfillment as the latter's presupposition and ground."[48]

In other words, Gilkey affirmed the liberal understanding of providence: God is the divine ground of all being that sustains the historical movement of being. But this conception of providence is not enough, he asserted. The crucial error of theological liberalism has been its tendency to interpret history solely in terms of the movement of freedom. Niebuhr's

---

47. Gilkey, *Reaping the Whirlwind*, 249.
48. Ibid., 253.

dialectic of sin stands as a judgment on all theologies that overemphasize providence. Niebuhr persistently warned that because evil is inextricably bound up with every good act and intention, the possibilities of evil grow with the possibilities of good.[49] Gilkey urged that for this reason, providence needs to be supplemented by redemption and eschatology. The crucial weakness shared by most forms of liberal and process theology is that they have not recognized that the persistence and pervasiveness of evil in history create a need for something "more" than providence. Christianity depends as much upon the redeeming work of Christ and the kingdom hope of eschatology as upon its faith in divine providence. As Augustine argued against Pelagius, freedom cannot be the determining ground of redemption because freedom shares in the corruption of a fallen humanity. For Gilkey, it followed that the same freedom that brings about the actualization of creative/divine possibilities in history must therefore *itself* be transformed by grace "if the possibilities of history are to be realized."[50] Without the redeeming work of Christ, freedom remains in estrangement, and the hope of a new age has no basis.

Gilkey's theology of providence thus retained the orthodox Protestant themes of preservation and concursus while rejecting the theme of governance. He argued that as a product (in part) of modern historical consciousness, modern theology requires an understanding of providence that eschews the sovereignty model of Protestant orthodoxy. God does not direct the wind or cause diseases to spread; neither does God direct our freedom or ordain us to will what we will. God makes process intelligible as the union of actuality and possibility in the present event of freedom. Yet Gilkey cautioned that human freedom and the openness of future possibility can exist only by virtue of God's self-limitation. Without a divine ground, the polarity of destiny and freedom would have no sustaining power, telos, or new possibilities; history would be meaningless. But without a divine power that is self-limiting, there would be no history at all; neither freedom or new possibilities would exist. Thus Gilkey argued that God acts in history through human freedom and is limited by human freedom.

The hope of the world is that providence and freedom will combine to create emancipating new possibilities in history. But because freedom is real, so is the possibility that freedom will be used to create even more evil forms of violence, exploitation, and oppression. As the power of being, God *preserves* the past by bringing it into the present as a factor that contributes to the continuity and order of life, but God's accompanying or *concurring* providence also "brings into being the present as self-determining in each

---

49. Niebuhr, *An Interpretation of Christian Ethics,* 60.
50. Gilkey, *Reaping the Whirlwind,* 266.

present."[51] God is the creative power of being through which the reality of each occasion arises and comes to be. Put differently, God is not only the ground of our freedom and destiny, but also the ground of our relevant possibilities. Gilkey explained elsewhere that God's creative providence is the "power of the continuing being of 'destiny,' the ground of our freedom, and the locus of possibilities to come."[52]

Reaping the Whirlwind thus presented answers to the theological problems of secularity described in *Naming the Whirlwind*. The four defining experiences of the modern spirit do not negate the possibility of a divine ground, Gilkey argued, but require it. Possibility can be real only if it is related to actuality, but it cannot be *possibility* if it is solely related to that which is already actual; otherwise the future would merely repeat the past. Genuine possibility can exist only "in relation to an actuality of transcendent scope, an actuality that is capable of holding within its power of envisionment the entire and so open realm of possibility." Moreover, if the actualization of possibility is to reshape or transform the inheritance of destiny, new possibilities must be related to actuality according to a graded structure of relevant options. Relevance is the test of the creativity, worthiness, and sheer reality of possibility in human affairs; it is the necessary condition of all historical change. But relevant possibility is itself only possible if it is grounded by "some actuality that spans achieved actuality and infinite possibility alike, giving to infinite possibilities both their locus in actuality and also their relevance to that actuality—for every event arises out of given actuality in union with relevant possibility."[53]

For Gilkey, this description of transtemporal actuality was one important way of renaming the whirlwind. As the creative power of being, God is transtemporal in the sense that God is transcendent over passage; God is the ground of all process without being subject to process. But as the ground of all process, God is also temporal in the sense that God is the condition of each moment and present in each moment of the movement of actuality into new possibilities. As the continuing source of being actualized in time, God is the unifying ground of past actuality, present realization, and future possibilities.[54] "God" is thus a way of naming the necessary creative power that transcends the temporal while working within it to ensure its continuation. "The becoming of reality calls for being, temporal passage calls for eternity, freedom and novelty for an ordered range of possibility, if a self-creative process is to be possible," Gilkey explained. The defining modern

---

51. Ibid., 305. See Gilkey, *Nature, Reality, and the Sacred*, 201–2.

52. Langdon Gilkey, *Message and Existence: An Introduction to Christian Theology* (New York: Seabury, 1981), 91.

53. Gilkey, *Reaping the Whirlwind*, 305.

54. Gilkey, *Message and Existence*, 96.

experiences of contingency, relativity, temporality, and autonomy do not negate the possibility of a divine ground, but are dependent upon God for their intelligibility and continuity. Just as we experience our contingent being as a self-actualizing process of uniting the past to future possibility, "so the infinite and absolute being of God unites past and future into those self-actualizing 'presences' which constitute process."[55]

The influence of Whiteheadian process philosophy in modern theology has been limited by its totalizing character. Because it presents a distinctively self-contained metaphysical system, the language and insights of process thought have been appropriated only rarely by theologians who do not adopt process thought as a system.[56] The general tendency over the past half-century is for theologians to either adopt Whitehead's metaphysical vision and proceed to work out some form of process theology *or* to pay little attention to the efforts of Whitehead and Charles Hartshorne to rehabilitate metaphysical reasoning.[57] Gilkey's theology of history presents the most significant exception to this pattern. Without adopting process thought as an alternative theological system, his theological perspective appropriates the process thesis that entities in process require a divine ground for their actualization. Without adopting Whitehead's doctrine of God, his account of the relationships between creativity and divine reality, or his interpretation of providence, Gilkey employs Whitehead's modal distinction between actuality and possibility and therefore reconceptualizes divine reality as the ground of all process. His claim that "providence is not enough" is crucial to his positioning as a Christian theologian who appropriates process thought as distinguished from a process theologian who translates Christian teaching into the language and system of neoclassical metaphysics.

This is a chief distinguishing quality of Gilkey's theological work. With a singularly open and dialogical spirit, his work has appropriated and built upon a remarkable variety of theological, historio-critical, and philosophical perspectives. Upon finishing *Reaping the Whirlwind*, he briefly considered the possibility of writing a major systematic theology that would have synthesized the thinking of Niebuhr, Tillich, Ricoeur, Eliade, and Whitehead, and which also would have appropriated the insights of current feminist and liberationist theologies. He later remarked that any serious

---

55. Gilkey, *Reaping the Whirlwind*, 306.

56. One important recent exception to this trend is Rosemary R. Ruether's appropriation of process thought in her ecofeminist work, *Gaia and God: An Ecofeminist Theology of Earth Healing* (San Francisco: HarperCollins, 1992), 246–53.

57. On process theology, see John B. Cobb Jr., *A Christian Natural Theology: Based on the Thought of Alfred North Whitehead* (Philadelphia: Westminster, 1976); John B. Cobb Jr., *Process Theology as Political Theology* (Philadelphia: Westminster, 1982); and John B. Cobb Jr. and David Ray Griffin, *Process Theology: An Introductory Exposition* (Philadelphia: Westminster, 1967).

contemporary theologian must address both the hermeneutical problem of the modern meaning of Christian symbols *and* the range of issues brought to the forefront of religious concern by liberation theology.[58] One concern that weighed upon him in contemplating the possibility of a theological system, however, was the example that Tillich's immense, intricate system set for him. A related problem was the weight of Tillich's influence over him. On various occasions he noted that his readings of Tillich nearly always produced the unsettling experience of rediscovering some insight or argument that he had long thought to be original to himself. In 1964, at the turning point of his theological career, he had shown Tillich the unpublished paper that later became the basis of *Naming the Whirlwind*. Tillich's somewhat deflating response to the paper was, "But Langdon, I said all this years ago." Gilkey replied that with the recent eclipse of neoorthodoxy, it was only now that he comprehended the significance of Tillich's work, "and I have, therefore, only now found myself saying it after you, but now in my own way."[59]

Later Works

Gilkey's work after *Naming the Whirlwind* outgrew some of Tillich's influence over his thinking. For example, *Reaping the Whirlwind* appropriated process theology and, to a lesser degree, the new eschatological theologies of Jürgen Moltmann and Wolfhart Pannenberg. In subsequent years, as Gilkey became increasingly interested in comparative religion and the problems of interreligious dialogue, he turned to Eliade for guidance.[60] Given the influence of Tillich's theology over him and the massive example that it set, however, Gilkey questioned whether he should devote himself to elaborating a new system. To commit himself to this project would prevent him from exploring various issues in the theology of culture, interreligious dialogue, and the dialogue between science and religion.[61] He finally decided that having a system wasn't worth the cost. "An unavoidable realism about the level of my own present learning and capacities, and the length of time remaining to improve either one, have together cautioned against such an

---

58. Langdon Gilkey, "Theology for a Time of Troubles," reprinted in *Theologians in Transition: The Christian Century "How My Mind Has Changed" Series,* ed. James M. Wall (New York: Crossroad, 1981), 31.

59. Langdon Gilkey, *Gilkey on Tillich* (New York: Crossroad, 1990), xiv.

60. See Langdon Gilkey, "Theology and Culture: Reflections on the Conference," *Criterion* (autumn 1989): 3. Tillich took up a serious interest in the theology of world religions near the end of his life; see Paul Tillich, *Christianity and the Encounter of World Religions* (Minneapolis: Fortress, 1994)

61. Langdon Gilkey, conversation with author, May 27, 1988.

ambitious and demanding project," he later explained.[62] His only systematic work, *Message and Existence,* was gauged as an introduction to theology for "interested beginners." It used the Tillichian method of phenomenological prolegomenon and existential correlation to articulate Christian answers (theological symbols) to the "religious" questions of ordinary experience.[63]

Thereafter his work turned almost exclusively to the essay form, addressing a wide variety of topics in the theology of culture, science, and world religions. Gilkey's later writings reflect his concern to relate Christian symbols to the problems of modern culture, science, politics, and religious pluralism, especially his desire to interpret the meaning of Christian faith in the context of what he calls "a time of troubles" and "a culture in decline." Through most of the 1980s the apparent intractability of the Cold War and America's support of oppressive dictatorships in the third world fueled his deep pessimism about the future of American culture and civilization. He saw little hope for a culture that invested its faith in scientific rationalism and devoted most of its scientific energy and resources to military ends.[64] Gilkey also wrote with evident sadness about the decline of the liberal Protestant churches in the United States and the erosion of spiritual practices and theological reflection in American churches.[65]

Gilkey's Synthesis

Gilkey's work, more than that of any theologian of the past half-century, appropriates and builds upon the major movements of modern theology, with the partial exception of recent feminist/liberationist and postmodern theologies. He has identified with and reinterpreted the liberal and neoorthodox traditions; he has appropriated process philosophy, eschatological theology, and history of religions comparativism without wholly adopting these perspectives; he has pursued the project of interreligious dialogue without giving up his Christian center. As an interpreter of the language and meaning of Christian myth, he has shown how theological liberalism can and must learn to appreciate myth as the primary mode of encounter with the sacred. His work has taken up and advanced the Tillichian understanding of myth as the essential language of religion. With distinctive powers of discernment, he has disclosed the character of myth as a historical language of action that expresses a relation to an ultimacy that transcends history and action. Gilkey's work teaches the value of addressing current

---

62. Gilkey, *Message and Existence,* 1–2.

63. Ibid., 3.

64. Langdon Gilkey, *Society and the Sacred: Toward a Theology of Culture in Decline* (New York: Crossroad, 1981), 4–5.

65. See Gilkey, *Through the Tempest* (Minneapolis: Fortress, 1991), 3–20, 35–47.

moral, religious, and social problems by thinking through the traditions of classical and especially modern Christian theology with an open, generous, and dialogical spirit.

Response to Professor Dorrien
Kent E. Robson

In his essay "Langdon Gilkey's Myth-Creative Liberal Theology," Professor Gary Dorrien explains carefully and in great detail the primary theological views of Langdon Gilkey. He casts Gilkey as a modern interpreter of thinkers such as Friedrich Schleiermacher, Paul Tillich, Reinhold Niebuhr, Mircea Eliade, Paul Ricoeur, and Alfred North Whitehead while, at the same time, showing how Gilkey reacted to Karl Barth, Emil Brunner, Rudolf Bultmann, and Dietrich Bonhoeffer. Dorrien also undertakes the heavy burden of not only interpreting all of these writers but also recounting Gilkey's views, reactions, and commentaries thereto. As such, Professor Dorrien's paper is a fine example of studious scholarship, and it is my hope that this response will be but one of many conversations kindled by his insightful paper.

As a self-proclaimed "scholastic" defender of neo-orthodoxy, Gilkey intended to share the responsibility of working out the theological principles established through this movement with other scholars. However, the Biblical Theology movement, the impetus of neo-orthodoxy, withered under critical accusations of its nonbiblical interpretations of history and bad semantic arguments. Neo-orthodoxy essentially came to an end in the 1960s (Dorrien, 385). But has it completely disappeared and have all of the neo-orthodox writers abandoned their themes? My guess is that they have not, for there are still writers today who reflect substantially neo-orthodox views. Still, as Dorrien indicates, Gilkey contributed significantly to the downfall of "American-style neo-orthodoxy," for which contribution he deserves high praise (Dorrien, 386). This collapse, however, left Gilkey searching for explanations, answers, and theological alternatives.

Aware of the issues that led to the downfall of neo-orthodoxy, Gilkey realized that any theology must be more sensitive to the tenets of what he described as the modern "secular mood" (Dorrien, 388). Gilkey argued that the need for such a secularly sensitive theology could be seen in the advent of the various liberation theologies, the most important of which were the

"Death of God" theologies.[66] For Gilkey, it was the work of these later theologians that both demonstrated the need for a new theology that could reinterpret traditional religious language for the secular age and illustrated the shortcomings of a completely secular theology.

Gilkey proposed following the "God is dead" theologians without accepting their conclusions (Dorrien, 388). Because these largely atheistic proponents asserted that Christian theology needed to be fundamentally revised in order to apply to a society that had outgrown its need for religion, Gilkey recognized that the "God is Dead" theologies could not be espoused. However, he did recognize the strength in their claim that religious language was no longer meaningful in the modern secular age. He affirmed that although they were right to take the modern secular mood seriously, they were wrong to endorse the modern secular understanding of human existence (Dorrien, 388–90).

According to Gilkey, there is a real and essential aspect of human existence that secular understanding simply cannot explain, a realm of ultimate concern that is reflected in both our fundamental anxieties and modern man's "secular" answers to these anxieties. "In our actual existence," he asserts, "we *are* religious whether we wish to be so or not." Gilkey argued that while the "God is dead" theologians generally want to interpret everything from a secular viewpoint, there is a symbolic and mythological element of religious language that, according to Gilkey, arises prior to language and reveals through experience a "dimension of ultimacy" that is the fundamental source of things.[67]

Gilkey described this dimension of ultimacy using four defining characteristics. First, ultimacy appears in our experience as the fundamental source of our being; it has neither the form nor feel of a finite entity amid other finite entities and, as such, conditions all other finite entities. Second, the dimension of ultimacy manifests itself as an awareness of our limits and as a limitation of an individual's formulation of limits (Dorrien, 392). By this Gilkey was referring to the threat of losing our existence—our meaning and autonomy—and the threat of our own temporality, both of which cause the infinite anxieties for which we seek infinite answers. Third, ultimacy determines our values and, as such, its loss spells the eradication of all being and meaning. Fourth, because ultimacy is revealed and defined through a dialectic of negation and affirmation—that is, recognition of both the meaninglessness and the excitement of life—and because it rests in a realm of transcendence, it takes on an air of mystery. It is precisely this

---

66. "One of the most telling symptoms of this new theological situation was the existence of . . . 'God-is-Dead' theology" (Dorrien, 389).

67. Donald W. Musser and Joseph L. Price, eds., *The Whirlwind in Culture: Frontiers in Theology* (Bloomington, Ind.: Meyer-Stone, 1988), 24.

transcendent paradoxical mystery that makes it impossible for the secular spirit to describe ultimacy.[68] And it is this mystery that drives us to look to the realm of the infinite to find answers for the ultimate anxieties of our finite existence. As Gilkey explained, this is all evident in observations of common experience, and it is the task of his prolegomenal book *Naming the Whirlwind* to explicate this dimension of ultimacy.

If theological discourse is to be true to the actual nature of lived existence in light of this ultimacy, it must at times dissent from the "implications of the secular spirit in which it lives."[69] However, if it is to be relevant for the modern man, it must also relate to and describe the realm of everyday, secular existence. The new theology must be grounded not in "contingency (or) relativity," but in the dictates of experience: it must be intelligible to the secular mood (Dorrien, 389).

Throughout all of this, Gilkey wanted to demonstrate that religious language is still meaningful in a secular age. He may fall short, however, for while Gilkey's views are religious, they also express experiences that are relational and can be grounded in sociological or social-psychological theories shaped by the language, customs, and symbols of a given community. Dorrien explains that a key element of myth is its "multivalence" (Dorrien, 396). Multivalent mythical symbols go beyond finite objects to refer to transcendent and unconditioned symbols. According to Gilkey, the sacred is never disclosed to us by itself, but rather it is a manifestation of the sacred unmediated object. Although Christianity shares these mythical elements with ancient religion, much has been lost in the modern, secular dithering of religion.

Despite the attempts of modern secular society to discount religious and mythical descriptions of actual existence, the inherent dimension of ultimacy requires society to nevertheless resort to mythical accounts in order to explain what secular language cannot.[70] The manner in which evil is dealt with in a secular society provides an illustrative example. Gilkey explains that the secular mind sees freedom as "freedom from evil," a view

---

68. Langdon Gilkey, *Naming the Whirlwind: The Renewal of God-Language* (Indianapolis: Bobbs-Merrill, 1969), 315.

69. Ibid., 251.

70. As Dorrien explains:

The rationalist image of the critical, scientific, "man of reason" is a mythical construct, as is the "authentic" self of existential philosophy, the unrepressed and loving self of humanistic psychology, the liberal democratic self of civic humanism, and the pragmatic manager of business culture. These images are clearly different from each other, Gilkey noted, yet all of them are distinctly modern ideal-types with common mythical features. (Dorrien, 397)

that always places evil "outside" of freedom (Dorrien, 397). But, Gilkey argues, proponents of this view say that "fate and sin arise from beyond the inward center of man: in ignorance, in repression, in the false objectification of things, in prejudice and false ideals."[71] They claim that with greater freedom, rationality, and control, man will not commit evil deeds. This view, however, is really false; freedom is just as often "freedom for evil" as it is "freedom from evil" (Dorrien, 397).

According to Gilkey, the modern secular man resolves the problem of evil by putting forth the myth that evil is the result of irrationality, ignorance, and repression. He claims that freedom is not always used to procure good and freeing man will not always make him better. Latter-day Saints would agree. It is incorrect to hold to an understanding of freedom that places evil outside its domain. Freedom can lead to sin, and, in fact, it is precisely the misuse of one's freedom that does lead to sin and evil. Furthermore, the possibility of freedom being used *for* evil cannot be avoided because in order for man to be free to exercise his agency for good, he must also be free to exercise his agency for evil.

Latter-day Saints would also largely agree with Gilkey regarding the ultimate dimension of one's existence. LDS leaders and scholars have long asserted that adopting the tenets of secular knowledge without the foundation of religious belief is crippling to one's faith and salvation.[72] Furthermore, LDS doctrine asserts that true science and true theology are essentially the same; when the world is understood correctly, there is no distinction between the secular and the religious.[73] LDS doctrine, however, moves a step beyond Gilkey in that it assigns the origin of this dimension of ultimacy. Whereas Gilkey explains that this dimension arises through a dialectic of negation and affirmation, the continual threat of the Void or possibility of nonbeing,[74] Latter-day Saints claim that the dialectic itself is caused by a more fundamental phenomenon. Ultimacy arises as an individual

---

71. Langdon Gilkey, "Modern Myth-Making and the Possibilities of Twentieth-Century Theology," in *Theology of Renewal*, vol. 1, ed. L. K. Shook (Montreal: Palm, 1968), 302.

72. Joseph Fielding McConkie, *Answers: Straightforward Answers to Tough Gospel Questions* (Salt Lake City: Deseret, 1998), 154–56; Mark E. Petersen, in *122nd Annual Conference of The Church of Jesus Christ of Latter-day Saints* (Salt Lake City: The Church of Jesus Christ of Latter-day Saints, 1952), 106; and Spencer W. Kimball, *Faith Precedes the Miracle* (Salt Lake City: Deseret, 1972), 280.

73. See *Discourses of Brigham Young*, ed. John A. Widtsoe (Salt Lake City: Deseret, 1954), 246, 258–59; John A. Widtsoe, *Joseph Smith as Scientist: A Contribution to Mormon Philosophy* (Salt Lake City: Bookcraft, 1964), 1–2; and Gordon B. Hinckley, in *135th Semi-annual Conference of The Church of Jesus Christ of Latter-day Saints* (Salt Lake City: The Church of Jesus Christ of Latter-day Saints, 1965), 52.

74. Gilkey, *Naming the Whirlwind*, 309–10.

struggles to understand his or her true nature as a being who is eternal and temporal, infinite and finite, free and determined. The ultimate in our experience arises from the eternal nature of man.

LDS theology makes the striking suggestion that persons are not created but have always existed: first as intelligences, then as spirits, and then as mortals with bodies received at mortal birth. According to LDS doctrine, man, like God, is eternal. In the King Follet Discourse of 1844, Joseph Smith explained:

> We say that God himself is a self-existent being. Who told you so? It is correct enough; but how did it get into your heads? Who told you that man did not exist in like manner upon the same principles? Man does exist upon the same principles.

Man is eternal, but in what sense? Joseph Smith continues by giving the following explanation:

> The mind or the intelligence which man possesses is co-eternal with God himself. . . . The intelligence of spirits had no beginning, neither will it have an end. . . . There never was a time when there were not spirits; for they are co-eternal with our Father in heaven. . . . Intelligence is eternal and exists upon a self-existent principle. It is a spirit from age to age, and there is no creation about it.

The primal identity of man—his intelligence—is eternal.[75] God placed man in this earthly realm, and although the knowledge of his prior existence has been veiled, he remains by nature an eternal being whose eternal nature is based on the same principles as God's eternal nature.

With this background, LDS theology is able to approach Gilkey's notion of ultimacy from a unique vantage point. It reveals the source from which his ultimacy dimension arises and illustrates why everyday life is continually

---

75. Joseph Fielding McConkie and Craig J. Ostler, *Revelations of the Restoration: A Commentary on the Doctrine and Covenants and Other Modern Revelations* (Salt Lake City: Deseret, 2000), 1094–95. It is important to note that God the Father is still very much the father of all humanity, and he plays the essential role in the development of man. Through his power we have come into the state of being that we know now. Joseph Smith also made this point clear in the King Follet Discourse: "The first principles of man are self-existent with God. God himself, finding he was in the midst of spirits and glory, because he was more intelligent, saw proper to institute laws whereby the rest could have a privilege to advance like himself." McConkie and Ostler, *Revelations of the Restoration,* 1096. God took intelligent, self-existing, primitive beings and set them on a path whereby they could come to be like their Father. Man exists eternally but only through God's divine will, his creative power, and his boundless grace does man have the potential and ability to progress beyond the state initially possessed.

saturated by ultimacy and why the secular mind never completely comprehends it.

Observations of human experience led Gilkey to believe that both the joy of our existence and the continual threat of our existence, which is slipping uncontrollably from us, are inherent in life. This is the ability of the individual to give meaning to life while battling the possibility of meaninglessness, the positive and negative nature of mortality, and the morally dynamic nature of personal autonomy. According to Gilkey, these characteristics of human experience—our contingency, relativity, temporality, and autonomy—reveal the dimension of ultimacy, which only mythical language can properly explain. However, when these characteristics are evaluated from an LDS perspective, Gilkey's emphasis on the need for explanatory myths becomes decidedly less justified.

The most obvious manner in which the LDS doctrine of the eternal nature of man differs from Gilkey's understanding of ultimacy is through the negation of the concept of human contingency. As an eternal being, man is not contingent; he cannot cease to exist. Thus, for the faithful adherent of this doctrine, the existential anxieties that, according to Gilkey, arise out of one's efforts to deal with his contingency are resolved. The area of ultimate concern, therefore, is not to secure existence but to secure a meaningful existence.

For Gilkey, however, "being" does not exist independent of God. He argues that "God is transtemporal in the sense that God is transcendent over passage: God is the ground of all process without being subject to process."[76] All calls for "contingency, relativity, temporality and autonomy . . . are dependent upon God for their intelligibility and continuity."[77] This contrasts with the LDS view in which there are other eternal beings and metaphysical realities (such as time) that influence what is happening in the universe. For Latter-day Saints, God is not the sole cause of everything. Therefore, while Gilkey and Dorrien say that "the divine being influences, through secondary causes, all self-actualizations of the present as well as the causal efficacy of the past upon the present,"[78] LDS theology argues that God influences only some of these self-actualizations, while different agents influence others, a fact that is true not only of our lives and of history but also of our existences in eternity. In response to Gilkey's claim that "God 'acts' in and through the secondary causes of destiny and freedom,"[79]

---

76. Gilkey, *Message and Existence*, 96, cited above (Dorrien, 408).
77. Gilkey, *Reaping the Whirlwind*, 306, cited above (Dorrien, 409).
78. Gilkey, *Reaping the Whirlwind*, 249, cited above (Dorrien, 406).
79. Gilkey, *Reaping the Whirlwind*, 249, cited above (Dorrien, 406).

Latter-day Saints would say God is only one of the many actors who can influence the secondary causes of freedom.

Although one of the fundamental aspects of secular self-understanding is the notion of complete relativity, Gilkey asserts the world is in reality a world

> where knowledge and understanding of [a] network of interaction is possible; a world also characterized by the search for meanings and values in what we do there and in the history in which we participate; a world filled with the urge both for freedom and community, for self-hood and its integrity, and for love in its mutual dependence.[80]

Latter-day Saints would again concur, claiming in addition that these characteristics arise because man's existence is assured, because he is not a contingent being whose goal is simply to exist. Man's search for meaning is an innate propensity of his eternal nature. Furthermore, this search for meaning is an area of ultimate concern for Latter-day Saints because scripture, both ancient and modern, attests that man's purpose in this mortal existence is to prepare to return to the presence of God (Alma 12:24; D&C 78:7). According to LDS theology, every individual has a purpose in life, and we must be free to use our agency to either fulfill this purpose or turn from it.

Accordingly, as in Gilkey's belief system, autonomy is a key principle of LDS theology. The doctrine of man's eternal nature ensures a strong sense of personal autonomy, and inasmuch as man's very happiness and eternal progression require the wise exercise of his free will, his eternal exaltation would not be possible without freedom and moral agency.

Although the prospect of eternal progression depends on God—man's agency is respected through God's choice to not intervene, and salvation can be found only through Jesus Christ—man's existence *per se* is guaranteed. This degree of self-existence provides for a sense of identity that is not a predicate of God's divine will, a fact that acts as the foundation for man's personal autonomy. The early LDS theologian B. H. Roberts concluded that because man is eternal, he must also possess the power of volition:

> It is of course possible to conceive of Intelligence and its necessarily attendant consciousness, existing without volition; but Intelligence so conceived is shorn of its glory, since under such conditions it can make no use whatsoever of its powers. Its very thinking would be chaotic; its consciousness distressing. If active at all its actions would be without purpose and as chaotic as its thinking would be, unless it could be thought of as both thinking and acting as directed by an intelligent, purposeful will external to itself; which would still leave the Intelligence

---

80. Gilkey, *Naming the Whirlwind*, 253.

a mere automation, without dignity or moral quality, or even intellectual value.[81]

For Latter-day Saints, man's first glory is his autonomy. And it is through God's plan that this autonomy is assured, man is granted agency, a world full of opposition is created, and man is placed on the path by which he may gain glory upon glory. By his very nature, man is personally autonomous; the freedom to exercise this agency is a gift of God, and to exercise his agency is his purpose on the earth.

Unfortunately, because both Gilkey and Dorrien apparently adhere to the Christian tradition based on the writings of St. Augustine, there seems to be no escape from our fated dependence on God, which would render the notion of freedom self-contradictory. This tradition is a result of St. Augustine's misunderstanding of Romans 5:12.[82] According to Elaine Pagels of Princeton University in her book *Adam, Eve, and the Serpent*, "Augustine read [this] passage in Latin, and so either ignored or was unaware of the connotations of the Greek original."[83] He therefore assumed that Adam brought universal and inevitable sin upon each of us prior to our individual sins. However, this is not what the passage in Greek says. Pagels points out that "the Greek text reads, 'Through one man sin entered the world, and through sin, death; and thus death came upon all men, *in that* all sinned.'"[84] Augustine's Latin version replaces the phrase "in that" with the mistaken phrase "in whom," which necessitated Augustine's conclusion that every human being is in bondage from the moment of conception. Only Christ, who was conceived of a virgin, is without sin. Thus, according to Augustine, all humans except Christ are fatefully and inescapably sinful from conception.

This account could explain why humans, according to Gilkey, are trapped by fate and ignorance and are therefore unavoidably fated to sin. Latter-day Saints, however, do not and cannot share this position with Gilkey or other Christians who draw from the Augustinian tradition. Latter-day Saints believe that no one is sinful at birth and that one cannot even begin to sin until he or she has acquired an awareness of what constitutes sin. Modern revelation has indicated that this awareness does not arise until eight years of age, and so Latter-day Saints do not perform baptisms until a person is at least eight years old. Latter-day Saints also believe that children

---

81. B. H. Roberts, ed., *Seventy's Course in Theology, Fourth Year: The Atonement* (Salt Lake City, Deseret News: 1911), 5.

82. Romans 5:12 reads: "Wherefore, as by one man sin entered into the world, and death by sin; and so death passed upon all men, for that all have sinned."

83. Elaine Pagels, *Adam, Eve, and the Serpent* (New York: Random House, 1988), 109.

84. Ibid., 109; emphasis in original.

are sinless prior to this age; if a child dies before the age of eight, that child is not encumbered by any sin or degradation.

It is critical here to note that, in Augustine's view, there can be no "freedom for evil" nor "freedom from evil" since humans do not have freedom in the first place. We are fated to be whatever God creates us to be; we have neither choices nor freedom. Human freedom is an illusion, and imagining that we have freedom is sinful. Thus humans are *necessarily* gripped by sin. Everyone who pays careful attention to Augustine must deal with this implication. As a result, for Augustine salvation is ultimately decided by God, and it is not in any way under our control. God, as our Creator, saves whom he wishes to save. We are saved by grace alone, as Augustine indicates. There is only fate.

LDS theology, on the other hand, accepts salvation through grace, but it also holds that God's extension of grace is dependent upon our individual acceptance thereof. As LDS scripture declares, "We know that it is by grace that we are saved, after all we can do" (2 Nephi 25:23). According to LDS doctrine, works of righteousness (including the performance of ordinances) are required for salvation, and these works are not fated. They are individually chosen. Therefore, freedom can be used either wisely or foolishly. If it is used foolishly, the individual, not God, is culpable. Furthermore, this culpability is dependent on what the individual has learned, for God will not punish those who sin in ignorance. On the other hand, an individual can and should be praised for using his or her freedom with real understanding, insight, and wisdom. This is a radical departure from Augustinian-Calvinistic theology. However, in this departure, Latter-day Saints find common ground with important pre-Augustine Christian thinkers.

According to Gilkey's understanding of time, "to be human is to be immersed in temporal change" (Dorrien, 402). Latter-day Saints resonate with this, given that they view time as eternal, preceding even the "organization" of the earth or even the universe. They would also likely agree with much of what Gilkey says about the manner in which our own temporality reveals the dimension of ultimacy. However, affirming again the notion of eternal existence, the ultimate anxieties arising from temporality are results of the possible eradication of the meaning we have struggled to give our lives rather than the role temporality plays in elucidating our contingency. Temporality becomes a concern not only because it drives us to find meaning, but because it threatens to wipe from history whatever meaning we have found.

However, there is no real time in the usual post-Augustinian view; temporality is only a burden imposed by the Creation. To avoid misunderstanding here, it would be well for Dorrien to clarify Gilkey's conception of time, either distancing it from or relating it to that of Augustine. Instead he seemingly bypasses the issue by focusing on "myth," which blurs the question as to whether there is real time, independent of creation and God. Gilkey says that we can understand history as being "based on a theologically formulated myth: a cluster of religious symbols concerned with the evident mystery—both transcendent and immanent, both of God and of man's freedom" (Dorrien, 403), but he is unable to go beyond myth to provide more illuminating theological explanations.

Gilkey believes theology needs "religious discourse that bridges the gap between religious experience and secular experience" (Dorrien, 399), and, throughout his work, he develops this assertion. I would personally question any claim that theology should be based on secular thought and culture, though I believe that any religion should be capable of relating the everyday experiences of human beings to the divine. Rather, I believe what the modern era needs is a theology that makes man more sensitive to the religious nature of his existence, or, as Gilkey would say, the dimension of ultimacy latent in common experience. In order to properly deal with the dimension of ultimacy arising out of man's eternal nature, people must gain a deeper understanding of who they are and why they are here. The new theology for which Gilkey articulated a need must indeed be capable of reaching the secular man; however, it must simultaneously require the secular man to recognize the inherently religious nature of his existence. A theology that fails to do this fails in its most fundamental goal: to articulate, clarify, and enhance man's relationship to God.

Finally, I must comment a bit on Gilkey's views as to the value and function of myth in Christian theologizing. In understanding Gilkey's theology, Dorrien says, we must "appreciate myth as the primary mode of encounter with the sacred" (Dorrien 409). In my judgment, Christian myth derives from a breakdown in understanding certain components of Christian philosophy. These components then become myths because they are based on an erroneous and mistaken interpretation of Christian theology that is grounded either in St. Augustine's misreading and mistranslation of key Christian passages or in other erroneous theological or philosophical concepts. Although myth may often help describe the truth and relate religious principles to the individual, it also often works as a subterfuge to remedy the lack of sufficient knowledge of the gospel of Jesus Christ. However, once gospel truths are revealed, the explanatory power of the doctrine of man's eternal nature eliminates the need for myth to explain the inherently religious nature of our existence. As a result, the theologies Gilkey discusses and his own efforts to formulate a new theology could be enormously improved by simply going back further than St. Augustine to the original sources of Christian belief found in the Bible.

Rejoinder

Gary Dorrien

Professor Robson devotes most of his attention to an issue that was not among the chief themes of my paper, though I can appreciate why, from his standpoint, the complexity of issues such as freedom and evil trump the rest of the present subject.

Two clarifications are in order before I turn to the subject that chiefly concerns Professor Robson. There is still such a thing as theological neoorthodoxy, as he suggests; prominent examples of neoorthodox theologians would be Thomas F. Torrance and Eberhard Jüngel. However, there are precious few theologians under the age of sixty who would call themselves neoorthodox, and this once-powerful movement claims few institutions today. Moreover, it was not liberation theology but the neoorthodox Biblical Theology movement of the 1950s to which the criticism of "contrived nonbiblical interpretations of history and bad semantic arguments" applied. The liberation theology movement has made its share of mistakes, but it never claimed a distinctive grammar for Hebrew religion.

Professor Robson moves quickly to the claim that all Christian theology except Mormonism is distorted by Augustine's faulty exegesis of Romans 5:12. It is true that Augustine's literalistic doctrine of original sin, which was connected to his failure to learn Greek, has been the source of immense harm in Western Christianity. However, Professor Robson's rendering of this legacy greatly exaggerates the influence of Augustine's arguments about original sin over "all the rest of Christianity." He ignores the doctrines of Eastern Orthodox churches as well as the import of four centuries of pre-Augustinian theology and a host of decidedly premodern and modern non-Augustinian Western Christian theologies. For example, Eastern Orthodoxy, various mystical theologies, pantheist and panentheist theologies, philosophical idealism, and romanticist theologies have always emphasized the unity of grace and nature. In Western Christianity, several theologies—all the way to the wilder shores of Arminianism, social gospel liberalism, and liberation theology—uphold positive conceptions of freedom, though I agree that the Mormon doctrines about God and freedom described by Professor Robson are distinctive to Mormonism. More pertinent to the present discussion is the Augustinianism of Reinhold Niebuhr, which Gilkey adopts. Since this was not the main subject of my original essay, but it is the main subject taken up by Professor Robson, I will try to explain what Niebuhr and Gilkey share with Augustine's thinking on the subject of evil while showing what they emphatically do not share with it.

Niebuhr's maxim about myth is a good starting point. Niebuhr and Gilkey regard myth as the essential language of religion, a view that Professor Robson treats as an obfuscating way of covering up theological confusion. Niebuhr's maxim was that good theology takes myth seriously but not literally. Niebuhr never tired of saying that the characteristic problem with theological liberalism was that it failed to take Christian myth seriously, while religious conservatism was beyond the pale because it persisted in taking Christian myths literally. For example, theological liberalism denigrated the very idea of a sinful human nature, while conservatives persisted in reading Genesis 2 as history. Niebuhr countered that the myth of the Fall in Genesis 2 is profoundly true as a description of the human condition. As creatures made in the image of God, Niebuhr reasoned, human beings possess capacities for self-transcendence that enable them to become aware of their finite existence in distinction from, though constitutive with, God's infinite existence. The same awareness, however moves human beings to attempt to overcome their finiteness by becoming infinite, like God. The root of human evil is the universal human pretension of being God. To Niebuhr, the biblical myth of the Fall was a true description of the tragic reality of life, for which the Enlightenment myth of progress and human perfectibility embraced by liberal Christianity was a pitiful substitute.

Niebuhr's thinking on this subject, like Gilkey's after him, had nothing to do with Augustine's literalistic theory of inherited corruption. Niebuhr explicitly disavowed not only every interpretation of the Fall as an account of the origin of evil but also every theory that conceptualized original sin as a biologically transmitted evil. For Niebuhr, and for Gilkey, the true meaning of original sin was existential, not biological. Just as the myth of the Fall is a description of the nature of evil rather than an account of the origin of evil, the reality of original sin is an inevitable fact of human existence, but not an inherited corruption of existence. The human capacity for self-transcendence makes sin inevitable. Sin is a reality in every moment of existence, yet it has no history.

This account of the human condition helped Gilkey make sense of his experience as a prisoner of war in China during World War II. He became a theologian in the process of reflecting on the puzzling and disturbing selfishness that he witnessed in an internment camp in Shantung Province. Faced with the task of organizing a mini-civilization under conditions of scarcity and confinement, he had expected his fellow inmates, many of whom were missionaries, to work out cooperative living conditions. What he found, instead, was that nearly everyone was much less rational and more selfish than he anticipated. They were not the nice people he was expecting; some were nothing like the nice people he thought he had known in Peking.

The worst cases were the moralistic Christians who always denied that their hoarding was motivated by self-interest.

Why was it so difficult to convince them that unyielding selfishness is self-defeating? Was the problem simply that the inheritance of animal instincts in human nature had not been brought sufficiently under rational control? That was the answer that Gilkey's liberal education gave him, but his camp experience convinced him that egotism is more than a consequence of instinct. The roots of human selfishness seemed to inhere in fears about the self's security, but these were fears that only a self-conscious being could experience. The fierce determination to hoard food for one's self while vulnerable and weaker neighbors starved was not an animal reaction; it was terribly human.

This is the biographical source of what Professor Robson calls "this distressing account." Gilkey told the story in his extraordinary memoir, *Shantung Compound*. He became a theologian out of his desire to comprehend the immense world-historical evils of the 1930s and 1940s and his own glimpse of human nature stripped of civilizing securities. Instinctive needs can be satisfied in a moment, he reflected, but it is only the human mind that looks far into the future, calculates the dangers to human existence, and moves to protect the self and its loved ones from every possible contingency. Human consciousness transforms the character of humankind's instinctive will to live. The instinctive will to live is transformed by consciousness into the aggressive, dynamic, and possessive will to power. Animals by comparison are innocent. Put differently, human beings are distinctively grasping, alienated, and destructive because of the demands of instinct accelerated by humankind's capacities of mind or spirit. There is no "really free" pure human spirit that is not implicated in this problem.

The realization that human beings are selfish is the starting point of a realistic understanding of the human condition. Yet human beings are confused and conflicted by the unnaturalness of their consuming self-regard. If human beings were *naturally* selfish, Gilkey reasons, they would be less conflicted about their egotism and certainly less driven to cover it up. Selfishness is pervasive in human relations and yet persistently denied, often for attractive moral reasons. For Gilkey and the neo-Augustinian Niebuhrians, this is the central clue to the superiority of Christian theology over humanistic and naturalistic accounts of the human condition. The truth of the Christian understanding of sin does not require belief in a historical Fall (as in fundamentalism) or in the transmission of original sin through procreation (as in Augustine). It is confirmed by every human interaction. The doctrine of the fallen condition of humankind is a true myth.

I trust that my paper makes clear why Gilkey and I are far removed from the doctrine of God expounded in Professor Robson's reply. And I hope that my response to Professor Robson sheds some light on Augustinianism in modern theology. The prospects for further dialogue on these subjects may be less promising than the myth question. The myth issue has a tendency to seem more threatening at first, but it has a fruitful way of opening up often-hidden presuppositions about what religious claims must be in order to be true. I follow Gilkey in affirming that the recognition of Christian myth is a distinguishing feature of modern theology. With C. S. Lewis, I believe that what myth communicates is not truth in the formal sense, but reality, that upon which truth *is*.

Response to Professor Dorrien

James E. Faulconer

Among other things, Langdon Gilkey[85] tells us that theology has moved from the question of the nature of religious language to the more radical question of the possibility of meaningful religious language. He suggests that if religious language is no longer a possible mode of meaningful discourse, it is because religious language is no longer related to experience and life: the triumph of secularism in the modern world has meant the loss of religious meaning. In response, Gilkey proposes to disclose "the meaning of religious language . . . by developing a hermeneutical phenomenology of experience" (Dorrien, 389). He argues, quite reasonably, that in rejecting the importance and meaningfulness of the conceptual/symbolic order, secularism is unable to recognize or explain the order that makes secularism itself possible.[86]

As Dorrien says, the secular mind "invariably resorts to mythical language in expressing its 'anti-mythical' world view," but it remains tone-deaf to the mythical character of that language. Examples from secular myth are the "image of the critical, scientific 'man of reason'" and the assumption that "the realization of freedom is always a moral good" (Dorrien, 397).

85. Though Gary Dorrien is the author of this piece to which I respond, it is about Langdon Gilkey's theology. As shorthand, therefore, I will usually refer to Gilkey, assuming that Dorrien's portrayal of Gilkey's position is correct.

86. Gilkey collapses the terms *myth* and *symbolic/conceptual order*. Though I think there are not only useful but important distinctions to be made between the two, to make the connection to Gilkey I will follow him and use the term *myth* to refer to both myth and symbolic/conceptual order.

With the triumph of secularism, the theologian's job cannot be to cast out secularism. Rather, says Gilkey, the theologian must give a better interpretation of myth for secular consciousness. He or she must reawaken secular consciousness to the mythic rather than argue against secularism *per se*. Thus, Gilkey's general strategy is to reinterpret Christian understanding in light of the myth of secularism but at the same time to show the inadequacy of the latter. Secularism, for example, cannot deal adequately with the inevitability of change. That requires reference to ultimacy, something missing in the secular myth but available in Christianity.

Following thinkers like Mircea Eliade and Paul Ricoeur, Gilkey argues that myth shapes human existence by giving us a structure on which we hang our understanding of society and the world: "The purpose of myth is to organize the [total 'world'] of one's desires, environment, and social situation into a reflective form that makes sense of the world" (Dorrien, 399).[87] Theology is a response to myth: "The purpose of theology is to explore reflectively the meaning and validity of mythical discourse" (Dorrien, 399) in order to "disclose the latent sacral elements of experience" (Dorrien, 391). The analysis required will necessarily be ontic rather than ontological,[88] for phenomenological analysis cannot prove that there is a dimension of ultimacy; it can only show that we experience that dimension. That dimension requires a phenomenological or hermeneutic analysis.

I am sympathetic to the general thrust of Gilkey's position, but he leaves important questions unanswered. Begin with a relatively innocuous one: how can ontic analysis show that a "dimension of ultimacy manifests itself as the source or ground of being" (Dorrien, 392)? To say that ultimacy reveals itself as the ground of being is to say something about being. It is to do ontology. It is not necessarily a problem to do ontology, but I wonder why Gilkey denies doing it. What problem does he think that denial will help him avoid, and does it? Since Gilkey knows Martin Heidegger's work (Dorrien refers to it when he denies that Gilkey does ontology [Dorrien, 389]), I also wonder why Gilkey does not deal with Heidegger's argument that God must be a being rather than being itself.[89] That argument brings

---

87. Here is a place where I believe that the distinction between myth and the symbolic order would be useful. The latter is the structure that organizes our concepts. Myth is the narrative in which we find that structure displayed.

88. The distinction between the ontic and the ontological is one that comes from the work of Martin Heidegger, *Being and Time: A Translation of* Sein und Zeit, trans. Joan Stambaugh (Albany: State University of New York, 1996), sec. 4.

89. For example, see Martin Heidegger, "Letter on Humanism," in *Basic Writings: from "Being and Time" (1927) to "The Task of Thinking" (1964)*, ed. David Farrell Krell, trans. Frank M. Capruzzi and J. Glenn Gray, 2d rev. ed. (San Francisco: HarperSanFrancisco, 1993), 251-53; and "Phenomenology and Theology," in *The*

Gilkey's method into question. For, if Heidegger is right, then the ultimacy that Gilkey proposes to reveal is not divine ultimacy.

A related question is how phenomenology can speak of transcendence and what kind of transcendence it can speak of. Heidegger's work shows that phenomenological analysis will allow us to speak of transcendence.[90] However, the transcendence of which that analysis speaks is not divine transcendence. It is neither a dimension of ultimacy nor the ground of being.[91] What kind of transcendence does Gilkey think divine transcendence is, and how can phenomenological analysis reveal that kind of transcendence?

Consider also Gilkey's claim that myth as well as theology is reflective. In a broad sense, as a response to the human condition, of course myth is reflective. However, if by *reflection* we mean "taking up something as an object of conceptual or intellectual inquiry" (and, presumably, that is the way theology is reflective), then given Gilkey's understanding of myth, it *cannot* be reflective in the same way that theology is. To say that both are reflective is to equivocate.

As a framework that makes understanding possible, the symbolic realm of myth and ritual is broader than that of philosophical and theological reflection. Given Gilkey's view, as a conceptual framework myth makes intellectual realms possible and so makes intellectual reflection on myth complicated. We can never have the whole myth before us as we reflect on it, *unless it is not the framework that we use for understanding that upon which we reflect.*[92] Thus, if myth is an organizing framework for understanding, it

---

Piety of Thinking, trans. James G. Hart and John C. Maraldo (Bloomington: Indiana University Press, 1976), 5–21.

90. Heidegger speaks of transcendence in many places, including, for example, *Being and Time* and "The Origin of the Work of Art," in *Basic Writings,* 145–46.

91. The questions of how to speak of transcendence and whether that transcendence can be divine transcendence continue to be central to much contemporary philosophy, particularly in Europe. For example, the work of Emmanuel Lévinas and Jacques Derrida can be understood to center around the first question and to touch on the second. Other contemporary French philosophers are also clearly engaging both questions. For a sample of this discussion in English, see the interchanges between several French philosophers by Dominique Janicaud, Jean-Francois Courtine, Jean-Louis Chrétien, Jean-Luc Marion, Michel Henry, and Paul Ricoeur, in *Phenomenology and the "Theological Turn": The French Debate,* trans. Bernard G. Prusak and others (New York: Fordham University Press, 2000).

92. This point is important to a criticism I make later in the paper. There is another objection, one that is related to my concern about *myth* and *conceptual or symbolic ordering:* If myth is not a conceptual ordering (it could be either a symbolic ordering or, more likely, a kind of narrative), then it is not the kind of thing that is concerned with reflection. Reflection involves at least conceptual analysis, and myth is not conceptual.

cannot also be the uncomplicated object of reflection except on the basis of some other myth or through a work of immanent critique. Gilkey's criticism of secularism is a form of such immanent critique, showing that secularism depends on the very thing it rejects. Presumably theology can also perform such a critique within a particular religion, but that is not how Gilkey deals with religion.

Given Gilkey's position, there can be no standpoint from which to analyze myth that does not depend on myth, but his assumption that myth is reflective tempts him to go beyond immanent critique. Gilkey says:

> What makes modern theology distinctive in religious history is the fact that modern theologians know that their myths are myths. Theology no longer claims to be able to make indicative statements about matters of fact. It is only as broken myth that Christianity's mythical inheritance can be appropriated. (Dorrien, 399)

Given Gilkey's understanding of myth, this claim about theology must depend on some conceptual structure. Which one? Is this a claim made possible by a position within religious myth or by a position within the myth of secularism? The fact that religious myth is said to be broken is evidence that the claim has its basis in secularism. Since Gilkey sees secularism as having completely triumphed over religion, that is not surprising. If the world is, indeed, irredeemably secular, then one can do theology and talk about religious myth only from a secular framework and one must, as Gilkey proposes to do, give a new interpretation of religious myth for secular consciousness.

To do so, however, is to undo the mythic function of religion, to rob it of its status as a way of understanding the world. Consider the biblical story of creation as an example. It is common to understand religious creation accounts as reflections on the origins of the cosmos, answers to the question "why?" that are in some sense parallel to the scientific question "why?" That is a mistake. There may be cases in which myth functions as a kind of primitive science, but the biblical story of creation is not one of them.[93] Of course, secularists are not the only ones to assume that the Bible story of creation is a case of primitive science. Some religious people also make that assumption, especially those who consider themselves literalists. Ironically, when people argue for creation science or for what is usually called a literal reading of the Bible, they are agreeing with the secular understanding of

---

93. Those unfamiliar with this view should see, for example, André LeCocque and Paul Ricoeur, *Thinking Biblically: Exegetical and Hermeneutical Studies* (Chicago: University of Chicago Press, 1998); and Northrop Frye, *The Great Code: The Bible and Literature* (New York: Harcourt Brace Jovanovich, 1982).

things.[94] They use conceptual structures taken from secularism, such as the necessity that explanation have a scientific form, to try to understand the Bible. Some give up or metaphorize the Bible when faced with the project of making the Bible and science answer the same questions, but some keep the Bible and insist that its account can be brought within the secular myth, though of course they would not say that is what they are doing. But both those who metaphorize and those who would make the Bible scientific do essentially the same thing: they begin from a secular understanding of the Bible. Thus, Gilkey shares the view of those we often refer to as "biblical literalists." Both assume that secularism gives us the basic structure of understanding and that all accounts must be hung on that structure. They disagree about what conclusions that leads one to, but they agree that the secular myth is the one that must be used for understanding.

However, when the Bible tells us how the world was created, it does so with interests, goals, and basic assumptions so different from those of science that we ought to be suspicious of claims that both the Bible and science are answering the same question, "How did the world come to be?" Such claims equivocate, for the question does not mean the same thing in a biblical context that it means in a scientific one. The great temptation is to assume that mythic accounts of creation are cases of primitive science. Perhaps some are. Surely we do not want to claim that all myth has the same goals. However, it is far from obvious that all creation myths are primitive science. In fact, in the case of the Bible, those who take it to be a scientific or quasi-scientific account have the considerable burden of proof. The interest of the biblical origin stories is much more on things like how the human condition came to be what it is, how evil came into the world, and why the covenant applies to each person than it is on the physical processes involved in creation. It is not clear that Genesis has any interest in the latter at all.

The result of this difference between the biblical story of origin and the scientific story is that comparisons of the two are problematic. Some wish to argue for creationism and some wish to treat the biblical story as at best metaphor and poetry, but it is not a simple matter to ask which interpretation is true. In fact, it is generally an impossible matter.[95] If I assume that the conceptual schema for deciding truth is the scientific, secular one, then

---

94. I quarrel with the description of "fundamentalist" readings of the Bible as literal readings. Such readings are exactly not literal—by the letter—readings; they are secularized readings, though in disguise. For more on this, see my "Scripture as Incarnation" in *Historicity and the Latter-day Saint Scriptures*, ed. Paul Y. Hoskisson (Provo, Utah: Religious Studies Center, Brigham Young University, 2001), 17–61.

95. For perhaps the best discussion of this issue available, see Peter Winch, "Darwin, Genesis, and Contradiction," in *Trying to Make Sense* (New York: Basil Blackwell, 1987), 132–39.

I assume that the questions and purposes of science are the relevant ones. Having done so, if I compare the claim that God created the heavens and the earth to a secular claim about the origin of the earth and then ask which is true, I will conclude that the secular account is true. On the other hand, if I assume that the relevant schema is that of the scriptural story with its questions and purposes, then when I compare the two claims about creation, I will conclude that the scriptural account is true.

However, to say that the scriptural account is true is not to say that the scriptural account is a good scientific account. It is not to assume that the two accounts are the same kinds of explanation and, therefore, that the scriptural account is better than the scientific one. Rather, it is to say that the scientific account doesn't deal with the questions of the biblical text in a fashion adequate to the project of the narrative in Genesis, assuming that the scientific account deals with them at all. Both accounts claim to tell us how things are, so they both make truth claims; I am not arguing for a naïve relativism. To the degree that the differing accounts make truth claims about the same things, they are comparable. It makes no sense to speak of a different kind of truth in one than in the other (as some, though not Gilkey, are tempted to do), unless by doing so one is covertly denying the truth of one or the other, perhaps by metaphorizing it. At least for biblical religions, it is far from obvious that myth and science make claims about the same things. Therefore, it is far from obvious that we can compare the truths of the scientific and the biblical accounts in order to decide which is superior.

Gilkey is willing to cede secularism the authority it demands and so to accept it as the story that determines truth. Thus, he says that although "myth refers to both the finite and the transcendent . . . its references to the finite must be understood to have no normative meaning as historical or scientific information" (Dorrien, 398). However, this can make sense only if he assumes that religious myth makes claims about matters of fact that are the same as the fact-claims of modern science. Though that assumption is common, it is incoherent. Gilkey recognizes the problem of assuming that myth is a primitive form of science, but he falls prey to the temptation of accepting the secular assumption that the mythic claims of secularism are the ones by which we will understand all claims to truth, in other words, all facts. Secularism tries to insist that there is no myth at all. Gilkey shows that to be self-contradictory. In other words, he shows that, in spite of what seems to be the case and in spite of the claims of secularism and its domination of our thought, secularism has not completely triumphed over religion because it shares religion's reference to a background myth. Why, then, grant the myth of secularism in thinking about religion? Doing so robs religion of its claims to truth and so of its power to have real effects. It makes religion only metaphorical. If only secularism can yield facts, then religion is an untrue though sometimes useful fable. Such a position takes the word *myth* to mean exactly what Gilkey denies that it means: merely a fable. Thus, the question is whether Gilkey has not given up too much, continuing Bultmann's demythologizing project without intending to.

If Gilkey's critique of secularism's rejection of myth is valid, as I believe it is, then the revelation of secularism's broken, self-contradictory character opens a space in which religious myth can be considered, not from the secular point of view, but from out of itself. Within a secular consciousness that considers itself whole, Christianity can be appropriated only as broken myth. However, the break in secularism to which Gilkey points opens a space for considering religious myth differently.[96]

One way to do so is to show, as Gilkey has tried to do, how the sacred manifests itself in and through the finite. The problem is how to deal with a phenomenology of religious experience in a way that will yield valid claims about divine transcendence. Though Gilkey has passed over that issue, at least two contemporary philosophers come to mind who have dealt with it extensively: Jean-Luc Marion and Michel Henry. To illustrate what attention to the issue might allow, let me briefly describe Marion's work as well as the criticism of it.[97] Then let me suggest an alternative that I believe takes up the insights of Marion's project and avoids the criticisms.

In both Kant and Husserl, a phenomenon must be understood within a horizon and according to an *I*. The impossibility of an unconditioned phenomenon, the impossibility of a pure experience of transcendence, results from this demand. As Kant's *Critique of Pure Reason* shows, to the degree that we deal only with conditioned phenomena we do not deal with what is transcendent. In response, Marion's project is to show that an unconditioned phenomenon is possible. His strategy is to argue for "saturated phenomena" rather than the "impoverished phenomena" of Kant (impoverished because they are constituted as phenomena by their horizon and subject, with little or nothing given by intuition).[98] Marion points out that his suggestion of this possibility is not as wild as it may seem at first glance. After all, we find something like this in Kant's aesthetic, in which the aesthetic idea is an intuition for which no adequate concept can be formed.

---

96. This possibility is one that might be undertaken in a deconstructive theology, something that Gilkey has, understandably, been unable to take up.

97. Jean-Luc Marion has made his case in work after work, from *L'idole et la distance: cinq études* (Paris: Grasset, 1977) to *De surcroît: études sur les phénomènes saturés* (Paris: Presses Universitaires de France, 2001). For an excellent version of the argument, see Jean-Luc Marion, "The Saturated Phenomenon," trans. Jeffrey L. Kosky and Thomas A. Carlson in *Phenomenology and the "Theological Turn": The French Debate* (New York: Fordham University Press, 2000), 176–216.

98. Marion, "Saturated Phenomenon," 180.

In Kant's aesthetic, the concept is impoverished, not the intuition, for the intuition gives too much to think. Kant says this excessiveness of intuition is "inexposable";[99] Marion uses, instead, the word *invisible*. The invisible phenomenon is "invisible, not by lack of light, but by excess of light."[100] The saturated phenomenon is invisible to the categories of understanding because it exceeds them. We do not have to think that excess in terms of enormity. All that is necessary is that it be impossible to apply a successive synthesis to the phenomenon so that one can see the sum of its parts. The invisible is excessive of understanding because no successive synthesis is possible.

However, in spite of the impossibility of performing a successive synthesis and thereby coming to a knowledge of the whole, it is possible to have an instantaneous synthesis of the saturated phenomenon. Amazement and bedazzlement are examples of such instantaneous syntheses. We look toward something when we are amazed or bedazzled, but it exceeds our understanding. What I see in the vision of the saturated phenomenon is not darkness but something so bright that it blurs my vision, something I *cannot* see clearly: "because the saturated phenomenon, due to the excess of intuition in it, cannot be borne by any gaze that would measure up to it ('objectively'), it is perceived ('subjectively') by the gaze only in the negative mode of an impossible perception, the mode of bedazzlement."[101]

For Marion, we do not find amazement and bedazzlement in only the exceptional case. With Martin Heidegger, Marion believes that such experiences are the fundamental modes of our experience with the world and so are determinative of phenomena. We can—indeed, must—"cover over" our amazement at and bedazzlement with things in order to get on in the world. I live most of my life as "one" lives life, shopping as one shops, for example. I do not look for some unique, authentic way for me to shop, perhaps refusing to use the check-out counter as one does and, instead, taking my eggs with me out the back door. To do so would be to shop in a way that may be authentically mine but, of course, is impossible to call *shopping*. What Heidegger calls inauthenticity *(Uneigentlichkeit)* is not a moral category and it is certainly not something that I should always avoid.

This covering-over is a way of proceeding that is not mine, it is a way that I have been given by my history, culture, and context, and it is necessary

---

99. Ibid., 196.

100. Ibid., 197.

101. Ibid., 201. The words *objectively* and *subjectively* are between quotation marks because bedazzlement is exactly not something constituted by the subject, in other words, not an object of a subject. Thus, the language of subjectivity and objectivity is inadequate.

to my existence as a person among other persons.[102] Nevertheless, the covering-over of ordinary life and experience is possible only on the basis of a "prior" encounter with things in which amazement and bedazzlement are essential. Marion's way of saying this is to say that because the saturated phenomenon is always "disfigured" by the horizon(s) in which it appears and the knowing subject who apprehends it, it is not recognized as what it is. Nevertheless, even this disfiguring is a manifestation of the thing.

Marion argues that because the experience of the saturated phenomenon is an experience of what I do not and cannot constitute, of what is excessive of understanding, it is an experience of my finitude and impotence. It is an experience in which I find myself constituted rather than constituting because I no longer have a dominant point of view over that which is intuited. Instead, the intuition overwhelms me: "The *I* loses its anteriority and finds itself, so to speak, deprived *(destitué)* of the duties of constitution, and is thus itself constituted: it becomes a *me* rather than an *I*."[103] I become a witness rather than a subject.[104]

For Marion's critics, this is where the problem arises. According to Marion, since the intuition of a saturated phenomenon is an intuition in which the *I* is constituted as *me,* that intuition is a *pure* intuition of transcendence, one unmediated by concepts and without structure.[105] But a pure intuition is, arguably, impossible. The idea of a pure intuition is the idea of an intuition with no content whatsoever; it is the idea of an experience to which no thought at all is attached, not just the experience of the overflow or excess of one's concepts but an experience in which all concepts are absent. As thought-provoking as Marion's analysis is, it goes too far.

---

102. See Heidegger, *Being and Time,* sec. 27. Note that he says, *"The 'one' is an existential and belongs as a primordial phenomenon to the positive constitution of Dasein"* (121, translation modified).

103. Marion, "Saturated Phenomenon," 211.

104. It is important to note that revelation is not the only kind of saturated phenomenon and that revelation is not only the revelation of the divine. Historical events are also saturated phenomena, and revelation includes the picture as spectacle (the "idol") and the particular face that bedazzles me (the "icon"), as well as the intuition of a gaze that envisages me and loves me (theophany). (Marion, "Saturated Phenomenon," 214–15.)

105. For examples of criticisms that focus on this point, see Dominique Janicaud, "The Theological Turn of French Phenomenology," in *Phenomenology and the "Theological Turn: The French Debate,"* 16–103; and his later work, *La phénoménologie éclatée* (Paris: L'Eclat, 1998). See also Marlène Zarader, "Phenomenology and Transcendence," 106–19; as well as Beatrice Han, "Transcendence and the Hermeneutic Circle: Some Thoughts on Marion and Heidegger," 120–44, both in *Transcendence in Philosophy and Religion,* ed. James E. Faulconer (Bloomington: Indiana University Press, 2003).

Quoting Marion, Dominique Janicaud asks, "What remains phenomeno-logical in a reduction that, 'properly speaking, *is* not,' and refers back to 'a point of reference [that is] all the more original and unconditioned as it is more restricted'?"[106] Janicaud's answer is pointed: nothing. A phenomenon requires that which makes it a phenomenon. It requires the *I*. A pure phenomenon is unintelligible.[107]

Does this mean that since there is no pure intuition of transcendence, every reference to transcendence remains trapped within the world of sub-ject and object, remains constituted and so not at all a reference to transcen-dence? No. To deny that there are unconditioned phenomena is not to assert that there is never anything of the unconditioned in phenomena. Intuition does not disappear. We experience the overflow of our concepts, the excess of intuition. As mentioned, without reducing transcendence to a phenom-enon and without arguing for pure intuition, Heidegger has already shown that transcendence is revealed in immanence. For example, he argues that the work of art reveals transcendence in immanence, revealing more than itself: "The work makes public something other than itself; it manifests something other; it is an allegory. In the work of art something is brought together with the thing that is made. To bring together is, in Greek, *symbal-lein*. The work is a symbol."[108]

Of course, Heidegger is hardly the only philosopher to have dealt with this problem or to have argued that we experience transcendence in immanence. The problem is how to talk about those experiences, for, at first glance, we seem unable to speak without speaking merely immanently and categorically. Our concepts are concepts of the phenomenal. How, then, can we use them to speak of what transcends the phenomenal, of overflow and excess, the unconditioned aspect of experience? This problem is an ancient one. Pseudo-Dionysus responds with negative theology. Plotinus speaks of the *trace*, a term that has been picked up and used in contemporary work, such as that of Emmanuel Lévinas and Jacques Derrida. Heidegger uses a variety of terms, among them words clustered around the word *Riß*: "rift," "tear," and as a root in words meaning "sketch," "design," "outline," "bound-ary."[109] Those in literature, such as Roland Barthes, speak of *subversion*, a term that Marléne Zarader borrows.

Finding a way to allow the subversion, interruption, supplementation, or tracing of the unconditioned to show itself in speech is the "solution"

---

106. Janicaud and others, "Theological Turn of French Phenomenology," 62, brackets in original.

107. Zarader, "Phenomemology and Transcendence," 118, makes this point very clearly.

108. Heidegger, "Origin of the Work of Art," 145–46.

109. See, for example, ibid., 188n.

to the problem.[110] Though there are interesting and important differences between these thinkers of interruption and subversion, one can make the general observation that all such talk points to the fact that we always find ourselves in a world that we constitute, and, at the same time, we find that something disturbs the horizon and the *I* that implicitly claim to account completely for things and the world.

Heidegger's discussion of the work of art and his frequent references to poetry are one way to understand such speaking: art and language cannot be reduced to their categorical content, and phenomenological analysis shows that. Marion has also used phenomenological analyses of the work of art to talk about our experience and communication of transcendence.[111] However, given that the experience of transcendence is not necessarily the experience of divine transcendence, being able to talk about transcendence is not enough. The work of art reveals what we might call the transcendence of things, but that is not necessarily the same as divine transcendence. In what do we find divine transcendence?

Like many, perhaps even all, religions, biblical religions call us to live in a certain way.[112] They may do so conceptually, but they need not. They can also do so by means of scripture and ritual and, especially, in their practices. As Kierkegaard points out, "The Christian thesis goes not: *intelligere ut credam,* nor is it *credere ut intelligam.* No, it is: Act according to the command and orders of Christ; do the will of the Father—and you will become a believing person."[113] In this view, the religious experience of transcendence is to be found in acts more than in concepts, whether mythic or rational. Just as works of art testify of the disruption of the ordinary world by transcendence, the acts, rituals, and scriptures of the religious testify of the disruption by divine transcendence. They testify of a call from beyond themselves and their horizon that the religious are bound to hear

---

110. This solution has much to do with the difficulty we find in reading such thinkers as Lévinas and Derrida, though it is not the only explanation.

111. See, for example, Jean-Luc Marion, *La croisée du visible* (Paris: PUF, 1996); and Jean-Luc Marion, *De surcroît: etudes sur les phénomènes saturés.*

112. There is considerable discussion of biblical religion as response and call. See, for example, Paul Ricoeur, "Experience and Language in Religious Discourse," in *Phenomenology and the "Theological Turn,"* 127–46; and especially Marlène Zarader, *La dette impensée: Heidegger et l'héritage hébraïque* (Paris: Seuil, 1990), 56–69. Zarader's discussion is replete with references both to biblical texts and to other authors.

113. Søren Kierkegaard, *Søren Kierkegaard's Journals and Papers,* vol. 3, trans. and ed. Howard V. Hong and Edna H. Hong (Bloomington: Indiana University Press, 1975), 363; emphasis in original. I am grateful to Keith Lane for this reference.

and obey.[114] Gilkey's understanding of religion seems to leave no room for such a call, for being called or chosen rather than choosing. But if there is no room for the call, then there seems to be no room either for testimony and witness.

The theologian is the person who responds to religious testimony reflectively. The materials for that reflection are the revelations of divine transcendence in religious immanence: acts, rituals, and scriptures. And the method of that reflection must be hermeneutic. As Ricoeur says, in the presence of revelation and the absence of universal religious phenomena, we are left "to run the gauntlet of a hermeneutic and more precisely of a *textual* or *scriptural* hermeneutic."[115] Unlike Ricoeur, I include religious ritual and practice among the things to be examined hermeneutically, but I do not think my inclusion changes Ricoeur's point much. A hermeneutic of these texts and practices can awaken us again to the witness they offer, the witness of a divine call.[116] Thus, faced with the "triumph" of secularism, the theologian can stand in the break opened in secularism by Gilkey's critique and read the rituals, practices, and scriptures of his or her religion reflectively, testifying hermeneutically of the divine transcendence witnessed in those texts, of the disruption of secular reality that they demonstrate. Testimony makes it possible for the secularist to hear something of the call to which the religious respond.

An understanding of theology as a hermeneutic of texts and practices is particularly appropriate in biblical religions, religions in which response and call rather than doctrine and dogma are fundamental. A theology that offers a hermeneutic analysis of the scriptural call that initiates religious practices and of the practices themselves not only analyzes the texts and practices to which it attends. Its analysis also testifies of the call of the divine heard in those texts and practices. Hermeneutic theology is, therefore, among the acts appropriate to religious life. It is testimony. The testimony of the hermeneutic theologian is a second-order testimony, for it testifies of the bedazzlement of the divine transcendence that reveals itself in religious life. Theological testimony can be meaningful in a secular

---

114. Of course, false and misleading or misunderstood testimony is always possible. That religious experience testifies of the divine is no proof of the divine. Neither does it follow that all testimony is of equal worth.

115. Ricoeur, "Experience and Language in Religious Discourse," 130. It is no stretch to include more than written, scriptural texts in this hermeneutic—to include, for example, ritual and practice.

116. Paul Moyaert, "The Sense of Symbols as the Core of Religion: A Philosophical Approach to a Theological Debate," in *Transcendence in Philosophy and Religion*, 53–69, is an excellent example of such a hermeneutic. In that essay the Catholic understanding of the sacrament of the Eucharist is the object of his analysis.

world, as Gilkey's critique of secularism shows. Hermeneutic theology cannot serve as the proof for God's existence that some may demand. Neither will it make biblical religion fit comfortably into a secular understanding of the world. Neither will it make it obvious to the secularist that religious language is meaningful. We do not escape the difficulty of being religious (and Kierkegaard is right that we should not). Nevertheless, a hermeneutic theology can speak in the space of secularism's self-contradiction. Testimony and attestation of religious experience, of the experience of divine transcendence, calls both to those who are presently religious, helping them hear the divine call again, and to those who are not religious, seeking to open their ears to the call of the divine. Like quotidian life, secularism washes everything in gray. Like art, hermeneutic theology can remove some of that gray, allowing light to shine through once again.

Rejoinder

D. Gregory Sapp

In his response to Gary Dorrien's essay, James Faulconer is presented with the daunting task of responding to a summary of one of the most important theologians of the twentieth century. Based on his reading of Dorrien's essay, Faulconer raises several issues that deserve further consideration and discussion. While I would like to respond to all of them, I will focus my response to Faulconer on what I perceive to be the most serious of the questions Faulconer raises concerning Gilkey: that Gilkey sees myth as an invalid way of understanding our reality in a secular context. While Faulconer claims that Gilkey has gutted myth of its importance for knowing truth in our scientifically minded world, it seems as though Faulconer has misunderstood Gilkey on this crucial point. A look at two of Gilkey's most popular works not treated by Dorrien should dispel any notion that Gilkey does not value the role of myth in understanding our reality. A consideration of *Shantung Compound* and *Creationism on Trial* reveals that Gilkey not only allows for myth, but considers myth vital to our understanding of the human condition.

Faulconer makes several claims regarding Gilkey's view of myth that reveal an incomplete understanding of Gilkey. First, Faulconer suggests that Gilkey equivocates by suggesting "that myth as well as theology is reflective" (Faulconer, 425). To be sure, Faulconer would be correct to fault Gilkey if this is what Gilkey meant (or even said). Faulconer seems to be drawing from Dorrien, who says in summary of Gilkey, "The purpose of myth is to organize the total 'world' of one's desires, environment, and social situation into a reflective form that makes sense of the world. It follows that the purpose of theology is to explore reflectively the meaning and validity of mythical discourse" (Dorrien, 399). The reflection Dorrien speaks of here is taking place at two levels. The story of myth makes sense of the world in an uncritical manner. Stories are told that explain the origins of facets of the human condition. Myth "makes sense" of one's world through story that is passed down from generation to generation and is taken on the authority of past generations until the myth is itself canonized by the community telling the myth. Theology (in Dorrien's sense here) done from within the religious community looks at myth critically, recognizing that myth is story, to determine whether the story is "true" in its ability to tell us something about the human condition. Theology done from outside the particular religious community can look at myth to determine any number of things, including internal consistency, historical context, or even comparing one community's myth to another's. Myth is the result of reflection on one's condition as it seeks to explain that condition or to speak to that condition. Theology is reflection on the myth itself as myth.

Faulconer also claims that Gilkey "sees secularism as having completely triumphed over religion," resulting in the need to "give a new interpretation of religious myth for secular consciousness" (Faulconer, 426). Because of this, he says, Gilkey has essentially undone "the mythic function of religion" and "[robbed] it of its status as a way of understanding the world"(Faulconer, 426). Nothing could be further from the truth for Gilkey. Gilkey did see the need for translating myth from one culture to the next, for without doing so myth loses its power to speak outside of its own context. Gilkey rightly understood that a scientifically based society cannot accept on its face a story that includes characters such as the walking, talking serpent of Genesis 3. Gilkey does not, however, dismiss such a story as irrelevant, having no voice in a postmodern world. On the contrary, he sees myth as a way of understanding one's world from a given perspective. For example, when the story of Adam and Eve was told, the community may well have believed in the possibility of such animals as described in Genesis 3, even if they had never encountered one. The point of that story, though, is not to show that snakes once walked around upright and were able to carry on extended conversations with humans. The point of the story is to explain that humans are in the condition they are in because the original parents of the human race chose themselves over their Creator as rulers of their lives. In that sense, they exercised a selfishness that seems to be characteristic of people even today. The story of the Fall seems to reflect the fact that many times most people act for themselves, even when warned that such actions will carry dire consequences. For Gilkey to believe that religious myths must be seen for what they are is not to deny them their power; it is to recognize their contextual nature and to recover the truth that is meant to be conveyed through the story. An example of how Gilkey used myth to help us understand our world is found in his theological reflection on his time in a Japanese-controlled internment camp during World War II.

As a young man Gilkey classified himself as a "classical liberalist," believing that humans were innately good. His experiences in an internment camp during World War II, however, created doubt in his mind regarding that view. In 1943 he was teaching English at Yenching University near Peking, China, when he and other Westerners were rounded up and sent to a Japanese-controlled internment camp in Shantung Province. His book, *Shantung Compound: The Story of Men and Women under Pressure,*[117] recounts his experiences of survival in the camp during the war. During his two and a half years at the camp, Gilkey and others had to somehow find a way to create a working community within the camp walls with only the barest of supplies. Creating this community required the cooperation of all the internees, and at first it seemed as if the goodness and ingenuity Gilkey expected of humans would show themselves as they began to organize and build camp life. On several occasions, however, the members of this forced community displayed a level of morality that was considerably lower than what Gilkey had expected.

Shortly after his arrival at camp, Gilkey became part of the leadership committee on housing. As with everything else in camp, space was extremely limited, and quarters were usually rather cramped. In one case, two rooms of equal size held different numbers of men. In one room were housed eleven men and in the other were housed nine. Initially, Gilkey was excited to have available a clear and simple solution:

> I must admit I felt elated. Here at last was a perfectly clear-cut case. Surely the injustice in this situation was, if it ever was in life, clear and distinct: since the rooms were next to each other, anyone who could (like Descartes) count and measure could see the inequity involved.
>
> The solution was so easy: if we did move one man, then each room would have ten persons. "Are not people rational and moral?" I asked myself.[118]

Gilkey's initial enthusiasm faded quickly when he met severe resistance on the part of the men in the room with nine. Offering their own "reasoning,"

---

117. Langdon Gilkey, *Shantung Compound: The Story of Men and Women under Pressure* (New York: Harper and Row, 1966).

118. Ibid., 77.

they refused to take the extra person willingly. Gilkey's belief in the inherent goodness of humanity and in the power of reason to provide the best course of action was significantly challenged:

> I came home that night confused and shaken. Everything that I had believed about "our sorts of people," about the ordinary civilized man, had said to me that his behavior would be fair and generous once he understood a situation. Most of our philosophers, educators, social scientists, and social psychologists had assumed this. For did not most of our modern culture hold that scientific knowledge and technical advance did lead to social progress? And did this not imply that the men who used this knowledge would be rational and just when they understood things clearly through organized inquiry?[119]

Gilkey noted that this kind of reaction was typical of all but one case with which he dealt in six months of trying to sort out housing issues.[120] He recalled that his ideas "as to what people were like and as to what motivated their actions were undergoing a radical revision."[121] His once-high view of humans had been drastically lowered.

Housing issues were not the only issues that challenged the people living in the camp. Food seemed always to be in short supply, giving rise for other displays of selfishness and low morality. One incident involving food occurred when the American Red Cross sent two hundred parcels (boxes) of food and supplies to the Americans in the camp. In addition to clothing and other supplies, these parcels held enough food to keep a person from being really hungry for four months, according to Gilkey.[122] The first shipment of parcels from the American Red Cross was clearly addressed to the two hundred Americans remaining in the camp in July of 1944 and not to any of the others of various nationalities. Gilkey noted that the Americans were, on the whole, generous with the supplies included in the first shipment of parcels. A problem occurred when a second shipment of parcels arrived from the American Red Cross.

The second shipment was of roughly 1,500 parcels but was not addressed to anyone in particular as had been the first shipment. Gilkey and a few others thought that the parcels should be distributed to all who were in the camp, regardless of nationality. One early solution to the problem was to give each of the 1,400 internees one parcel with the remaining 100 parcels divided among the 200 Americans. Just before this plan was go into effect, though, some of the Americans protested that all of the parcels should be given to the Americans who could then share as they wished. This meant

---

119. Ibid., 78–79.
120. Ibid., 79.
121. Ibid., 89.
122. Ibid., 98–100.

that each American would receive seven and a half parcels each with their non-American neighbors receiving nothing. In speaking with those who favored such a plan, Gilkey discovered a deep selfishness that refused to consider any solution that did not put all of the parcels in American hands.

Rather than allow for this selfishness to be explained by the mere animal drive to survive that lies within us, as though humans were composed of both a reasoning (human) and animalistic side, Gilkey noted that the desire to have all of the parcels was based in the reasoned notion that without all of the parcels they might not survive the length of their internment. An animal might fight for food that is present because of present hunger, but only "the human mind could look far into the future and see that four or five parcels would run out over several months' time; then, noting that distant peril, decide that at least seven would be needed for its security."[123] Gilkey came to conclude that this act of selfishness was *human*, not animal, and that it represented a flaw in the human condition that was characteristic of humans alone.

His confidence in the inherent goodness of humans shaken, Gilkey turned to the myth of the Fall of humans as told in Genesis 3. Referring to the story of Adam and Eve's sin, Gilkey says:

> In all probability there was no such single pair of progenitors as the man Adam and his wife Eve; in any event, this is a matter for the biological and anthropological sciences to determine. Few of us wish to or can believe that their one act of disobedience brought about a Fall for the whole race continued in us by inheritance. Blaming our troubles on an inheritance from Adam is as futile and evasive as blaming them on our evolutionary animal predecessors!
>
> Yet, when one looks at the actual social behavior of people, this theological notion of a common, pervasive warping of our wills away from the good we wish to achieve is more descriptive of our actual experience of ourselves than is any other assessment of our situation. What the doctrine of sin has said about man's present state seemed to fit the facts as I found them.[124]

Gilkey's dismissal of the story as literal indicates his interpretation of the story as myth. His acceptance of the story as "true" indicates his acceptance of myth as a valid way of communicating truth about the human condition. The story of the Fall and the doctrine of pervasive sin to which it leads tell us something that is true about the human condition. Gilkey experienced the reality of this truth through his experiences in camp and noted that the best way to explain his experiences was by referring back to

---

123. Ibid., 114.
124. Ibid., 115–16.

the myth of the Fall. In *Shantung Compound*, Gilkey rightly recognizes the value of religious myth as a means of helping us determine truth in our reality.

Gilkey also saw the limitation of myth as a means of knowing, as seen in his work *Creationism on Trial: Evolution and God at Little Rock*.[125] In this work, Gilkey recounts his participation in the 1981 Little Rock trial that was held to determine the constitutionality of Act 590 of the Acts of Arkansas of 1981.

Act 590 was passed and signed into law in Arkansas in 1981 and required the teaching of so-called "creation science" alongside "evolution science" in public school classrooms. A lawsuit was filed against the state by local clergy in Little Rock, claiming that the act crossed the line of separation between church and state and so was unconstitutional. Gilkey was called in as a witness for the plaintiffs to demonstrate that what the act required in the teaching of creation science was actually the teaching of a particular form of religion based on the Bible. While it may seem that, as a witness for the plaintiffs, Gilkey believed that the mythological language of creation was invalid and, thus, had no place in the secular classroom, his arguments against Act 590 demonstrate a clear appreciation for the validity of symbolic[126] language in its proper arena.

There are, primarily, two arguments Gilkey makes to show that Act 590 established a particular religious tradition in the classroom. First, Gilkey noted, the creation-science account requires a creator and is unintelligible without one. According to Gilkey, in the creationist model, God alone was present at creation, for nothing that has been created could have been there to witness the creation itself. Gilkey says:

> Here, at creation, *only* God is present. And, let us also note, only *God* could be present, all alone like that: underived, eternal, necessary, self-sufficient. Above all, only *God's* power and intelligence are capable of bringing all things into being where nothing at all was, and giving them the order and the reality to last. Only God can create out of nothing. Therefore, the idea of creation, as stated in the Act, *must* speak of God,

---

125. Langdon Gilkey, *Creationism on Trial: Evolution and God at Little Rock* (Charlottesville: University Press of Virginia, 1998).

126. I appreciate Faulconer's distinction of symbol from myth. In Gilkey's usage, however, a myth such as the story of the Fall, can itself serve as *a symbol* conveying a truth that goes beyond the story itself. In other words, the story of Adam and Eve's sin is a story without historical basis and so can be regarded as a myth. The story, though, has one major point and so can be seen as a self-contained, singular story that acts as a symbol pointing to a truth beyond itself. It becomes, in Gilkey's understanding at least, a symbol for the brokenness and self-centeredness of humans.

or else it speaks of nothing, it makes no sense at all. It is a religious statement, or it is not a statement at all.[127]

Further, since only God could be present at this creation, knowledge
of the act of creation can be known only through revelation by God to
humans.[128] There is no way for any human to observe the act of creation as
humans are, themselves, a result of that act. For a human to have "knowledge" of the act of creation, the creator would have to impart that knowledge
after the fact. The receiving of such knowledge through revelation is religious and not scientific, as the recognition of revelation is necessarily a
matter of faith and not of scientific verifiability. While all statements of
truth originate within the realm of the secular inasmuch as they are made
and understood by finite human beings, to believe that the origin of the
universe lies outside the universe necessarily requires that knowledge of
that origin come from outside the universe, that is, outside the observable
workings within the universe itself. Such knowledge must be believed rather
than demonstrated and is, thus, religious knowledge.

A second problem with the creation-science position is that it fails to
differentiate between ultimate and proximate causation. As Gilkey explains,
ultimate causation refers to the primary act of causation, that is, that which
caused all that is to be. This is the first act of creation. As noted above, any
statements about ultimate causation—creation—are necessarily religious in
their nature. Secondary, or proximate, causation has to do with causation
within the enclosed system that is the result of primary causation. Once a
system is in place, then statements of causations within the system can be
made by observation of the system itself. This is the arena of science. Gilkey
is careful to separate these two spheres and shows that the sphere of ultimate causation is the sphere of the religious while that of secondary causation is the sphere of science. The language of the two spheres is necessarily
different and should be recognized as such.

Creation-science, however, does not distinguish between ultimate and
proximate origins[129] and so does not distinguish between scientific arguments and philosophical arguments.[130] Gilkey spends more time on this
in his deposition.[131] There, he says, "[All] direct analogies from experience,
all ordinary sequences of secondary causes, are here transcended, even
negated, in the religious symbol expressing the origin in God of that whole
experience and that whole system of causes."[132] Gilkey clearly recognizes

---

127. Gilkey, *Creationism on Trial*, 103; emphases in original.
128. Ibid., 102.
129. Ibid., 34.
130. Ibid., 35.
131. Ibid., 49–61.
132. Ibid., 60.

the need for mythological language and the use of symbols to speak of that which lies outside the secular realm of observation. A problem occurs when the language of the two realms is confused such that the mythological language of religion is mistaken as scientific language of the secular.

Creationists, however, believe they have as much right to speak of creation as science as evolutionists have to speak of evolution as science. Since the creationists make no distinction between ultimate and secondary causes, hence, between scientific and philosophical arguments, creationists believe that when an evolutionist claims evolutionary forces were at work in bringing our present reality to be, the evolutionist is claiming there is no God and so claim that evolutionary theory is religious itself. The obverse of this is the real issue, though: the creationists claim that creation-science is just as scientific as evolutionist-science because both take positions with regard to the existence or nonexistence of a creator.

Gilkey rebuts this position in his trial testimony by showing that the realm of science is necessarily limited to what can be observed within the natural world and cannot go beyond the observable, natural world to make supernatural claims:

> Science is, in short, *secular*; it deals with the worldly world: with nature and its forces, with human bodies, and—by extension into the social and psychological sciences—with social, historical, and possibly psychological forces. It cannot go beyond this "secular" level because then it leaves the observable, sharable, quantitative, measurable, the natural or finite, level. Thus it leaves out a lot: my intentions, decisions, values, and commitments, as well as God's; it omits the human and divine *person*.
>
> Thus, scientific discussions of origins are significantly different from religious discussions of origins. The first trace out the finite processes by which things arose and came to be; the second witnesses to the ultimate origin and purpose of these processes. Scientific accounts of development in astronomy, geology, and biology, are, therefore, not at all incompatible with religious views, even though they do not speak of God. The fact that science omits God is a result of the *limitation* of science, not of its atheism: Science is limited to finite causes and *cannot* speak of God without making God into a finite cause.[133]

Creationists are at a disadvantage in their arguments, then, in that they do not understand where the lines should be drawn between the two realms. In confusing science for a philosophy, they confuse their philosophy for science.

Gilkey addresses the other side of this problem as well. When science does speak to primary causes it ceases to be science and instead becomes

---

133. Ibid., 115; emphasis in original.

religious.[134] In chapter 7 of *Creationism on Trial,* Gilkey speaks to the danger of science becoming a religion in the form of scientism. In this case, science oversteps its limits as religion oversteps its limits when it attempts to speak authoritatively of secondary causes. To be sure, Gilkey realizes "that all thought *is* 'theory-laden,'"[135] and he spends a great deal of energy in this account showing that science is full of presuppositions as is religion.[136]

For Gilkey, then, mythological language clearly has its place in the description of our reality. Dorrien is correct to show that Gilkey emphasized the necessity of recognizing mythological language as inextricably tied to the secular, but this does not indicate a dismissal on Gilkey's part of myth as pointing beyond itself to truth beyond the secular. Influenced by Tillich (as well as Whitehead, Bultmann, and others), Gilkey recognized the power of symbolic language in the form of myth to offer true descriptions of the human condition as well as to communicate truth from the sacred to the secular. He was careful, though, to emphasize the proper realm and limit of mythological language to the realm of ultimate causation. Mythological language, though valid in its own realm, cannot speak intelligibly with regard to issues of proximate causation. This may be why Gilkey is sometimes misunderstood as saying that myth has no place in our world. Nothing could be further from the truth.

On a final note, Faulconer also wonders "why Gilkey does not deal with Heidegger's argument that God must be a being rather than being itself" (Faulconer, 426). There are at least two reasons for this. First, Gilkey, like most Protestant and Catholic theologians, is unwilling to limit God to a particular time and place as is necessary when one refers to God as "a being." Second, Gilkey recognizes that all language about God is metaphorical language and does not want to fall into speaking of God as "a being" like we understand other beings to be. To do so makes God nothing more than a projection of our own imaginations from within our own contexts and places us squarely in the sights of Feuerbach's criticism of the very existence of God. Gilkey, following Tillich, prefers to speak of the symbol of God, recognizing that our language is inadequate to capture the essence of God by itself. Unlike contemporary Christian fundamentalists who have no qualms about making positivist statements about God, Gilkey is more

---

134. Ibid., 64–65.

135. Ibid., 134; emphasis in original.

136. While the philosophy of science is a terribly interesting topic, it is beyond the scope of this essay, so I omit most of Gilkey's intriguing discussion here. For a more thorough treatment of the relationship of science to religion, I suggest Gilkey's *Religion and the Scientific Future, Society and the Sacred* and his *Nature, Reality, and the Sacred.*

cautious and prefers to see our speech of God as *pointing to* God and not as *descriptive of* God.

This is the very reason Gilkey sees so much importance in mythological language for bridging the gap between us and that which we cannot directly experience. The danger lies in mistaking the mythological language for the truth itself rather than seeing the language as pointing to the truth. As quoted above, Gilkey cannot accept the historicity of two original parents—Adam and Eve—who caused a break in the relationship between God and humans by one act of disobedience. However, the story of the Fall does, in fact, represent a truth about what appears to be a universal human condition, i.e., that at some point to be human means to make decisions for the self that are contrary to whatever authority has determined for us so far. The story of the Fall tells us that we usually make decisions based on what we think is best for ourselves rather than taking the larger picture into consideration. This truth was borne out time and time again in Gilkey's experience in the internment camp, and the story of the Fall helped him make sense of his experiences there. Gilkey recognized the language of the Fall as mythological and the Fall itself as a symbol that points to a truth of the human condition that is beyond the story itself. One does not have to take the story of the Fall as historical to accept the truth of the Fall as real. This is the beauty of mythology.

Gilkey in no way dismisses myth as irrelevant in a scientific world. He argues, instead, for an understanding on the part of both religionists and secularists that myth is a means to an end and not the end itself. Further, myth should be seen as conditioned by its cultural context, not to dispel it, but to understand and to be able to apply it to a contemporary setting. An unfortunate, and unnecessary, altercation has arisen since the Enlightenment between those who insist on the historical truth of the myths of religions and those who would dismiss the religions on their mistaken interpretation of the religions' myths. Understood correctly for what it is, myth still serves as a viable way for helping us make sense of our world and of ourselves.

Reply to Professor Sapp

James E. Falconer

D. GREGORY SAPP SAYS THAT MY CRITICISMS OF LANGDON GILKEY "reveal an incomplete understanding" of his work and, specifically, that I have misunderstood Gilkey when I argue that he has gutted myth of its importance for knowing the truth. Since I was responding to Gary Dorrien's précis of Gilkey's position and I do not have a first-hand knowledge of Gilkey himself, that is quite possible. It is always dangerous to argue against someone based on another person's account because doing so at least doubles the opportunities for misunderstanding. I would not be surprised to be shown that I have gotten something wrong about Gilkey, even something important. Nevertheless, if Sapp's response gives a reasonably accurate account of Gilkey's position, I do not think that the overall argument I made is fundamentally flawed. Reviewing that argument against the backdrop of Sapp's response will allow me to bring my criticisms of Gilkey into relief.

As I understand Gilkey, via Dorrien, he argues that myth organizes the world as a totality "into a reflective form that makes sense of the world" (Dorrien, 399). It is the expression of a way of being in the world, and it follows that the self-understanding of the secular world is mythic. Sapp seems to agree with that description of myth and the conclusion which follows from it. In spite of that agreement, however, Sapp follows Gilkey in distinguishing between myth and a critical understanding of the world and in privileging the latter (Sapp, 436–40). My point was that if a critical understanding of the world is part of a reflective form that makes sense of the world, then it, too, is mythic. That complicates the relation between religion and secularism considerably.

My major criticism of Gilkey is that he does not deal with the complication sufficiently: we can criticize a myth, but doing so involves either a different framework, one outside the myth being criticized (which will beg the question), or it is a work of immanent criticism. Using secular reason to criticize myth is using one form for understanding the world as a whole to make sense of another. However, since understanding the world as a whole is myth, and legitimate criticism requires a view of the world as some whole, the privilege given to any one form of understanding is given by the form of understanding itself, the form of understanding from within which one makes the criticism. There is no neutral realm from which to make our criticisms. Thus, when secular reason criticizes myth, it begs the question. Nevertheless, it does not follow that it is impossible to criticize myth. Criticism is possible with a hermeneutic, immanent criticism. (I take

Gilkey's criticism of secularism as unable to deal with ultimacy to be such an immanent criticism.)

According to Sapp, Gilkey recognizes that theology looks at myth from within the mythic community: "theology is reflection on the myth itself as myth" (Sapp, 436). That reveals the problem: either such reflection begs the question—if, for example, it uses the tools and methods of the secular world—or it is a hermeneutic, immanent criticism. In many ways, my criticism of creationism overlaps with Gilkey's. In spite of that, his response to the story of the Fall, reducing it to an idea that can be understood even outside of religion and theology, "a common, pervasive warping of our wills away from the good" (Sapp, 439), is good evidence that he accepts the ability of secular myth to criticize religious myth. So does his description of the Genesis story as nonliteral but true, ignoring the question of truth by assuming that it is defined by the secular myth. I acknowledge Gilkey's recognition that lines must be drawn between science and religion and that one ought not to confuse science for a philosophy or philosophy for a science. Nevertheless, Gilkey allows for the criticism of religious myth from outside the mythic community without explaining how that is possible. Gilkey does not tell us what gives the secular myth its explanatory privilege. Though it appears that Gilkey, Dorrien, and Sapp say that there is truth in myth, they believe that "all statements of truth originate within the realm of the secular" (Sapp, 441), which is part of the secular myth. The truth of myth itself is not real truth, not even for those supposedly reflecting on it from within the community.

As to the question of why Gilkey is willing to use Heidegger's thought but ignores Heidegger's argument that God is a being: the issue is one of consistency, not whether Heidegger knew the traditional arguments for why God cannot be a being. Given the fact that Heidegger began his career as a Catholic theologian, it is difficult to imagine that he did not. Nevertheless, as he understood his own thinking, it requires that we understand God as a being—a provocative claim, to be sure, but not one ignorant of the counterarguments. What does it mean for a theology to appropriate Heidegger's thinking but to ignore that Heideggerian provocation? One could argue that Heidegger's conclusion does not follow from his understanding of the question of being. However, without such an argument, a reader is entitled to conclude that the appropriation is inconsistent, appropriating what it wishes but ignoring the conclusions that purportedly follow. Implicated in this problem is the question of what kind of transcendence Gilkey ascribes to God, a knotty issue and an issue that one cannot avoid if one takes a Heideggerian view, but an issue that it seems Gilkey ignored, as have many other theologians.

Sapp is right to tell us that the metaphorical character of religious language "is the very reason Gilkey sees so much importance in mythological language for bridging the gap between us and that which we cannot directly experience" (Sapp, 444). I am not opposed to understanding the language of religion in mythic terms, nor do I disagree that they are metaphorical, but as I understand Gilkey's view, religious language is *merely* mythic and *merely* metaphorical. If it is to be more than that, it must be translated into the terms of secularism. Thus, I think that, in spite of himself, Gilkey follows Bultmann's program of demythologizing.

Consider a particular claim: "This theological notion of a common, pervasive warping of our wills away from the good we wish to achieve is more descriptive of our actual experience of ourselves than is any other assessment of our situation" (Sapp, 439). Though religion may have helped us see that point, having been translated into secular language, it is no longer religious. The myth of secularism can replace that of religion (even if science cannot replace religion) because it is fundamental in a way that the religious myth is not. If we accept Gilkey's view, then the meaning of religion and religious experience is ultimately secular and the language and ritual of religion are merely primitive means for pointing at what secularism gives us more directly.

About the Authors

Gary Dorrien (Ph.D. Union Graduate School) received an M.Div. from the Union Theological Seminary and an M.A. and Th.M. from Princeton Theological Seminary. He is Professor of Religion at Columbia University and Reinhold Niebuhr Professor of Social Ethics at Union Theological Seminary. An Episcopal priest, he is the author of eleven books and over one hundred articles that range across the fields of theology, philosophy, social theory, politics, ethics, and history. He recently completed the third volume of a trilogy titled *The Making of American Liberal Theology* (Westminster John Knox Press).

Kent E. Robson (Ph.D. Stanford University) did considerable work in theology during his doctoral studies in philosophy and did postdoctoral work at the University of Warsaw, Poland. He is a professor of languages and philosophy at Utah State University.

James E. Faulconer (Ph.D. Pennsylvania State University) has published on the philosophy of psychology and the philosophy of religion, as well as on contemporary European philosophy. He is the editor of *Transcendence in Religion and Philosophy* (Indiana University Press, 2003) and, with Mark Wrathall, *Appropriating Heidegger* (Cambridge, 2000). He is a professor of philosophy at Brigham Young University, where he is also the Associate Director of the Faculty Center.

D. Gregory Sapp (Ph.D. University of Virginia) earned an M.Div. from the Princeton Theological Seminary and a B.A. from Stetson University. He has published and presented papers in the areas of philosophical theology and in the history of Christian thought. He is the author of *A New Testament Curriculum* and *An Old*

Testament Curriculum, used by the Texas Baptist Laity Institute. He is Associate Professor of Religious Studies and Hal S. Marchman Chair of Civic and Social Responsibility at Stetson University.

A Dialogue on Theology as Hermeneutics

A Catholic View of Philosophy: Revelation and Reason

David Tracy

In the history of Christian theology, philosophy has played many roles. The crucial factor, from the theological side, is some notion of revelation as well as the divinely engifted reception of that revelation called "faith"—a knowledge born of revelation. A familiar Catholic (and possibly Mormon?) theological position is this: if there is divine self-revelation and if there is a form of human knowledge constituted by that revelation, then theology can neither ignore nor be sublated by philosophy. Many modern philosophies focus on the category "religion," and any claims to divine self-revelation will be philosophically interpreted under a philosophical construal of religion. Indeed, philosophy of religion is a discipline invented by modern thinkers. Its most characteristic moves are twofold: first, to religionize the traditional question of God and revelation and thereby any understanding of divine self-revelation; second, to render philosophically intelligible the cultural and empirical category of religion. Philosophy of religion is the discipline most clearly allied to theology in modernity. And yet, the two disciplines are constituted differently.

Philosophy of religion must clarify the category "religion" and, through that strictly philosophical clarification, any further philosophical notion of "revelation" or even "God." Theology must clarify the strictly theological category "revelation" and, through that clarification, any theological claim to a form of knowledge constituted by a divine self-disclosure ("faith"). As an interested reader of the distinguished history of Latter-day Saint philosophical reflection, I have found it fascinating but difficult to try to understand the complex relationships between philosophy and theology in Mormon thought. I write this article to clarify certain opinions in Catholic thought on philosophy and theology with the hope that this inner-Catholic clarification may encourage a similar articulation of the relationship of philosophy and theology in the Mormon tradition, the one Christian tradition grounded in the revelation attested to in not only the first or Old Testament and the second or New Testament but also in the third testament of the canonical works attesting to the new revelation to the Latter-day Saints. Only after a self-clarification of their distinct subject matters (and therefore methods) can a philosophy of religion and a theology of revelation clarify their further relationships to each other. Such, at least, is my basic hypothesis for Catholic theologies. Since I have elsewhere written on the "origins" of modern philosophy of religion and how the category "religion" (not "God" or "revelation") began to play the major philosophical role in Hume, Kant, and Hegel, I will here turn to the second discipline in conversation, Catholic theology. My hope is to clarify one way in which a theology grounded not in religion but in revelation may nonetheless relate in significant ways to philosophy insofar as a revelation-constituted understanding of faith as knowledge is a meaningful cognitive claim.

First, however, it is important to eliminate two often employed models as not useful for understanding, much less assessing, the relationship of philosophy and theology. These models are fideism and rationalism. These models are almost never used by a Catholic thinker for a self-description but are often used by other thinkers in describing what is judged to be an inadequate alternative. But since such ideal types are used so widely in both philosophical and theological forms, it is well to eliminate, at the very beginning, at least the "vulgar" (both as intellectually unsophisticated and, alas, also as popular—especially in the textbooks) understanding of these two much used and much abused models.

I admit that just as Leslek Kolakowski claims that what is often called "vulgar Marxism" may, in fact, be Marxism (however unhappy that thought may be to revisionary Marxists), so too what I am here naming "vulgar fideism" and "vulgar rationalism" may actually prove in some rare individual cases of Catholic theologies to be fideism and rationalism. Even if that proves to be one case, it would not remove the need to develop some further distinction for the large majority of theological options between something like the vulgar and revisionary forms of each option. Indeed, when one observes the fuller complexity of a position like that of Hans Urs von Balthasar on the one hand or George Tyrell on the other, the labels "fideism" (von Balthasar) and "rationalism" (Tyrell) begin to seem entirely inappropriate.

Strictly speaking, a fideist position insists that faith is the only relevant form of knowledge on matters of revelation. Philosophy, therefore, may be useful on other topics like science (or even religion) but is irrelevant for understanding faith and revelation except in relatively trivial ways. It is difficult to find a pure form of fideism (hence its ideal-type status) since even pure traditionalist fundamentalists usually admit that every believing theologian uses some philosophical categories at least for the expression of one's understanding of faith. Therefore, at the very least, philosophy as clarificatory conceptual analysis of some categories (for example, causality) inevitably used by theologians is necessary even for a fideist perspective. But this conceptual analysis position, on strictly fideist grounds, cannot play the more ambitious (if still philosophically modest) role that several analytical "Christian philosophers" accord their philosophy of understanding Christian faith as knowledge. For these Christian philosophies after all include both defensive moves against philosophical critiques of faith and constructive (or better, reconstructive) moves to clarify and sometimes even to develop the understanding and thus intelligibility of Christian beliefs as forms of knowledge. The better position (like its theological counterparts of Hans Urs von Balthasar in Catholic theology and Karl Barth in Reformed theology) is far more complex than the usual meaning that "fideism" allows.

The same kind of intellectual difficulty holds for the category "rationalism." Strictly speaking, a rationalist position holds that only reason is relevant for understanding and judging any cognitive claims implicit in Christian faith. Just as there are some strict fideists, so too there are some strict rationalists. However, the very turn to religion as the central category needing analysis in modern philosophies of religion has occasioned a hesitation in assuming that religion can be adequately interpreted and thereby assessed or judged by reason. This move to acknowledge the complexity of religious phenomena as not reducible to other phenomena, as understood by Kant in *Religion within the Limits of Reason Alone,* is in various forms a now familiar position in modern philosophies of religion. No more than Kant can be considered a strict rationalist in relationship to religion (as D'Holbach or Brand Blanshard can be), so too most philosophers of religion and most liberal or revisionary theologians employing some philosophical analysis of "religion" (beginning with Schleiermacher) cannot be construed as rationalist. Something more complex is at stake in the positions often named fideism or rationalism by their adversaries.

This complexity can be viewed by observing it in two familiar Catholic theological candidates for these labels: Hans Urs von Balthasar (sometimes called a fideist) and George Tyrell (sometimes called a rationalist). Von Balthasar's position is well known: Catholic theology must be based in God's self-revelation and theologians should not search, via philosophy or any other discipline, to ground theology in human experience or knowledge. At the same time, von Balthasar insists that reason and all human culture should be reconstructed from the viewpoint of the new knowledge gained through the gift of faith. In short, faith as knowledge, clarified through the discipline of theology and precisely as *theological* knowledge, can reconstruct philosophical knowledge in such a manner that philosophy too can acknowledge the reasonableness, although not the truth (which is constituted by faith alone), of the knowledge constituted as faith by revelation.

At the other end of the spectrum, George Tyrell, in the Catholic modernist crisis early in this century, held that theology is accountable to the "right, correct, modern [for Tyrell, 'personalist'] philosophy" in order to develop criteria of credibility or intelligibility for assessing the cognitive claims of Christian faith. However, the strictly existential character of faith, in Tyrell's view, does not allow faith to be existentially reducible to philosophy. Philosophy, in this view, provides a personalist metaphysics for understanding and assessing all relevant cognitive claims. God—existentially the God of Christian faith—is the God experienced through Jesus Christ as existentially revelatory and salvific. To understand and assess this existential relationship to God, therefore, demands explicitly theological criteria, including criteria of appropriateness to scripture and the classical Catholic tradition, including a Christology, not merely a Jesusology. The existential criteria, moreover, need include, but are not exhausted by, an understanding of "religion" as a category for human wholeness.

There can be little doubt that Hans Urs von Balthasar inclines to fideism but opens up to a reconstruction of philosophy by theology in such manner that "Christian philosophers" can employ his work for their own strictly philosophical purposes. At the same time, George Tyrell and the other Catholic modernists, however dependent upon and indeed philosophically creative in their use and development of modern philosophy, remain distinct from rationalism by their strictly Christological (and thereby strictly theological) interpretation of the use of philosophy in theology. After all, strictly Enlightenment rationalisms, when interpreting and assessing Christian faith, needed something like a theory of religion (or "natural religion") but surely no Christology!

My point in recalling so briefly the main outlines of the complex positions of von Balthasar and Tyrell is not to suggest that there are no fideists or rationalists on the issue of the relationship of philosophy and theology. Clearly, there are. But the more interesting and influential theological positions—that is, complex positions like those of von Balthasar and Tyrell—are, I believe, too complex and too nuanced to lend themselves to so wooden a designation as fideism or rationalism.

This is even more the case for the mediating positions on the theological spectrum, especially but not solely the main Roman Catholic and Anglican positions. There are real differences, for example, between Karl Rahner and

Hans Urs von Balthasar on the relationship of theology and philosophy.[1] But those real differences are not clarified, despite the claims of some of their followers, by such terms as fideist or rationalist. Indeed, von Balthasar was far more open to the reconstructive task of philosophy's use in theology than was Karl Barth. This is partly dependent on von Balthasar's use of the Catholic model of grace and nature as distinct from Barth's understanding of grace as power and his Reformation model of grace-sin and gospel-law. There should be little surprise that von Balthasar remains analogical in language and in his construal of basic continuities involved in the relationship of philosophy and theology while Barth, even after writing his commentary *Romans* and developing his "analogy of faith" positions, remains dialectical in his analysis of that relationship. Those classical nature-grace (Catholic) and grace-sin (Reformed) differences remain real and deeply influential upon the use of philosophy by a particular Catholic or Reformed theology.

Moreover, Karl Rahner's transcendental reformulation of both philosophy and theology does insist that philosophy can show that the condition of the possibility of human beings is that we are none other than contingent, temporal, and historical hearers of a possible word of revelation. But that Word comes to us as pure gift, sheer grace, and as a categorical revelation which correlates with but is not equivalent to transcendental revelation. This transcendental position frees Rahner to a greater intrinsic use of philosophy in his theology than von Balthasar. But both work within the same grace-nature Catholic model, so the differences, although real, are not mutually exclusive.

Revelation and the Knowledge of Faith

The first need, from the viewpoint of Catholic theology, is to clarify the category "revelation," not "religion." Theologically construed, revelation is an event of divine self-manifestation in the event and person of Jesus the Christ.[2] Each of these categories demands clarification:

Event

"Event" language in contemporary theology is indicative of the gratuitous or gracious character of divine revelation. The very fact that God reveals Godself is grace, event, happening. Theologically, revelation is never a

---

1. For a good study, see Rowan Williams, "Balthasar and Rahner," in *The Analogy of Beauty: The Theology of Hans Urs von Balthasar*, ed. John Riches (Edinburgh: T. and T. Clark, 1986), 11–34.

2. For an expanded version of my hermeneutical analysis here, see my essay to the former conference on "Word, Language, and Religion" in the volume edited by Marco Olivetti entitled *Religione, Parola, Scrittura* (Padova: CEDAM, 1992).

human achievement, work, or necessity; revelation must be understood as event, happening, gratuity, grace. Hermeneutically, the category event (*Ereignis* in German) is applicable even to word as Word-event (*Sprach-Ereignis*) as a happening of language itself and as therefore not under the control of the modern subject.

The Event of Divine Self-Manifestation

The language of divine self-manifestation indicates, theologically, that revelation is not construed primarily (as in the older Catholic manual scholastic traditions) as propositional truths that would otherwise be unknown (that is, "supernatural" or "revealed" truths). Rather, in modern Catholic theologies revelation is primarily construed on an interpersonal or encounter model as an event of divine self-manifestation to humanity. This interpersonal model of revelation further assumes that some person-like characteristics (namely, intelligence and love) must be employed to understand the reality of God as God manifests Godself as Wisdom and Love. The dangers of anthropomorphism here are real but finally unavoidable (as Buber insisted in his critique of Spinoza and his insistence on designating the biblical God as Thou). Indeed, despite some strong qualifications on the use of personal language for God (for example, Schleiermacher), all modern Catholic theologians who employ the category of revelation as divine self-manifestation must, if they wish to be hermeneutically faithful to scripture, at some point also employ (biblical) personal language and thereby interpersonal models for God as Wisdom and Love.

Hermeneutically, this use of the category "manifestation" is also, as we shall see below, suggestive of the hermeneutical notion of truth as primordially an event of manifestation (or disclosure-concealment). The subjective correlate to the objectivity of manifestation is "recognition." In an analogous manner, the theological counterpart to the event-gift-grace of revelation as divine self-manifestation is the gift, grace, happening (never "work" or personal achievement) of faith as reorientation of trust in and loyalty to the God disclosing Godself in the Word, Jesus Christ.

Event of Divine Self-Manifestation in the Word, Jesus Christ

The decisive event of God's self-manifestation is not merely an event, but a person, that is, the person of Jesus of Nazareth proclaimed and manifested as the Christ and thereby as the decisive Word-event of divine self-manifestation. In and through this Jesus Christ, the Christian learns the identity of the God disclosing Godself in Jesus Christ. Here one cannot find a strict hermeneutical correlate but rather the possibility of hermeneutically clarifying the nature of Word as divine self-expression. In Catholic Christian theism, the ultimate understanding of the Word is as the second person of the Trinity. Any full Catholic theological understanding of God would need that further Trinitarian clarification in order to understand both the intrinsically relational character of the doctrine or symbol of revelation and the intrinsically relational (that is, explicitly Trinitarian) reality of the Christian understanding of God.

For present purposes these further important questions on the Trinitarian nature of God as clarified by the Christian understanding of revelation in the Word, Jesus Christ, need not be pursued further here. Rather, there is a prior need to clarify how Word enters the Catholic Christian understanding of revelation as an entirely dialectical reality that determines the Catholic understanding of Word.

The dialectic of the Word in Christian theological self-understanding begins with the hermeneutical insight that Word may take the form of either *Logos* or *Kerygma*. Hermeneutically, Word is, therefore, both disclosure-manifestation (Word in the Form of Logos) and proclamation-disruption (Word in the Form of Kerygma). In history of religion terms, Logos becomes "religion as manifestation," especially the manifestation of primordial correspondences obtaining throughout all reality. The archaic, meditative, and mystical traditions analyzed by Mircea Eliade and others are the clearest illustrations of these Logos traditions, just as sacrament, nature, creation, and cosmos are the clearest Christian analogies of Word in the form of Logos manifesting all reality (God-cosmos-history-the self) as a vast system of disclosive and participating analogical correspondences. The reality of participating symbol (sacrament) is crucial for the Word as Logos.

In history of religion terms, Word in the form of Kerygma or Proclamation also becomes word as interruption, disruption; that is, word as a distancing from a sense of manifestory participation. Where Word as Logos discloses a vast system of participatory and analogical correspondences, Word as proclamation both discloses and conceals Word as proclamatory interruption of all senses of continuity, participation, and rootedness (all now labeled "paganism"). When the German Catholic political theologian Johann Baptist Metz (here, following Walter Benjamin) describes religion with the one word "interruption," he well describes this classical trajectory of the prophetic, apocalyptic, proclamatory Word in Judaism and Christianity.

In Christian theology the dialectic of Word in the form of Logos and Word in the form of Interruptive Kerygma can be found in all the classic dichotomies and become dialectical antinomies of Christian theological self-understanding. Consider the contrast between Logos Christologies beginning with the disclosive manifestory Gospel of John and apocalyptic Christologies like Mark's or proclamatory and disruptive Christologies of the Cross like Paul's Christology of Christ crucified. Or consider the contrast in Christian theologies between the Comprehensible-Incomprehensible Logos traditions' understanding of God in Aquinas and Rahner and the Hidden-Revealed proclamatory God of Luther and Calvin. Recall Paul Tillich's formulation of the dialectic of Protestant principle (word as disruptive, critical, suspicious proclamation) and of Catholic substance (word as participatory Logos). Or recall, in conceptual terms, the differences between the analogical languages of classical Orthodox, Anglican, and Roman Catholic theologies and the negative dialectical theologies of classical Protestant theologies.

Even in terms of the symbols of incarnation-cross-resurrection, Word as Logos instinctively appeals to the symbol of incarnation whereas Word as Kerygma instinctively appeals to the cross. Both find the need for one another in their distinct appeals to the symbol of resurrection to complete the dialectic of Christian symbols. Only the fuller symbol system of incarnation-cross-resurrection clarifies the dialectic of Jesus the Christ as the Word; that is, as both Logos and Kerygma, both John's Word of Glory and Paul's Crucified Christ, both Mark's Word of the cross and Luke's Word of resurrection-ascension.

It would be possible to clarify further the Christian understanding of Word through a further exposition of one or another of the classical dialectics noted above: incarnation-cross; sacrament-word; cosmos-history; symbol-allegory; icon-idol; analogy-dialectic; Comprehensible-Incomprehensible God or Hidden-Revealed God; creation-redemption; nature-grace or grace-sin; love-justice; participation-distance; continuity-discontinuity; continuity-interruption. Pervading all these dialectics is the originating Christian dialectic of revelation as Word: Jesus the Christ as Word—Word in the form of Logos and Word in the form of Proclamation. It would also be possible to see this same dialectic continued in the two distinct readings of the tradition: either the prophetic-apocalyptic reading of the Word-as-proclamation tradition beginning with Mark and Paul or the meditative tradition which yields wisdom and mystical and archaic (cosmic) readings of Word-as-disclosive Logos beginning with John.

As anyone familiar with the history of Catholic theological reflection can readily see, all these formulations of the Christian dialectic of Word have been tried and reformulated over and over again in the history of Catholic reflection in both philosophy and theology. Each of them has yielded genuine fruit. However, too many of those theological formulations of the dialectic of the Christian revelation as Word have ignored the fact that Jesus Christ as Word is both disclosive (Logos) and disruptive (Proclamation) of God and humanity, of cosmos and history. Word therefore manifests both nearness and distance, both participation and interruption.

To ignore this dual function of Jesus as the Christ is to ignore the fact that the fuller Christian description of revelation, the event of divine self-manifestation in the Word, Jesus Christ, is testified to and indeed rendered in written words and written forms like narratives in scripture. This singular fact of revelation as written and there informed by forms in scripture cannot be hermeneutically and theologically irrelevant. Christianity must affirm its self-understanding in its scriptural-biblical base and its Jewish, not Greek, roots. Catholic theology, moreover, must leave behind both naïve and Gnostic notions of the Letter and the Spirit in order to understand the place of written scripture in Christian self-understanding. Only by a focus on scripture as written word may any adequate hermeneutics of the Christian understanding of revelation through Word in writing occur.

For Catholic Christianity, the Christian Testament (New and Old) is scripture: the written original witness to the revelation. The decisive revelation for all Christians occurs in the event and person of Jesus Christ as true Word of God. The Word, Jesus Christ, is affirmed as present to the community and the individual Christian in two principal forms: word (proclamation) and sacrament (those disclosive signs which render present what they signify). Even the common confession of most Christian churches (including the Latter-day Saints)—"We believe in Jesus Christ with the apostles"—is dependent on this notion of the Word's presence to the community. The rule for the *lex credendi* is the *lex orandi*. The present worshipping community renders present the same Jesus Christ in word and sacrament to all Christian believers. The Scripture remains the authoritative *normans non normata*. The written texts called Scripture assure that the Christ of the present Christian community is the same Christ witnessed to and testified to by the apostolic witnesses as the decisive self-manifestation of God and humanity. Neither "Scripture Alone" nor "Scripture and Tradition" clarify this important hermeneutical role of scripture for the Christian. Rather one may speak of Scripture-in-tradition; that is, the rendering present in word and sacrament of the Word witnessed to in the scriptures as decisively present in Jesus Christ.

The recent recovery of the import of the genre "gospel" as a proclamatory narrative has clarified this form's peculiar, indeed unique, role as indispensable in the written narrative and confessional scriptural texts for Christian self-understanding. If gospel is both proclamation and narrative, gospel is both a proclamatory confession of faith and a disclosive narration of the identity of this Jesus as the Christ and thereby ultimately as God. *Lex credendi* is based on the presence of the Word as Logos and Kerygma to the worshipping community *(lex orandi)*. Both are held together by what may be named the peculiar role of narrative writing as rendering present what is absent, the identity of the God manifesting Godself in Jesus Christ.

Faith as Knowledge: Event, Manifestation, Possibility, Exercise

In Catholic Christian self-understanding, faith is a gift. Faith is the gift-grace for the reception of revelation. Faith is constituted by God's own self-manifestation. In and through the Spirit, Jesus is recognized in faith as the very Christ of God. Jesus Christ is acknowledged as God's own self-manifestation. Who God is—Love (1 Jn. 4:16)—is known by faith in and through knowing God's identity as that identity is manifested primarily in the form of the passion narrative of Jesus Christ. Who Christians may become—those commanded and empowered to love—is known by those Christians in and through their faith in Jesus Christ. Bernard Lonergan, the great contemporary Catholic theologian, understood faith as "a knowledge born of love," which is surely a correct, if somewhat cryptic, description of the kind of knowledge which Catholic faith is.[3] For faith is a knowledge born of revelation, and that revelation in Jesus Christ manifested to those engifted to faith by the Spirit is Love: God is love and human beings are loved and are therefore commanded and empowered to love in their turn. Indeed, all being is now known as gracious. Here, as Lonergan suggests, is the one great exception to the dictum: *non amatum nisi cognitum.*

What kind of knowledge is this knowledge of faith? Here the traditional analogy of love seems entirely appropriate. What love fundamentally gives is a new understanding of possibility. What once seemed "reality," more exactly "actuality," now seems in the light of love's new understanding relatively narrow in scope and small in spirit. The new knowledge born of all human love is the knowledge, above all, of new possibility. The knowledge born of Christian revelation, the knowledge of God as Loving Father and Mother, a knowledge obtained through Jesus Christ in the Spirit, is a knowledge in and through the manifold forms of revelation, beginning with and grounded in the form of the passion narrative—that narrative which identifies who this Jesus is and thereby who Christ is. In identifying Jesus as the Christ, the narrative also identifies the God manifesting Godself in Jesus Christ as none other than Pure Unbounded Love.

The knowledge born of that revelation of God as Love is the new knowledge of faith—the gift/power/grace of faith. Such faithful knowledge (knowledge as disruptive proclamation) disrupts our sinful, self-deluding grasp of what we consider "reality" and "realistic" knowledge. The new knowledge of faith also gives the gift of Love now understood to permeate the reality within which we, as thus engifted to love, now understand the possibility to love beyond even our best actualities. The further development of such knowledge—the knowledge born of revelation that has now

---

3. For Bernard Lonergan, see *Method in Theology* (New York: Herder and Herder, 1972), 115.

become the new knowledge of new possibility (faith, hope, and love)—also demands, as the ancient philosophers knew, the discernment and development of what Pierre Hadot nicely named "spiritual exercises" (to be discussed below).

It is little wonder that so many ancient Christian thinkers found Platonism in its many forms so natural a philosophical ally to the new knowledge of the revelation of Jesus Christ. For Platonism, in its many forms, does live in and by a sense of sheer wonder at the engifted, gracious possibilities within which we live and move and have our being. From Plato's own vision of Beauty occurring "suddenly" (as event, happening) in the *Symposium* to his "Good beyond Being" (and beyond the achievements even of dialectic) in the *Republic* to his final mythic-philosophical vision of all reality in the *Timaeus,* one cannot but sense in Plato, as in his Platonist successors, a sense of the sheer wonder of existence as a feeling of genuine participation in the possibilities opened by Beauty, by the Good, by the One, by Intelligence, and by all the Forms.

The Christian Platonists, moreover, sensed this wondrous, participatory reality in Plato and the Platonists. The Christian thinkers did not hesitate to transform the forms of Platonism, when necessary, to cohere with *the* form of God, the Form where God is manifested in and through Form, Jesus the Christ. This incarnational Christology freed Dante to understand the necessity for the particularity of Beatrice; that is, the necessary particular form in and through which essence manifests itself and without which the manifestation could not occur. Thus can a new ethic of the Good be worked out through manifold forms in the theology of Augustine. Thus could a new understanding of truth itself as manifestation in and through Christological form occur for Christian thinkers from Bonaventure to von Balthasar. Plato and Platonism, once reconstructed or transformed through the possibilities disclosed by a new form of forms and Jesus Christ as proclamatory and manifesting Word, were far more religiously available to Christians than was either Aristotle or Stoicism.

Today, in the twilight of Platonism, other philosophies may seem more appropriate to the Catholic insight into faith as knowledge of possibility born of that love empowered by the revelation of Christ in the Spirit. Among contemporary philosophies, I continue to believe that hermeneutical philosophy provides the kind of contemporary philosophy needed by a revelational theology.[4] Although I have argued the case elsewhere, for the

---

4. *Inter alia* see Hans-Georg Gadamer, *Wahrheit und Methode* (Tübingen: J. C. B. Mohr, 1965); Martin Heidegger, *Zur Sache des Denkens* (Tübingen: Max Niemeyer, 1969); and Paul Ricoeur, *Hermeneutics and the Human Sciences* (Cambridge: Cambridge University Press, 1981).

present purposes the following summary statement of why hermeneutics aids theology in its understanding of revelation can be stated as follows:

1. Hermeneutics, philosophically, accords a priority to "possibility" over "actuality" analogous to revelation's disclosure of new divine possibility over present actuality.

2. Hermeneutics (unlike Platonism) takes history and historicity with full philosophical seriousness. For Judaism and Christianity, with their revelation in and through historical events, this need is crucial.

3. As Paul Ricoeur argues, truth is primordially, on the hermeneutical vision, an event of manifestation (Ricoeur) or disclosure (Gadamer) or disclosure-concealment (Heidegger). This defense of how manifestation (not correspondence or coherence) is the primary, indeed primordial, notion of truth in hermeneutics is clearly fruitful for a philosophical clarification of the meaning of revelation as the self-manifestation of God in and through form as event.

4. Hermeneutics, by its concentration on text (or even action as text), provides philosophical clarification of how essential form is for rendering manifestation. Form is not dispensable but crucial for understanding the manifested essence. Moreover, precisely the interest in the informing of text by such strategies of form as composition, genre, and style (Ricoeur) opens to exactly what a theology of revelation needs: an understanding of the text disclosing in and through form *(Darstellung)* a possible mode of being in the world. Philosophically, the hermeneutical world of possibility[5] is an appeal to the productive imagination. Theologically, it is persuasive, not argumentatively coercive, as a Christian revelation's appeal to new possibility, and the self-manifestation of this hermeneutical understanding of imagination is analogous to God in and through the indispensable and unsubstitutable Form of Jesus Christ as witnessed to in all the scriptural forms, especially the passion narratives that render that self into three identities: Jesus, Christ, and God.

5. Hermeneutics, through its dialogical model for understanding, encourages the philosopher, in my judgment, to develop an ethics of the Good since the Good transforms reality by theologically understanding all being as gracious.

All these moves suggest that philosophy (here, hermeneutical philosophy) has two central roles in a theology grounded in revelation: first,

---

5. For the spectrum of reception of this possibility, see Hans Robert Jauss, *Toward an Aesthetic of Reception,* trans. Timothy Bahti (Minneapolis: University of Minnesota Press, 1982).

to reconstruct the hermeneutical categories (possibility, event, historicity, manifestation, form, dialogue) in accordance with the Form of Christian revelation in and through Jesus Christ. This theological reconstruction, moreover, will itself be informed by hermeneutical philosophy by finding categories (via hermeneutics) which genuinely clarify and develop the meaning of revelation itself. Second, hermeneutical philosophy—especially through its development of the notion of the productive imagination in and through forms—provides a new way to clarify and, when necessary, challenge and correct theology's own self-understanding of revelation as manifestation of *reasonable* even if formerly unimagined possibility. Whether such correlation occurs in an ad hoc or more general (inevitably transcendental) way is a further question that demands both further philosophical and further theological analysis. For the moment, it is enough to see that a correlation can and does occur between revelational theology and hermeneutical philosophy even without prior decisions on the general or ad hoc question.

Like Platonism before it, contemporary hermeneutical philosophy keeps alive the sense of wonder and participation crucial to revelation and philosophy alike. Unlike Platonism, moreover, hermeneutical philosophy can open philosophy itself to its ancient heritage by uniting theory to the praxis of spiritual exercises.

As theology struggles to bridge the nearly fatal separation (not distinction) between theology and spirituality, perhaps theology may also suggest new ways for philosophy itself (including hermeneutical philosophy) to abandon all modern separations of theory and practice and retrieve the ancient philosophers' understanding of the role of spiritual exercises in and for theory itself. As Pierre Hadot's work has shown,[6] the ancients, whether in the schools of Stoics, Epicureans, Aristotelians, Platonists, or in the non-institutionalized movements of skepticism and cynicism, all insisted on philosophy as a way of life. As such, philosophy united theory to praxis (and vice versa) partly by means of the regular, systematic use of spiritual exercises (for example, exercises of a tensive attentiveness to the Logos for the Stoic, exercises for letting go for the Epicureans). The loss of such exercises—even the classical use of mathematics for understanding pure intelligibility in Pythagoras and Plato, much less the exercise of ancient dialectic and the Hellenistic spiritual exercises of the Platonists—is peculiar to modern Western philosophy and theology. As our Western philosophy and theology learns to acknowledge the cognitive point of such exercises in, for example, Buddhist philosophies, perhaps at least "Christian philosophers" might join their theological colleagues in new, if tentative, attempts to recover what

6. See Pierre Hadot, *Exercices spirituels et philosophie antique,* 2d ed. (Paris: Études augustiniennes, 1987).

was once held together in both our disciplines—spiritual practice and theory, theory and a way of life. Such a remarkable union seems clearly present in Mormon philosophies. The new global cross-cultural understanding of both disciplines can encourage all responsible thinkers to that new intellectual journey back to the future of both theology and philosophy as thoughtful ways of life. I would be thankful to hear any further reflections from Mormon thinkers on philosophy and theology.

Response to Professor Tracy

Jim Siebach

In HIS INSIGHTFUL ESSAY, DAVID TRACY requests an articulation of the relationship between philosophy and theology in the LDS tradition.[7] However, to put it most bluntly, such an articulation, to the extent it represents official LDS church doctrine, could properly be made only by a prophet, for in the LDS tradition, talk about God rests in the domain of prophecy and decidedly not in the domain of natural or systematic theology. Simply put, LDS theology lies more in the mantic than the sophic mode; it is more Hebrew than Greek. God's nature, will, mind, and covenant are known, not through rational analysis or rational discovery, but through God's direct communication with a chosen prophet, who, in turn, reveals that kerygma to God's children.

While there are occasional official LDS church declarations of doctrine,[8] few of these are couched in the language of systematic theology. There are no official LDS church theologians, no certificates required by the LDS church to teach theology, and there aren't even degrees in religious studies at LDS church–sponsored schools. In place of all such theological activities and institutions, the LDS church claims prophecy and revelation.

---

7. "I have found it . . . difficult to try to understand the complex relationships of philosophy and theology in LDS thought. I write this article . . . in the hope that . . . clarification may encourage a[n] . . . articulation of the relationship of philosophy and theology in the LDS tradition" (Tracy, 449–50).

8. See, for example, "The Family: A Proclamation to the World," *Ensign* 25 (November 1995): 102; and "The Living Christ: The Testimony of the Apostles of The Church of Jesus Christ of Latter-day Saints," *Ensign* 34 (December 2004): 9. For a more extensive documentation of official proclamations by LDS church leaders, see James R. Clark, *Messages of the First Presidency*, 2 vols. (Salt Lake City: Bookcraft, 1965).

Thus, in the *traditional* sense of natural or systematic theology, the LDS church is profoundly atheological. The following definition of theology is typical of early LDS religious writings: "[Theology is] the science of communication, or of correspondence, between God, angels, spirits, and men, by means of visions, dreams, interpretations, conversations, inspirations, or the spirit of prophecy and revelation."[9] The definition exemplifies the decidedly prophetic and apocalyptic (in the sense of revelatory) character of LDS theological understanding. To the extent that theology is a science, it is one of communication between God and human beings, and talk about God is almost exclusively a matter of hearing what God has to say.

While the prophet ultimately determines the LDS church's official stand on every fundamental issue, it *is* possible for someone other than a prophet to articulate why Latter-day Saints are so deeply atheological. Such an articulation must begin with an astonishing event that is known as "the First Vision."

In 1820, Joseph Smith, a young man of fourteen years, sought to know which Christian sect to join. He resided in upstate New York, where sectarian activity and the recruitment of new members was intense. Unable to decide which sect to join on the basis of their espoused doctrines, Joseph read in the New Testament book of James, chapter 1 verse 5: "If any of you lack wisdom, let him ask of God, that giveth to all men liberally and upbraideth not; and it shall be given him." Joseph resolved, in accordance with this promise, to put the question of which sect he should join to God himself. He thus retired to a small grove of trees and there began to pray. The response he received is stunning:

> I saw a pillar of light exactly over my head, above the brightness of the sun, which descended gradually until it fell upon me. . . . When the light rested upon me I saw two Personages, whose brightness and glory defy all description, standing above me in the air. One of them spake unto me, calling me by name and said, pointing to the other—*This is My Beloved Son. Hear Him!*

Upon asking the Lord his question, Joseph says he was told he must join none of the sects, for they were all wrong. He continues, "And the Personage who addressed me said that all their creeds were an abomination in his sight; that those professors were all corrupt; that 'they draw near to me with their lips, but their hearts are far from me, they teach for doctrines

---

9. Parley P. Pratt, *Key to the Science of Theology*, 5th ed. (Salt Lake City: George Q. Cannon and Sons, 1891), 1.

the commandments of men, having a form of godliness, but they deny the power thereof."[10]

This description is profoundly informative of theological practice in the LDS tradition. The experience began what the LDS church calls "the restoration" of the gospel. That is, the Latter-day Saints believe, on the basis of the epiphany of the Father and the Son and their instructions to Joseph Smith, that the Christian tradition had departed profoundly from the gospel taught in the New Testament and that the Lord had to again personally inaugurate the purity of his gospel along with the ecclesiastical structure of the church present in New Testament times (that is, a church headed by a prophet and twelve apostles). The reasons for such a departure, or apostasy, in the early church include the synthesis of Platonic metaphysics with Christian theology affected in the first five centuries A.D. Professor Tracy acknowledges this synthesis. He writes, "It is little wonder that so many ancient Christian thinkers found Platonism in its many forms so natural a philosophical ally to the new knowledge of the revelation of Jesus Christ. For Platonism, in its many forms, does live in and by a sense of sheer wonder at the engifted, gracious possibilities within which we live and move and have our being" (Tracy, 459).

While Platonism did, indeed, seem an attractive alliance for early Christian theologians, the LDS church, on the basis of epiphany to Joseph Smith and the instructions given to him then, regards such a synthesis as ultimately deleterious to a true understanding of the divine nature. In place of the New Testament descriptions of God as Father, the LDS church believes that Nicea I substituted confused concepts of *hypostasis* and *ousia*. These concepts obscure rather than illuminate the divine nature. By way of contrast, the LDS church points to the First Vision with its clear description of the Father and the Son as distinct and separately embodied persons.

The LDS church further argues that the First Vision establishes the fundamental manner in which God is known (by revelation) and not known (by disputation and rational enquiry). The LDS church regards the practice of speculating about the divine nature, among both early Christians and contemporary theologians, as quickly prone to error and misunderstanding. As Professor Tracy says, "The Christian thinkers did not hesitate to transform the forms of Platonism, when necessary, to cohere with the form of God, the Form where God is manifested in and through Form, Jesus the Christ" (Tracy, 459). The Latter-day Saints believe this transforming of Platonism also transformed Christianity; it was not simply that Platonism was made to cohere with the Form of God, but that the Form of God was made to

---

10. See Joseph Smith Jr., *History of The Church of Jesus Christ of Latter-day Saints,* ed. B. H. Roberts, 2d ed. rev., 7 vols. (Salt Lake City: Deseret, 1976), 1:1–8, for a complete account.

cohere with Platonism. And this coherence with Platonism estranged the understanding of God from its biblical basis. The reason for such belief, however, is not rational argument (though one could adduce rational arguments in support of the view) but the content of the First Vision.

The First Vision evidences that both God the Father and the Son are embodied persons, humanlike in form.[11] Such a view is scandalous to most philosophy and rational speculation. But it must be noted that this idea became scandalous *only* when early Christian theologians began appropriating philosophical concepts in order to both explain the nature of God and apologize for Christianity to the philosophers who accused Christians of resembling, in their polytheism, the pagans. The Latter-day Saints also believe that Christ's appraisal of Christian sectarian beliefs—"Their creeds were an abomination in his sight"—applies not only to the contents of the creeds, but also to the manner in which early Christian theologians formulated such creeds. Therefore, in place of Nicea I and the disputational manner in which it arrived at a doctrine of the Trinity, the LDS church asserts pure revelation.

The theological significance of the First Vision in the LDS church is not only in the content of Christ's message to Joseph Smith—none of the Christian sects is to be joined—but also in the procedure by which the communication came to Joseph. That is, Joseph was unable to determine, by his own reason, which church was right. The answer to that question, along with all other fundamental questions about dogma, liturgy, and ecclesiastical structure, must be received by revelation, by hearing the word of God. The First Vision thus establishes a precedent and procedure. From the time of the First Vision, the LDS church asserts an uninterrupted, ongoing stream of revelation from God to his people through a prophet who leads and guides the LDS church. The prophet hears and then informs the people, whose obligation is to hearken.

The revelatory basis of LDS God-talk made clear, I hasten to add that the LDS church does not, in any way, object to or discourage apologetic use of reason; for example, the use of science or philosophical argument to support the truths of the faith.[12] The LDS church insists only that rational enquiry must, where possible, be enlightened by revelation and certainly not contradict revealed truths. Thus, while reason as an authority is acknowledged and promoted, it is always secondary to and dependent on the truths of scripture and revelation.

---

11. It is more accurate to say that human beings are Godlike in form, since God created man in his own image.

12. See, for example, David Paulsen, "The Doctrine of Divine Embodiment: Restoration, Judeo-Christian, and Philosophical Perspectives," *BYU Studies* 35, no. 4 (1995–6): 7–94.

Furthermore, the LDS church encourages the rational pursuit of knowledge in all its forms, whether philosophical, scientific, historical, technological, and so on. "The glory of God is intelligence," LDS scripture states (D&C 93:36). One of the particular features in which human beings are created in God's likeness and image is in their capacity to know, and the act of knowing is imitative of the divine life. The LDS church teaches, extraordinarily, that "whatever principle of intelligence we attain unto in this life . . . will rise with us in the resurrection. And if a person gains more knowledge and intelligence in this life through his diligence and obedience than another, he will have so much the advantage in the world to come" (D&C 130:18–19). The increase of knowledge through reasoning, scientific inquiry, or faith, therefore, is not only encouraged, but is part and parcel of the Christian life, both here and hereafter.

All truth is worth knowing. Scientific inquiry, for example, may increase our understanding of God's creation and may thus be spiritually valuable as well as valuable for the improvements it can bring to human life. Philosophical analysis and reasoning can surely contribute substantially to human understanding. But again, where scientific or philosophical conclusions appear to contradict those of scripture or revelation, intellectual assent is to be given to revelation as the superior authority. "To be learned is good if [the learned] hearken unto the counsels of God," states LDS scripture (2 Nephi 9:29). The usefulness of "mundane knowledge" to knowing God more fully and to communicating his gospel is emphasized elsewhere in LDS scripture. "Teach ye diligently . . . of things both in heaven and in the earth, and under the earth; things which have been, things which are, things which must shortly come to pass; things which are at home, things which are abroad; the wars and the perplexities of the nations, and the judgments which are on the land; and a knowledge also of countries and of kingdoms—that ye may be prepared in all things" (D&C 88:78–80). Such teaching and learning must take place within the larger framework of revealed knowledge. Passages such as those above drive the extraordinary LDS emphasis on acquiring knowledge as part of Christian discipleship. Truths not addressed by God's revelation are to be pursued through learning, study, and rational enquiry. But when reason discovers theological truths, they have no official standing within the church unless their veracity is confirmed by revelation.

The view that reason can discover truths about God's nature that nevertheless have no official status as doctrine or dogma in the LDS church may strike those accustomed to a rich theological tradition, such as Catholicism, as crude and simplistic. But such distancing is a matter of protection and prudence. The history of natural theology is often one of continuing syntheses between philosophical metaphysics and scripture. Such marriages are always, in the LDS view, transformative of both philosophy and scripture and, as such, a departure from revealed truth, for philosophical systems are relative to culture in a manner that revelation is not, even though revelation takes place in a particular culture and time.

Professor Tracy concludes his essay by calling for a closer tie between hermeneutical philosophy and a theology of revelation: "I continue to believe that hermeneutical philosophy provides the kind of contemporary philosophy needed by a revelational theology" (Tracy, 459). The role that such a tie between hermeneutical philosophy and theology grounded in revelation could play is "to reconstruct the hermeneutical categories . . . in accordance with the Form of Christian revelation in and through Jesus Christ. This theological reconstruction, moreover, will itself be informed by hermeneutical philosophy by finding categories (via hermeneutics) which genuinely clarify and develop the meaning of revelation itself" (Tracy, 461). Though such a tie may produce fruit at the personal or individual level, it is not the procedure by which LDS doctrine is to be established or clarified.

Indeed, the LDS church would greet Dr. Tracy's proposal with great caution. On the one hand, any effort to infuse one's philosophical thinking with the revelation of Jesus Christ is not only encouraged but expected. But on the other hand, it is a distraction, if not a misguidance, to assume that systematic philosophical thought—even the application of hermeneutical categories—ought to be employed in order to clarify the content of revelation. The confidence of the LDS church is that the content of revelation is to be understood by further revelation; it is to be clarified, when obscure, by more fasting, prayer, and study. But the study that clarifies is scriptural and moral, not philosophical. Those who live the life of holiness place themselves in a position to hear clearly, and hearing is refined by hearkening.

In conclusion, then, it is clear that the LDS tradition of theology, or atheology, with its emphasis on prophetic hearing and its refusal to incorporate philosophical analysis into the formulation of LDS church doctrine, is quite different from the Catholic tradition. Such differences, though, should not obscure the enormous profit all may derive from studying the spiritual achievements of both traditions.

Response to Professor Tracy

James E. Faulconer

D AVID TRACY POINTS OUT THAT THE DIFFERENCE between philosophy of religion and theology is that the latter requires "some notion of revelation as well as divinely engifted reception of that revelation called 'faith'—a knowledge born of revelation" (Tracy, 449), while the former does not. One can examine religious beliefs philosophically, including a belief in revelation or a claim to faith, without assuming the reality of either revelation or faith. However, the consequence of assuming divine revelation and knowledge based on that revelation is that "theology can neither ignore nor be sublated by philosophy" (Tracy, 449). It cannot be sublated by philosophy because by beginning with revelation and knowledge produced by that revelation, it contains an element that philosophy cannot take into itself. Presumably, theology cannot ignore philosophy because philosophy is that discipline by which we examine knowledge. However, that it cannot ignore philosophy does not mean that theology can be reduced to philosophizing about a particular subject matter. Tracy's question for Mormons is how we understand the relation between philosophy and theology.

The easy answer is that, as he suggests, the situation in Mormonism is similar to that in Catholicism: theology cannot ignore philosophy but is not subsumed by it, and the theology of Latter-day Saints most often tends toward one of two forms, rationalism or fideism, neither of which can be neatly separated from the other. Like Tracy, most Mormons would agree that theology must be grounded in revelation. However, that agreement is complicated by Tracy's separation of revelation and religion, a separation that most Mormons cannot make and that may be contradicted by Tracy's turn to hermeneutics. Though Tracy does not explicitly tell us what he means by religion, he seems to mean something like "the practices and institutions of a particular religious tradition." I doubt that many Latter-day Saints would allow the distinction of revelation from religion since revelation is assumed to be part of religion's practices and institutions. As I will argue, theology must take up religion and belief as part of a way of life. Since that way of life includes revelation, revelation cannot be distinguished from it.

Latter-day Saints are primitivists: we believe that the original Christian church was restored in 1830 through the Prophet Joseph Smith. The Restoration began in a literal revelation to Smith: just as Jesus-God made himself manifest in first-century Palestine, God and Jesus Christ appeared to Joseph Smith and spoke to him. Later, angels—embodied angels with whom one could shake hands—appeared to him and others, speaking with them, relaying divine counsel, and ordaining them to the priesthood by putting their angelic hands on the mortal heads of Joseph Smith and Oliver Cowdery. The primary revelation of early Christianity repeats itself at the founding of Mormonism. As a result, the events that led to and included the founding of the Church of Jesus Christ of Latter-day Saints are called by Mormons the "Restoration."

Mormon primitivism means that Smith's encounter with transcendence was not an encounter with a metaphysically transcendent world, but with a world that most Mormons assume is ontologically like our own.[13] Though few Mormons claim to have had a similar experience (I have met none), the possibility of that kind of revelation—direct, unmediated, physical encounter—remains permanently open.[14] Jesus Christ is present not only in the "word (proclamation) and sacrament (those disclosive signs which render present what they signify)" (Tracy, 457). It is also always possible that Jesus will be present in physical person. Indeed, we generally assume that kind of revelation did not cease with Smith but continued with some succeeding prophets as well as other people.

Mormons also recognize forms of revelation that are much more like what other Christians speak of; we assume that revelation most often comes as inspiration and impression, "the whisperings of the Spirit,"[15] rather than as voice, vision, or visitation. Nevertheless, for Latter-day Saints, revelation is assumed to be a common as well as a fundamental religious experience, and it is an experience that has at its base the possibility of an unmediated encounter with God, an encounter that is ontologically comparable to that of the first Christians.

The Book of Mormon is explicit about the importance of revelation:

> And when ye shall receive these things, I would exhort you that ye would ask God, the Eternal Father, in the name of Christ, if these things are not true; and if ye shall ask with a sincere heart, with real intent, having faith in Christ, he will manifest the truth of it unto you, by the power of the Holy Ghost.

---

13. However, see my "Divine Embodiment and Transcendence: Propaedeutic Thoughts and Questions," *Element: An E-Journal of LDS Thought*, vol. 1, no. 1 (2005): 1–14, for a discussion of some of the ways in which the divine world and our world differ and some theological questions those differences raise.

14. One of many examples: "Revelation may come through dreams or visions, the visitation of angels, or, on occasion such as with Moses, by face-to-face communication with the Lord." Hugh B. Brown, *131st Semi-annual Conference of The Church of Jesus Christ of Latter-day Saints* (Salt Lake City: The Church of Jesus Christ of Latter-day Saints, 1961), 95.

15. Gordon B. Hinckley, *Teachings of Gordon B. Hinckley* (Salt Lake City: Deseret, 1997), 364.

And by the power of the Holy Ghost ye may know the truth of all things. (Moroni 10:4–5)

This passage has become more and more doctrinally important among Mormons—it is, for example, an important element in the proselytizing program of the Church—and I think we find it implicitly behind Terryl Givens' argument that the Mormon understanding of revelation is unique in that it is "dialogic." According to Givens, revelation allows Mormons to appeal to God for answers to questions and problems without the restraints of a closed canon, resulting in revelation as knowledge with a propositional content given directly to particular individuals by God rather than (but not excluding) revelation as the experience of divine grace, the content of scripture, or the self-disclosure of God.[16] As mentioned, revelation need not come in the form of propositions literally heard or understood, but one form of revelation, perhaps the form most often referred to when Latter-day Saints speak of revelation, does have a propositional content, though not necessarily a propositional form. Little scholarly work has been done on what the term *revelation* means to Mormons, but there is sufficient discussion of it in nonscholarly contexts to give us a reasonable idea: it includes an unmediated response from God in a form that can often be given a propositional exposition. This understanding goes a long way toward explaining the dominant Mormon understanding of theology as rational, in other words, propositional.

Nevertheless, Mormons today, intellectuals or otherwise, do not use the word *theology* in a consistent way. From the beginning of the Church to the present, Latter-day Saints have often assumed that theology means "rational or systematic theology" (by *systematic* I mean a theology in which the doctrines are assumed to be interrelated and capable of structured exposition rather than a theology which is divided into the traditional branches of Christology, Pneumatology, etc.). The nineteenth-century work *Lectures on Faith*,[17] arranged in a catechetical format and, for a while, included in

---

16. Terryl L. Givens, "The Book of Mormon and Dialogic Revelation," *Journal of Book of Mormon Studies*, vol. 10, no. 2 (2001): 16–27. See also the relevant portions of Terryl L. Givens, *By the Hand of Mormon* (Oxford: Oxford University Press, 2002). I think that whether Givens is right that the LDS understanding of revelation as dialogic differs significantly from the experiences of personal revelation by other Christians, such as evangelicals, remains a question.

17. Traditionally *The Lectures on Faith* have been attributed to Joseph Smith. However, there is disagreement over its authorship. See Noel B. Reynolds, "The Authorship Debate Concerning *Lectures on Faith*: Exhumation and Reburial," in *The Disciple as Witness: Essays on Latter-day Saint History and Doctrine in Honor of Richard Lloyd Anderson*, ed. Stephen D. Ricks, Donald W. Parry, and Andrew H. Hedges (Provo, Utah: FARMS, 2000), 355–82. I suspect it was removed from the canon

the LDS canon, is an excellent example of a work that makes this assumption. We find another example in the controversial writings of Orson Pratt, also in the nineteenth century. John A. Widtsoe's *A Rational Theology* (1915), first used as a manual in weekly classes for the Church's lay priesthood and later in adult classes of the Church's Mutual Improvement Association, is yet another. We see contemporary examples in Bruce R. McConkie's *Mormon Doctrine*[18] (more of an encyclopedia than a theology and self-described as a compendium, but nevertheless an attempt at systematic exposition) and Blake Ostler's series *Exploring Mormon Thought*.[19] Thus, when in 1995 Chieko Okazaki equated theology and "theorizing about the gospel,"[20] I doubt that anyone found that usage unusual.

Our widespread understanding of theology as rational theology seems to spring from our interpretation of claims we find in scripture, such as "The glory of God is intelligence" (D&C 93:36). Widtsoe characterized the Mormon understanding of theology as rational theology this way:

> Whether knowledge be obtained by any or all of the methods indicated [namely, the senses, inward feeling, transmitted knowledge], it should be carefully examined in the light of reason. . . . A man should therefore use his reasoning faculty in all matters involving truth, and especially as concerning his religion.[21]

Brigham Young called theology his favorite study, comparing it to law, "physic," and astronomy.[22] An impetus for identifying theology with rational theology can be found in a Mormon belief that truth is ultimately "one great whole,"[23] a whole that has, for historical and broad cultural reasons, been assumed to be rational. Surely the fact that, for Mormons, revelation is often, if not exclusively, propositional is largely responsible for the general understanding of theology as rational: reflection on revelation is a matter of making the propositions of revelation rationally coherent.

However, from early in Church history, and still today, the word *theology* has also been used more loosely, as a synonym for belief or teaching.

---

because its teachings about the Holy Ghost do not cohere with early-twentieth-century proclamations by the LDS church's First Presidency.

18. Bruce R. McConkie, *Mormon Doctrine* (Salt Lake City: Bookcraft, 1966).

19. Blake T. Ostler, *Exploring Mormon Thought*, 2 vols. (Salt Lake City: Greg Kofford, 2001).

20. Chieko N. Okazaki, *Aloha!* (Salt Lake City: Deseret, 1995), 54.

21. John A. Widtsoe, *A Rational Theology*, 4th ed. (Salt Lake City: Deseret, 1937), 7–8.

22. Brigham Young, in *Journal of Discourses*, 26 vols. (Liverpool: F. D. Richards, 1855–1856), 6:315, April 7, 1852.

23. See, for example, Howard W. Hunter, *The Teachings of Howard W. Hunter*, ed. Clyde J. Williams (Salt Lake City: Bookcraft, 1997), 182.

George Q. Cannon, of the Council of Twelve, spoke of his children's favorite study as theology.[24] Marion D. Hanks, speaking to Brigham Young University students in 1960, described theology as "religious doctrine and knowledge."[25] And in 2002 Neal Maxwell, another member of the Twelve, speaking in the Church's General Conference, equated "the restored gospel" and theology.[26] My anecdotal experience is that Mormons seldom distinguish between these two different meanings: sometimes *theology* means "what we believe" or something like that, and sometimes *theology* includes explaining what we believe by giving it a rational structure. Often it is not obvious which of those is intended.

This broadness in the meaning of theology is at least partly the result of the fact that there has not yet been anything like an official Mormon theology. If *theology* means "beliefs," then there is a widely accepted theology, though there is considerable variability in even that. However, if *theology* means formal reflection about religious beliefs and practices, then Mormonism does not even have a widely accepted theology, much less an official one, though it has and has had several practitioners.

In spite of the prevalence of equating the terms *theology* and *beliefs* in Mormonism, when I use the term *theology* I will not use it that way. Though I intend to continue to use the word broadly, whatever else theology is, I assume that it includes a reflective, explanatory component. It is more than "what most Mormons believe." When *theology* is used in that way, we can accurately say that few Mormons have done it.[27] We could describe those who come closest today, such as David Paulsen and Ostler, as doing either the philosophy of religion or theology, though I believe that one hears their

---

24. George Q. Cannon, "Education of Children, Tithing," *Collected Discourses Delivered by Wilford Woodruff, His Two Counselors, Twelve Apostles, and Others*, ed. Brian H. Stuy, 5 vols. (Burbank, Calif.: B. H. S., 1987–1992), 2:39.

25. Marion D. Hanks, "Steps of Learning," *BYU Speeches of the Year, 1959–1960* (Provo, Utah: Brigham Young University, 1960), 2.

26. Neal A. Maxwell, "Encircled in the Arms of His Love," *Ensign* 32 (November 2002): 16.

27. Indeed, there is considerable interest in the philosophy of religion among LDS intellectuals. Paulsen's classes at BYU are always full, and Ostler's books sell well. There is an e-mail discussion group, LDS-Phil, dedicated to discussions of Mormonism and philosophy that, for obvious reasons, often discusses topics in the philosophy of religion. Clark Goble has a website devoted to his philosophical reflections on that topic ("Mormon Metaphysics" at http://www.libertypages.com/clark/—read August 1, 2006). One can find nonacademic discussions of the philosophy of religion fairly regularly on LDS blogs such as the group blog, Times and Seasons (http://timesand-seasons.org—August 1, 2006.). But I think few, if any, of these would call what they do theology, and this constitutes a small group within Mormonism as a whole, even within educated or intellectual Mormons.

work referred to most often as "philosophy of religion." Though there are notable exceptions, Mormons have not done much theology, and since about the beginning of the twentieth century, we generally avoid calling what we do theology.

One obvious reason for the relative absence of theology among Mormons is that the Church is still young. A tradition that is not yet two hundred years old has not had time to develop the kind of theological discussions that one finds in much older Christian traditions, such as Catholicism. Furthermore, though deciding cause and effect here is difficult (assuming it is relevant), the absence of theological work in the LDS Church today is also probably related to the fact that fideism seems to have grown in popularity among contemporary Church leaders. For example, speaking of church history and the origins of Mormonism, Maxwell said, "Reason, the Greek philosophical tradition, dominated, then supplanted, reliance on revelation," but with the Restoration, "Revelation thus replaced the long and inordinate reliance on reason."[28] Though this more fideistic approach has become more obvious during the last half of the twentieth century, it is not a completely original development.[29] Among other precursors, we find Joseph Smith saying things like, "Without a revelation, I am not going to give them the knowledge of the God of heaven"[30] and, speaking of the rest of Christianity, "[they] are bound apart by cast-iron creeds, and fastened to set stakes by chain-cables, without revelation."[31] Revelation trumps reason.

Let me briefly offer three additional reasons for the dearth of theology among Latter-day Saints: the belief in continuing revelation, the nature of scripture, and the fact that, like many Jews, Mormons understand their religion primarily in terms of practices and attitudes rather than in terms

---

28. Neal A. Maxwell, "From the Beginning," *Ensign* 23 (November 1993): 19–20. Taking a somewhat ameliorated position, Dallin H. Oaks has said, "The source of the ancient conflict between (1) reason or intellect and (2) faith or revelation is the professor's rejection of revelation, not the prophet's rejection of reason." *The Lord's Way* (Salt Lake City: Deseret, 1991), 50.

29. One would have to do a more thorough study of the documents to decide, in fact, whether this movement from more focus on rational theology to more focus on fideism is as pronounced as I take it to be. I have not made that study, so I rely on my intuition that it is.

30. Joseph Smith, *Discourses of the Prophet Joseph Smith*, comp. Alma P. Burton (Salt Lake City: Deseret, 1977), 36.

31. Joseph Smith Jr., *History of the Church of Jesus Christ of Latter-day Saints*, ed. B. H. Roberts, 7 vols. (Salt Lake City: The Church of Jesus Christ of Latter-day Saints, 1950), 6:75.

of beliefs.[32] Of these, of course, perhaps only the first is unique to Mormons. The other two reasons can also be found in other religions. Indeed, Tracy argues that the nature of scripture requires us to rethink theology (Tracy, 452, 457), and he also sees the importance of practice, arguing explicitly that theory and a way of life ought to join themselves and recognizing that "such a remarkable union seems clearly present in Mormon philosophies" (Tracy, 462).

Continuing revelation makes theology more challenging—if theology means rational theology—because, as Spencer J. Condie says, "Change is an inevitable consequence of continuous revelation."[33] Two iconic events in Mormon history, the 1890 prohibition of polygamy and the 1978 declaration that blacks were to be given the priesthood, remind Latter-day Saints of the fact that a belief in living prophets who give continuing revelation means that, not only is our canon not closed, but what has been an authoritative teaching can become radically nonauthoritative, even when the original authority was direct revelation from God. Our religion requires that we always recognize the possibility that we will have to give up doctrines and practices that we thought central and authoritative.

The first of the two iconic practices, the practice of polygamy, was supported by a well-developed theology, a theology based on official teachings, scriptural and prophetic, that made polygamy a religious requirement for some.[34] In the second case, though there was neither authoritative revelation nor explanation for why blacks were not ordained, there was a great deal of speculation, speculation that many Mormons took as quasi-authoritative. The belief that there was a doctrinal basis for the exclusion of blacks from the priesthood was so strong in the Church that, even among those Mormons who, prior to 1978, refused to give revealed status to the practice, few thought that the practice would be discontinued in the foreseeable future. Many Mormons assumed that the practice could be explained in terms of authoritative Church teachings, even if no one seemed able to say what that explanation was. However, in spite of their authoritative place within Church belief and theology, revelations from prophets overturned

---

32. See my "Why a Mormon Won't Drink Coffee but Might Have a Coke: The Atheological Character of Mormonism" (unpublished) for an expanded discussion of these three claims.

33. Spencer J. Condie, *In Perfect Balance* (Salt Lake City: Bookcraft, 1993), 106.

34. Perhaps the experience of having a thorough theological justification for the necessity of polygamy only to have polygamy abandoned is also at the root of less and less theology in the twentieth century and afterward—not in absolute numbers, but in relation to the membership of the Church: there are substantially fewer people doing theology as a percentage of Church membership than there were in the nineteenth century prior to the abandonment of polygamy.

both practices and their associated beliefs and explanations. (In the first case, the overturning took a while to complete; in the second, the effect was essentially instantaneous.) It is difficult for any rational theology to contain the proposition, "Important authoritative propositions in this theology could be authoritatively denied at any moment, requiring the complete rerationalization of the propositions that remain." As a result, some modes of rational theology have been difficult for Mormons, but we have seldom recognized other kinds of theology, except theology as a set of beliefs.

As I pointed out, the second reason that we find little theology among Latter-day Saints, the nature of scripture, is not unique to us. My point about the effects of the nature of scripture on theology is similar to one that Tracy has made: we often speak of and use scripture as if it were a set of propositions that are poorly expressed or, at best, poetic. We then try to discover the propositional content (doctrine) that we assume is behind those poorly expressed or poetic expressions. But scripture is not like that. Instead, it is an inspired resource that allows us to question ourselves and our world through reading and reflection. Scripture requires our response in interpretation and mediation: the appropriation of scripture—in Mormon terminology, likening it to ourselves (1 Nephi 19:23)—more so than its rational exegesis. Still, the appropriation proper to scriptural understanding is inherently theological, albeit not strictly rational.[35]

Few Mormon academics have taken up the task of this appropriation, but why? Part of an answer is, I think, the belief in continuing revelation combined with the cultural assumption that scripture is to be understood as collected prophetic declarations that set forth a particular, unique set of propositions, though those propositions are often only implicit. (That is, of course, not an assumption found only among Mormons.) Whatever the reason, in spite of the dearth of theology among Latter-day Saints, a theology of appropriation fits well with our insistence on continuing revelation. I assume that a theology of appropriation would be a hermeneutic theology similar in many respects to that argued for by Tracy—and that it would together bring our reliance on scripture and our belief in continuing revelation.

Of the three reasons (continuing revelation, the nature of scripture, and the fact that religion is primarily a matter of practice rather than propositional belief), the latter seems to me to be the most important. To say that Mormons focus primarily on practices is, of course, not to say that beliefs are irrelevant to Latter-day Saint religion. Rather, it is to say that they are what they are and have their importance only in terms of the practices of which they are part. To use Heideggerian language, it is to say that beliefs

---

35. See David Tracy, *The Analogical Imagination* (New York: Crossroad, 1981), 104.

have their importance only as they are part of a way of being.[36] Latter-day Saints are more concerned with whether they have paid their tithing, visited an ill fellow congregant, done their home or visiting teaching,[37] and performed vicarious ordinances in the temple than they are with how to explain the grace of God or the Word of Wisdom.[38] (Of course, that one thing is more important than another does not mean that the second is unimportant.) Perhaps the most important reason that Latter-day Saints have done little toward giving an intellectual clarification of revelation is that our experience of religion is fundamentally practical and, so, does not lend itself readily to theological reflection as most Mormons understand that term. The faith-knowledge engifted by revelation, perhaps most obviously seen in the faith-knowledge of scripture, is practical rather than theoretical knowledge, so one theology that can deal appropriately with that knowledge would be a hermeneutic theology, a theology of listening for the word of God and saying what one hears and how one hears it. Naturally, like the hermeneutical theology described by Tracy, this hermeneutic would be more than a hermeneutic of texts. It would especially be a hermeneutic of relations, practices, and events.

Indeed, there is an important sense in which, without calling it theology, Latter-day Saints have practiced hermeneutical theology since shortly after the founding of the Church. They have been intensely interested in and written much about Church history, understanding Mormon history—the things we have done and experienced—as the key to understanding what it means to be a Mormon; understanding the interpretation of Latter-day Saint history as disciplined reflection on what it means to be a Latter-day Saint, in other words as quasi-theological, even if only implicitly. Perhaps this explains why the *Encyclopedia of Mormonism*,[39] though it contains articles on traditional theological questions such as God's foreknowledge, devotes proportionally much more space to articles on Church history. It also explains why Latter-day Saint academics and students, as well as Church members outside the academy, often have an avid interest in Mormon history, even though they are not themselves historians. Finally,

---

36. For more discussion of this point see my "Myth and Religion: Theology as a Hermeneutic of Religious Experience," in this volume (423–35).

37. Home and visiting teaching are Church programs in which members of the Church are assigned to visit each other each month in pairs—men for home teaching, women for visiting teaching—to encourage and to watch over the members of the congregation.

38. The Word of Wisdom is a revelation forbidding the use of coffee, tea, and alcoholic drinks, and urging moderation in meat-eating. See Doctrine and Covenants 89.

39. Daniel H. Ludlow, ed., *Encyclopedia of Mormonism*, 4 vols. (New York: Macmillan, 1992).

understanding Mormons as doing hermeneutical theology by doing history explains why the dispute over how history should be done—a dispute that was resolved only by the participants changing topics and, so, a dispute that remains implicit in much Mormon discussion of our history—was so strong.[40]

Thinkers including Mark Wrathall and myself have made the hermeneutical approach more explicit, using philosophical rather than historical hermeneutics to think about our faith. Though thinkers like Martin Heidegger, Hans-Georg Gadamer, and Paul Ricoeur are not among the philosophers to whom most Mormons are likely to refer, that seems to be changing. Of course, hermeneutical theology is not the only Mormon alternative to rational theology and its offspring. Though less well known than the work in the philosophy of religion done by Paulsen and Ostler, there are a number of contemporary Mormon thinkers who are exploring alternatives. Kathleen Flake has taken the Mormon interest in history and used it to think about Mormon faith through narrative theology.[41] Some Mormon thinkers, like Brian Birch and Keith Lane, use D. Z. Phillip's Wittgensteinian understanding of theology as a basis for their reflections. One Latter-day Saint thinker, Adam Miller, takes his theological cue from the work of Alain Badiou. It is interesting that all of these alternative approaches, even Miller's, assume as fundamental that practice, belief, and reflection on practice and belief are temporal and situated.

Thus, the answer to Tracy's question, "How do Mormons understand the relation between philosophy and theology," turns out to be complicated. Traditionally, we have taken theology to be strongly rationalistic, though there has also been an important and growing fideistic strain in Latter-day Saint thought, a strain that may be a reaction against rationalist theology more than a positive assertion about the nature of reason and faith. But, because the practical rather than theoretical understanding of religion is fundamental to Mormonism, perhaps the most important Mormon theological work to date has been the work of Mormon historians. Though people like Paulsen and Ostler continue to labor for theological understanding in a more systematic fashion, it appears that the theological work traditionally done by attention to history is beginning to be supplemented by theologies of scriptural appropriation, narrative, Wittgensteinian analysis,

---

40. See, for example, the essays in George D. Smith, ed., *Faithful History: Essays on Writing Mormon History* (Salt Lake City: Signature, 1992).

41. Kathleen Flake, "Translating Time: Joseph Smith's Translation of the King James Bible," unpublished manuscript delivered at "God, Humanity, and Revelation: Perspectives from Mormon Philosophy and History," New Haven, Yale University, March 24, 2003. Notice that *history* takes the place in the title of the conference where one would expect to find *theology*.

and hermeneutics, theologies that cannot take the implicitly objective view of rational theology and theologies for which continuing revelation plays a more central role than it does in rational theology. Mormon theology is beginning to take part in the larger theological discussion, moving more in the direction of multiple theologies and, particularly, theologies that, as Tracy so well puts it, "accord priority to 'possibility' over 'actuality,'" "take history and historicity with full seriousness," and recognize truth as manifestation, disclosure, or disclosure-concealment (Tracy, 460).

Theology in the Light of Continuing Revelation

Benjamin Huff

THERE ARE GOOD REASONS WHY DAVID TRACY finds it "difficult" to understand the relationship of philosophy and theology in Mormon thought (Tracy, 449). One reason is that Mormons hold a range of views as to what this relationship should be. Yet many of the same considerations that bear on this question for Catholics arise for Mormons as well, and I find both the way Tracy develops his question and his suggestions toward an answer very helpful. Between the vocabulary of typical Mormon discourse and Tracy's vocabulary of Catholic hermeneutic theology there is a gap which I will not attempt to fully bridge, but I will respond to Tracy's provocative question by articulating a sympathetic Mormon view of theology. I will set out some reasons why Mormons might particularly sympathize with Tracy's view in contrast to some other Catholic views. I take a more optimistic view of the value of rational theology, however, because of Mormon beliefs about the potential for humans to approach and understand God.

The word *theology* can be used in a number of ways, but as Tracy uses the term for the bulk of his essay, theology is an activity or process by which we develop and clarify our understanding of God in response to revelation, in part using philosophical methods.[42] Of course, as Tracy observes, spiritual practices are crucial in the Mormon view of how one comes to know God (Tracy, 462). While we spend time studying and discussing scripture and its import, it is primarily through serving one another as neighbors and friends, parents and spouses, in various roles within our congregations,

---

42. On this view as I understand it, theology never aims to take the place of revelation; rather, theology is a kind of active listening to the message of revelation.

and through Sabbath and temple worship that we not only qualify for the spiritual guidance that opens our understanding, but more importantly we experience and participate in the kind of life God leads. We come to know God best through serving him in action. These actions are guided and enhanced by our understanding, however, and so theology has significant value.

I. Commonalities with Tracy

Tracy asks about the relationship of philosophy to theology in Mormon thought. He then discusses factors that bear on this question as it arises for Catholics, particularly in light of dialectics between rationalism and fideism, Logos and Kerygma, which a Catholic must navigate. Rather than fixing on rationalism or fideism, he argues that a proper Christian response to God must appropriately integrate both faith and reason, just as Christian revelation involves both Logos and Kerygma as necessary aspects. Tracy then argues that Platonic and hermeneutic philosophy are particularly appropriate supplements to theology in light of this task. Both Platonic and hermeneutic philosophy "[keep] alive the sense of wonder and participation crucial to revelation and philosophy alike" (Tracy, 461).

Tracy's recommendation of Platonic and hermeneutic philosophy should have real force for Mormons as well as for Catholics and other Christians, as Christians are called not only to believe but also to understand. Philosophy can be of use as we try to understand what has been revealed to us. Some modes of philosophy may overemphasize comprehension and hence miss or even conceal how far the content of revelation exceeds what we are prepared to comprehend.[43] This would clearly cause problems for authentic faith. Similarly, some modes of philosophy emphasize detached objectivity, which is quite opposed to a faithful response to God in hope and love. In fact, philosophy is sometimes seen as the ultimate effort to eliminate wonder and longing. For Stoic, Epicurean, and Skeptic philosophy such an effort is explicit and central to their self-understanding,[44] and certainly the same impulse has resurfaced regularly in the practice

---

43. I discuss the limits of our comprehension more carefully in sections 2 and 3 of this paper.

44. Epicureans and Sceptics took *ataraxia,* or "untroubledness," as their goal. This included freedom from strong desires and from intellectual puzzlement. Similarly, for the Stoics virtue requires essentially eliminating emotion (see, e.g., Julia Annas, *The Morality of Happiness* [New York: Oxford University Press, 1993], 351), including subduing one's response to uncertainty. The effort to eliminate, or at least minimize, wonder and longing in these traditions grounds distinctive spiritual exercises, habits of body and heart as well as mind. In such a form, philosophy is a similar type of project to religion and may easily compete with it.

of philosophy since. Platonic (as Tracy construes it) and hermeneutic philosophy, however, expect and embrace wonder and longing in the course of their search for improved understanding. This seems exactly fitting for a Christian: a Christian seeks reunion with God, when wonder will presumably be at a maximum, while doubt is extinguished.

Of course, the Stoic and Skeptic movements in philosophy drew much of their strength from Plato,[45] and there are reasons why Mormons are typically quite wary of Platonic philosophy. Tracy focuses on certain themes of Plato's multifaceted thought which have not always received the same emphasis.[46] A Platonic view of embodiment encouraged Christians to deny that God the Father is corporeal, whereas Joseph Smith affirmed this. Platonic and Aristotelian reasoning about God led to the traditional understanding of the Trinity in terms of one metaphysical substance, a view with sketchy support in the scriptures and of questionable relevance to the concrete life of faith. More broadly, Mormons believe that after the deaths of the original apostles Christians fell into errors grave enough to require that the church be restored through Joseph Smith. While Mormons have no official account of the details of how error arose, they worry that an excessive reliance on reason led early Christians to discount or distort the message of revelation on many points.[47] To recommend Plato while maintaining appropriate caution about the reliability of human speculation, one must see the Socrates of Plato's dialogues as a deeply ironic figure. Yet Tracy seems to agree on the limits of rational speculation about God, as he distances himself from the "older Catholic manual scholastic traditions" (Tracy, 454), though of course they dominated for centuries, and emphasizes the truth found in a narrative over the truth one might find in

---

45. The Academic Skeptics explicitly took Socrates as their model, focusing on themes like his claim to know nothing, the skeptical implications of his dialectical mode of argument, and his argument that the happy person has few desires. Annas, *Morality of Happiness*, 23. The Stoics defined themselves more independently, but developed Socratic themes such as the conception of virtue as a skill and the idea that virtue is self-sufficient for happiness.

46. Plato's thought is very rich and complex, offering a range of resources from which various later philosophers draw selectively. Tracy seems more interested in the ideas on philosophical method and goals which appear in Plato than in particular philosophical claims. Of course, because Plato wrote dialogues, there is also room for widely different interpretations of Plato.

47. That Christians put human ideas ahead of divine teachings is one natural way of reading the words of Christ in Joseph Smith's account of his First Vision, of the religious leaders of the day: "they teach for doctrines the commandments of men, having a form of godliness, but they deny the power thereof" (Joseph Smith—History 1:19).

a philosophical system (Tracy, 458–59).[48] The doubts Mormons usually have about Catholic philosophical theology are out of place with Tracy and with the work of many other recent Catholic thinkers.

Indeed, Tracy even criticizes Plato on the point of God's corporeality, if not in exactly the way Mormons often do. Tracy asserts that Platonism has to be corrected in light of the Incarnation, in which God fully revealed himself in the (corporeal) Form of a man, Jesus Christ. According to this "incarnational christology" it is necessary that there be a "particular form in and through which essence manifests itself and without which the manifestation could not occur" (Tracy, 459). Further, Tracy seems to indicate that God's corporeality in Christ is not merely one theological fact, but instead reveals deep truth about the nature of being. A similar principle is reflected in the Catholic understanding of the Eucharist, according to which Christ again becomes present in the offered bread and wine,[49] and seems to be reflected in Tracy's remarks on scripture, a concrete expression and record of eternal truths including God's love.[50] In my view as a Mormon, the Platonic rejection of incarnation and, more broadly, of the finitude of which corporeality is a species are some of Platonism's most important problems, but Tracy breaks decisively with Plato on these.

Mormons believe that God is a particular person and that humans' birth into an embodied state is a crucial step toward becoming closer to God and more like him, not less. God is also profoundly passible, as portrayed in the Pearl of Great Price.[51] Further, while not all Mormons embrace

---

48. Even Plato's Socrates has a tendency to launch into mythic narrative after exhausting the power of dialectical argument, e.g., in *Republic, Gorgias, Phaedo*, and others.

49. Mormons often see the Catholic belief in the real presence, when explained in terms of Aristotelian substance and accident, as a key example of how philosophy corrupted the Christian tradition. In fairness, however, they should appreciate the deeply un-Platonic nature of some contemporary Catholic sacramental theology.

50. Tracy's comments on the particular form of divine teaching in scripture suggest he might sympathize with my point in section 3 about God's willingness to work with human rational limitations.

51. Consider not just the extended passage in which God weeps over the wickedness of his children (Moses 7:28–40), but also God's statement that "my work and my glory [is] to bring to pass the immortality and eternal life of man" (Moses 1:39; compare John 15:8, 17:10). God's glory in this view depends on us, his children, who may or may not choose the eternal life he calls us to. As Clark Pinnock has observed, the Incarnation in which all Christians believe is itself naturally read as the most eloquent possible rejection of standard Platonism, but traditional Christians have carefully avoided this message by such claims as that it was only Christ's human nature that suffered, while his divine nature remained impassible. Clark Pinnock, *Most Moved Mover* (Grand Rapids: Baker Academic, 2001), 7, 27–28.

this teaching, Joseph Smith clearly taught that God increases in glory and perfection over time—that is to say, he *becomes*.[52] In a standard reading of Plato, however, the Good is universal, timelessly perfect, and unaffected by anything. Thus if God is himself the highest good, then the Mormon conception of God implies as direct a rejection of standard Platonism as can be. Reciprocally, from a Mormon standpoint, standard Platonism appears a direct inversion of the truth. Yet Tracy embraces embodiment and particularity as fitting for God and, by implication, at least certain kinds of finitude. Further, the hermeneutic philosophy Tracy recommends breaks with Plato in prioritizing possibility over actuality (Tracy, 459). Hence I suggest Mormons should greet Tracy's mode of philosophy not with suspicion but with a warm welcome.

II. Implications of Continuing Revelation

Mormons must consider many of the same factors as Catholics in determining how to combine reason and revelation. Hence some Mormon thinkers, such as James Faulconer, feel a hermeneutic theology is appropriate for reasons similar to Tracy's. One may even regard much of traditional Mormon theological discourse as a kind of hermeneutic theology based on narrative, which bears fruit especially by motivating and informing spiritual practices. Indeed, Mormons may have more reasons than Catholics for approaching theology hermeneutically.

A key difference between Mormons and Catholics in answering this question is the Mormon belief in continuing revelation. This belief precludes any simple adoption of the method of the "Catholic manual scholastic traditions" and gives Mormons strong additional reasons to consider a hermeneutic approach to theology. After developing the implications of continuing revelation, however, I argue that a modified systematic approach to theology can play a positive role in Mormons' approach to understanding God.

When Mormons speak of continuing revelation, they do not mean simply ongoing contact with God. For Tracy, the prime revelation is God's

---

52. There is a range of views among Mormons regarding in what sense(s) God continues to progress now and in the future. A moderate view is that he grows in glory and dominion only, as his works continue, and more of his children are faithful to him. Such growth could be construed as purely external or relational, a growth in his works but not in God himself. However, in sermons such as the King Follett Discourse, Smith teaches that God was not always God, but became the sort of being he now is. Joseph Smith, *Teachings of the Prophet Joseph Smith* (Salt Lake City: Deseret, 1961), 342–62. This is sufficient to assure that God represents a radically different ideal of the Good than the standard Platonic view.

self-revelation in Jesus Christ.[53] For Mormons, too, contact with God is both the origin and goal of faith. However, by *continuing revelation* Mormons mean that through ongoing contact with God, the church and its members acquire new knowledge. If faith is the knowledge acquired through revelation in Tracy's terms, then the Mormon belief in continuing revelation translates to a belief in continual augmentation of the deposit of faith which the church has received.

In one sense it would seem that all the knowledge one could need would have been available to Christ's original disciples, since they walked and talked with him for years, and he is the Truth. One might suppose something similar about Joseph Smith after his many heavenly visitations. Yet the human capacity to absorb the truth manifest in revelation is limited, due to imperfections of both heart and mind. Even after years of companionship, Christ's disciples fell far short of understanding him and his words, as they showed in what they said and did during the time of his death and resurrection. According to Mormon scripture, God responds dynamically to this limited human capacity to assimilate truth. He grants

> [a] portion of his word . . . unto the children of men, according to the heed and diligence which they give unto him. And therefore, he that will harden his heart, the same receiveth the lesser portion of the word; and he that will not harden his heart, to him is given the greater portion of the word. (Alma 12: 9–10)

God often gives us a portion of truth and then waits for us to assimilate it before giving us more. Further, it is not merely through intellectual development that one becomes ready for more truth, but through what one does, through spiritual practices performed in "heed and diligence." One must allow one's heart to be moved and molded in order to receive more truth.

Like Christ's preaching in parables to one audience and more openly to another, God's dynamic revelatory response to our limitations is not only described but illustrated in several places within the Book of Mormon: some receive glorious visions because of their faith, others are commanded not even to teach to particularly wicked people, and several authors of the book are told by God to write no more on certain topics.[54] The doctrine of continuing revelation thus underscores the fact that human knowledge of God is incomplete and will continue to be incomplete this side of the eschaton. Hermeneutic theology proceeds with a keen awareness of the limits of our knowledge and of the ways in which we must be transformed in order

---

53. Perhaps in this sense of revelation, the real presence of Christ in the Eucharist at each mass would count as a kind of continuing revelation.

54. Consider for example 1 Nephi 11:4-6, 14:28; Ether 3:9, 21; Ether 13:13; Mormon 8:12; and a number of passages in the Doctrine and Covenants and Pearl of Great Price.

to grow in understanding. The doctrine of continuing revelation gives clear reasons to approach theology in this way.

III. Human Rational Potential

Mormons have many reasons to approach theology hermeneutically. There are some tensions worth noting, however, between a hermeneutic emphasis on the limits of rational knowledge and Mormon views of human potential and eschatology. Mormons take very seriously the New Testament promises that "when [Christ] shall appear, we shall be like him; for we shall see him as he is" (1 John 3:2), and that "then shall I know even as also I am known" (1 Cor. 13:12). A completion of knowledge is a key part of the heavenly reward God has in mind for us. Doctrine and Covenants 42:61 promises the faithful "revelation upon revelation, knowledge upon knowledge, that thou mayest know the mysteries and peacable things—that which bringeth joy." While one's capacity to assimilate revealed truth may be limited at any given moment, by accepting and heeding what one receives one can surpass all limits. With God's help, human understanding is ultimately unlimited: "He that keepeth [God's] commandments receiveth truth and light, until he is glorified in truth and knoweth all things" (D&C 93:28). In receiving this knowledge, humans become like God, for "the glory of God is intelligence" (D&C 93:36). Nor is it necessary to wait until the next life to aspire to such knowledge: "Whatever principle of intelligence we attain unto in this life, it will rise with us in the resurrection. And if a person gains more knowledge and intelligence in this life through his diligence . . . he will have so much the advantage in the world to come" (D&C 130:18–19). Though God will normally reveal only limited amounts to any given group of people, a faithful individual may eventually receive "the mysteries of God until he know them in full" (Alma 12:10). In light of the promise of knowing all things, it would seem that hermeneutic modesty itself should be subject to limits.

Further, Mormon scripture gives an optimistic view of reason's role in the human approach to God, when reason is supported by revelation and the Holy Spirit. Though the reasoning and conceptual abilities of mortal humans are normally very limited, God is quite willing to work with those limitations: "the Lord God giveth light unto the understanding; for he speaketh unto men according to their language, unto their understanding" (2 Nephi 31:3; see also D&C 1:24). Reasoning is portrayed as an appropriate means of teaching divine truths. Paul "reasoned in the synagogue . . . and persuaded the Jews and the Greeks" (Acts 17:2, 18:4). William McLellin is told by revelation, "Go unto the eastern lands, bear testimony . . . reasoning with the people" (D&C 66:7), and similarly Orson Hyde is told to go, "reasoning with and expounding all scriptures unto them." God himself says, "let us reason together, that ye may understand," and proceeds to reason through an extended passage in D&C 50:10–25. Chapters 1–10 of the book of Hebrews are an extended, reasoned exposition of Christ's mission in relation to the Law of Moses and the new logic of salvation under the new law. The Book of Mormon includes many extended passages of reasoning and reasoned exposition such as 2 Nephi 2, 9:1–27, and 31; Alma 34:8–16; Alma 41–42; and Moroni 8. D&C 76 and 88:1–45 show less overt reasoning but take the form of detailed and systematic explanation of a set of related aspects of the process of salvation.

A systematic theology along the lines of the scholastic tradition cannot be squared with the Mormon belief in continuing revelation. Such an approach aims to fit all relevant knowledge into a single coherent conceptual system, adjusting each element to reflect the others. New revealed knowledge then would likely require wholesale revision of such a system. Perhaps more importantly, the very idea of constructing a seamless whole, when one believes that important aspects of the relevant truth have not yet been revealed, is incoherent. By doing so one might seem rather to be investing in the hope that no new revelation will come after all!

These difficulties notwithstanding, I argue that a systematic approach to theology can play an appropriate role within a larger, broadly hermeneutic process. The effort to fit all knowledge into one system we may call a monosystematic approach. While I reject this mode of theology, I believe it may be valuable to build one system to a certain point of completion, with the expectation that in time it will fail or be rendered obsolete, and hence be superseded by a more adequate system of understanding. This system would be developed with a similar expectation that it too would eventually be superseded, and so on. We may call this a polysystematic mode of theology. Such a mode is quite ambitious as regards its eventual goal, but modest in its claims at any given stage along the way.

Illustrations of polysystematic progress in understanding appear in the history of science.[55] For example, an Aristotelian conception of the heavens was developed and refined over time, but then gave way to the Copernican conception, which in turn was replaced by the Newtonian and then the Einsteinian conceptions. While nothing has yet replaced Einstein's conception of heavenly motion, it seems clear that it also is neither complete nor final, and alternatives are in the works. Today, of course, a student of astronomy may progress in understanding through several of these systems in the course of a few years. Newton's view is still taught as a helpful one, sufficient in its own right for most people, and a step toward being ready to study Einstein's general theory of relativity.

---

55. Of course, the history of science was not widely conceptualized in this way until Thomas Kuhn's *The Structure of Scientific Revolutions* (Chicago: University of Chicago Press, 1970), and then not using this word.

This comparison of theology with the history of science is a bit baroque, but I believe it illustrates a pattern we can also see in the history of Judeo-Christian revelation. Some progress in understanding is a matter of simply adding or extending knowledge, but at times progress requires the replacement of one system of concepts with another. The Law of Moses was a kind of "schoolmaster to bring us unto Christ" and the new law (Gal. 3:24). The revelation to Moses included commandments but also conceptual content. Implicit in the Mosaic practices was a logic of sin, justice, and compensation for and forgiveness of sin. Salvation was understood primarily in terms of enjoying, as a nation, health, fertility, material prosperity, and victory over enemy nations. Christ satisfied the old logic of justice while introducing a new logic of justice and salvation, new commandments, a new nation, and a new victory.[56] He introduced a new, though substantially analogous system of concepts in terms of which humans are to understand their relationship with God. Yet we have reason to expect that these concepts too will fail and be superseded by a fuller understanding: "For we know in part, and we prophesy in part. But when that which is perfect is come, then that which is in part shall be done away" (1 Cor. 13:10).[57]

Though this historical progression provides the clearest example of the succession of views I have in mind, one need not necessarily wait for centuries to see a plurality of systematic views appear. Revelation as it stands is susceptible to multiple strands or levels of interpretation, especially revelation that takes the form of narrative. A single narrative can often be conceptualized in a number of ways. Further, the parables and analogies used in much New Testament teaching are not conceptually homogenous. For example, Jesus' parables compare divine judgment to an accounting for debt, a trial of one's preparation, and a division between crops and weeds. Each of these comparisons suggests a quite different logic of justice and atonement, worth developing in its own right.

Mormons are wary of systematic theology because the most conspicuous examples of it include many claims that we do not accept. However, since these were propounded without access to (what Mormons understand to be) revelation, similar errors would likely have appeared regardless of theological method. Where revealed truths are available, but neglected in favor of human constructs, this is not a result of systematic thought but

---

56. He satisfied the old justice through his sacrifice on the cross (Heb. 10:1–4, 11–14), thus preparing the way for a new justice (see, e.g. Matt. 20:1–16). He replaced a nation defined by biological descent with a nation defined by faith (John 8:39), and so forth.

57. Presumably Christ had a more unified understanding of justice and atonement, only partially reflected in any one of these parables or analogies. However, we must work with what he gave us.

rather of the elevation of human judgment over revealed truth. Moreover, if theology is understood to be a method of coming to better understand revelation and prophetic deliverances, as I suggest it should be, then it is by nature subordinate and attentive to revelation. In the history of science, careful study of the ways in which a theory broke down often led to a breakthrough. Similarly, theological practice that truly seeks to understand should welcome the disruption of new revelation.

Narrative and practice are vital to proper knowledge of God. Still, as humans we inevitably understand these through rational concepts. That some of these concepts defy explicit definition and hence require judgment or *phronesis* to be properly applied does not prevent their being systematically related. If one set of concepts is inadequate, then we should work toward a better set. The new set may also be inadequate, yet still be an improvement. To refuse to think through one's understanding systematically at all, I suggest, is to risk simply consigning oneself to confusion. Thus appropriate attention to narrative, practice, and conceptual framework, including systematic considerations, should be combined in the best approach to theology.

Errors will occur in the process of interpreting and assimilating revelation, as in any other mode of human thought. These should be corrected over time through due attention to the source of truth. In the meantime errors are unfortunate, but the potential for error is not a reason to abandon the project. Of those who build on the foundation of Christ, Paul says, "the fire shall try every man's work of what sort it is . . . If any man's work shall be burned, he shall suffer loss: but he himself shall be saved; yet so as by fire" (1 Cor. 3:13, 15). What matters most in theology, as in any enterprise of faith, is that one labor, and build on the true foundation.

About the Authors

David Tracy (S.T.D. Gregorian University) is the former editor of *The Journal of Religion*, *The Religious Studies Review*, and *Concilium*. His professional memberships include the American Academy of Religion, the American Theological Society, and the Catholic Theological Society of American, of which he was the president from 1977 to 1978. He is currently the Andrew Thomas Greeley and Grace McNichols Greeley Distinguished Service Professor of Catholic Studies and professor of theology and philosophy of religion at the University of Chicago Divinity School, where he is also on the Committee of Social Thought.

James L. Siebach (Ph.D. University of Texas, Austin) received his Ph.D. in classics and philosophy. He is an associate professor of philosophy at Brigham Young University. He has published on Plato, St. Augustine, Gregory of Nyssa, and Didymus the Blind. He recently completed a translation and commentary, along with Daniel W. Graham, on Didymus the Blind's *Commentary on the Psalms*.

James E. Faulconer (Ph.D. Pennsylvania State University) has published on the philosophy of psychology and the philosophy of religion, as well as on contemporary European philosophy. He is the editor of *Transcendence in Religion and Philosophy* (Indiana University Press, 2003) and, with Mark Wrathall, *Appropriating Heidegger* (Cambridge, 2000). He is a professor of philosophy at Brigham Young University, where he is also the Associate Director of the Faculty Center.

Benjamin Huff is Assistant Professor of Philosophy at Randolph-Macon College (Ashland, Virginia). He received a B.A. from Brigham Young University in 1996 and a Ph.D. from the University of Notre Dame in 2006, with a dissertation entitled, "Friendship and the Shared Life of Virtue." His research and teaching interests include ethical theory, especially virtue ethics; ancient Greek philosophy; social/political philosophy; and philosophy of religion. Interests within Mormon thought include ecclesiology, justice and atonement, and the unity of God.

A Dialogue on Openness Theology

Open and Relational Theologies

Clark H. Pinnock

For all of us God is a great mystery and a major challenge to speak about. Therefore, a humble spirit is required if we wish to attempt it, which (of course) we do, because we must talk about God, who is the first and principal topic of Christian doctrine. Augustine sets the tone for any inquiry into the mystery of God when he begins a tract entitled "On the Holy Trinity" by asking readers to keep him company when they are in agreement, to dialogue with him when they are hesitant, and to call him back when they think he is in error. Augustine hopes that such practices will ensure that we will advance together toward God. He also adds that there is no "inquiry more laborious" nor where "error [is] more dangerous," but also none where the "discovery of truth [is] more profitable."[1]

When I refer to open and relational theologies in the title of this chapter, I have in mind a cluster of models of the divine that strive to bring out the personal nature of God and want, in their own distinctive ways, to lift up the conviction that God is "open" and that he exists in a significant relationship with the creature. Open and relational theologies envisage a situation where there is genuine interaction between God and his creations, where God enters into reciprocal give-and-take relations with his creations, and where God responds to what his creations do, willingly (sometimes necessarily) accepting a degree of conditionality and risk taking. Although these theological themes are quite old, traditionalists have not usually allowed such models to hold sway. But many theologians are adopting similar models today. These theologians are keen to recover such relational themes as God's loving, God's risking, God's suffering, God's changing, and so forth.

---

1. Augustine, "On the Trinity," in *A Select Library of Nicene and Post-Nicene Fathers*, ed. Philip Schaff, vol. 3, bk. 1 (Grand Rapids: Eerdmans, 1956), chap. 3.

The desire to formulate a more relational model is widespread among theologians across the spectrum of Christian thought. As for myself, I have worked with a relational model that has been named "the openness of God"—sometimes called free-will theism—and have done so in the evangelical context.[2] As hinted at above, this model is by no means limited in time or number. Relational non-determinist theology is as old as Christianity itself. One finds it in the Eastern church; in Justin Martyr, John Wesley, and Karl Barth; among contemporary Roman Catholics like Walter Kasper and Norris Clarke; and among Reformed thinkers like Vincent Brümmer, Adrio König, and Nicholas Wolterstorff. One sees it consistently in the Wesleyan/Arminian and Methodist traditions; in Boston personalism and process thought (which come out of Methodism); in the recent Trinitarian theologies; in liberation theologies; in scientists like John Polkinghorne; in philosophers like Richard Swinburne; and last but not least, in LDS thought. Although I am a relational theist who swims in the streams of tradition flowing from Wesley, I believe that there are different ways of approaching relational theism and that subscribers to these various approaches need to be in touch with one another and conversing. Who knows—we may learn something from the methodologies of others and from the discoveries that they have made. The fact is that we know the things of God only "in part" (1 Cor. 3:12), which should make us open to insight from whatever direction.[3]

From my standpoint, I perceive several "sisterly" relational models that develop their ideas in slightly different ways. And since this is a book where members of The Church of Jesus Christ of Latter-day Saints are finding a voice, I can give these sisterly models a relevant spin. I have an opportunity not possible in most of the other chapters to include LDS theology in my presentation and to invite Latter-day Saints to clarify their beliefs for a wide spectrum of readers. I am not presenting something alien to the Latter-day Saints but something familiar and agreeable to them. In this book, Latter-day Saints are finding their voice, and I can help to draw it out by being conscious of them throughout. I will put them in the center of my exposition, not leave them cheering from the sidelines. I am confident in thinking that progress can be made in the theological development of us all.

Relational theists have a lot in common with Latter-day Saints, commonality that should lead to fruitful interaction. Social Trinitarianism, the

---

2. See the manifesto written by Clark Pinnock, John Sanders, Richard Rice, William Hasker, and David Basinger, *The Openness of God: A Biblical Challenge to the Traditional Understanding of God* (Downers Grove, Ill.: InterVarsity, 1994). John Sanders filled out the picture in *The God Who Risks: A Theology of Providence* (Downers Grove, Ill.: InterVarsity, 1998).

3. See Sanders, "Divine Relationality in the Christian Tradition," in *The God Who Risks,* chap. 5.

view that the Godhead is best understood by starting from the threeness of the persons, is one example. Another is my own personal openness to considering the idea of a divine embodiment, taboo in traditional theology but central to LDS thinking. Then there is a mutual dissatisfaction with classical theism, the espousal of libertarian freedom, the denial that God has a monopoly on power, the belief that God experiences pathos in interaction with creatures, and the belief that God prefers to exercise persuasive rather than coercive power. There may be more. And of course there will be divergences alongside the convergences.[4]

As a non-Mormon but not an anti-Mormon, I am not as familiar as I ought to be with LDS thinking, but I have enjoyed researching it and will do my best to be fair in my interaction. I have been helped by perusing the five volumes of *The Encyclopedia of Mormonism*, by dipping into the work of FARMS and BYU Studies, and by reading Blake T. Ostler's *The Attributes of God*, which was written for non-Mormons like me who are interested in comparing LDS thought with traditional Christian theology.[5] In this connection, David Paulsen eased my mind when he admitted in the preface to Ostler's book that "LDS insights on the nature of God remain among the world's best kept secrets—at least, in scholarly circles."[6] I hope I will not be judged too harshly for any errors I may make, and I hope that more scholars outside of the LDS faith will increasingly consider the theological insights Latter-day Saints have to offer.[7]

In this chapter, I will present open and relational theologies in an attempt to call attention to possible points of contact with LDS thought and to open up lines of communication. As a non-Mormon who is not an anti-Mormon, I am genuinely interested both in hearing and learning from what Latter-day Saints have to say on the matters I will present and am hopeful that the interaction will be enriching. Beyond that, I cherish the hope that the Holy Spirit will open doors to dialogue between Latter-day Saints and

---

4. In the dialogue book *How Wide the Divide? A Mormon and an Evangelical in Conversation,* co-authored with Craig Blomberg (Downers Grove, Ill.: InterVarsity, 1997), 195–96, Stephen E. Robinson lists the most important points of agreement and disagreement that were discovered.

5. Daniel H. Ludlow, ed., *Encyclopedia of Mormonism,* 5 vols. (New York: Macmillian, 1992; Blake T. Ostler, *The Attributes of God,* Exploring Mormon Thought, (Salt Lake City: Greg Kofford, 2001).

6. David Paulsen, preface to *Attributes of God,* xvi.

7. Let me be frank. When I think about the LDS church, I think of an indigenous form of Christianity outside the Western orbit, like (for example) in Africa, The Church of Jesus Christ on Earth by the Prophet Simon Kimbangu. I also relate it to the Montanist movement of the second century with its visions and prophets who helped to renew the church.

traditional Christian believers. Obviously there will be differences and limits to agreement at this stage, but there may be areas promising of growth also.

I know that Latter-day Saints debate with each other as to what ideas are necessary beliefs in their faith and as to how these beliefs are best articulated. I know that they do not now follow some practices that were followed by LDS in the nineteenth century (for example, the practice of polygamy or the practice of denying priesthood to blacks). LDS thinking does not stand still, and we should not impute to them things that they do not now hold or practice. I will give David Paulsen the opportunity to clarify things that puzzle me.

In this conversation, of course, we are coming from very different places. The Latter-day Saints will be appealing to the broad canon of their scriptures and standard works and to the restoration gospel contained therein, and I will not be. But I think the simple fact that we both accept the Holy Bible completely means that there will still be a lot in common. On the subject of canon, let me add this: I freely grant that, were there to have been a restoration of Christianity through Joseph Smith, there would have been fresh scriptures to bear witness to it. Scriptures arise in such contexts. I find the existence of the Book of Mormon and other uniquely LDS scripture to be consistent with religious tradition and entertain no dogma of a closed canon that would rule out such modern revelation.[8] As for a restoration, this is a familiar theme in American church history. One thinks of the Anabaptists, the Campbellites, and the Pentecostals, who rival even the Latter-day Saints in world outreach. But all of these organizations think of themselves in these restorationist terms, and it seems to this Canadian that the Americans have a flair for restoring, rectifying, and renewing religion!

Relational Theology in General

A distinguishing feature in the doctrine of God today is the debate surrounding the traditional absolutist model of God, a model which was developed in the ancient and medieval periods of church history and that is inclined to employ abstract and deterministic categories for understanding the nature of God and God's relationship to the world. Many theologians today, including some who think of themselves as classical theists, are critical of this approach. A great many find themselves tending to emphasize the perfections of a personal God, who engages in give-and-take relationships with creatures. There is a trend in contemporary theology toward relational

---

8. Stephen Robinson has expressed the wish that some evangelical would say that the Book of Mormon could be inspired by God. Blomberg and Robinson, *How Wide the Divide?*, 71. I would say this. Of course it could be. But the possibility does not prove that it is or that there may not be some explaining to do.

theism, a shift in doctrine toward more dynamic categories and away from the more static categories. Open theists think (and I believe that Latter-day Saints agree) that this does greater justice to the revelation of God in Jesus Christ, who is not an apathetic and immobile God but a compassionate, loving, and responsive person.

Donald G. Bloesch, a leading evangelical theologian, expresses this strongly when he writes,

> A compelling case can be made that the history of Christian thought shows the unmistakable imprint of a biblical-classical synthesis in which the ontological categories of Greco-Roman philosophy have been united with the personal-dramatic categories of biblical faith. The attempt at synthesis began already with the early apologists, who sought to vindicate the claims of Christianity to the pagan culture of their time. The Hellenising of Christian faith was particularly apparent in Clement and Origen, who introduced "elements of religious speculation and intellectualistic spirituality belonging to a world altogether different from that of the Gospel."[9]

The God of biblical faith interacts with people in the drama of history, whereas the God of the Hellenistic ethos is a self-contained absolute, characterized by imperturbability and impassibility. But believers do not want a cold, immutable, and philosophical kind of God. They want a God who reveals himself, listens to prayer, and can (to some extent) be grasped in human terms. Shay Cohen writes,

> The God of the Hebrew Bible is for the most part an anthropomorphic and anthropopathic being, that is, a God who has the form and emotions of humans. He (it is a he) walks and talks, has arms and legs, becomes angry, happy, or sad, changes his mind, speaks to humans and is addressed by them, and closely supervises the affairs of the world. The God of the philosophers [perhaps we should add, of certain philosophers] is a different sort of being altogether: abstract (the Prime Mover, the First Cause, the Mind or Soul of the universe, etc.), immutable,

---

9. Donald G. Bloesch, *God the Almighty: Power, Wisdom, Holiness, Love* (Downers Grove, Ill.: InterVarsity, 1995), 205–6, quoting Vladimir Lossky, *The Vision of God,* trans. Asheleigh Moorhouse (Crestwood, N.Y.: St. Vladimir's Seminary Press, 1983), 67. Curiously, the critics who rail against open theists for talking like this are silent when it comes to criticizing this Reformed scholar, who says the very same things. Thomas F. Torrance also thinks in these terms and even coined the term "openness of God" long before we took it up in his book *Space, Time, and Incarnation* (New York: Oxford University Press, 1969), 74–75. Notice, however, that Bloesch wants a relational theism but not quite an open theism (254–60). He complains that we "make the revealed mysteries too transparent." Bloesch, *God the Almighty,* 259. Like prominent evangelical theologian J. I. Packer, perhaps, Bloesch would postulate an antinomy in place of an explanation at the point of sovereignty and freedom.

and relatively unconcerned with the affairs of humanity. The tension between these rival conceptions of the Deity is evident in the work of Philo, who is able to find a philosophically respectable God in the Torah only through allegorical exegesis (see chapter 6). Philo is particularly careful to sanitize the anthropomorphic and anthropopathic passages.[10]

This kind of criticism is made by many. It is made by liberals like Adolph von Harnack, by Reformed scholars like Vincent Brümmer, by open theists like John Sanders,[11] and by LDS academicians like Stephen Robinson. In *How Wide the Divide?* Robinson writes, "There isn't a single verse of the Bible that I do not personally accept and believe, although I do reject the interpretive straightjacket imposed on the Bible by the Hellenized church after the apostles passed from the scene." Thus Robinson accepts the Bible, but not what he calls the theological and philosophical "add-ons" of tradition.[12]

Robinson's statement clearly converges with the beliefs of other varieties of relational theology. Belief in some kind of mistake by certain theologians of absolutism is not limited to Latter-day Saints, although they see it radically. But even here we need not exaggerate the difference. Robinson writes, "Informed Latter-day-Saints do not argue that historic Christianity lost *all* truth or became *completely* corrupt. The orthodox churches may have lost the 'fullness' of the gospel, but they did not lose all of it nor even most of it."[13] This is a remarkable concession and a conciliatory tone that is seldom heard among the sometimes vicious evangelical critics of LDS thought. At the same time, as in so many matters, there may be a difference of opinion between Latter-day Saints on this point, given the fact that Joseph Smith expressed strongly negative opinions about traditional Christianity in his account of the First Vision of 1820. However, Robinson warns against our misinterpreting Joseph Smith's intent, and Benjamin Huff warns that Latter-day Saints ought to be careful how they see the precise nature of the apostasy and should not distort things.[14]

---

10. Shaye J. D. Cohen, *From the Maccabees to the Misnah* (Philadelphia: Westminster, 1987), 86–87.

11. Sanders, *The God Who Risks,* chap. 2.

12. Blomberg and Robinson, *How Wide the Divide?* 59, 138.

13. Blomberg and Robinson, *How Wide the Divide?* 61; emphasis in original.

14. Blomberg and Robinson, *How Wide the Divide?* 161–62, 165–66; Benjamin Huff, "How Polemics Corrupted Latter-day Saint Apologetics," *FARMS Review* 15, no. 1 (2003): 273–309, believes that Richard R. Hopkins is too unnuanced in Hopkins's book *How Greek Philosophy Corrupted the Christian Concept of God* (Bountiful, Utah: Horizon, 1998).

Open Theism in Particular

Open theism, which also associates itself with the evangelical movement in North America, belongs to the family of relational approaches. Sharing themes with others, we open theists too are in pursuit of a personal God who is dynamically related to the world. We hold that God by grace has granted humans significant freedom to cooperate with or work against God's will for us and that God enters into dynamic give-and-take relationships with us. We also espouse the belief that the future is not settled in every respect and that God knows both what will be and what might be. Open theism is a biblical theology rather than a metaphysical construct, though open theists are not averse to or disinterested in its philosophical, scientific, and existential credibility. In their efforts to engage in biblical theology, the Latter-day Saints are closer to open theism than they are to process thought (Griffin, 161–87) and, like open theists, are something of a *via media* between classical and process theism; however, they tend more to process theism in some matters (for example, when it comes to creation out of nothing).

The openness version of the relational models has been marketed under that "openness" logo to the evangelicals because the chief proponents of open theism are themselves evangelicals and because there are so many other evangelicals whom we can reach. We present it as a biblical theology and one that is in sync with our relational piety. In spite of opposition, mostly from the paleo-Calvinist strongholds in the evangelical movement, the message has been getting out. (Indeed their vociferousness in criticism has given us a great deal of free publicity as well as sympathy.) Whatever the disadvantages in marketing open theism in this way (for example, having new theological thoughts, however biblical, that challenge tradition can be suspect in such circles), we also have a few advantages. For example, it is hard to find an evangelical who does not believe in a relational God that responds freely to prayer. For another thing, young people often gravitate toward open theism because it encourages them to believe that they can make a difference in the future, which is not altogether settled.

In terms of publicity again, putting open theism out onto evangelical turf has resulted in its being much more widely noticed than it would have been if it were just circulating in the mainline/old line/sideline church contexts. For example, do you think the *Washington Post* would have done an article on open theism if we had tossed it onto the floor of the annual conference of the Presbyterian Church, USA instead? There it would have gotten eclipsed by something else, such as the debate over gay marriage. Sowing the seed among evangelicals, then, has been strategically effective because these people profess to care and, I think, do care about what the Bible says.

Of course, open theism is a little controversial because it challenges tradition in the way it appeals to scripture, causing some conservative Christians to balk. But ought we not place scripture above tradition, and ought we not welcome new light that shines forth from God's holy word? We are critical, for example, of traditionalism, which seems to be conditioning evangelicals not to grow as hearers of the word of God. At the same time, we do not want to dismiss all catholic traditions and do not actually consider open theism to be a major innovation. Critics exaggerate the degree of innovation in order to stir up passions against us, but we do not see open theism as highly untraditional. We see it as a not-too-large modification of Wesleyan/Arminian thinking.[15] Of course, if one's view is that any adjustments to tradition are forbidden, then it is radical. But that is an extreme position—the best theologians accept the need of at least some theological fine-tuning and redefining of concepts.

What we have named "the open view of God" is a particular flowering of relational theism. We gave it this name because it expressed our vision and because it was not already in use and thus was available. We wanted evangelicals in particular to encounter relational theism as a scriptural paradigm, unencumbered by any existing and possibly tired-out labels. Eventually, of course, critical examination will locate it in the flow of tradition, likely as a development of Wesleyan thinking. Meanwhile, one way to get a perspective on it is to see it as a mediating position, a *via media* between classical theism on the one hand and process theism on the other. This gives us three explanatory models to compare, offering us a well-rounded explanation of God's nature and God's relation to the world.[16]

To start with, classical theism is an absolutist understanding of the nature of God in which God has no need of the world and is not internally related to it. God's joy is not increased by the world's beauty or diminished by its pain. God's being is perfect and fully actualized apart from the world. Any alteration to God's character would only decrease it. In this understanding, God is immutable in a static sense, essentially unrelated to the world and unaffected by what happens in it and to it. Classical theists see absoluteness and impassibility as basic attributes of God that determine how the revelation of God in Christ is understood. This model has dominated Christian thinking through most of church history and defines the God that atheists love to hate. One wonders how many people have rejected

---

15. John Sanders, "Open Theism: Radical Revision or Miniscule Modification of Arminianism?" *Wesleyan Theological Journal* 38 (2003): 69–102. See also Roger Olson, *The Mosaic of Christian Belief: Twenty Centuries of Unity and Diversity* (Downers Grove, Ill.: InterVarsity, 2002), 192–96.

16. For this format, see John S. Feinberg, *No One Like Him: The Doctrine of God*, (Wheaton, Ill.: Crossway, 2001), 62–73.

faith in God because of such a definition of him. It presents God as, in the words of Dallas Willard, "a great unblinking cosmic stare."[17]

At the other extreme stands process theology. Here God and the world are coeternal, reciprocally related, and interdependent. According to process theology, God created the world and the world creates God. He is evolving along with the universe and dependent on the world for the content of his life experience. The creature continually adds value to the divine experience. God is immanent in the life of the world and the world is immanent in the life of God. In effect, as the saying goes, God proposes, man disposes. Not at all distant and aloof, God is always involved in the world. There are possibilities for change and improvement. God has a physical pole and is thereby thoroughly passible. God cares about us all and is always trying to lure us toward what is best for us. Being mutable and involved in the process of becoming, his knowledge is finite and undergoes changes. He cannot know the future exhaustively. He knows all possibilities, not which possibility will become actual. God and the world are ultimate. Creativity is everlasting. God is always with us and cares about us deeply. He never gives up on us. Ultimately, all entities receive their life from God and return their life to God. God is the power that inspires the creative becoming of all things through tender persuasion and that treasures their achieved values in his own everlasting life.

Open theism, as I have said, takes a position between these two extremes, and I believe that LDS thought does also. Open theism appeals to those who like aspects of process theism and cannot accept classical theism but want a more mediating corrective. I am not presenting something alien to the Latter-day Saints but something familiar and agreeable to them. One might say that these individuals want a neo-classical, not a non-classical, view. Openness thinking has affinities to both process theism and classical theism, plus real differences. Open theists embrace the one God, maker of heaven and earth, who at the same time self-limits to make room for significant creatures. In sovereign freedom, the triune God chooses to create. In particular, he makes a world capable of receiving and returning love and grants the kind of freedom necessary for this. God also decides to make some of his actions contingent on us, on our prayers and actions. He lets himself be affected by what we do, and he responds to what we do. God does not tightly control everything that happens but gives space for us to operate and cooperate in. God is also creative and resourceful in how he works with

<hr>

17. Dallas Willard, *The Divine Conspiracy: Rediscovering Our Hidden Life in God* (San Francisco: HarperSanFrancisco, 1998), 244–45. Francis Beckwith and Stephen E. Parrish are classical theists who have written about LDS thought: *The Mormon Concept of God: A Philosophical Analysis* (Lewiston, N.Y.: Edwin Mellen, 1991).

us. As Sanders puts it, "God has divine purpose with open routes."[18] We reject the blueprint worldview. History is not a scripted play in which our decisions are simply what God has decided.

Controversially, open theists also say that God knows all that it is possible to know, that God knows what will be but also what might be. He knows what he has decided to bring about, but he also knows the possibilities that he has left open. Graciously, God invites us to collaborate with him in bringing the as-yet-open part of the future into being. Open theists do not want a God as impotent and finite as the process God, so they posit omnipotence but see God as choosing not to use his full power out of respect for libertarian freedom. I realize that this exposes a point of vulnerability for me in that a God who can self-limit can also un-self-limit, but I can live with it.[19] As a *via media,* open theism wants to preserve the classical emphasis on the greatness of God while at the same time highlighting the relational aspects.

Being a pilgrim in theology, I have experienced changes in my thinking over the years, and one such change lies in God's relationship to humans. Over a period of thirty years, I have moved away from the paleo-Calvinist system typified by the canons of Dort to a post-conservative, evangelical Wesleyan standpoint. In terms of the doctrine of God, I moved from thinking of God as "an unmoved mover" to thinking of him as "a most moved mover." And it has taken effort over a lifetime to work out the implications of this one thing: what does it mean to believe in a relational God of unbounded love?[20]

Belief in a loving triune God took center stage in my thinking, and I began to see God not as a solitary God, but as a communion of love marked by overflowing life. I got the sense of a totally shared life at the heart of the universe, not of God the monarch, ruling from isolated splendor, but of God the perfect sociality, which embodies the qualities of mutuality,

---

18. Sanders, *The God Who Risks,* 230–35.

19. Tyron L. Inbody, *The Transforming God: An Interpretation of Suffering and Evil* (Louisville, Ky.: Westminster John Knox, 1997), 67–78, 142–43, 148–49.

20. The story is told in my biography by Barry L. Callen, and the shift is documented in the following writings: Barry Callen, *Clark H. Pinnock: Journey Toward Renewal—An Intellectual Biography* (Nappanee, Ind.: Evangel, 2000); and Pinnock, "The Need for a Scriptural, and Therefore a Neo-Classical Theism," in *Perspectives on Evangelical Theology,* ed. Kenneth S. Kantzer and Stanley N. Gundry (Grand Rapids: Baker, 1980), 37–42. See also Pinnock, "God Limits His Knowledge," in *Predestination and Free Will: Four Views of Divine Sovereignty and Human Freedom,* ed. David and Randall Basinger (Downers Grove, Ill.: InterVarsity, 1986), 143–62; "From Augustine to Arminius: A Pilgrimage in Theology," in *The Grace of God, the Will of Man: A Case for Arminianism,* ed. Clark H. Pinnock (Grand Rapids: Zondervan, 1989), 15–30; and "Systematic Theology," in *The Openness of God,* 101–25.

cooperation, and reciprocity—a unity with genuine diversity.[21] I began to see that relationality is central to who God is, in that ours is a personal God, carrying out a project and acting for the sake of others. God is the maker of heaven and earth, of all things visible and invisible, and the source of everything, but God is also one who limits himself in ways that preserve his eternal nature while relating to us. God takes a stance of openness toward the world. He chooses to be God for the world and allows himself to be affected by it and opens himself up to vulnerability. God sovereignly restricts his power and risks the pain of rejection. The relationship is a two-way street. Humans can choose for or against God's love, and their decisions genuinely affect him. Thus we gather that God must to some extent be limiting the exercise of his power to give us space to act in.[22]

Thus God, though unchangeable in his qualities, is open to change in other ways. Who God is does not change, but what God experiences does change. So, too, God is not impassible, as the tradition has mostly insisted. The God who loves us is open to experiencing delight as well as anguish. God does not experience fickle emotions or suffer inappropriately as we do. But there is pathos and suffering in God. Similarly, God is not timeless, since he accompanies us in time as we act and he responds. Such interaction reveals that God experiences sequence. God is not in time as we are, but his experience is sequential like ours. As a result of thinking through the truth of the love of God, I was led to the open view of God.

A dozen years ago, five colleagues put together a multi-authored book, written in understandable terms, that would make a case for open theism. We knew that some people already held this view (especially some of the Christian philosophers) but that far more people were unaware of it, at least formally. So we became a team to cover the bases, methodologically following the Wesleyan quadrilateral.[23] We asked ourselves questions like the following: What do the scriptures say? (Richard Rice, an Adventist); How well have we done theologically? (Sanders and Pinnock); What perspective might philosophy contribute? (William Hasker); and Are there practical implications? (David Basinger). Now to be more specific and to bring to the surface issues of interest both to openness and LDS thought, let us scout out the territory that we mapped out and, at the same time, interact with the LDS doctrine of God. I will share what open theists found and open the

---

21. Clark H. Pinnock, *Flame of Love: A Theology of the Holy Spirit* (Downers Grove, Ill.: InterVarsity, 1996), chap. 1.

22. John Polkinghorne, ed., *The Work of Love: Creation as Kenosis* (Grand Rapids: Eerdmans, 2001).

23. For the use in theology of multiple sources, see Donald A. D. Thorson, *The Wesleyan Quadrilateral: Scripture, Tradition, Reason and Experience as a Model of Evangelical Theology* (Grand Rapids: Zondervan, 1990).

door to critical feedback. I hope it is possible that, as friends, we may agree and/or disagree amicably.[24]

A Dialogue between Open Theism and Latter-day Saint Thought

First, and foremost, open theists appeal to the Bible, which is for us a basic commitment and one that motivates us to be respectful of its truth and to be wary of alien assumptions. Our primary commitment is to the scriptures rather than tradition, reason, or experience. And, in our appeal to scripture, we have brought neglected truth to light and offered a plausible mode of its interpretation. We give particular weight to the narrative quality of the Bible and to the language of personal relations. The sacred story involves real drama and bears witness powerfully to the interactivity of God. We accept diversity in the biblical witnesses, too, and recognize the dialogical character of the text. The Bible does not speak with a single voice but fosters dialogue between different voices. The writings contain a long and complex search for the mind of God. We listen to the Bible as we would listen to a conversation between testimony and counter-testimony, aware of the fact that scripture is inexhaustibly rich and that, when approached prayerfully and with good questions, it will yield ever new insights.[25]

Open and relational theists find in the Bible a witness to a triune personal God who seeks relationships of love with creatures. He enters into partnerships, he self-limits, he experiences vulnerability, he undertakes risks, he enters into conflict, he participates in a real drama, and so on. Here is the self-disclosure of a personal God in the history of Israel and in the life, death, and resurrection of Jesus Christ. We try not to burden the text with our presuppositions but learn from God's self-revelation. We do not presume the absolutist hermeneutic but listen to the scriptures when they tell us that God changes for our sake and even suffers on our behalf. The scriptures lead us to speak of God as one who humbles himself and who shows his perfection by changing as well as by not changing. We celebrate God's compassionate, suffering, and victorious love. We think that Augustine was wrong to have said that God does not grieve over suffering in the world, that Anselm was wrong to have said that God does not experience compassion, and that Calvin was wrong to have said that the biblical

---

24. From my standpoint, Joseph Smith had stimulating and even prophetic insights that I can appreciate in dialogue with Latter-day Saints even though I do not hail him as the Prophet of the latter days.

25. Walter Brueggemann features the motif of testimony and counter-testimony in his work. See *Theology of the Old Testament: Testimony, Dispute, Advocacy* (Minneapolis: Fortress, 1997).

metaphors are merely accommodations to our finite understanding. For much too long, pagan assumptions about the divine nature have skewed our exegetical reflection.[26]

Thus we note in the text such things as God's testing of Abraham (and many such texts of testing) as God's way of knowing what is in man's heart. After testing Abraham, God says, "Now I know that thou fearest God" (Gen. 22:12). By testing Abraham, God learned what kind of fellow he was. On one occasion, God had decided to set aside the people of Israel and try some other approach, but, in response to Moses's prayer, he chose not to. The text says, "The Lord changed his mind about the disaster that he planned to bring upon his people" (Ex. 32:14). Jeremiah visited a potter's house and noted how the potter would rework the clay when it did not suit him. God says it is thus with the nations. God will bring judgment or not, depending on the circumstances. What God will do or not do depends in part on what his people do or do not do (Jer. 18:4–10). Isaiah the prophet likens Israel to a vineyard that God planted, one in which he worked hard but that still disappointed him. He had expected good grapes but received only wild grapes. God asks rhetorically why it yielded a bad harvest (Isa. 5:1–5). It was not what he had expected and not what he had wanted. In a word to Hosea, God speaks of his compassion despite Israel's ingratitude and even describes his inner feelings: "My heart recoils within me; my compassion grows warm and tender" (Hosea 11:8). We find many texts that seem to support an openness rather than a classical hermeneutic.

At this point, I wish to put on the table specific items that will foster conversation between open and LDS theists.

Item 1: Divine Embodiment

In the course of searching out the truth of scripture, I stumbled onto what was to me an unfamiliar and not very congenial idea (though not unfamiliar or uncongenial to LDS thinking or the patristic sources). This was evidence of divine embodiment.[27] Divine embodiment has not been something that open theists, much less other evangelicals, have been comfortable with. Thus it happened that, as one who wanted to take biblical imagery seriously, I found myself having to reckon on the possibility of God's having—or at least assuming, in the case of Jesus—embodied ways.[28] (What a good illustration this is of how influential on the results of our interpretations is the community in which the texts are read.) So I had to ask myself why I had

---

26. Pinnock, "Overcoming a Pagan Inheritance," *Most Moved Mover,* chap. 2.

27. See, for example, Terence E. Fretheim, *The Suffering of God: An Old Testament Perspective* (Philadelphia: Fortress, 1984), chap. 6.

28. See Pinnock, *Most Moved Mover,* 33–35.

just let this lie before and had never pursued it. It was not as if some of the early fathers of the church, like Tertullian, had not taken it seriously—he did so, and strongly. Nevertheless, "the idea that God is not embodied has been the stock-in-trade of Theological orthodoxy" for centuries.[29] John Macquarrie observes, "That God is a purely spiritually being, immaterial, invisible, intangible, is assumed to be a basic truth by the great majority of those who believe in God. To suggest that God might have a body would seem absurd to virtually all of those believers."[30] But divine embodiment cannot be ruled out so long as one is prepared to elucidate the idea responsibly, which is what Jantzen was trying to do with the suggestion that the universe itself is somehow God's body. I think that relational theists can accommodate this idea under our belief in God's omnipresence.

After I regained my bearing, I remembered a wise question of C. S. Lewis's: "What soul ever perished from believing that God the Father really has a beard?"[31] In other words, maybe corporeality is a funny idea to many Christians and not one that we can easily entertain, but why rule it out when it has scriptural backing and when it forms no boundary issue for Christianity? Christians are entitled to peculiar beliefs without its robbing them of salvation, aren't they?

More substantially, I also remembered how Donald G. Bloesch makes room for the idea of divine embodiment when he writes, "[God] stands infinitely beyond materiality, but he has his own divine nature, his own supernatural body." Again he writes, "God is not a material being, but he can assume a material form, and he has done so in the incarnation of his Son."[32] This is extraordinary—here we have the premier evangelical systematic theologian speaking of divine embodiment! Granted, LDS theology is not his likely source, but Latter-day Saints are entitled to a bit of "we told you so" to more traditional Christians. Then add these comments by Richard Swinburne, a world-class Christian philosopher and open theist: "By saying that God is essentially bodiless, I mean that, although he may sometimes have a body, he is not dependent on his body in any way." In other words, while we need our bodies in order to exist, God does not, though he has one.[33]

---

29. Grace Jantzen, *God's World, God's Body* (Philadelphia: Westminster John Knox, 1984), 21; and David L. Paulsen, "The Doctrine of Divine Embodiment: Restoration, Judeo-Christian, and Philosophical Perspectives," *BYU Studies* 35, no. 4 (1995–96): 7–94.

30. John Macquarrie, forward to Jantzen, *God's World, God's Body*, xi.

31. C. S. Lewis, *Letters to Malcolm: Chiefly on Prayer* (New York: Harvest-Harcourt Brace Jovanovich, 1964), 22.

32. Bloesch, *God the Almighty*, 50, 89.

33. Richard Swinburne, *The Christian God* (New York: Oxford University Press, 1994), 127.

Whatever we make of this, I think we have to say that it is God *as personal*, not God *as spiritual*, that dominates biblical thinking. The writers did not worry as much as we do about approximating God too closely to the human. The tradition has wanted to emphasize the spirituality of God but in doing so has obscured the personal nature of God. So a corrective is needed, but a careful one, because there are dangers. Surely God is not subject to human limitations such as needing to sleep or going to the toilet.[34]

In this area, I was helped by something Stephen Robinson said: "Latter-day Saints affirm only that the Father has a body, not that his body has him."[35] And I also appreciated Blake Ostler's writing that "the sense in which the Father's body is like a human body must be qualified."[36] We have to remember that a glorified body would be very different from what we know of bodies (see Philip. 3:21 and 1 Cor. 15:50). The idea does not have to be taken in a crude way—there may be ways of understanding it that are intellectually viable.[37] It is easier, however, to understand how the Son acquired a body now in glory (we all celebrate that fact) than to understand how the Father acquired a body (if he did) or how the Spirit will (if he or she does). So there are issues to work on here. Meanwhile, in saying that God has a body, the Latter-day Saints have raised an issue for Christian theology and philosophy at large that should not be swept under the rug anymore. Are we traditionalists willing to give them a little credit for that? Can we not let them come in out of the cold?

Item 2: Gods other than Yahweh

A similar example of an unexpected result of exegesis among open theists, and of interest to Latter-day Saints, crops up in the work of Gregory A. Boyd. While examining the motif of spiritual warfare in the Bible, he says he is comfortable with biblical references to other gods existing alongside Yahweh.[38] Boyd does not think that these other gods can successfully challenge the creator, since their power is "on loan," but he does think that they have significant power to thwart God's will and can inflict suffering on others. This is a different take on monotheism, which dictates that God is the only god in existence. Boyd sees other "gods" as created but fallen beings

---

34. Walther Eichrodt, *Theology of the Old Testament,* vol. 1 (Philadelphia: Westminster, 1961), 206–20.

35. Blomberg and Robinson, *How Wide the Divide?* 88.

36. Ostler, *Attributes of God,* 352.

37. For example, David Paulsen, "Must God Be Incorporeal?" *Faith and Philosophy* 6, no. 1 (January 1989): 76–87.

38. Gregory A. Boyd, *God at War: The Bible and Spiritual Conflict* (Downers Grove, Ill.: InterVarsity, 1997), chap. 4. I have spoken of other gods myself: Clark H. Pinnock, *A Wideness in God's Mercy* (Grand Rapids: Zondervan, 1992), chap. 4.

and comes close, I think, to the LDS idea of subordinate gods. The Bible does not take the view that there are no gods apart from Yahweh. It presents a more practical kind of monotheism. The Bible says that the nations have their "gods," but Yahweh is the only God one needs to deal with if one is an Israelite (or a Christian). We believers are unimpressed by rival deities—for us, the Lord, not Baal, is God. The other gods are subject to God, who is surrounded by powers that praise and serve him. The psalmist says, "God has taken his place in the divine council; in the midst of the gods he holds judgment" (Ps. 82:1).[39] In this arena, Western theology tends to think of God and the world but neglects to consider the celestial middle world, that is, the powers in between heaven and earth. This cannot be said about churches in the third world nor about the Latter-day Saints.[40] I am unsure whether Mormons also develop, as Boyd does, a scenario of spiritual warfare that may contribute to a relational theodicy, helping to explain why the world often has the appearance of a battlefield.

Item 3: Theosis

Yet another exegetical surprise, also in the realm of "the gods," arose in the idea of "theosis" drawn from Eastern Orthodox thinking, to which both Latter-day Saints and open theists appeal. Theosis is the idea that believers will share the glory of God and become partakers of the divine nature (2 Pet. 1:4). Evangelicals accept this notion too and indeed are thrilled by it; however, they have not taken "theosis" so literally that they call it deification. Open theists have thought of it as believers sharing the glory of God without ceasing to be creatures.[41] We have not felt comfortable saying that humans "become gods," as Latter-day Saints have, even though we know that early Christians did speak of our human destiny in such terms. For example, Irenaeus writes, "Christ became what we are so that we might become what he is,"[42] and Athanasius writes, "He became man that we might become divine."[43] However, I wonder whether these Greek theologians thought of it quite in Latter-day Saint terms. Bridging the gap a little, Ostler makes the point that these "gods" are not to be identified with the supreme God. Lesser deities can partake of the divine nature but cannot surpass God, who is ruler of the universe and the God of gods.[44] Robinson

---

39. Ostler, *Attributes of God*, quoting an observation by Hans-Joachim Kraus.

40. Walther Eichrodt, "The Celestial World," in *Theology of the Old Testament*, 2 vols. (Philadelphia: Westminster, 1967), 2:186–209.

41. Compare Robert B. Rakestraw, "Becoming like God: An Evangelical Doctrine of Theosis," *Journal of the Evangelical Theological Society* 40 (1997): 257–69.

42. Irenaeus, *Adversus Haereses*, book 3, chapter 10.

43. Athanasius, *De Incarnatione*, paragraph 54.

44. Ostler, *Attributes of God*, 9–10.

too writes, "Latter-day Saints do not, or at least should not, believe that they will ever be independent in all eternity from their Father in heaven or from their Savior Jesus Christ or from the Holy Spirit." They "will always be subordinate to the Godhead."[45] This narrows the gap between open theists and Latter-day Saints. With these comments in mind, how far apart are we really? (I suspect that the exponents of theosis in the early church and even in modern exponents like C. S. Lewis would have held onto a gap remaining between the uncreated God and a created humanity, even a humanity in this blessed condition.)[46]

Item 4: God's Omniscience

When it comes to God's omniscience, there is a discussion among Latter-day Saints, much as there is among evangelicals, with some holding to exhaustive definite foreknowledge and others holding to present knowledge, that is, to a foreknowledge that considers the future as not completely settled and, therefore, as not completely foreknown.[47] Belief in libertarian freedom beckons both groups to move in this direction. For instance, open theists hold to a self-limitation on God's part, one aspect of which involves God's making a world with a future that would not be foreknowable in its entirety. Open theism takes self-limitation one step further than classical Arminians, who believe in libertarian freedom but maintain exhaustive foreknowledge, do. This is an important step but not a huge one. It sounds to me as if in this matter the two communities are in just about the same place.

Item 5: God and Gender

A delicate point and a point of divergence concerns God and gender. If God is personal, even embodied, one might conclude that God would have to be either male or female. And, since God is our "Father," he is presumably male. And, if God is male and begets offspring, there must be a goddess, a Mrs. God, somewhere. (Unless God were male and female, since humankind, male *and* female, was made in God's image.) So what, if any, sexual characteristics apply to God?

Open theists assume that none literally do, except in sociological ways. That is, we have taken the term "Father" not to indicate a sexual being so much as a patriarch, pointing to God's qualities of leadership, headship, and transcendence. We have not and do not think of God as having a consort.

---

45. Blomberg and Robinson, *How Wide the Divide?* 86.

46. This point is discussed in Richard N. Ostling and Joan K. Ostling, *Mormon America: The Power and the Promise* (San Francisco: HarperSanFrancisco, 1999), chap. 18.

47. Ostler, *Attributes of God,* chap. 10.

True, Jesus is the "Only Begotten" of the Father, but we have not thought of this in sexual terms either. I have always thought of the Father/Son relation not in terms of physical patriarchy but in terms of intimacy and mutual fidelity. We think of God as male-like in depiction but also as female-like—that is, as manifesting feminine qualities like nurturing and tenderness (for example, God's feeling the pangs of childbirth on behalf of his people in Isa. 42:14). Similarly, activities of the Holy Spirit are taught with the use of feminine images—activities like comforting, encouraging, yearning, and birthing. Some prefer the masculine traits in God, which bring out ideas of initiating, commanding, and establishing. But open theists, along with many others, are drawn in the direction of balancing both male and female traits in God.

On the other hand, Latter-day Saints seem to believe in a literal male deity. This being the case, I wonder why we hear practically nothing of a female deity. Is she everlasting too? Can she be prayed to? Do Latter-day Saints speak of goddesses? Is there procreation among God and Goddess? Evangelicals have great difficulty imagining God in this way. We have heard of such things in the religions of the Ancient Near East, where gods are begotten and come into being, but we have not seen it in the Bible. Might it be that, just as classical theism was influenced by Hellenism (as open theists and Latter-day Saints agree), LDS theism runs the risk of buying into a different kind of paganism, a paganism not from Athens but from Ugarit? I mean, is it possible that in their tradition of a procreating God and Goddess, Latter-day Saints have let some pagan Semitic ideas exercise undue influence?[48]

Issues such as this one suggest certain questions about the role of tradition in theology. While openness theologians are perhaps unwilling to partake in the drastic revision of tradition that a notion like God's gender would require, certain theological revisions need to be made in light of the openness view, revisions which Latter-day Saints presumably could agree with. For open theism, certain of the divine attributes need to be redefined so as to bring out the perfections of a personal God. We need to introduce such categories as God's changeable faithfulness, God's self-limitation, God's relationality, the divine pathos, the divine temporality,

---

48. Jim Adams puts his finger on this issue in "The God of Abraham, Isaac, and Joseph Smith? God, Creation, in the Old Testament and Mormonism," in *The New Mormon Challenge: Responding to the Latest Defenses of a Fast-growing Movement*, ed. Francis J. Beckwith, Carl Mosser, and Paul Owen (Grand Rapids: Zondervan, 2002), 153–91. This is an informative book, but it is too negative and unsympathetic to the Latter-day Saints, not even acknowledging that they are Christians and never granting that they have things to contribute to the theological conversation.

the divine foreknowledge, and the divine wisdom and resourcefulness.[49] New categories need to come into play, and some may need to be retired or, if not retired, at least reworked. For example, there is no love without openness to rejection, suffering, and loss. To believe in the triune God is to believe in a God who shares our suffering, a suffering that is not a sign of impotence but of strength and that leads to final victory. God's unity is not a mathematical oneness but a living unity with diversity. God's steadfastness is not a dead immutability but a dynamic constancy of character and purpose that includes movement and change. Here is a power that is not raw omnipotence but that reigns with a sovereignty of love that is strong even in weakness. Here is an omniscience that is not a trivial know-it-allness but a wisdom that includes the foolishness of the cross. An openness hermeneutic requires revision in the ways we think about and define some of the divine attributes. It requires subtle changes across the spectrum of the attributes, if they are to be the perfections of a personal God.[50]

Item 6: Tradition and Interpretation

So what about tradition and the influence it exercises upon our interpretations? The two groups see themselves differently. Open theists see themselves as belonging to the "one, holy, catholic, and apostolic church," whatever the differences among members. They want to be in continuity with history and the community, even though they recognize that there are reforms to be undertaken.[51] Thus they speak of "great tradition," of the Vincentian canon (what has been believed by "everyone, everywhere, at all times"), and even of "mere Christianity," as referred to by C. S. Lewis.[52] Admittedly, the great tradition is a nebulous concept and one that open theists do not take uncritically, though we receive it respectfully. It serves as a kind of a subordinate third testament and map to the terrain, a canon outside the canon, and a way to identify error. It is a *norma normata* (a norm that is

---

49. Consider Hendrikus Berkhof, *Christian Faith: An Introduction to the Study of the Faith* (Grand Rapids: Eerdmans, 1979), chaps. 18–22.

50. I appreciate Daniel L. Migliore's treatment of this in *Faith Seeking Understanding: An Introduction to Christian Theology* (Grand Rapids: Eerdmans, 1991), 72–74.

51. We are part of a living tradition, two thousand years old: see Thomas C. Oden, *The Rebirth of Orthodoxy: Signs of New Life in Christianity* (San Francisco: HarperSanFrancisco, 2003).

52. I have noticed an appreciation by Latter-day Saints of C. S. Lewis and thought to myself what an important factor that might prove to be, if in fact he is a friend to us both. Certainly he is quoted more often by the LDS leadership than any other non–Latter-day Saint writer. A friend of a friend is a friend of ours. See Nathan Jensen, *Restored Gospel according to C. S. Lewis* (Springville, Utah: Bonneville, 1998).

itself normed by scripture), which directs but does not control us.[53] Open theists differ from Latter-day Saints in holding to God's promise not to let the gates of hell prevail against the church. We take it as a promise to help her to remain in the truth and not to fall into irremediable ruin. We do not find the New Testament warning us of a completely ruinous apostasy.

In contrast, Latter-day Saints do speak of an apostasy and of a restoration, similar in some ways to a reformation, but much more radical. This restoration has been the source of some radical new ways of thinking. For instance, it supplies what Robinson calls "the different ontological frame or view of the nature of the universe" in which Latter-day Saints place "the basic gospel of Christ." This includes the literal fatherhood of God, God and humans belonging to the same species of being, and God's having spiritual offspring in a pre-mortal existence.[54] Reading the Bible in this context is bound to take interpretation in a certain direction, just as respect for the "great tradition" would in the case of open theists. Still, there is room for us to relate. LDS traditions from the early days until now, current developments in LDS thinking, and respect for the prophetic office—all of this is likely to produce differently nuanced interpretations over time and to open up points of contact, maybe even surprisingly so. I think both groups, Latter-day Saints and open theists alike, must ask ourselves what is really binding in our positions and what is open to re-examination.[55]

Item 7: The Trinity

Remarkably, both Latter-day Saints and open theists hold to a social Trinity. Open theists believe in one God and three persons. We see God's eternal life as personal life in relationship. God exists in community and constitutes a *koinonia* of persons joined in love. The divine life is social and the basis of community among creatures. (Indeed, our human experience of community is the best clue we have for understanding God's triune life.) The three persons find their identity in their relationship with one another. They "indwell" each other, they make room for each other, and they are united in a divine dance. But what is the nature of the unity? The Trinity seems to be quite unlike anything on earth. It involves a rich and complex

---

53. On scripture and tradition, see Olson, *The Mosaic of Christian Belief,* chaps. 1–2.

54. Blomberg and Robinson, *How Wide the Divide?* 18–19.

55. Latter-day Saints enjoy the luxury of having living prophets and therefore need depend less than evangelicals on written texts. What God said in the past is somewhat secondary to what God is saying now. And who knows where that will take them? The evangelical fixation on the past makes it hard for them to change and reform. It happens, but it is undisciplined.

oneness and is closer to an organic than to a mathematical unity.[56] Open theists do not think of the Trinity as a self-enclosed group of divine beings (like Peter, James, and John in Gregory of Nyssa's analogy), which smacks of tritheism. Instead, open theists are dealing with a mysterious symbol of a God who saves us and whose triune nature is something incomprehensible in theory but intimate in relational terms. God is a community of persons knit together in a bond of love and beyond complete understanding. It calls believers to enter the dance and to love without judging.

For Latter-day Saints, the Trinity is a little differently understood. It consists of three individual personal and separate beings, collectively constituting the object of faith. They are distinct persons. Yet Latter-day Saints use the term "God" to refer to the Godhead, which the three comprise, and which is close to what open theists believe. For Latter-day Saints, as for open theists, there is a three-in-oneness and a plurality of persons united by being in relationship with one another. Neither of us really knows exactly how the three are one, but it is LDS doctrine and openness doctrine that they *are* one. What Latter-day Saints do not hold is that the three persons are ontologically one being, as the creed says. Their emphasis is on a functional rather than on an essential Trinity. At the same time, I hear Robinson denying polytheism and affirming that the three are only one God.[57] Are we not both trying to retain belief in one God (Deuteronomy 6:4) with a trinitarian structure that is faithful to the gospel narrative? On the other hand, the LDS idea makes membership in the Trinity somewhat voluntary and therefore potentially subject to breaking up (for example, if Jesus had succumbed to temptation)—an unsettling thought that takes God's risking to a much higher level.

Item 8: God and World

The ultimate metaphysical fact—is it God-and-world or is it God, period? For process thought (and LDS thought), the ultimate metaphysical fact seems to be God-and-world. Without a world, God would have no actuality and no real existence. Thus God needs the world almost as much as the world needs God. So God is inherently limited. For open theists, the situation is different. For us, the ultimate metaphysical fact is not God-and-world but God only. We believe that God could exist without creation, even though he chooses not to. Thus the world owes its existence to God's free choice, not to any metaphysical necessity.

---

56. On twentieth-century efforts to understand the Trinity, see Roger E. Olson and Christopher A. Hall, *The Trinity* (Grand Rapids: Eerdmans, 2002), 95–115.

57. Blomberg and Robinson, *How Wide the Divide?* 131–32.

Both open theists and process theists appeal to the logic of love to explain creation but do so differently. For process theists (and perhaps Latter-day Saints), the divine love entails a necessary world—God must have creatures to love and care for. For open theists, on the other hand, God's love excludes a necessary world because love must be a voluntary commitment. Love requires a degree of divine independence and a creation freely chosen. Open theism is thus neo-classical in certain ways (for example, creation by the word of God and not the result of some other power). Nor do open theists believe that God began creation with something pre-existing, as Latter-day Saints do. As Langdon Gilkey puts it, "God is the source of all that there is"; "creatures are dependent but real and good"; and "God creates in freedom and with purpose."[58]

The term *creatio ex nihilo* (creation out of nothing) was meant by theologians to lift up the notion of a sovereignly chosen creation. I myself would rather speak of creation *ex amore*, that God in the act of creating acted out of love for creatures. I believe this is the most important point to make in discussing creation.[59] Still, open theists are impressed by God's creating "all things, visible and invisible" (Col. 1:15). We believe that "God calls into existence things that do not exist" (Rom. 4:17). We hold to creation by God's word such that "what is seen was made from things that are not visible" (Heb. 11:3). The key issue here is whether there is reality that is a given for God and that God is stuck with. Open theists believe that everything is ontologically dependent on God and has not existed everlastingly. At the same time, I have never thought that Genesis chapter one taught "creation out of nothing." Genesis 1:2 seems to describe a situation pre-existing when God begins the six-day work. So I do not draw the idea of *creatio ex nihilo* from there and would not even claim that my texts prove *creatio ex nihilo* outright. I would also admit that, even with the *creatio ex nihilo*, God soon finds himself confronted by serious opposition in the world we have to live in. So what difference does it really make in practice?

For Latter-day Saints, there seem to exist several metaphysical factors that, in their interaction with each other, have helped to produce the present world. It seems as if there is a struggle involving a diversity of ultimate principles. In that case, what do we make of the structurally unified character of the world that makes it an object of knowledge? It does not seem to be something on the verge of breaking up, there being no all-embracing

---

58. Langdon Brown Gilkey, *Maker of Heaven and Earth: The Christian Doctrine of Creation in the Light of Modern Knowledge* (Garden City, N.Y.: Doubleday, 1959), chap. 3.

59. Eichrodt, *Theology of the Old Testament,* 2:99–106. Consider Paul Copan and William Lane, *Creation out of Nothing: A Biblical, Philosophical and Scientific Exploration* (Grand Rapids: Baker, 2004).

unity that holds it together. The world does not seem to be suffering this defect, because there are, open theists believe, no metaphysical first principles alongside God, having their being from themselves and not from him. We see creation as God's decision and the meaningful expression of his will, not the outcome of struggles between gods or primary principles. I am not denying that, at the present moment, real conflict exists between God and the gods, owing to the freedom they have been given, which can be used to frustrate God's will. The gods do have a certain autonomy without being radically independent from God. However, they were created by God and are sustained by him and are gradually being lured, in spite of themselves, to a future that God has planned.

I sense that Latter-day Saints may feel that, were God to have created the world out of nothing, it would put God far away from us and jeopardize his interactions with us. It's almost as if God has to be a mortal being in order to relate to mortals. Surely not. God could have created the world by his word alone without being totally beyond it himself. God is exactly as far from it and as near to it as he wants to be. He can behold the world from his heavenly glory and, at the same time, enter into its life as fully as he wants to. God decides what his relations with creation will be.

Item 9: God's Power

Concerning omnipotence, open theists and Latter-day Saints agree that there are limitations on God's power but do not explain it in quite the same way. Open theists use the language of voluntary self-limitation, while Latter-day Saints think of God's being limited by uncreated matter and intelligences, which are entities external to himself.[60] To my understanding, Joseph Smith saw such inherent limitations as entities coeternal with God, chaotic matter that God has to deal with and built-in law-like structures.[61] But Ostler adds this: "God could prevent an intelligence or natural substance from *exercising power* freely by overpowering it through coercive power. . . . [However,] God will generally refrain from such coercive power because it is not consistent with his loving nature."[62] Ostler seems to be saying that God has obstacles to overcome but that he can overcome them. This would approximate the view of open theism that God is not so much limited in power as he restrains its exercise. As in his loving relations with us, God does not force himself on us. Open theists see a restraint of power for the sake of love, and I think that Latter-day Saints do, too.

---

60. On divine self-limitation, see Sanders, *The God Who Risks*, 224–28.

61. See David L. Paulsen, citing D&C 93:23, 29, in "Joseph Smith and the Problem of Evil," *BYU Studies* 39, no. 1 (2000): 58.

62. Ostler, *Attributes of God*, 132.

By accepting some limitations and conditionality within God, both open theists and Latter-day Saints make room for a more modern understanding of the world and its processes. This understanding and the powers of reason that helped formulate it also have a role to play in theology, if we value coherence and intelligibility in our work and if we want the message to be timely and compelling. Philosophers can help us if they have good data to work with. Relational philosophies and theologies are good at relating to the dynamic understanding of reality that is characteristic of our time. Reason gives us a metaphysics of love and offers a dynamic understanding of the world. It can help us negotiate the shift we are seeing from a static to a more dynamic understanding of reality. The old Newtonian assumption that the world moves forward in a deterministic fashion is being replaced in quantum theory and by an understanding of causation that includes an intrinsic element of indeterminism. The old assumption that the world is a stable, solid, deterministic, thoroughly rational, and utterly predictable system is being replaced by a view of the world as a dynamic process that is to some extent indeterministic and unpredictable. The more it shifts this way, the less classical theism will have anything to say and the more relational theism will have to offer.

Item 10: Theodicy

The next item is the issue of theodicy, or the issue of God's causing or allowing evil. Open theists think that light is shed on this issue from the direction of God's voluntarily, not essentially, limited power. This contrasts with LDS thought, which sees the limit on God's power to be not the result of God's decision but in the nature of things. This means that there is a limitation on the power of God that is inherent in the structure of the world. In this regard LDS theory is closer to process theism than it is to open theism.[63]

This is how the Latter-day Saints see it. If God's power is inherently and not only voluntarily restrained, then God cannot be blamed for many of the evils that happen because God is already doing the best that he can in the face of stubborn resistance. On the other hand, open theists do not solve the problem of evil by making God seemingly powerless, so that he cannot be held responsible for what happens in the world because he can't do much about it. We prefer to say that God does have the power to overturn evil but rarely does so because he values human freedom. (Latter-day

---

63. See Paulsen, "Joseph Smith and the Problem of Evil," 53–65. Discussing the doctrine of "eternal progression," David Paulsen recognizes the similarity between process theory and LDS theory and asks whether process theorists like Alfred North Whitehead, Charles Hartshorne, John Cobb, and David Griffin have impacted LDS understandings of God. He says yes, almost with a tone of confession. But I see nothing wrong in that—open theism too is appreciative of aspects of process thought.

Saints agree with us that God can perform miracles, which puts them closer to us than to process theorists.) It seems to us that God has set himself a limit that he will not cross in taking away freedom. God's problem (if I may speak thus) is that God loves. Love complicates his life, as it does ours. So there is a reason (a creation covenant) why he does not prevent certain evils. Hence there are psalms of lament in the Bible where believers ask God why he is not doing more, on the assumption that he *could be*. We have to trust God when things do not seem to be lining up in our understanding. In the last analysis, however, we agree that God does not cause or will our suffering; rather, we believe that God identifies with our suffering and works faithfully and everlastingly to transform that suffering into the highest possible good.[64]

Item 11: United Belief

Relational theologies have tremendous practical appeal. Open theism supplies "existential fit" in the way we handle our walk with God and the life of prayer. It energizes us by imputing real "say so" to human beings. (Remember that Latter-day Saints and open theists are both strongly Arminian.) Open theology confirms our deepest intuitions that our choices are not predetermined and the future is not altogether settled. Thus it enjoys an "as if not" advantage. That is, we notice that people act "as if" the relational gospel were true even when they do not believe that it is, which is a fine compliment. Open theology is a theology where our lives really matter and where what we do or do not do makes a real difference. Thus it is a theology for revival and for missions (a passion to evangelize the world is yet another factor that Latter-day Saints and open theorists share). I resonate with William James, who wondered what difference divine aseity or God's self-love or God's simplicity or God's pure act make, without agency. James wrote, "if they severally call for no distinctive adaptations of our conduct, what vital difference can it possibly make to a man's religion whether they be true or false?"[65] The pragmatic test for truth may not be everything, but it counts for something. Open theism works in the lives of those who espouse it. Here the open and LDS views seem indistinguishable.

Conclusion

Open theism is part of a larger movement of relational theologies, which include LDS theology and which seek to recover the perfections of a personal

---

64. Blake Ostler presses the critique of openness theodicy: "Evil: A Real Problem for Evangelicals," *FARMS Review* 15 (2003): 201–13.

65. See William James, *The Varieties of Religious Experience: A Study in Human Nature* (Mineola, N.Y.: Dover Publications, 2002), 445.

God and the dynamic relationships into which God enters with his creatures. It is a biblical theology that seeks to bring our definitions of God's attributes into line with the perfections of a personal God. It celebrates God's true glory, which is not static perfection but loving relationships with his creatures and partnerships in which God allows himself to be made vulnerable.

Open theism is being discussed widely, and its prospects seem promising.[66] It is scripturally compelling. Its doctrine of God appeals in a context where classical theism can be a hard sell. It promotes intimacy with God and posits a real "say so" to human beings. In the evangelical context, it needs to overcome the paleo-Calvinist charge that it is heretical and the classical Arminian intuition that it goes too far. In terms of connecting with other relational theologies, a beginning has been made in our interaction with process theology. For example, John B. Cobb Jr., and I issued a book, *Searching for an Adequate God*, which brought process and free will (or open) theists into dialogue. And, in this chapter, we are exploring another relationship: how open theism relates to LDS thought and vice versa. For many of us, this is new territory. I myself have not had Latter-day Saints as dialogue partners before, but I welcome it. I look for ways that we can help one another. Of course, not everyone approves of our talking to Latter-day Saints, process theists, and others. They see it as proof positive that we are not evangelical ourselves and perhaps not even Christian. But we do not believe in closing doors that God has opened and do not allow ourselves to be governed by our fears.

I close with this: none of us controls the outcomes of our deliberations, and God's providence will see to it that what is valid is sorted out from what is invalid and what is significant from what is insignificant. As St. Paul says, "Now we know in part—then we will know as we are known" (1 Cor. 13:12). Meanwhile, our work is tentative, though we hope it is worthwhile.

---

66. See William C. Davis, "Why Open Theism Is Flourishing Now," in *Beyond the Bounds: Open Theism and the Undermining of Biblical Christianity*, ed. John Piper, Justin Taylor, and Paul Kjoss Helseth (Wheaton, Ill.: Crossway, 2003), 111–45.

Response to Professor Pinnock

David L. Paulsen

THIS RESPONSE IS OFFERED IN THE SAME AUGUSTINIAN SPIRIT that Clark
Pinnock exemplifies in his addition to this book. I will at times "keep him
[Pinnock] company" when I am in agreement, at other times I will "dialogue with him" when I am hesitant, and I will not be reluctant to respectfully "call him back" when I think he is in error (Pinnock, 489). Given
Pinnock's definition of a "relational" theology, I wholeheartedly concur
with his classifying Mormonism as a "sisterly model." At the outset of his
essay, Pinnock identifies the essential elements of a relational theology, all
of which LDS theology, indisputably, affirms.[67]

In regard to open theism in particular, Mormonism shares unique
theological convergences as well as important divergences that ought to be
explored with the shared goal that "progress can be made in the theological
development of us all" (Pinnock, 490). Joseph Smith would undoubtedly
agree with such an exchange as he emphatically declared before the Saints
in Nauvoo that "we should gather all the good and true principles in the
world and treasure them up, or we shall not come out true 'Mormons.'"[68]

With the preceding as the groundwork, I offer the following in response
to the several varied issues that Pinnock introduces as "possible points of
contact" between open and LDS thought (Pinnock, 491). In doing so, I follow Pinnock in applying reason, tradition, and experience to what Latter-
day Saints believe to be the "revelation of God in Jesus Christ" contained in
scripture (Pinnock, 493), both biblical and Latter-day Saint–specific.

Divine Embodiment

To be frank, it is particularly refreshing to see a theologian from the
Wesleyan tradition seriously considering the many biblical passages that
apparently take divine embodiment for granted. While I will refrain from
taking the "I told you so" attitude regarding this particular issue, I will say
that the Latter-day Saints have waited a long time for competent Christian

---

67. Pinnock identifies four essential elements of relational theology models. First,
they "strive to bring out the personal nature of God." Second, they want "to lift up the
conviction that God is 'open' and existing in significant relationships with creatures."
Third is the element of divine conditionality and risk taking. Fourth, and finally, in
order for a theology to be considered "relational" it should privilege scripture over
tradition (See Pinnock, 489, 496).

68. Joseph Smith Jr., *History of The Church of Jesus Christ of Latter-day Saints*, ed.
B. H. Roberts, 2d ed., rev., 7 vols. (Salt Lake City: Deseret, 1971), 5:517.

theologians to release explicitly anthropomorphic and anthropopathic biblical passages from the shackles of merely figurative interpretation.

Pinnock addresses the issue of divine embodiment at greater length in
his book *Most Moved Mover,* where he writes,

> There is an issue that has not been raised yet in the discussion
> around the open view of God. If he is with us in the world, if we are to
> take biblical metaphors seriously, is God in some way embodied? Critics
> will be quick to say that, although there are expressions of this idea
> in the Bible, they are not to be taken literally. But I do not believe that
> the idea is as foreign to the Bible's view of God as we have assumed. In
> tradition, God is thought to function primarily as a disembodied spirit
> but this is scarcely a biblical idea. For example, Israel is called to hear
> God's word and gaze on his glory and beauty. Human beings are said
> to be embodied creatures created in the image of God. Is there perhaps
> something in God that corresponds with embodiment? Having a body
> is certainly not a negative thing because it makes it possible for us to be
> agents. Perhaps God's agency would be easier to envisage if he were in
> some way corporeal. Add to that fact that in the theophanies of the Old
> Testament God encounters humans in the form of a man. They indicate
> that God shares our life in the world in a most intense and personal
> manner. For example, look at the following texts. In Exodus 24:10–11
> Moses, Aaron, Nadab, Abidu and seventy of the elders of Israel went up
> Mount Sinai and beheld God, as they ate and drank. Exodus 33:11 tells
> us that "the Lord used to speak to Moses face to face, as one speaks to
> a friend." Moses saw "God's back" but not his face (Exod.33:23). When
> God chose to reveal his glory, Isaiah saw the Lord, high and lifted up (Is.
> 6:1). Ezekiel saw "the appearance of the likeness of the glory of the Lord"
> (Ezek. 1:28). John saw visions of one seated upon the throne (Rev. 4:2) and
> of the Son of Man in his glory (Rev. 1:12–16). Add to the fact that God
> took on a body in the incarnation and Christ has taken that body with
> him into glory. It seems to me that the Bible does not think of God as
> formless. Rather, it thinks of him as possessing a form that these divine
> appearances reflect.[69]

Latter-day Saints have often made similar biblical cases for the doctrine, agreeing with Pinnock's own declaration, "We need to let God's own
self-revelation dominate our thinking rather than what natural reason and
tradition tell us that God must be like."[70] Pinnock's statement echoes that
of LDS scholar B. H. Roberts in *The Mormon Doctrine of Deity* wherein
Roberts cites Jesus Christ as being "both premise and argument" for divine

---

69. Clark Pinnock, *Most Moved Mover: A Theology of God's Openness* (Carlisle,
Cumbria: Baker, 2001) 33–34; see also 80–81.

70. Pinnock, *Most Moved Mover,* 79.

embodiment.[71] Is Jesus God? Was he resurrected with a tangible, though glorious, incorruptible body of flesh and bones? In describing to his apostles the nature of his resurrected body, Jesus uses straightforward declaration rather than allegory, imagery or parable. "Behold, my hands and my feet, that it is I myself: handle me, and see; For a Spirit hath not flesh and bones as ye see me have" (Luke 24:39).

Will Jesus ever lose or discard His resurrected body?[72] James describes death as "the body without the spirit," and Paul affirms that Christ's resurrected body is incorruptible (1 Cor. 15), "that Christ being raised from the dead dieth no more" (James 2:26; Rom. 6:9); Latter-day Saints hold to a social model of the Godhead consisting of three distinct persons, Father, Son and Holy Ghost, who together constitute one God or one mutually indwelling divine community. Did not Jesus declare himself to be the fullest and clearest revelation of God the Father when he declared, "He that hath seen me hath seen the Father" (John 14:9)? Paul is even more explicit in his letter to the Hebrews: "God . . . hath in these last days spoken unto us by his Son . . . Who being the brightness of his glory, and the express image of his person" (Heb. 1:1–3). *Strong's Concordance* explains "express image" as denoting "a graver, i.e., engraving, the figure stamped, i.e., an exact copy or representation."[73] Therefore, the LDS *biblical* case for divine embodiment can be succinctly stated as follows:

1. Jesus Christ is God.

2. Jesus Christ was resurrected with an incorruptible body.

3. The separation of the spirit from the body is death.

4. Jesus Christ will never die again.

5. Thus, Jesus Christ will be embodied everlastingly (from 2–4).

6. Therefore, Jesus Christ is both God and embodied everlastingly (follows from 1, 2, and 5).

7. Jesus is the express image of the Father (Heb. 1:1–3)

8. Therefore, God the Father is embodied everlastingly (from 5 and 7).

Pinnock states that divine embodiment cannot be "ruled out so long as one is prepared to elucidate the idea responsibly" (Pinnock, 502). What could be more responsible than relying on "the revelation of God in Jesus Christ" as our premise, argument and understanding for the way in which

---

71. B. H. Roberts, *The Mormon Doctrine of Deity* (Salt Lake City: Signature, 1998), 119.

72. Paul uses the word "spiritual" body to mean resurrected body in 1 Cor. 15:44.

73. *The New Strong's Exhaustive Concordance of the Bible* (Nashville: Thomas Nelson, 1990), paragraph 5481, page 77 of Greek Dictionary of the New Testament.

God is embodied? Is it so "peculiar" to believe that one member of the Godhead has the same properties (physical as well as moral) as another (Pinnock, 502)?

In *Most Moved Mover*, in addition to making a biblical case for divine embodiment, Pinnock proposes (without developing) three arguments for the same conclusion. First, Pinnock opines that God's agency would be easier to envisage if he were in some way corporeal.[74] Second, Pinnock suggests that embodiment may be a necessary condition of personhood. "The only persons we encounter are embodied persons and, if God is not embodied, it may prove difficult to understand how God is a person. What kind of actions could a disembodied God perform?"[75] Finally, Pinnock hypothesizes that corporeality may be a necessary condition of God's being passible.[76] Each of these suggestions is provocative and each merits further development. Latter-day Saints should be eager to join in the task.

In regard to tradition, while Latter-day Saints would agree with Pinnock that "the idea that God is not embodied has been the stock-in-trade of orthodoxy for centuries," they might question how *many* centuries Christians have believed in an incorporeal God (Pinnock, 502). Indeed, divine simplicity and incorporeality were not included in the faith once delivered to Christians, but were introduced into Christian thought from Greek philosophy (Pinnock, 493). Pinnock concedes that it is Platonism rather than Biblicism which damns the idea of a corporeal God when he writes, "I do not feel obliged to assume that God is a purely spiritual being when his self-revelation does not suggest it. It is true that from a Platonic standpoint, the idea is absurd, but this is not a biblical standpoint."[77] In a previous paper, I provide evidence that ordinary Christians for at least the first three centuries of the current era commonly (and perhaps generally) believed God to be corporeal.[78] It is the tradition of the early centuries, as close to the apostolic era as possible, to which the Latter-day Saints (and maybe openness?) would rather associate.

Finally, I will mention two issues in regards to the existential meaning of a belief in an embodied God. First, belief in an embodied God replaces the duality of Greek philosophy wherein the body is relegated to an evil regression from the purely spiritual[79] with an abiding reverence for the body, which finds a divine parallel in God. Thus, as LDS philosopher Truman

---

74. Pinnock, *Most Moved Mover*, 34.

75. Pinnock, *Most Moved Mover*, 34; see. 80–81.

76. Pinnock, *Most Moved Mover*, 81; 81 n. 54.

77. Pinnock, *Most Moved Mover*, 34.

78. David L. Paulsen, "Early Christian Belief in a Corporeal Deity: Origen and Augustine as Reluctant Witnesses," *Harvard Theological Review* 83, no. 2 (1990): 105–16.

79. The work of St. Thomas and the Scholastics revolved around this issue, with Platonic and Aristotelian premises—the relegating of the "heavenly" to

Madsen says, "There are levels of consciousness, powers of expression, ways of fulfillment in thought, feeling, and action that come only when the threefold nature of man is harmoniously combined. To cultivate the soul is to cultivate both the body and spirit."[80] LDS apostle Charles W. Penrose summarizes this existential implication of believing in divine embodiment in this way, "The body of flesh is . . . essential to its [the spirit of man's] progress, essential to its experience on the earth and ultimately in its glorified condition, essential to its eternal happiness, and progress and power in the presence of the Father."[81] Second, understanding the literalness of being created "in the image" of God is tremendously ennobling and empowering as one seeks to overcome the trials and temptations of the flesh (Gen. 1:26–27). Current LDS apostle Thomas S. Monson expressed this idea when speaking to a group of Latter-day Saints in Helsinki, Finland:

> When we realize that we have actually been made in the image of God, all things are possible. John Mott, a recipient of the Nobel Prize, indicated that this particular knowledge, a knowledge that we have been created in the image of God, is the single greatest segment of knowledge that can come to man in mortality. Mr. Mott, who is not a member of our church, indicated that that knowledge would give man a profound new sense of power and strength. We know that such is the case. We know that in and of ourselves we can do but little, but motivated with the spirit and knowledge that we have been created in the image of God, we can accomplish great things.[82]

In conclusion, it is important to keep in mind here that while the Latter-day Saints *do* find considerable biblical evidence and rational support for the doctrine of divine embodiment,[83] their affirmation of the doctrine is grounded most fundamentally neither on biblical exegesis nor theological argument. Joseph declared that the Father and Son have tangible bodies, humanlike in form, because this is how these two divine personages revealed themselves to him in a series of divine disclosures beginning with their appearance to Joseph in a tradition-shattering theophany known

---

immateriality, (the angels, for example, are "pure species") and the "earthly" to materiality or corporeality.

80. Truman G. Madsen, *Eternal Man* (Salt Lake City: Deseret, 1966), 47.

81. Charles W. Penrose, in *Journal of Discourses,* 26 vols. (Liverpool: F. D. Richards, 1855–86), 26:21, November 16, 1884. For a recent article discussing the existential implications for the LDS view, see Russell M. Nelson, "We Are Children of God," *Ensign* 28 (November 1998): 85–87.

82. Rulon T. Burton, comp., *We Believe: Doctrines and Principles of The Church of Jesus Christ of Latter-day Saints* (Salt Lake City: Tabernacle, 1994), 429.

83. Gen. 1:27; 5:1; 9:6; 32:30; Ex. 24:10; 31:18; 33:11; Luke 24:39; John 14:9; 2 Cor. 4:4; Philip. 3:21; 1 John 3:2; Rev. 22:4; D&C 130:22.

as the First Vision.[84] These disclosures have served to greatly illuminate anthropomorphic biblical passages. Modern revelation is thus the bedrock for LDS belief in divine embodiment.

Spiritual Warfare, Creation, God's Limitation, and Theodicy

Pinnock is unsure whether Mormons develop "a scenario of spiritual warfare that may contribute to a relational theodicy" (Pinnock, 504). Very simply, yes, they do. However, the LDS understanding of "spiritual warfare" is a result of the conjunction of two foundational doctrines both of which are addressed by Pinnock. The first is the belief in the eternality of intelligences[85] (or primordial individuals[86]) while the second is the LDS belief in libertarian free will.

These two beliefs lay the foundation for LDS belief in a pre-mortal "war in heaven." Since individuals have always existed and have always possessed free will, it is possible that there have always been wills in opposition to the divine will, and hence the possibility of "spiritual warfare" is something that God has always had to deal with. Latter-day Saints believe this battle of competing agencies was what John the Revelator was describing when he wrote,

> And there was war in heaven; Michael and his angels fought against the dragon; and the dragon fought and his angels, and prevailed not; neither was their place found any more in heaven. And the great dragon was cast out, that old serpent, called the Devil, and Satan, which deceiveth

---

84. See Joseph Smith—History 1:15–17.

85. The term "eternalism" was coined by B. H. Roberts to describe the Mormon position. See B. H. Roberts, *A Comprehensive History of The Church of Jesus Christ of Latter-day Saints, Century One*, 6 vols. (Provo, Utah: Corporation of the President, The Church of Jesus Christ of latter-day Saints, 1965), 2:410.

86. Even within the LDS church, opinions vary regarding this particular point. That "intelligence" is coeternal with God is universally held, but the question of whether or not the term "intelligence" refers to individuals has been the cause of much debate. The issue became a matter of wide discussion in the early 1900s. B. H. Roberts' Seventy's Yearbook, vol. 4, assumed the co-eternity of individuals. Later, he published the article "The Immortality of Man," *Improvement Era* 10, no. 6 (April 1907): 419. This article teaches the "existence of independent, uncreated, self-existent intelligences" which, though they differ, are "alike in their eternity and their freedom." Bruce R. McConkie has most recently argued that "the intelligence or spirit element became intelligences after the spirits were born as individual entities." This view implies that all of God's children, *qua animo*, had a beginning in time—including Christ. Bruce R. McConkie, *Mormon Doctrine*, 2d ed. (Salt Lake City: Deseret, 1979), 387. See also, the King Follet Discourse by Joseph Smith in Andrew Ehat and Lyndon Cook, comps. and eds., *The Words of Joseph Smith* (Orem, Utah: Grandin, 1991), 341–62.

the whole world; he was cast out into the earth, and his angels were cast out with him (Rev. 12:7–9).

Scriptures revealed to Joseph Smith are even more explicit in describing the rebellion of Lucifer and his attempt to persuade the children of God to follow him (see Moses 4:1–6). This belief in pre-mortal war is congruent with the LDS conception of mortal life as a testing and trial period (see Abraham 3:25). Jude records that there were angels "which kept not their first estate" (Jude 1:6). LDS theology recognizes mortality as man's second estate and the next phase in the battle, which started in the pre-mortal realm, to overcome evil and develop Godlike qualities. This insight becomes especially profound when one attempts to develop a relational theology that effectively deals with the problem of evil, for if intelligences (or spirits) are self-existently eternal and autonomous, then God cannot determine or control the choices that these intelligences may make. His only option is persuasion. Thus, God is relational not solely by choice but by ontological necessity. He must, in order to accomplish his plans and purposes, resort to persuasion, longsuffering, and loving relationships when dealing with others.

Openness theology, on the other hand, accepts libertarian free will but then rejects the eternality of spirit or intelligence (and matter) in favor of creation ex nihilo, a move to which I will turn my attention. Creation out of nothing (ex nihilo) is one of the core doctrines of conventional Christianity with which Openness has no quarrel. Indeed, according to Pinnock, they have "resisted tossing out creation *ex nihilo*."[87] Why is this? It even seems as if some of Pinnock's statements about creation are incongruous with creation ex nihilo. For example, Pinnock states, "The acts of creation as recorded in Genesis chapter 1 brought chaos under control and reintroduced God's order, but they did not eliminate the threat of this mysterious 'formless void' factor. It is a situation where, although God has the upper hand, he is not now totally in control."[88] If God brought all things out of nothing, only extreme self-limiting in regards to the processes of nature would allow him to be not totally in control. For a theology that holds to the primacy of scripture, it is interesting for Pinnock to admit, "I have never thought that Genesis chapter one taught creation out of nothing. Genesis 1:2 seems to describe a situation pre-existing when God begins the six day work. So I do not draw the idea of 'creatio ex nihilo' from there and would not even claim that my texts prove 'creatio ex nihilo' outright" (Pinnock, 510). Thus, it seems pertinent to question why openness clings to idea of creation ex nihilo when they have rejected many other concepts because they

87. Pinnock, *Most Moved Mover,* 78.
88. Pinnock, *Most Moved Mover,* 36.

conflict with the Bible.[89] Pinnock recognizes that the idea of a self-limiting God "exposes a point of vulnerability" of open theism yet is willing to "live with it" in order to retain the doctrine of classical omnipotence (Pinnock, 498). Yet, elsewhere, Pinnock concurs with John Sanders that "sometimes the attributes of God are derived on the basis of the *dignum deo* (what it is dignified for God to be according to natural theology)."[90] Furthermore, Pinnock speaks negatively about theology which "think[s] of God abstractly as a perfect being and then smuggle[s] in assumptions of what 'perfect' entails."[91] Pinnock's unyielding defense of conventional conceptions of creation out of nothing and its corollary that God is subject to no nonlogical conditions or constraints appears to be an expression of *dignum deo,* not biblical, theology. This is puzzling. Perhaps openness is concerned about its relationship to the evangelical movement and is therefore wary of departing too far from conventional Christian thought.

Nevertheless, Pinnock does offer a subtle defense of the openness interpretation of creation when he criticizes the LDS conception of the doctrine by saying that in LDS theology, "without a world, God would have no actuality and no real existence" (Pinnock, 509). This statement seems to indicate that the creator-God of openness/conventional Christianity is superior to that of the LDS faith because of his ability to have "real" existence without a world which, if true, might provide a rationale for openness thinkers to stick to the doctrine of creation ex nihilo. However, I believe this is a mischaracterization of LDS thought. Joseph Smith affirmed that God is a self-existent being and further elaborates, "God himself found Himself in the midst of spirits and glory. Because he was greater He saw proper to institute laws whereby the rest, who were less in intelligence, could have a privilege to advance like Himself."[92] In LDS theology God does *not* depend on the world for his "actuality" or "real existence." As we have seen, God and the world (or, rather, the elements from which God organized the world) are both "actual" and "real" *metaphysically.* Matter is eternal and cannot be created nor destroyed. God likewise is eternal, existing *independently alongside* matter, and neither is dependent on the other for "actuality" or "real existence."

---

89. For example, in the Openness publication *The Openness of God* (Downers Grove, Ill.: InterVarsity, 1994), 101–25, Pinnock himself argues against the traditional conceptions of omnipotence, immutability, impassibility, and omniscience on biblical grounds.

90. Pinnock, *Most Moved Mover,* 67, quoting John Sanders.

91. Pinnock, *Most Moved Mover,* 67.

92. Stan Larson, "The King Follett Discourse: A Newly Amalgamated Text," *BYU Studies* 18, no. 2 (1977–78): 204.

Thus, in LDS thought, God *could exist* without creation. Pinnock questions whether for LDS thought the divine love entails that God engages in creative activity. I believe it does. Indeed, while in conventional Christianity, God's nature forbids that he should have equals, in LDS theology God's very nature entails that he seeks to share with others all that He is and has.

Conversely, the openness view is that "*God does not need a world in order to experience love.*"[93] Hence, according to openness theology, the world becomes "not something God needs, but something he wants. . . . A world would provide for God an external expression of his own perfect goodness." To me this appears to differ but little from conventional Christianity's claim that God created in order to provide himself with creatures who would worship him. Although openness theology attempts to change this motivation from "the desire for adoration" to "the need for love," for me their argument ultimately fails because, in short, given an openness worldview, *we are not necessary in the eternal scheme of things.* God would be just fine without us! Finally, I must say that LDS view the causal/teleological order of the cosmos in the same light as conventional Christians: namely as a testimony of the reality of a Supreme Creator or Organizer. While process theology might argue for "a struggle involving a diversity of ultimate principles" (Pinnock, 510), LDS theology holds that "All kingdoms have a law given; And there are many kingdoms; for there is no space in the which there is no kingdom" (D&C 88:36–37). God's creative power, therefore, is not only reflected in chaos, but also stems from his knowledge of the eternal laws and principles by which the universe is inherently structured! The application of "higher laws" can overcome "lesser laws" (just as Bernoulli's principle can in a sense overcome gravity) and through their application God was able to "create" or "organize" what we see today. Thus it seems that both LDS and openness theologies view creation as God's decision and the meaningful expression of his will, not as the outcome of struggles between gods or primary principles.

Pinnock is right when he comments that in the LDS perspective "God is inherently limited" (Pinnock, 509) (which may be another reason why openness theology accepts ex nihilo creation). Indeed, the difference between LDS and openness theology is quite clear: for the Latter-day Saints this limitation is a *metaphysical* reality, while openness thinkers claim that God *voluntarily* limits himself. This assertion by open theism of self-limitation on the part of God is for me the greatest point of divergence between LDS and open thought, especially in view of the fact that self-limitation combined with creation ex nihilo does not succeed in exonerating God from the responsibility of creating evil. For if God did create the world ex nihilo, as openness theology holds, then is not God still, at least ultimately, responsible for all

---

93. John Sanders, *The God Who Risks: A Theology of Providence* (Downers Grove, Ill.: InterVarsity, 1998), 185.

the evil (both natural and moral) in the world since He produced by fiat the natural structure of the world and gave his creatures agency? Could he not, for instance, have created humans with a nature far less prone to gross sinfulness? I am not sure that the openness "solution" to the problem of evil would survive an attack such as Dostoevsky's and still be able to justify that such a risk was "worth it."[94] God really could prevent genuine evils; he really could possess exhaustive specific foreknowledge.

Pinnock deserves commendation once more for his lucid portrayal of LDS belief on the subjects of creation, theodicy, and the ultimate constituents of being. Joseph rejected the idea that God is the "ground of all being." Instead, he taught that a plurality of original entities exist coeternally with God, including matter and human beings. In the words of the Prophet: "We say that God himself is a self-existent being. Who told you so? It is correct enough; but how did it get into your head? Who told you that *man did not exist in like manner upon the same principles?* Man does exist on the same principles."[95] Thus, in LDS thought God *is* ultimately limited by the structure of uncreated reality, and hence there are ontological (not merely logical) limits on what he can do or bring about (e.g., he cannot force free intelligences to act against their wills or impart knowledge that can only be gained through personal experience). However, this does not mean that Latter-day Saints should have less confidence in God than their Christian counterparts have—Latter-day Saints believe in the same Bible, which constantly testifies that God is able to accomplish *all* of his plans and purposes. In fact, the Lord gave us this promise through Joseph Smith: "I, the Lord, am bound when ye do what I say, but when ye do not what I say, ye have no promise" (D&C 82:10), meaning that when we are obedient, the Lord *will* do what he has promised, whatever that may be. Hence the Latter-day Saints take seriously each and every promise God makes in the Bible, and look forward to their fulfillment. This fact not only makes a difference theoretically, but also existentially. Does the open view of God have similar positive existential consequences? For example, can petitionary prayer affect God to the extent that He will un-self-limit in order to meet the needs of humans? The biblical narrative speaks of a God who does *all He can* to benefit His children who are endowed with agency. If God *could* un-self-limit at any time, then He is not doing all he can. Why would God then allow evils to occur that do not serve some greater good, for surely openness thinkers do not consider *all* evil to be logically necessary for a greater good? It seems much easier to relate to a loving God who does all he can to prevent seemingly

---

94. Fyodor Dostoyevsky, *The Brothers Karamazov* (New York: Penguin, 1993), 271–83.

95. Roberts, *Comprehensive History of the Church*, 2:393; emphasis added; see also Ehat and Cook, *Words of Joseph Smith*, 346, 352, 359.

pointless evil than to one who deliberately chooses, for personal reasons, to do less than he can.

I have asked relevant and difficult questions concerning creation ex nihilo and the implications of holding to it. Joseph Smith's revelations present a viable alternative to this troublesome doctrine. Is Joseph's doctrine not both scripturally as well as practically sound? Indeed, there are many scriptures that testify that man is the offspring of God (see Deut. 14:1, Ps. 82:6, Hosea 1:10, Mal. 2:10, Acts 17:29, Rom. 8:16), created in his image (Gen. 1:27) and endowed with His knowledge (Gen. 3:22), and from my understanding of the openness model it seems like a rejection of creation ex nihilo would be a more consistent position to hold for three reasons. First, it would be *much* easier to explain God's desire to enter into relations with us as well as his ability to interact with us dynamically. Second, it would extricate the open model from the problem of evil by attributing ontological self-existence and agency to entities other than God, thereby making evil an eternal possibility or something that God has always had to deal with. Finally, it would make the existential appeal already enjoyed by the open model even greater by elevating the status of human persons from brute creations to sons and daughters of God, who, through obedience and the grace of God might one day become "joint heirs with Christ" (Rom. 8:17).

The Celestial Middle World and Deification

This observation leads us to consider the next item, namely the LDS conception of deification. Pinnock seems to accept theosis to a point, yet maintains an ultimate and inherent "gap" between "the uncreated God and a created humanity" even in a blessed condition (Pinnock, 505). Latter-day Saint tradition holds that there exists no ontological barrier preventing mankind from becoming all that God is and enjoying the *same* kind of life that God lives, and I have been puzzled by scholarly claims to the contrary.[96]

The logic behind such a concept is quite simple: man is an eternal intelligence, and so is God. God has advanced (staggeringly) far beyond man, and thus, in the words of Joseph Smith,

---

96. For example, in *How Wide the Divide?* 86, Robinson wrote:

What do Latter-day Saints mean by "gods"? Latter-day Saints do not, or at least should not, believe that they will ever be independent in all eternity from their Father in heaven or from their Savior Jesus Christ or from the Holy Spirit. Those who are exalted by his grace will always be "gods" (always with a small g, even in the Doctrine and Covenants) by grace, by an extension of his power, and will always be subordinate to the Godhead. In the Greek philosophical sense—and in the "orthodox" theological sense—such contingent beings would not even rightly be called "gods," since they never become "the ground of all being" and are subordinate to their Father.

God himself, finding he was in the midst of spirits and glory, because he was more intelligent, saw proper to institute laws whereby the rest could have a privilege to *advance like himself.* The relationship we have with God places us in a situation to *advance* in knowledge. He has power to institute laws to *instruct* the weaker intelligences, that they may be exalted *with Himself,* so that they might have one glory upon another, and all that knowledge, power, glory, and intelligence, which is requisite in order to save them in the world of spirits.[97]

Thus God, our Father in Heaven, analogously to an earthly father, becomes our mentor, our confidant, and our guide as we pass through the experiences of our mortal lives. We are dependent upon Him for the means and guidance to *survive* physical and spiritual death and to flourish spiritually, but not because we are of a different ontological species—we simply lack the requisite knowledge, experience and spiritual strength to do so on our own. Thus God's purpose becomes the immortality and exaltation of the "weaker intelligences." Indeed, in a revelation to Joseph Smith, Jesus Christ promises, "you may come unto the Father in my name, and in due time receive of his fullness. For if you keep my commandments you shall receive of his fullness, and be glorified in me as I am in the Father" (D&C 93:19–20). Elaborating upon this promise, Joseph taught,

> What is it [to be joint heirs with Christ]? To inherit the *same* power, the *same* glory, and the *same* exaltation, until you arrive at the station of a God, and ascend the throne of *eternal* power, *the same as those who have gone before.* What did Jesus do? Why; I do the things I saw my Father do when worlds came rolling into existence. *My Father worked out his kingdom with fear and trembling, and I must do the same;* and when I get my kingdom, I shall present it to My Father, so that he may obtain kingdom upon kingdom.[98]

In short, God's purpose is to help man realize his divine potential, and until recently LDS thought has recognized no limits upon this potential. One of the biggest differences between LDS and openness theology is that in LDS theology there is no inherent or unbridgeable ontological gap between human beings and God. Pinnock notes this while talking of the differing "ontological frame" from which Mormons view the world (Pinnock, 508). If this is the case, the question for open theism is what to do with the overwhelming biblical evidence that humans are offspring of God, not creatures merely.[99] If humankind is of the "same species" as God, then it is rational to believe in a more ennobling version of theosis or deification (Pinnock, 508).

---

97. Smith, *History of the Church,* 6:312; emphasis added.
98. Smith, *History of the Church,* 6:306; emphasis added.
99. See for example, Acts 17:28–29, Deut. 14:1, Ps. 82:6, Hosea 1:10, Mal. 2:10, Eccl. 12:7, Rom. 8:16, Eph. 4:6, and Heb. 12:9.

For traditional Christianity, the doctrine of deification[100] has a unique history. Biblically, Peter, John, and Paul all spoke of the idea that man can become God (2 Pet. 1:4, John 14–17, Rom. 8). In the writings of Irenaeus of Lyons, Clement of Alexandria, Athanasius, and Cyril of Alexandria, one can find references to the idea that "God became man, that man might become God."[101] Consequently the doctrine of *theosis* has always played a distinctive role in the East; Vladimir Lossky refers to theosis as the "very essence of Christianity."[102] By contrast, however, acceptance or enumeration of an explicit doctrine of deification in Western theology has been minimal, if not absent. D. B. Clendenin says,

> Western theologians in general and Protestants in particular have given only scant attention to the central importance of theosis in Orthodox thought. Nor do they address the doctrine as an important biblical category in its own right. New Testament theologies such as those by George Ladd (1974) and Leon Morris (1986), for example, do not even mention theosis. On the other hand, as early as Gregory Palamas's fourteenth-century work *On Divine and Deifying Participation*, Orthodox thinkers have systematically analyzed the doctrine at length.[103]

---

100. To follow suit with recent theologians, I will use the terms *deification* and *theosis* as synonyms in this paper. Carl Mosser points out however that traditionally, the term *theosis* "has been uniquely associated with the classical tradition of Byzantine theology represented by such figures as Pseudo-Dionysius, Maximus Confessor, and Gregory Palamas." Carl Mosser, "The Earliest Patristic Interpretations of Psalm 82, Jewish Antecedents, and the Origin of Christian Deification," *Journal of Theological Studies*, n.s. 56 pt 1 (April 2005): 31 n. 3.

101. See Norman Russell, "'Partakers of the Divine Nature' (2 Peter 1:4) in the Byzantine Tradition," in *Kathegetria: Essays Presented to Joan Hussey for Her 80th Birthday* (Camberley, UK: Porphyrogenitus Publications, 1998), 51–67, for arguably the best treatment of deification in the Patristic Fathers. See also "Deification," *Oxford Dictionary of the Christian Church*, 3d ed., ed. F. L. Cross and E. A. Livingstone (Oxford: Oxford University Press, 1997), 467.

102. Vladimir Lossky, *In the Image and Likeness of God* (Crestwood, N.Y.: St. Vladimir's Seminary Press, 1974), 97. Also, D. B. Clendenin, *Eastern Orthodox Christianity: A Western Perspective*, 2d ed. (Grand Rapids: Baker Academic, 2003), 120–21.

103. Clendenin, *Eastern Orthodox Christianity*, 121. Also see "Deification," *Oxford Dictionary of the Christian Church*, 465. Contemporary Western theologians agree that a marginal amount of attention has been paid to deification. See A. N. Williams, "Deification in the Summa Theologiae: A Structural Interpretation of the Prima Pars," *Thomist* 61 (1997): 219–55; Carl Mosser, "The Greatest Possible Blessing: Calvin and Deification," *Scottish Journal of Theology* 55, no. 1 (2002): 36–57; Robert Rakestraw, "Becoming Like God: An Evangelical Doctrine of Theosis," and *Journal of the Evangelical Theological Society* 40, no. 2 (June 1997): 257–69.

But things are changing. The past 50 years reflect a steadily increasing amount of interest in the issue of deification.[104] Some scholars are asserting that deification is not only compatible with Augustinian theology, it is central to it.[105] References to deification have even been found in Aquinas's *Theologica*.[106] The result of this awakening has been a virtual explosion of research, dialogue, and publication regarding the doctrine of deification. A relatively current bibliography[107] of articles, books, chapters in books, and dissertations reveals 222 publications. 195 (or 88% of these) were published since 1950. One hundred four (nearly half of the total) were published by 1990, and at least twenty more have come off the press since then. Interest in deification remains high, indeed. And it crosses every denominational line. Latter-day Saints are eager to continue the conversation.

As to the existential meaning of belief in theosis, Latter-day Saints identify with Catholic theologian Mark O'Keefe. After noting that "reference to deification is virtually absent from the major Roman Catholic ascetical and mystical manuals of this century," O'Keefe mourns its loss and the fact that it "could not regain a central place in Roman Catholic spiritual theology."[108] He speaks repeatedly of "retrieving" the idea of theosis and believes that this doctrine contains a powerful pragmatic punch that should be vital in spurring believers to live a more moral and spiritual life. He explains,

> To understand the Christian life as a path of *theosis* is to suggest that the human person is called not "merely" into relationship with God—as truly incredible as that is in itself—but that human persons are

---

104. Reasons why this may be are varied. Some suggest that the rise of the Soviet Union may have engendered increased study of deification. As scholars came out of the Soviet Union to settle in Europe and other places, they had access to Western publications in which they were able to contribute. As Russian scholars of Orthodox background, they were able to introduce the doctrine of deification to a wider audience. Yet others suggest that the fall of the Soviet Union contributed to greater awareness of deification. Protestant missionaries were able to enter historically Orthodox land, and, as a result of increased exposure to Orthodox theology, specifically deification, these missionaries were able to research the teaching more fully.

105. David L. Balas, "Divinization," *Encyclopedia of Early Christianity*, 2d ed., 2 vols., ed. Everett Ferguson (New York: Garland, 1997), 1:339; Gerald Bonner, "Augustine's Conception of Deification," *Journal of Theological Studies* n.s., 37, no. 2 (1986): 369–86.

106. Williams, "Deification in the Summa Theologiae," 219–55. "Where the conventional wisdom errs, however, is in locating the break in the Middle Ages, for the greatest of all medieval Western theologies, the Summa theologiae of Thomas Aquinas, contains a highly developed doctrine of deification" (219).

107. Bibliography in author's possession.

108. Mark O'Keefe, "Theosis and the Christian Life: Toward Integrating Roman Catholic Ethics and Spirituality," *Eglise et Théologie* 25 (1994): 56.

invited and called into a share in the divine life itself, into the very inner life of the triune God. . . .

Because *theosis* is a present reality—though only partially realized—Christians strive to live a life in conformity to the awesome dignity to which they are called. . . .

To believe that one already shares in the divine life demands of the Christian an authentic response to the divine life and love, especially as this has been revealed in Jesus Christ. Christians strive to model in their lives those perspectives, dispositions, virtues, attitudes, intentions, and affections that seem authentically conformed to the deified life which they have already begun to live, although as yet incompletely and imperfectly. Believers strive to decide and to act in a way consistent with their new life and with the character which flows from it. Christian ethics—both of doing and of being—must be profoundly rooted in the reality of *theosis*.[109]

While I believe that scripture, tradition, and reason compel us to this stronger formulation of deification, I do think Stephen Robinson is essentially correct when he said that deified humans "will always be subordinate to the Godhead"[110] as long as such subordination is not held to be an ontological necessity. Deified humans will forever be subordinate to the Godhead because, as Charles Hartshorne argues, God is unsurpassable in certain respects, but eternally self-surpassing in others. But never is God to be surpassed by something else.[111] Hence even those who reach the status of god will never catch up to God himself because he is continually progressing with respect to these great making attributes. Furthermore, I think B. H. Roberts had it right when he taught that

Exalted intelligences who have become "partakers in the one Divine Nature," being united in brotherhood with others of like nature may be regarded as available for *assignments* to presiding stations among the Presiding Intelligences of the universes of the Gods—the sons of Gods, to preside in worlds or systems of worlds as may be required. . . . Of such may be chosen sons to preside *as Deities* over worlds and world systems as the Gods of eternity may determine or appoint.[112]

God will continue to direct the future of the cosmos, but within a community of those who possess the same nature and attributes rather than as a solitary, "unmoved mover."

---

109. O'Keefe, "Theosis and the Christian Life," 60–61.

110. Blomberg and Robinson, *How Wide the Divide?* 86.

111. Charles Hartshorne, *Man's Vision of God and the Logic of Theism* (Hamden, Conn.: Archon, 1964), 46.

112. B. H. Roberts, *Discourses of B. H. Roberts* (Salt Lake City: Deseret, 1948). 95–96; emphasis added.

Omniscience and the Future

Pinnock's fourth item deals with the apparent conflict between God's omniscience and libertarian free will, or in other words whether the future has been "settled" in God's mind via his access to exhaustively specific foreknowledge or if God holds the future to be "open" or "unsettled."

Pinnock challenges the traditional understanding of omniscience by contending that although God knows "everything that could exist in [the] future," he does not possess exhaustive specific foreknowledge.[113] For Pinnock, "exhaustive foreknowledge would not be possible in a world with real freedom."[114] Critics of the openness model are quick to contend that any qualification of the notion of God's complete knowledge of the future diminishes his power and worshipability. To the contrary, openness theologians argue, this only makes God more praiseworthy for his wisdom and resourcefulness in responding to emerging contingencies. I would agree with Pinnock's assessment that in the area of divine foreknowledge the LDS and open "communities are in just about the same place" (Pinnock, 505).

Latter-day Saints differ among themselves in their understandings of the extent of God's foreknowledge.[115] Some, including Presidents Brigham

---

113. Pinnock, *Most Moved Mover,* 100.

114. Ibid.

115. David L. Paulsen, "Omnipotent God; Omnipresence of God; Omniscience of God," in *Encyclopedia of Mormonism,* ed. Daniel H. Ludlow, 4 vols. (New York: Macmillian, 1992), 3:1030. Also, in the early days of the Church, Elder Orson Pratt was reprimanded by the First Presidency and Quorum of the Twelve (see "Instructions to the Saints, January 29, 1860," and "Proclamation of the First Presidency and Twelve, October 21, 1865," *Messages of the First Presidency,* comp. James R. Clark, 6 vols. (Salt Lake City: Bookcraft, 1965), 2:222–23, 235–40, for teaching that progression in knowledge ceases once we become "one" with the Father. He had stated: "When they [the Saints] become one with the Father and the Son and receive a fulness of their glory, that will be the end of all progression in knowledge, because there will be nothing more to be learned. The Father and the Son do not progress in knowledge and wisdom, because they already know all things, past, present and to come." Orson Pratt, *The Seer* 1 (August 1853): 117. Compare such a statement with those of Brigham Young, Lorenzo Snow, and George Q. Cannon: "All organized existence is in progress, either to an endless advancement in eternal perfections, or back to dissolution. . . . All things that have come within the bounds of man's limited knowledge—the things he naturally understands—teach him that there is no period, in all the eternities, wherein organized existence will become stationary, that it cannot advance in knowledge, wisdom, power and glory." Brigham Young, in *Journal of Discourses,* 1:349–50, July 10, 1853. "We will continue on improving, advancing and increasing in wisdom, intelligence, power, and dominion, worlds without end." Lorenzo Snow, "opening Address," in *71st Annual Conference of The Church of Jesus Christ of Latter-day Saints* (Salt Lake City: The Church of Jesus Christ of Latter-day Saints, 1901), 2. "There is progress for

Young and Wilford Woodruff, have thought that God increases endlessly in knowledge and, hence, presumably, at every time lacks exhaustive fore-knowledge. Brigham Young stated that "the God I serve is progressing eternally, and so are his children; they will increase to all eternity, if they are faithful."[116] And, in agreement with Young, Wilford Woodruff explained: "If there was a point where man in his progression could not proceed any further, the very idea would throw a gloom over every intelligent and reflecting mind. God himself is increasing and progressing in knowledge, power, and dominion, and will do so, worlds without end. It is just so with us. We are in a probation, which is a school of experience."[117]

Other Latter-day Saints hold to a more traditional view that God's knowledge, including the foreknowledge of future free contingencies, is exhaustively complete. Joseph Fielding Smith asserted: "Do we believe that God has all 'wisdom'? If so, in that, he is absolute. If there is something he does not know, then he is not absolute in 'wisdom,' and to think such a thing is absurd. . . . It is not through ignorance and learning hidden truth that [God] progresses, for if there are truths which he does not know, then these things are greater than he, and this cannot be."[118] Bruce R. McConkie expressed a similar sentiment: "There are those who say that God is progressing in knowledge and is learning new truths. This is a false teaching which grows out of a wholly twisted and incorrect view of the King Follett Sermon. . . . God progresses in the sense that his kingdoms increase and his dominions multiply—not in the sense that he learns new truths and discovers new laws. God is not a student. He is not a laboratory technician. He is not postulating new theories on the basis of past experiences. He has indeed graduated to that state of exaltation that consists of knowing all things."[119]

Despite these differing views within the LDS tradition, there is accord on three fundamental points: (1) Man is an agent with power to choose other than what he, in fact, chooses; (2) Whatever the extent and nature of God's foreknowledge, it is not inconsistent with man's freedom—God's

our Father and for our Lord Jesus. There is no such thing as standing still in the eternal work of our God. It is endless progress, progressing from one degree of knowledge to another degree." George Q. Cannon, *Gospel Truth: Discourses and Writings of President George Q. Cannon,* sel., arr., and ed. Jerreld L. Newquist (Salt Lake City: Deseret, 1987), 92.

116. Brigham Young, in *Journal of Discourses,* 11:286–87, January 13, 1867.

117. Wilford Woodruff, in *Journal of Discourses,* 6:120, December 6, 1857; emphasis added.

118. Joseph Fielding Smith, *Doctrines of Salvation,* comp. Bruce R. McConkie 3 vols. (Salt Lake City: Bookcraft, 1954) 1:5.7.

119. Bruce R. McConkie, *Sermons and Writings of Bruce R. McConkie,* ed. Mark L. McConkie (Salt Lake City: Bookcraft, 1998), 24–25.

knowledge does not causally determine human choices; and (3) God's knowledge, like God's power, is maximally efficacious. No event occurs that he has not anticipated at least *qua* possibility or has not taken into account in his planning.

Pinnock's statement concerning the attractiveness of open theism could well describe Mormonism: "Young people gravitate toward open theism because it encourages them to believe that they can make a difference in the future, which is not altogether settled" (Pinnock, 495). Libertarian free will contains tremendous emotional and practical appeal. We find it ennobling to understand ourselves as agents, free to choose, and thus to accept responsibility for our choices. It is motivating to believe that our futures are not yet settled and that our present choices will impact the world's outcomes. Indeed, we live as if these self-understandings were true, no matter what our theological creeds may say.

God and Gender

The next item Pinnock raises concerns the issue of God and gender for, as Pinnock astutely notices, "if God is personal, even embodied, one might conclude that God would have to be either male or female" (Pinnock, 505).

In regards to the "delicate point" of God and gender, I return once again to Jesus Christ as both premise and argument.[120] Was Jesus Christ literally a man? Is Jesus Christ God? The same argument asserted in favor of divine embodiment may be used again in regards to God being literally male. Assuming God is male (as Latter-day Saints do) Pinnock asks a variety of questions, including, "Do Latter-day Saints speak of goddesses?" and "Is there procreation?" (Pinnock, 506). To both of these questions, LDS theology answers yes. The idea of a Mother in Heaven is deeply enshrined in LDS thought and even hymnology. Indeed, the idea found its clearest and most moving expression in a poem written by Eliza R. Snow, first published November 15, 1845, in the *Times and Seasons*. It was subsequently set to music and included in an LDS hymnal first published (without a title) in 1851 in Liverpool.[121] Titled now "O My Father," it has been one of the Latter-day Saints' most beloved hymns for over 150 years. Besides affirming belief in a Heavenly Mother, it sets out the LDS belief that each of us existed premortally. It is partially quoted here:

> O my Father, thou that dwellest
> In the high and glorious place,

---

120. B. H. Roberts, *The Mormon Doctrine of Deity* (Salt Lake City: Signature, 1998), 119.

121. Jill Mulvay Derr, "The Significance of 'O My Father' in the Personal Journey of Eliza R. Snow," *BYU Studies* 36, no. 1 (1996–97): 98.

When shall I regain thy presence
And again behold thy face?
In thy holy habitation,
Did my spirit once reside?
In my first primeval childhood
Was I nurtured near thy side?

I had learned to call thee Father,
Thru thy Spirit from on high,
But, until the key of knowledge
Was restored, I knew not why.
In the heav'ns are parents single?
No, the thought makes reason stare!
Truth is reason; truth eternal
Tells me I've a mother there.[122]

---

122. Eliza R. Snow, "O My Father," *Hymns of The Church of Jesus Christ of Latter Day Saints* (Salt Lake City: Deseret, 1985), 292. For an early Christian parallel to Snow's poem, see John W. Welch and James V. Garrison, "The 'Hymn of the Pearl': An Ancient Counterpart to 'O My Father,'" *BYU Studies* 36, no. 1 (1996–97): 127–38. The authors write, "One of the most endearing writings found in early Christianity is known as the 'Hymn of the Pearl.' This text has immediate appeal to readers of all levels and resonates a beautiful message of a soul's journey from a pre-mortal home, through mortality, and back to heavenly parents. To this extent, the poem can be seen as an early Christian counterpart to the early Latter-day Saint hymn 'O My Father.' The Hymn of the Pearl is quoted in an apocryphal work entitled *The Acts of the Apostle Thomas*. . . . The composition begins with the soul as a young boy in his primeval childhood, being nurtured in the royal house of his parents, the King of Kings and the Queen of the East. One day his parents instruct him that he is to leave home and his glittering robe and garments and take a journey down into Egypt to find there a pearl guarded by a terrible serpent. The parents covenant with him that, if he recovers the pearl and returns home with it, he will be allowed to put his glorious robes back on and will be made heir in the kingdom together with his oldest brother, the second in command. Accordingly, he leaves home with a bundle of provisions prepared for him, and with a pair of guides, he makes his way for Egypt." (Welch and Garrison, "Hymn of the Pearl," 127–28.)

The following is a possible partial LDS interpretation of the parable.

Hymn of the Pearl symbols	An LDS interpretation
"King of Kings"	Heavenly Father
"Queen of the East"	Heavenly Mother
"The East"	Our heavenly home—pre-mortal existence
"sent me out . . . [of] our homeland"	Mortal birth
"The Pearl"	Purpose of life—moral and spiritual development; deification.

The belief that we have a Mother in Heaven was officially accorded doctrinal status in 1909 when the Church's First Presidency, in a statement called "The Origin of Man," declared: "All men and women are in the similitude of the universal Father and Mother, and are literally the sons and daughters of Deity."[123] The doctrinal status of a Heavenly Mother was again officially reaffirmed in the "Proclamation on the Family" issued in 1995 by the Church's First Presidency and Quorum of the Twelve Apostles:

> All human beings—male and female—are created in the image of God. Each is a beloved spirit son or daughter of heavenly parents, and, as such, each has a divine nature and destiny. Gender is an essential characteristic of individual premortal, mortal, and eternal identity and purpose.[124]

Perhaps more surprising than present Christian theological interest in a divine feminine is the emerging body of scholarship which indicates that the idea of a Heavenly Mother is no modern innovation but has biblical support. The least that can be said is that a great many Bible scholars believe that ancient Israel believed in a goddess named Asherah. Mark S. Smith goes further than this, suggesting that perhaps the majority of experts in this field agree that ancient Israel believed in this goddess.

> Does the biblical and extrabiblical evidence support the view that Asherah was a goddess in ancient Israel and that she was the consort of Yahweh? Or, alternatively, does the data point to the asherah as a symbol within the cult of Yahweh without signifying a goddess? The first position perhaps constitutes a majority view, represented by the older works of H. Ringgren, G. Fohrer, and G. W. Ahlstrom, and the more recent studies of W. G. Dever, D. N. Freedman, R. Hestrin, A. Lemaire, and S. Olyan.[125]

Hymn of the Pearl symbols	An LDS interpretation
"devouring dragon"	Satan
"hard and terrible way"	Opposition, trials, temptations of mortal life
"two guides"	Earthly parents
"land of the Babylonians"	Worldly temptations that distract us on our journey

123. "The Origin of Man, November, 1909," in Clark, *Messages of the First Presidency,* 4:203. In 1925, the First Presidency in another official declaration reaffirmed the Mother in Heaven doctrine using the exact language of the 1909 statement. "'Mormon' View of Evolution, September, 1925," in Clark, *Messages of the First Presidency,* 5:244.

124. "The Family: A Proclamation to the World," *Ensign* 25 (November 1995): 102.

125. Mark S. Smith, *The Early History of God* (New York: Harper and Row, 1990), 88–89. Smith himself holds to a minority position held by B. Lang, P. D. Miller, J. Tigay,

LDS leadership and scholars have said much by way of the existential meaning of Joseph's doctrine. In speaking to the women of the church, President Spencer W. Kimball said, "God made man in his own image and certainly he made woman in the image of his wife-partner.... You [women] are daughters of God. You are precious. You are made in the image of our heavenly Mother."[126] President Harold B. Lee spoke of the influence of our Mother in Heaven in this way: "Sometimes we think the whole job is up to us, forgetful that there are loved ones beyond our sight who are thinking about us and our children. We forget that we have a Heavenly Father and a Heavenly Mother who are even more concerned, probably, than our earthly father and mother, and that influences from beyond are constantly working to try to help us when we do all we can."[127] Another church leader, Vaughn J. Featherstone said, "Women are endowed with special traits and attributes that come trailing down through eternity from a divine mother. Young women have special God-given feelings about charity, love, and obedience. Coarseness and vulgarity are contrary to their natures.... Theirs is a sacred, God-given role, and the traits they received from heavenly mother are equally as important as those given to the young men."[128] This existential meaning is deeply significant to Latter-day Saints.[129]

Pinnock's curiosity concerning "Mrs. God" is valid and his honest inquiries deserve reasoned responses.

"Is she everlasting?" As we have already seen, the Latter-day Saints hold that *all* intelligence is "everlasting" in the sense that it cannot be created or destroyed, and hence the intelligence possessed by "Mrs. God" is just as everlasting as that possessed by us as well as that of God the Father.

"Can she be prayed to?" In their prayers the Latter-day Saints, like their fellow Christians, follow the pattern outlined by the Savior in the Lord's Prayer: they begin by addressing the Father, they give thanks, they

and U. Winter, who maintain on the paucity of evidence that asherah neither referred to a goddess nor symbolized the goddess of Israel.

126. Spencer W. Kimball, *The Teachings of Spencer W. Kimball* (Salt Lake City: Bookcraft, 1982), 25.

127. Harold B. Lee, *The Teachings of Harold B. Lee* (Salt Lake City: Bookcraft, 1996), 70.

128. Vaughn J. Featherstone, "A Champion of Youth," *Ensign* 17 (November 1987): 28.

129. Carol Lynn Pearson, "Healing the Motherless Home," in *Women and Authority: Re-emerging Mormon Feminism,* ed. Maxine Hanks (Salt Lake City: Signature, 1992), 231–46; "Emerging Discourse of the Divine Feminine," in Hanks, *Women and Authority,* 257–296; Cheryl B. Preston, "Feminism and Faith: Reflections on the Mormon Heavenly Mother," *Texas Journal of Women and the Law* 2 (1992): 337–86; and Margaret Merrill Toscano, "Is There a Place for Heavenly Mother in Mormon Theology?" *Sunstone* no. 133 (July 2004), 14–22.

ask for blessings and close in the name of Jesus Christ. This pattern holds true for all prayers in the LDS tradition, both public and private, as well as those offered within the confines of LDS temples. President Gordon B. Hinckley reiterated this pattern to the Church on September 28, 1991, when he taught,

> Logic and reason would certainly suggest that if we have a Father in Heaven, we have a Mother in Heaven. That doctrine rests well with me.
>
> However, in light of the instruction we have received from the Lord Himself, I regard it as inappropriate for anyone in the Church to pray to our Mother in Heaven.[130]

However, he hastens to add that "the fact that we do not pray to our Mother in Heaven in no way belittles or denigrates her." In our prayers we simply strive to follow the example that Jesus Christ set for us.

"Do the Latter-day Saints speak of goddesses? Is there procreation?" While the Latter-day Saints admittedly do not often speak of "gods and goddesses" in their Church meetings, this idea *does* occupy a central place in LDS theology as well as in temple ceremonies—of which eternal marriage is one. And as noted before, the ability to enjoy an "eternal increase" is one of the main characteristics by virtue of which God is considered to be divine. Hence, the LDS notion of deification holds that this divine, procreative power can be communicated to those who qualify for exaltation in the celestial kingdom. Thus it is clear that deification requires *both* the male and female genders, and that *both* are to be considered "gods" and "goddesses" respectively, and the doctrines of the eternality of families and the ability to exercise procreative powers beyond the grave are cherished by the Latter-day Saints.

Finally, since the doctrine of a Heavenly Mother is explicitly stated neither in any LDS scripture that came to or through Joseph Smith[131] nor in any of his writings or sermons, Pinnock's suggestion that there may have been some theological borrowing from Ugarit is understandable.[132] However, the

---

130. Gordon B. Hinckley, "Daughters of God," *Ensign* 21 (November 1991): 100.

131. Latter-day Saints accept four books as scripture (or authoritative canon): the Holy Bible, the Book of Mormon, the Pearl Great Price, and the Doctrine and Covenants. The Book of Mormon and the Pearl of Great Price consists of ancient revelations that came through Joseph Smith. With a few exceptions, the Doctrine and Covenants consists of revelations that came directly to Joseph Smith.

132. At least one LDS scholar has questioned whether the doctrine can be ascribed to Joseph. See Blake T. Ostler, "The Idea of Pre-existence in the Development of Mormon Thought," *Dialogue: A Journal of Mormon Thought* 15 (spring 1982): 59–78, 76. Ostler raises the issue in a footnote to his study of the development of the doctrine of premortal existence. He says, "Although Joseph Smith may have secretly taught the doctrine of Mother in heaven, he did not bifurcate the pre-existent state of man into a

doctrine was implicit in Joseph's revelations regardless whether he explicitly drew it out.[133] Indisputably, the idea of a Mother in Heaven was openly

---

period of existence as intelligences and existence as spirits after spirit birth through a heavenly mother. All sources attributing the idea of a heavenly Mother to Joseph Smith are late and probably unreliable." Ostler, "The Idea of Pre-existence," 75 n. 28. Others find convincing the total evidence—circumstantial, testimonial and otherwise—that Joseph taught the doctrine. Among the scholars who attribute this idea to Joseph Smith are Jill Mulway Derr, Charles R. Harrell, and Linda P. Wilcox. Derr argues that Eliza R. Snow could not have been the originator of the idea, pointing out, among other data, that W. W. Phelps had written a poem referencing our Mother in Heaven and presented it publicly before Snow wrote "O My Father." She concludes that Joseph Smith was the source for the Mormon belief of a Mother in Heaven. See Derr, "Significance of 'O My Father,'" 98–101. Harrell addresses the issue in the context of tracing the development of the doctrine of the preexistence in Mormon theology. He concludes that the circumstantial evidence points to Joseph possibly being responsible for the doctrine. He argues that since "spirit birth" was known and taught by close associates of Joseph like Orson Pratt who had a book published at the printers with the doctrine contained therein as early as June 22, 1844, and since "spirit birth" presupposes a mother, the doctrine could have been known and taught by the Prophet prior to his death. Charles R. Harrell, "The Development of the Doctrine of Preexistence, 1830–1844," *BYU Studies* 28, no. 2 (1988): 75–96. Linda Wilcox provides a comprehensive study of the subject of a mother in heaven in Mormon history, doctrine, and theology. She sets out the testimonies of those close to the prophet who affirm that he taught it and concludes Joseph did. These witnesses include Susa Young Gates, who was told by Zina Diantha Huntington of a time when Zina was consoled by Joseph on the death of her mother in 1839, when Zina asked whether she would know her mother again on the other side. Joseph said, "More than that, you will meet and become acquainted with your eternal Mother. . . ." David McKay (father to the later president of the church David O. McKay) "recorded that during a buggy ride on which he accompanied Eliza Snow, he asked her if the Lord has revealed the Mother in Heaven doctrine to her. She replied, 'I got the inspiration from the Prophet's teachings; all that I was required to do was to use my Poetical gift and give that Eternal Principle in Poetry.'" We have a third hand account, from the journal of Abraham H. Cannon, of a vision Zebedee Coltrin had with Joseph Smith, in which they saw "the Father seated upon a throne; they prayed again and on looking saw the Mother also; after praying and looking the fourth time they saw the Savior added to the group." Linda P. Wilcox, "The Mormon Concept of a Mother in Heaven," in *Women and Authority*, 5–6.

133. "The Mother in Heaven concept was a logical and natural extension of a theology which posited both an anthropomorphic god, who had once been a man, and the possibility of eternal procreation of spirit children." Wilcox further explains that the idea of a Mother in Heaven was considered by the leaders of the church in the nineteenth century to be "commonsensical." Wilcox quotes Brigham Young as saying that God "created man, as we create our children; for there is no other process of creation. . . ." She quotes the apostle Erastus Snow as saying, "Now, it is not said in

expressed and published within months of Joseph's death. W. W. Phelps[134] referred to the idea in a poem,[135] which he composed and read at the dedication of the Nauvoo Seventies Hall on December 26, 1844. The poem was published in the church newspaper the following month. It seems especially significant that this *first known* publication of the idea was presented the doctrine matter-of-factly, as if commonplace, not novel. Several months later, in October 1845, Eliza R. Snow published her poem "O My Father."

A Social Trinity

Another point on which LDS understanding and openness thought converge is their view of the Christian Godhead. Both reject the conventional view that the Father, Son, and Holy Ghost constitute one metaphysical substance, affirming rather that they are so lovingly interrelated as to constitute one perfectly united community. This understanding of the Godhead is known in contemporary Christian discourse as "social trinitarianism" or as "the social analogy of the Trinity."

Pinnock's brief treatment of the LDS understanding of the Godhead was very straightforward, perceptive, and correct. In 1842, in response to a Chicago newspaperman's inquiry as to what Mormons believed, Joseph penned thirteen basic beliefs, which have come to be known as "The Articles of Faith." They remain the closest LDS analogue to a creed. The first of these articles affirms LDS belief in the New Testament Godhead. It states simply: "We believe in God, the Eternal Father, and in His Son, Jesus Christ, and in the Holy Ghost."

Complicating the matter are Joseph's revelations, replete with the statement that the Father, the Son, and the Holy Ghost, are one God (2 Nephi

---

so many words in the Scriptures, that we have a Mother in heaven as well as a Father. It is left for us to infer this from what we see and know of all living things in the earth including man. . . . To our minds the idea of a Father suggests that of a Mother." Wilcox, "Mormon Concept of a Mother in Heaven," 4, 6.

134. W. W. Phelps was closely associated with Joseph Smith, serving as both clerk and scribe to Joseph in Nauvoo, and, earlier, as counselor in the first stake in Missouri. He is well-known for his talents in setting gospel doctrines to both music and poetry. Sydney Marie Hughes, "Phelps, William W.," in Cannon, Garr, and Cowan, *Encyclopedia of Latter Day Saint History*, 917–18.

135. This poem in part reads:

Come to me; here's the myst'ry that man hath not seen:
Here's our Father in heaven, and Mother, the Queen,
Here are worlds that have been, and the worlds yet to be:
Here's eternity,—endless; amen: Come to me.

From W. W. Phelps, "A Voice from the Prophet. 'Come to me,'" *Times and Seasons* 6 (January 15, 1845), 783.

31:21; Mosiah 15:2–5; Alma 11:44; 3 Nephi 11:27, 36; Mormon 7:7) and his declaration that "we have three Gods anyhow, and they are plural."[136] Thus, as Cornelius Plantinga puts it in writing about the Creed of the (Eleventh) Council of Toledo, "the main problem or puzzlement here is that of three-ness and oneness. What are the referents of these numbers? Three what? One what? And especially, how are these three and this one related?"[137]

Joseph revelations respond to each of these questions. Three what? Joseph answers, "I have always declared God to be a distinct personage, Jesus Christ a separate and distinct personage from God the Father, and that the Holy Ghost was a distinct personage and a Spirit: and these three constitute three distinct personages."[138] One what? Joseph answers, "and he [Jesus] possesses the same mind with the Father."[139] The Book of Mormon also helps to answer "one what?" with words like "doctrine," "judgment," "baptism," and "record."[140]

And especially, how are these three and this one related? Joseph answers: "The Son, who was *in the bosom of the Father,* . . . possessing all the fullness of the Father, or *the same fullness* with the Father. . . . And he being the *Only Begotten of the Father,* full of grace and truth, and having overcome, received a fullness of the glory of the Father."[141] Further, Joseph taught, "everlasting covenant was made between three personages [Father, Son and Holy Ghost] before the organization of this earth."[142] In short, the persons of the Trinity are bound by genetics, by "everlasting covenant," and by "the same fullness" or set of divine attributes.

Thus, Joseph explicitly rejected the traditional belief that the Godhead, or Trinity, constituted one metaphysical substance.[143] Rather, Joseph understood the Trinity to be constituted by three distinct persons who together

---

136. *History of the Church,* 6:474; Larry E. Dahl and Donald W. Cannon, eds., *Encyclopedia of Joseph Smith's Teachings* (Salt Lake City: Bookcraft, 1997), 297.

137. Cornelius Plantinga Jr., "Social Trinity and Tritheism," in *Trinity, Incarnation, and Atonement,* Ronald Feenstra and Cornelius Plantinga Jr., eds. (Notre Dame, Indiana: University of Notre Dame Press, 1989), 21.

138. *History of the Church,* 6:474; Dahl and Cannon, *Encyclopedia of Joseph Smith's Teachings,* 297.

139. Dahl and Cannon, *Encyclopedia of Joseph Smith's Teachings,* 345.

140. 2 Nephi 31:21, Alma 11:44, 3 Nephi 11:27, and 3 Nephi 11:36, respectively.

141. Dahl and Cannon, *Encyclopedia of Joseph Smith's Teachings,* 344–45; emphasis added.

142. Dahl and Cannon, *Encyclopedia of Joseph Smith's Teachings,* 712.

143. Christopher Stead writes, "Theologians have been rightly convinced that the ultimate effect of Nicaea has been to assert, not merely the equality, but also the essential unity, of the three Persons; and they have attempted, I think incautiously, to represent this as the original and express intention of the Nicene fathers. In support of this view, it has been argued that homoousios was adopted at Nicaea to express

form one mutually indwelling divine community, perfectly united in mind, will, work and love.[144] In his revelations, the word *God* is used to designate the divine community as well as to designate each individual divine person.[145] In order to avoid misunderstanding, it is imperative to keep this dual use of the word *God* in mind. Thus, consistent with his revelations, when Joseph declares there are "three Gods," he means that there are three distinct personages, each of whom is divine. When he affirms that there is "one God," he means that there is one perfectly united mutually indwelling divine community.[146] There is no contradiction here. Perhaps the late LDS apostle Elder James Talmage provided the clearest formulation of Joseph's understanding of the Godhead when he wrote,

> This unity is a type of completeness; the mind of any one member of
> the Trinity is the mind of the others; seeing as each of them does
> with the eye of perfection, they see and understand alike. Under any
> given conditions each would act in the same way, guided by the same
> principles of unerring justice and equity. The one-ness of the Godhead,
> to which the scriptures so abundantly testify, implies no mystical union

---

the form of trinitarian theology prevailing in the West." Christopher Stead, *Divine Substance* (Oxford: Clarendon, 1977), 251.

144. "Many men say there is one God; the Father, the Son and the Holy Ghost are only one God. I say that is a strange God anyhow—three in one, and one in three! It is a curious organization. 'Father, I pray not for the world, but I pray for them which thou hast given me.' 'Holy Father, keep through Thine own name those whom thou hast given me, that they may be one as we are.' All are to be crammed into one God, according to sectarianism. It would make the biggest God in all the world. He would be a wonderfully big God—he would be a giant or a monster. I want to read the text to you myself—'I am agreed with the Father and the Father is agreed with me, and we are agreed as one.' The Greek shows that it should be agreed. 'Father, I pray for them which Thou hast given me out of the world, and not for those alone, but for them also which shall believe on me through their word, that they all may be agreed, as Thou, Father, are with me, and I with Thee, that they also may be agreed with us' and all come to dwell in unity, and in all the glory and everlasting burnings of the Gods." Joseph Smith, *Teachings of the Prophet Joseph Smith,* comp. Joseph Fielding Smith (Salt Lake City: Deseret, 1976), 372–73. See also John 17:21 in *The Message Bible* and *Worldwide English Bible,* for other variant translations.

145. Joseph said, "The heavens declare the glory of a God, and the firmament showeth His handiwork; and a moment's reflection is sufficient to teach every man of common intelligence, that all these are not the mere productions of chance, nor could they be supported by any power less than an Almighty hand" (*History of the Church,* 2:14; Dahl and Cannon, *Encyclopedia of Joseph Smith's Teachings,* 291; emphasis in original).

146. See my interview, "Are Mormons Trinitarian?" in *Modern Reformation* (November/December 2003), 40–43, wherein I answer common questions concerning the LDS understanding of the Godhead.

of substance, nor any unnatural and therefore impossible blending of personality. Father, Son, and Holy Ghost are as distinct in their persons and individualities as are any three personages in mortality. Yet their unity of purpose and operation is such as to make their edicts one, and their will the will of God.[147]

Joseph held and his successors hold to a "one perfectly united, mutually indwelling divine community" model of the unity of Godhead rather than a "one metaphysical substance" model. As stated in the LDS Bible Dictionary, *mystery* "denotes in the New Testament a spiritual truth that was once hidden but now is revealed, and that, without special revelation, would have remained unknown."[148] Thus, the Latter-day Saints recognize the doctrine of the Trinity as a mystery, a spiritual truth re-revealed through Joseph Smith.

It is to *scripture* rather than the historic creeds of Christianity that the Latter-day Saints wish to conform, which is precisely the criticism openness theology is making. Christianity should be defined by God's own revelatory disclosures rather than by our rational constructions of what he *must* be. In the words of Pinnock,

> For too long pagan assumptions about God's nature have influenced theological reflection. Our thinking needs to be reformed in the light of the self-revelation of God in the gospel and *we must stop attributing to God qualities that undermine God's own self-disclosure*. Let us not treat the attributes of God independently of the Bible but view the biblical metaphors as reality-depicting descriptions of the living God, whose very being is self-giving love.[149]
>
> [For] what we are doing, in effect, is seeking to correct the Bible; to derive truth about God not from biblical metaphors but from our own intuitions of what is "fitting" for God to be.[150]

The Latter-day Saints claim that "God's own self-disclosure" continues through living prophets today, and when God the Father and his Son, Jesus Christ, appeared to Joseph Smith in the spring of 1820 as *separate individuals* the LDS conception of the Trinity began its development.

Conclusion

Latter-day Saint church president John Taylor once said,

---

147. James E. Talmage, *The Articles of Faith* (Salt Lake City: Deseret, 1988), 37.

148. LDS Bible Dictionary, *Holy Bible* (Salt Lake City: The Church of Jesus Christ of Latter-day Saints, 1979), s.v. "Mystery," 736. (Compare Rom. 16:25–26; Eph. 1:9; 3:3–10; Col. 1:26; 4:3; 1 Tim. 3:16).

149. Pinnock, *Most Moved Mover*, 27; emphasis added.

150. Pinnock, *Most Moved Mover*, 67.

When "Mormonism" was presented to me my first inquiry was, "Is it Scriptural? Is it reasonable and philosophical?" This is the principle I would act upon today. No matter how popular the theories or dogmas preached might be, I would not accept them unless they were strictly in accordance with the Scriptures, reason, and common sense.[151]

I think that these words offer a summation of the success of both "Mormonism" and other relational theologies: they are scriptural, reasonable, and practically appealing. Indeed, both find an "existential fit" within the lives of their adherents and even within the lives of their enemies, as Pinnock astutely notices. Neither theology claims to have all the answers, yet both believe that these answers are within our reach and it is *this* belief that keeps the conversation alive. I have learned much from responding to Pinnock's well-crafted essay, and I hope that what I have said will be of benefit to others as we progress towards a greater understanding of each other's beliefs. With that I wish to close with the words of Joseph Smith, who said,

The inquiry is frequently made of me, "Wherein do you differ from others in your religious views?" In reality and essence we do not differ so far in our religious views, but that we could all drink into one principle of love. One of the grand fundamental principles of "Mormonism" is to receive truth, let it come from whence it may.[152]

Rejoinder

Clark H. Pinnock

TIME PERMITS ONLY A BRIEF REPLY owing to publishing deadlines, and yet the opportunity to say something in closing must not be missed since the issues are so many and so profound. Let me say first that I appreciate interacting with Dr. Paulsen very much, both in person and in print, and am the richer for it as a theologian and as a person. I appreciate both the convergences and the divergences of our positions and detect room for growth in myself and (I think) in Dr. Paulsen. Unless I am much mistaken, there is a good deal of room in both LDS and evangelical thinking about God to make a dialogue between us worthwhile. I hope that this volume will make sure that it continues.

151. John Taylor, *Journal of Discourses*, 13:14, March 14, 1869.
152. *History of the Church*, 5:499.

Reading Dr. Paulsen's extensive and well-written essay, literally "just now," allows me to register some closing thoughts, if only briefly. It will be apparent to readers that the two of us come at things from very different localities, theologically and spiritually. We come at the material from different angles, which makes a world of difference. A concept of God is a system of ideas of what God is like and how God is related to the world. The concepts that we hold concerning the divine nature will influence the interpretation of many matters, even matters of the utmost importance. I come to the issues from the standpoint of a modified classical trinitarian monotheism while Dr. Paulsen comes at them from the insights (nay, revelations) found in the LDS standard works and later documents, which make parts of his theology very firm and other parts open to revision. The result is that when I encounter this LDS concept of God, I am amazed, that is, I find myself scratching my head and asking myself: "What did he just say?" Partly this is due to my not having come across some of the ideas before and partly it is due to what seems to me to be its fantastic aspect. You know what I mean: the golden bible, a radical doctrine of deification, private temple rituals, the remarkable history, Joseph Smith's King Follett Discourse, and so on. I am only trying to register the point that the intellectual and cultural distance between us is considerable and the evangelical/LDS dialogue is at an early stage. We are not going to get things altogether right the first time round, and the best thing for us to do is just to get on with it. We agree that God is very good and very great and that we can trust him to use such conversations to bring us closer to the truth, closer to one another, and closer to God.

Hear me then as I walk through David's paper and register some of the items that catch my eye. First, as regards the divine embodiment, David was encouraged when he found that I had noticed this idea in the Bible and was willing to take it seriously, if not literally. He is right—it is time for self-styled Bible-believing evangelicals to stop sweeping under the carpet biblical ideas that they disapprove of. For my part, I do not mind giving credit where credit is due. Latter-day Saints take this concept very seriously! The difference between us two on this issue is (I think) what we imagine it means for God to be embodied. I am much less sure about it than David is, but I celebrate the truth that God loves to be embodied and to come to us in human and (therefore) in a vulnerable form. Besides, I agree with C. S. Lewis—that no soul (read, no LDS soul) will perish for having thought that God had a beard. Let's stop nitpicking and start asking, How is it that God can do the things that the Bible plainly says he does? Surely in that discussion, the Latter-day Saints will have useful things to contribute, as one can see in David's paper.

Second, as regards divine limitations and the problem of evil, I believe that God is not limited by anything outside of himself but that he loves to constrain himself voluntarily especially where love is concerned. God gives room to creatures to love him freely. In a one-sided emphasis, classical theologians have overstudied God's transcendence, while neglecting God's condescendence. This has resulted in the image of an omnipotent God and an impotent man and lacking the "strength in weakness" motif that took our Lord to the cross. Unlimited power fosters subservience and not the loving fellowship that God desires. God is, as it were, unwilling to be omnipotent without us, because he wants partners, not slaves. Now as regards the vexed question of theodicy, open theism (we grant) does not resolve the theodicy problem completely. But who (pray tell) has the full solution? Surely, only God himself can shoulder that burden. There can be no complete theodicy without eschatology, that is, without the hope of a great victory over the reality of evil and the resurrection of the dead. It is to these divine promises and not to human speculations that I look. I am not much comforted by LDS speculations about God/gods that are too weak to put a stop to evil because they are inherently limited. I will go this far, though, and say that Genesis 1:1–2 ("when God created the heavens and the earth, the earth was without form and void") describes not an ex nihilo creation, but a reworking of elements then present. This takes the ex nihilo off the table somewhat and allows both of us to take seriously the reality of spiritual warfare and the resistance that God faces.

Third, as regards human deification, the similarity between what St. Athanasius was teaching and what Joseph Smith was saying may be more apparent than real. I think that the Orthodox theologians longed for the day when believers will share God's glory but not for the day when, through a process of perfection, they will become gods themselves just like God. A real difference here is my belief in the ontological gap between God and the creation and David's denial of it. The God I worship was not once a man like me. We are not (God and I) of the same species. I am created—God is uncreate.

Fourth, as regards the divine omniscience, David and I are quite close and find debating partners within our own groups on this subject. Were it the case that God possessed exhaustive definite foreknowledge, it would mean that the future is completely settled and no issues need to be resolved. It leaves no room for the historical biblical drama or to our own dignity to make contributions as co-labourers with God. It prevents us from being possibility thinkers and makes us into a people of resignation, as if whatever will be will be.

Fifth, as regards the divine gender, I in my innocence prodded David to talk about it a little, and he for his part put a number of interesting ideas on the table. His discussion of the hymnody, for example, revealed how proud Latter-day Saints are of their doctrine of divine gender. They love to think that they have a Mother in Heaven who models for them what it means to be female, including the conception and rearing of children. But questions arise in my curious mind. Do the gods and goddesses have sexual intercourse? Do their bodies eliminate waste? Did Yahweh have a wife and consort? In David's response we learn that he may have had one and that her name was possibly Asherah. One marvels at how literal the Latter-day Saints are willing to be in working out their beliefs in divine embodiment and human theosis. They really mean it when they say that we are "like God" and God is "like us," whiskers and all. I think that non–Latter-day Saints will take a while to come round to these ideas. On the other hand, it could stir up a new wave of feminist theology because it brings to the table some really new ideas.

Sixth, as regards the social Trinity, Latter-day Saints are tritheists, which fits their polytheistic outlook in general. The Father, Son, and Spirit refer to three individual and separate deities who collectively constitute a Trinity or the cosmic committee of three. This is not what I have taken the social Trinity to be. By the term, I have meant to affirm that the eternal life of the one and only God is personal life in relationship. They are three ways in which God is God. It is like, but not exactly like, a *koinonia* of persons in love. It is like, but not exactly like, a loving community and the picture of hospitality. Obviously I am assuming monotheism when thinking of the persons, while David is not.

Latter-day Saint thought challenges evangelical thought in its complacency toward other varieties of Christian faith. Latter-day Saint scholars are working hard at the defence of their faith. The opposite is also true. The quality and quantity of evangelical work is improving and could benefit from the interaction we are seeing. Let the iron sharpen iron. May God lead us all into the fuller truth of what Jesus brought into the world.

Reply to Professor Pinnock

David L. Paulsen

I AM LEARNING MUCH AS A RESULT OF MY DIALOGUE with Professor Clark Pinnock. He is an ideal conversation partner. He takes my ideas seriously, and his responses are always respectful yet thought-provoking and challenging, compelling me to rethink and refine my ideas. I too am richer both as a person and as a thinker for our interactions.

We do, as Clark points out, come to our understanding of God from distinctly different perspectives: he from the standpoint of what he calls a "modified classical" trinitarianism (Pinnock, 543) and I from the standpoint of what I believe to be modern revelation, beginning with the First Vision of Joseph Smith. We are not, however, without common ground. We both believe in the Bible and in the possibility of divine guidance in our search for fuller understanding. These can indeed bring us closer to the truth, closer to one another, and closer to God. To these ends I continue our conversation, focusing principally on the specific issues Clark raises in his rejoinder.

Social Trinity

My understanding of the Godhead appears to be what contemporary theologians refer to as "a social Trinity," but Clark labels my view "tritheistic." At the same time, Clark's view seems closer to classical trinitarianism than to a social model inasmuch as Clark seems to pull away from affirming the real distinctness of the three divine persons when he says, "The eternal life of the one and only God is personal life in relationship. They are three ways in which God is God" (Pinnock, 545). While this may be his understanding of the social Trinity, others present a stronger model. In his lucid presentation on the subject, Cornelius Plantinga specifies three conditions a view of the Godhead must satisfy in order to be a "strong or social theory":

> (1) The theory must have Father, Son, and Spirit as distinct centers of knowledge, will, love, and action. Since each of these capacities requires consciousness, it follows that, on this sort of theory, Father, Son, and Spirit would be viewed as distinct centers of consciousness or, in short, as *persons* in some full sense of that term. (2) Any accompanying sub-theory of divine simplicity must be modest enough to be consistent with condition (1), that is, with the real distinctness of trinitarian persons.... (3) Father, Son, and Spirit must be regarded as tightly enough related to each other so as to render plausible the judgment that they constitute a particular social unit.[153]

---

153. In regard to how the three divine persons are one, Plantinga outlines three ways. "There is only one font of divinity, only one Father, only one God in that sense of God," there is "only one generic divinity" or "set of excellent properties severally necessary and jointly sufficient for their possessor to be divine," and there is "only one divine family or monarchy or community, namely, the Holy Trinity itself." Cornelius Plantinga Jr., "Social Trinity and Tritheism," in *Trinity, Incarnation, and Atonement: Philosophical and Theological Essays,* ed. Ronald Feenstra and Cornelius Plantinga Jr. (Notre Dame, Ind.: University of Notre Dame Press, 1989), 22, 31. Latter-day Saints also affirm that there is only one God in each of these senses. Compare

The LDS understanding of the Godhead clearly satisfies Plantinga's criteria of a social model. So when I say that Latter-day Saints are social trinitarians, it is to these conditions that I appeal. It is not clear to me that Clark's model satisfies Plantinga's condition (2). If not, then given Plantinga's criteria, it is Clark's view, not the LDS view, of the Godhead that fails to constitute a social model of the Trinity. There is, of course, much more to consider here. Would Clark endorse Plantinga's criteria for a social model? If not, what would he offer as alternative criteria? Perhaps a more important question is: what model coheres best with the New Testament? Plantinga acknowledges that his model might be considered tritheistic by Christians who hold to a strong simplicity theory. But if so, Plantinga says, he is in good company, for, by the same criteria, Paul and John would also be tritheists. Latter-day Saints would also be proud to be in this company.

It is obvious that more dialogue on this issue is needed. For this dialogue to meaningfully proceed, I need a much fuller and clearer understanding of Clark's model of the Godhead. I look forward to being so informed and to the ensuing discussion.

Divine Embodiment

On this issue our views converge considerably, although Clark is much less certain than I as to the nature and mode of God's embodiment. The divergence in our views is again a function of our initial standpoints. The biblical data on which Clark relies is not sufficient to resolve the issue. Canonized modern revelation accepted by Latter-day Saints is more definitive: the Father and the Son have bodies "of flesh and bones as tangible as man's," while the Holy Ghost is "a personage of Spirit" (D&C 130:22–23).[154] Spirits

---

Jürgen Moltmann's, *The Trinity and the Kingdom of God* (London: SCM, 1981), 177–78, account of the unity of the triune God:

> In respect of the constitution of the Trinity the Father is the "origin-without-origin" of the Godhead. According to the doctrine of the two processions, the Son and the Spirit take their divine hypostases from him. So in the constitution of the Godhead, the Father forms the "monarchial" unity of the Trinity.
>
> But in respect of the Trinity's inner life, the three Persons themselves form their unity, by virtue of their relation to one another and in the eternal perichoresis of their love.
>
> Finally, the mutual transfiguration and illumination of the Trinity into the eternal glory of the divine life is bound up with this.

154. Doctrine and Covenants 130:22–23. Compare the words of the resurrected Lord to his apostles: "Behold my hands and my feet, that it is I myself: handle me, and see; for a spirit hath not flesh and bones, as ye see me have" (Luke 24: 39).

are also bodies. A "spirit" is a person with a body that is humanlike in form (Ether 3:6–16). "All spirit is matter," but matter so rarefied and pure that it cannot be discerned by normal visual perception (D&C 131:7–8). The conventional idea that spirits are immaterial substances, I believe, is not biblical but a borrowing from Platonist philosophy.[155]

In the context of discussing LDS belief in a Mother in Heaven, Clark "marvels at how literal Latter-day Saints are willing to be in working out their beliefs in divine embodiment and human theosis" (Pinnock, 545) and poses some of the questions to which these beliefs give rise. "Do the gods and goddesses have sexual intercourse? Do their bodies eliminate waste?" (Pinnock, 545).

Very simply, we do not know. Of course, it is fallacious to assume that since God is like us in some respects—for example, in having a body that is humanlike in form—he must be like us in all respects—for example, in having a body that is exactly like ours in all of its operations and functions.[156] To make such an assumption is to be guilty of "reverse anthropomorphism."

Scriptures, both biblical and LDS-specific, definitively mark out ways in which a divine or resurrected body differs from ours. In his first letter to the Corinthians, Paul provides the fullest biblical account of different modes of embodiment; he sharply distinguishes the mortal or natural body from a resurrected or divine body:

---

155. Rabbinic anthropology, for instance, does not consider the soul to be immaterial or radically distinct from the body. As Alon Goshen Gottstein explains, "Rabbinic anthropology differs . . . from Hellenistic and later Christian anthropology. The distinction between spirit and matter is not known in rabbinic literature . . . [M]etaphysically soul and body form a whole, rather than a polarity. Crudely put, the soul is like the battery that operates an electronic gadget. It may be different and originally external to the gadget, but the difference is not one of essence." Alon Goshen Gottstein, "The Body as Image of God in Rabbinic Literature," *Harvard Theological Review* 87, no. 2 (April 1994): 176–77.

It is Platonism that supplies the idea that soul and body are radically different, as J. N. D. Kelly notes, "Philosophy was the deeper religion of most intelligent people; what is more important for our purpose, its concepts provided thinkers, Christian and non-Christian alike, with an intellectual framework for expressing their ideas." That Plato's philosophy contradicts Rabbinic anthropology is stated by Kelly, "The transition to Plato's psychology and theology is easy. In his view the soul is an immaterial entity." J. N. D. Kelly, *Early Christian Doctrines,* 5th rev. ed. (London: Adams and Charles Black, 1977), 14, 16.

156. But compare Luke's account of the appearance of the resurrected Christ to his apostles where after showing them his hands and his feet "he said unto them, Have ye here any meat? And they gave him a piece of a broiled fish, and of an honey-comb. And he took it, and did eat before them" (Luke 24:41–43).

So also is the resurrection of the dead. It is sown in corruption; it is raised in incorruption: It is sown in dishonour; it is raised in glory: it is sown in weakness; it is raised in power: It is sown a natural body; it is raised a spiritual body. . . . For this corruptible must put on incorruption, and this mortal must put on immortality. So when this corruptible shall have put on incorruption, and this mortal shall have put on immortality, then shall be brought to pass the saying that is written, Death is swallowed up in victory. (1 Cor. 15:42–44, 53–54)

Similarly, in his epistle to the Philippians, Paul again strikingly contrasts these two kinds of body when he affirms that Christ "shall change[157] our vile[158] body that it may be fashioned like unto his glorious body, according to the working whereby he is able even to subdue all things unto himself" (Philip. 3:21). James Faulconer has reminded us that "Luke 24:31 tells us that Christ is able to disappear immediately from view and Luke 24:36 tells us that he can enter a ["shut", John 20:19] room just as suddenly."[159] This ability is also shown in Acts 1:1–11 when Christ ascends bodily into heaven.

---

157. The word *change* means to transfigure. It has been suggested that we have here the thought of metamorphosis, which is a remarkable change in the form and structure of a living body. When Jesus took Peter, James, and John up into the Mountain, we read that he "was transfigured before them" (Matt. 17:2). Christ appeared during that brief period of time in his glorified body. He was transfigured (or metamorphosed) before them. He had a body like his postresurrection body when he appeared to his disciples behind shut doors (John 20:19). The change of the believer at the resurrection has to do with his body, wherein resides the sin principle, for even the Christian must admit, "I know that in me (that is, in my flesh,) dwelleth no good thing" (Rom. 7:18). The word change could not refer to the spiritual part of man, for, as Kenneth Wuest says, "The word 'change' is the translation of a Greek word which speaks of an expression which is assumed from the outside, which act brings about a change of outward expression." Kenneth S. Wuest, *Philippians in the Greek New Testament* (Grand Rapids: Eerdmans, 1942), 103.

158. The Greek word used here means literally "an unpretentious state or condition, lowliness, humility, humble station." Paul is referring to "the humble body, of the material body in contrast to the glorified body." *A Greek-English Lexicon of the New Testament and other Early Christian Literature,* rev. and ed. Frederick William Danker, 3d ed. (Chicago: The University of Chicago Press, 2000), 990. Many Bible translations reflect the real meaning better than the KJV. Examples include, The New International Version, "lowly body"; New King James Version, "lowly body"; New American Standard Bible, "the body of our humble state"; The Message, "earthy bodies"; and New Living Translation, "weak mortal bodies."

159. James E. Faulconer, "Divine Embodiment and Transcendence: Propaedeutic Thoughts and Questions," *Element: An E-journal of Mormon Philosophy and Theology* 1 (2005): 1. Faulconer provides a fuller explanation of these differences and examines the philosophical implications of divine embodiment.

Mortal and divine bodies are also contrasted in modern revelations. For instance, in Joseph Smith's account of his First Vision, he describes the Father and the Son as standing above him in the air—apparently divine bodies are not subject to the laws of gravity in the same way ours are. He reports that their "brightness and glory" was beyond "all description" (Joseph Smith—History 1:17). And in the report of Moses' face-to-face encounter with God,

> the presence of God withdrew from Moses, that his glory was not upon Moses; and Moses was left unto himself. And as he was left unto himself, he fell unto the earth. And it came to pass that it was for the space of many hours before Moses did again receive his natural strength like unto man; and he said unto himself: Now, for this cause I know that man is nothing, which thing I never had supposed. But now mine own eyes have beheld God; but not my natural, but my spiritual eyes, for my natural eyes could not have beheld; for I should have withered and died in his presence; but his glory was upon me; and I beheld his face, for I was transfigured before him. (Moses 1:9–11)

So glorious is God's personage that Moses had to undergo a temporary transfiguration of his own body simply to withstand God's presence. Notwithstanding the fact that our knowledge of divine bodies is scant, it is clear that they are not subject to all of the limitations of mortal bodies.[160]

---

160. For instance, Grace Dyck (now Jantzen) has shown there is no incoherence in holding a divinely embodied person to be omnipresent. She correctly points out that the claim that an embodied being cannot be omnipresent is ambiguous between "His body cannot be everywhere," which, she says, is true but harmless, and "He cannot be everywhere," which, she argues, is not necessarily true. The former follows analytically from the meaning of the word *body*, the latter does not. Grace M. Dyck "Omnipresence and Incorporeality," *Religious Studies* 13, no. 1 (March 1977): 90–91. See also David L. Paulsen, "Must God be Incorporeal?" *Faith and Philosophy* 6, no. 1 (January 1989): 81. Stephen Robinson makes a similar point in a published dialogue with an evangelical scholar, Craig Blomberg. Robinson says, "Latter-day Saints affirm only that God the father has a body, not that his body has him." Robinson goes on to explain,

> The only real question is whether God can be present without being materially present, and both Evangelicals and Latter-day Saints say yes. If an immaterial God can be immaterially omnipresent, then a material God can also be immaterially omnipresent (even where his body is not), in the same way. Similarly, I would agree with 1 Kings 8:27 that God cannot be contained by an earthly temple or by heaven and earth themselves. (Craig L. Blomberg and Stephen E. Robinson, *How Wide the Divide: A Mormon and an Evangelical in Conversation* [Downers Grove, Ill. Intervarsity, 1997], 88.)

The Problem of Evil

Open Theism

Belief in ex nihilo creation greatly exacerbates the logical problem of evil. For it posits God as the ultimate cause of all things, making him an accessory before the fact and, thus, seemingly ultimately omniresponsible for all the world's evils. While Clark hedges on the biblical standing of ex nihilo creation, he does acknowledge that it is not supported by the Genesis account of creation:

> I will go this far though and say that Genesis ch. 1:1–2 ("when God created the heavens and the earth, the earth was without form and void") describes, not an ex nihilo creation, but a reworking of elements then present. This takes the ex nihilo off the table somewhat and allows both of us to take seriously the reality of spiritual warfare and the resistance which God faces. (Pinnock, 544)

However, I don't understand how this admission serves to exculpate God from ultimate responsibility for the world's evil, for elsewhere Clark suggests that "elements then present" (and, indeed, all things) were ultimately ex nihilo creations of God (Pinnock, 544). I hope Clark and other openness theologians will address this issue more directly as our conversations continue.

Mormonism

In its rejection of ex nihilo creation, modern revelation provides Latter-day Saints resources for resolving the logical problem of evil.[161] These revelations indicate that intelligences (or primal persons), chaotic matter (D&C 93:29, 33), and "the laws of eternal and self-existent principles"[162] are realities coeternal with God. Given a plurality of coeternal realities, it follows that God is neither an accessory before the fact to all the world's evils nor ultimately responsible for them. Further, given this plurality of coeternal realities, it follows that God is not unlimitedly powerful. There are limits and conditions as to what he can bring about. B. H. Roberts has proposed that Latter-day Saints understand divine omnipotence as the power to bring about any state of affairs consistent with the natures of eternal existences.[163] From these theological premises, it does not follow that the existence of God and the existence of evil are logically incompatible. On the other hand,

---

161. See David L. Paulsen, "Joseph Smith and the Problem of Evil," *BYU Studies* 39, no. 1 (2000): 53–65.

162. Ehat and Cook, *Words of Joseph Smith*, 60.

163. See B. H. Roberts, *The Seventy's Course in Theology*, vol. 2 (Dallas, Texas: S. K. Taylor, 1976), Fourth Year, Lesson 12, 70.

neither does it follow, as Clark infers, that God is "too weak" to prevent the evils that occur in the world (Pinnock, 546). It does follow that he cannot prevent all evils without an overriding diminution in the overall value of the world. Lehi, a Book of Mormon prophet, sets out some of the eternal principles to which even God is subject. Lehi teaches that "men are that they might have joy" (2 Nephi 2:25). But, Lehi explains, not even God can bring about joy without moral righteousness, moral righteousness without moral freedom, and moral freedom without an "opposition in all things" (2 Nephi 2:11, 13).[164] Insights gained from modern revelation shed considerable light on the unavoidability of evil in our present existence.

Nonetheless, Clark does well to remind us that even with the light of modern revelation Latter-day Saints also "see through a glass darkly" (1 Cor. 13:12) in our attempt to understand the "why" of many of the world's actual evils. We, too, must look to the eschaton for fuller light. Latter-day Saints, like openness thinkers, believe that God is redemptively sovereign. We trust that he can and will fulfill all of his purposes and promises. As Joseph Smith reassured the early Saints, "All your losses will be made up to you in the resurrection, provided you continue faithful."[165]

Deification

Clark is correct, I believe, in pointing out that Latter-day Saints hold a more robust view of deification than most Orthodox theologians, owing to a difference in their theological anthropology. Clark says that "the God I worship was not once a man like me. We are not (God and I) of the same species. I am created—God is uncreate" (Pinnock, 544). Given Clark's premise that man is create and God uncreate, it follows logically that man can never be exactly like God for that which is create can never become uncreate.

Aside from this trivial implication of Clark's premise, I ask what conceivable limits are there in eternity to human development and transformation with God as guide, sanctifier, and enabler? Is God unable or unwilling to share with faithful saints all that he is? John, Peter, and Paul all affirm that in the eschaton Christ will transform man into his likeness. Paul, as we have seen, writes that Christ "shall change our vile body, that it may be fashioned like unto his glorious body" (Philip. 3:21); Peter declares that faithful saints might "be partakers of the divine nature" (2 Pet. 1:4); and John writes, "Beloved, now are we the sons of God, and it doth not yet appear what we shall be: but we know that, when he shall appear, we shall be like him; for we shall see him as he is" (1 Jn. 3:2). Sacred scripture affirms that God is both able and willing to transform us into his likeness. Why then should we call

---

164. I call this passage "Lehi's theodicy."

165. Joseph Smith, *Teachings of the Prophet Joseph Smith*, 296.

such transformation impossible or even qualify God's promises in ways he does not?

The Divine Feminine

Pinnock appears quite surprised, nay almost shocked, by the disclosures provoked by his "innocent" prodding on the subject of divine gender. He "marvels" at how literal Latter-day Saints are in their beliefs on the subject, asks "curious" questions and, in an obvious understatement, says, "I think that non-Mormons will take a while to come round to these ideas" (Pinnock, 545).

Yet without doubt, LDS beliefs in a Heavenly Mother and in eternal marriage and family relationships have tremendous existential appeal. Perhaps Clark was serious when he said that "on the other hand" the LDS view "could stir up a new wave of feminist theology because it brings to the table some really new ideas" (Pinnock, 545). Time will tell. In the meantime, I hope openness and other Christian theologians will give more thought to the divine feminine and to gender as an eternal property of resurrected persons. For me, personally, these ideas make the eschaton all the more inviting and exciting.

Without doubt, LDS and Evangelical scholars are hard at work in more clearly articulating and defending their faith. Both can benefit from the interaction we are seeing. I thus say "Amen" to Clark's concluding appeal: "Let iron sharpen iron. May God lead us all into the fuller truth of what Jesus brought into the world" (Pinnock, 545).

About the Authors

Clark H. Pinnock (Ph.D. University of Manchester) has authored, edited, or coauthored fifteen books. He taught at the University of Manchester, New Orleans Baptist Theological Seminary, Trinity Evangelical Divinity School, and Regent College in Vancouver. He, along with four other authors, wrote The Openness of God (InterVarsity, 1994), more recently publishing The Most Moved Mover (Baker, 2001), a publication of his 2000 Didsbury Lectures, and presented at the Third Annual Mormon Theology Conference in 2004. He is an emeritus professor of Christian interpretation at McMaster Divinity College, Hamilton, Ontario.

David L. Paulsen (Ph.D. University of Michigan) is professor of philosophy at Brigham Young University, where he specializes in the philosophy of religion. His doctoral thesis explored the comparative coherency of classical and Mormon theism. Paulsen has published widely, exploring the bearing of LDS revelation on issues in the philosophy of religion. He held the Richard L. Evans Chair for Religious Understanding at Brigham Young University from 1994 to 1998.

Index

Scripture Index